Security Policies and Implementation Issues

THIRD EDITION

Robert Johnson | Chuck Easttom

JONES & BARTLETT
LEARNING

World Headquarters
Jones & Bartlett Learning
25 Mall Road
Burlington, MA 01803
978-443-5000
info@jblearning.com
www.jblearning.com

Jones & Bartlett Learning books and products are available through most bookstores and online booksellers. To contact Jones & Bartlett Learning directly, call 800-832-0034, fax 978-443-8000, or visit our website, www.jblearning.com.

Substantial discounts on bulk quantities of Jones & Bartlett Learning publications are available to corporations, professional associations, and other qualified organizations. For details and specific discount information, contact the special sales department at Jones & Bartlett Learning via the above contact information or send an email to specialsales@jblearning.com.

Production Credits

VP, Product Management: Amanda Martin
Director of Product Management: Laura Pagluica
Product Manager: Edward Hinman
Content Strategist: Melissa Duffy
Content Coordinator: Paula-Yuan Gregory
Development Editor: Ginny Munroe
Technical Editor: Rob Shimonski
Project Manager: Lori Mortimer
Project Specialist: John Coakley
Digital Project Specialist: Rachel DiMaggio
Marketing Manager: Michael Sullivan
Production Services Manager: Colleen Lamy
Product Fulfillment Manager: Wendy Kilborn
Composition: Exela Technologies
Project Management: Exela Technologies
Cover Design: Briana Yates
Text Design: Kristin E. Parker
Media Development Editor: Faith Brosnan
Rights Specialist: James Fortney
Cover Image (Title Page, Part Opener, Chapter Opener):
    © obpcnh/Shutterstock
Printing and Binding: LSC Communications

Library of Congress Cataloging-in-Publication Data
Names: Johnson, Rob (Robert), author. | Easttom, Chuck, author.
Title: Security policies and implementation issues / Robert Johnson, Chuck Easttom.
Description: [Third edition] | Burlington, MA : Jones & Bartlett Learning, [2021] | Includes bibliographical references and index.
Identifiers: LCCN 2020018594 | ISBN 9781284199840 (paperback)
Subjects: LCSH: Computer security.
Classification: LCC QA76.9.A25 J64 2021 | DDC 005.8–dc23
LC record available at https://lccn.loc.gov/2020018594

6048

Printed in the United States of America
26 25 24 23 22   10 9 8 7 6 5 4 3

Brief Contents

Contents

CHAPTER 8   ## IT Security Policy Framework Approaches   199

CHAPTER 11

Data Classification and Handling Policies and Risk Management Policies   283

To my wife Teresa, who is always very supportive of all I do.
—Dr. Chuck Easttom

Preface

Purpose of This Book

This book is part of the Information Systems Security & Assurance Series from Jones & Bartlett Learning (*www.jblearning.com*). Designed for courses and curriculums in IT Security, Cybersecurity, Information Assurance, and Information Systems Security, this series features a comprehensive, consistent treatment of the most current thinking and trends in this critical subject area. These titles deliver fundamental information-security principles packed with real-world applications and examples. Authored by Certified Information Systems Security Professionals (CISSPs), they deliver comprehensive information on all aspects of information security. Reviewed word for word by leading technical experts in the field, these books are not just current, but forward thinking—putting you in the position to solve the cybersecurity challenges not just of today, but of tomorrow, as well.

Implementing IT security policies and related frameworks for an organization can seem like an overwhelming task, given the vast number of issues and considerations. *Security Policies and Implementation Issues* demystifies this topic, taking you through a logical sequence of discussions about major concepts and issues related to security policy implementation.

It is a unique book that offers a comprehensive, end-to-end view of information security policies and frameworks from the raw organizational mechanics of building to the psychology of implementation. This book presents an effective balance between technical knowledge and soft skills, both of which are necessary for understanding the business context and psychology of motivating people and leaders. It also introduces you in clear, simple terms to many different concepts of information security, such as governance, regulator mandates, business drivers, legal considerations, and more. If you need to understand how information risk is controlled, or are responsible for oversight of those who do, you will find this book helpful.

Part 1 of this book focuses on why private and public sector organizations need an information technology (IT) security framework consisting of documented policies, standards, procedures, and guidelines. As businesses, organizations, and governments change the way they operate and organize their overall information systems security strategy, one of the most critical security controls is documented IT security policies.

Part 2 defines the major elements of an IT security policy framework. Many organizations, under recent compliance laws, must now define, document, and implement information security policies, standards, procedures, and guidelines. Many organizations and businesses conduct a risk assessment to determine their current risk exposure within their IT infrastructure. Once these security gaps and threats are identified, design and implementation of more-stringent information security policies are put in place. This can provide an excellent starting point for the creation of an IT security policy framework.

Policies are only as effective as the individuals who create them and enforce them within an organization. Part 3 of this book presents how to successfully implement and enforce policies within an organization. Emerging techniques and automation of policy enforcement are also examined.

This book is a valuable resource for students, security officers, auditors, and risk leaders who want to understand what a successful implementation of security policies and frameworks looks like.

Learning Features

The writing style of this book is practical and conversational. Step-by-step examples of information security concepts and procedures are presented throughout the text. Each chapter begins with a statement of learning objectives. Illustrations are used both to clarify the material and to vary the presentation. The text is sprinkled with Notes, Tips, FYIs, Warnings, and sidebars to alert the reader to additional helpful information related to the subject under discussion. Chapter Assessments appear at the end of each chapter, with solutions provided in the back of the book.

Chapter summaries are included in the text to provide a rapid review or preview of the material and to help students understand the relative importance of the concepts presented.

Audience

The material is suitable for undergraduate or graduate computer science majors or information science majors, students at a two-year technical college or community college who have a basic technical background, or readers who have a basic understanding of IT security and want to expand their knowledge.

New to This Edition

- Covers additional standards:
    - ISO 38500
    - ISO 27007
    - ISO 30105
    - GDPR
    - ETSI
- Updated NIST Special Publication (SP) 800-53 for the 2019 changes
- Updated COBIT for COBIT 2019
- Added the CIS Critical Security Controls for Effective Cyber Defense
- Added coverage of mobile devices in the workplace (BYOD, COPE, CYOD)
- Included additional models like McCumber Cube
- Updated statistics and case studies

Theory Labs

This text is accompanied by Cybersecurity Theory Labs. These hands-on labs provide guided exercises and case studies where students can learn and practice foundational cybersecurity skills as an extension of the lessons in this textbook. For more information or to purchase the labs, visit go.jblearning.com/johnson3e

Acknowledgments

We would like to thank Jones & Bartlett Learning for the opportunity to work on this book and be a part of the Information Systems Security & Assurance Series project. It is always a pleasure to work with a high-quality publisher who pushes for the best book they can create.

About the Authors

ROB JOHNSON has more than 22 years of experience in information risk, IT audit, privacy, and security management. He has a diverse background that includes hands-on operational experience, as well as providing strategic risk assessment and support to leadership and board-level audiences. He is currently a Senior Vice President at Bank of America in the Global Technology Organization.

Johnson has held senior roles in large global companies, in large domestic banks, and as product architect for an international software company. Several of the key risk-related roles he has held include Head of Information and Operations Risk Management for ING U.S. Financial Services, Senior Partner at Aegis USA Executive Consulting, First Vice President and IT Senior Audit Director for WAMU, Vice President/CISO for Security Services at First Bank Systems, and Product Owner and Architect for SAP/ERP solutions at Bindview.

Johnson lives in the Seattle area with his wife and children. He holds a BS in interdisciplinary studies from the University of Houston with a concentration in computer science and mathematics. He is a Certified Information Systems Auditor (CISA), Certified Information Security Manager (CISM), Certified Information Systems Security Professional (CISSP), Certified in Risk and Information Systems Control (CRISC), and Certified in the Governance of Enterprise IT (CGEIT). Rob has served on several international education and standards committees, including as 1 of 19 former members of the prestigious international C5 Task Force that developed COBIT 2019.

DR. CHUCK EASTTOM is the author of 29 books, including several on computer security, forensics, and cryptography. His books are used at over 60 universities. He has also authored scientific papers (over 60 so far) on digital forensics, cyber warfare, cryptography, and applied mathematics. He is an inventor with 22 computer science patents. He holds a Doctor of Science (DSc) in cyber security (dissertation topic: "A Study of Lattice-Based Cryptographic Algorithms for Post Quantum Computing") and three master's degrees (one in applied computer science, one in education, and one in systems engineering). He also holds a Doctor of Philosophy (PhD) in nanotechnology. and is currently working on a PhD in computing from the University of Portsmouth (dissertation topic: "On the Application of Algebraic Graph Theory to Network Forensics"). He is a Senior Member of the Institute of Electrical and Electronics Engineers (IEEE) and a Senior Member of the Association of Computing Machinery (ACM). He is also a Distinguished Speaker of the ACM, a Distinguished Visitor of the IEEE Computer Society, and a frequent speaker at conferences. He is a reviewer for six scientific journals and the Editor in Chief for the American Journal of Science and Engineering. He also currently holds 55 industry certifications (CISSP, CASP, CEH, etc.). More details are available at www.ChuckEasttom.com

PART ONE

The Need for IT Security Policy Frameworks

Information Systems Security Policy Management

FOR AN ORGANIZATION TO ACHIEVE ITS GOALS, business processes must be reliable, affordable, and legal. Reliable policies require clearly defined processes. Most organizations use policies and procedures to tell employees what the business wants to achieve and how to perform tasks to get there. This way, the business can achieve consistent quality in delivering its products and services.

Though policies and procedures need to be reliable, affordable, and legal, policies are not perfect. Even if a policy is inherently perfect, perfect implementation of it would require employees to follow policies and procedures at all times; however, we do not live in a perfect world. Neither policies nor procedures are always perfect, nor do employees always follow them. Anyone who has cashed a check at a bank understands what a basic procedure looks like. A check-cashing procedure includes checking the person's identification and the account balance. The bank's policy states that when a teller follows the check-cashing procedure and the account has sufficient funds, the teller may give the cash to the account holder. The teller must follow this procedure to protect the customer and the bank from fraud. Failure to do so can be a substantial breach and can have significant deleterious consequences.

Business processes are highly dependent on timely information. It's also challenging to find an organization that does not rely on technology, whether it sells hamburgers, cashes checks for people, or is building the next-generation airliner. Processes use technology and information to make business decisions, keep food safe, track inventory, and control manufacturing, among other things. The more complex these technologies become, the more vulnerable they become to disruptions. The more people rely on them in their daily lives, the more vulnerable they become when these technologies do not work.

You can also think of a policy as a business requirement of actions or processes performed by an organization. An example is the requirement that a customer provide a receipt when returning an item to a retail store for a refund. That may be a simple example, but essentially, it places a control on the return process. In the same manner, security policies require placement of controls in processes specific to the information system.

One of the challenges organizations face is the cost of keeping pace with ever-changing technology. This includes the need to update policies at the same time the organization updates technology. Failure to do so can create weaknesses in the system. These weaknesses make business processes and information vulnerable to loss or theft.

Many factors drive the policy requirements of **information systems security policies**, also called *security policies*, *IS policies*, or *ISS policies*. These requirements include the organization's size, processes, the types of information the business deals in, and the laws and regulations that may affect the policies. Once an organization creates policies, it will face both technical and human challenges implementing them. The keys to implementing policies are employee acceptance and management enforcement. A policy is worth little or nothing if no one follows it.

Chapter 1 Topics

This chapter covers the following topics and concepts:

- What information systems security is
- How information assurance plays an important role in securing information
- What governance is
- Why governance is important
- What information systems security policies are and how they differ from standards and procedures
- Where policies fit within an organization's structure to effectively reduce risk
- Why security policies are important to business operations, and how business changes affect policies
- When information systems security policies are needed
- Why enforcing, and winning acceptance for, security policies is challenging

Chapter 1 Goals

When you complete this chapter, you will be able to:

- Compare and contrast information systems security and information assurance
- Compare and contrast quality control and quality assurance
- Describe information systems security policies and their importance in organizations
- Describe governance and its importance in maintaining compliance with laws
- Explain what policies are and how they fit into an organization
- Compare and contrast threats, vulnerabilities, and risks

What Is Information Systems Security?

A good definition of **information systems security (ISS)** is the act of protecting information and the systems that store and process it. This protection is against risks that would lead to unauthorized access, use, disclosure, disruption, modification, or destruction of information. The first thing that should be clear from this definition is that ultimately it is the information that requires protecting. Usually, information is on digital devices such as computers, tablets, routers, and similar devices. Those devices' primary value is the information on them.

It is important to remember that it is not just the information inside a computer you need to protect. Information needs to be protected in any form. Some examples include print and removable storage such as optical DVD drives. In fact, well-structured security policies ensure protection of information in any location and in any form. Many organizations come up with effective ways of protecting buildings, people, and other physical resources. Most people understand the need to lock their doors at home at night. Yet they may not always have the same instincts or habits when it comes to handling their data.

Sometimes the rules for dealing with information are unclear. Suppose your business knows a person's name, phone number, and email address. How much privacy should that person expect from your business? What are you obligated by law to protect? What's the right thing to do ethically? These are just some of the questions businesses struggle with daily. Not every employee is an expert in these matters. So, organizations create policies and procedures for their employees to follow.

Sometimes these same organizations fail to properly protect the information they process. Some do not consider information important to their operations. Some believe that security measures designed to protect buildings and people will protect information. Some just do not want to spend more money. However, protecting information is vital to business operations.

Information Systems Security Management Life Cycle

Generally, in any process of importance, you would use some type of life cycle process to reduce errors and make sure all requirements are considered. It is no different for implementing security policies. Information security controls and processes use common approaches that simplify the build and reduce mistakes. A typical life cycle process breaks up tasks into smaller, more manageable phases. The Information Systems Audit and Control Association (ISACA) developed a widely accepted international best practices framework. This framework, called Control Objectives for Information and related Technology (COBIT), was first released in 1996. The next major version, 5.0, was released in April 2012. This version is still in use; however, in 2018, COBIT 2019 was released. COBIT 2019 includes:

- Design factors and focus areas that offer more transparency on building a governance system
- Improved compliance with global frameworks
- Consistent updates on a rolling basis
- An open-source model that enables feedback from the external governance community for quicker enhancements
- Better instructions and a broader toolkit to assist enterprises with creating a top-notch governance system
- An improved tool for measuring Capability Maturity Model Integration (CMMI) alignment and IT performance
- Greater support for decision making

COBIT 2019 is made up of the following elements that differentiate it from previous versions of COBIT:

- Design factors and focus areas that offer more transparency on building a governance system
- Improved compliance with global frameworks
- Consistent updates on a rolling basis
- An open-source model that enables feedback from the external governance community for quicker enhancements
- Better instructions and a broader toolkit to assist enterprises when creating a top-notch governance system
- An improved tool for measuring CMMI alignment and IT performance
- Greater support for decision-making

COBIT is more than just a life cycle; it's a framework for managing and governing IT processes. These types of frameworks allow businesses to align themselves to outcomes that they and their customers expect. At its core are four domains that collectively represent a conceptual **information systems security management life cycle**:

- Align, Plan, and Organize
- Build, Acquire, and Implement
- Deliver, Service, and Support
- Monitor, Evaluate, and Assess

 NOTE

You can read more about **COBIT** at *https://www.isaca.org/resources/cobit.*

The life cycle process can use these simple domains, or phases, to build policies or controls. Each phase builds on the other. A failure in one phase can lead to a weakness or vulnerability downstream. For the purposes of discussion, you will learn about the four domains from a high-level life cycle view. The COBIT framework goes into great depth to further break down these domains into detailed tasks and processes. Many organizations look at the richness of a framework like COBIT to tailor a life cycle management approach that makes sense for their business.

In 2012, COBIT 5.0 was released to the public. This version of COBIT introduced the idea that good business processes make it possible for organizations to do the following:

- Deliver value to internal and external stakeholders.
- Meet organizational goals.
- Practice life cycle management: building, maintaining, supporting, and disposing of products and other assets.
- Learn from others to keep abreast of industry best practices.

COBIT 5.0 was a departure from other frameworks in that it put emphasis on what enables processes to work well. In fact, COBIT calls these *process enablers*. For example, think of a teller cashing a check. What does a bank have to think about to align, plan, and organize to achieve stakeholder value? Clearly the bank wants the customer, as the external stakeholder, to have a good experience. This will build loyalty and repeat business. But the customer needs must be balanced with the business goal of making a

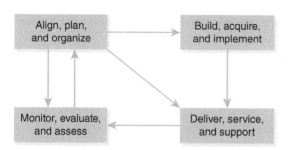

FIGURE 1-1

A simplified ISS management
life cycle using COBIT 5.0.

profit. The bank must also be aware of changing industry standards and new technology
such as mobile devices.

As was already discussed, COBIT 2019 expanded and built on COBIT 5.0, but most of the
fundamentals remain.

FIGURE 1-1 depicts one simplified example of an ISS management life cycle.

Align, Plan, and Organize

The COBIT Align, Plan, and Organize domain includes basic details of an organization's
requirements and goals. This domain answers the questions "What do you want to do?" and
"How do you want to get there?" The information in this phase is still high level. Even at a
high level, it is important to understand the risks and threats clearly. You review how you
are going to manage your IT investment such as contracts, **service level agreements (SLAs)**,
and new policy ideas. An SLA is a stated commitment to provide a specific service level.
For example, an SLA could state how often a supplier will provide
the service or how quickly the firm will respond. For managed
services, the SLA often covers system availability and acceptable performance measures. It's also important to look at where
or how the system will operate to determine the SLA. SLAs are
important to ensure that all parties know their obligations. There
are different types of service levels that apply to contracts versus
what you need to deal with day to day. The Deliver, Service, and
Support domain helps you define and manage day-to-day SLAs. In
the Align, Plan, and Organize domain, you are primarily concerned
with the type of equipment and services you are acquiring and
how to hold a supplier accountable for those deliveries.

 NOTE

Notice in Figure 1-1 that the Align, Plan,
and Organize domain touches all the
other domains. This is because you will
determine how the project will be managed in the Align, Plan, and Organize
domain. This means you need to initially
decide and then adjust management
and staff throughout the project.

A contract must provide the ability to ensure a supplier meets its obligations. The SLA
language in a contract must provide clear monitoring and enforcement rights. For example, consider the 2013 breach of Target stores. Although this is an older breach, it is one
of the major events in cybersecurity history and still worthy of consideration. Between
November 27 and December 15, 2013, hackers accessed the credit card information of
40 million customers. Later it was discovered that an additional 70 million customers'
personal information was also accessed by hackers. It's been widely reported the hacker
gained access through the supplier who maintained the company's heating and air condi-
tioning systems. Simply having a contract with the supplier wasn't enough. Target had an
obligation both to limit the supplier's access while on its network and to monitor access

sufficiently to ensure the contract was being enforced. These are general industry norms. Either one or both of these did not occur.

A key understanding in this life cycle phase is the understanding of threats, vulnerabilities, and risks. These three concepts are addressed in different forms throughout this text; however, a basic understanding is essential to scope the build effort. To understand these concepts, consider the following high-level definitions:

- **Threat**—A human-caused or natural event that could impact the system
- **Vulnerability**—A weakness in a system that can be exploited
- **Risk**—The likelihood or probability of an event and its impact

As an example, a common IS **threat** would be a hacker trying to break into a system. A **vulnerability** would be a weakness in a system that allows the hacker to gain unauthorized access. A vulnerability could be a misconfiguration, bug, or flaw in the system. A **risk** is a combination of the likelihood that such a misconfiguration could happen, a hacker's exploiting it, and the impact if the event occurred. Consider a non-Internet-facing system for ordering office supplies. Why might you think the risk is low? Although a misconfiguration may be possible, systems not on the Internet are less likely to be hacked. Additionally, unauthorized access to the office supply system would most likely have little long-term impact on a company.

> **NOTE**
>
> Generally, regardless of threat or vulnerability, there will always be a chance a threat can exploit a vulnerability. Consequently, whenever you have a threat or vulnerability, you will have a risk. The key is understanding whether that risk is small (unlikely) or large (probable).

Other examples may be of higher risk and require significant investment. An example of a natural threat would be a hurricane. A vulnerability may be a lack of a recovery site. If your main data center, for example, is damaged, where would you go? The risk may be high for a business that relies on Internet orders, especially if the business is located in Florida, which is prone to hurricanes.

Build, Acquire, and Implement

The COBIT Build, Acquire, and Implement domain addresses schedules and deliverables. The basic build occurs within this phase. The *build* is where the security control is built and policies and supporting documents written. The build is based on the requirement created in the Align, Plan, and Organize phase. The quality of the security controls that are built depends on the understanding of the threats, vulnerabilities, and risks. The deeper this understanding, the better the controls. The more detailed the requirements, the more easily the build will go. The more details included in the Align, Plan, and Organize phase, the easier the Build, Acquire, and Implement phase will be. The SLA becomes an important consideration of the build because it determines the type of solutions that will be selected.

Additionally, the ability to manage change is critical in this phase. Often, changes known as *upgrades* are made to existing systems. That means changes have to be timed perfectly. This is to avoid disrupting current services while new services are added. Often this will occur during off-hours such as weekends or overnight. Plans have to be put in place to back out the change in the event of a major problem. Understanding the impact of change and knowing how to recover if something goes wrong are parts of **change management**.

By the end of the Build, Acquire, and Implement phase, you have acquired and implemented your equipment. You have controls built into the systems. You have policies, procedures, and guidelines written. You have teams trained.

Deliver, Service, and Support

In the COBIT Deliver, Service, and Support domain, the staff tunes the environment to minimize risks. It is in this phase that you collect lessons learned. By running the systems, you learn what's working and what isn't. This is where you apply those lessons learned to improve operations. This could mean adjusting controls, policies, procedures, contracts, and SLAs. It is here you analyze data from the prior phase and compare it with day-to-day operations. You also perform internal and external penetration testing and, based on the results of those tests, make critical adjustments in areas such as perimeter defense, remote access, and backup procedures. You review contracts and SLAs for validity and modify them as needed.

This phase requires regular meetings and good communication with your vendors. You must quickly identify any issues with the vendors' capabilities to meet SLAs. Typically, a vendor provides its record for meeting SLAs. You compare the vendor's report to your organization's internal reports. If you rely heavily on the vendor, you should meet monthly to compare records and recap incidents during the month. It is important that SLAs also be explicit. Failure to clarify precisely what services are provided and how they are provided can lead to confusion and dissatisfaction from both the customer and the vendor.

In this phase, the day-to-day operations are managed and supported. You manage problems, configurations, physical security, and more. If you plan correctly and implement the right solution, your organization sees value.

Monitor, Evaluate, and Assess

After evaluating the ISS management life cycle, you can see that ISS focuses on specific types of controls at specific points within the system. Testing and monitoring of controls occur, and the results are analyzed for effectiveness. The oversight of the COBIT Monitor, Evaluate, and Assess domain looks at the big picture. Are your controls and supporting policies and procedures keeping pace with changes in technology and in your environment? This phase looks at specific business requirements and strategic direction and determines whether the system meets these objectives.

Internal and external audits occur during the evaluation phase. Audits also take place through all testing in this and prior phases to ensure requirements are being met. This may include penetration testing by a third-party trusted agent. The testing performed during this phase must be comprehensive enough to encompass the entire ISS environment. The level of additional security testing will depend on business requirements and complexity; for example, if your requirements include regulatory compliance, include appropriate control tests. You should also evaluate the incident response process.

Audits are independent assessments. The more robust the self-assessment process, the fewer the problems that will be discovered by an audit. Independence is a relative term. No one is truly independent. Consider this: Everyone belongs to a family. Everyone lives in a town or city. Everyone has a multitude of private and business relationships. People may feel comfortable criticizing politicians but suddenly uncomfortable criticizing a teacher who has the power over their final grade. It's human nature that the closer the relationship, or the more control someone has over your well-being, the less likely you are to criticize. Yet in business, this honest view of mistakes is essential to success.

The concept of independent audits (or assessments) is that the further one is away from the actual transaction, the more unbiased and independent the opinion that can be obtained. In other words, it's hard to criticize your own work. However, the more you understand the work, the better your chances are, generally, of finding out what went wrong. To balance these potentially competing interests, there is usually a series of assessments and audits. The following lists the most common types of assessments and audits:

- **Self-assessment**—This is typically in the form of quality assurance (QA) and quality control (QC).
- **Internal audit**—This consists of reports to the board of directors and assesses the business.
- **External audit**—This is done by an outside firm hired by the company to validate internal audit work and perform special assessments, such as certifying annual financial statements.
- **Regulator audit**—This is an audit by government agencies that assess the company's compliance with laws and regulations.

ISO/IEC 38500

Although COBIT is widely used and respected, it is not the only standard relevant to the information systems security management life cycle. The International Standards Organization publishes ISO 38500, "Information Technology—Governance of IT for the Organization," which provides guidance for managing IT governance. This standard is broader than just information systems security, but it includes and is applicable to information systems security management.

This standard was last revised in 2015. It specifically addresses monitoring of resources and auditing, both of which are clearly information systems management functions. This framework sets out six principles for corporate governance of information technology:

- Responsibility
- Strategy
- Acquisition
- Performance
- Conformance
- Human behavior

Clearly, each of these is as applicable to information security systems as it is to IT in general.

What Is Information Assurance?

Too often you will hear the terms *information systems security* and *information assurance* used interchangeably; however, they are not the same thing. **Information assurance (IA)** grew from information systems security. The high-level difference is that ISS focuses on protecting information regardless of form or process, whereas IA focuses on protecting information during process and use. You can see some of these differences as you examine the security tenets, also known as the "five pillars of the IA model":

- **Confidentiality**—Generally accepted as ISS and IA tenets
- **Integrity**—Generally accepted as ISS and IA tenets
- **Availability**—Generally accepted as ISS and IA tenets
- **Authentication**—Generally accepted as an IA tenet
- **Nonrepudiation**—Generally accepted as an IA tenet

The first three—confidentiality, integrity, and availability—are bedrock principles throughout information security. These are often referred to as the *CIA triangle*. (Some sources refer to this as the *CIA triad*; the two terms are synonymous.) This is not to suggest that authentication and nonrepudiation are not information security concerns. The goals are similar; however, the approach and focus are different. IA imposes controls on the entire system regardless of the format or media. In other words, IA ensures data is protected while being processed, stored, and transmitted. This ensures the confidentiality, integrity, availability, and nonrepudiation of the data.

Confidentiality

Confidentiality is the goal of ensuring that only authorized individuals are able to access information. A user should be granted access only to the specific information necessary to complete his or her job.

Typical users do not need unlimited access to all systems and all data. In fact, in regulated environments, if ordinary users had such access, this would be viewed as a compliance issue and a violation of law. Many organizations have adopted the **need-to-know principle**. In brief, this means that you gain access only to the systems and data you need to perform your job. For example, payroll personnel may need your employee and personal information, such as salary and Social Security number. Your manager may need access to your salary for budgeting but not your Social Security number. By restricting access, you maintain confidentiality.

FIGURE 1-2 depicts the confidentiality tenet. The figure represents three users—two are regular users; one is a privileged user. User A and User B have limited access rights to data. User A can read only data stored in the product list, whereas User B can read and update all data in the database. The privileged user has elevated database administration privileges; however, even he or she might not have access to all data.

> **NOTE**
>
> Another consideration of confidentiality is how to protect data in the event of a breach or unauthorized access. One way to resolve this issue is to use encryption. This is considered a security layered approach. A breach in one layer will be caught by another. In this case, even if data is improperly accessed, it still cannot be read.

Integrity

Integrity ensures that information has not been improperly changed. In other words, the data owner must approve any change to the data or approve the process by which the data changes. There are several ways to ensure that data is protected. Many operating systems allow permissions on data files and directories to provide restricted access. These

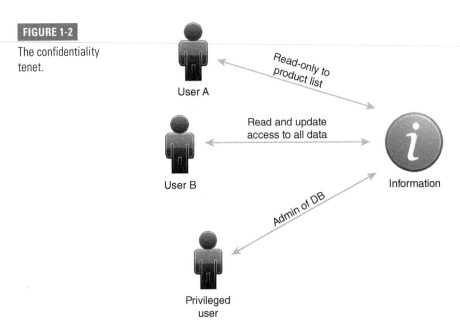

FIGURE 1-2

The confidentiality tenet.

User A

Read-only to product list

Read and update access to all data

User B

Information

Admin of DB

Privileged user

containers typically reside on a server that requires users to log on and authenticate to gain approved access. This ensures that only users who have the data owner's permission can change the information. Often, access is limited to an application. In this way, a user does not access data directly. The user accesses the application. The application accesses the data. So, the application acts as a gateway. This allows for more fine-grained granting of access, often referred to as **entitlement**. With entitlement, you can restrict the type of access a user has. For example, the application can allow a user to approve a payment but limit the amount to less than $1000. Encryption also ensures integrity as well as confidentiality. Encryption protects data from being viewed or changed by unauthorized users. Only users with the proper key can change or view encrypted data. Encryption is often used to protect data being transmitted or moved. Encryption can also be used to protect data at rest.

FIGURE 1-3 depicts the integrity tenet. There are two users, an application, a database management system (DBMS), and the data. The application control limits the type of change a user can make. The DBMS rules prevent unauthorized changes to data. User A can change data. User B can only retrieve data.

Authentication

Authentication is the ability to verify the identity of a user or device. You probably see authentication in use every day. For example, you might use an online email system such as Google Gmail or Yahoo! Mail. What protects your email is your user ID and password, which you selected when you signed up for the service. This user ID and password are your authentication approach to accessing your email service.

It's not just humans who need their identities verified. Computers often exchange information or process transactions on our behalf. While you are asleep, a computer system may by printing your payroll check. Many of these functions are sensitive. As a security professional, you should ensure that only these authorized processes are accessing this sensitive

FIGURE 1-3

The integrity tenet.

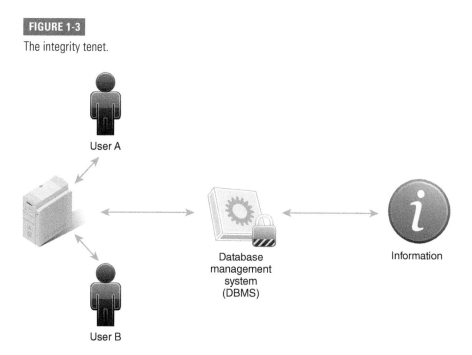

User A

Database
management
system
(DBMS)

Information

User B

information. This means these computers and automated processes need to be authenticated. Just like an individual, their identity is verified before being granted access to data. For example, services running in Microsoft Windows Server could have an ID assigned. Network devices can exchange information at a network protocol level to verify identity. These nonhuman IDs typically have elevated rights. This means they have lots of authority to access data across multiple systems. It's important that access to these nonhuman accounts be tightly controlled.

There is a lot involved in maintaining good authentication processes, such as forcing users to change their passwords periodically and forcing rules on how complicated passwords should be. These housekeeping tasks are becoming easier and more automated. One of the more critical keys to success is having credentials that are hard to forge or guess. A good example is a strong password known only to the user. Additionally, these credentials must not be transmitted in the clear over the network. Passwords sent over the network in plaintext, for example, can be observed with network sniffers. In a typical business environment, if these two goals are accomplished as well as many of the housekeeping items previously discussed, you begin to have reasonable assurance you know who is accessing your computer systems.

Availability

Availability ensures information is available to authorized users and devices. A major challenge to availability is the spread of *denial of service (DoS) attacks*. The technological sophistication and intensity of DoS attacks have increased significantly in recent years. These attacks flood a server with information that overwhelms its ability to process, causing the server to crash. Thus, the service becomes unavailable. The point of the attack is not to steal information but to crash the system. DoS attacks are often measured by the amount of information flooding the server. The typical measurement is in Gbps (gigabits per second). The size of DoS attacks keeps growing. In 2018, it was reported that the average DoS attack was bigger than 26 Gbps, and the maximum attack size was 359 Gbps.[1] However, in 2019, the average size decreased by 85 percent, and the maximum attack size decreased by 24 percent.[2]

Initially, the information owner must determine availability requirements. The owner must determine who needs access to the data and when. Is it critical that data be available 24/7, or is 9 to 5 adequate? Does it need to be available to remote or only local users? The raw business requirements then need to be translated into technical and operational commitments, such as hours of operations for when the systems would be available.

After availability requirements are determined, you must assess the threats and implement appropriate controls. Associated with the servers is all the network equipment that provides interconnectivity and remote access. Proper configuration of these devices will allow access to the information when needed.

Nonrepudiation

Nonrepudiation is both a legal term and a concept within information security. The idea is simple—nonrepudiation is the assurance that an individual cannot deny having digitally signed a document or been party to a transaction. As a legal concept, it is the sum total of evidence that proves to the court's satisfaction that only one person could have executed that transaction.

Before the Internet, individuals struggled with the question. When you sign a legal document, often you need a notary. That notary is there to be part of the nonrepudiation process of gathering evidence. He or she takes copies of your identification and matches signatures. Some even take a thumbprint. All this effort is so that later you cannot claim it wasn't you who signed.

So how do you sign a document electronically? A leading method is to use a digital signature. If used properly, the electronic signature cannot be forged and is digitally timestamped. Most important, the receiver of the document can verify it is your digital signature. But even a digital signature relies on a private key that must be protected. It's worth noting that these digital signatures are legally binding under the U.S. Federal ESIGN Act of 2000.

However, many final electronic transactions do not use digital signatures. In fact, often online banking transactions, money transfers, or buying and selling stock rely on other technology, including strong authentication. Ultimately you want to prove that only that person could have executed that transaction. A leading vendor in this space is IBM, whose flagship product for secure messaging is called Websphere. IBM defines nonrepudiation as an end-to-end service that "can be viewed as an extension to the identification and authentication service." Although secure messaging ensures the collection and delivery of the transaction, the application that consumes the message still has to be proven as secure.

> **NOTE**
>
> The Federal ESIGN Act defines an electronic signature as an "electronic sound, symbol, or process, attached to or logically associated with a contract or other record and executed or adopted by a person with the intent to sign the record." To learn more, go to *https://www.fdic.gov/regulations /compliance/manual/10/x-3.1.pdf*.

It should be noted that the CIA triangle, although widely used in information security, is a somewhat simplistic model, and there have been expansions to it. The McCumber cube is one such expansion of the CIA triangle that is worth discussing. It was described in detail in 2004 in the book *Assessing and Managing Security Risk*

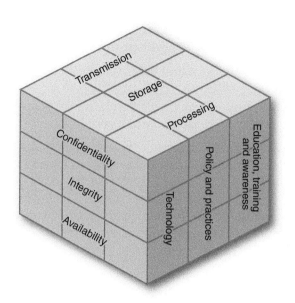

FIGURE 1-4

The McCumber cube.

in IT Systems: A Structured Methodology. It looks at security as a three-dimensional cube. The concept is to add more dimensions to the traditional CIA triangle. In addition to the three aspects of the CIA triangle, the location of information is addressed. Is the information in transmission, storage, or processing? Then the security aspect is addressed. Is the issue technology, policy and procedure, or education training and awareness? Thus, one might examine the policy and procedure aspects of confidentiality of data in transmission. Or one might address the technological issues of maintaining integrity of information in storage. The McCumber cube can be seen in **FIGURE 1-4**.

No one technology is foolproof, so many security experts believe that applying multiple security services collectively that tie the transaction back to a single individual is the best way to meet business needs. The simple fact is the more evidence you gather, the harder it is for that person to deny it. Ideally, businesses want to prove it was your computer, your ID, your digital signature, and your transaction that cannot be repudiated.

What Is Governance?

Governance is both a concept and a set of specific actions an organization takes to ensure compliance with its policies, processes, standards, and guidelines. The goal is to meet business requirements; however, the focus of governance is ensuring everyone is following established rules. What is assumed in governance is that these business objectives were well understood and baked into the rules. Thus, by following the rules, you achieve these business goals. Good governance should include a good understanding of the business, so when enforcement of a rule doesn't make sense, adjustments to the governance process can take place.

Governance in the real sense is much more than a concept. An organization puts formal processes in place and creates committees to act as gateways. These are tangible acts that collectively define the governance structure of an organization. Governance is a collection of checkpoints that perform either a **quality control (QC)** or **quality assurance (QA)** function. In this context, if the governance body must approve an action, then it's a QA function. If the governance body reviews actions after the fact, then it's a QC function. This distinction is critical in understanding how controls are managed. These terms are often misunderstood:

- Quality *assurance* functions act as a preventive control. When QA works well, it prevents mistakes from happening.
- Quality *control* functions act as a detective control. When QC works well, it improves the quality over time by affording opportunities to learn from past mistakes.

Think of this from the perspective of the forest and the trees. When you think about QA, think about looking at each tree to see if its healthy. In contrast, when you think about QC, you check to see if the forest is healthy.

Governance includes a series of oversight processes and committees. Collectively, governance ensures accountability, monitors activity, and records what is going on. What is also implied is that the governance structure will take action when the rules are ignored or not properly applied.

Why Is Governance Important?

Good governance provides assurance and confidence that rules are being followed. Who needs that assurance? First, senior management needs to know that its business objectives are being met. If the rules are being followed, there is some assurance the value promised to the business is being delivered. Also, senior management needs to know that the investment the organization has made is being properly managed. Second, regulators look at the governance structure for assurance that risks to shareholders, customers, and the public are being properly managed.

Effective governance embraces QA and QC as part of the culture. By embedding these concepts throughout, the organization promotes awareness and provides evidence of control. This is particularly important to regulators. Regulators want to see controls applied consistently. They want to know that management is aware of problems and that the company does not take shortcuts than can lead to breaking the law. Generally, the more confidence regulators have that a company has strong governance, the less regulatory oversight is used. This is especially true in highly regulated industries like healthcare and financial services. Failure to have strong governance means less opportunity to expand into new markets. Conversely, good governance means expanded business opportunities.

It's not unusual to assess the governance process of an organization. These assessments can be either self-assessments, internal audits, or regulatory reviews. For example, operational risk or compliance functions within an organization may perform a review.

The importance of governance is evident in a configuration management process. By controlling system configuration, previously mitigated vulnerabilities remain in check. This results in greater uptime rates. Change management often employs both QA and QC functions. QA governance routines review and approve each change. Whereas the QC function reviews the number of the outages caused by change and tries to improve the record, the QA function benefits from lessons learned. Governance is important to the daily operation of an organization and should not be viewed as an occasional occurrence. Integrating the annual cost of governance into **business as usual (BAU)** budgets keeps the benefits governance provides from being viewed as an unexpected expense.

What Are Information Systems Security Policies?

Security policies are actually a collection of several documents. They generally start with a set of principles that communicate common rules across the enterprise. It is these principles that governance routines use to interpret more detailed policies. Principles are expressed in simple language. An example may be an expression of risk appetite by employing the "need-to-know" approach to the granting of access. From these security principles flow security policies that detail how the principles are put into practice.

When combined, these policy documents outline the controls, actions, and processes to be performed by an organization. An example is the requirement that a customer provide a receipt when returning an item to a retail store for a refund. That may be a simple example of a policy, but essentially, it places a control on the return process. In the same manner, ISS policies require placement of controls in processes specific to the information system. ISS policies discuss the types of controls needed but not how to build the controls. For example, a security policy may state that some data can be accessed only from the office. How the security control would be built to prevent remote access, for example, would not appear in the policy.

ISS policies should cover every threat to the system. They should include protecting people, information, and physical assets. Policies should also include rules of behavior such as acceptable use policies. The policies must also set rules for users, define consequences of violations, and minimize risk to the organization. Enforcement will depend on the clarity of roles and responsibilities defined in policies. Remember, you need to hold people accountable for policies. When it's unclear who is accountable, a policy becomes unenforceable. Other documents in the **policy framework** provide additional support.

There are typically six different types of documents in a framework:

- **Principles**—Establish the tone at the top and the authority by which policies are enforced
- **Policy**—A document that states how the organization is to perform and conduct business functions and transactions with a desired outcome
- **Standard**—An established industry norm or method, which can be a procedural standard or a technical standard implemented organization-wide
- **Procedure**—A written statement describing the steps required to implement a process
- **Guideline**—A parameter within which a policy, standard, or procedure is suggested but optional
- **Definitions**—Statements that define the terms used in the policy documents and set the context in which the policies documents are interpreted

Many people refer to all these documents as "security policies," but they aren't necessarily. **FIGURE 1-5** depicts the relationship among these six types of documents. The figure shows that procedures and guidelines support policies. In addition, the figure indicates that

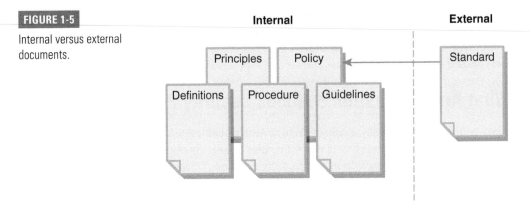

FIGURE 1-5

Internal versus external documents.

standards influence policies. The six documents fall into two groups: internal and external. Standards are external documents. The other five are internal documents.

A **standard** can be a process or a method for implementing a solution. This involves technology, hardware, or software that has a proven record of performance. This can be a procedural or implementation standard or a technical deployment standard implemented company-wide. For the purposes of ISS, a standard is the set of criteria by which an information system must operate. Standards exert external influence on the creation of policies. An organization can have internal standards. Often these standards are tailored to the organization based on some external best practice. The proper application of standards provides assurance that lessons learned within the industry have been considered.

NOTE

Standards become the measuring stick by which an organization is evaluated for compliance. The Federal Information Processing Standards (FIPS) publications are examples of standards. You can view FIPS publications online at *https://www.nist .gov/itl/publications-0/federal-information -processing-standards-fips.*

A **policy principles document** communicates general rules that cut across the entire organization. Principles are written in plain English and focus on key risks or behaviors. When reading security principles, think of them as senior executives expressing their goals and objectives. They express core values of the organization that often include the areas where there will be zero tolerance for transgression.

A **policy** is a document that states how the organization is to perform. It describes how to conduct business functions and transactions with a desired outcome. It sets the stage for secure control of information. It is the "who does what to whom and when" document. It should reflect what leadership commitments are to protecting information. Defined roles and responsibilities lay the foundation for enforcing the policy.

NOTE

A policy is often approved by the most senior levels of management. A procedure or guideline is often approved by lower-level management responsible for the implementation of policies.

A **procedure** is a written statement describing the steps required to implement a process. Remember that procedures support policies and standards. Procedures describe how to accomplish specific tasks. A more detailed procedure produces a more error-free result. Procedures are not written just for humans to follow. Well-written procedures are often used to document requirements for automated processes.

A **guideline** sets the parameters within which a policy, standard, or procedure can be used. A guideline is optional. It is a policy-support document. Similar to procedures, guidelines help businesses operate more smoothly. They are not as rigid. Although optional, they set a direction to be taken whenever possible. Once the new approach has been widely adopted, a guideline can transition into a policy.

A **policy definitions document** is often overlooked, yet it's enormously important. It's often used by auditors and regulators when evaluating the soundness of controls. Think of it this way: If you and someone else were speaking two different languages, you might recognize some of the other person's words. Yet, the depth of the meaning of these words could easily get lost. Even common words can have many meanings in the context of a policy. For example, if a policy refers to a user ID, does the policy apply to nonhuman and human IDs equally? If the term *platform* is used, does it mean desktop or server or router? Words in policies must be rich in meaning, clear, and concise. A well-constructed policy dictionary is key to achieving this goal.

How Policies and Standards Differ

Now that you know what policies are, let's discuss the difference between policies and standards. Policies implement controls on a system to make it compliant to a standard. Standards influence the creation of policies. Standards often determine a minimum requirement but can be very detailed in nature. Laws or agreed-upon practices produce standards. Standards then become the criteria for governance or certification and accreditation.

Standards often start with industry norms. Over time, organizations that represent the industry develop and publish standards. These standards often become the measuring stick by which regulators judge organizations. It's not uncommon for a company to adjust standards to meet specific needs, and then republish them internally as a company standard or internal policy.

Be cautious when deviating too far from industry standards. There are both civil and legal penalties for not following them. Consider the Payment Card Industry Data Security Standard (PCI DSS). It calls for the following penalties:

- Fines of $500,000 per data security incident
- Fines of $50,000 per day for noncompliance with published standards

How Policies and Procedures Differ

In a similar manner, you can contrast the difference between policies and procedures. As a reminder, policies are requirements placed on processes. Procedures are the technical steps taken to achieve those policy goals. Procedures can contain step-by-step instructions on the performance of a task. They can also identify how to respond to an incident.

Within a policy framework, there could exist a policy stating the requirement for disaster recovery planning. A separate procedural document would call out specific tasks to provide recovery services. In other words, procedures are the how-to document.

Creating Policies

Clearly, policies are a key part of information systems security. Thus, creating policies is an important task that must be executed in an effective manner. In addition to the previously mentioned COBIT, other tools aid in creating policies. The International Organization for Standardization (ISO) created the standard ISO 17799, which is titled "Information Technology—Security Techniques—Code of Practice for Information Security Management." This standard establishes best practices of control objectives and controls, including security policies. This is an excellent starting point for guidance on creating information system policies.

Another source is National Institute of Standards and Technology (NIST) 800-12, titled "An Introduction to Information Security." Chapter 5 of this standard is entirely about information security policy. It provides general guidelines for developing policies. Specific policy issues such as email privacy, bring your own device (BYOD), and social media are also covered. Reviewing NIST 800-12 in conjunction with ISO 17799 will provide you with a solid understanding of policy standards.

In addition to standards such as ISO 17799 and NIST 800-12, there are several other sources for policy information. For example, the SANS organization has a number of templates you can download; these are located at *https://www.sans.org/security-resources /policies*. If you are new to developing policies, reviewing templates and the policies of other organizations is helpful.

Where Do Information Systems Security Policies Fit Within an Organization?

Governance over information security policies fits at more management levels. Consequently, both business and technology leaders work closely together to ensure value is delivered. However, the actual implementation of information security policies is far more complex and requires deep technical knowledge. The implementation of ISS policies often falls to the technology teams of an organization. With technology ingrained into today's society, protecting information is everyone's concern. As you discovered about information systems security, there is more to consider than just the wires and computers.

Organizations rely as much on information systems as they do on human resources. In a production facility, computers control most manufacturing devices. In a nuclear power plant, electrical generation and contamination containment rely on controlling systems to ensure the flow of power keeps the lights on safely. In a legal office, an aide researches thousands of documents and case law through a remote vast online database. These are just a few examples of the impact information systems have on a daily basis. As you can see, technology continues to become a greater part of our daily lives.

FIGURE 1-6 shows the seven domains of a typical IT infrastructure. Each domain provides unique policy requirements. Within each domain, ISS policies are vital to maintaining a secure work environment that protects the information resources critical to their individual requirements. It is becoming harder and harder to understand and protect networks when outside vendors are involved, such as a cloud service provider. You may not have direct access to vendor systems that support your network, so you may not have the assurance that your network is fully protected.

FIGURE 1-6

The seven domains of a typical IT infrastructure.

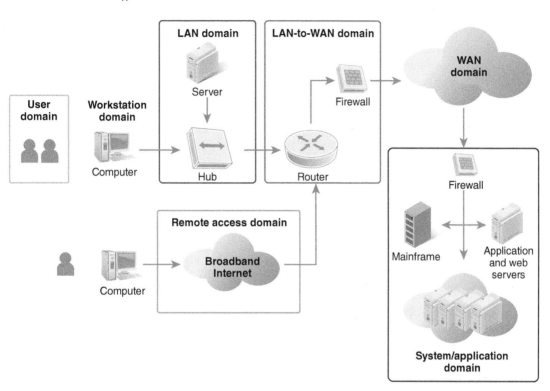

Why Information Systems Security Policies Are Important

ISS policies ensure the consistent protection of information flowing through the entire system. Information is not always static and often changes at it is processed. The information must be protected throughout the process at all times. Physical and logical access controls must work together to protect the data; however, that is not always the case. What about a disgruntled employee with elevated access privileges? How do you protect resources from someone with this kind of authorized access? Physical security has limits and should be viewed as one of several layers of control.

The following are foundational reasons for using and enforcing security policies:

- **Protecting systems from the insider threat**—The "insider threat" refers to users with authorized access. These are privileged users who would have the ability and access to wreak havoc on the system. The insider threat is probably the most significant threat to any information system. Policies help monitor authorized user activity.
- **Protecting information at rest and in transit**—Data is generally in one of two states— **data at rest**, such as on a backup tape, or **data in transit**, such as when traveling across a network. Essentially, policies help to protect data all the time.

- **Controlling change to IT infrastructure**—Change is good. Managing change is better. This reduces the risk of vulnerabilities being introduced to the system.
- **Defending the business**—Ensuring that the business can deliver reliable products and/or services will protect the company's brand.

Security polices strengthen an organization's ability to protect its information resources at all times while providing secure access to employees when they need it. Policies allow for control of the system, changes to the system, and reduction of much of the risk to the system.

Policies That Support Operational Success

The definition of operational success may vary from one organization to another. Governments may view stakeholder success differently from private industry. However, all kinds of organizations have a common concern: Is there a cost involved? Cost can be measured by either the cost of deploying policies or the cost of not having the policy in place. The cost of lacking a policy is often measured in terms of fines and legal expenses.

An effective way of expressing cost is through risk. By spending X, you can reduce Y amount of risk. For example, it would be reasonable to spend $50,000 to reduce a high risk of getting a $500,000 fine. This also allows for change in a controlled manner. It ensures that only policies that add true value are adopted. A good policy includes support for incident handling. Containing an incident can help reduce an exposure time to the organization. Identification of the reason for the incident can begin immediately and attackers potentially determined. A solution is more forthcoming, allowing the resource to be made available in a shorter amount of time. As most business folks will tell you, "Time is money."

By controlling costs and focusing on the most important risks, an organization can eliminate waste and support operational success. The key risks to the organization are reduced over time through continuous improvement achieved in part by having a good postincident handling process.

Challenges of Running a Business Without Policies

When an organization lacks policies, its operations become less predictable. Individuals will operate based on what they think is a good idea at the time. Imagine a rowing team without direction. Everyone has an oar and tries to arrive at a destination and avoid obstacles along the way. Even if you managed to arrive, think of the waste of going in circles as one side of the boat rows faster and with more urgency than the other. This assumes you can get the team to row at the same time. It's no different with policies. Policies allow an organization to row in the same direction applying the same rules, priorities, and business goals across the teams.

Here are a few challenges you can expect without policies:

- **Higher costs**—Due to wasted efforts and a lot of rework
- **Customer dissatisfaction**—Unable to produce quality because individuals make their own judgment as to what is right or good

- **Lack of regulatory compliance**—Individuals decide when and how to follow legal mandates

The result may well be legal action amounting to fines and loss of business. Depending on the industry, regulators may have the authority to close a business.

Let's look at a typical credit card breach. Assume a hacker gains access to data for 1 million credit cards. Additionally, assume the hacker accesses personal information such as Social Security numbers. Also, assume the company was out of compliance with industry norms in protecting its systems. The lack of security policies and resulting lack of methodical ways to manage risks allow vulnerabilities to these systems to go undetected. This could lead to lawsuits by customers and shareholders.

Dangers of Not Implementing Policies

If security policies are to ensure information is properly protected, failing to implement policies leaves information vulnerable. The information may be vulnerable to an attack or mishandling. Some employers say, "Our employees are the smartest in their fields," or, "We've been operating like that for years without a single problem (knock on wood)." These are also responses to the question, "Why implement policies?"

The dangers of not implementing policies are unexpected and undesirable outcomes. In the event of an ISS incident, employees will not know what to do, how to react, or whom to notify. This will lead to general confusion. As they're trying to figure out the answers to those questions, an attacker may be copying more information from the system.

Good security policies include creating awareness of security's benefits. This includes benefits to the employee. When good policies are implemented, they protect both customer and employee. With good policies in place, even if there is a data breach, the damage may be limited.

Dangers of Implementing the Wrong Policies

Similar to not implementing policies is implementing the wrong policies. You should create policies to address the proper processes, or detrimental consequences can occur. For example, consider a policy that states all employees should be granted administrator privileges to a system. Under this policy, the basic tenets of information assurance cannot be guaranteed. Users will have access to all information, which is probably not intended, nor is it a best security practice. Security policy is often a family of policies, so be sure they do not conflict with one another. In the event of a data breach, all employees with access immediately become suspect. This can often delay investigations.

When Do You Need Information Systems Security Policies?

"Timing is everything." This is most likely the No. 1 tenet of comedians. The same applies to the timeliness of policies. Why implement a policy on milking cows when your business model raises chickens? The possibility exists that your farm will expand operations one day, but there is no reason to write policies until that expansion occurs.

There will be times when the need for an ISS policy is evident. There is always a need for foundational security policies. This includes defining basic data handling and acceptable use policies. Security policies need to ensure that new technology is not introduced without a supporting set of policies in place. Another consideration is that you may have a process that occurs daily and all the involved employees are aware of that process. The employees may modify the process. But without configuration management control, modifications can make secure systems nonsecure. Or an important process may be undocumented, even though employees know all the steps. This is the perfect opportunity to formalize a written procedure.

Business Process Reengineering (BPR)

Business processes are constantly under scrutiny for improvement. As that business process life cycle is accomplished, the process is improved and changed; however, the associated policies must also be changed and updated. Typically, the associated policies and procedures recognized during the life cycle are operational in nature. Policies that support operations, like security policies, are not always considered. Failing to update those policies and procedures leaves a window of opportunity for error or disaster.

The process change could be dramatic enough to introduce new security vulnerabilities. If the equipment operating within the process completely changes, old security vulnerabilities reappear. Therefore, it is imperative to ensure that when reengineering any business process, you also review security. This will ensure that **business process reengineering (BPR)** includes ISS concerns, and those policies and procedures are updated as needed.

FIGURE 1-7 shows the four phases of BPR. Phase 1 is the planning phase. Phase 2 sees the creation or modification of the process baseline. Research and benchmarking happen in Phase 3. Phase 4 develops the future process; it is during this phase that new policies are written or current ones are updated. Phase 5 adds to governance routines.

Continuous Improvement

You can view **continuous improvement** as finding a better way or as a lesson learned. As employees find new ways to improve a system or process, you need to have a way to capture their ideas. The concept of continuous improvement applies to all aspects of ISS and IA. For example, when looking at availability issues, you may come across an authentication weakness. Regardless of how the weakness or risk was found, you need to capture the

FIGURE 1-7

Basic business process reengineering.

| Plan | Create/refine process baseline | Research and benchmarking | Develop the future process | Add to governance routines |

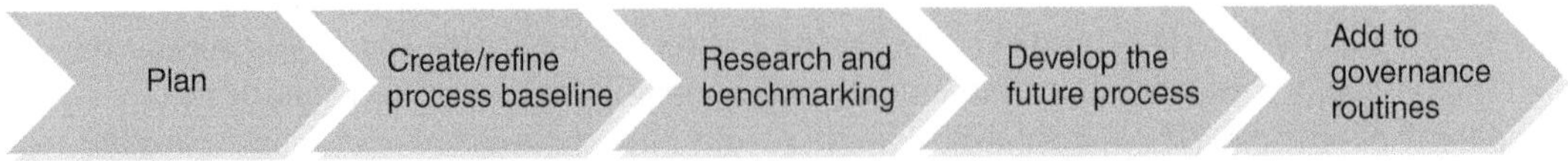

information, assess the importance, and apply an improvement. Often, lessons learned flow from effective governance. Quality control will reflect what worked well and what didn't. The part that didn't work well represents the lessons learned. Sometimes this means changing policy. When policy goals cannot be achieved, enforcement becomes impossible, and the overall security policy framework is weakened.

The driver for "finding a better way" should not be a system crash or breach. In those cases, you may have to deal with lessons learned from the incident. Think of continuous improvement as a suggestion box. Employees identify needed changes and write a suggestion. The suggestion is either accepted or rejected. If accepted, it enters the formal reengineering process.

Making Changes in Response to Problems

Even with a sound policy framework, issues will occur. Depending on the criticality of the issue, policy implementation or change can occur at any time in the process. Policy changes brought about in this manner help avoid future incidents. In a perfect environment, policies fall into place before incidents occur; however, most organizations do not operate in a perfect environment. Once an event not covered by a policy occurs, an event analysis takes place, and a recommendation is drafted. For events that are noncritical in nature, policy drafting comes about in concert with the remediation process. If it is more critical in nature, remediation should occur prior to writing the policy.

Why Enforcing and Winning Acceptance for Policies Is Challenging

There are many barriers to policy acceptance and enforcement. Without acceptance and enforcement of policies, employees could operate in a laissez-faire state. This runs counter to the business goals. It will inevitably lead to an employee not taking policy seriously. Employees taking shortcuts or ignoring policy can have serious impacts. Within an organization, there must be support at all levels, from the top to the bottom. Employees must have a stake in ISS. They must understand how those policies and procedures affect them and their business area. If they have a stake in creating or approving policies, they will be more likely to accept those policies. The following is a list of policy acceptance challenges:

- **Organizational support at all levels**—Without cohesive support from all levels of the organization, acceptance and enforcement will fail.
- **Giving employees a stake**—There must be something to motivate employees to buy in to the process. This could be some kind of award for participating, or disciplinary action if they don't.
- **Policy awareness and understanding**—Employees must know a policy exists and understand what it means. Crafting the document to make this easy can be challenging.

 NOTE

The biggest hindrance to implementation of policies is the human factor. Human beings must first fully understand the policy. Then the policy must be implemented and adhered to. Both of these activities can fail due to human error.

- **Rewarding and recognizing behavior**—Employees must see good examples to model their behavior after.
- **Hold individuals accountable**—Employees must know there is a consequence for repeated noncompliance.

Enforcement of policies can be just as difficult as policy acceptance. There are several reasons why enforcement is challenging. The language in which policies are written can be vague enough to be unenforceable. Infractions are not reported, which is often a key contributor to the lack of enforcement. Other business areas in the organization, such as human resources or the legal department, might not be part of the enforcement process. This can give employees license to either disregard the policies or perform actions contrary to them. The following list recaps policy enforcement challenges:

- Poorly written policies
- Failure to report infractions
- Lack of involvement in enforcement of key departments and management
- Lack of clearly defined roles and responsibilities

CHAPTER SUMMARY

This chapter defined foundational ISS concepts and key terms. You learned about the key tenets of ISS management to ensure confidentiality, integrity, availability, authentication, and nonrepudiation. Additionally, you read that information systems security (ISS) and information assurance (IA) are two separate but similar concepts. Associated with IA and ISS is governance. Governance ensures people are following the rules, such as policies, regulations, standards, and procedures. You also read about the importance of quality control and quality assurance.

There are several situations when security policies are to be considered. Opportunities include:

- New business processes
- Changes in current business processes
- Business process reengineering (BPR)
- Incident occurrence

You read about where policies fit within an organization to meet operational and governance requirements. These include all seven domains, across the business spectrum. ISS policies are important for several reasons. A primary reason is controlling authorized access to information. Another reason is to control change to systems. You read about how to express risk in terms of threats and vulnerabilities. Finally, you learned about policy acceptance and enforcement, and factors that make those processes difficult. Employee support is required at all levels for policy buy-in and enforcement. Enforcement also hinges on effective policy writing.

KEY CONCEPTS AND TERMS

Authentication

Availability

Business as usual (BAU)

Business process reengineering
(BPR)

Change management

Confidentiality

Continuous improvement

Data at rest

Data in transit

Entitlement

Governance

Guideline

Information assurance (IA)

Information systems security
(ISS)

Information systems security
management life cycle

Information systems security
policies

Integrity

Need-to-know principle

Nonrepudiation

Policy

Policy definitions document

Policy framework

Policy principles document

Procedure

Quality assurance (QA)

Quality control (QC)

Risk

Service level agreement
(SLA)

Standard

Threat

Vulnerability

CHAPTER 1 ASSESSMENT

1. John works in the accounting department but travels to other company locations. He must present the past quarter's figures to the chief executive officer (CEO) in the morning. He forgot to update the PowerPoint presentation on his desktop computer at the main office. What is at issue here?

A. Unauthorized access to the system

B. Integrity of the data

C. Availability of the data

D. Nonrepudiation of the data

E. Unauthorized use of the system

2. Governance is the practice of ensuring an entity is in conformance to policies, regulations, _____, and procedures.

3. COBIT is a widely accepted international best practices policy framework.

A. True

B. False

4. Which of the following are generally accepted as IA tenets but not ISS tenets? (Select two.)

A. Confidentiality

B. Integrity

C. Availability

D. Authentication

E. Nonrepudiation

5. Greg has developed a document on how to operate and back up the new financial section's storage area network. In it, he lists the steps required for powering up and down the system as well as configuring the backup tape unit. Greg has written a _____.

6. When should a wireless security policy be initially written?

A. When the industry publishes new wireless standards

B. When a vendor presents wireless solutions to the business

C. When the next generation of wireless technology is launched

D. After a company decides to implement wireless and before it is installed

7. A toy company is giving its website a much-needed facelift. The new website is ready to be deployed. It's late October, and the company wants to have the site ready for the holiday rush. The year-end holiday season accounts for 80 percent of its annual revenue. What process would be of particular importance to the toy company at this time?

A. Continuous improvement

B. Business process reengineering

C. Change management

D. Information security system life cycle

8. Implementation and enforcement of policies is a challenge. The biggest hindrance to implementation of policies is the _____ factor.

9. Information systems security policies should support business operations. These policies focus on providing consistent protection of information in the system. This happens by controlling multiple aspects of the information system that directly or indirectly affect normal operations at some point. Although there are many different benefits to supporting operations, some are more prevalent than others. Which of the following are aspects of ISS policies that extend to support business operations?

   A. Controlling change to the IT infrastructure
   B. Protecting data at rest and in transit
   C. Protecting systems from the insider threat
   D. B and C only
   E. A, B, and C

10. Trina is an administrator in the server backup area. She is reviewing the contract for the off-site storage facility for validity. This contract includes topics such as the amount of storage space required, the pickup and delivery of media, response times during an outage, and security of media within the facility. This contract is an example of information security.

    A. True
    B. False

11. A weakness is found in a system's configuration that could expose client data to unauthorized users. Which of the following best describes the problem?

    A. A new threat was discovered.
    B. A new vulnerability was discovered.
    C. A new risk was discovered.
    D. A and B
    E. B and C
    F. A, B, and C

ENDNOTES

1. Fadilpašić, Sead, "DDoS Attacks Are Getting Even Larger," ITProPortal, September 13, 2018, *https://www.itproportal.com/news/ddos-attacks -are-getting-even-larger/,* accessed April 14, 2020.

2. Help Net Security, "Average DDoS Attack Sizes Decrease 85% Due to FBI's Shutdown of DDoS-for-Hire Websites," March 21, 2019, *https://www.helpnetsecurity.com/2019/03/21 /average-ddos-attack-sizes-decrease/,* accessed April 14, 2020.

Business Drivers for Information Security Policies

WITH EACH PASSING YEAR, technology is more integrated into business. It is common for businesses to use technology for data management, financial transactions, advertisement, customer service, and a host of other activities. Almost all businesses and governments use technology to support their operations, from the most basic to the most complex. Dependence on information technology has grown so rapidly over the past decades that it's hard for people to envision their lives without it.

Consider what it would be like to disconnect from technology for a week. No cell calls. No GPS to find that new restaurant. No Internet. It's not only the products people use or consume, but also the way they get these products. Without technology, delivery of products and services often would not be possible. However, this integration of technology into our lives also introduces new threat vectors to our information. Whether in the public or private sector, the threat of information being stolen and the threat of unauthorized access are major concerns. When you reduce these types of risks to information assets, you reduce risks to the business as well. Security policies let your organization set rules to reduce risks to information assets.

The goal of information security is not to eliminate all risk. That is not possible. The goal is to effectively manage risk so the risk is at or below an acceptable level. What an acceptable level is varies between organizations and even within different segments (departments, teams, workgroups, etc.) in the same organization. A good policy can reduce the likelihood of risk occurring or reduce its impact. This is the essence of risk management. A business must find a way to balance a number of competing drivers. Some of these drivers include:

- **Cost**—Keep costs as low as practical.
- **Customer satisfaction**—Keep customer satisfaction high.
- **Compliance**—Meet regulatory obligations.
- **Measurement**—Be self-aware and avoid surprises.

Security policies define how to protect and handle information. These security policies should be brief and concise. They should define in simple terms how information should be handled and processed to meet business goals. Aligning security policies with business objectives makes policies easier to understand and more likely to be followed.

This chapter provides an overview of concepts that can reduce business risk. Although the term *business* is used, the concepts apply equally to both public and private organizations, and for-profit as well as nonprofit entities. When the term *risk* is used, it refers only to the risk to information assets. It is impossible to discuss all potential business drivers to reduce risk for every organization. This chapter focuses on key risk areas.

Chapter 2 Topics

This chapter covers the following topics and concepts:

- What a business driver is and why business drivers are important
- What it means to maintain compliance
- What business risk exposure is
- What business liability is
- What operational consistency is and why it is important

Chapter 2 Goals

When you complete this chapter, you will be able to:

- Describe basic business risks
- Explain the difference between business risk exposure and business liability
- Describe some techniques the business uses to reduce risk
- Explain the important issues related to operational consistency
- Describe the relationship between business risks and security policies

Why Are Business Drivers Important?

Computer systems continue to evolve and become more complex. This makes it hard for the business to understand the technology that supports it. Yet a security **breach** can have a significant impact on the bottom line. The following are three examples of why organizations need good security policies:

 NOTE

The business refers to the operations of either a public or private sector organization.

The national retailer Target Corporation, with more than 1800 stores in the United States, suffered a major data breach during the 2013 holiday shopping season. This breach put at risk the financial information of an estimated 40 million customers. The costs incurred to companies involved in this fiasco reached upwards of US$200 million.

In September 2018 it was discovered that British Airways had been breached, and the attacker injected malicious code into an insecure website, capturing customers' personal and payment data. The breach was believed to have impacted about 500,000 customers. In addition to the direct damage, British Airways faced fines based on the General Data Protection Regulation (GDPR) of US$230 million. GDPR is explored in Chapter 3.

In 2019, Capital One experienced a large data breach in which an attacker gained access to more than 100 million accounts and credit card applications. In addition to the direct damage from this attack, it also caused substantial harm to the company's reputation. As of this writing, this breach is still being investigated, and full remediation steps have not yet been made public.

One could argue that these cases resulted from a security policy failure. Each of these breaches is attributable, at least in part, to a failure either to have an appropriate policy or to enforce it. In 2019, Egress conducted a survey of data breaches.[1] Seventy percent of respondents believed that employees put the company data accidentally at risk in the last 12 months. In 2018, the Ponemon Institute conducted a survey of cybersecurity in small and medium-sized businesses. In this survey, respondents indicated that the risk of negligence leading to a data breach was getting worse. Sixty-one percent stated that negligent employees put the company at risk for ransomware, an increase from 2017 when 58 percent of respondents identified employee negligence as a proximate cause of ransomware attacks.[2] Although the exact percentage may vary each year, the point is that having good policies isn't enough. Businesses must be self-aware and measure whether those policies are being followed. Businesses cannot afford data breaches resulting from employees' failure to follow good policies.

Organizations are increasingly concerned with how information risks are managed and reduced. Security policies are not considered solely a technology issue anymore. Organizations also expect security policies to reflect how they want information handled. An organization's security policies, taken collectively, show its commitment to protect information. Good security policies keep the business healthy. Some of the basic concerns with implementing such a policy include:

- **Cost**—Cost of implementing and maintaining controls
- **Impact**—Impact on the ability of the business to serve the customer
- **Regulation**—The organization's capability to defend its policies and practices before regulators, should the need arise
- **Adoption**—The degree to which employees understand and are willing to follow policies—"to make them their own," in other words

Policies are effective only if they are enforced. Managers dislike surprises. Finding out later that security policies are too costly or that they negatively impact customers is not acceptable. To avoid this, management needs to take part in creating and implementing security policies. Even in the best of situations data can be stolen. By having good security policies, the organization is better positioned to defend its actions to the public and in the courts. For example, an email security policy that warns employees that their messages may be monitored can help defend against a lawsuit for violation of privacy.

Maintaining Compliance

The term *compliance* refers to how well an individual or business adheres to a set of rules. **Security policy compliance** means adhering to security policies. It is difficult to know whether an organization complies with every security policy. To state that an organization is compliant, you must be able to validate that the requirements within security policies have been applied to security controls and information. Difficulties arise due to the sheer volume of digital information. Even a relatively small business with only a few hundred employees could have tens of thousands of files. These files travel between servers, desktops, laptops, backup media, universal serial bus (USB) drives, and more. The issue becomes even more complex in large organizations with thousands of employees and millions of files. Knowing exactly what data is captured where and how it is used in an ever-growing complex environment is difficult. Businesses are concerned not only with files that employees can access, but also with files exposed to vendors and suppliers. A common issue with security in many organizations is that there may be adequate policies, but there is no effective mechanism to ensure compliance with those policies. Even the best policies are almost useless without some compliance assurance.

Compliance Requires Proper Security Controls

The key to security policy is being able to measure compliance against a set of controls. Security controls define *how* you protect the information. The security policies should define *why* you set the goal. This effectively bridges business requirements with security controls. The security policies also define *what type* of protection will be achieved. How you implement the security policy can vary. For example, implementing strong authentication depends on several factors. Do you understand what is meant by "strong authentication"? Are you aware of the technology choices available given your specific application? Within those choices, does your organization prefer to keep things standardized? Has the choice you made been properly approved? How do you measure that the right choices were made? How do you measure whether both the policy and the right processes were followed?

TABLE 2-1 provides a conceptual example of a high-level security policy and control statement. A policy must describe a clear set of actions needed to be compliant. Vague or open-ended statements create confusion. They may lead people to make incorrect choices. However, policies that are too detailed cannot be applied broadly. So, some situations can arise to which no policy applies. Again, this can be confusing and lead people to wrong choices. A well-written policy should follow a few basic guidelines. It is critical that a policy strike the right balance. It must be clear and concise. It must lead to specific outcomes and embody principles that can be applied broadly. Writing good policy is an art as much as a science.

 TIP

Make your security policies relevant to business needs. They stand a better chance of being followed.

To know whether an organization is complying with security policies, you must measure the level of compliance. The level of compliance can change depending on what exactly is measured. Consider the example in Table 2-1. You could perform a simple measurement of compliance by verifying that firewall rules exist; however, simple measurements can be less accurate or misleading. For example, assume four firewalls allow the traders access to the Internet. You check each firewall and find that three contain the proper firewall rule described in Table 2-1. At first glance, a simple measurement indicates the business is 75 percent compliant with this policy. On further inspection, you discover that the fourth firewall does not follow the required rule. This firewall represents 70 percent of the traders' Internet traffic. This new fact could mean the business is only 30 percent compliant.

TABLE 2-1 An Example of Security Policy and Control Components

POLICY OR CONTROL	ANSWERS	ISSUE
Security policy	Why	The Securities and Exchange Commission (SEC), under rule 17A-4, requires stock traders' conversations with clients to be recorded and retained. In this case, the purpose is to ensure a detailed record of transactions with the client. Establishing a record allows regulators to audit for compliance with disclosure rules.
Security policy	What	To ensure compliance, all traders should communicate with clients only through company telephones or the company's email system.
Security control	How	Using the firewall, stop all traffic for traders to the Internet except for web browsing and company email. For all security policies, the how is a critical component.
Security control	Measurement	All attempts by traders to use the Internet should be logged. Each trader's log should be reviewed by a manager at least monthly to ensure compliance. Effective metrics are the clearest way to assure compliance with policies.

A more accurate measurement gives the business more confidence to understand its risks. This clarity of thought on risk often leads to a consensus on a solution. Even when no solution is available, this strong understanding of risk can help an organization prepare if an incident occurs. It is not possible to measure compliance to each individual policy. With thousand or millions of transactions daily, not every employee action can be logged. So, taking measurements and reviewing logs often focus on high-risk activities— those activities that would lead to significant impact if the policy was not followed.

TABLE 2-2 illustrates what can be achieved with good policy compliance measurements.

 NOTE

Employees must be aware of and formally educated on all company policies. Awareness is the first step in ensuring policies are followed.

Security Controls Enforce Information Security Policies

Security controls are the means of enforcing security policies that reflect the organization's business requirements. These controls ensure the confidentiality, integrity, and availability of the information. They can be used to protect physical resources, including worker safety. They are also the means to measure security compliance. You should build security controls based on the security policies. If you know the security controls work, you know you are complying with security policies.

TABLE 2-2 Control Measurement Benefits

CONTROL MEASUREMENT CONSIDERATION	BENEFIT TO THE BUSINESS
Determine which security controls to measure.	Defines the scope of the compliance being measured
Determine appropriate metrics.	Defines precisely what metrics will be recorded and why. Measurement is only effective if the appropriate metrics are measured.
Verify these controls are working.	Defines the effectiveness of the controls being measured
Express compliance in terms of adherence to policy, not controls.	Defines what business goals are to be achieved
Express compliance in terms of potential impact to the business.	Defines the impact to the business if the goals are not achieved
Ensure there is a way to measure compliance.	Defines how the policy will be enforced

> **TIP**
>
> Reducing the frequency of security policy changes makes policies easier to enforce. It's also easier to train employees.

Security policies do not contain security controls; however, a security control may have to change if the related security policy changes. By treating them separately, you can change the control to meet the security policy. This is an advantage as technology evolves. For example, suppose you have six separate IDs and passwords to access six different systems. Let's assume technology is introduced to allow all six systems to recognize one ID and password. Much of the security policy on password controls may not change: You still know to keep your password a secret and how to select a complex password. When security policies are well established and understood by employees, they are more easily enforced. When policies change too frequently, they become confusing.

A number of classifications can be applied to security controls. The three most common are:

- **Physical control**—As the name implies, this refers to some physical device that prevents or deters access. A locked door, a camera, an electric fence, and a security guard are all examples of physical controls.
- **Administrative control**—Also known as a *procedural control*, this relies on a human to take some action. Some examples of a procedural control could be providing security awareness training or having a manager check an employee's work.
- **Technical control**—This refers to software that creates a logical control. Passwords and antivirus software are examples of technical controls. Dedicated hardware, such as a firewall, would be considered a technical control because it contains the necessary software to create the logical control.

Security controls also follow three unique design types—preventive, detective, and corrective—as shown in **FIGURE 2-1**.

FIGURE 2-1

Three unique security control design types.

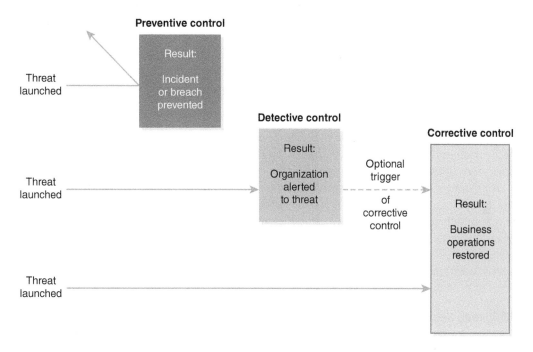

Preventive Security Controls

A **preventive control** stops incidents or breaches immediately. As the name implies, it's designed to prevent an incident from occurring. A firewall ideally would stop a hacker from getting inside the organization's network. This kind of control is an automated control.

An **automated control** has logic in software to decide what action to take. With an automated control, no human decisions are needed to prevent an incident from occurring. The human decisions occurred when designing the security control.

Detective Security Control

A **detective control** does not prevent incidents or breaches immediately. Just as a burglar alarm might call the police, a security control alerts an organization that an incident might have occurred. When you review a credit card statement, your review is a detective control. You review the statement for unauthorized charges. The process of reviewing the statement did not prevent the unauthorized charge from occurring. The review, however, triggers corrective action if needed.

Perhaps the most obvious information security detective control is an intrusion detection system or intrusion prevention system (IDS/IPS). Such systems observe network activity for anomalies that appear to be related to either an attack or a violation of specific policies/rules. Then, when anomalies are detected, they are logged, and the appropriate personnel are notified. In the case of the IPS, an additional step occurs: the anomalous traffic/activity is terminated.

NOTE

If human action is required, the control is considered manual. If no human action is required, the control is automated.

Some detective controls are considered **manual controls**. A manual control relies on a human to decide what action to take. Still, manual controls can have automated components. For example, a system administrator could automatically receive a cell phone text when the number of invalid logon attempts reaches some threshold on a server. The administrator still needs to take some manual action. However, the aforementioned IDS/IPS are automatic controls that operate without human intervention, and then inform a human operator.

Corrective Security Control

A **corrective control** does not prevent incidents or breaches immediately. It limits the impact to the business by correcting the vulnerability. How quickly the business can restore its operations determines the effectiveness of the control.

For example, backing up files to enable data restoration after a system crash is a corrective security control. A corrective control is either automated or manual. For instance, you may automatically mirror (create exact copies of) files and then restore them in the event of hard drive failure. This is an automated control. If a human is required to decide when to restore the backup, that is a manual control. As a general rule, automated controls are preferred when feasible because when a control is automated, it is no longer subject to human error or even forgetfulness.

Mitigating Security Controls

To appreciate and understand how data is protected, you must look beyond a single control. It is important to look at how preventive, detective, and corrective controls work together. For example, assume someone entered the wrong Social Security number by accidentally reversing two of the digits. There may not be a control in place to catch this mistake as it's entered; however, later in the process, a corrective control may catch and correct it. When considering how well protected the system is, look at the process end to end. Although there may be a lack of control on the front end, there may be something that stops it on the back end. That back-end control would mitigate any negative impact and so would be considered a mitigating control. Mitigating controls can be preventive, detective, or corrective. Just keep in mind that anything meant to mitigate an issue is a control. Controls can be technical, they can be policy, and they can be behavioral.

Beyond having all three areas of controls, it is often advantageous to have multiple controls of the same type. For example, in preventing viruses, an organization should have policy controls in addition to technical controls. To continue this example, policies regarding opening email attachments, downloading from the Internet, plugging in external devices, and the implementation of antivirus software are four separate controls, all designed to mitigate the occurrence and impact of malware.

Mitigating Risk Exposure

As previously stated, it is impossible to eliminate risk. The goal is simply to mitigate risk. More specifically, the goal is to mitigate risk such that the residual risk is at or below acceptable levels. How can information security policies help? Well-defined security policies balance business requirements and limit behavior. The policy reflects how the business wants to manage its risks. The importance placed on such issues as customer privacy and protecting company secrets directly influences employee behavior.

Security policies must drive a culture that mitigates risk exposure. Policies, and the way they are enforced, reflect the business perception of risk. They are more than just simple business requirements that translate into security controls. Policies can reduce business risks by setting the tone at the top and promoting a risk-aware culture.

 NOTE

Tone at the top refers to a company's leaders making sure every employee knows the priorities. In this case, it means senior management's stated commitment to security policies. Beyond words, the actions taken by senior managers to implement and enforce policies build trust with the public and with regulators.

Educate Employees and Drive Security Awareness

Security is ultimately a function of people, processes, and technology working well together. A well-educated employee goes a long way toward reducing risk. Policies cannot define every risk. Unlike automated security controls, which look only for specific risks, an aware employee can better detect unusual activity. This ability to detect and deal with the unexpected makes employees extremely valuable in reducing business risk.

A good **security awareness program** makes employees aware of the behaviors expected of them. All security awareness programs have two enforcement components, the carrot and the stick. The carrot aims to educate the employee about the importance of security policies. You can use rewards to motivate compliance. The stick reminds the employees of the consequences of not following policy. Motivation is a powerful tool in any environment. Positive reinforcement often yields better results than negative consequences. Unfortunately, you may need both components to implement a successful security policy program.

 NOTE

If policies are optional, employees might treat them simply as guidelines. If you never enforce a policy, employees might perceive it as irrelevant or unimportant.

You can implement a security awareness program in many ways. Here are some generally accepted principles:

- **Repetition**—Most employees do not deal with risk daily, so they need to be reminded.
- **Onboarding**—New employees should be told of their responsibilities immediately.
- **Support**—Leaders should provide visible support.
- **Relevance**—Rules that show awareness of the business context are more likely to be followed.
- **Metrics**—Measure the effectiveness of policies.

The presentation of security awareness training is also critical. Security awareness is about good communication. It's not about memorizing policy word for word. You need to focus on key concepts and teach employees when to ask for help. An employee should know what to do when encountering something suspicious or unexpected. Be sure to point out resources such as intranet sites within the organization. Most important, a security

 TIP

Refresh your security awareness training program at least once a year. Retrain employees after revising the program. It is important to connect with your audience. Just like a commercial, you are selling a message. Use whatever approach works. Humor works well.

awareness program should teach an employee where to go for help. New employees espe-cially need to know they are not alone in dealing with unexpected issues.

Leaders need to provide visible support for the program. Training takes time away from employees' regular work. Leaders need to walk the talk. They themselves need to take the training and reinforce the message with their teams. How leaders reward when policies are consistently followed or react when they are not sends a strong message. The daily message sent by leaders determines the **risk culture** of an organization.

A security awareness program gains credibility when the business sees a reduction of risk. Each employee plays a role in the business process. Multiple benefits come with a secu-rity awareness program that emphasizes the business risk, including:

- **Value**—Policies relevant to business are more likely to be followed by the business.
- **Culture**—Well-understood and enforced security policies promote a broad risk culture.
- **Resiliency**—Policies provide a basis for dealing with the unexpected.

Competence is difficult to measure. At a minimum, most programs track names of those who attended classes; however, simply taking roll is not a good way to measure competency. Many awareness programs have short quizzes to test key areas of knowledge. The challenge is that an employee may need to apply the knowledge long after the class ends. Often the best measure is noting real-world problems that occurred by not following policy. That way you can go back and continuously improve the training.

A risk-aware culture may be the critical success factor that affects the business the most. This means a culture that shares a common set of values, beliefs, and knowledge about the importance of managing risks. When you develop a risk-aware culture, people want to do the right thing all the time. It is second nature to follow the rules and support one another. This translates into an increased likelihood of policies being followed. When this behavior is modeled every day by everyone, it becomes the norm and defines the risk culture.

Prevent Loss of Intellectual Property

The Legal Information Institute, created by Cornell Law School, defines **intellectual property (IP)** as "any product of human intellect that is unique and un-obvious with some value in the marketplace. Intellectual property laws cover ideas, inventions, literary creations, unique names, business models, industrial processes, computer program code, and more."[3] Intellectual property can include patents, copyrights, and trademarks; however, IP is not limited to those three categories. In business, IP is a term applied broadly to any company information that is thought to bring an advantage. For instance, you need to protect secrets in order to protect your advantage over competitors. IP comes in many forms and can be electronic or physical. Security policies should state how to protect that information regardless of format.

Certainly, there are technological measures that can aid in protecting IP, but the focus in this text is policies. Protecting IP through security policies starts with human resource (HR) policies. The first step is screening employees to try and reduce the likelihood of an employee disclosing IP. However, these HR policies also establish a code of conduct. They should give employees clear direction as to what the organization owns with respect to IP. The issue of IP ownership can be confusing when a new employee brings to the workplace IP acquired or created while he or she was at another firm. Employment agreements may even attempt to enforce the confidentiality of IP after an employee leaves the organization or for work performed during the employee's spare time. These HR policies and employment agreements may or may not be enforceable, depending on current law and location. Nonetheless, when building security policies, you should take a close look at HR policy. You want to be sure there are no conflicts between HR policy and security policy.

Labeling Data and Data Classification

The first step is labeling intellectual property. Is this data confidential? Is it proprietary? Once an organization clearly defines its intellectual property (IP), the security policies should define how to label or classify the information. There is a difference between labeling and classifying data. In both cases, a label identifies the level of protection needed. A **label** is typically a mark or comment placed inside the document itself; for instance, putting a "confidential" label in the footer of a document. When you classify a file in a process known as **data classification**, a label may or may not be applied. When data classification is applied, the sensitive file is placed in a secured location.

Some organizations can have difficulty inventorying their intellectual property. IP material comes in many forms. Consider a simple document labeled as sensitive IP. Portions of the document may be cut and pasted to create new material. How much of that new material should be considered IP? Although this can be difficult, the generally accepted approach is to label what you can. Restrict access based on the label. Treat any new document containing any portion of the original IP with the same restrictions you placed on the original material. Unfortunately, there can be a merging of confidential data with nonconfidential data. Thus, there is a need to clearly label and classify data.

One of the most important deliverables of security policies is the labeling and data classification approach. The approach selected will drive the cost of handling data. An employee needs to know how to handle both kinds of information—labeled and classified. Security policies instruct an employee on the proper handling depending on the business requirements. The combination of the following is a widely accepted practice to help prevent loss of IP:

- Label and classify IP data.
- Restrict access.
- Filter email and other communication tools for IP data.
- Educate employees on handling IP material.

Even civilian organizations can take some direction from Department of Defense data classifications. The U.S. Department of Defense classifies data as confidential, secret, or top secret, and there are a few other special classes of top-secret data (such as sensitive compartmented information [SCI] and special access program [SAP]). Although a civilian organization may not require that much fine-tuning, a minimum of confidential vs. public classification is necessary. Then confidential data can be further labeled as patent, trade secret, business process, customer data, or whatever data labels are appropriate for the organization. Whatever methodology the organization selects, the most important thing is consistent labeling of data.

Protect Digital Assets

Digital assets are any digital content an organization owns or has acquired the right to use. *PC Magazine* defines digital assets as "Any digital material owned by an enterprise or individual including text, graphics, audio, video and animations. A digital asset is owned by an organization if it was created on the computer by its employees or if it was custom developed for and purchased by the organization. Images scanned into the computer are also a digital asset if the original work was owned by the company."[4] The term *digital assets* is often inaccurately applied to all computer-related resources. This chapter will use the strict definition.

It is also important to inventory the various assets. You can protect digital assets with a good inventory. Only at the moment you identify a specific digital asset and apply a label or data classification do you know where the data is. The challenge is keeping track of the information as it is moved, changed, created, and deleted. A good inventory of digital assets allows you to design security controls where the data resides. Security policies define what an asset is. They also define what label or classification should be applied. You can see these key relationships needed to protect information in **FIGURE 2-2**.

The ability to protect information starts with well-defined security policies. The definition of digital assets is so broad it is difficult to create a complete inventory. Many organizations rely on tools that scan servers, desktops, and laptops. They try to inventory sensitive information based on patterns such as Social Security numbers (SSNs). When they see a pattern match, they can determine the level of security control to apply.

To protect digital assets, you need to know where your data is. You need good tools to inventory information and networks. You will need to refresh this inventory often. Finally, you need to be able to label or classify data quickly. The sooner data is labeled or classified, the sooner it is protected. The ability to inventory digital assets is a major policy implementation issue.

FIGURE 2-2

Key components in protecting digital assets.

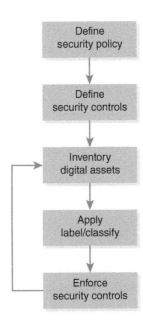

Once data is inventoried, it's fairly straightforward to apply a label or classify the data. But you need to be sure the security policies clearly define the handling for each label and data class. It's almost impossible to classify every data file. Think of the thousands of files on a single personal computer or laptop: data in the form of documents, essays, screen shots, pictures, tax returns, and much more. Much of this is considered unstructured data. The data was not predefined or as well organized as you would find in a production environment such as a bank, which will have defined processes for transactions such as taking deposits. Production systems organize data in a well-defined manner. Their processes are unambiguous and repeatable.

Applying data classification to unstructured data is a major challenge. Often data classifications are applied to where data is stored. In other words, you may not know all the files within a user's laptop, but you know it's a user's laptop. Based on that knowledge, any data placed on a laptop may have a certain data classification. This is a good technique when assessing data classification at a file level is not possible.

> **WARNING**
>
> Creating an accurate inventory is a major problem, given the speed at which data files are created, deleted, moved, and changed. Not knowing where your highly sensitive data is at any point in time is a major risk. Mobile devices such as USB drives and smartphones that can receive email compound the problem. And how do you protect information when it leaves your network? An organization should prioritize the inventory of assets, starting with the most sensitive.

2

Business Drivers for
Information Security Policies

Technical TIP

Whenever possible, you should put inventory tools that automatically classify data into *log mode*. In log mode, the security control records only what it would have done but does not take the action. Then, by reviewing the logs with management, you can assess the impact of classifying data in that way. It is not unusual for automated tools to overclassify, locking the business out of key systems. For example, let's assume you highly restrict access to customer addresses. Potentially, the logs would show that the customer care desk could not access the data to verify customers' identity when they call in for help. You can avoid upset users by rehearsing log use before applying preventive controls. In this example, no actual customers or business functions would be affected. The security control could then be adjusted to include access for the customer care desk. Log mode is a good way to gain business support for implementing more restrictive security controls.

Secure Privacy of Data

It is human nature to crave privacy when it comes to our personal matters. People want their highly personal information to be secure—whether it is their medical or financial records. What many do not realize is that this information can be stored in digital files in computers anywhere in the world. Your personal information might be found with an offshore vendor in China. Regardless of where your personal data travels, securing and protecting this information is both a trust and a legal obligation. This chapter focuses on U.S. privacy obligations; however, all developed countries throughout the world have some form of privacy laws.

NOTE

Different states have varying laws that define what is included as PII. For instance, one state may consider a person's home address a **public record**, whereas another may not. States vary also in how they require data to be handled to protect privacy. Most large companies adopt a single policy that can be applied to multiple states.

The concept of protecting privacy starts with data that identifies people as unique individuals. The U.S. Government Services Organization cites the Office of Management and Budget (OMB), which defines **personally identifiable information (PII)** as:

> Information which can be used to distinguish or trace an individual's identity, such as their name, social security number, biometric records, etc. alone, or when combined with other personal or identifying information which is linked or linkable to a specific individual, such as date and place of birth, mother's maiden name, etc.[5]

Security policies need to define PII data by business type and location. A bank, for example, follows different federal regulations than a local check-cashing service or medical clinic. The state in which you operate could have different requirements than a neighboring state. Widely accepted practices help businesses navigate the maze of privacy regulations. For example, most states consider the combination of a person's name and SSN as PII. With identity theft, a major concern for both businesses and consumers, you should be careful of any combination of information that could be used to open or access an account. Depending on the business, these types of data have a good chance of falling within the PII definition.

NOTE

The chief privacy officer provides direction on how to handle legal requirements regarding PII data, including how to report incidents.

Because organizations must follow many different privacy regulations, some organizations have established a **chief privacy officer (CPO)** position. This is the most senior leader responsible for managing an organization's risks. The CPO is responsible for keeping up with privacy laws. The CPO also needs to understand how the laws impact business. Due to the nature of the work, many CPOs are lawyers. Although they are generally not technology people, they work closely with technology teams to create strong security policies.

You should consider the following guidelines when developing policy to secure PII data:

- **Examine**—Understand local state and federal requirements.
- **Collaborate**—Work closely with the CPO.
- **Align**—Coordinate privacy policies with data classification policies.
- **Educate**—Conduct awareness training on handling of PII data.
- **Retain**—Ensure proper controls around data retention and destruction.
- **Limit**—Collect only the data you need from an individual to provide the service or product.
- **Disclose**—Fully disclose to the individual what data is being collected and how it will be used.
- **Encrypt**—Consider using encryption when storing or transmitting PII data.

Full Disclosure and Data Encryption

Privacy regulations involve two important principles. *Full disclosure* gives the consumer an understanding of what data is collected and how the data is used. *Data encryption* provides a standard for handling consumer information.

The first principle—**full disclosure**—is the idea that an individual should know what information is being collected. They should also be told how that information is being used. Many people use the Internet as a quick-and-easy way to buy products and services. It seems like just as quickly your email inbox fills with offers from other companies. Did the online service collect and sell your information? Did the company fully disclose how that data was to be used? These are the issues that a privacy policy needs to address.

> **NOTE**
>
> Some regulations allow companies to sell customer data if the individual gives permission through an *opt-in* process. Other states allow for the sale of information but require that the consumer be given a choice through an *opt-out* process.

The second principle—**data encryption**—recognizes that even with the best efforts, data can fall into the wrong hands. This happens when data is stolen, lost, or accidentally accessed. Encrypted data can be read only when the user has the correct decryption key. For example, Roy has an encrypted hard drive containing his business ledgers. Moss finds Roy's laptop, but Roy's financial information is still secure because the hard drive cannot be read without an encryption key. This provides an additional layer of security.

Encryption is a preventive security control. But encrypting data and managing encryption keys can be complicated and expensive. Although expensive, it's often a lot less expensive than having to notify millions of customers that their personal information has been lost or stolen. Beyond loss of trust, companies may face legal penalties.

Encryption is considered an effective practice. Encrypting data when transmitting over the Internet is commonplace today. Encrypting data at rest on a server's hard drive or mass storage array is far more complicated if multiple technologies are involved. Sometimes, encrypting data at rest is not technically possible.

Technical TIP

Payment Card Industry Data Security Standard (PCI DSS) mandates the use of encryption for transmitting and storing credit card information. Companies and vendors have created materials to support these PCI requirements. Even if your organization does not process credit cards, this material could provide helpful guidance on encryption for protecting PII data. The Cisco PCI Solution for Healthcare Design and Implementation Guide, for example, outlines a conceptual model for protecting data, including encryption components. The guide is located at https://www.cisco.com/c/en/us/solutions/enterprise/design-zone/compliance.html

Lower Risk Exposure

Well-defined and enforced security policies lead to well-defined controls. These controls, in turn, protect the information. So how do you achieve lower risk exposure? The concept of exposure relies on a calculation that estimates the losses to the business in the event the risk is realized. First you need a scale that allows you to measure risk against predicted business losses. Over time, you invest in people, processes, and technology to lower that risk to an acceptable level. That acceptable level is sometimes called your "risk appetite."

What a risk appetite tells you is how much loss an organization is willing to accept in the normal course of business. These calculations are made in many different businesses and industries. Credit card companies estimate losses from fraud and invest in countermeasures. As the fraud rises, so does the spending to stop it and lower the risk exposure. You calculate the loss if these events occur and invest in programs to lower the risk exposure. For example, most banks today have changed their security policies to require much more rigorous screening of calls to the customer service desk. It's not unusual for a customer to be asked more detailed questions than just their name, account number, and SSN. A customer could be asked about current balances, last transactions, and other details in an attempt to reduce risks of fraud.

There is no easy way to calculate risk to the business in the event of a security breach. Ideally, you should calculate risk exposure in terms of total potential losses in financial terms. Given that security breaches could also result in reputation damage, it is hard to calculate that in financial terms.

Some organizations take an easier approach. They calculate risk exposure in terms of security policy compliance. This approach takes a leap of faith that if you comply with good security policies, you are adequately controlling the risk. This approach lets you lower risk exposure to the business by measuring and improving policy compliance over time.

Regardless of approach, you cannot rely exclusively on risk score. A risk score is quantitative and as such is a numerical representation of multiple factors. It does not replace risk judgment. Nor can it replace a person making a qualitative judgment through experience and common sense. Risk scores are based on factors people think they understand at a moment in time; however, the risk scores may not keep up with changes in the environment, technology, or the market. The danger is in blindly following the numbers (the quantitative judgment) when common sense and experience (the qualitative judgment) say the risk is much higher. Think of the financial crisis of 2007–2008, with trillions of dollars in losses and millions put out of work. Many risks were considered low. This is an oversimplified example, but generally quantitative scores for many banks assumed that housing prices would continue to rise forever. So, it didn't matter how much you loaned, there would always be buyers for properties and homeowners would always have equity. The qualitative side, the human judgment and common sense, was missing. As a result, the United States endured the worst financial crisis since the Great Depression of the 1930s.

Minimizing Liability of the Organization

A *business liability* emerges when an organization cannot meet its obligation or duty. Business liability is a subset of an organization's overall risk exposure. An obligation can be either a legal or a promised commitment.

If a business fails to follow the law, it has violated its *legal obligation*. This liability leaves the organization open to potential fines or limits how it conducts business. In rare cases, an organization can be found to have engaged in criminal conduct. Its officers could then face criminal charges.

A business not living up to promised commitments loses the trust of customers. When a business fails to deliver the product or service it promised, the liability is lost business. Customers post complaints on the Internet, creating the potential for lawsuits and more business loss. Customer opinions are easily and widely spread today via social media, postings on product review sites, and the like. It is increasingly important that businesses live up to their commitment to customer service.

NOTE

Business liability occurs when a company fails to meet its obligation to its employees and community. A business's *legal obligation* is an action it is required to take in compliance with the law.

The role of security policies is to reduce these liability risks. When hackers breach a company's security, for example, you often have both trust and regulatory issues to deal with. Each event has potential liabilities. Reviewing past events to predict future situations will help you gauge overall risk exposure and specific business liabilities. Policies must define the proper handling of each of these types of events.

Separation Between Employer and Employee

It is important that an employer act quickly when a known violation occurs. The employer may not be responsible for an employee's action, but the employer's failure to act will create the impression that, despite written policy, the employer condones the employee's action. This could create legal liability for the employer. It's not enough just to have a written policy. The policy must be enforced. Employees must be held accountable and, as needed, disciplined for noncompliance. This protects the customer and the employer.

Policies make clear to an employee what acceptable behavior is. Policies also provide a degree of separation from employees who fail to follow rules. A business can point to its policies as a statement of what should have occurred. The ability to defend the organization's position to the public and regulators is an important byproduct of security policies.

However, just having security policies will not create this separation. The business is obligated to take steps to implement and enforce the policy. Some of these reasonable steps include:

- **Policy**—Have clear security policies on the handling of customer information.
- **Enforce**—Express strong disapproval when policy is not followed.
- **Respond**—Quickly respond to incidents to minimize the impact to customers.
- **Analyze**—Understand what happened.
- **Educate**—Improve employee training.

These steps will minimize losses and show a commitment to customers. When challenged by the public or regulators, this will also help separate the employer's actions from a rogue employee.

TIP

Be sure to work with in-house legal counsel on policy strategies to lay the foundation for defending the organization in the event of an incident.

Acceptable Use Policies

Acceptable use policies (AUPs) are formal written policies describing employee behavior when using company computer and network systems. Most AUPs outline what is acceptable and unacceptable behavior. They also need to outline the disciplinary process when an employee violates policy. Because the disciplinary process could lead to termination, the policy must be clear and concise. Many companies require the employee to sign the AUP to acknowledge receipt of the rules. Both the legal and HR departments always approve final draft policies. It is important that an AUP keep up with technology changes. It must be clear when personal devices are allowed during business hours. In particular, many company policies today cover mobile phone use. Often, these policies also include an overview of the use of cameras. However, few policies today cover the use of the wearable devices that are becoming available. Google Glass, for example, can take a picture with a blink of an eye.

The AUP is an important tool to create a legal separation between the employer and employee. Little tolerance exists for employees who create unnecessary liability for the organization. For example, using company computers to harass or threaten others, or view obscene materials, could result in termination.

Confidentiality Agreement and Nondisclosure Agreement

A **confidentiality agreement (CA)**, also known as a **nondisclosure agreement (NDA)**, is a binding legal contract between two parties. It is a promise not to disclose any information covered by the agreement to a third party. The agreement needs to clearly define the information covered. This reduces problems that may arise between the two parties or any other party asked to resolve legal disputes.

These types of employment agreements are often made at the time of hire. They outline what information should not be disclosed outside the company. These agreements could bind the employee from disclosing company information after employment terminates. If the organization did not have an NDA as part of the hiring process, this can be an issue later. It is important to begin implementing NDAs.

 NOTE

Not all CAs and NDAs are written the same way. They can be one-sided, granting excessive rights or penalties to one side. They should be reviewed by the legal department before being signed.

NDAs are not used only with employees. They are often used with business partners. The CA or NDA is often used to explore business opportunities before buying a product or service. Let's say a company wants to hire a consultant to redesign a major computer application. Both parties would sign a CA. The company could then disclose its problems and the consultant would have more precise information on which to base an estimate. The CA would bind both parties even if the company decided not to hire the consultant.

Security policies typically include guidance regarding when a CA or an NDA should be required. Most security policies require such agreements to be in place before any data can be exchanged. This includes requiring such agreements to cover employees and nonemployees, such as temporary or contract workers. This is especially important for nonemployees who may not go through the company's normal security awareness training.

Business Liability Insurance Policies

Business liability insurance lowers the financial loss to the business in the event of an incident. Even when a business has well-defined security policies, problems can still occur. Business liability insurance will pay for losses within the limits of the policy.

Business liability insurance can be issued to both organizations and individuals. For
example, a computer engineer performing consulting services could obtain professional
liability insurance. Such a policy would cover any successful claims that the engineer was
negligent or made errors. The same type of coverage would apply to large companies facing
claims that their product or services were negligent or in error. The provisions of the coverage need to be examined closely. For instance, coverage may be dependent on the company
complying with industry norms. What does that mean? Let's say you are maintaining a
company website. Standards in your particular industry may dictate that you must perform
annual penetration testing. Failure to perform the test or to comply with your own policies
could lead to your insurance claim being denied.

An important benefit of this insurance coverage is the payment of legal fees. Even when
a company is found innocent, the legal costs can be substantial. These policies do have limits, conditions, and requirements that the policyholder must meet. These policies also have
exclusions. They do not protect a company that has committed illegal acts. Overall, these
policies are another tool to further reduce risk.

Implementing Policies to Drive Operational Consistency

Operational consistency means ensuring that an organization's processes are repeatable and
sustainable. The business goal is to have these processes executed each time with the same
consistency and quality. This reliability allows the business to continuously improve quality.
Processes evolve over time, and the more repeatable a process can be, the more likely it is
that risks can be detected and removed.

You can implement security policies in the same way. This ensures that the same consistency and quality are applied to protection of information. What is meant by "a repeatable
process" or "consistency"? It means when a particular risk is found again and again, the
same process is used to address it each time. This consistent execution is often referred to as
operational consistency.

Forcing Repeatable Business Processes Across the Entire Organization

Operational efficiency means lower costs to the business. By applying this principle
across the enterprise, greater quality results can be achieved at a lower cost. For
organizations with multiple divisions, developing processes once and repeating them
saves time and resources. This approach also allows the organization to develop centers of excellence. These centers are typically small teams with very deep knowledge
of a subject area.

An *enterprise view* allows senior leaders to understand how risk affects the entire organization. Someone with an enterprise view can see past the individual part to the entire structure. Such a person can see the forest and not just the trees. A single tree or group of trees
might have root rot; however, the overall health of the forest may be good. This means you

have a problem, but it is localized. Conversely, individual process failures may seem insignificant, but collectively they may indicate a systemic problem.

This is particularly important when it comes to security policies. Leadership needs a high level of certainty that there is operational consistency in how information is protected. Leadership is often asked by regulators to attest to security controls. For example, the chief information officer (CIO) under the Sarbanes-Oxley (SOX) Act is required to describe IT security controls goals. Many CIOs point to their company's enforced security policies.

To achieve this repeatable behavior, you must measure both consistency and quality. Additionally, you will need to measure whether the implemented policy is achieving the desired results. It is not surprising to find processes that run for years while providing no real value. A typical example might be a report that was specially designed for an executive who has since left the company. The new executive continues to receive the report. He or she may even occasionally review it out of curiosity. But the executive never leverages its content for any real purpose. This report might be highly repeatable and sustainable, but it does not provide value.

TIP

Be sure to interview the individuals who created or manage the process. They will have insights beyond the measurements.

Security policies drive operational consistency by enforcing how information is handled the same way within business processes. Policies also force close oversight and measurement of the processes. Security policies often outline oversight requirements. They explain which measurements should be captured and how often reporting is required. The following oversight phases are typically found when trying to achieve operational consistency:

- **Manage**—Manage process execution and note exceptions to standard procedures.
- **Measure**—Measure volume, consistency, and quality.
- **Review**—Periodically assess to ensure desired results are achieved.
- **Track**—Track defects, errors, and incidents.
- **Improve**—Improve quality continuously by making adjustments as needed.

Differences Between Mitigating and Compensating Controls

A **mitigating control** limits the damage caused by not having a control in place. It assumes the absence or breakdown of a primary control. It is a control after the fact. For example, suppose someone enters an invalid account number. Either a control did not exist to prevent this or that control did not work. Either way, as long as the account number is validated before further action can be taken, there is a mitigating control in place. A mitigating control, however, may not achieve the full intent of a policy.

In contrast, a **compensating control** achieves the desired outcome and policy intent. It doesn't necessarily achieve it the way the policy says to do it, but the outcome is the same. Back to the example: Suppose before the account number can be entered, a master list of accounts is checked manually. Ideally the error would be caught immediately, but the manual check is still a preventive control. If the policy required an automated validation of all account numbers at time of entry, the system would be out of compliance; however, the manual check is a compensating control, and the risk is mitigated.

Understanding mitigating and compensating controls is essential in granting exceptions. What you must figure out is how much risk is left and whether that risk is acceptable.

Policies Help Prevent Operational Deviation

Operational deviation is inevitable. It's important the intent be clear in a policy. From clearly communicated intent comes a better understanding of the desired outcome. Intent also helps employees know better what risks the company is not willing to take. It is impossible to foresee every possible circumstance. For one thing, security policies tend to cover broad topics. Second, technology is always evolving. Good policies allow the employee to apply the intent and understanding of risk to situations not explicitly outlined.

Operational deviation from policy in itself may not be a problem when there is a solid business reason. However, as the number of exceptions grows, the policy's credibility is potentially reduced. Security policies are put in place to reduce risk. Deviating from those policies could increase the risk and prevent meeting legal obligations.

To balance these interests, most organizations have an exception process. This is also called a *waiver process*. Typically, you submit a waiver request to a centrally managed team that reviews and approves the deviation. The waiver process examines the business rationale and tries to determine whether the exception is necessary. When implementing a waiver process, the following should be considered:

- **Independence**—Be independent of the business unit seeking approval.
- **Impact**—Examine the risk to the entire organization.
- **Benefits**—Understand the business benefits.
- **Mitigation**—Identify security controls outside of policy.
- **Approvals**—Residual risk should be formally accepted by management.

Residual risk is the risk that remains after security controls have been applied. When the business cannot comply with policy, the residual risk needs to be measured and compensating controls considered. A compensating control can reduce the same risk identified by policy but in a different way from what is outlined in policy. Ideally you want to implement compensating controls that reduce the same amount of risk identified in policy. If not, they should at least reduce some of the risk. When you cannot implement a preventive control as required by policy, consider using a detective control. These compensating controls may be outside policy but may be able to reduce some or all of the risk. Any remaining risk would then have to be properly approved. Proper approval includes vetting residual risk with those leaders who would be held accountable in the event the risk is realized. For example, if the application could not meet security policy requirements on protecting PII data, the CPO needs to approve the exception. Ultimately, if PII data is lost or stolen because of the policy exception, the CPO may have to explain to regulators why the exception was permitted.

CHAPTER SUMMARY

People manage risk every day of their lives. They choose when to go bed, when to wake up, what foods to eat, what route to drive their cars, and much more. Each decision has risk and rewards attached. This is no different in the business world. People face many decisions daily. They often operate with incomplete information. They are faced with critical deadlines that could be more easily met by sharing information outside policy guidelines. As you gain experience, these decisions become more instinctive.

For business, it is daily processes and decisions that control risk. Policies provide guidance on how to think about risk. Policies and their related controls detail how to prevent, detect, and correct errors. This landscape of controls and processes makes risk management real for every employee. Most important, it encourages behavior that positively drives the organization's risk culture.

KEY CONCEPTS AND TERMS

Acceptable use policies (AUPs)
Automated control
Breach
Chief privacy officer (CPO)
Compensating control
Confidentiality agreement (CA)
Corrective control
Data classification
Data encryption

Detective control
Digital assets
Full disclosure
Intellectual property (IP)
Label
Manual controls
Mitigating control
Nondisclosure agreement (NDA)
Operational deviation

Personally identifiable information (PII)
Preventive control
Public record
Residual risk
Risk culture
Security awareness program
Security policy compliance

CHAPTER 2 ASSESSMENT

1. What is policy compliance?

   A. The effort to follow an organization's policy
   B. When customers read a website policy statement
   C. Adherence to an organization's policy
   D. Failure to follow an organization's policy

2. What is an automated control?

   A. A control that stops behavior immediately and does not rely on human decisions
   B. A control that does not stop behavior immediately and relies on human decisions
   C. A control that does not stop behavior immediately but automates notification of an incident
   D. A control that stops behavior immediately and relies on human decisions

3. Which of the following is *not* a business driver?

   A. Ability to acquire the newest technology
   B. Cost of maintaining controls
   C. Ability to legally defend
   D. Customer satisfaction

4. A firewall is generally considered an example of a _____ control.

5. What is an information security policy?

   A. A policy that defines acceptable behavior of a customer
   B. A policy that defines what hardware to purchase
   C. A policy that defines how to protect information in any form
   D. A policy that defines the type of uniforms guards should wear

6. Which of the following is *not* a type of security control?

   A. Preventative
   B. Correlative
   C. Detective
   D. Corrective

7. *Tone at the top* refers to:

   A. A company's leaders making sure every employee knows the priorities
   B. Senior leaders implementing and enforcing policies
   C. Senior managers building trust with the public and with regulators
   D. All of the above

8. Privacy regulations involve two important principles: full disclosure and data encryption.

   A. True
   B. False

9. What are the benefits to having a security awareness program emphasize the business risk?

   A. Risk becomes more relevant to employees.
   B. Security policies are more likely to be followed.
   C. It provides employees a foundation to deal with unexpected risk.
   D. All of the above

10. Which of the following is *not* a guideline to be considered when developing policy to secure PII data?

   A. Align—Coordinate privacy policies with data classification policies.
   B. Retain—Ensure proper controls around data retention and destruction.
   C. Disclose—Fully disclose to the individual what data is being collected and how it will be used.
   D. Resiliency—Policies provide guidelines for the unexpected.

11. Information used to open or access a bank account is generally considered PII data.

   A. True
   B. False

12. Which of the following is *not* a benefit of having an acceptable use policy?

   A. Outlines disciplinary action for improper behavior
   B. Prevents employees from misusing the Internet
   C. Reduces business liability
   D. Defines proper behavior while using the Internet

13. Mitigating controls always meet the full intent of the policy.

   A. True
   B. False

14. Which of the following do you need to measure to achieve operational consistency?

   A. Consistency
   B. Quality
   C. Results
   D. All of the above

15. Well-defined and properly implemented security policies help the business in which of the following ways?

   A. Maximize profit
   B. Reduce risk
   C. Produce consistent and reliable products
   D. All of the above

ENDNOTES

1. Egress.com, "IT Leaders and Employees Differ on Data Ethics, Ownership and Root Causes of Insider Breaches," May 22, 2019, *https://www.egress.com/en-US/news/insider-data-breach-survey-2019-na*, accessed April 15, 2020.

2. Keeper Security, "2018 State of Cybersecurity in Small & Medium Size Businesses," Ponemon Institute, 2018, *https://keepersecurity.com/assets/pdf/Keeper-2018-Ponemon-Report.pdf*, accessed April 15, 2020.

3. Legal Information Institute, "Intellectual Property," *https://www.law.cornell.edu/wex/intellectual_property*, accessed April 15, 2020.

4. MediaValet, "What Is a Digital Asset," *https://www.mediavalet.com/blog/what-is-a-digital-asset-2/*, accessed April 15, 2020.

5. https://www.gsa.gov/reference/gsa-privacy-program/rules-and-policies-protecting-pii-privacy-act

Compliance Laws and Information Security Policy Requirements

I N RECENT YEARS, **globalization** has been driven by technology and the growth of the Internet. Internet usage statistics show that as of 2019, 57.3 percent of the world's population, or 4.4 billion people, have Internet access.[1] In North America and Europe, that number is above 85 percent. Several other sources report similar numbers.[2,3]

The expansion of Internet access continues to grow rapidly in developing countries. The Internet's explosive reach has created global economic opportunity never seen before. You can see this in products you buy every day. Technology has helped create a global supply chain that delivers to consumers worldwide an array of low-cost goods that would have been unimaginable just a few years ago.

But the speed with which the Internet has expanded has come at a price. Privacy is an issue. People may feel, not unreasonably, that every action they take is being captured. Cellphones leave computer records of who called whom. Social media provides channels for cyberbullying in schools. Hackers have been able to steal massive amounts of credit card information through the Internet. Countries have used the Internet to launch attacks on other countries.

In February 2014, President Obama declared, "Cyberterrorism is [the] country's biggest threat."[4] In general, **cyberterrorism**, or *cyberwarfare*, refers to an attempt to cause fear or major disruptions in a society through hacking computers. The idea is to attack government computers, major companies, or key areas of the economy. Such attacks can come from terrorist groups or individuals, as well as **nation-states** (sovereign countries).

President Obama's statements still ring true. In 2019, there was an attempt to attack U.S. power companies that many sources believe was sponsored by the Chinese government.[5] The Center for Strategic and International Studies reported that in May 2019, Iran was using a network of websites to launch a disinformation campaign against several nations, including the United States, Israel, and Saudi Arabia.[6] Clearly, these threats have not abated since 2014.

With so much at stake, governments cannot sit on the sidelines. In the United States, the federal and state governments establish laws that define how to control, handle, share, and process the sensitive information that this new economy relies on. Much of that information is about you. It's personal data about your finances, health, buying habits, and more. To these laws are added *regulations*, typically written by civil servants to implement the authority of the law. *Regulators* are the individuals or entities who help enforce these rules. Industry groups also try to *self-regulate*, which means they create standards their members must follow. Failure to follow regulations or industry standards can result in fines or limits placed on a company's ability to operate. Gross violations of regulations can be seen as violation of criminal law. These violations can result in the arrest of officers of the company and possible jail time.

This chapter discusses major government laws and their compliance requirements. When the term *regulation* appears in this chapter, it relates to either U.S. laws or laws that are widespread around the globe. You will read about how requirements influence security policies. You will also learn about major drivers for the regulations and the importance of protecting personal privacy. You will see how to create compliant policies, standards, procedures, and guidelines. The chapter also examines industry standards that drive security policies. Any one of these laws or standards could take up the pages of an entire book. The focus here is on high-level principles that drive security policies and controls.

This chapter will focus primarily on U.S. laws and regulations; however, specific non-U.S. laws are also explored due to either their significance to U.S. businesses or their exemplary content. For example, the Global Data Protection Regulation (GDPR), although a European Union (EU) law, also affects any business operation in the EU. This includes e-commerce platforms with European customers. Thus, it is important for even U.S. businesses to be aware of this regulation.

Chapter 3 Topics

This chapter covers the following topics and concepts:

- What U.S. compliance laws are, and why they are important
- Who is protected by these laws
- How security policies are influenced by the laws
  - Non-U.S. laws
- What approaches are used to make security policies, standards, procedures, and guidelines comply with regulations
- What industry leading practices are
- Why industry standards are important

Chapter 3 Goals

When you complete this chapter, you will be able to:

- Compare and contrast different U.S. compliance laws
- Describe regulations and their importance in organizations
- Describe government drivers to implement regulations and their importance in maintaining compliance with laws
- Define cyberterrorism and the nation-state threat
- Explain approaches to align policies with regulations
- Explain leading practices and how they fit into the industry

U.S. Compliance Laws

Tremendous economic benefits flow from private markets. These benefits often rely on the use of technology. There is no single way of looking at government's role in regulating or intervening in these markets; however, government is concerned with consumer protection, promoting a stable economy, and maintaining a reliable source of tax revenue. The government must balance these needs against the threat of cyberterrorism. All of these drivers are linked. If people feel safe using the Internet to buy goods and services, a stable economy emerges. People also have to trust the government to keep them safe. When you have a stable sector of the economy, government has a reliable source of tax revenue.

It is good to understand what drives government regulations. In the end, government regulations are mandates. Security policies must achieve their goals while balancing business needs. Organizations put stronger security in areas where the perceived threats to resources or employees are greater.

When you implement security policies, remember that there are business and regulatory pressures that can lead to tradeoffs. For example, you may have to place restrictive controls on data to comply with a regulation that limits how your business operates. If your company is part of the country's critical infrastructure, there may be certain security policies it must comply with. As you balance competing interests, you must talk to business leaders to understand their priorities and issues. Security policies reflect how the business wishes to balance competing interests.

> **NOTE**
>
> Key elements of the country's transportation, energy, communications, and banking systems are referred to as its **critical infrastructure**. Examples are power companies, oil and gas pipelines, and large banks.

Shareholders of a company are investors who expect to make money. Maximizing profit and maintaining a healthy stock price are business concerns. The government focuses more on fairness, health, and safety issues. One of the challenges organizations face is the cost of keeping pace with ever-changing technology. This includes the need to update policies at the same time the organization updates technology. Failure to do so could create weaknesses in the system. These weaknesses could make business processes out of compliance with industry and government regulations. The role of well-defined security policies is to be clear and concise on how these goals and vulnerabilities will be addressed. **FIGURE 3-1** illustrates these competing interests—shareholder value, technology vulnerabilities and limitations, and regulations.

Government agencies that regulate information handling exist at the federal and state levels. These agencies sometimes have competing interests. As a result, laws often overlap requirements but are written from different perspectives. A federal banking regulation, for example, might define **data privacy** differently than a state law does. Competing regulatory agencies may have different missions and use different enforcement tools. Compliance can be difficult and costly with conflicting language and different interpretations; for example, a large U.S.-based bank needs to comply with hundreds of regulations.

Staying compliant means incurring the cost to keep up with changes in many laws, continually documenting evidence of compliance, and dealing with onsite visits of regulators. Staying compliant with regulations can be a distraction for businesses and the technology teams that support them. Yet they are very important. In large companies, compliance teams act as a go-between for the technical staff and regulators. These compliance teams know

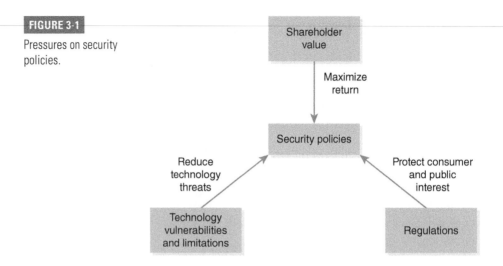

FIGURE 3-1

Pressures on security policies.

the regulations and requirements. They obtain information from the technical teams. The compliance teams meet with regulators. These are usually specially trained individuals who know company policy, the company's technological capability, and the law. This allows the technical staff to stay focused primarily on delivering technological solutions.

What Are U.S. Compliance Laws?

What are the major concerns of U.S. regulations? How do you manage competing interests in security policies? As much as these regulations might differ, there are also common concepts. In recent years there has been increased partnership between the U.S. government and private companies. This partnership comes in many forms, such as the sharing of good security policies and the sharing of resources to investigate hacking incidents. Most notably, the government now shares intelligence information about threats and the type of attacks that might occur. In February 2013, the White House issued an executive order for key agencies to share cyberthreat information with private companies.[7] This sharing of cyberthreat information helps companies better defend themselves.

The best approach to regulatory compliance is common sense. Rather than building rules into security policies for each regulation, you should build in the key control concepts found in many regulations. By mapping these key control concepts to specific security policies, you can quickly demonstrate compliance across a broad set of regulations. If you can master these concepts, you can learn how to recognize these principles in regulations. This gives you the basic tools needed to keep your security policies compliant.

It's not possible to discuss all key concepts for information security in every U.S. regulation. This chapter discusses several major regulations that deal with consumer rights and personal privacy. These laws protect consumers from potential scams and ensure the privacy of personal information. **Consumer rights** in e-commerce broadly deal with creating rules on how to handle a consumer's transaction and other information. **Personal privacy** in e-commerce broadly deals with how to handle personal information and what it is used for. **TABLE 3-1** identifies key concepts found in many regulations that influence what will appear in your security policies.

TABLE 3-1 Key Concepts Contained in U.S. Compliance Laws Affecting Information Security Policies

CONCEPT	OBJECTIVE
Full disclosure	The concept that individuals should know what information about them is being collected. A company must give written notice on how it plans to use your information.
Limited use of personal data	The concept that the company can use the information collected only for the immediate service provided or transaction made, such as a purchase. For example, assume a bank just approved your credit card purchase of ski equipment. In most states, the bank could not then share that information with someone who will try to sell you a ski vacation.
Opt-in/opt-out	The practice of asking permission on how personal information can be used beyond its original purpose. For example, a real estate company might ask permission of someone who sold their home if their information can be shared with a moving company.
Data privacy	A company must tell an individual how personal information will be protected, and limits are placed on how the data will be shared.
Informed consent	The concept that someone is of legal age, has the needed facts, and is without undue pressure to make an informed judgment.
Public interest	The concept that an organization has an obligation to the general public beyond its self-interest. It's a vague term, but it's not unusual for regulators to look at the impact an organization has on the industry or the economy in general.

Federal Information Security Management Act (FISMA)

The federal government is unique in that it can identify the standards it wants to follow and passes laws requiring the standards to be followed. The Federal Information Security Management Act (FISMA) of 2002 is a good example of government self-regulation. FISMA requires government agencies to adopt a common set of information security standards. Some parts of the government, such as the military, go beyond these standards. For many government agencies, FISMA creates mandatory requirements to ensure the integrity, confidentiality, and availability of data. If your organization processes data for the government, you may be required to follow these same standards. FISMA also requires that agencies send annual reviews to the Office of Management and Budget (OMB). For example, an audit of the Veterans Affairs (VA) Department in 2012 found 15,000 security policy violations. As a result, the VA was found to be noncompliant with FISMA. In 2018, a report was released of the FISMA audit of the Securities and Exchange Commission (SEC). It recommended 20 different corrective actions.[8] These two case studies would tend to indicate that FISMA compliance is still not where it should be with many federal agencies.

The National Institute of Standards and Technology (NIST) is responsible for developing FISMA-mandated information security standards and procedures. Each agency is then responsible for adopting them as part of their agency's information security policies. NIST standards, processes, and guidelines are available at *http://csrc.nist.gov /publications/sp/*.

NIST publications outline a complete set of security standards and processes. To be compliant, your policies must include key security control requirements. Some of these key requirements include:

- **Inventory**—An inventory of hardware, software, and information identifies the type of information handled and how data passes to the systems, and pays special attention to national security systems.
- **Categorize by risk level**—Inventory needs to be classified. The idea is that this classification will highlight higher-risk areas that need more protection.
- **Security controls**—The NIST standards outline which controls should be applied and when. They also outline how these controls are documented and approved. The approach is risk-based, which gives some flexibility to the agency to tailor controls to meet its operational needs.
- **Risk assessment**—Risk assessments are also required. **Risk assessments** are an essential part of a risk-based security approach. The risk assessment results drive the type of security controls to be applied.
- **System security plan**—A formal security plan for major systems and for the system or application owner is also required. The security plan serves as a road map. It is updated to keep current with threats and is an important part of a certification and accreditation process.
- **Certification and accreditation**—This process occurs after the system is documented, controls are tested, and risk assessment is completed. It is required before going live with a major system. Once a system is certified and accredited, responsibility shifts to the owner to operate the system. This process is also referred to as the *security certification* process.
- **Continuous monitoring**—All certified and accredited systems must be continuously monitored. Monitoring includes looking at new threats, changes to the system, and how well the controls are working. Sometimes a system has so many changes that it must be recertified.

⬛ **NOTE**

The difference between opting in and opting out generally refers to clicking a box on a webpage. In an **opt-in** process, unless the consumer clicks the "Yes" box, no additional service is offered. In an **opt-out** process, the consumer is automatically enrolled in a service unless he or she clicks the "No" box or deselects the "Yes" box.

Health Insurance Portability and Accountability Act (HIPAA)

The Health Insurance Portability and Accountability Act (HIPAA) became law in 1996. The law protects a person's privacy. If you handle someone's health records, you must adhere to HIPAA. This includes doctor's offices, hospitals, clinics, and insurance companies. The law recognizes that digital data exchange of health records, such as between insurance companies and doctor's offices, is a necessity. But in 2013, new restrictions were placed on access to health records by subcontractors and vendors. The law wants to make sure that patient privacy is maintained.

3

Compliance Laws and Information
Security Policy Requirements

FYI

The U.S. Department of Health and Human Services has several publications on HIPAA privacy and security standards at *https://www.hhs.gov/hipaa/index.html.*

The HIPAA law defines someone's health record as protected health information (PHI). The term PHI refers to both digital and physical paper copies of health records. Electronic PHI (EPHI) refers to the electronic form of PHI records. HIPAA establishes privacy rules that outline how EPHI can be collected, processed, and disclosed. There are significant penalties for violating these rules. In 2013, these fines were increased to a maximum of $1.5 million per violation. This regulation applies to any covered entity that manages health records, including:

- **Healthcare providers**—Doctors, hospitals, clinics, and others
- **Health plans**—Those that pay the cost for the medical care, such as insurance companies
- **Healthcare clearinghouses**—Those that process and facilitate billing
- **"Business associates"**—Vendors and subcontractors of any covered entity

For your security policies to be HIPAA-compliant, they must include the following key control requirements:

- **Administrative safeguards**—Refers to the formal security policies and procedures that map to HIPAA security standards. It also refers to the governance of the security policies and their implementation.
- **Physical safeguards**—Refers to the physical security of computer systems and the physical health records.
- **Technical safeguards**—Refers to the controls that use technology to protect information assets.
- **Risk assessment**—Refers to a standard requirement of a risk-based management approach to information security.

 NOTE

In January 2013, new HIPAA rules were issued to improve privacy rights. Key provisions of these new rules are:

- Increased fines of up to $1.5 million per violation
- New requirements on sharing information with contractors
- Stricter requirements on reporting breaches
- Requirements for improved privacy notices

HITECH

HIPAA was enhanced in 2009 with the Health Information Technology for Economics and Clinical Health (HITECH) Act.[9] Among other enhancements, HITECH imposes data breach notification requirements for unauthorized uses and disclosure of unsecured or unencrypted PHI. HITECH also expanded HIPAA compliance requirements to business associates of medical providers.

Gramm-Leach-Bliley Act (GLBA)

The Gramm-Leach-Bliley Act (GLBA) became law in 1999. The law is not focused on technology; rather, it was meant to repeal existing laws so that banks, investment companies, and other financial services companies could merge. Prior to GLBA, banks, for example, were restricted on the types of products they could offer. However, in addition to this, under what is known as Section 501(b), the law outlines information security requirements for the privacy of customer information.

The law is enforced through regulators who are members of the Federal Financial Institutions Examination Council (FFIEC). The FFIEC publishes booklets of what type of computer security policies and controls must be in place for an institution or company to be compliant with GLBA. These booklets define availability, integrity, confidentiality, accountability, and assurance as key objectives.

FYI

The FFIEC booklets are used by many government agencies. They are available to the public. Aligning security policies to these booklets will help keep a company compliant with government regulations. See *https://ithandbook .ffiec.gov/it-booklets.aspx.*

FYI

GLBA applies to any financial institution, defined as "any institution the business of which is engaging in financial activities as described in section 4(k) of the Bank Holding Company Act (12 U.S.C. § 1843(k))." This is broadly defined to mean any organization that lends, exchanges, transfers, invests, or safeguards money or securities. Generally, any company that deals in credit or loans would be covered. This includes businesses offering payment plans, such as those that car dealerships commonly offer.

The FFIEC booklets are publicly available through the council's website. The following website introduces the 501(b) rules: *http://ithandbook.ffiec.gov/it-booklets.aspx.*

To be GLBA-compliant, your security policies must include the following key components:

- **Governance**—Requires a strong governance structure in place. This includes designating someone in an organization as accountable for information security. This is often the **chief information security officer (CISO)** or **chief information officer (CIO)**. Most boards receive formal GLBA reporting through the audit committee. The head of information security usually writes this report each quarter.
- **Information security risk assessment**—Requires a well-defined **information security risk assessment** to identify threats, potential attacks, and impacts to the organization.
- **Information security strategy**—Requires a formal security plan to reach compliance.
- **Security controls implementation**—Requires a process to properly design and install security controls that meet the security plan objectives.
- **Security monitoring**—Requires continuous monitoring of security controls. This is to ensure that the design meets the objectives. This is event-based monitoring and includes incident response.
- **Security monitoring and updating**—Requires monitoring of trends, incidents, and business strategies, and appropriate updates to the security plan.

Sarbanes-Oxley (SOX) Act

The Sarbanes-Oxley (SOX) Act became law in 2002. The law was enacted in reaction to a series of accusations of corporate fraud. Some companies were accused of "cooking the accounting books" or making illegal loans to their top executives. Companies such as Enron and WorldCom became symbols of corporate greed and corruption. Enron filed for bankruptcy in 2001 amid accusations of cooking the books to inflate its stock price. WorldCom filed for bankruptcy in 2002 amid accusations of illegal loans to its chief executive officer (CEO), as well as billions in accounting fraud to inflate the stock price. These two highly visible corporate fraud cases shook shareholder and public confidence. SOX was enacted to restore confidence in the markets.

SOX goes well beyond information security policies. It also describes how a company should report earnings, valuations, corporate responsibilities, and executive compensation. The act is intended to improve the financial accuracy and public disclosure to investors. In fact, some argue the act goes too far and is too costly. This chapter focuses on those portions that affect security policies known as SOX 404.

The basic idea behind SOX 404 is to require security policies and controls that provide confidence in the accuracy of financial statements. In other words, security policies must ensure the integrity of the financial data. Independent testing of these controls is required. Additionally, top executives are required to sign off quarterly that these controls meet SOX 404 requirements or explain why they do not.

One of the challenges of SOX is cost. It is expensive and nearly impossible to test *all* a company's controls. The requirement to test all possible controls drew many complaints from companies, so in 2007, the government changed the rules for SOX. The change allowed companies to limit testing to only the most important controls—those in areas of high risk. This lowered costs for many companies. It also made it easier for a company to prove it was compliant. All security controls are important. Well-written security policies highlight key controls to indicate which are most important.

> **NOTE**
>
> SOX requires annual testing of controls. It is not enough, under SOX, to have security policies. SOX also requires that the controls in the security policies be tested to ensure they are working. Remember, SOX only applies to publicly traded companies; it does not apply to privately held companies.

The act created the Public Company Accounting Oversight Board (PCAOB). The PCAOB sets accounting and auditing standards. The Securities and Exchange Commission (SEC) is responsible for enforcing SOX. The challenge for information security is that SOX 404 sets broad IT objectives. It does not define how to comply. Rather than developing new information security and control standards, the PCAOB and SEC have endorsed using industry best practice frameworks. The following are endorsed frameworks that companies commonly use to meet SOX 404 requirements. These frameworks are widely used by external auditors as well to certify SOX compliance:

- **Committee of Sponsoring Organizations (COSO)**—As it relates to security policies, this organization creates rules for implementing internal controls and governance structures.
- **Control Objectives for Information and related Technology (COBIT)**—Created by ISACA, formerly known as the Information Systems Audit and Control Association, this framework is an internationally recognized best practice. Keep in mind that although many are still using COBIT 5.0, there is a newer version, COBIT 2019, that has some additions.

In many ways, COBIT is "one-stop shopping" for SOX security policies and controls. The controls within COBIT are a rich range of activities: strategic planning, governance, life cycle, implementation, production support, and monitoring. The framework fits in and supports the COSO framework. The COBIT framework allows COSO to focus on the business side while COBIT focuses on the IT side. By leveraging both, you are able to bridge control requirements, technology issues, business risk, and shareholder concerns. The reason the framework is so popular among regulators, auditors, and IT risk professionals is that if you implement the COBIT framework, you are most likely SOX 404–compliant.

FYI

ISACA has a number of publications publicly available through its website. You can find an executive summary of COBIT 2019 at *https://www.isaca.org/resources/cobit/*.

Family Educational Rights and Privacy Act (FERPA)

The Family Educational Rights and Privacy Act (FERPA) was put into law in 1974. This law applies to educational institutions such as colleges and universities. Any educational institution must protect the privacy of its student records and must provide students access to their own records. This gives students a way to correct errors and control disclosure of their records.

The Family Policy Compliance Office of the U.S. Department of Education enforces the act. The law broadly defines education records as any information related to the educational process that can uniquely identify the student. This has been widely interpreted as any student information, from financial means to class lists to grades. The student records can be in any form, from handwritten notes to digital files. There are exclusions such as law enforcement or campus security records. For the purpose of this discussion, the important point is that this broad set of student records (in any form) must be protected.

To be FERPA-compliant, security policies must contain the following key elements:

- **Awareness**—The school must post its FERPA security policies and provide awareness of them.
- **Permission**—Generally, schools must have recorded permission to share the student's education records.
- **Directory information**—The school can make directory information (such as name, address, telephone number, and date of birth) about the student publicly available but must provide the student with a chance to opt out of such public disclosure.
- **Exclusions**—The school can share information without permission for legitimate education evaluation reasons as well as for health and safety reasons.

Security policies must ensure records are kept when student permissions are not obtained under the exclusions. In addition, policies must ensure that opt-in and opt-out records are properly maintained for historical purposes to record student permissions.

FYI

The U.S. Department of Education provides a general and detailed FERPA publications website at *http://www2.ed.gov/policy/gen/guid/fpco/ferpa/index.html*.

In January 2013, two important changes were made to the law. First, it became easier to share records with child welfare agencies; for example, child welfare agencies would be able to confirm that children in foster care are actively attending school. Second, the change eliminates some requirements to notify parents when school records are being released—to a court, for example.

Children's Internet Protection Act (CIPA)

The Children's Internet Protection Act (CIPA) was put into law in 2000. The law tells schools and libraries that receive federal funding that they must block pornographic and explicit sexual material on their computers. The law attempts to limit children's exposure to such material.

The Federal Communications Commission (FCC) establishes the rules that schools and libraries must follow. The CIPA regulation was challenged in a lawsuit heard by the Supreme Court. The basis of the challenge was that restricting access to information is unconstitutional. Additionally, there were questions about whether the technology would end up blocking sites not originally intended by the law. The result of the court challenge was mixed. The court held that the CIPA law was constitutional; however, the courts do require schools and libraries to unblock sites when requested by an adult. The FCC has several publications on CIPA available at *http://www.fcc.gov/cgb/consumerfacts /cipa.html.*

Here are key CIPA components that your security policies must include:

- **Awareness**—The school or library must post its CIPA security policies and provide awareness of them.
- **Internet filters**—Best efforts must be made to keep **Internet filters** current so that only the targeted material intended by CIPA is blocked.
- **Unblocking**—There must be a process to allow the filter to be unblocked or disabled for adults who request access to blocked sites.
- **Education**—Children must be provided education on Internet safety and on cyberbullying and how to respond.

FYI

In 2012, the CIPA was changed to include requirements to educate young people about Internet safety. The changed law said, "Beginning July 1, 2012, schools' Internet safety policies must provide for educating minors about appropriate online behavior, including interacting with other individuals on social networking websites and in chat rooms and cyberbullying awareness and response."

Why Did U.S. Compliance Laws Come About?

These laws recognize the power of information. The more personal the data, the more powerful the information. Many changes in law relate to privacy. These changes range from how personal information is collected to how it is used and what type of written notice must be given. The power comes from the impact that personal information has on our lives. It affects what type of job we can get, the car we can buy, and the home we can afford. It also determines the quality of medical care we receive. The misuse and abuse of this information is equally powerful and can make our lives miserable. Identity theft is a major problem. It can take years of effort to restore a credit rating. You've surely heard stories of millions of credit cards stolen each year. Although slow to react, the government does respond to emerging national threats and public pressure.

Many of these laws have come about to protect our personal privacy and to limit how companies can use the information they collect. On the other hand, the sharing of information across government agencies has increased. When millions of citizens' personal data is lost or stolen, many questions are raised. It's hard to know exactly how many breaches occur each year. It is estimated that in the United States alone, there were over 3800 data breaches in 2019 alone. This has resulted in more than 3.2 billion records containing personal information being stolen. A host of personal information is associated with these records, including Social Security numbers, bank account information, health records, and more. Even if these numbers are wrong (and many believe they are too low), they reflect the real danger facing society. The cost to business is high, and so is the cost to individuals. As a result, a number of regulations in recent years have come about to require organizations to do what they can to prevent such breaches. These regulations hold an organization accountable when breaches occur.

Whom Do the Laws Protect?

Is an individual's privacy the government's sole concern? No, it is not. These laws have four major beneficiaries:

- **Individuals**—A number of laws focus on protecting an individual's private information.
- **Shareholders**—A number of laws are designed to provide confidence in the markets. When investors believe that a company's financials and risks are properly managed, they feel they can make informed judgments. This promotes a healthy economy.
- **The public interest**—This term reflects the idea that an organization has an obligation to the general public beyond their self-interest. Although this is a vague term, regulators often look at the impact a company has on the industry group or the economy in general.
- **National security**—The idea is that cyberterrorism threatens not only the company being targeted, but also the country's critical infrastructure.

To be clear: The world is not perfect, and the goals of regulations are not always achieved. Regardless of the value you place on regulations, you shouldn't treat them as abstract concepts. Regulations do affect security policies. They limit how business can collect, store, and process information. Security policies are looked to as a way to ensure compliance with government mandates.

It's an accepted concept that when everyone has to follow the same rules, the playing field is level. Without regulations, companies feel the pressure to take shortcuts to maintain competitive advantage. Regulations remove some of this pressure because everyone must comply. In other words, doing the "right thing" becomes not a matter of cost or advantage, but part of the business culture and the law.

Which Laws Require Proper Security Controls to Be Included in Policies?

You cannot design effective security controls without good security policies. It's important to create and enforce policies that demonstrate compliance with regulations. This is true of organizations of all types, including business and government. But there is no cookie-cutter approach—each entity will have its own way of implementing and enforcing policies.

Regardless of the information being protected, a security control needs to be designed and implemented to enforce the policy. If a law requires any type of information protection, it also requires proper security controls. This includes physical security controls to protect information in physical form such as paper reports.

> **NOTE**
>
> Every regulatory requirement on the handling of data should map to one or more security policies.

Which Laws Require Proper Security Controls for Handling Privacy Data?

Asking which laws require proper security controls for handling privacy data is a trick question. As a general rule, you should consider that all laws in some way require controls over the handling of data. They may vary, though, in their requirements and specific obligations. Well-written policies, rather than focusing on one law, will tend to satisfy regulatory requirements by fostering sound security practices across the enterprise. You should also always remember that you have both a legal and an ethical responsibility to your customers. And you have an obligation to shareholders to protect the company. This includes protecting customers' personal information, even when a law doesn't explicitly call for privacy controls.

As a practical matter, a breach of customer information could leave a company facing a long and costly lawsuit. Consequently, it's simply good business to protect customers' personal information. Security policies should reflect this thinking—for example, a need-to-know policy, which would limit access to data to just those employees who require the information to perform their jobs. This is a simple security principle that shows customers you protect their interest.

A good rule of thumb is whenever your organization handles personal information, you should be sure your security policies and controls protect privacy. If the company is not currently obligated to follow a privacy law or regulation, there's a good chance at some point it will be, whether at a state or federal level. Over time, it's far less expensive and easier to implement core privacy principles, such as those in Table 3-1, than to implement specific controls to keep pace with each changing law. One can also argue it's simply the right thing to do.

The only conflict comes when an organization wants to use the information beyond the scope of these core principles. At that point, management should determine whether using the information violates current law. Another key consideration is whether the use of the data violates the trust agreement with the customer. This includes both the privacy notice given to the customer and the organization's core values. If the law allows, and customer trust is deemed not at risk, then a determination can be made to either change the

TIP

An organization's privacy or compliance officer is a good source for determining what should be in security policies to meet regulatory requirements.

core principles or make an exception. This pushback from business to use information beyond the core principles is healthy. It results in a candid conversation with the business about current regulations and the values the organization wants to embrace. The approach results in better understanding of the law, greater awareness of core organizational values, and a stronger foundation of controls.

Aligning Security Policies and Controls with Regulations

You have reviewed six major laws at a high level and their effects on security policies and controls. Depending on your organization, you may have hundreds of laws to deal with. So how do you cope? There are many factors you must consider to ensure security policies and controls align with regulations, such as the following:

- **Inventory**—Make sure you have a solid inventory of hardware, software, and information. You need know to where the information is collected, stored, and processed.
- **Business requirements**—Your business is ultimately accountable to regulators. Ensure the business understands the data-handling requirements of each regulation. Ensure that there is an acceptable use policy for the handling of different kinds of data; for example, is the customer presented with an opt-in or opt-out check box? Even these simple choices may have regulatory implications.
- **Security policies**—Security policies need to reflect business requirements. It's equally important to establish a core set of principles, such as those in Table 3-1. These core principles allow you to educate the entire business and address a significant number of regulations.
- **Security framework**—The selection of a security framework allows you to show regulators that you are using best practices. Use widely accepted standards, procedures, and guidelines.
- **Security control mapping**—When you build security controls, be sure to map them to the related policy or policies. Policies also map to regulations. **Security control mappings** are important to demonstrate coverage of regulatory requirements. They show the importance of each security control. Ideally, you also want to map security controls to the security framework. This will provide a comprehensive end-to-end overview of security.
- **Monitoring and testing**—Your organization must monitor and test any security control related to regulatory compliance. You should try to monitor and test all security controls. If you cannot, prioritize the controls starting with the most important ones.
- **Evidence**—At some point you will be required to provide regulators with **evidence**. Regulators want to see a well-thought-out approach to compliance. The security policies, framework, and control mapping are a good start. The mapping demonstrates a thorough understanding and intent to comply. Your monitoring and testing efforts also provide evidence that things are working as planned.

You learned earlier in the chapter that COSO and COBIT are widely accepted frameworks. Other frameworks are equally important. You should also be familiar with the publications from the International Organization for Standardization (ISO). Another important framework is the **Information Technology Infrastructure Library (ITIL)**. ITIL is a set of practices and predefined procedures for managing specific IT services such as change management. You will learn about ITIL later in this chapter.

Next, we look at how these frameworks help you build security policies and controls. Make sure you understand the security requirements for each regulation and your business. Also be sure to work with your compliance and legal department. It's important that the policies reflect current regulatory requirements. Specialists in the compliance and legal department usually keep track of changing laws. Then you can start building or updating security policies, standards, controls, and procedures. The following is one approach:

1. Document the concepts and principles you will adopt.
2. Apply them to security policies and standards.
3. Develop security controls and procedures.

The typical approach involves moving from core security principles to implementing specific controls. **FIGURE 3-2** illustrates this point using COSO, COBIT, and ITIL. In this example, COSO provides the necessary governance structure. Although COBIT defines policies and controls requirements, you can then define your procedures using ITIL predefined libraries.

The ability to map to existing standards and frameworks is powerful. This approach leverages years of experience across industries. It also provides confidence to regulators and auditors that you are properly managing risks. Even if you fail to document a risk, there's a strong likelihood that the layered nature of the controls will mitigate the threat. It also reduces implementation time and produces high-quality policies, procedures, and security controls.

The approach is straightforward. The ability to implement quickly is not. The challenge is not in the approach, but in volume. As mentioned, you might have hundreds of regulations to follow. Even a small company may have hundreds of applications, and *Fortune* 500 companies will have thousands of applications. Multiply that by the number of users, the number of files, the number of devices, and the number of Internet connections, and you begin to see the difficulties. You might have an untold number of controls. Suddenly the volume can get overwhelming. That's why it's important not to take shortcuts with the key considerations

FIGURE 3-2

Security policies and controls mapping to frameworks.

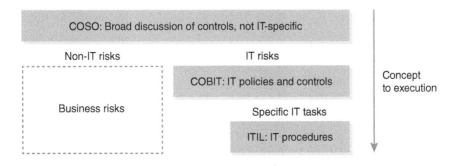

listed previously. It's important that a policy outline the governance and oversight require-ments for maintaining those controls. You also need a rigorous process for building, inventorying, and maintaining security controls.

Industry Leading Practices and Self-Regulation

You learned how news stories and public pressure drive government regulations. They also drive many industries to more self-regulation. The hope is to demonstrate to the government and the public that these industries are aware of the problem and are taking action. An industry prefers to self-regulate for two key reasons, cost and flexibility. There's a perception that regulations increase cost because they can be restrictive and require lots of compliance evidence to be collected. Additionally, regulations can require specific solutions to a problem. Retaining the flexibility to select from an array of solutions and apply new technology is one reason given to avoid regulations. The counterargument is that, without laws, industries won't fully address problems.

> **NOTE**
>
> Most information security professionals belong to associations or regional groups. There are also online communities. These communities share solutions and publish survey results. It's important to take advantage of this knowledge to understand if you are using leading practices.

Regardless of your viewpoint on the merits of regulation, the result is that industries create standards over time that may become best practices. The term *best practice* is commonly understood; however, it can be confusing when trying to understand industry standards. The term is overused and difficult to quantify. What does "best" compare with? Is a simple solution best because it costs the least? Or, is a solution better because it is more reliable? Another term with more precision is *leading practice*, which is easier to quantify. If most members of an industry adopt a method, it's considered to be "leading." It might be the best solution, but that's not always the case.

Regulated companies look to leading practices as one way to shield themselves from regulators. If regulators have confidence in a leading practice by virtue of adopting it, a company should be confident it is complying with the law. You may not always be able to apply the best solution, but it's important to be able to tell a regulator that you do conform to industry norms.

Some Important Industry Standards

Payment Card Industry Data Security Standard (PCI DSS)

The **Payment Card Industry Data Security Standard (PCI DSS)** is a worldwide information security standard that describes how to protect credit card information. If you accept Visa, MasterCard, or American Express, you are required to follow PCI DSS. These card companies formed the Payment Card Industry Security Standards Council to create the standard. The PCI DSS standard was released in 2004. The current version of PCI DSS is 3.0, released in 2013. There was a revision to 3.2.1 in 2018. The standard applies to every organization that stores, processes, or exchanges cardholder information.

> **NOTE**
>
> In February 2014, PCI DSS 3.0 was released in nine languages. PCI is considered a global standard.

The standard requires an organization to have specific PCI DSS security policies and controls in place. The organization must also have these controls validated. If you are a small merchant, you can perform a self-assessment questionnaire (SAQ). Large-volume merchants must obtain their validation through a qualified security assessor (QSA). Failing to validate, or failing the validation, can result in fines from the credit card companies. In extreme cases of noncompliance, you may be prevented from handling credit cards. Taking credit cards away could put you out of business.

The PCI DSS is an information security framework, so it contains a lot of technical requirements. Two have been a challenge for organizations to implement: network segmentation and encryption. PCI DSS strongly encourages isolating credit card systems at a network layer. For many open network designs and shared systems, this is a challenge. If you cannot segment the systems that contain cardholder data, PCI DSS requires that all systems on that segment must comply with PCI DSS. This means if you have 20 systems on a segment and one processes credit card information, all 20 systems should comply with PCI DSS standards. This could be expensive. The second major challenge is encrypting data at rest. Encrypting data in transit is common over the Internet and public networks. Encrypting data at rest, however, can be technically challenging and at times not feasible.

There are six control objectives within the PCI DSS standard. To be compliant, you need to include these control objectives in your security policies and controls. These control objectives are:

- **Build and maintain a secure network**—Refers to having specific firewall, system password, and other security network layer controls.
- **Protect cardholder data**—Specifies how cardholder data is stored and protected. Also sets rules on the encryption of the data.

> ▶ **TIP**
> The PCI DSS materials are free and publicly available through the PCI Security Standard Council website at *https://www.pcisecuritystandards.org*.

- **Maintain a vulnerability management program**—Specifies how to maintain secure systems and applications, including the required use of antivirus software.
- **Implement strong access control measures**—Refers to restricting access to cardholder data on a need-to-know basis. It requires physical controls in place and individual unique IDs when accessing cardholder data.
- **Regularly monitor and test networks**—Requires monitoring access to the cardholder. Also requires periodic penetration testing of the network.
- **Maintain an information security policy**—Requires that security policies reflect the PCI DSS requirements. Also requires these policies are kept current and an awareness program is implemented.

Clarified Statement on Standards for Attestation Engagements No. 18 (SSAE18)

The American Institute of Certified Public Accountants (AICPA) created the **Statement on Standards for Attestation Engagements No. 18 (SSAE18)**. It was issued in April 2010, replacing the widely accepted auditing standard referred to as SAS 70. An SSAE16 audit examines an organization's control environment. This usually includes an audit of the information security controls. An SSAE16 allows an independent auditor (called a *service auditor*) to review an organization's control environment. The service auditor then issues an independent opinion in a cover letter. The actual audit report and opinion is provided to the organization being examined. Then SSAE 18 was released to further clarify and update the standard.

The popularity of an independent audit comes from the use of the opinion letters. Anyone trying to buy services from a vendor should ensure the data is protected. Organizations often request an opinion letter from a vendor to help build that confidence. Vendors often promote how well they passed an SSAE16 audit as a way of selling their services.

NOTE

The AICPA has free publications available at *http://www.aicpa.org/Research /Standards/AuditAttest/Pages/SSAE.aspx.*

There is a mutual benefit in having an independent audit performed. To the customer, it provides some assurance that their vendor's control environment has been audited. And the vendor can say there's been independent opinion that the customer's data is protected. A key area of examination is security policies. Having well-defined policies and evidence of their effectiveness is required as part of an SSAE16 review.

Technical TIP

The opinion of the auditor depends in part on the scope of the SSAE16 review. When requesting the opinion, be sure to ask for the scope of the examination. This helps you understand the context of the opinion. For example, if you are concerned with whether a vendor can recover the system in case of an outage, be sure to ask whether backup and recovery controls were in the scope of the SSAE16 review. Simply obtaining an opinion that controls are working is not enough. You need to know which controls were tested.

Does an SSAE16 truly test if controls provide adequate safeguards to protect data? That depends in part on the type of SSAE16 audit performed. There are two types of SSAE16 audits:

* **Type I**—This is basically a design review of the controls. The auditor's opinion would note if the controls are designed well. The audit also looks at documented policies and procedures. The opinion states if the policies, controls, and procedures could meet the control objective stated. This doesn't mean the controls are working. It simply says that if the controls are executed, then they should work.
* **Type II**—Includes everything in Type I. In addition, the controls are tested to see if those controls are properly installed and working effectively.

Information Technology Infrastructure Library (ITIL)

The **Information Technology Infrastructure Library (ITIL)** is a series of books that describe IT practices and procedures. The collection of books originally came from a British government initiative. The first version was published in 1989 as ITIL v1.0. The current version as of this writing is ITIL v4.

ITIL has evolved over time from over 30 booklets on different topics to a unified IT service management (ITSM) approach. ITIL focuses on the entire service life cycle. It outlines goals, activities, tasks, inputs, and outputs. It is seen as outlining the best management practices for IT.

The ITIL official website states "ITIL provides a cohesive set of best practices, drawn from the public and private sectors internationally."[10] The concept behind ITSM is to use ITIL to optimize the IT infrastructure, lower costs, and improve quality.

FYI

ITIL is not free, and it can be expensive to buy the entire library. You can purchase just the ITIL books of specific interest. The official website has some free material at *https://www.axelos.com/best-practice-solutions/itil.*

ITIL has five core books called volumes. The following outlines each of the five volumes:

- **Service Strategy**—Relates to how to define the governance and portfolio of services. This includes aligning to the business and IT finance requirements.
- **Service Design**—Relates to the actual design of the service and controls. Here is where you take into account all the business and technology concerns. For example, risk management, capacity management, availability, information security, and compliance are among the elements considered.
- **Service Transition**—Relates to the transition of services into production. For example, validation testing, release management, and change management are among the elements considered.
- **Service Operation**—Relates to ongoing support of the service. For example, incident and problem management, and access management, are among the elements considered.
- **Continual Service Improvement**—Relates to continuous improvement of the service. For example, measuring, reporting, and managing service level agreements (SLAs) are among the elements considered.

International Laws

Although the focus of this chapter is on U.S. laws, there are laws and regulations from outside the United States that are worth mentioning. It would be impossible to cover every privacy or information security management regulation in the entire world; however, some regulations apply to such a broad range of nations that at least a basic description is important.

General Data Protection Regulation (GDPR)

The most important non-U.S. regulation is the General Data Protection Regulation (GDPR). This was passed in 2016 by the European Union (EU) and has sweeping regulations regarding data privacy. The full scope of GDPR would occupy an entire book (and in fact, several books have been written on it). A brief overview of critical points is provided here.

This law applies to any organization that collects data from EU residents, even if that organization is outside the EU. The primary goal of GDPR is to protect personal data. One of the bedrock principles of GDPR is informed consent. Any data collected or used must have been given with informed consent explicitly for the purposes for which the data is used. That consent can be withdrawn by the data owner/subject at any time. The process for opting out cannot be any more difficult than was the process to opt in. Importantly, a service provider may not refuse service to users who decline consent to processing that is not strictly necessary in order to use the service.

European Telecommunications Standards Institute (ETSI)

The European Telecommunications Standards Institute (ETSI) established a cybersecurity committee in 2014 to establish cybersecurity standards for all of Europe. This committee has published a wide range of standards on topics ranging from consumer Internet of Things (IoT) security to Quantum-Safe Virtual Private Networks.[11]

Asia-Pacific Economic Framework (APEC)

In Asia, 21 member countries have adopted a voluntary privacy framework called the Asia-Pacific Economic Framework.[12] APEC consists of nine principles regarding privacy. It defines personal information as any information that can be used to identify an individual. The nine principles in the APEC privacy framework are preventing harm, notice, collection limitations, uses of personal information, choice, integrity of personal information, security safeguards, access and correction, and accountability.

CHAPTER SUMMARY

This chapter described how important it is to conform to U.S. compliance laws and examined how technology and the Internet are driving globalization. With broad use of the Internet comes new threats. You also learned the importance of compliance to the economy and how it serves the public interest. The chapter examined a number of major compliance regulations. From these examples, you can see an increasing government need to regulate. Sometimes regulations result from public pressure when something goes wrong. The chapter examined these pressures and the motivations of both the government and the industry. The chapter also discussed how the industry tries to self-regulate to avoid government regulation to keep costs down and retain flexibility. The United States faces new threats continuously from nation-states trying to attack the country's critical infrastructure.

This chapter also examined how security policies, controls, and procedures need to align with regulations, and demonstrated how to create this alignment. The chapter also examined how to show evidence of compliance to a regulator. You read about the challenges to comply with regulation and industry standards, as well as the need to align security policies to both legal requirements and the company's core values.

Finally, a key lesson in this chapter is not to chase laws by building specific security policies and controls tailored to each new regulation. Rather, you should base policies on key concepts that address a broad range of regulatory concerns such as consumer protection and privacy.

Also, this chapter touched on several international laws. Obviously, it is not possible to cover every law in every country. One will need to consult the laws in one's own nation. However, a brief introduction to international laws was covered.

KEY CONCEPTS AND TERMS

Chief information officer (CIO)
Chief information security officer (CISO)
Consumer rights
Critical infrastructure
Cyberterrorism
Data privacy
Evidence
Globalization

Information security risk assessment
Information Technology Infrastructure Library (ITIL)
Internet filters
Nation-states
Opt-in
Opt-out

Payment Card Industry Data Security Standard (PCI DSS)
Personal privacy
Risk assessment
Security control mapping
Shareholder
Statement on Standards for Attestation Engagements No. 18 (SSAE18)

CHAPTER 3 ASSESSMENT

1. When creating laws and regulations, the government's sole concern is the privacy of the individual.

   A. True
   B. False

2. Which of the following are pressures on creating security policies?

   A. Shareholder value
   B. Regulations
   C. Technology vulnerabilities and limitations
   D. B and C only
   E. A, B, and C

3. Which of the following laws require(s) proper security controls for handling privacy data?

   A. HIPAA
   B. GLBA
   C. FERPA
   D. B and C only
   E. A, B, and C

4. Which of the following are control objectives for PCI DSS?

   A. Maintain an information security policy
   B. Protect cardholder data
   C. Alert when credit cards are illegally used
   D. A and B only
   E. None of the above

5. Nation-state attacks that try to disrupt the country's critical infrastructure are sometimes referred to as _____.

6. Healthcare providers are those that process and facilitate billing.

   A. True
   B. False

7. The law that attempts to limit children's exposure to sexually explicit material is _____.

8. The only consideration in protecting personal customer information is legal requirements.

A. True
B. False

9. You should always write new security policies each time a new regulation is issued.

A. True
B. False

10. What should you ask for to gain confidence that a vendor's security controls are adequate?

A. An SSAE16 Type I audit
B. An SSAE16 Type II audit
C. A list of all internal audits
D. All of the above

11. Why is it important to map regulatory requirements to policies and controls?

A. To demonstrate compliance to regulators
B. To ensure regulatory requirements are covered
C. To demonstrate the importance of a security control
D. All of the above

12. Who typically writes a report to the board of directors on the current state of information security within a company?

A. Chief risk officer
B. Chief information officer
C. Chief information security officer
D. A and B
E. B and C
F. A, B, and C

ENDNOTES

1. Internet World Stats, *https://www.internetworldstats.com/stats.htm* accessed December 2019

2. Kemp, Simon, "Digital 2019: Global Internet Use Accelerates," We Are Social, *https://wearesocial.com/blog/2019/01/digital-2019-global-internet-use-accelerates,* accessed April 10, 2020.

3. "Internet Stats and Facts (2020)," HostingFacts, *https://hostingfacts.com/internet-facts-stats/,* accessed April 10, 2020.

4. Harress, Christopher, "Obama Says Cyberterrorism Is Country's Biggest Threat, U.S. Government Assembles 'Cyber Warriors,'" *International Business Times,* February 18, 2014, *http://www.ibtimes.com/obama-says-cyberterrorism-countrys-biggest-threat-us-government-assembles-cyber-warriors-1556337,* accessed March 9, 2014.

5. Goodin, Dan, "New Advanced Malware, Possibly Nation Sponsored, Is Targeting US Utilities," Ars Technica, *https://arstechnica.com/information-technology/2019/08/new-advanced-malware-possibly*

-nation-sponsored-is-targeting-us-utilities/, accessed April 10, 2020.

6. Center for Strategic and International Studies, "Significant Cyber Incidents," *https://www.csis.org/programs/technology-policy-program/significant-cyber-incidents,* accessed April 10, 2020.

7. "Executive Order—Improving Critical Infrastructure Cybersecurity," The White House, Office of the Press Secretary, February 12, 2013, *https://obamawhitehouse.archives.gov/the-press-office/2013/02/12/executive-order-improving-critical-infrastructure-cybersecurity,* accessed April 11, 2020.

8. U.S. Securities and Exchange Commission, Office of Inspector General, Office of Audits, "Audit of the SEC's Compliance with the Federal Information Security Modernization Act for Fiscal Year 2017," *https://www.sec.gov/files/Audit-of-the-SECs-Compliance-with-FISMA-for-Fiscal-Year-2017.pdf,* accessed April 10, 2020.

9. American Speech-Language-Hearing Association, "Health Information Technology for Economics and Clinical Health (HITECH) Act," *https://www.asha.org/Practice/reimbursement /hipaa/HITECH-Act/,* accessed April 10, 2020.

10. ITIL, *http://www.itil-officialsite.com/home/home .asp,* accessed March 22, 2010.

11. ETSI, "Cyber," *https://www.etsi.org/committee/1393-cyber,* accessed April 11, 2020.

12. Asia-Pacific Economic Cooperation, "APEC Privacy Framework," *https://www.apec.org/Publications/2005/12 /APEC-Privacy-Framework,* accessed April 11, 2020.

Business Challenges Within the Seven Domains of IT Responsibility

THE VOLUME OF DATA handled in many organizations is tremendous. Organizations of any size can have millions of transactions occurring every day among customers, employees, and suppliers. Today, many systems are automated. They generate their own transactions in the form of online product queries, searches, inventory checks, authorization checks, and log entries. Tracking of product, pricing, invoicing, service calls, email, instant messages, support tickets, and order processing all require data. One touch of a keyboard generates potentially hundreds of transactions in today's complex business environment. All of this information needs to be protected. Whether the data is stored at rest on a hard drive or in transit over the network, regardless of form or method of access, threats to the information must be considered.

Reports predict that over 40 zettabytes of data will be stored digitally worldwide by the end of the year 2020. A zettabyte is a unit of measure equivalent to 10^{21} bytes of data. In context, 42 zettabytes are equivalent to storing every word spoken by every human in history. In 2018, *Forbes* magazine reported that there are 2.5 quintillion bytes of data created each day.[1] A quintillion in U.S. units is 1,000,000,000,000,000,000. That is 2.5 exabytes per day. To give you some idea of scope, consider **TABLE 4-1**.

TABLE 4-1 Data Units

UNIT	SIZE	COMPARISON
Kilobyte	1000 bytes	A typical JPEG image is from 50 kilobytes to 2 megabytes.
Megabyte	1,000,000 bytes	
Gigabyte	1,000,000,000 bytes	As of 2019, an average thumb drive can hold 32 to 128 gigabytes.
Terabyte	1,000,000,000,000 bytes	As of 2019, the largest external hard drive for commercial purchase is about 12 terabytes; 2 to 4 terabytes is common.
Petabyte	1,000,000,000,000,000 bytes	A petabyte of MP3 or MP4 recorded songs would take roughly 2000 years to play.
Exabyte	1,000,000,000,000,000,000 bytes	Some sources claim that 42 zettabytes would be equal to all of the words ever spoken by mankind.

Table 4-1 should give you some concept of just how much data is being generated. All of that data requires some level of security. The precise level varies based on the nature of the data. The expanded use of social media, more widespread cloud and mobile computing, and the widespread adoption of smart devices and the Internet of Things (IoT) are a few of the factors contributing to this growth. Technologies just now being envisioned mean this growth trend will not stop in the foreseeable future.

The large accumulation of data is often referred to as *Big Data*. The global society is wired. Among the items going into the vast global store of data may be a tweet, a copy of an email, an Internet search, or a copy of a receipt from a retail store. This vast array of data is often unstructured, and for a market researcher or a government snoop, it may be a treasure trove of information that reveals a lot about an individual: his or her habits, interests, gender, associations, opinions, and much more.

FYI

The term *Big Data* is somewhat nebulous. There is not a precise demarcation line between standard data and Big Data. In general, Big Data refers to data sets that are large enough that typical methodologies for searching, categorizing, or dealing with the data are not effective.

What does this mean for business? It means new opportunities and new challenges. Businesses that understand how to mine this data will understand their customers' needs. Companies that lose control over their data will put their customers and businesses at risk. This data is accumulated over years and is relatively static. Yet the law is not static. For example, as privacy laws change, what was once considered acceptable business use may now be illegal. Security policies must keep up with these ever-changing legal requirements or run the risk of exposing the business to legal penalties.

This chapter divides the IT environment into seven logical domains. Each domain represents a logical part of the technology infrastructure. You will follow the data through these seven domains to understand the business challenges of collecting, processing, and storing information. You will also consider the business, technical, and security policy challenges that affect organizations.

Chapter 4 Topics

This chapter covers the following topics and concepts:

- What the seven domains of a typical IT infrastructure are
- How security policies mitigate risk within the seven domains
- What the different methods of building access control are

Chapter 4 Goals

When you complete this chapter, you will be able to:

- Identify the seven domains of typical IT infrastructure
- Identify the risks and concerns involved with the various domains
- Describe the top business risks within each of the seven domains
- Understand the difference between role-based access control (RBAC) and attribute-based access control (ABAC)
- Understand how security policies map to business requirements
- Understand the role security policies play in mitigating business risks within the domains

The Seven Domains of a Typical IT Infrastructure

Examining risk from a data perspective involves following data through an end-to-end process. As you move through your technology infrastructure, you'll find similar risk and policy issues. There are many ways to group security policies. A common method is to group common risks and related policy issues into domains. These domains share similarities but are distinctive enough to allow logical separation into more manageable security areas. An advantage of this method is that each **domain** typically focuses on a different target audience. This means security awareness and training can be more precisely targeted. Recall the McCumber cube introduced in Chapter 1; it looked at security from multiple perspectives including data at rest, data in transit, and data in processing.

In this section, you will learn the definition of these domains. This section examines the attributes of each domain so you can gain a better understanding of the issues. Later in the chapter, you will examine the business issues and policy challenges of these problems, along with risk mitigation techniques.

FIGURE 4-1 illustrates seven typical domains of an IT infrastructure, which include:

- **User**—This domain refers to any user accessing information. This includes customers, employees, consultants, contractors, or any other third party. These users are *end users*.
- **Workstation**—This domain refers to any endpoint device used by end users. This can mean any smart device in the end user's physical possession. For the purposes of this chapter, it's any device accessed by the end user, such as a smartphone, laptop, workstation, or mobile device.
- **LAN**—This domain refers to the organization's local area network (LAN) infrastructure. A LAN connects two or more computers within a small area. The small area could be a home, office, or group of buildings.
- **WAN**—A wide area network (WAN) covers a large geographical area. The Internet is an example of a WAN. A private WAN can be built for a specific company to link offices across

FIGURE 4-1

The seven domains of a typical IT infrastructure.

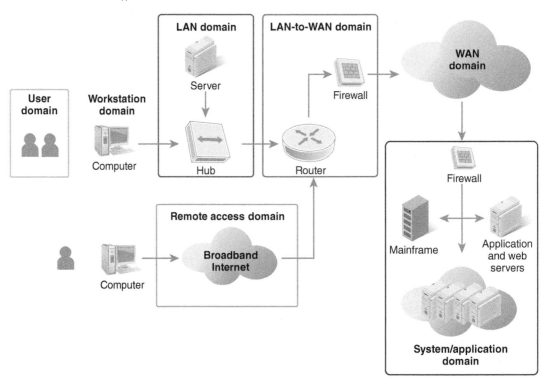

the country or globally. Many businesses use the Internet for communicating between offices and regions. The Internet has become so inexpensive and reliable that it is often the first choice of businesses. Communications are typically secured through the use of encryption.

- **LAN-to-WAN**—This domain refers to the technical infrastructure that connects the organization's LAN to a WAN. This allows end users to access the Internet. Communications flow in both directions in the LAN-to-WAN domain.

- **Remote Access**—This domain refers to the technologies that control how end users connect to an organization's LAN. A typical example of remote access is someone connecting to the office network from a home computer. End users can use a WAN to access a LAN; for example, an end user could use the Internet to create a private and secure session to connect with the office through a virtual private network (VPN) connection.

- **System/Application**—This domain refers to the technologies needed to collect, process, and store information. The System/Application domain includes hardware and software.

Although there are many advantages to grouping policies in this way, it can be hard to understand how data is controlled. In other words, it could be challenging to understand the end-to-end layers of controls. One way to overcome this challenge is to map business requirements by examining each of these logical segments. These requirements provide constraints upon end users and ultimately determine how security controls are designed.

Take a look at each of the seven domains to better understand how data is treated and how many common constraints are placed on them by the business.

User Domain

The **User domain** refers to any end user accessing information in any form. This includes how end users handle physical information such as printed reports. Control of physical information starts well before someone ever touches a keyboard. It must start with end user awareness of policies and on-the-job training. As good as an awareness program is, formal education programs are no substitute for the experience gained from on-the-job training. *Onboarding* refers to new employee training. Even if your organization doesn't have a formal on-the-job training program, something as simple as giving someone a "buddy" to show him or her how the area operates often achieves many of the same goals.

> ⚠ **WARNING**
>
> How coworkers treat data can significantly influence an employee's behavior beyond any formal awareness training. Regardless of training, if coworkers and management treat policies as unimportant, a new employee might also treat policies as unimportant.

An end user must be familiar with several key policies before accessing company information. Some of the more important policies you should include in an awareness training program include:

- **Acceptable use policy**—An acceptable use policy (AUP) establishes a broad set of rules for acceptable conduct when a user accesses information on company-owned devices. For example, this policy may set rules on what type of website browsing is permitted or if personal emails over the Internet are allowed.
- **Email policy**—An **email policy** discusses what's acceptable when using the company email system. The policy is much more specific than the broad statements found in an AUP policy.
- **Privacy policy**—A **privacy policy** addresses the importance the organization places on protecting privacy. It also discusses the regulatory landscape and government mandates. This policy discusses how to handle customer data as well as the individual obligation to protect the information.
- **System access policy**—A **system access policy** includes rules of conduct for system access. This policy covers end user credentials like IDs and passwords. The policy may also be specific to the business or application.
- **Physical security and clean desk policy**—The physical security and clean desk policy outlines conduct in the workplace. It typically covers the expectation that employees will lock up sensitive information before going home at the end of the workday. This is what the term *clean desk* refers to.
- **Corporate mobility policy**—An organization's corporate mobility policy sets expectations on the use and security of mobile devices. This policy could also set requirements on using personal devices to access company systems. For example, there is a growing trend of allowing personal smartphones to access company email systems. This reduces costs

because the company does not have to issue phones. But it also creates new risks, because companies have less control over devices they do not own.

- **Social networking policy**—The social networking policy has emerged as a type of code of conduct. With the rise of social media, many businesses are concerned about employees posting information about the company on these sites. This policy provides guidance to employees. For many organizations, posting any information about the business beyond the employee's name and title is strictly forbidden.

Authentication is one of the most important components of the User domain. You must determine an authentication method that makes sense for your organization. Your authentication method must also meet business requirements.

The use of user IDs and passwords as authentication methods remains a minimum standard for many organizations. It is considered a foundational control for many businesses. The ID and password can be widely used, and a password can be easily reset in the event an end user forgets it. The low cost and high efficiency of this method of authenticating users also represent its greatest weakness. Because IDs and passwords have been used throughout the history of modern computing, exploits of this authentication method continue to be refined. More advanced mechanisms, such as two-factor authentication, are being implemented more widely. These methods are designed to overcome the weaknesses of bad passwords or of someone guessing a password. For many businesses, however, IDs and passwords alone are not enough. In addition to two-factor authentication, there are many methods to improve the authentication process. Authenticating the end user device in combination with the ID and password provides a stronger authentication method. For example, access may be restricted only to work hours on devices issued by the business for employees with a valid ID and password. Although the ID and password may be compromised, the risk is reduced because access would be denied on noncompany computers.

The best and most common method for ensuring you know who is being authenticated is to restrict access to an ID and password to a single individual and force individuals to change their password often. The key lesson is that authentication must make sense in the business context in which you use it.

Another key component is authorization. Authorization is especially important in large, complex organizations with thousands of employees and hundreds of systems. Authorization is what takes place once the user is authenticated. The next step is to determine what the user has access to. The single most important concept, regardless of the authorization method used, is to obey the principle of least-privileges. Any users should only be authorized to access data/take actions directly required by their job role and no more. No matter how trusted and how well trained the user is, he or she should be given access to *only* enough to do his or her job. The authorization method must clearly define who should have access to what. One popular method is **role-based access control (RBAC)**. In this method, instead of granting access to individuals, you assign permissions to a role. Then you assign one or more individuals to that role.

The huge advantage of RBAC is speed of deployment and clarity of access rights. Let's assume you hire an accountant named Nikkee and you grant her access to 12 systems, many spreadsheets, email folders, and more. If you had to grant that access to her individual ID, it could take you days or even weeks. Given the complexity of a system, you may need to grant hundreds of permissions. The volume of permissions means there is a good chance of an error by missing something or granting too many rights. Now let's assume you hire a second accountant named Vickee. You would have to start the process over again to grant her rights to the systems, spreadsheets, and so on. What's even more time-consuming is if one of these individuals leaves, you must go through a similar process to remove her access.

Instead, let's assume you previously set up a role called "Accountant" and granted all necessary permissions to this role. Creating a new account would take the same time as creating a single user without RBAC. But creating a role is a one-time event. When you hire Nikkee and Vickee, you can connect their IDs to the Accountant role, quickly giving them access to the systems, spreadsheets, and email folders they need to perform their jobs. Now let's say Vickee is promoted. You can quickly remove her ID from the Accountant role and place her ID in a Senior Accountant role. You reduced deployment time for these individuals from days or weeks to hours or minutes. By listing the people connected to the roles and the permissions within the roles, you can clearly see who has access to what business resources. This clarity of access helps an organization control access to its critical processes, manage its risk, and prove to regulators that it manages customer data properly. **FIGURE 4-2** illustrates the RBAC concept.

RBAC is effective, but other methods have been developed. In January 2014, NIST issued publication 800-162, entitled "Guide to Attribute Based Access Control (ABAC)." **Attribute-based access control (ABAC)** relies on specific attributes associated with the login. For example, if a loan officer logs in from a bank computer during normal business hours, he may

FIGURE 4-2

Role-based access control concept.

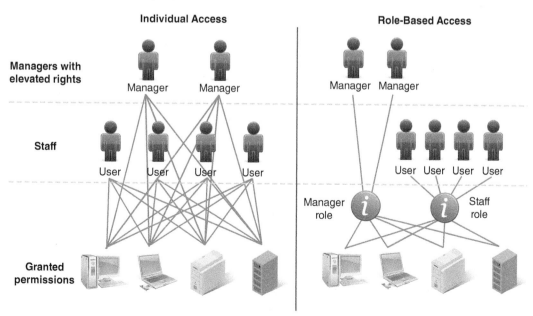

be given broader access than if the same loan officer logs in from a remote computer in a foreign country from an IP address he has never used before. The attributes are all the properties about the login. The source of the login, the time of day, and the nature of the activity are all considered.

You might allow a travelling salesperson to log in from Malaysia, but not your accountant. Or, you may allow the accountant to log in, but only to read files, not to delete data. Clearly, setting up ABAC is a bit more complicated, but well worth the effort. You may have encountered a primitive version of ABAC when logging in to your bank's website. If you log in from a different machine, one that has not been previously used to log in, there might be additional login steps. A common step is to text a code to the user's phone that must also be entered. This is a primitive, rather limited version of ABAC.

To add a bit more detail to ABAC, the model essentially looks at attributes and then applies a simple Boolean logic. The attributes can be user attributes, resource attributes (what is being accessed and how), environmental attributes (where is the access from, what time of day, etc.), or any other attribute that is relevant. These systems are sometimes called claims-based access control (CBAC) or policy-based access control (PBAC). The term *PBAC* is used due to the fact that the decision-making process is often governed by policies. A policy might state that users can be granted access only within the continental United States or that remote users have limited rights and increased logging/monitoring.

Workstation Domain

 NOTE

For the purposes of this chapter, the term *workstation* refers to any end user device that accesses information.

The **Workstation domain** includes any computing devices used by end users. Usually, the term *workstation* refers to a desktop or laptop computer; however, a workstation in the context of this chapter can be any end user device that accesses information. Control on your handheld device, like a smartphone, would fall within this domain.

Usually, when an end user seeks to access information, he or she authenticates in the User domain. Once he or she is known, the end user is often authorized to the workstation itself. Each workstation has an identity much like an end user. Not only can you restrict end users to specific workstations, but you can also restrict what workstations are allowed on your network. This is important when connecting to a network wirelessly because wireless access may be available to the public. Most wireless access points restrict which devices can access the internal network. Wireless access points should also encrypt the traffic between the authorized wireless device and the entry point for the LAN.

 NOTE

Authentication of a workstation and encryption of wireless traffic are Workstation domain and LAN domain issues. The assignment of a workstation identity and configuration of the wireless protocol is a Workstation domain issue. The authentication and encryption of the traffic is a LAN domain issue.

The Workstation domain defines the controls within the workstation itself, such as limiting who can install software on the workstation. Some end users share a workstation; therefore, it is important that settings be stable and that one end user not be able to affect another. To achieve this, end users often have limited rights on workstations. That means they can typically access the software that's been installed, and they have some rights to configure the software to their needs, but they do not have unlimited rights to make changes that could affect another user. This also ensures that an end user does not inadvertently infect the workstation with a virus or malware. Most domain controls ensure that appropriate antivirus software is loaded and runs on each workstation.

A central management system typically manages workstations such as Microsoft System Center Configuration Manager (SCCM). Note that although many still use the old name, Microsoft has changed it to Microsoft Endpoint Configuration Manager. The Microsoft Endpoint Configuration Manager combines System Center Configuration Manager and Systems Management Server. These management systems have evolved over time and help an organization save time and money, and greatly improve response time. Can you imagine having to visit hundreds or thousands of desktops individually to apply a patch or install a piece of software? Fortunately, those days are long over.

Regardless of the management software used, different brands all generally share many of the same capabilities. The key functionalities to look for are these:

- **Inventory management**—An **inventory management** system tracks devices as they connect to the LAN. This builds an inventory of which devices are on the network and how often they connect to the LAN. Information inventories are useful for investigating security incidents and ensuring regulatory compliance.
- **Discovery management**—A **discovery management** system detects software that is installed on a device. It can also detect information on a workstation. This is highly specialized software that is not routinely used.
- **Patch management**—A **patch management** system ensures that current patches are installed on devices. It's important to apply security patches in a timely manner to address known vulnerabilities.
- **Help desk management**—A **help desk management** system provides support to end users through a help desk. Help desk technicians may remotely access a device to diagnose problems, reconfigure software, and reset IDs.
- **Log management**—A **log management** system extracts logs from a device. Typically, log management software moves logs to a central repository. Typically, the volume of logs is so large that it takes special software to automatically search and highlight potential risks. Administrators scan these logs to find security weaknesses or patterns of problems.
- **Security management**—A **security management** system manages workstation security. This may include ensuring end users have limited rights and that new local administrator accounts are not present. The unexpected addition of local administrator accounts may be an indication that a security breach has occurred.

With the widespread adoption of personal handheld devices, a number of issues have become important in the Workstation domain. It is likely that users within your organization have their own devices. These devices, if allowed to connect to your network, become workstations. This brings up several questions regarding security, but the most important is whether or not to allow such devices to connect. The common approaches are:

- **Bring your own device (BYOD)**—With **bring your own device (BYOD)**, users are allowed to bring their own device to work and to connect to the network. This is sometimes augmented with specific security requirements, and in some cases Network Access Control (NAC). NAC scans the device to ensure it complies with security requirements.

- **Choose your own device (CYOD)**—Users are given a list of approved devices, and if the user purchases one of those, they can connect it to the company network.
- **Company-owned and -provided equipment (COPE)**—The company or organization provides devices. This has the advantage of allowing greater control over security, but it can be cost prohibitive.

Whatever the choices made, the issue of personal devices must be addressed. Currently, these are primarily smartphones; however, implantable medical devices, smart eyewear, exercise/fitness devices, and other networked devices are becoming increasingly common.

LAN Domain

The **LAN domain** encompasses the equipment that makes up the LAN. A LAN typically has network devices that connect a local office or buildings. A LAN can be either simple or complex. If you have a wireless network device at home, you have a simple LAN. Let's say you have a home cable modem connected to a wireless device, which is usually called a wireless router. The wireless router creates a LAN, bridging your cable modem to your home computer. This wireless router is your LAN access point to the Internet.

The following are definitions for common network devices found on LANs:

- **Switch**—A **switch** is similar to a hub, but it can filter traffic. Hubs are old technology that don't really exist today. A hub would simply send copies of all traffic out all ports. That quickly proved inefficient and was replaced by switches. You can set up rules that control what traffic can flow where. Unlike hubs, which duplicate traffic to all ports, a switch is typically configured to route traffic only to the port to which the system is connected. This reduces the amount of network traffic, thus reducing the chance that someone will intercept communications. Switches direct traffic based on the destination media access control (MAC) address. Thus, they are only used internally in networks.
- **Router**—A **router** connects LANs, or a LAN and a WAN. Routers direct traffic based on the destination IP address, as well as rules programmed into the router.
- **Firewall**—A **firewall** is a software or hardware device that filters traffic into and out of a LAN. Many can do deep-packet inspection, in which the firewall examines the contents of the traffic as well as the type of traffic. You can use a firewall internally on the network to further protect segments. Firewalls are most commonly used to filter traffic between the public Internet WAN and the internal private LAN.

A LAN in the business world is far more complex than a home LAN and has many layers of controls. This chapter looks at two general types of LANs, flat and segmented networks.

A **flat network** has few controls, or none, to limit network traffic. When a workstation connects to a flat network, the workstation can communicate with any other computer on the network. Think of a flat network as an ordinary neighborhood. Anyone can drive into the neighborhood and knock on any door. This doesn't mean whoever answers the door will let the visitor in; however, the visitor has the opportunity to talk his or her way in. In the case of flat networks, you can talk your way in by being authorized or by breaching a server, for instance, by guessing the right ID and password combination. Flat networks are considered less secure than segmented networks because they rely on each computer (i.e., each home on the block) to withstand every possible type of breach. They are also less secure because every computer on the network can potentially see all the network traffic. This means a computer with a **sniffer** can monitor a large portion of the communication over a LAN. A sniffer can capture the traffic on a network. This includes recording IDs and passwords in the clear. So, if there's a special code, secret knock, or handshake at the door, it has also been recorded. That's why most security policies require passwords to be encrypted when passed through the network.

NOTE

Many standards require network segmentation. Payment Card Industry Data Security Standard (PCI DSS), for example, requires network segmentation to further protect credit cardholder information. Segmented networks allow different security policies for different segments. Your database servers probably require higher level security than does the front desk workstation.

A **segmented network** limits what computers can say to each other and how they are able to talk to each other. By using switches, routers, internal firewalls, and other devices, you can restrict network traffic. Continuing the analogy from the previous paragraph, think of a segmented network as a gated community. To access that neighborhood, you must first approach a gate with a guard. The guard opens the gate only for certain traffic to enter the community. Once inside, you can knock on any door. A segmented network acts as a guard, filtering out unauthorized network traffic. Frankly, any network that is more than trivial in size should be segmented.

LAN-to-WAN Domain

The **LAN-to-WAN domain** is the bridge between a LAN and a WAN. A LAN is efficient for connecting computers within an office or groups of buildings; however, to connect offices across the country or globally you need to connect to a WAN. Generally, routers and firewalls are used to connect a LAN and WAN. The Internet is a WAN. Like many WANs, the Internet is public and considered unsecure. **FIGURE 4-3** illustrates the basic LAN-to-WAN network layers.

How do you move data from an unsecure WAN to a secure LAN? Typically, you begin by segmenting a piece of your LAN into a **demilitarized zone (DMZ)**. The military uses the term *DMZ* to describe a buffer between two opposing forces. The DMZ sits on the outside of your private network facing the public Internet. Servers in the DMZ provide public-facing access to the organization, such as public websites. By definition, you must allow more people to access your web server than you would allow to access your internal network. The DMZ will allow public access to servers such as web servers, while preserving the more robust access control within your network. Sitting between the DMZ and internal network are firewalls that filter traffic from the DMZ servers to the private LAN servers. Often, the DMZ sits between two layers of firewalls. The first firewall allows limited Internet traffic into the DMZ, and the second highly restricts traffic from the DMZ servers into the private network.

There are a number of different network architecture designs that can be used to connect your internal private LAN with the external Internet WAN. The key point is to understand that you need some layer of firewalls to limit traffic between these domains. Creating a network segment like the DMZ as a buffer between the LAN and WAN is a good way to protect your private network.

In recent years, some firewalls have added behavior and heuristic checks. Basically, this means the firewalls learn over time what "normal" looks like. By recording volume and type of traffic, they create a pattern. When these behaviors change dramatically, firewalls can

FIGURE 4-3

Basic LAN-to-WAN network layers.

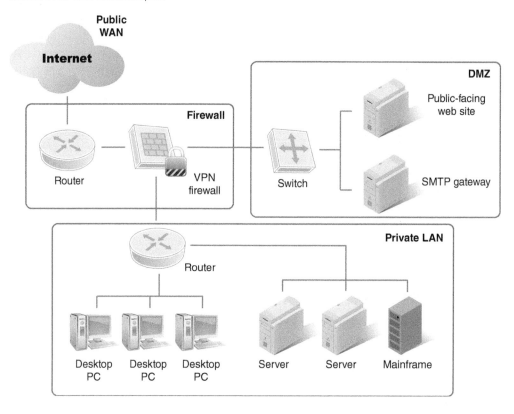

limit traffic and alert the security teams. For example, assume typical overseas customers represent 3 percent of your website's traffic, but then suddenly turn into 99 percent of your traffic. This could be an indication of a potential breach, especially if that country of origin is known to be a source for hacks. Although each individual transaction looks valid, collectively the pattern can trigger firewall rules to restrict access.

WAN Domain

The **WAN domain**, for many organizations, is the Internet. Alternately, large organizations can lease dedicated lines and create a private WAN. However, as connectivity to the Internet has become more reliable, many organizations have switched from private WANs to using the Internet to connect offices all over the world.

A challenge for companies using the Internet to connect offices is how to keep communications secure and private. A common solution is a **virtual private network (VPN)**. By setting up network devices at both offices, you can create an encrypted tunnel through the Internet. The tunnel protects communication between the offices from eavesdropping. You can use a dedicated network device whose only function is to create and manage VPN traffic. These devices are *VPN concentrators*. Many firewalls also have the capability to create and maintain a VPN tunnel.

Organizations can lower communication costs by using VPN tunnels instead of leasing private lines for WANs. Beyond cost, there's also the issue of time. Leased lines for WANs can take weeks to months to order, contract for, install, and set up. Most companies already have an Internet connection. They can add VPN-compatible devices at both ends to establish a VPN tunnel in days. For small and medium-size companies, it's the only practical solution given the cost and technical complexities.

Cloud computing has emerged as a major technology. Sources predict cloud computing in the United States will reach $150 billion by the end of 2020.[2] *Forbes* predicts it will be over $300 billion by the end of 2022.[3] Eighty-one percent of all enterprises are already implementing or working on cloud computing strategies. McAfee reports that the average employee actively engages with over 30 cloud services.[4] By any measure, cloud computing is becoming ubiquitous. Most projections show that this will continue to grow in coming years.

Think of cloud computing as a way of buying software, infrastructure, and platform services on someone else's network. You rent this capability when you need it and stop paying when you are done. It's like renting a car: If you have out-of-town guests, you might rent a large van while they are in town. Your costs are incurred during their stay. When your guests leave, you return the van and go back to driving your two-seat sports car. Likewise, cloud computing allows you to rent additional computing power when you need it and release it when the demand is low. Access to cloud computing is typically through the WAN (i.e., Internet).

Remote Access Domain

The **Remote Access domain** is nothing more than an enhanced User domain. The only difference is that you are traveling from a public unsecure network into the private secure company network. You have all the issues you have in the User domain plus special remote authentication and network connectivity issues.

Remote authentication has always been a concern because the person is coming from a public network. Do you truly know that individual is an employee, or is he or she a hacker pretending to be an employee? There's less of a concern when accessing the network within the office. The office might have guards at the entrance, locked doors, badges, and visibility of people sitting at workstations. Over the Internet, how do you know who's on the other side of the wire? Most organizations today feel that an ID and password combination is not an adequate authentication method for remote access.

Many companies require **two-factor authentication** for remote access. Two-factor authentication requires an end user to authenticate his or her identity using at least two of three different types of credentials. The three most commonly accepted types of credentials are as follows:

- **Something you know**—Refers to something only you are supposed to know, such as your ID and password combination. You should never share your password with anyone.
- **Something you have**—Refers to a unique device that you must have in your physical possession to gain access. This physical device could be your computer itself. In general

terms, all devices have identities, from your laptop to your phone. The physical device you are logged on with can be used as a way of verifying your identity.

- **Something you are**—Refers to some sort of biometric feature such as a fingerprint scanner.

Technical TIP

There are many ways to verify a computer's identity. A common method is using digital certificates. In general terms, the certificate acts like a digital fingerprint. Of course, this requires issuing digital certificates to all computers you wish to have connect to your system. This is useful in verifying that the user is on a specific computer. For example, suppose a bank wants to make sure any money wired is sent from only one computer in a locked room. That would provide both a physical and logical control over sending money. The wire application could verify the digital fingerprint of the remote computer to verify that any wire request is coming from a specific authorized computer.

NOTE

In 2012, the Federal Financial Institutions Examination Council (FFIEC) issued guidance entitled "Authentication in an Electronic Banking Environment." It requires financial institutions go beyond using just IDs and passwords. It requires banks to use **multifactor authentication** more widely.

Many organizations today require two-factor authentication for remote users. The authentication factors may be an ID/password combination (something you know) plus some type of token or smart card (something you have) to authenticate remote access. This provides a high level of confidence that the remote user is an employee. Some tokens can be loaded directly to the company laptop. The laptop becomes something you must have to connect remotely.

Remote network connectivity has the issues previously discussed with WAN domains: how to keep communications secure and private. A VPN is typically the solution. You can configure a VPN to permit only predefined workstations to be connected. Each site has a dedicated hardware device that creates an encrypted tunnel through the Internet. This is typically called a site-to-site VPN connection. A remote user can also create a VPN tunnel. Instead of having VPN hardware at home, you have a desktop or laptop with software called a VPN client. This VPN client communicates with the VPN hardware to create the same type of encrypted tunnel through the Internet. This is typically called a client-to-site VPN connection. In both cases, VPN is used to secure the communication through the Internet. **FIGURE 4-4** illustrates the site-to-site and client-to-site connectivity.

The combination of enhanced remote authentication and network connectivity can be a powerful tool to ensure a network's protection. Yet these tools also extend the business network anywhere in the world. Consider this scenario: Shelly, an executive, receives a call on a Saturday to approve a change to a vital business shipment. For Shelly to approve the shipment, she must review the changes on an internal system and electronically sign off on the changes; however, she is away for the weekend with her family.

Fortunately, Shelly has her laptop in the hotel, and she has an Internet connection. She signs on to her company laptop and connects to the network using her ID/password and a

FIGURE 4-4

Basic types of VPN connectivity.

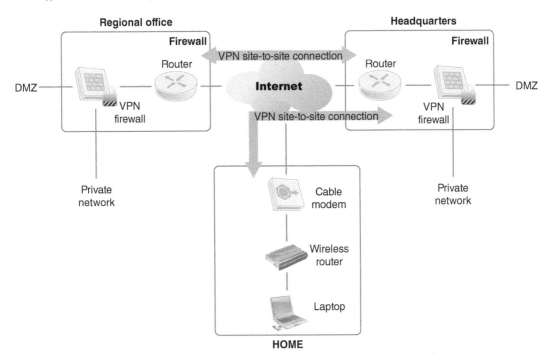

token she carries on her keychain. A VPN tunnel is established, and her laptop is authorized onto the network. Shelly can now access the system the same way she does from her desk in the office. The encrypted communications are secure and private. She can review the shipment change and approve its release. The use of the ID/password and token achieves authentication and nonrepudiation for any transactions Shelly decides to execute. The confidentiality and integrity of the communication is achieved through encrypting the tunnel.

System/Application Domain

As complex as networks are, they essentially secure communication between an end user and some application software. What collects, processes, and stores data is ultimately software. Business software is typically an *application*. **System software**, such as a server operating system, runs business applications. The **System/Application domain** refers to all the system and application software-related issues.

Application software is at the heart of all business applications. Application software can run on a workstation or server. For example, an application can display a screen by which customers and employees can select products and enter data. Once the information is collected, the application transmits the transaction to a server. The server stores the information in a database to be processed later or instantly processes the transaction, stores the results, and displays information back to the end user. Later an employee can extract data from this ordering application into a spreadsheet to track the total number of orders each month by product type. The application that took the orders, the spreadsheet that tracked the orders, and perhaps the email client used to announce record sales for the month are all examples of application software.

FYI

People often use the terms *system software* and *application software* interchangeably. They are not the same. Generally, any business software that an end user (including customers) touches is an application. This includes email, word processing, and spreadsheet software. The operating system, which is the software that runs applications, and software that allows a computer to communicate over a network are system software.

Information Security Business Challenges and Security Policies That Mitigate Risk Within the Seven Domains

The previous section provided a foundational understanding of each of the seven domains. In this section, you will examine the business challenges and risks in each domain. You will also learn how the proper application of security policies can mitigate many of these risks.

User Domain

For an organization to be efficient requires the proper alignment of people, processes, and technology. As with most technology problems that are enormous in size, scope, and complexity, the best approach to finding a solution is to break down the problem into manageable pieces. In this case, the goal for business is to have this alignment to produce consistent, repeatable, high-quality results. The challenge is that humans are not always predictable and consistent. So, any process that relies on humans must reinforce good behavior and verify results often. This reinforcement of education, monitoring, and adjusting behaviors is a never-ending cycle in implementing security policies.

Employee efficiency starts with well-defined policies that reflect the organization's reasonable expectations. Security policies must closely align with business requirements. This situation allows employees to understand the importance of the policy to the organization. It also ensures that security policies support business goals. One of the major business challenges is getting employees to follow policies. There are several ways good security policies can mitigate this risk, as follows:

- **Awareness**—Policies require employees to receive formal security awareness training. Most importantly, this training lets employees know where to go for help when the unexpected arises. The training also sets expectations on the handling of sensitive information that needs to be protected, such as ensuring customer privacy.
- **Enforcement**—Security controls flow from security policies. These controls are designed to enforce how the business wishes to operate. Among the most important security

controls are those that enforce segregation of duties. *Segregation of duties*, or *separation of duties*, means a single person cannot execute a high-risk transaction, for example, wiring large sums of money out of a bank. Typically, this requires one person to request the wire and a manager to approve the transfer.

- **Reward**—Refers to how management reinforces the value of following policies. An organization should put in place both disciplinary actions for not following policies and recognition for adhering to policies. This could be as simple as noting the level of compliance to policies in the employee's annual review.

- **Monitoring**—It's not enough to publish well-defined security policies. You have to know they are working. Monitoring can take many forms. Typically, it is a combination of quality assurance and quality control. Quality *assurance* is about verifying and approving actions before they occur. Quality *control* is about sampling work that has already been done to ensure that, collectively, actions meet standards. This combination of two types of monitoring can be used to drive enforcement and improve awareness.

Another business concern is handling sensitive information in physical form, such as reports. As noted earlier, many organizations have a *clean desk policy*. This policy generally requires employees to lock up all documents and digital media at the end of a workday and when not in use. Compliance checks are relatively easy because any report or CD left out overnight is a violation of policy. This protects customer privacy and reminds employees of the sensitivity of company information. It also sets the right image for customers and vendors who may be visiting the office.

Security policies also ensure that contractors and consultants are properly vetted before gaining access to company information. This includes performing background checks. Employees and nonemployees alike must follow security policies.

Not all business processes can be standardized. Employees sometimes transfer knowledge by word of mouth, such as how to run some nonstandard transaction. The potential for significant failure in these processes may exist. At a minimum, when a failure occurs, the security policies ensure the process and related data can be restored.

Workstation Domain

Locking your front door but leaving your window wide open is not good security. Let's assume you have good authentication and you know who is signed onto your network. However, if a workstation is breached, you could have malicious software compromising your network whenever the authorized user connects.

The ramifications of a security breach are more severe for some organizations that are regulated. The expectation is that leading practices are being applied to prevent such breaches. Security policies help identify those practices and ensure they are applied to protecting the workstation. That includes ensuring that all workstations that access the network are patched and have antivirus software installed. The business may not be aware of many of these basic common controls expected by regulators. The security policies ensure such controls are in place and help ensure regulatory compliance.

Effective security is often a matter of determining some basic security configuration rules and applying them consistently across your enterprise. Applying such security without disrupting the business is a concern. For most organizations, the days of sending a technology person to each desk to configure a workstation are long past. Security policies can help establish a reliable automated patch management process. Security policies can specify the type and frequency of patches to apply. The policies often require IT to test patches in a lab setting before applying them to workstations. Changes are made at night so there is a minimal impact on the company's day-to-day operations.

Security policies also reduce the risk of malware by limiting access to workstations. Usually an end user does not have administrative rights on a workstation. This means the end user cannot inadvertently install programs like malware that could launch a botnet attack.

FYI

A *botnet* is a collection of computers infected by malware loaded onto them by hackers without the knowledge of the computers' owners. What distinguishes this type of attack from others is its ability to create a vast array of computers that all communicate for a single purpose. For example, a botnet can be used to launch a distributed denial of service (DDoS) attack from millions of points across the globe.

If they cannot breach your company's network directly, hackers often attempt to breach a workstation and infect it in some manner. The attempt is to either capture information from the workstation or use the workstation as a way to access the protected network. Security policies are good at outlining the rules for protecting workstations. One good example is encrypting laptop hard drives. This has become standard practice in many industries. With the increase in mobile computing, sensitive data leaves networks more easily and more often. As a result, many companies that handle sensitive information encrypt their employees' laptop hard drives. In that way, if the laptop is lost or stolen, the sensitive data is protected.

Many security policies require the encryption of data whenever the information leaves the protection of the network. This include encrypting data over the Internet; in emails; and on mobile devices such as universal serial bus (USB) drives, CDs, smart phones, tablets, and laptops. Despite these efforts, 2019 was a record year for data losses due to breaches, according to a study published in February 2020. The study noted 3800 recorded incidents, resulting in 4.2 billion records being exposed. This illustrates the need to have strong policies, monitoring, and enforcement.

Security policies that set encryption standards need to ensure the vendors and contractors follow the same policies that employees are required to follow.

LAN Domain

Many organizations have discovered that granting mobile access to business applications can increase productivity and revenue. A LAN is all about connectivity for the business. The more easily you can be connected to a LAN, the faster you can start accessing and exchanging data. Wireless and mobile computing have changed the way people understand LANs. This new view affects the perception of LAN and Remote Access domain issues.

Wireless connectivity allows you to view the LAN more broadly than the computer on your desktop. Handled devices allow you to extend your LAN network out of the office and into the business. In other words, you can connect to the network and access or exchange information where the product or service is being made or delivered. Here are a few examples of how using wireless technology can extend the LAN into the business:

- **Health care**—Healthcare providers can access real-time patient information or medical research from a patient's bedside. These devices enhance collaboration for more accurate diagnoses. These devices can also track medical equipment to ensure availability at critical times.
- **Manufacturing**—Wireless connectivity allows employees to share real-time data on the factory floor.
- **Retail**—Wireless access to a LAN helps retailers place intelligent cash registers where there is no network wiring. This network access allows retailers to manage inventory, check customers out faster, and print the latest promotion coupons from the register.

Extending the LAN has many advantages over just connecting a standard PC. LANs today can carry voice, video, and traditional computer traffic. Voice over Internet Protocol (VoIP) allows you to place and receive phone calls over a LAN or WAN. This has become popular for both home and business because of the cost savings over traditional telephone systems. Rather than incurring high flat-rate fees and per-minute call charges, most VoIP services charge a low flat-rate fee. New companies continue to enter the market offering less expensive voice and video solutions over the Internet.

Organizations often view LANs much like utilities such as electricity, water, or gas. The organization expects the LAN to always be available and always have capacity. It's also thought of as a commodity that should be inexpensive to install and run. This puts tremendous pressures on LAN resources. Bandwidth within the LAN, for example, decreases as new services such as VoIP and video are offered.

It's not uncommon to have security policies limit the use of live video, music feeds, and social media sites. They can represent hours of lost employee and contractor productivity. These feeds also take up significant bandwidth. For example, as far back as 2012, Procter & Gamble, with 129,000 employees, used security policies to stop video and music feeds. Many such policies can be enforced at the firewall, cutting off the source of video and music from the Internet. However, with the Covid-19 pandemic in 2020, many companies depended on video for remote workers.

Even with these business challenges, the benefits of extending a LAN beyond the workstation are enormous and include enhanced productivity, collaboration, and responsiveness.

> **NOTE**
>
> LANs today often carry physical security information, such as video feeds. With this expanded capability, you can see the growing integration of logical and physical security. For example, employee card access is tightly aligned with an individual's logical security access. These work together both to control the room one can access and to restrict the computers one can access once one is in the room.

> **NOTE**
>
> Bandwidth is a measurement that quantifies how much information can be transmitted over the network. When a LAN reaches its maximum bandwidth, it becomes susceptible to many kinds of transmission errors and delays.

LAN-to-WAN Domain

A major concern of organizations is protection of the servers in the DMZ. In other words, are the website servers protected? Organizations are particularly concerned about website availability

NOTE

An organization's reputation can be diminished by the appearance of **web graffiti** on its website. Web graffiti is a result of **website defacement**, in which a website is breached and its content altered, usually in a way that embarrasses the website owner. Web graffiti can contain abusive language or even pornographic images.

and integrity. The websites for many organizations represent their public image and, for companies, their major sales channel.

Security policies set strict rules on how DMZ traffic should be limited and monitored. Security policies outline how the DMZ server should be configured and how often security patches should be applied. Security policies also outline how often external penetration testing is conducted. Penetration testing probes the network for weaknesses and vulnerabilities from the outside looking in. Penetration testing is required by many standards and is considered a best practice; for example, if you accept or process credit cards, PCI DSS requires penetration testing.

However, these rules and limitations put onto the DMZ create their own risks. DDoS attacks typically attempt to overwhelm the DMZ capability, resulting in the servers crashing and becoming unavailable. So, the more limits put on the traffic, the more you have to test whether the systems can withstand a DDoS attack. It's not enough just to limit traffic; the policy must also ensure that systems stay available.

WAN Domain

When it comes to WANs, an organization is generally concerned about cost, reliability, and speed. As discussed earlier in the chapter, many organizations use virtual private networking to protect and secure communications over the Internet. With most organizations having already incurred the cost of Internet connectivity, the use of secure communications over the Internet is now seen as a de facto standard.

 NOTE

With virtual private networking, you "tunnel" through the public Internet to reach a specific site. Typically, two VPN devices establish a site-to-site VPN tunnel. Both devices are usually preconfigured with keys so only these devices communicate with each other. Once the tunnel is established, it can link entire LANs. A remote office, for example, can link to headquarters.

Cost-wise, a VPN over the Internet is the right choice. The cost is modest. Because most organizations already have Internet connectivity, IT can quickly deploy VPN technology. It could be as easy as installing devices and synching keys to establish a VPN tunnel.

The reliability of a VPN depends on your Internet service provider (ISP). You can experience reliability issues even if your ISP guarantees a level of service while you're traveling over a public network. Think of the Internet like a road system. You have local roads, main arteries, and superhighways. Some ISPs advertise how many hops away from the Internet backbone they are. The *Internet backbone* represents the superhighway in our road system and can handle the fastest traffic. In theory, the fewer hops it takes to get to the backbone, the faster your access. A *hop* is a term meaning generally how many routers you have to pass through to get to your destination. If you have to go through a lot of back roads to get to your destination, it takes a lot longer than if you live close to a superhighway. The same holds true for the Internet traffic. Many large organizations will connect to multiple ISPs. This will give the redundancy needed in the event a single ISP fails to deliver the needed connection speed.

Although speed over the Internet continues to improve, it's not an unlimited resource. To control usage, many ISPs limit bandwidth. As upper limits are reached, some customers may be transferred to slower network connections. This may be acceptable for a home user;

however, for a business this could be devastating. Businesses often require consistent response times for the customer. To achieve that, they pay a premium to the ISP. This premium places the business on a less crowded network connection that has excess capacity to ensure the response level does not fall below a prescribed level. This makes predicting reliability less of a challenge.

> **NOTE**
>
> Private WANs are point-to-point solutions that are not publicly shared and thus are usually not encrypted. Service providers of private WANs can guarantee upload and download bandwidth consistency.

Deciding on a public or private WAN solution for your organization depends on your requirements and budget. Small organizations have few options. For large enterprises, both WAN options are available.

Security policies outline how each connection type should be configured and protected. The security policies also outline roles and responsibilities. Keep in mind that the service provider typically configures private WAN security. Therefore, your security policies need to include how to deal with the vendor and how to validate the security configuration. Companies of any size can manage security for Internet-based VPN solutions in-house.

Remote Access Domain

When it comes to remote access, organizations are concerned about flexibility, reliability, and speed. As discussed, extending the LAN into the business where products are produced and services delivered has tremendous benefits. This is also true for extending the LAN anywhere in the world. This is where remote access concerns need to be addressed.

When it comes to flexibility, employees cannot be tethered to their desktops. Laptops have broken that tie, allowing employees to connect to the company network wherever there is an Internet connection. Wireless connections further extend the flexibility of laptops. Today, travelers and mobile employees often use a laptop with a mobile hotspot to access the Internet and work network. A mobile hotspot can be a personal device that acts like a cell phone for a laptop, allowing the end user to obtain a broadband Internet connection. These personal hotspots often support connections for typically four to eight devices. *Hotspot* can also refer to a fixed Internet access point available to the public; for example, coffee shops often provide hotspot access to the Internet for their customers.

Mobile devices and broadband are becoming very reliable; however, the speed and reliability with which they can access and exchange data depend on location and carrier. Much like cell phone coverage, mobile broadband coverage is spotty at times. Despite their drawbacks, mobile devices offer many business benefits, including:

- Increased customer responsiveness
- Quick reaction to news and business-related events
- Advantage of real-time data access

Bring your own device (BYOD) was mentioned previously in this chapter and is a current trend within many organizations. Recall that BYOD refers to allowing employees to bring their own devices to work to access the organization's data. For example, it could allow employees to access their company email through their personal smartphones. Businesses embrace BYOD to reduce cost and expand connectivity options. Costs are reduced because a company does not have to buy and deploy company-owned mobile devices.

Security depends on your business requirements—how much data you need to send and how fast you need it to arrive. Some good examples are the use of smartphones and iPads and other tablet computers. They are very efficient for gaining access to well-defined applications such as email; however, they do introduce risks and policy questions that must be addressed. Some security policy questions that must be addressed for handheld device use include:

- Who owns the device?
- Who has the right to wipe the device if it's lost or stolen?
- How do you encrypt data on the device?
- How do you apply patches?
- Who's allowed to have such a device connected to the company network?

With any emerging technology, well-defined security policies help an organization think through these risk decisions. Security policies ensure risk assessments are performed and leading practices are reviewed. This is vital so the organization can understand not only the benefits of new technology, but also the risks.

Security policies should not focus on specific products, but on broader capability. A smartphone can access email but also has a camera. Rather than addressing smartphones, a well-defined policy deals more broadly with mobile email access and acceptable use of digital recordings. By taking this approach as new technology is introduced, the organization covers the capability in the policy. Perhaps the most effective way to address BYOD is through the use of Network Access Control (NAC), which was also briefly mentioned earlier in this chapter.

System/Application Domain

An organization has two main concerns when it comes to information collected, stored, and processed: Is the information safe? Can you prevent confidential information from leaving the organization? These seem like fairly easy questions, but they are complicated to answer.

This chapter has discussed many ways to keep information safe. Security policies ensure risks are evaluated throughout the seven domains. Security policies ensure alignment to business requirements. When risks exist, security policies ensure a risk assessment is performed so that management can make a balanced decision.

In this section, you will focus on the second business concern of how to prevent confidential information from leaving the organization. Security policies define what's often called either a **data loss protection (DLP)** program or a **data leakage protection (DLP)** program. Both terms refer to a formal program that reduces the likelihood of accidental or malicious loss of data.

Company managers worry about secret business information ending up in competitors' hands. Managers must also protect customer privacy as required by law. A hacker does not have to be physically present to steal your business secrets, especially if he or she is a disgruntled employee who might work in a data-sensitive area of the company. Your top salesperson might leave the company to work for a competitor and email your entire sales database to his home Internet account. These are not theoretical losses to a business. You must ensure that all of your potential data leaks, both physical and digital, are plugged.

The concept of DLP comes from the acknowledgment that data changes form and often gets copied, moved, and stored in many places. This sensitive data often leaves the protection of application databases and ends up in emails, spreadsheets, and personal workstation files. Business is most concerned about data that lives outside the hardened protection of an application.

A typical DLP program provides several layers of defense to prevent confidential data from leaving the organization, including:

- Inventory
- Perimeter
- Device management

Inventory

The DLP inventory component attempts to identify where sensitive data may be stored. This includes scanning workstations, email folders, and file servers. The process requires actually inspecting the content of files and determining if they contain sensitive information such as Social Security numbers. Once data locations are identified, reports can be created to compare the security of files with security policies. For example, this helps prevent private customer information from accidentally being stored in a public email folder. Although this is an important capability, it has its limitations. The ability to understand the sensitivity of a file is very difficult to automate. Either you end up having too many false positives or you end up missing the identification of sensitive data.

Perimeter

The DLP perimeter component ensures that data is protected on every endpoint on your network, regardless of the operating system or type of device. It checks data as it moves, including the writing of data to email, optical devices, USB devices, instant messaging, and print. If sensitive data is written to an unauthorized device, the technology can either stop and archive the file or send an alternate. It stops data loss initiated by malware and file sharing that can hijack employee information. Through the logging and analysis server, the DLP perimeter monitors real-time events and generates detailed forensics reports.

You can also establish and manage security policies to regulate and restrict how your employees use and transfer sensitive data. It uses the same basic technology that is applied with the inventory component. It has the same limitations. Because you are dealing with data movement, you can add rules not often found in the inventory process, such as not permitting large database files to be emailed. Regardless of content, these rules can stop a hacker from sending a large volume of data out the door.

Device Management

In many ways, mobile devices like smartphones and tablets are mobile external hard drives. They carry the same information that can sit on a workstation or server. When an executive receives an email on an upcoming merger or a doctor gets a message about a patient, the information needs the same protection as if it were on a workstation or server. The information on mobile devices is subject to the same regulatory requirements. This means you must also apply the same level of controls, such as encryption.

The ability to manage these devices from a central service is essential. As new threats are identified, this device management capability is essential to push out patches and ensure controls are working well.

You need a DLP program because loss of confidential data hurts the reputation of a business, discloses competitive secrets, and often violates regulation. Well-defined security policies establish a formal DLP program within an organization.

CHAPTER SUMMARY

You learned in this chapter how to break up policies into seven domains. You examined each of the domains to learn why they exist, looked at related business concerns, and learned how to mitigate common risks. Security policies have to be aligned to the business. Most important, security policies can highlight regulatory and leading practice to guide the business in controlling these risks.

This chapter examined the changing nature of business through technologies such as wireless and handheld devices. You read about the differences between access methods such as RBAC and ABAC. It is important that security policies keep pace with changing technologies. You also saw what happens when security policies are not effective, as when more than 4.2 billion customer records were exposed in 2019. You should better understand the expanding role of the LAN to establish global connectivity through WANs. You also learned about techniques that keep this communication protected and private, such as VPN. Finally, you learned about the importance of having a DLP program defined in your security policies and about the drivers for DLP, including BYOD programs. DLP programs help organizations reduce the likelihood of data loss.

KEY CONCEPTS AND TERMS

- Application software
- Attribute-based access control (ABAC)
- Bring your own device (BYOD)
- Data leakage protection (DLP)
- Data loss protection (DLP)
- Demilitarized zone (DMZ)
- Discovery management
- Domain
- Email policy
- Firewall
- Flat network
- Help desk management
- Inventory management
- LAN domain
- LAN-to-WAN domain
- Log management
- Multifactor authentication
- Patch management
- Privacy policy
- Remote Access domain
- Remote authentication
- Role-based access control (RBAC)
- Router
- Security management
- Segmented network
- Sniffer
- Switch
- System access policy
- System/Application domain
- System software
- Two-factor authentication
- User domain
- Virtual private network (VPN)
- WAN domain
- Web graffiti
- Website defacement
- Workstation domain

CHAPTER 4 ASSESSMENT

1. Private WANs must be encrypted at all times.

A. True
B. False

2. Which of the following attempts to identify where sensitive data is currently stored?

A. Data leakage protection inventory
B. DLP encryption key
C. Data loss protection perimeter
D. DLP trojans

3. Voice over Internet Protocol (VoIP) can be used over which of the following?

A. LAN
B. WAN
C. Both
D. Neither

4. Which of the following is *not* one of the seven domains of typical IT infrastructure?

A. Remote Access domain
B. LAN domain
C. World Area Network domain
D. System/Application domain

5. Which of the seven domains refers to the technical infrastructure that connects the organization's LAN to a WAN and allows end users to surf the Internet?

6. One key difference between RBAC and ABAC is which of the following?

A. ABAC is dynamic, and RBAC is static.
B. ABAC is static, and RBAC is dynamic.
C. No difference; these are just different terms to mean the same thing.

7. A _____ is a term that refers to a network that limits what computers can say and how they are able to talk to each other.

8. A LAN is efficient for connecting computers within an office or groups of buildings.

A. True
B. False

9. What policy generally requires that employees lock up all documents and digital media at the end of a workday and when not in use?

A. Acceptable use policy
B. Clean desk policy
C. Privacy policy
D. Walk out policy

10. What employees learn in awareness training influences them more than what they see within their department.

A. True
B. False

11. What kind of workstation management refers to knowing what software is installed?

A. Inventory management
B. Patch management
C. Security management
D. Discovery management

12. Always applying the most strict authentication method is the best way to protect the business and ensure achievement of goals.

A. True
B. False

13. Generally, remote authentication provides which of the following?

A. Fewer controls than if you were in the office
B. The same controls as if you were in the office
C. More controls than if you were in the office
D. Less need for controls than in the office

14. Remote access does not have to be encrypted if strong authentication is used.

A. True
B. False

15. Where is a DMZ usually located?

A. Inside the private LAN
B. Within the WAN
C. Between the private LAN and public WAN
D. Within the mail server

16. Dedicated network devices whose only function is to create and manage VPN traffic are called VPN _____.

17. What is a botnet?

    A. A piece of software the end user loads onto a device to prevent intrusion

    B. A piece of software a company loads onto a device to monitor its employees

    C. A piece of software a hacker loads onto a device without user knowledge

    D. A piece of software used to communicate between peers

18. The minimum standard in authentication for businesses is the use of _____.

ENDNOTES

1. Marr, Bernard, "How Much Data Do We Create Every Day? The Mind-Blowing Stats Everyone Should Read," *Forbes*, *https://www.forbes.com/sites/bernardmarr /2018/05/21/how-much-data-do-we-create -every-day-the-mind-blowing-stats-everyone -should-read/#3ad8b75b60ba*, accessed April 13, 2020.

2. Ch., Radoslave, "Cloud Computing Statistics 2020," Techjury, March 28, 2019, *https://techjury.net/stats-about/cloud -computing/*, accessed April 13, 2020.

3. Columbus, Louis, "Public Cloud Soaring to $331B by 2022 According to Gartner," *Forbes*, *https://www.forbes.com/sites/louiscolumbus /2019/04/07/public-cloud-soaring-to-331b -by-2022-according-to-gartner/#39bdacfb5739*, accessed April 13, 2020.

4. McAfee, "12 Must-Know Statistics on Cloud Usage in the Enterprise," March 9, 2017, *https://www.skyhighnetworks.com/cloud-security -blog/12-must-know-statistics-on-cloud-usage-in -the-enterprise/*, accessed April 13, 2020.

Information Security Policy Implementation Issues

SUCCESSFUL IMPLEMENTATION of information security policies starts before the policies are even written. Implementation depends on how well the policy is integrated into existing business processes and how well it is understood and embraced by leadership and employees. Implementing information security policies often results in putting in controls that slow the exchange of data. Creating, implementing, and maintaining adequate security control can seem burdensome, but is entirely necessary. Successful implementation of policies, therefore, must be viewed as a journey from conception to implementation. You must start with engagement, with creating awareness within the organization, and by building consensus on the need to implement the policy. As difficult as the technological side of information security can be, the human side, because it's so unpredictable, can be even more challenging.

Once a security policy is created or revised and agreed upon, the implementation process starts. The process of implementing security policies can be harder than creating the document itself. You should not underestimate this effort. Implementing security policies successfully takes a combination of soft skills in dealing with human nature and company culture and hard skills in project management. The number of tasks and considerations can seem overwhelming. It's important to take a systematic approach that keeps the implementation moving forward and supporters engaged.

A new policy or one that changes a common operation can make implementation difficult. Resistance to a policy viewed as restricting some necessary or desired operation can occur. Ensuring all personnel are informed and educated on the new or changed policy is critical. Educating personnel on policy issues is one of the more challenging aspects of policies.

Security policies specify ways to control risk and reflect the core values of the organization. This means security policies are as much about promoting a risk-aware culture and motivating workers as they are about implementing technical business requirements. Therefore, it's important to keep in mind that a successful implementation must motivate, gain consensus, and compete with an individual's priorities. Gaining executive support is one of the keys to success. This means you must be able to communicate the value of the security policies. You must be able to explain why the business and individuals should care. This takes skill in influencing others and marketing the value of the security policies.

In this chapter, you will review many of the issues and problems faced when implementing security policies. The chapter gives pointers on how to overcome these challenges and how to deal with human nature in the workplace. The chapter also gives guidance on how to manage security policy changes in your organization.

Chapter 5 Topics

This chapter covers the following topics and concepts:

- How to deal with human nature in the workplace
- What various organizational structures are
- How to overcome user apathy
- Why executive management support is important
- Why support from human resources policies is important
- How security policies influence roles, responsibilities, and accountability
- What happens when policy fulfillment isn't part of the job description
- How an entrepreneurial approach affects productivity and efficiency
- Why it's important to find the right measure of employee performance and accountability in implementing security policies

Chapter 5 Goals

When you complete this chapter, you will be able to:

- Describe what a control partner is
- Describe how people are motivated in the workplace
- Describe different workplace personality types
- Compare advantages and disadvantages of different organization structures
- Describe the basic characteristics of organizational structure
- Explain how user apathy affects security policy implementation
- Explain the importance of executive and human resources support
- Describe the importance of a change model in implementing security policies
- Describe key tasks within a change model
- Explain key roles and responsibilities in implementing security policies
- Describe attributes of an entrepreneurial business unit

Human Nature in the Workplace

A successful security policy implementation depends on people understanding key concepts and embracing the material. Understanding and influencing different personalities in the workplace will be important to achieving that success. But it's not just the needs of the internal employee you need to consider. A variety of stakeholders will have an interest in information security policies, including external parties such as vendors, customers, and regulators. As competition grows globally, new channels of sales and products appear. These factors are usually accompanied by a change in technologies. Enormous efforts and resources are spent to document, debug, and map an organization's processes to these technologies. Over time, technology, frameworks, and standards evolve to become best practices. Success does not come by technology or process alone. Successful security policy implementation depends on the correct alignment of people, processes, and technology.

How much time and resources are placed on the people element? Too often, not enough.

This section explores human nature in the workplace. More precisely, it looks at different personality types and how they affect the adoption of security policies. A successful security policy implementation is defined in part when an employee understands the key concepts and can apply them broadly to situations that are not anticipated. Going beyond what one is told helps define a successful implementation of security policies.

One practical method of gaining support and educating staff is storytelling. At a previous position, this author would make a habit of sending out a brief story each month to the employees of that company. The story briefly told of a salacious security breach, then explained that this is why a given policy or policies were in place. The communication was both brief and interesting to employees. This proved to be an effective method for communication.

Basic Elements of Motivation

What is motivation? What makes a help desk employee work persistently to fix your problem? It's being enthusiastic, energized, and engaged to achieve a goal or objective. A lack of motivation can be measured in poor customer service and doing the minimum to get by, with mediocre results.

There are several possible sources of motivation: pride, self-interest, fear, desire, and success. Some of these are appropriate for the workplace, others less so. Fear is not usually recommended. Clearly, there are consequences for failing to adhere to policies, but the primary motivation to follow policies should not be fear. Having employees take pride in their work and understand their own interest is served by policies, and employees' desire to perform well in the workplace are positive methods of motivation and should be used.

Good leadership can motivate employees. Consider, for example, when information security policies are implemented effectively across all teams but one. A review of differences between the teams would be in order. Suppose that review indicates that all teams across the enterprise use the same technology and received the training, and that all other factors were the same, except that, of course, different teams have different leadership. Then the unsuccessful implementation could be attributed to lack of effective leadership.

An important first step is ensuring that leadership at all levels of the company values security. It begins, of course, at the top executive levels, but valuing security must permeate all levels of management, including midlevel and lower-level managers.

Pride

Pride is part of human nature. Individuals are more likely to become motivated when they are working on something that is important. If your work is discarded or trivialized, you're less likely to put in a high-quality effort the next time. Conversely, if you understand the goals and objectives of the team and see how your individual efforts contribute, you will likely feel a sense of obligation. It also builds team pride and spirit, which are important for future successes.

An important component of pride involves an understanding of the overall goals and objectives. Management is responsible for informing employees of their roles and how their efforts contribute to the larger goal. This is where good leaders can motivate, and poor leaders can derail a good security policy. A manager's comment, "You must do it because the security department says to" is a good indication of poor leadership. In this case, management may not embrace the policy, and more important, staff might perceive the policy as a burden. That perception can lead to the staff doing only the bare minimum. Conversely, a manager could approach the employees and outline the problem being solved. He or she might add their personal endorsement of the action taken. The manager could position the policy change as an opportunity to expand staff skills and to stress the importance of protecting the customer.

Pride can be a powerful motivator. It can also create competition and a sense of self-worth. Managers must control competition so that the sole measure of success is not simply completing the task first. Managers must also promote helping each other so the "team" can succeed. Measuring success needs to include all the values important to the organization, including quality of service, customer satisfaction, and teamwork.

In order to utilize pride as a motivating factor in security, it is important to accurately communicate the value of security to the entire organization. This begins with a realistic understanding of the threats. The entire organization needs to understand the dangers, so that they understand the countermeasures and the reasons for policies. Then employees can be motivated to excel at security. The security goals must be integrated with the business goals. For example, a sales team that is only evaluated on sales volume, without any concern for security, won't take pride in exceeding security goals.

Self-Interest

Self-interest, and sometimes self-preservation, is also part of human nature. Humans tend to repeat behavior that is rewarded. Having well-defined goals and objectives for individuals helps them understand what they must achieve. Those who achieve these goals receive rewards. Those who exceed these goals typically receive bigger or better rewards. Those individuals are "high achievers" or high performers. High achievers receive promotions more often and are models for others to emulate. To promote the importance of information and adherence to information policies, you should gain the support of high performers.

In a declining economic market, there's significant pressure on companies to cut jobs to save money. Employees who feel their jobs are at risk will not take chances. This could lead to individuals doing the minimum to stay out of trouble. Worse yet are individuals who feel they will be next to be let go. They may be angry and try to undermine management efforts. When an organization lays off employees, it's often called a **reduction in force**. Generally, it's not a good idea to implement significant policy changes during a force reduction.

Discipline also has an important self-preservation effect on our behavior. When an employee fails to perform, disciplinary action might be required. How management handles disciplinary actions either motivates or demotivates an employee. Unfortunately, discipline must be an element of security policy enforcement.

Everyone has strengths and weakness. Most people make mistakes, and at some point, they will do something foolish. One management approach is to look at an employee's pattern of behavior more than at individual errors in judgment. This approach has its limits, as in a case of sexual harassment or fraud. Except for these extreme cases, though, when management accepts failures as part of individual and team growth, a culture of taking chances emerges. More important, this approach creates the trust that encourages employees to report policy failures and breakdowns. Not only the individual employee, but also the whole organization can learn from such failures. This experience is often referred to as "lessons learned." Making it easier to record and track these lessons learned will allow the information security team to improve policies to prevent future problems.

> **NOTE**
>
> Disciplining employees can be risky if you don't do it right. You need to make sure that you do not discipline different employees differently for the same policy violation. Your inconsistency could lead to a lawsuit or a claim of employment discrimination. Always work through your human resources department and strictly follow company procedures in disciplining employees.

Taking chances and going beyond what's expected define high achievers and high-performance teams. Because security policies cannot define every event, their success depends on employees taking action by applying core principles to new situations. For example, you may have a clear policy and related process for setting up administrator accounts. Assume a vendor provides support for your organization. Assume it's not unusual for the vendor to request to change access to devices they support. Historically, it requests access changes once or twice a year. Now let's assume you receive a request from the vendor representative (in accordance with established processes) to remove all existing administrator accounts and replace them with new accounts. The request follows established processes.

However, those employees who understand the risks associated with administrator accounts and those who feel empowered might challenge the request and ask for additional authorization, even though additional approvers are not required by policy. And it might turn out that the vendor representative asking to make those highly unusual changes has just been fired or has just been the victim of some form of identity theft. In this scenario, the high-achieving employees who had the systems knowledge and the confidence to challenge the vendor rep could be what protect the organization.

Success

Wanting to be successful is part of human nature. Anyone who has played on a winning team knows the feeling. It's simply a lot more fun being on the winning team than on the team that always comes in last. Even if you are a high performer, it's hard to get motivated if your team as a whole keeps losing. It is no different in the workplace. Individuals build confidence when frequently recognized for their successes. These individuals quickly become highly motivated. Equally important, they can motivate others and support others to win. This is an essential element in creating a winning team. They can also afford to take chances and are more likely to build on their success by going beyond what's required.

Success is measured as the perception of how well you perform your work. This can, in turn, be defined by how you work as part of the team, ethical behavior, and the perception of your customers. There are certainly other definitions of success that are more narrow. Whatever one's definition, the desire for something we label as success seems universal.

You need to have some proficiency in soft skills to convince an organization to adopt security policies. *Soft skills* refer to certain social personality traits such as the ability to communicate and project optimism. Mastering these soft skills is essential to influencing others. This is particularly important when trying to sell new security policy and control concepts. More and more, business relies on the agility of its workforce to adapt to the unexpected. These skills are just as highly valued as technical knowledge. In other words, the "people" part of the equation is also critical to implementing security policies. Soft skills help turn people into high performers who apply their own knowledge effectively and draw out the best from others. Successful implementation of security policies over time will change individual attitudes. If that success continues throughout the organization, a culture that is more security and risk aware may emerge. This culture shift makes it much easier in the future to identify and mitigate risk.

Pride, self-interest, and success issues overlap and interact. Sustaining motivation comes by creating the right balance among these basic elements. When you achieve balance, you motivate not only individuals, but also teams, departments, and entire organizations. FIGURE 5-1 depicts these three basic elements of motivation and their intersections.

Motivated employees are far more likely to embrace the implementation of security policies. This leads to more risks being identified and mitigated for the organization.

Personality Types of Employees

It's easy to see firsthand that individuals react differently in the workplace. What motivates one person does not always work for another. Understanding different personality types within a team is key to understanding how to motivate people. It's important to understand

FIGURE 5-1

Three basic elements of motivation.

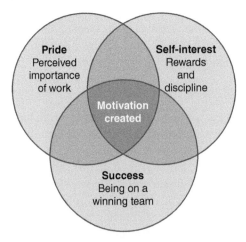

and appreciate the differences. This understanding allows you to leverage talents more effectively.

Let's illustrate this point with a simple example. Assume you're dealing with two key stakeholders in the Finance and Audit departments. The financial analyst may be analytical and want to know about the financial impact of implementing the new security policy. The auditor may be more focused on the outcome. What risks will be reduced after the policy is implemented? There may also be a host of individuals with a wide variety of motivations. Being able to recognize these differences will allow you to speak to the points of interest that will be most persuasive. Talking to financial analysts about threats might be good background to justify a project, but it doesn't address their potential concern about going over budget.

> **NOTE**
>
> Understanding personalities is particularly important in dealing with stakeholders. *Stakeholder* is a term referring to individuals who have an interest in the success of security policies. During the early stages of implementing a policy, the stakeholders play a critical role. If you understand their personalities and needs, you can motivate them to support the implementation.

HR Magazine identified eight classic personality types in the workplace. They are commanders, drifters, attackers, pleasers, performers, avoiders, analyticals, and achievers. In many ways, the personality names speak to the individual traits of each type. The following is a high-level summary of each of these traits:

- **Commanders**—Are demanding and not tactful. They might come across at best as impolite and at their worst as rude and abrupt. They are forceful when attempting to achieve stated goals. They can be agents for change, breaking from the past and overcoming barriers within the organization.
- **Drifters**—Are uncomfortable with structure and deadlines. They might be great with people and communications because what they lack in discipline may be offset by their creativity and thinking outside of the box.
- **Attackers**—May seem angry or even hostile toward ideas and others on the team. They are critical of others' ideas. They may know why things fail but offer no alternative solutions. They can be helpful in understanding the risks associated with a new policy, but don't expect them to offer solutions to make the policies better.
- **Pleasers**—Are very kind and thoughtful to others. They want everyone to "feel good" and will put their own self-interest aside for the good of the whole. They may shy away from enforcing rules that offend others. These individuals would not affect enforcing security policies.
- **Performers**—Like to be center stage. They like to entertain and be the center of attention. They develop over time a wit and charm to capture people's attention. They may not be the highest producers and may be in the habit of self-promotion. These individuals are good candidates to promote awareness of and training in security policies. Their wit and humor, when harnessed, are effective in communicating why the security policy is important.
- **Avoiders**—Like to fly under the radar and be in the background. They tend not to take chances or do anything that brings attention on them. They will do precisely what's asked of them but not much more. Although not good as leaders at looking beyond the letter of the policy, they will execute the security policy and related processes consistently.

- **Analyticals**—Like structure and deadlines. They measure their success in precise terms of the number of widgets produced in a given time at a given quality level. They tend to be obsessed with precision and attention to detail. They may not be the best at understanding human dynamics, so working with customers and emotions may be a problem. They would be well suited for measuring the effectiveness of the information policy, such as by being part of the quality control function.
- **Achievers**—Are result-oriented. They may have several traits of the other personality types; for example, they may be self-confident but not at the expense of others. They genuinely want the best result and may seek different ways to achieve it. Achievers are well suited to listening to all stakeholders and crafting security policies that meet both security and business needs.

FYI

Personality assessments have existed for a long time. The Myers-Briggs Type Indicator (MBTI), for example, was first published in 1962. Assessments of personality types have become more widely used recently because computer-based testing makes them easier to deliver and their perceived accuracy has grown. Such an assessment should not, however, be the sole basis for hiring someone. A test can simply help you better understand a job candidate. Personality tests are also helpful when forming teams for long-term or highly important projects. Human resources (HR) books and websites are also good sources for personality type models.

It's rare that an individual is just one of these personality types. Typically, personality types blend and mix depending on many factors. Dominant traits over time can become your safe zone. A *safe zone* refers to the skills you are comfortable with to achieve a predictable outcome.

Understanding these personality traits is an advantage in implementing security policies. Often, new security policies represent change. You can use the strengths of these personality traits to overcome objection to the change. For example, analyticals could review detail logs and network designs to identify potential security threats. There is no set rule of how to tap the talent of each of these personality types. Understanding these types allows you to leverage people's strengths to more quickly implement security policies.

Leadership, Values, and Ethics

Given all the material that has been written on the subject, entire libraries can be built around leadership, business values, and ethics. They are discussed in this section to help you better understand human nature in the workplace. This section focuses on how leadership affects employee behavior and how good leadership can help ensure that employees adhere to policies.

Leaders must require proper behavior from employees and exhibit the same qualities in their own actions. A leader who demonstrates ethical behavior every day is more likely to see that behavior emulated by employees. Good leaders recognize the need to work within these personality types, guide their energy and passion, and get results. A leader's job is to work through others to achieve specific goals. Implementing security policies is all about working through others to gain their support and adhere to the policies.

There is no secret formula for motivating individuals. Some widely accepted leadership rules that also apply to security policies include:

- **Values**—Good leaders have core values. Leaders share their core values with employees. Good leaders will seek to understand and convey the importance of security policies. Core values can also apply to the organization.
- **Goals**—Good leaders have clear vision and set goals. They communicate these goals both to the team and to individuals. They communicate how contributions lead to success. People want to know they are working on something that matters. Good leaders will be able to communicate the importance of the policy to the organization and to individual team goals.
- **Training**—Good leaders train their team to focus on goals and support each other's work. A good leader will make sure the team is ready to take on the additional responsibilities outlined in the policy. Training is also a key component of security. All of the policies and technology you can possibly imagine will be ineffective without properly trained employees.
- **Support**—Good leaders accept failures. Things will go wrong. People will make mistakes. How a leader reacts to these mistakes sets a tone that can be healthy or destructive. The trust a good leader creates is essential in encouraging accurate reporting of whatever is not working. This, in turn, is essential in improving the control environment. When employees trust that they can report noncompliance without repercussions and can report the reason the mistake was made, it's more likely that the problem can be corrected and kept from recurring. In fact, the practice of candid reporting of problems should be the norm and should be rewarded when it occurs.
- **Reward**—Good leaders reward results, not personalities. A quick way to demoralize a team is to reward individuals based on who is liked versus who produces. What's commonly referred to as "company politics" can never be eliminated; however, the more a leader can measure real risk reduction because of security policies and controls, the less interference from office politics will be encountered.

Part of understanding human nature in the workplace is recognizing its complexity. You need to understand what motivates individuals and yourself. A leader can't simply issue commands and expect good results time after time. Nor can an **executive** simply mandate information security policies and expect staff to follow them. Good leaders demonstrate core values in their own actions, and they communicate their expectations. They understand the human personality, ignite passions, and inspire people to achieve common goals. Managers and employees must understand these dynamics to approach implementation of security policies in a realistic and thoughtful manner.

Being thoughtful about the implementation of security policies and controls means balancing the need to reduce risk with the impact to the business operations. It could mean phasing security controls in over time or simply aligning security implementation with the business's training events.

> **NOTE**
>
> Implementing security policy means continuous communication with stakeholders. It means being transparent about what's working and what's not working. In this way, the control environment can be continuously improved over time.

Organizational Structures

The way an organizational structure evolves over time affects the way people behave. Management must determine the behaviors and values it wants to promote; then it can design an appropriate structure. The organizational structure chosen by management influences how security policies are put in place. It creates complex relationships and personal dynamics between different leaders, layers of approvals, and core values. An organization's structure reflects the relationship between teams (or departments), their responsibilities, and lines of authority. TABLE 5-1 highlights some common types of stakeholders. It is not an exhaustive list. The list of stakeholders will vary depending on the policy being implemented. For example, data center security policies will typically include physical security. Consequently, data center security policies will include building managers to ensure all doors are secure and cameras are well placed. But Table 5-1 does illustrate the broad and competing interests that must be addressed when implementing a security policy.

An organizational structure clearly indicates who's in charge and who reports to whom. FIGURE 5-2 depicts a typical U.S. company organizational chart. You can learn a lot from an organizational structure. In this example, notice two lines of business. Assume that these businesses are distinct enough that they require a separate focus and leadership. This could be because the products are distinctive or because the customer base has unique needs. For example, a bank typically separates its retail banking functions (including services such as personal checking accounts and lines of credit) from its commercial banking (business loans and checking accounts, among other services). Although both are banking functions, the products, customers, and regulations can be very different.

TABLE 5-1 Common Stakeholders

STAKEHOLDERS	KEY FOCUS AREAS
Lines of business	Timely delivery of high-quality products and services at competitive prices
Information security	Protection of the company and the customer
Compliance	Compliance with laws and regulations
Operational risk	Keeping operations within risk tolerances
IT architects	Setting of technical standards
IT developers	Building solutions to meet business and technical standards
IT operations	Operationalizing
Audit	Effective comprehensive assurance policies
Finance	Effectively managed budgets
Human resources	Hiring, management practices, and related activities
Executives	The leadership that ultimately approves all business decisions or approves which subordinate can make such decisions

FIGURE 5-2

Typical organizational chart.

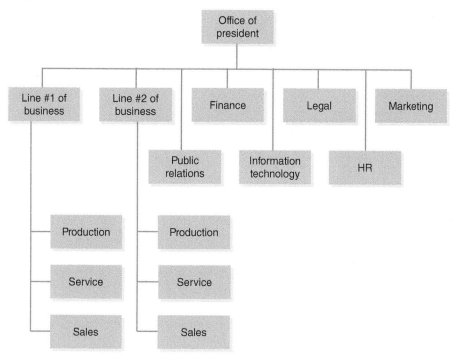

The key point is that an organizational structure provides insight into leadership's perspective on the business and the types of challenges faced. You also get a sense of priorities. You can see in Figure 5-2 that the business has decided to centralize the information technology (IT) function. This is typically called *shared services*. This term relates to a department or team that provides similar services across an entire organization. By centralizing services, a business can reduce operating costs. For example, rather than building two almost identical data centers to service two business lines, both can share the same data center operated by the IT department. Within the IT department's structure, you find a further breakdown on how services are provided to the two lines of business. Also notice how some departments report directly to the office of the president. This gives them greater influence and perceived authority.

Let's examine how these dynamics influence the implementation of security policies. Assume the **chief information security officer (CISO)** reports directly to the chief finance officer (CFO),

 TIP

Consider the regulatory mandates, too, when understanding organizational influences. The higher the reporting of information security issues, the more influence. For example, the Gramm-Leach-Bliley Act (GLBA) requires the board of directors of an organization to be briefed on information security programs. GLBA requires many other things of corporate boards as well, but the point is that regulations requiring senior leadership engagement create visibility and opportunity to advocate for information security.

FIGURE 5-3

CISO reporting directly to CFO.

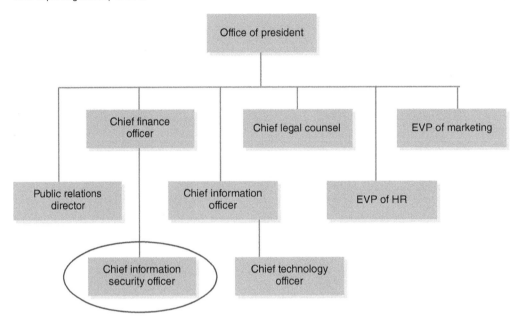

as shown in **FIGURE 5-3**. The CFO's role is traditionally a powerful position. Consequently, it's more likely that information security is perceived as a business concern rather than solely a technology issue. This allows information security policies to be given a higher priority across the enterprise.

Conversely, let's assume the CISO role reports three or four layers deep inside the IT department, as shown in **FIGURE 5-4**. The CISO would not have the organizational muscle to implement security policies with the same perceived influence or authority. This does not mean security policies couldn't be implemented effectively. The difference would be the approach used given the organizational realities. In this case, the CISO would most likely seek greater executive involvement rather than relying on the CFO's influence and authority.

Ultimately, an organization has to determine how it wants to manage the division of labor and span of control. The **division of labor** means how you group various tasks. It's sometimes more effective to divide tasks into specialties. This way, the depth and quality are higher. As more tasks are divided into separate jobs, more specialties are created. As more specialties are created, more teams are formed. The result is the organization grows, along with operating costs. Employees are the most valuable resources, but they are also expensive. They require salaries, training, supplies, facilities, benefits, and leadership support. An organization needs to divide labor in a way that yields quality and keeps it competitive while controlling operating costs.

FIGURE 5-4

CISO organizational chart—CISO role appears several layers deep.

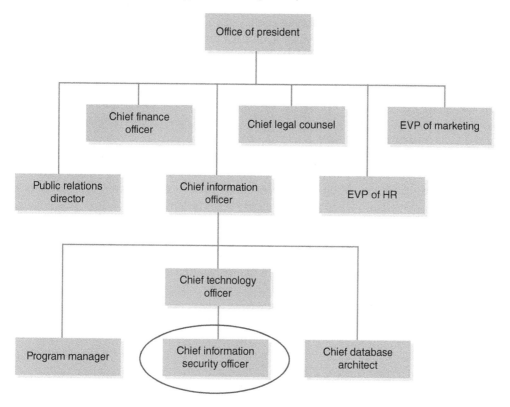

FYI

The larger the organization, the more diverse a set of relationships will exist within it. This means potentially more stakeholders will need to be engaged. It is important to understand that the stakeholders in this matrix are not just communicating with the security team, but also with each other. This is why transparency is a necessary part of the policy implementation process. The interaction of leadership and the different personalities can significantly impact a policy deployment. The more you can create a unified view, the greater the likelihood of success.

Another consideration is **span of control**, which relates to the number of layers and number of direct reports found in an organization. The span of control widens when a leader has many direct reports. This tends to flatten an organization. This is called a **flat organizational structure**. When the span of control widens, the leader is less connected to the details of what's going on. If a leader has to deal with a dozen direct reports, for example, it's doubtful he or she would have time to address many details. The leader would tend to focus on the big picture and the big risks.

There's no magic rule on the right number of direct reports. The appropriate span of control depends on the nature of the business, complexity of the issues, and number of problems needing the leader's attention. As the span narrows, the organization gains layers. This is called a **hierarchical organizational structure**. More layers tend to make an organization bureaucratic. Hierarchical organizations are necessary. They allow specialties to thrive and produce high-quality products and services.

Having multiple layers isn't necessarily bad. There needs to be separation, though, not just for efficiency, but also to create segregation of duties. **Segregation of duties (SOD)**, also referred to as **separation of duties**, refers to a requirement that a task be performed by more than one person. This approach is often used to prevent fraud and reduce errors. The point is to create the minimum number of organizational layers needed to achieve a specific business purpose. An organization can have an overall hierarchical structure with pockets of flat organizational structure for specific teams and departments. An example of SOD would be to separate the ability to set up a new vendor account and ability to authorize payment to a vendor. The ability both to set up and to authorize a vendor creates an opportunity for fraud. The SOD controls reduce the likelihood that a fake vendor is set up and paid.

The difference between a flat and hierarchical organization is relative to its size and business model. Figure 5-2 indicates that an organization can be perceived as either flat or hierarchical. To understand the difference, you need to understand the number of layers between managers controlling the business and workers delivering products and services. For example, assume Figure 5-2 represents a carpet cleaning business with 20 workers. The two lines of business could be commercial and residential customers. The organization could be perceived as hierarchical. This is because the number of layers between the president of the company and workers could be perceived as excessive. Given the size and complexity of the business, one would expect a much smaller and flatter organization. Yet the same figure when applied to a larger business would be relatively flat. For example, assume Figure 5-2 represents a major domestic bank that offers retail banking and credit cards as lines of business. A major bank could have tens of thousands of employees. Yet Figure 5-2 reflects a relatively flat organization.

Flat Organizations

In a flat organization, the leaders are close to the workers that deliver products and services. A flat organization is generally defined as one with a limited number of organizational layers between the top and bottom ranks. As a result, leaders know their customers' and employees' needs and problems firsthand. This tends to produce faster decisions and more confidence to innovate. The right leader within this type of structure can be inspiring. This structure gives the leader the ability to connect with the workers and build trust.

In a flat organization, leaders can bring their knowledge about customers and products to the creation and implementation of security policies. Security policies are not abstract concepts in a flat organization. They are seen through the lenses of individuals directly accountable for the delivery of product and services. In a hierarchical organization, leaders are also responsible for product and services; however, the accountability is indirect through several layers of leadership. Having firsthand knowledge of the company's products and services is always valuable in implementing security policies.

Flat organizations often have decentralized authorities. This can quickly become a negative for flat organizations when the span of control becomes too wide. With wide span of control, there is no time to bring every problem to management for resolution. In some ways, you need higher caliber teams that feel comfortable making independent decisions. Yet these decisions can lead to problems, especially when dealing with information security. Some problems include conflicting statements to regulators by the subordinate and senior leadership. It's important when defining security policy in a flat organization to decide clearly how issues are to be identified, catalogued, debated, and escalated. This includes clarity about who has the authority to speak to and present the full risk story to the regulator.

Hierarchical Organizations

For large organizations, hierarchical models are a necessity. The complexity required to keep a large organization running effectively requires a hierarchy of specialties. This means senior leaders are more detached from day-to-day operations. Can the same tone at the top be sent to all employees in a hierarchical organization? Yes, but it's more difficult than in a flat organization. The dynamics are different in a hierarchical organization.

Consider a help desk worker in an organization with 10,000 employees. The help desk worker is engaged with management within the team and department. Receiving a message on the importance of information security from the president of the company may have far less impact in a hierarchical organization. The message must still be sent, but it needs to be reinforced throughout the layers.

FYI

When rolling out information security policies, make communications a priority. Be sure your approach includes these points:

1. Be clear—Avoid technical jargon when possible.
2. Set the **tone at the top**—Ask your leaders to help deliver the message.
3. Use many channels—Reinforce the message as many times as possible.
4. Be forthcoming—Be honest and candid about any impact the policy will have.
5. Say "thank you"—Acknowledge the efforts both to create and to implement the security policies.

This list is not exhaustive, but it highlights key points.

To be successful in implementing security policies in a large organization, you must continually sell the message at each layer. You must build support at the top, middle, and bottom ranks. You must choreograph the review, approval, and release process so you continue to be part of the messaging. Remember, the message can change as it moves through the layers of the organization. For example, when dealing with senior leaders, a core part of the message could be cost avoidance and reduction in operating risks. Messages to other layers might have greater emphasis on regulatory compliance or meeting customer expectations of privacy. It's important to tailor the benefit message to resonate with the audience. If workers can connect with the importance and priority, they are more likely to follow the policy.

Advantages of a Hierarchical Model

There are some distinct advantages to a hierarchical model. The importance of specialization has been discussed. In a hierarchical model, communication lines are more clearly defined. When you encounter a problem, there is most likely a group that specializes in that area that can help solve it. The depth of knowledge in a subject area tends to be greater. This allows managers to predict and avoid problems before they occur.

Managers can also create "centers of excellence." These are small, specialized teams that focus on specific problems within an organization to help provide high-quality products and services. Large organizations often have teams dedicated to identifying the next big threat. These teams examine industry breaches and analyze if the company would be vulnerable to those types of attacks. In a small, flat organization, these specialties and skills may not be available.

Disadvantages of a Hierarchical Model

There are also some disadvantages in a hierarchical model. One such disadvantage is accountability. A hierarchical model relies on work passing between a number of teams to ultimately produce a product or service. A communications breakdown between these groups could cause errors or delays.

Accountability could also be a problem. When many component teams are involved, whose fault is it if something doesn't work? This becomes even more difficult when teams cross organizational boundaries such as between large departments.

There's no one structure that fits all organizations. The right type of structure for an organization depends on multiple factors, such as the organization's goal and the individual styles of its managers. A mature organization, moreover, may tend to be more hierarchical than flat. And an individual manager may be more comfortable establishing layers of controls, leading to a more hierarchical rather than flat organization.

In the end, it's people within the organization who will make the implementation of security policies and controls successful. How they are motivated to adopt the security principles within these policies indicates how easily you can introduce change. The inherent disadvantage of a hierarchical model is the number of touch points and personalities that must be engaged to successfully implement a security policy. As the number of touch points increases, the number of complex matrix relationships also increases. **Matrix relationships** are the complex relationships between stakeholders. For example, a line of business and data center operations may be two stakeholders. The relationships involved in discussing a proposed policy might be between the security team and the line of business, the security team and data center

WARNING

The larger the organization, the faster it can grow. For example, the more teams involved in producing a product or service, the more teams will be needed to coordinate their activity. It's important that an organization does not grow for the sake of growth. It's especially important that security policies keep pace with organization growth, which drives a greater exchange of information sharing.

operations, and data center operations and the line of business. Conversations also get more complex as these discussions occur lower in the organizations. Conversations and relationships between senior leaders would be different from those at a staff level. The point here is that you should expect that a complex set of relationships will influence and drive policy conversations. Successful implementation of security policies will depend on how well you can navigate these people issues.

The Challenge of User Apathy

In its basic form, **apathy** is indifference and lack of motivation. An employee who is apathetic often "goes through the motions." This attitude results in poor performance and doing the minimum to get by. In the case of information security, it's hard to imagine that doing the minimum keeps information safe. In security, user apathy renders the entire organization vulnerable.

Policies by their nature cannot anticipate every situation. Talented and trained individuals will always be needed to deal with the unexpected. The combination of an apathetic worker with an unexpected security incident can result in disaster. A simple delay in reporting a potential incident, for example, could mean the difference between preventing an incident and having to deal with its aftermath. An apathetic worker can miss the opportunity to prevent sensitive information from getting into the wrong hands, leaving thousands of angry customers whose personal privacy has been breached.

Well-defined security policies assume a certain level of non-compliance and even worker apathy. You build redundancy into security policies to detect and react to security breaches. In this way, you don't have to rely on any one individual to maintain security. A good example is automated escalation. If an administrator is paged about a potential security breach and fails to respond within a given time limit, an escalation page is sent to a supervisor. Security policies can require such escalation.

 TIP

Assigning a security liaison within a department or group can often be a way to effectively engage a group of workers. Someone who knows the personalities and language of the group can convey the security message in a positive way.

Overcoming the effects of apathy on security policies is a combination of the following:

- **Engaged communication**—Get leaders to listen to reasons for worker apathy. Adjust the implementation strategy to better explain the importance of the policy within the context of the individual role.
- **Ongoing awareness**—Continually reinforce the message of the value and importance of information security. Good security awareness can be a preventative measure against apathy.
- **Setting the right expectations**—Ultimately workers are expected to follow policy as part of their jobs. Compliance must be monitored, and individuals must be held accountable.
- **Creating some layers of redundancy**—Some layers of redundancy are good. Avoid, whenever possible, sole reliance on any individual or single technology. Frankly, the more redundancy an organization can afford, the better. However, redundancy is expensive.

- **Recognize and reward compliance**—Seek opportunity to spotlight individuals who model the desired behavior. This can be as simple as public recognition by a senior executive or a small gift card reward. Rewards are a fantastic motivational tool.

The Importance of Executive Management Support

Implementing security policies starts with executive management. Without executive support, policies are just words. To have meaning they must be given the right priority and be enforced. That's when the benefits and value of security policies are realized for an organization. Implementing security policies creates a culture in which risk awareness takes work and resources. Unfortunately, some executives see involvement with security policies and risk awareness as an IT issue, and a distraction given their other priorities. However, executive management support is critical to the success of security policy implementation and acceptance throughout the organization.

Be cautious if the security policy depends on the executive management support to implement large, complex IT systems. Not even large IT projects with large budgets have any guarantee of success. In fact, there are numerous examples to indicate that the larger the IT deployment, the greater the risk of failure. A study by McKinsey in 2012 revealed that 17 percent of IT projects with budgets greater than $15 million fail so badly that the company involved almost goes out of business. Consider the rollout of HealthCare.gov, the government website for people needing to sign up for medical insurance under the Affordable Care Act. The site's early months were a disaster, marked by system crashes and lack of functionality, despite a budget of more than $600 million.

Selling Information Security Policies to an Executive

Understanding executive perception of these successes and failures is important. These perceptions must be overcome when soliciting support from executives. The online business site Allbusiness.com reported that projects fail due to eight common perceived missteps:

- **Unclear purpose**—Unclear purpose refers to the clarity of value a project brings. In the case of security policies, it's important to demonstrate how these policies will reduce risk. It's equally important to demonstrate how the policies were derived in a way that kept the business cost and impact low.
- **Doubt**—Doubt refers to the need for change. You need to explain why what's in place today is not good enough. Change is perceived as a distraction from the core business. You need to convince the executive that the benefits outweigh disruption. Doubt may also be a factor if an organization has had several false starts. If several attempts have been made to implement a security policy with little success, you must convince them that this time is different. Even when the message and benefits are clear, it is also a matter of credibility with the executive.
- **Insufficient support from leadership**—Insufficient support from leadership refers to the broad support for the project. In the case of policies, a leader doesn't like surprises and wants to know he or she is not alone. You need to explain both the depth and breadth of support for the policies. To avoid surprises, be sure to articulate any pushback you are getting from other leaders. This will help avoid surprises, and the executive can be an

advocate to sway his or her peers. When problems are encountered, be sure to anticipate where your support will emerge or evaporate.

- **Organizational baggage**—Organizational baggage refers to how the organization executes, as judged on the basis of past unsuccessful efforts. Unlike doubt, which is a personal credibility issue, this category focuses on the organization's capacity to execute. If an organization continues to have problems implementing policies of any kind, how will security policies be any different? This type of organization usually fails to stay on course. Organizations that reorganize twice a year or have frequent leadership changes fall within this category.
- **Lack of organizational incentives**—Lack of organizational incentives refers to the inability to motivate behavior. Value is only derived from policies when they are enforced. An organization must have the will and process to reward adherence. The organization must have a low or zero tolerance for security policy violations.
- **Lack of candor**—Lack of candor refers to not having open, candid conversations. In the case of policies, you need to be clear what can and cannot be achieved. You need to listen and explain how the business's input was considered and adopted or rejected. Executives need a sense that they were part of a process and not just the recipients of the result.
- **Low tolerance for bad news**—Low tolerance for bad news refers to how executives react to missteps. You can count on an error in judgment at some point in implementing security policies. You need to prepare executives for the inevitable. You also need to gauge how they will react.
- **Unmanageable complexity**—Unmanageable complexity refers to how complex and realistic the project is. The ability of the organization to support the security policies will be an important topic of conversation.

Before, During, and After Policy Implementation

There's an art and science to obtaining support from executives for security policies. It's as much about confidence and credibility as it is about the facts. It's important to stay engaged and in communication with executives before, during, and after security policy implementation.

One pitfall you want to avoid is trying to turn an executive into a knowledgeable security expert. Executives generally have neither the time nor interest, and they need to rely on your expertise. What they do expect is that you have packaged the implementation steps into clearly understood and manageable tasks that minimize costs and effort. Their staff will also report back to them the results of your efforts. Therefore, you must be clear about what you expect and what the business must deliver.

The following is a checklist for packaging implementation tasks and to help stay on point when discussing security policies:

- **Clarity of objectives**—What goals and benefits are to be achieved?
- **Things to do**—What exact tasks are to be performed and by whom?
- **Things to pay attention to**—How does the business know if it is successful?

 TIP

Establish relationships with key stakeholders well in advance of creating security policies. Building confidence and credibility early makes implementing security policies later that much easier.

5

Information Security Policy Implementation Issues

- **Things to report**—What should be reported and when?
- **Roles and responsibilities**—Who's responsible for what?
- **Things to be aware of**—Why is the security policy in place?
- **Things to reinforce with employees**—What is the messaging to the staff?

Investing in planning prior to implementation will build a strong relationship with executives. It should also build true support. Executives who truly support you will continue their support when things do not go as planned. Messaging to executives needs to include their accountability for information security. Their role is essential to create a genuine effort to protect information. In the end, it's their organization that is affected when a breach occurs.

The Role of Human Resources Policies

Well-defined HR policies provide the framework that governs employee relations. HR policies state core business values and what is expected. They can also prevent misunderstandings. Managers are more likely to engage a worker on sensitive topics, such as lack of performance, when there's a clear process they can follow to stay out of trouble. Like any written record, the HR policies can be used against an organization in a lawsuit. Poorly drafted policies become evidence to support an employee's contention that he or she acted within company expectations.

Although HR policies must demonstrate commitment to secure business practices and clearly state values, they must be flexible and defensible in a court of law while meeting business objectives. They must also establish processes for management to follow. You often find HR policy language intentionally vague. This avoids language that could be interpreted as an employment contract or unintended promise. Although they may be flexible in their language, HR policies must be applied consistently across individuals. For example, disciplining two individuals differently for the same security policy violation could result in a lawsuit. In contrast, security policies must be precise, establishing clear expectations of behavior that can be enforced.

Consequently, automated enforcement of security policies shows consistency and often leads to a higher compliance rate than manual controls. It's also better to stop a security policy violation immediately through automation than to deal with its aftermath. However, how do you enforce security policies when automated controls are not available or ineffective? A classic example is when a worker views inappropriate sexual material on a company computer. Let's assume it can clearly be shown as willful versus accidentally stumbling onto an inappropriate website. This example starts to show the reliance that security policies have on HR policies to define acceptable behavior and to enforce adherence through disciplinary actions.

 NOTE

The acceptable use policy (AUP) is often based in part on HR policy. It establishes expected behavior such as prohibiting access to social networking sites from company computers.

Relationship Between HR and Security Policies

Security policies must be well grounded within HR policies. Don't look for precision in HR policies. They are better viewed as a foundation on which to build. They establish broad rules of acceptable behavior. These rules cover such topics as expectation

FIGURE 5-5

Conceptual relationship between HR policies and security policies.

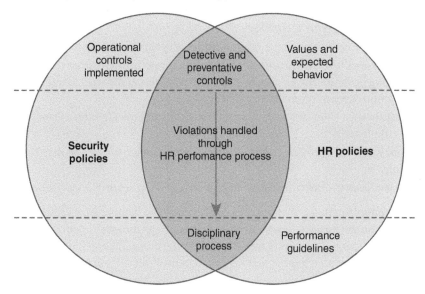

of privacy when using company computers to zero tolerance for certain inappropriate behaviors. Security policies can then operationalize these core values and define controls to enforce them. Just as security policies must align to business processes, they must also align to HR policies.

The relationship between HR and security policies can be seen in **FIGURE 5-5**. This figure depicts several key touch points. Let's use the previous example of viewing inappropriate material on a company computer. Figure 5-5 illustrates the relationship between HR and security policies. First, an HR policy would state the core value. This could be as simple as "Computers are for company use only." Or it could detail the type of material prohibited. The security policies could then align by outlining acceptable uses of the Internet. Preventative security controls can be designed to block unacceptable sites. A worker who finds a way around these controls may be discovered through detective controls that scan company computers for unauthorized software and information. If such material is found, management can determine what disciplinary action, if any, is necessary. Management would look to HR policies for guidance. After working with HR, management might decide a formal warning or even termination is appropriate. This illustrates the close alignment needed between HR and security policies.

Lack of Support

The ability to take disciplinary action to enforce security policies is not the only reason to seek support from HR. A lack of support can also make implementing security policies difficult or impossible. You need to remember that HR is a primary point of contact with workers. It can serve as a point of communication with the employees and a place to resolve conflicts. The following outlines several key areas of support provided by HR regarding security policy implementation:

- **HR policy and values**—Establishes a baseline of permitted behavior, including the acceptable use of company technology.
- **Security awareness**—Promotes understanding of security policies.
- **Exit interview**—Allows departing employees to express how effective security controls are in enabling or inhibiting employee productivity. This candid expression allows for the continued improvement of security policies.
- **Event monitoring**—Allows a broader understanding of how effective security policies have been implemented.
- **Disciplinary action**—Provides a process to adjust behavior to align with security policy expectations.
- **Source of authority**—Provides authority for establishing security controls.

You need HR support to make sure you are interpreting the language correctly. These interpretations become the basis of key security policies such as monitoring employee behavior on company equipment. If you don't have the right interpretation of HR policies, it's difficult or impossible to design effective security controls to prohibit certain behavior.

Security policies rely on employees understanding and cooperating with the rules. Security awareness is one of the best ways to achieve this understanding. A good security awareness program starts when a new employee walks in the door. It's reinforced at least annually and as an employee is promoted into new responsibilities. A lack of HR support makes it impossible to provide security awareness to new employees, when they are first hired or when their jobs change.

Continuous improvement relies on people telling you what is and isn't working. A good source for this information is an employee departing a company. You ask current employees what they think. But do you know if they are just telling you what you want to hear? They may not want to make waves. Individuals departing a company tend to be more candid with less to lose. Most HR departments conduct an exit interview. They ask basic questions about the work environment and why the person is leaving. It's also a good opportunity to ask a few well-selected questions on security. This could help you understand the strengths and weaknesses of the information security program. A lack of HR support means you never get to ask the question to know where your security weaknesses may lie.

An important part of HR's job is to field complaints from employees. No matter how good you are at explaining security policies, at some point you will ruffle someone's feathers. Count on them calling HR to complain. To get HR staff on your side, you need to let them know exactly how and why you are implementing security policies. They are skilled in listening and communicating with employees on sensitive matters. They can support you to help defuse problems. They can explain how the policies align with company values. They can reinforce key security awareness messages. A lack of support has the opposite effect. Complaints can escalate and get out of hand. Worse yet, if HR takes the employee's side, you may find yourself backing down on security policies or weakening the security awareness message.

You have learned how HR support relates to disciplinary action. If security policies are not enforced, employees inevitably perceive them as unimportant. Management needs the broad mandates within HR policies to assess employee performance. This includes how well people follow security policies. Without this HR support, security policies become optional and unenforceable.

Security policies, like any policy, must have a mandate. Someone in authority has to say, "This is important" and "You have to do it." Often this comes from executive leadership. On occasion you can point to key values within HR policies as an additional source of authority. Doing so also provides a perceived mandate that helps gain support among executives. A lack of HR support makes it more difficult to obtain executive approval for security policies and easier to have them challenged.

In summary, it's difficult or impossible to implement security policies without HR support. Fortunately, HR in most organizations understands its role in helping implement security policies. It's rare to find an HR department that attempts to hinder implementation of security policies. More likely, you will find different degrees of support. The relationship with HR is an important one for the information security team to develop.

Policy Roles, Responsibilities, and Accountability

It's important to note that change is inevitable. The implementation of security policies is just one of a vast array of changes employees must absorb. Understanding this is important when creating security policy roles, responsibilities, and accountability. The closer you can align employees' current roles with their current job responsibilities, the easier it will be to implement. For example, assume a security policy requires a certified security trainer for a specific team. Now assume that team already has a trainer for a nonsecurity purpose such as office safety. Combining these roles and responsibilities could create the opportunity to combine training requirements and make it easier for the business to accept the security policy.

Many players are involved in the process of security policy implementation. The roles and responsibilities are different depending on where you are in the life cycle of a security policy. The term *life cycle* in this chapter refers to the creation, implementation, awareness, and enforcement of security policies. These different tasks require different roles and responsibilities.

There are many theories on how to approach change and an individual's role in the change process. The key point is to understand everyone's role from the perspective of a change model. You need to clearly define everyone's role when developing and changing policies. You also need to recognize different roles when it comes to enforcing policies after they have been implemented.

 TIP

When you implement security policies, you are implementing change. This can include implementing business perspectives and organizational values. This means sometimes you are implementing culture change as much as security controls. Be sure to select a change management model that speaks to the need to influence leaders as much as to technical implementation of controls.

Change Model

There are many change models to choose from. You may be able to adapt some when implementing security policies. This section focuses on Kotter's Eight-Step Change Model. John Kotter, a professor at Harvard Business School, developed the model and introduced it in 1995 in a book titled *Leading Change*. The model has been widely adapted for a number of purposes. It addresses the need to create executive support for implementing change. This is a critical success factor in implementing security policies.

Professor Kotter states that to be successful in implementing change in a company, at least 75 percent of management needs to "buy into" it. The early stages of creating vision and urgency around the need for security policies will be critical later to build the coalition of executives needed to make change happen.

Let's examine the model in relation to implementing security policies. The model divides an effective change process into eight steps:

1. **Create urgency**—For change to happen, there must be an urgent need. Helping people understand information security threats and risk to the business can help build this sense of urgency.
2. **Form a powerful coalition**—For change to happen, leadership must back you. Establish early a tone at the top for the need for the security policy.
3. **Create a vision for change**—Change needs to be understandable. It must be clear what you are asking of people and what measurable benefit the security policy will bring.
4. **Communicate the vision**—Once you have support, you need to communicate your intent widely. Communicate the security message through as many channels as possible.
5. **Remove obstacles**—There will be barriers to your success. Empower individuals to be change agents. A **change agent** is someone tasked with challenging current thinking.
6. **Create short-term wins**—Success, no matter how small, breeds more success. Focus on small, well-defined goals that collectively build toward larger long-term goals.
7. **Build on the change**—Real change takes time and continued effort. Build a process of continuous improvement of the security policies.
8. **Anchor the changes in corporate culture**—To make anything stick, it must become habit and part of the culture. Find opportunities to integrate security controls into day-to-day routines.

FIGURE 5-6 shows how this model can be adapted to implementing security policies. You would cycle through this model each time you add a new security policy or make a major change to an existing policy. This model ensures that before you start a formal implementation, you have the leadership support needed to succeed. It also highlights the separation between informal and formal tasks. When we adapted Kotter's model for the purposes of this chapter, we created a separation between informal and formal implementation tasks. This is to emphasize the importance of preparing for policy implementation through informal discussions versus starting a formal project approach right away. There are two major benefits to having these informal tasks. First, you gain executive support. Having a formal project before you have executive support is presumptuous and will create unnecessary resistance. Second, it establishes a collaborative setup that allows you to change and modify your approach. It also builds ownership into the process for the executive giving you advice.

Responsibilities During Change

Implementing security policies is easier if you manage it from a change model perspective. It helps you establish a collaborative style that allows business leaders to understand and buy into what you are trying to accomplish. The process starts with an informal set of steps

FIGURE 5-6

Basic policy implementation approach.

Informal discussions

Transition from informal to formal Implementation tasks

Formal implementation project

Build security policy

Implement security policy

Step four: Communicate the vision

Step one: Create urgency

Step five: Remove obstacles

Step two: Form a powerful coalition

Step six: Create short-term wins

Step three: Create a vision for change

Step seven: Build on the change

Step eight: Anchor the changes in corporate culture

that builds awareness and understanding. With a clear purpose beyond your security policies, you can build the executive support needed to succeed.

Using the steps in Kotter's Eight-Step Change Model, the following sections explain the roles and responsibilities involved in the change process.

> **⚠ WARNING**
>
> Be candid and transparent with leaders. Explain clearly what information security policies can and cannot achieve. Equally important, be upfront about the impact on the business; otherwise, you risk losing credibility.

Step 1: Create Urgency

It is the responsibility of the CISO, who may simply be called the *information security officer (ISO)*, to convey urgency to business leaders. This is selling the need for information security. An effective way of doing this is to understand the business risk the security policy addresses and convey the need in business terms. The greater the business risk reduction, the greater the urgency perceived by the business.

Step 2: Create a Powerful Coalition

It's important to get executive support. Leaders are responsible for reducing risk to their organization. It's the responsibility of the ISO to know who the key stakeholders are. It's also the responsibility of the ISO to reach out to stakeholders, explain the policy change, and listen to concerns. Many organizations have what are called **control partners**. It's the responsibility of a control partner to offer an opinion on the soundness and impact of the security policy. Many organizations require control partners' input before a policy change can be made. The following are examples of control partners found in many large organizations:

* Internal auditors
* Operational risk managers

- Compliance officers
- Legal professionals

The size of the stakeholder group varies depending on the scope of the policy change and the size of the organization. When the number of stakeholders in any group is too large, the ISO can take a sampling approach. For example, assume a policy change affects the entire organization, which is composed of more than 1000 managers. It's not practical to ask each manager how the policy would affect every team. Therefore, the ISO would sample a population of managers. The ISO can target those types of managers who would be more affected than others.

Step 3: Create a Vision for Change

The security policy must be understandable. It is the ISO's responsibility to write the policy in terms the business understands. The ISO can tune the message so the value of implementing the policy makes sense. After compiling everyone's input, the ISO creates a coherent security message and policy. The message should include high-level explanations of the policy to sell the vision. It is the responsibility of the stakeholder to validate the ISO's assumptions and raise objections.

It's not appropriate for a stakeholder to wait until just before a security policy is implemented to object. The ISO is responsible for ensuring all objections are transparent and either resolved or escalated. The ISO must make every effort to resolve an objection. The objection could be pointing out a legitimate problem that requires a change to the security policy or control.

It might not be possible to make everyone happy; however, everyone needs to have a say. Remember, success depends on a genuine effort to implement the spirit of the policies. Everyone reports to someone in an organization. It is the ISO's role to escalate conflicts to some authority who can resolve them. In the end, you are trying to get the majority of leaders on your side.

> **TIP**
>
> Find a leader in your organization who can be an agent of change. These are leaders who don't always follow the pack and can think outside of the box. They can guide you through the organizational politics involved in implementing change.

Step 4: Communicate the Vision

The policy change must be widely communicated. It is the ISO's responsibility to create the message. The ISO must also formally lay out communication plans. A communication plan outlines the messages to be conveyed, how they will be conveyed, and to whom they are conveyed. Communication starts before the policy is published. For example, establishing a comment period for a new or changed policy can generate awareness. The ISO also needs to transition the implementation of security policies from informal discussions to a formal project plan. The project plan needs to outline dates, timelines, resources, and organizational support needed to be successful.

Stakeholders, particularly executive leaders, are responsible for communicating the change with their endorsement. Whether a leader raised an objection or not, leaders have an obligation to communicate and endorse any approved policy. This tone at the top is an important responsibility for an executive to perform. Executives are also responsible for setting team priorities to implement security policies.

> **TIP**
>
> The collateral created to sell the policy vision should be used in security awareness training. It will express the business need for the policy as well as the technical security components.

Step 5: Remove Obstacles

Obstacles to implementation must be identified and removed. It is the ISO's responsibility to be the central point of contact and to track implementation problems. It is the stakeholder's responsibility to collect and report problems with the implementation. It is everyone's responsibility to report problems with security policies to their leadership. Many information security teams set up intranet sites so security issues can be reported directly to the security team.

Step 6: Create Short-Term Wins

It's important to demonstrate value as early as possible. The ISO is responsible for identifying how success is measured. The ISO works with line management to collect metrics for assessing the policies' effectiveness. It is usually the responsibility of these line managers to make sure such metrics are captured and are meaningful.

Step 7: Build on the Change

It takes time to change an organization's culture. The ISO must continually monitor security policy compliance. The ISO reports to leadership on the current effectiveness of the security policies. The ISO will also have to ask the business to accept any residual risk or come up with a way to reduce it. Residual risk is the amount of risk that remains after you implement security controls. For example, let's assume a virus scanner can catch 99 percent of all known viruses. That leaves 1 percent of the viruses undetected. The business needs to know about this risk. The business leaders are then responsible for accepting this risk or paying for more technology to stop the remaining 1 percent.

Step 8: Anchor the Changes in Corporate Culture

Make the values in the security policies part of the culture. This takes time and is achieved by changing employees' attitudes. The ISO needs to be a strong communicator. It is his or her responsibility to come up with ways to reinforce the security message without creating a distraction for the business.

Roles and Accountabilities

The organization is ultimately accountable for information security. When something catastrophic occurs, with lawyers and regulators engaged, the organization's leaders have to explain what happened. In fact, officers of the organization may be held personally liable. They may pull the top technology executive (the CIO) along for the ride. But executives are the ones who fund technology and determine how much risk they are willing to pay to reduce.

Setting expectations for leaders quickly becomes a matter of budget. If there aren't dollars to spend to implement controls, then it's hard to hold executives accountable. IT spending varies greatly by industry. Deloitte found that on average, companies spend 3.28 percent of their revenue on IT. This percentage changes if you focus on specific industries. Banks tend to spend around 7.16 percent and construction 1.51 percent. Of those companies that consistently outperform the S&P 500, 57 percent increased their IT budget from 2016 to 2017.[1]

Companies that spend more on IT have more resources to deploy for information security. Thus, the expectations for information security in a financial services company may be different from those in a manufacturing company.

Although business leaders may be ultimately responsible, they rely on key technology roles to keep them out of trouble. These roles are accountable for implementing security policies, monitoring their adherence, and managing day-to-day activities. Although their titles may vary within an organization, typically you find different individuals accountable for each of the following roles:

- **Information security officer (ISO)**—The individual accountable for identifying, developing, and implementing security policies. The ISO is also accountable for ensuring that corresponding security controls are designed and implemented.
- **Executive**—A senior business leader accountable for approving security policy implementation. An executive is also responsible for driving the security message within an organization and ensuring the security policy implementation is given appropriate priority.
- **Compliance officer**—An individual accountable for monitoring adherence to laws and regulations. A **compliance officer** often uses adherence to security policies as a measure of regulatory compliance.
- **Data owner**—Typically someone in the business who approves access rights to information. **Data owners** are accountable for ensuring only the access that is needed to perform day-to-day operations is granted. They would also be responsible for ensuring there is a separation of duties to reduce risk of errors or fraud.
- **Data manager**—An individual typically responsible for establishing procedures on how data should be handled. **Data managers** also ensure data is properly classified.
- **Data custodian**—An individual responsible for the day-to-day maintenance of data. **Data custodians** back up and recover data as needed. They grant access based on approval from the data owner. You can view their accountability as generally maintaining the data center and keeping applications running.
- **Data user**—The end user of an application. **Data users** are accountable for handling data appropriately. They are accountable for understanding security policies and following approved processes and procedures. Data users have an obligation to understand their security responsibilities and not to violate policies.
- **Auditor**—An individual accountable for assessing the design and effectiveness of security policies. An **auditor** can be internal or external to the organization. They offer formal opinions in writing. These opinions review the completeness of the policy design and how well it conforms to leading industry practices. Auditors also offer opinions on how well the policies are followed and how effective they are. Auditors do not report to the leaders they are auditing. This allows them to provide a valuable independent second opinion. For example, internal auditors in publicly traded companies typically report findings to the audit committee and line management. External auditors may issue findings to executive management and the audit committee. The audit committee is a subcommittee of the board of directors.

ISOs need to make sure they build security policies collaboratively. The key is to create an open and candid conversation on risk. If the discussions on risk are perceived as valuable, executives are more willing to commit their time. This means the ISO needs to hold stakeholders accountable to participate. No one should be able to opt out. Accountability changes once the security policies are implemented. End users are accountable for following policies. The ISO's central role is to coordinate these activities.

When Policy Fulfillment Is Not Part of Job Descriptions

There is no rule of thumb about how often an employee's performance should be appraised. Many organizations perform annual assessments, although some perform assessments twice a year. This is in addition to individual appraisals between employees and their managers.

The basis for these appraisals starts with the employee job description. When a job description does not include adherence to policies, it's more challenging to implement security policies. When an employee intentionally violates any policy (including security policy), the matter can be treated as an HR issue; that is, regardless of the job description, there's an expectation that an employee will follow established policies as a term of his or her employment.

However, if a job description does not include policy fulfillment, the employee could perceive it as someone else's problem. This is particularly important given that many employees are overworked. They have constant limits on their time and resources. Too often in today's challenging business climate there's little or no mention of security policies during an employee's appraisals. The exception is when a gross violation of policy or a major incident occurs. Minor violations may be overlooked. Even major security policy and control deployments may not be considered important. Security policy fulfillment is an abstract concept to many. Given a choice, most employees will focus on what their manager thinks is important instead of learning an abstract concept.

You learned earlier in the chapter how self-interest is a powerful motivator of behavior. When there's no reward associated with promoting security policies, such activity competes with other interests. The unfortunate reality is that many times the effort given is the bare minimum. It's not because executives or managers don't believe it's important. It's because there's little time and no perceived benefit.

There's no easy answer on how to overcome this. If you can't change job descriptions, you need to create a perceived benefit. The culture of compliance can help by creating peer pressure. Also, it's useful to engage employees so they feel some ownership in the security policies' success. This can be as simple as soliciting ideas for improvement and publicizing those suggestions selected. Provide public recognition for individuals who exhibit the desired behavior. This could be as simple as a thank-you letter from a top executive in the organization. In short, create a reward outside the job description.

Impact on Entrepreneurial Productivity and Efficiency

Entrepreneurship can be defined in many ways. Let's talk about some key attributes. Entrepreneurship focuses on innovation and growth. Startup companies are full of entrepreneurial spirit out of necessity. They must innovate to enter a crowded market, and they must grow to survive. Well-established organizations have long passed this stage. As an organization matures, so does its business model. Those true entrepreneurs that started the company, or saw it through its high growth periods, often leave. They are usually replaced with very talented professional managers.

Therein lies the struggle between how to manage a business versus how to "grow" it. This is not an abstract problem. It has significant implications for security policies that must reflect the core values of the business.

A company in its early startup stages or in high-growth mode focuses on agility and innovation, and it tends to have a greater acceptance of risk. This is when you see a dominant entrepreneurial culture emerge. When a business has a large percentage of leaders who share this entrepreneurial mindset, you will also see a greater level of risk acceptance. They challenge the status quo and push the limits of policies to achieve their goals.

Conversely, as the company matures and this population of entrepreneurs leaves the company, they are often replaced with professional managers. These may be talented individuals coming from the finest business schools. But you do see a different culture emerge with a greater focus on how to sustain and manage a business. This translates into less risk taking and a clearer definition about how business should be run. During this latter maturity stage, the business starts growing its bureaucracy.

It's not suggested that one approach is better than the other. That will depend on the business and situation. But an information security professional must recognize which attitude dominates his or her organization. All organizations have dominance of one over the other. Security policies must be written and implemented to accommodate this mindset and tolerance for risk.

Although there is always a dominant culture, an organization can by design be a mix of these two mindsets. The mix typically comes in when a mature company is "testing the waters" into a new business line.

Consider, for example, a company that has little or no sales presence on the Internet. It wants to start a new unit to test for feasibility by selling a limited number of products online. Let's assume the test period is 24 months. The business intends to evaluate the success or failure of the effort. The business wants to keep costs low—it may completely disband the new unit and abandon the idea within the next 24 months. It brings in leaders with startup experience, and a clash of cultures occurs almost immediately. The new unit's staff is under tremendous pressure to demonstrate small successes quickly. They have little tolerance for delays. They face pressure to get their applications onto the Internet quickly and to have access to information on demand. This situation promotes a tendency to take shortcuts within existing processes, which can increase risk.

Security policies need to reflect the dominant view of risk within an organization. This is often referred to as **risk tolerance**. You need to establish security policies that reflect the overall tolerance for the enterprise. Establish through policy those tolerances as acceptable behavior. Then create risk acceptance processes and mitigating controls for behavior that falls outside the tolerance area.

That's exactly what is called for in the example of an entrepreneurial unit startup in a more mature organization. Although the policies would apply to this unit no differently than any other unit, their execution and mitigating controls may be different. For example, you could segment the network in a way that isolates those systems and applications being placed on the Internet. You could also grant them the elevated privileges necessary for them to create, change, and deploy experimental products. The acceptance of risk in this environment would be greater than that in the environment of well-established products and services.

This does not mean that the controls associated with an entrepreneurial unit are bypassed or disabled. A business cannot accept unreasonable risks or risks that place the company in noncompliance to regulations. It does mean that your service model to an entrepreneurial unit must change. You must adopt a service model that reflects the same agility that the unit needs to stay in business. This could mean assigning an ISO directly to that business unit. Dedicating resources to the business would improve responsiveness. It would also increase costs.

Entrepreneurial businesses, like any other, need the discipline that comes with security policies to control risks. The service model associated with these businesses needs to be responsive and agile to avoid impacting their productivity. The security policies also need to support processes that can quickly escalate risks to the business for acceptance or mitigation.

Tying Security Policy to Performance and Accountability

Measuring the effectiveness of security policies is essential to maintaining leadership support. The quality control function is a good place to obtain these measurements. Typically, a quality control function will sample security controls and test their effectiveness. These measurements are often shared with leadership, stakeholders, control partners, and regulators. They are a good indication of the health of the system and level of adherence to information security policies within it.

To ensure accountability, you need to measure if employees are following the policies. Selecting the right performance measurement can be tricky. A common pitfall is to measure success as a percentage of implemented policy coverage. It's easier to demonstrate the value security policies bring to the business when the business sees its operational risk being reduced. Therefore, the best measurement of whether employees are following policies is the actual reduction in risk that occurs.

For example, let's say you have a security policy that requires all servers to be patched. More precisely, all critical security patches must be applied within so many days of their release. For this discussion, assume you know what a critical security patch is and can measure when it's applied. Reporting that 90 percent of your servers have received the patch may sound good. But how much of the risk has been reduced? If 80 percent of your business runs through the 10 percent that has not been patched, your business is very much at risk. When measuring performance or effectiveness of policies, always ask, "How much actual risk to the business has been reduced?"

Measuring effectiveness is easier than measuring accountability. As in the prior example, the organization can quickly

 TIP

When tying policy adherence to performance measurement, focus on measuring risk to the business as opposed to implementation of policies and controls.

determine if the level of patch management is compliant with security policy. But suppose it is not. Who is accountable? It is often much harder to measure the percentage of employees that either follow or fail to follow policy. One method is to use effectiveness measurements to identify areas of high or low effectiveness. Then analyzing *why* certain areas were successes while other areas were failures leads you to accountability.

You can get a basic understanding if individuals are being held accountable for adherence to security policies by examining policy violations, incidents, and security awareness. These basic measurements are as follows:

- **Number of security violations by employees reported**—You should investigate any unexplained increase in this number to determine why an abnormal number of security violations occurred. One reason could be lack of training.

- **Number of incidents that could have been avoided**—When a security breach occurs, you need to determine the root cause. This root cause can tell you if a contributing factor was a policy failure.

- **Completion and competency rate for security awareness**—You should track which individuals have completed security awareness training. Additionally, the training should measure the level of competency with the material. This training needs to be refreshed and redone at least annually.

 TIP

When reporting trends, explain how the numbers were collected and the business context. For example, an increase in security policy violations may be expected if a new policy was just released or if the reporting capability was recently improved.

CHAPTER SUMMARY

This chapter discussed complex relationships and personality types in the workplace and how they can affect how you implement security policies. It's important to understand different personality types in the workplace to better motivate and influence workers to embrace security policies. Proper motivation can overcome user apathy. Executive support is important to get resources and to drive the security message and visibility needed for the implementation to be successful. The chapter also discussed the importance of pulling stakeholders and control partners into the policy implementation process. This chapter also discussed the Kotter model and a minor variation of it.

Post-implementation activities are just as important as those leading to policy implementation. Success is measured by the value the security policies bring in alignment with the company's risk tolerance. The chapter also examined how security policies are effective only if they are used. This means they must be enforced. The core values and ways to look at risk within security policies can be applied to a wide array of business situations and new technologies. Successful security policy implementations can change mindsets and an organization's culture. They can further reduce risks as individuals are better equipped to deal with the unexpected threats.

KEY CONCEPTS AND TERMS

Apathy	Data managers	Matrix relationships
Auditor	Data owners	Reduction in force
Change agent	Data users	Risk tolerance
Chief information security officer (CISO)	Division of labor	Segregation of duties (SOD)
	Executive	Separation of duties (SOD)
Compliance officer	Flat organizational structure	Span of control
Control partners	Hierarchical organizational	Tone at the top
Data custodians	structure	

CHAPTER 5 ASSESSMENT

1. Which of the following is a basic element of motivation?

  A. Pride
  B. Self-interest
  C. Success
  D. B and C
  E. All of the above

2. Which personality type often breaks through barriers that previously prevented success?

  A. Attackers
  B. Commanders
  C. Analyticals
  D. Pleasers

3. Avoiders like to _____ and will do _____ but not much more.

4. As the number of specialties increases, so does _____.

5. In hierarchical organizations, the leaders are close to the workers that deliver products and services.

  A. True
  B. False

6. User apathy often results in an employee just going through the motions.

  A. True
  B. False

7. Which of the following is a method for overcoming apathy?

  A. Avoiding redundancy
  B. Issuing company directives
  C. Engaging in communication
  D. Requiring obedience to policies

8. Why is HR policy language often intentionally vague?

  A. To avoid being interpreted as an unintended promise
  B. To start lawsuits
  C. To avoid being too severe for new hires
  D. To provide flexibility for interpretation

9. In the case of policies, it is important to demonstrate to business how policies will reduce risk and will be derived in a way that keeps costs low.

  A. True
  B. False

10. An ideal time to refresh security policies is during a reduction in force.

  A. True
  B. False

11. Kotter's Eight-Step Change Model can help an organization gain support for _____ changes.

12. When a catastrophic security breach occurs, who is ultimately held accountable by regulators and the public?

    A. Company officers
    B. The CIO
    C. The ISO
    D. The data owner

13. Which of the following are attributes of entrepreneurs?

    A. Innovators
    B. Well educated in business management
    C. More likely to take risks
    D. A and C
    E. B and C

14. A control partner's role includes analysis of proposed policy changes and providing an opinion on their viability.

    A. True
    B. False

15. Which of the following is the best measure of success for a security policy?

    A. The number of security controls developed as a result
    B. The number of people aware of the policy
    C. Reduction in risk
    D. The rank of the highest executive who approved it

16. A change agent typically will:

    A. Ensure current processes are working
    B. Ensure application code changes are well understood
    C. Challenge whether a company's existing processes represent the best approach

ENDNOTES

1. Leapfrog, "What Percentage of Your Company's Budget Should Be Allocated for IT Operations," July 30, 2019, *https://leapfrogservices.com/percentage-companys-budget-allocated/*, accessed April 14, 2020.

PART TWO

Types of Policies and Appropriate Frameworks

IT Security Policy Frameworks

AN INFORMATION TECHNOLOGY (IT) security policy framework is the foundation of an organization's information security program. The framework consists of a library of documents. A policy framework is much more than "just" a collection of documents. Organizations use these documents to build process, determine acceptable technologies, and lay the foundation for enforcement. The security policy framework documents and their implementation express management's view of the importance of information security.

Security policy frameworks can be large and complex, with significant impacts to the organization. Implementation requires strong management support and good planning. There are many individual tasks and issues to resolve along the way. Maintaining a clear line of communication with the executives who demonstrate support for and, ideally, personal commitment to the implementation is important. The implementation is not complete when a policy framework is published. The framework must define the business as usual (BAU) activities and accountabilities needed to ensure information security policies are maintained. You can measure success by how well the framework helps reduce risk to the organization. Implementing the framework is one of the first steps in managing information security risks.

Organizations cannot afford to be reactive or operate in an ad-hoc fashion regarding information security. There's increased accountability and liability with regulations. There's increased demand from senior leadership to demonstrate value. There's a push from security professionals to measure success. However, before you can measure anything, you need a benchmark. A benchmark allows you to gauge if you've reasonably covered the risks. It's something you can measure against to demonstrate value. The benchmark, and that gauge of success, is a part of the security framework. It captures the experience and knowledge of security professionals from all over the world. It provides a road map to guide an organization through the maze of security issues.

This chapter covers the components of an IT security policy framework. It also helps you understand how to create a framework that meets your organization's needs. The chapter covers the business and assurance consideration, and also discusses the issues with unauthorized access and their ramifications. Through these discussions you will better learn the value and construction of security frameworks.

Chapter 6 Topics

This chapter covers the following topics and concepts:

- What an IT security policy framework is
- What a program framework policy or charter is
- Which business factors you should consider when building a policy framework
- Which information assurance factors and objectives to consider
- Which information systems security factors to consider
- What best practices are for IT security policy framework creation
- What are some case studies and examples of IT policy framework development

Chapter 6 Goals

When you complete this chapter, you will be able to:

- Describe the role of a policy framework in an information security program
- Describe the different types of policies used to document a security program
- Describe what a dormant account is
- Explain the role of policies, standards, guidelines, and procedures
- Explain the organization of a typical standards and policies library
- Explain the personnel roles in a typical security department
- Explain what the C-I-A triad is and why it is important

What Is an IT Policy Framework?

An **IT policy framework** includes policies, standards, baselines, procedures, guidelines, and a taxonomy. Many frameworks resemble a hierarchy or tree. At the top of the tree is a charter or program framework policy, followed by additional policies. Then there are several standards. Under standards are many guidance and procedure documents. Getting the framework right is key to a successful security program.

FIGURE 6-1 offers one view of how you might structure an information security policy and standards library. For the framework to be useful, it must be accessible and understandable. Although most frameworks are available online, it's not enough just to provide access. It's equally important to ensure the documents are written at a level that is well understood and

NOTE

You will often hear the framework documents referred to as *policies*. In practice, the framework includes policies, standards, and other documents. Each type of document has a specific purpose.

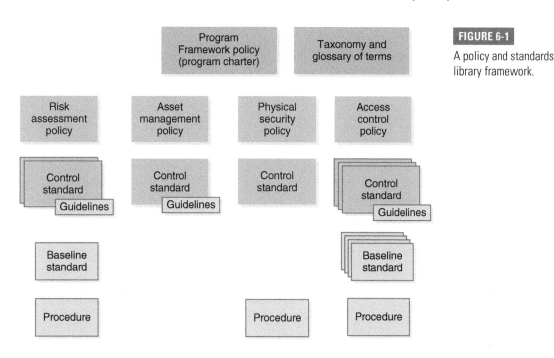

FIGURE 6-1

A policy and standards library framework.

can be navigated easily. The documents must be well organized, so that users can find what they are looking for quickly.

Building a policy framework is also like growing a tree. The roots and branches of the tree are established; then, you water the tree and allow it sufficient time to grow. Eventually it provides coverage for everyone. Over time, tree branches die off, leaves fall to the ground, new branches grow, and the tree needs pruning. A policy framework works in the same way. You give it ongoing attention to nurture the process and document content. This assures that it provides the coverage your organization needs and demands. What this means from a practical standpoint is that a policy framework does not have to be comprehensive on Day One. For example, you might have a policy that outlines the security requirements for managing encryption keys. As mobile technologies are introduced for the first time, these requirements may not provide adequate guidance or simply may not work with these new technologies. It may become clear that you need to create a separate mobile technology encryption policy.

An organization's security posture is often expressed in terms of **risk appetite** and risk tolerance. These two terms are sometimes misused and assumed to mean the same thing. They are not the same. Although they both are used to measure how much risk an organization is willing to accept, they have two very different purposes. *Risk appetite* generally refers to how much risk an organization is willing to accept to achieve its goal. This is often expressed by the impact on the organization and the likelihood of something bad happening. **FIGURE 6-2** illustrates this point. Ideally you would like to face only risks in which the likelihood of the negative event is low, and even if it did happen, the impact to the organization would be minimal. But this is not an ideal world. Many security risks will have significant impact on customers and the profits of a business, so they must be understood and managed.

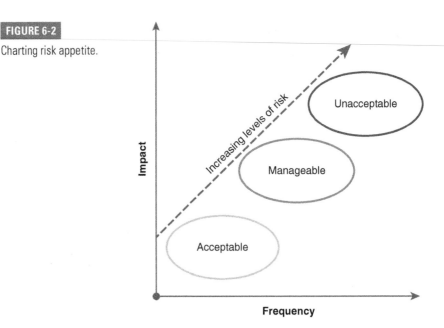

FIGURE 6-2

Charting risk appetite.

Typically, the security risks are managed by adding controls. Eventually a set of risks becomes simply too great for an organization to accept. These risks may relate to life and safety, or their potential impact would put the organization out of business. A security framework must have policies that clearly draw the lines to define acceptable behavior that ensures activities fall within the limits of risk appetite. As the levels of risk increase, so must the levels of control.

Risk tolerance relates how much variance in the process an organization will accept. This is often expressed in term of a percentage, such as plus or minus 10 percent. For example, assume you own a company that buys, renovates, and sells real estate. Assume your company special-izes in residential real estate. As a result, there may be no risk appetite for buying a commercial office building. That is because your company, lacking expertise in the commercial sector, is at greater risk of making a mistake if it tries to make a commercial deal. The higher costs of com-mercial properties and fluctuations in the market could result in huge losses that put your com-pany out of business. Consequently, commercial properties may be outside your risk appetite. Within the residential properties you do control, you set a budget for renovations. You watch every dollar spent and put in controls to ensure you come in within 10 percent of budget. You're comfortable that as long as you manage to this risk tolerance, you can make a healthy profit.

In an information security context, it's not always clear when and how to apply these concepts. You cannot apply risk appetite and risk tolerance to every control. You must select those controls (or group of controls) where key risk decisions must be made. For example, consider the group of controls related to security patch management. A decision must be made balancing information security and business needs over how much risk will be accepted to allow systems to run without patches to close security vulnerabilities. A risk appetite may not allow any systems with critical patches to run in production beyond five days. This would address immediate threats, and there could be a risk tolerance of 30 days (plus or minus 10 percent) established for all remaining security patches to be applied.

What Is a Program Framework Policy or Charter?

The program framework policy, or **information security program charter**, is the capstone document for the information security program. The charter is a required document that establishes the information security program and its framework. This high-level policy defines:

- The program's purpose and mission
- The program's scope within the organization
- Assignment of responsibilities for program implementation
- Compliance management

The chief executive officer (CEO) usually approves and signs the charter. The charter establishes the responsibility for information security within the organization. It's important that senior leadership of an organization express support for the information security program. This support comes in many forms. For instance, it's not unusual for the CEO to attach a personal message to the release of an information security program charter, or as part of an annual information security awareness effort. This responsibility is often placed on an individual known as the chief information security officer (CISO). The CISO is responsible for the development of the framework for IT security policies, standards, and guidelines. The CISO also approves and issues these documents. One of the CISO's primary roles is to ensure adherence to regulations. The regulations may be at the local, state, or federal level. The CISO also sets up a security awareness program. The program helps employees understand and live up to the organization's information security policies, standards, guidelines, and procedures.

FYI

The CISO may also be known by many other titles, depending on the culture of the organization. The CISO role is functionally aligned to the top-ranking individual who has full-time responsibility for information security. Some examples include:

- Director of information security
- Chief security officer
- Director of risk and compliance
- Information security program manager

Information security teams must ensure that security policies comply with laws and regulations; however, information security personnel are not lawyers. They work with their organizations' compliance and legal teams to gain an understanding of legal requirements. That is different from determining whether an organization is violating a law. That is the task of the legal department—and if it's not done properly there, the matter may be settled in court. In other words, the information security team must determine violations of an organization's *security policy* but should never express an opinion on violations of *law*. If a law appears to have been broken, a host of complex issues may arise, such as: What was the intent behind the actions taken? Was anyone's behavior reckless?

It's best for information security teams to express violations in terms of security policies. Information security leadership should ensure policies comply with legal requirements, and there should be a process for reporting major violations to compliance and/or legal departments.

Purpose and Mission

This part of the policy states the purpose and mission of the program. You should define the goals of the IT security program and its management structure. The needs can form the basis of the program's goals. Integrity, availability, and confidentiality are common security-related needs. Most e-commerce systems maintain confidential personal data. In this case, the goals might include stronger protection against unauthorized disclosures.

You should create a structure that addresses alignment with program and organizational goals. Your policies should mirror your organization's mission and goals. They should describe the operating and risk environment of the organization within this structure. Important issues for the structure of the information security program include:

- Management and coordination of security-related resources
- Interaction with diverse communities
- The ability to communicate issues of concern to upper management

TIP

Align scope with your annual information security budget. If scope and budget are not in alignment, you may be committing to something you cannot deliver.

TIP

Distinguish the responsibilities of computer services providers from those of the managers of applications who use the computer services. This policy can also serve as the basis for establishing employee accountability.

Scope

A policy's scope specifies what the program covers. This usually includes resources, information, and personnel. In some instances, a policy may name specific assets, such as major sites and large systems.

Sometimes, you must make tough management decisions when defining the scope of a program. For example, you may need to decide how the program applies to contractors who connect to your systems. The same concept applies to external organizations.

Responsibilities

A policy should state the responsibilities of personnel and departments related to the program. This includes the role of managers, users, and the IT organization. This is also referred to as the program's delegation of authority.

Compliance

Compliance is the ability to reasonably ensure conformity and adherence to both internal and external policies, standards, procedures, laws, and regulations. A program-level policy should address enforcement of the policy; for example, what happens if someone doesn't comply with computer security policies?

The program-level policy is a high-level document. It usually does not include penalties and disciplinary actions for specific infractions; however, this policy may authorize the creation of other policies or standards that describe violations and penalties. One common strategy for handling this issue is to have the information security policy refer to disciplinary procedures found elsewhere, such as in a human resources (HR) policy that broadly covers disciplinary actions.

 NOTE

An employee can unintentionally violate a policy. For example, an employee may lack knowledge or training. This can result in noncompliance.

Some organizations create a specific *consequence model* for information security policy violations. A consequence model does not replace the broader HR polices that deal with disciplining individuals. A consequence model is not intended to be punitive for the individual. Its purpose generally is to remove the risk introduced by the policy violation. For example, suppose a security policy has strict control requirements for coding applications that face the Internet. Assume an information security scan of a newly deployed interfacing application found a security weakness in direct violation of the policy. A consequence model (based on level of risk) could give the developer x days to fix the code to be in compliance. The consequence of failing to fix the code within the prescribed time would be to take the application offline and remove the risk.

Industry-Standard Policy Frameworks

Policy frameworks provide industry-standard references for governing information security in an organization. They allow you to leverage the work of others to help jump-start your security program efforts. The following areas determine where framework policies are helpful:

- Areas where there is an advantage to the organization in having the issue addressed in a common manner, such as shared IT resources
- Areas that affect the entire organization, such as personnel security
- Areas for which organization-wide oversight is necessary, such as compliance
- Areas that, through organization-wide implementation, can result in significant economies of scale, such as unified desktop computer management

No two organizations are alike. For-profit companies may have different goals and concerns than nonprofit organizations or government agencies. Different needs require different solutions. Therefore, security professionals have a wide variety of policy frameworks to work with. It's up to each organization to determine the best policy framework that meets the needs of the organization and the threats they face.

Three frameworks stand out because of their scope and wide acceptance within the security community:

- **Control Objectives for Information and related Technology (COBIT)**—A widely accepted set of documents that is commonly used as the basis for an information security program. COBIT is an initiative from ISACA, formerly known as the Information Systems Audit and Control Association, and is preferred among IT auditors. Keep in mind that COBIT was updated in 2019 to COBIT 2019.

- **ISO/IEC 27000 series**—An internationally adopted standard, the **ISO/IEC 27000** series can be found in the information security management program of virtually any organization.
- **National Institute of Standards and Technology (NIST) Special Publications, such as (SP) 800-53, "Recommended Security Controls for Federal Information Systems and Organizations"**—Geared to U.S. government agencies and their subcontractors.

Many of the regulatory bodies use these standards to develop security guidance and auditing practices. By relying on those who have paved the way for you, you can help to assure compliance with regulations that affect your organization without reworking all of your compliance processes. The following sections offer details on how to use the ISO/IEC 27002, 30105, and 27007 standards and the NIST SP 800-53 standard to describe your policy framework.

ISO/IEC 27002 (2015)

The International Organization for Standardization (ISO) and the International Electrotechnical Commission (IEC) develop and publish international standards. These standards are published as ISO/IEC numbered designations. It's common to see these standards abbreviated as ISO. For example, the **ISO/IEC 27002** standard is often shortened to ISO 27002.

 NOTE

ISO is actually not an acronym. It is short for *isos*, which is the Greek word for *equal*.

ISO/IEC 27002 is titled "Information Technology—Security Techniques—Code of Practice for Information Security Controls." This is a popular industry standard for establishing and managing an IT security program. ISO/IEC 27002 outlines 15 main areas that compose the framework:

1. **Foreword**—Describes the overall purpose and key references for the document. This includes the following key areas:
   - Scope
   - Terms of reference
   - Structure of the document
2. **Information security policy**—Describes how management should define an information security policy. Organizations usually maintain detailed security policies in a library. Information security standards, procedures, and guidelines support the library.
3. **Organization of information security**—Describes how to design and implement an information security governance structure. This section describes the need for an internal group that manages the program, including the governance of business partners.
4. **Human resources security**—Describes security aspects for employees joining, moving within, or leaving an organization. The organization should manage system access rights. The organization should also provide security awareness, training, and education. Section 4 covers these employment phases:
   - Prior to employment
   - During employment
   - Termination or change of employment

5. **Asset management**—Describes inventory and classification of information assets. The organization should understand what information assets it holds, and manage their security appropriately. This section covers responsibility for assets and information classification.

6. **Access control**—Describes restriction of access rights to networks, systems, applications, functions, and data. This section addresses controlled logical access to IT systems, networks, and data to prevent unauthorized use. The following topics are covered:
   - Business requirements for a control
   - User access management
   - User responsibilities
   - Network access control
   - Operating system access control
   - Application and information access control
   - Mobile computing and remote employee access

7. **Cryptography**—Describes the use and controls related to encryption. This includes the following key control areas:
   - Cryptographic authentication
   - Cryptographic key management
   - Digital signatures
   - Message authentication

8. **Physical and environmental security**—Describes protection of computer facilities. Valuable IT equipment should be physically protected against malicious or accidental damage or loss, overheating, loss of main power, and so on. This section covers:
   - Secure areas
   - Equipment security
   - Critical IT equipment, such as cabling and power supplies

9. **Operations security**—Describes operational management of controls to ensure that capacity is adequate and performance is delivered. This section includes these key topics:
   - Operational procedures and responsibilities
   - Protection against malicious and mobile code
   - Backups
   - Logging and monitoring
   - Information systems audit coordination

10. **Communications security**—Describes securing the network and controlling access to information by third parties. This section includes these topics:
    - Third-party service delivery management
    - Network security management

11. **Systems acquisition, development, and maintenance**—Describes building security into applications. Information security must be taken into account in the systems development life cycle (SDLC) processes for specifying, building/acquiring,

testing, implementing, and maintaining IT systems. These activities include the following:

- Security requirements of information systems
- Correct processing in application systems
- Cryptographic controls
- Security of system files
- Security in development and support processes
- Technical vulnerability management

12. **Supplier relationships**—Describes the policy and procedures needed to monitor suppliers' information security controls. This includes but is not limited to:

- How suppliers access company information
- How suppliers access the company network
- Monitoring access and activity of suppliers when they are on the organization's network
- Managing access rights when supplier personnel change roles
- Auditing suppliers to service level agreements

13. **Information security incident management**—Describes anticipating and responding appropriately to information security breaches. Information security events, incidents, and weaknesses should be promptly reported and properly managed. This section of the standard covers:

- Reporting information security events and weaknesses
- Managing information security incidents and improvements

14. **Information security aspects of business continuity management**—Describes protecting, maintaining, and recovering business-critical processes and systems. This section describes the relationship among IT disaster recovery planning, business continuity management, and contingency planning, ranging from analysis and documentation through regular exercising/testing of the plans. Controls are designed to minimize the impact of security incidents that occur despite the preventive controls from elsewhere in the standard.

15. **Compliance**—Describes areas for compliance, which include:

- Compliance with legal requirements
- Compliance with security policies and standards, and technical compliance
- Information systems audit considerations

ISO/IEC 27002 covers the three aspects of the information security management program: managerial, operational, and technical activities. All three must be present in any IT security program for comprehensive coverage. For more information about ISO/IEC 27002, visit *http://www.iso27001security.com/html/27002.html*.

ISO/IEC 30105

ISO/IEC 30105, "Information Technology—IT Enabled Services-Business Process Outsourcing (ITES-BPO) Lifecycle Processes," covers outsourced processes. Some processes are outsourced in every organization. There must be clear policies that govern the entire outsourcing process, including methods, procedures, and operations.

There are five parts to this standard:

- Part 1: Process reference model
- Part 2: Process assessment model
- Part 3: Measurement framework and organization maturity model
- Part 4: Terms and concepts
- Part 5: Guidelines

In relationship to frameworks, clearly Part 3 is of interest, but so is Part 5. This standard specifies all the steps in outsourcing, including planning, establishing, operating, monitoring, reviewing, maintaining, and improving services. Given the ubiquitous nature of outsourcing at least some business functionality, it is worthwhile to have at least a general understanding of this standard.

ISO 27007

The ISO 27007 standard, "Information Technology—Security Techniques—Guidelines for Information Security Management Systems Auditing," was first published in 2011 and was revised in 2017. When it was revised again in 2020 the name was changed to "Information Security, Cybersecurity, and Privacy Protection — Guidelines for Information Security Management Systems Auditing". This standard governs compliance auditing for information technology. This may seem far removed from frameworks; however, it provides a basis for any framework. Looking at the security policy framework from the perspective of compliance with audit requirements can be an effective approach for many organizations.

NIST Special Publication (SP) 800-53

NIST is an agency of the U.S. Department of Commerce. NIST develops information security standards and guidelines for implementing them. **NIST SP 800-53**, "Security and Privacy Controls for Federal Information Systems and Organizations," is the primary standard for federal systems.

Organizations often rely on NIST publications for reference and to develop internal IT security management programs. NIST SP 800-53 uses a framework similar to ISO/IEC 27002; however, NIST SP 800-53 includes 18 areas that address managerial, operational, and technical controls. **TABLE 6-1** summarizes NIST SP 800-53 rev. 4.

For more information about NIST SP 800-53, visit *https://nvd.nist.gov/800-53*

Version 4 of this standard was published in February 2012. The fifth version of this standard had a final draft release in March 2020 and is set for publication in late 2020. The basics of the standard are the same, but have been enhanced in the following ways:

- Making the security and privacy controls outcome-based
- Integrating privacy controls into the security control catalogue
- Deemphasizing the federal focus of the publication to encourage greater use by nonfederal organizations
- Promoting integration with different risk management and cybersecurity approaches
- Incorporating new, state-of-the-practice controls based on threat intelligence and empirical attack data

TABLE 6-1 A Summary of NIST SP 800-53

CONTROL AREA	DESCRIPTION
Access Control	Limit information system access to: • Authorized users • Processes acting on behalf of authorized users • Devices (including other information systems) • The types of transactions and functions that authorized users are permitted to exercise
Awareness and Training	Ensure that managers and users of information systems are aware of the security risks associated with their activities. Ensure adequate training for personnel to carry out their assigned information security–related duties and responsibilities.
Audit and Accountability	Create, protect, and retain information system audit records. Records include those for monitoring, analysis, investigation, and reporting of unlawful, unauthorized, or inappropriate information system activity. Users are accountable for their actions.
Security Assessment and Authorization	Periodically assess the security controls in information systems to determine if the controls are still effective. Develop and implement plans of action that correct deficiencies and reduce or eliminate vulnerabilities in information systems. Continually monitor information system security controls to ensure their effectiveness.
Configuration Management	Establish and maintain baseline configurations and inventories of information systems throughout their life cycles. Establish and enforce security configuration settings for devices in use.
Contingency Planning	Establish, maintain, and implement plans for: • Emergency response • Backup operations • Postdisaster recovery
Identification and Authentication	Identify information system users. Verify the identities of those users, as a prerequisite to allowing access to information systems.
Incident Response	Establish an incident handling process for information systems. Track, document, and report incidents to appropriate officials and/or authorities.
Maintenance	Perform periodic and timely maintenance on information systems. Provide effective controls to conduct information system maintenance.
Media Protection	Protect information system media, both paper and digital. Limit access to information on information system media to authorized users.

Physical and Environmental Protection	Limit physical access to information systems, equipment, and operating environments to authorized people.
	Protect the support infrastructure for information systems.
	Protect information systems against environmental hazards.
	Provide environmental controls for all information systems.
Planning	Develop, document, periodically update, and implement security plans for information systems. Describe the security controls in place or planned for the information systems. Include the rules of behavior for accessing the information systems.
Personnel Security	Determine that individuals in positions of responsibility are trustworthy and meet established security criteria for those positions, including third-party service providers.
	Maintain the protection information systems during and after terminations and transfers.
	Employ consequences for people failing to comply.
Risk Assessment	Periodically assess the risk to operations, assets, and people when using information systems or transmitting information.
System and Services Acaquisition	Allocate sufficient resources to protect information systems.
	Employ system development life cycle processes that incorporate information security considerations.
	Ensure that third-party providers employ adequate security measures to protect information, applications, and/or services.
System and Communications Protection	Monitor, control, and protect information transmitted or received by information systems at perimeter and important boundaries of the information systems.
	Employ architectural designs, software development techniques, and systems engineering principles for effective information security.
System and Information Integrity	Identify, report, and correct information and information system flaws in a timely manner.
	Provide protection from malicious code at appropriate locations within information systems.
	Monitor information system security alerts and advisories and take appropriate actions in response.
Program Management	Ensure the ongoing operation of the Information Security program.

What Is a Policy?

Policies are an important part of an information security program. They are best defined as high-level statements, beliefs, goals, and objectives. Policies help protect an organization's resources and guide employee behavior. Security policies help you address critical computer security issues. With effective policies in place, your organization will have better protection of systems and information.

Security policies also provide the "what" and "why" of security measures. Procedures and standards go on to describe the "how" of configuring security devices to implement the policy. The lack of information security policies and enforcement leaves an organization vulnerable to data breaches, business interruptions, and legal liabilities. In fact, in many states, not having or not enforcing information security controls in accordance with industry norms could lead to jail time for business owners and executives. There's a lot at stake. Yet, despite the urgent need and potential legal liabilities, many organizations do not have the defined security policies they need. As far back as 2012, a study by Symantec reported that of 1015 small and midsize companies in the United States, 83 percent had no cybersecurity plan. A more recent report, from 2019, states that on average a breach will cost a company 200,000 US dollars.[1] This can put many smaller businesses out of business. Implementing a good set of security policies can be a major competitive advantage. It ensures the protection of customer information and the stability of the business systems, and it protects the company from legal liabilities. These formal definitions of policies versus procedures are not always so clear in practice. In some organizations, what are actually procedures may be referred to as policies.

The IT security program begins with statements of management's intentions. These intentions are documented as policies. Policies describe the following:

- Details of how the program runs
- Who is responsible for day-to-day work
- How training and awareness are conducted
- How compliance is handled

The following is an example of a high-level policy that establishes an IT security program:

> Executive Management endorses the mission, charter, authority, and structure of Information Security. The Company's Executive Management has charged Information Security with the responsibility for developing, maintaining, and communicating a comprehensive information security program to protect the confidentiality, integrity, and availability of Company information resources.

Write policies as broad statements that describe the intent of management, defining the direction for the organization. Make these statements nonspecific as to *how* that will be accomplished. You should include details about how to meet the policy in a family of documents below the high-level policy.

What Are Standards?

You have many choices when deciding how to protect your computer assets. Some choices are based on quantifiable tradeoffs. Other choices involve conflicting tradeoffs and questions related to your organization's strategic directions. When making these choices, the policies and standards you establish will be used as the basis for protecting your resources—both information and technology—and for guiding employee behavior.

---

[1]https://www.cnbc.com/2019/10/13/cyberattacks-cost-small-companies-200k-putting-many-out-of -business.html

Standards are formal documents that establish:

- Uniform criteria that you can evaluate and measure
- Methods to accomplish a goal
- Repeatable processes and practices for compliance with policies

Security standards provide guidance towards achieving specific security policies. Although security policies are written at a high level, there's insufficient detail to explain how people should support them.

Security standards are often related to particular technologies or products. They are used as benchmarks for audit purposes and are derived from:

- Industry best practices
- Experience
- Business drivers
- Internal testing

Standards can come in different forms. Two common forms are control or issue-specific standards and system-specific technical or baseline standards.

Issue-Specific or Control Standards

An **issue-specific standard** focuses on an area of current relevance and concern to your company. Be prepared for frequent revision of these standards because of changes in technology and other related factors. As new technologies develop, some issues diminish in importance while new ones continually appear. For example, it might be important to issue a standard on the proper use of a cutting-edge technology even if the security vulnerabilities are still unknown.

A useful structure for issue-specific or baseline standards is to break the document into basic components. The components are described in the following sections.

Statement of an Issue. This section defines a security issue and any relevant terms, distinctions, and conditions. For example, an organization might want an issue-specific policy on the use of Internet access. The standard would define which Internet activities you permit and those you don't permit. You may need to include other conditions, such as prohibiting Internet access using a personal connection from an employee's desktop PC.

Statement of the Organization's Position. This section should clearly state an organization's position on the issue at hand. To continue with the example of Internet access, the policy should state which types of sites are prohibited. Examples of these sites may be pornography, brokerage, and/or gambling sites. The policy should also state whether further guidelines are available, and whether case-by-case exceptions may be granted, by whom, and on what basis.

Statement of Applicability. This section should clearly state where, how, when, to whom, and to what a particular policy applies. For example, a policy on Internet access may apply only to the organization's on-site resources and employees and not to contractors with offices at other locations.

Definition of Roles and Responsibilities. This section assigns roles and responsibilities. Continuing with the Internet example, if the policy permits private Internet service provider

(ISP) accesses with the appropriate approvals, identify the approving authority in the document. The office or department(s) responsible for compliance should also be named.

Compliance. This section gives descriptions of the infractions that are unacceptable and states the corresponding penalties. Penalties must be consistent with your personnel policies and practices and need to be coordinated with appropriate management.

Points of Contact. This section lists the areas of the organization accountable for the policies' implementation. These are typically the subject matter experts (SMEs). They interpret the policy. Often they are also in charge of ensuring the controls are in place to enforce the policy. This section may also identify other applicable standards or guidelines. For some issues, the point of contact might be a line manager. For other issues, it might be a facility manager, technical support person, systems administrator, or security program representative.

System-Specific or Baseline Standards

A **system-specific standard**, or baseline standard, is focused on the secure configuration of a specific system, device, operating system, or application. Many security policy decisions apply only at the system level.
   Examples include:

- Who is allowed to read or modify data in the system?
- Under what conditions can data be read or modified?
- What firewall ports and protocols are permitted?
- Are users allowed to access the corporate network from home or while traveling?

What Are Procedures?

A procedure is a written instruction on how to comply with a standard. A procedure documents a specific series of actions or operations that are executed in the same manner repeatedly. If properly followed, procedures obtain the same results under the same circumstances. Procedures support the policy framework and associated standards by codifying the steps that are proven to yield compliant systems.
   Procedures should be:

- Clear and unambiguous
- Repeatable
- Up to date
- Tested
- Documented

Examples of procedures include:

- Incident reporting
- Incident management
- User ID addition/removal
- Server configuration

- Server backup
- Emergency evacuation

A single standard often requires multiple procedures to support it. The people responsible for supporting or operating technical equipment in compliance with a standard are often the same people who document procedures to meet compliance requirements. Security department personnel may assist with documenting procedures. Once approved, the procedures are published within the policy and standards library with appropriate controls over who has access to them. Procedures are usually where metrics are collected to monitor compliance. Consequently, it's important to understand how these new procedures impact any governance and oversight. For example, assume there's a weekly oversight meeting to review the volume of user ID changes such as adding and deleting accounts. Also assume there's a dashboard that breaks down weekly activity to itemize the types of changes that occurred. This type of dashboard is common to try to proactively identify problem areas and detect unusual activity.

A new procedure may be introduced to remove dormant accounts. A **dormant account** is typically one that has not been used for an extended period of time. When this new procedure was put in place to remove dormant accounts, it would directly impact the weekly oversight meeting. In other words, you need to not only implement the new security procedure, but also update the weekly dashboard. Additionally, you need to discuss with the members of the weekly oversight meeting the ramification of the process change made.

FIGURE 6-3 illustrates an example of an extract of a policy and standards library. The figure highlights an access control policy, which is one of many security-related policies.

NOTE

Some procedures may be proprietary or contain trade secrets. They may also contain sensitive information on how security is monitored and controlled. These procedures may not be suitable for broad access by all employees.

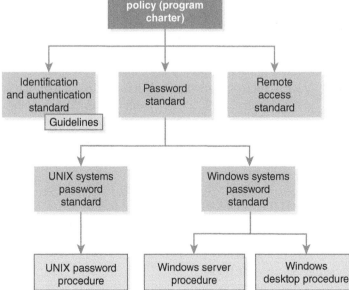

FIGURE 6-3

A possible access control policy branch of a policy and standards library.

Exceptions to Standards

Situations arise in which your organization cannot meet one or more standards immediately. You must recognize an **exception** to standards to determine where problems may exist.

Periodic reviews of these exceptions can also lead to improvements to the standards when many exceptions point to a general inability to meet compliance goals. Paying attention to exceptions is vital to ensuring that the policy framework remains relevant and current.

Exceptions are seldom approved "forever." Typically, they are reexamined annually. This allows leadership to discuss whether they are willing to accept the risk for another year or fund the changes needed to ensure compliance with security policies. Exceptions often include a discussion of compensating controls and mitigating controls. Compensating controls mean that although you cannot meet the letter of the policies, you can still achieve their goals through other means. Mitigating controls mean that although you cannot meet all the policies' goals, you can still achieve partial compliance. It's important to understand when you are approving a security exception how much risk you are accepting.

What Are Guidelines?

IT security managers often prepare guidelines, or guidance documents, to help interpret a policy or a standard. Guidelines may also present current thinking on a specific topic. Guidelines are generally not mandatory—failing to follow them explicitly does not lead to compliance issues. Rather, guidelines assist people in developing procedures or processes with best practices that other people have found useful. A guideline can also clarify issues or problems that have arisen after the publication of a standard.

NOTE

You usually do not invent best practices—you adopt them from others. Following best practices helps you avoid making mistakes that others have already learned from. This is a primary reason for being fully involved in the IT security industry. You can learn from peers about concerns and problems that led them to improved processes and technologies.

You can think of guidelines as "standards in waiting." They are used where possible, and feedback on guidelines is given to IT security managers responsible for policy and standards maintenance. Guidelines provide the people who implement standards or baselines more detailed information and guidance (hints, tips, processes, etc.) to aid in compliance. These documents are optional in a library but are often helpful.

Eventually, a guideline may become a standard when its adoption is widely accepted and implemented. For example, assume you have guidelines outlining five acceptable encryption techniques. Of the five, assume three become so widely adopted by the development teams that they are used in 95 percent of all applications. A decision could be made to make those three the standard for all new development. You can then treat the other two techniques, used in 5 percent of the application, as exceptions, or you can budget to upgrade them.

TIP

Joining an association focused on IT security is a good way to meet peers and develop skills. There are many associations you can join, including ISACA (*isaca.org*), ISC² (*ISC2.org*), and ISSA (*issa.org*).

Business Considerations for the Framework

An organization's collection of security policies, and therefore the entire security framework, shows its commitment to protecting information. As with security policies in general, a couple of considerations for implementing a framework are:

- **Cost**—Cost of implementing and maintaining the framework
- **Impact**—Impact of the controls required by the framework on employees, customers, and business processes

Creating a policy framework from the ground up takes time and effort. It's important for management to budget for these expenses. In addition, as the number of documents in the framework grows, you may need a content management system to manage the documents. Many organizations already use Microsoft SharePoint Server or a similar product to manage all business-related documents. You can use the same system to manage documents in a policy framework.

Employees often resist change, especially changes that affect how they need to perform their jobs. However, a comprehensive policy framework can help employees do their jobs more efficiently. The framework includes guidelines that employees can follow and procedures that specify how to perform tasks. Essentially, a policy framework provides a structure within which employees can work more efficiently.

Adding a taxonomy and glossary of terms is critically important. A well-formed taxonomy becomes the "Rosetta stone" for the framework's policy documents. It's used to interpret the meaning of the policies and scope efforts. Let's assume your policies include the terms *platform* and *network infrastructure*. What does *platform* mean? Do platform requirements include a firewall? Maybe. Maybe not. Yes, a firewall sits on a platform. There's a physical box with an operating system. But the taxonomy and glossary of terms may define *platform* as devices upon which an application resides, such as application and database servers. All other nonapplication networked devices may fall under the definition of *network infrastructure*. In this case, for firewall controls, you would go to the framework's network infrastructure documents. This distinction is not academic. Most likely the control requirements

Complying with the Sarbanes-Oxley Act

As technology further expands, laws and regulations eventually follow to compel positive action to protect information systems. In 2002, the U.S. Senate passed the Sarbanes-Oxley (SOX) Act, which gained the attention of U.S. corporate CEOs. The act passed in the wake of the collapse of Enron, Arthur Andersen, WorldCom, and several other large firms. SOX requires publicly traded companies to maintain internal controls. The controls ensure the integrity of financial statements to the Securities and Exchange Commission (SEC) and shareholders. The act also requires that CEOs attest to the integrity of financial statements to the SEC.

Because of this mandate, controls related to information processing and management are now highly scrutinized. Since the law took effect, the need for a comprehensive library of current operating documents is underscored.

for platforms would be different from those for network infrastructure. And it is critically important to get the right controls for the different devices.

A policy framework also helps management adhere to compliance requirements. Your security policy framework enables you to show regulators that you are using best practices. Many regulations provide specific details that must be included in your security policies. It's often helpful to create a "cheat sheet" that cross-references your security documents with the standards. For example, an entry might state that "HR Policy 2010-033 entitled 'Pre-Employment Screening' satisfies PCI DSS requirement 12.7." This will come in very handy if you are ever audited; you can use the cheat sheet to show auditors the exact sections of policy that implement each requirement. The challenge is maintaining these cheat sheets. It's important to build in a process of updating the cheat sheets whenever you revise the policies they're based on.

Roles for Policy and Standards Development and Compliance

Developing and maintaining a policy framework is a major undertaking. In large organizations, it usually requires many people. TABLE 6-2 lists roles commonly found in the development, maintenance, and compliance efforts related to a policy and standards library.

TABLE 6-2 Roles Related to a Policy and Standards Library

ROLE	ACTIVITY
CISO	Establishes and maintains security and risk management programs for information resources
Information resources manager	Maintains policies and procedures that provide for security and risk management of information resources
Information resources security officer	Directs policies and procedures designed to protect information resources, identifies vulnerabilities, and develops security awareness program
Owners of information resources	Responsible for carrying out the program that uses the resources. This does not imply personal ownership. These individuals may be regarded as program managers or delegates for the owner.
Custodians of information resources	Provide technical facilities, data processing, and other support services to owners and users of information resources
Technical managers (network and system administrators)	Provide technical support for security of information resources
Internal auditors	Conduct periodic risk-based reviews to ensure the effectiveness of information resources security policies and procedures
Control partners	Typically in areas such as compliance and operational risk. Ensure that security policies result in operational compliance with risk appetite and regulatory requirements.
Users	Have access to information resources in accordance with the owner-defined controls and access rules

Information Assurance Considerations

To develop a comprehensive set of security policies, start with the goals of information security: confidentiality, integrity, and availability. Information assurance (IA) tenets also include nonrepudiation and authentication.

One of the prime objectives of the information security program is to assure that information is protected. Ensuring confidentiality means limiting access to information to authorized users only. The integrity of the information must also be maintained so that it can be trusted for decision making. A system is considered to have integrity when you can trust that any modifications to the data were intentional changes made by authorized users or business processes. Availability ensures the information is accessible to authorized users when required. Nonrepudiation ensures that an individual cannot deny or dispute being part of a transaction. Finally, authentication is the ability to verify the identity of a user or device.

FYI

The goals of information security—confidentiality, integrity, and availability—are often referred to as the C-I-A triad. However, if you use the abbreviation C-I-A, make sure people understand you're referring to "confidentiality, integrity, and availability."

To meet information assurance needs, your framework should include policies for the following:

- Automation of security controls, where possible.
- Implementation of appropriate accounting and other integrity controls.
- Controls that handle potential conditions that appear while a system is operating. This should include error handling that won't reduce the normal security levels it's expected to support. Fail-secure rather than fail-safe is better for protecting information systems.
- Development of systems that detect and thwart attempts to perform unauthorized activity.
- Assurance of a level of uptime of all systems.

The following sections address the tenets of IA from a policy framework perspective.

Confidentiality

Confidentiality broadly means limiting disclosure of information to authorized individuals. This could include protecting the privacy of personal data and proprietary information. To meet confidentiality requirements, your security objectives must be specific, concrete, and well defined. Consider the goal of confidentiality as applied to email as an example. You might have an objective of ensuring that all sensitive information is protected against eavesdropping. You implement this by requiring that users

 NOTE

The more fine-grained a policy is, the easier it is to automate enforcement. For example, if an email server requires a specific configuration to be considered secure, a monitoring tool or agent on the server can report on the configuration and relay this to compliance personnel.

encrypt all emails containing sensitive information and ensuring that only authorized individuals have access to the key to decrypt the messages.

Write objectives so they are clear and achievable. Security objectives should consist of a series of statements that describe meaningful actions about specific resources. These objectives are often based on meeting business functions. In addition, they should state the security actions needed to support the requirements.

Integrity

Integrity refers to guarding against improper modification or destruction of data. One way to meet integrity requirements is to define operational policies that list the rules for operating a system. Access control rules in the form of permissions are often used to achieve this goal. Integrity can be achieved by limiting the type of permission to only certain accounts. For example, you might have a file that is widely accessible to read but that only a few individuals have permission to modify.

Managers must make decisions when developing policies because it is unlikely that all security objectives will be fully met. Consider the degree of granularity needed for operational security policies. **Granularity** indicates how specific the policy is regarding resources or rules. The more granular the policy, the easier it is to enforce and to detect violations. A more granular policy involves security controls over a specific element of technology. It might describe all the settings needed to configure a device or system securely. Checking it only requires ensuring that the settings are still in place. A less granular policy does not provide many details about a specific control, which allows people to determine how to comply. With less granular policies, it's more difficult to prove compliance, because each situation differs.

It's important to find and maintain the right level of granularity in security policies. The advantage of less granular policies is that they can be applied to broad sets of circumstances. Yes, they are subject to more interpretation. But when unknown conditions arise, they can be used broadly to control emerging risks. In contrast, very granular policies most likely will not address emerging risks precisely. They may be less helpful to users trying to figure out how to deal with new threats.

A formal policy is published as a distinct policy document. A less formal policy may be written in a memo. An informal policy might not be written at all. Unwritten policies are extremely difficult to follow or enforce. On the other hand, very granular and formal policies are an administrative burden. In general, best practice suggests a granular formal statement of access privileges for a system because of its complexity and importance.

Availability

Availability is the timely and reliable accessibility of information. To meet requirements for availability, your policy framework may include documents specifying when and how systems must be accessible to internal and external users. This can lead to different solutions for different needs; for example, external users require different forms of access than internal users. An external user might be required to use a virtual private network (VPN), for instance, to access the internal network.

Information Systems Security Considerations

The success of an information security program depends on the policy produced and on the attitude of company management toward securing information technology (IT) systems. The policy framework helps ensure that all aspects of information security are considered and controls are developed. As a policymaker, it's up to you to set the tone and the emphasis on the importance of information security.

Unauthorized Access to and Use of the System

The proliferation of technology has revolutionized the ways information resources are managed and controlled. Long gone are the days of the "glass house," full of mainframe computers under tight centralized control. Internal controls from yesteryear are inadequate in controlling today's decentralized information systems. Relying on poorly controlled information systems brings serious consequences, including:

- An inability of the organization to meet its objectives
- An inability to service customers
- Waste, loss, misuse, or misappropriation of scarce resources
- Loss of reputation or embarrassment to the organization

To avoid these consequences, risk management approaches are needed. Risk is an accepted part of doing business. Risk management is the process of reducing risk to an acceptable level. You can reduce or eliminate risk by modifying operations or by employing control mechanisms.

The dollars spent for security measures to control or contain losses should never be more than the estimated dollar loss if something goes wrong. Balancing reduced risk with the costs of implementing controls results in cost-effective security. The greater the value of information assets, or the more severe the consequences if something goes wrong, the greater the need for control measures to protect it.

Unauthorized Disclosure of the Information

Maintaining the confidentiality of information is critical to many organizations in the age of knowledge workers. When you consider the economic activity of the world's more advanced nations, most of the productive output of workers is information, rather than the widgets of yesterday. Consider two examples:

- Market research companies spend thousands of dollars and countless hours gathering business intelligence for their clients. Often, the sole output of these projects is a report summarizing the results. If this got into the hands of the client's competitors, it would destroy the competitive advantage created by the report. It could also reduce the economic value of the information to the client, and potentially jeopardize the market research firm's client relationship.
- Manufacturing companies may now produce many of their products in overseas factories where labor is inexpensive. However, they still do the "knowledge work" of developing

product plans, formulas, and other trade secrets in developed nations. If those plans got into the hands of competitors, it would be quite simple for the competitor to ship the plans to an overseas factory and produce the same product without any of the research and development expense.

Disruption of the System or Services

The demands for timely and voluminous information are increasing. One major protection issue is the availability of information resources. In some cases, service disruptions of even a few hours are unacceptable. Think about how much revenue Amazon or eBay loses for every hour of downtime. Reliance on essential systems requires a plan for restoring systems in the event of disruption. Organizations must first assess the potential consequences of an inability to provide their services and then create a plan to assure availability.

Modification of Information

If information is modified by any means other than the intentional actions of an authorized user or business process, it could spell disaster for the business. This underscores the importance of integrity controls, which prevent the inadvertent or malicious modification of information. Consider, for example, a product-testing firm that spends many hours testing the optimal settings for a piece of safety equipment used in factories. If a power surge alters the data stored in the testing database, the company might use the incorrect data to recommend equipment settings, jeopardizing the safety of factory workers.

Destruction of Information Resources

In addition to unauthorized modification of information, security controls should also protect against the outright destruction of information, whether intentional or accidental. The most common control used to protect against this type of attack is the system backup. By storing copies of data on backup tapes or other media, the company has a fallback option in the event data is destroyed. Consider the case of an insurance company that stores policy information on servers in a data center. If that data center is destroyed by fire, off-site backup tapes can be used to re-create it. Without those backup tapes, the company would have no way of knowing which policies it had issued, putting the entire business in jeopardy.

Best Practices for IT Security Policy Framework Creation

Your policies need high visibility to be effective. When implementing policies, you can use various methods to spread the word throughout your organization. Use management presentations, videos, panel discussions, guest speakers, road shows, summits, question/answer forums, and newsletters. Introduce computer security policies in a manner that ensures that management's support is clear, especially where employees feel overwhelmed with policies, directives, guidelines, and procedures.

Remember that the work of building awareness and gaining acceptance of security policies does not start when the framework is published. Its success will be determined by how it is put together and who is involved. Every organization is different, and differences play out in many ways. Organizations vary as to their industry or field, their regulatory requirements, their culture, and their leadership personalities.

All are necessary considerations as you start to develop a framework. In general, you should state core principles in the form of goals upfront. This defines "what" the framework must achieve. These goals are typically nonnegotiable security requirements. First get buy-in on the "what," and then get others to work together with you on the "how." You can be more flexible on the "how" than the "what." Gain ownership from key user groups by offering them choices on how to achieve policy goals. Executives and end users know the business and can usually find ways to integrate security processes while minimizing operational impact.

Formulating viable computer security policies is a challenge and requires communication and understanding of the organizational goals and potential benefits that will be derived from policies. Through a carefully structured approach to policy development, you can achieve a coherent set of policies. Without these, there's little hope for any successful information security systems.

Case Studies in Policy Framework Development

This section provides three case studies that help you understand how to develop or implement a policy framework. You will look at cases from the private sector, the public sector, and the critical infrastructure protection area.

Private Sector Case Study

Alberta Health Services established a policy development and document management framework in 2016.[1] Its policy framework began with a clear statement of the purpose and mission. The mission statement is:

> Alberta Health Services' (AHS) mission is to provide a patient-focused, quality health system that is accessible and sustainable for all Albertans. The Policy Development Framework and the Policy Development Steps are essential components in achieving this mission. The Policy Development Framework and Policy Development Steps are based on best practices and reflect organizational feedback.

The framework clearly describes processes, stakeholders, and committees that are involved in policy formulation. The framework also identifies principles that guide policy development. Chapter 1 and section C provide step-by-step processes for developing plans for policies, drafting policies, consulting with subject matter experts, and policy approval.

The framework established by Alberta Health Services goes beyond policy creation and approval. It has a whole section on policy implementation. It also has a section on how to review the policy and evaluate its efficacy. In addition to clear processes, the final step of review and evaluation of policy are worth study and emulation. The framework specifically states, "The review and evaluation process provides a regular opportunity for careful consideration of existing policy documents. The scheduled periodic review period is typically every 3 years, or as directed by the Sponsor or Approval Authority. A policy may be re-confirmed with no changes of content, modified, or a decision may be made that the policy is no longer needed."

Private Sector Case Study Two

Policy development is an international concern. Thus, it should come as no surprise that frameworks for developing policies can be found around the world. The University of Huddlesfield in England published a policy development framework for its 2017/2018 school year.[2] The University of Huddlesfield policy framework is less detailed than that for Alberta Health Services, but does provide essentials.

The university framework describes a policy owner responsible for the development and dissemination of the policy as well as maintenance and review. This framework also suggests, when needed, consultation with subject matter experts. A large section of the framework is devoted to approval of policies and policy changes. Unlike the Alberta Health framework, this framework has only a small section devoted to compliance.

Public Sector Case Study

This case study is a bit older, but still worthy of study as an example of a policy development framework. In 2006, the State of Tennessee determined the need for a comprehensive information security program. One of the main goals was to protect the state's revenues, resources, and reputation. The state accomplished this by researching, selecting, and implementing risk management methodologies, security architectures, control frameworks, and security policies.

The policies for Tennessee were based on the ISO/IEC 17799 (now ISO/IEC 27002) standard framework. The policies comply with applicable laws and regulations. The policies in the framework are considered the minimum requirements to provide a secure computing operation for the state.

The framework defines the information security policies for the State of Tennessee and the organizational structure required to communicate, implement, and support these policies. The policy framework was developed to establish and uphold the controls needed to protect information resources against unavailability, unauthorized or unintentional access, modification, destruction, or disclosure.

The policies and framework cover any information asset owned, leased, or controlled by the State of Tennessee. They control the practices of external parties that need access to the State of Tennessee's information resources. The policies were developed to protect:

- All state-owned desktop computing systems, servers, data storage devices, and mobile devices
- All state-owned communication systems, firewalls, routers, switches, and hubs
- Any computing platforms, operating system software, middleware, or application software under the control of third parties that connect to the State of Tennessee's computing or telecommunications network
- All data stored on the State of Tennessee's computing platforms and/or transferred by the state's networks

Private Sector Case Study Three

Target is a major retailer with more than 1800 stores in the United States and 133 in Canada. Target employs more than 360,000 people. Since 1962 it has built its reputation as a trusted member of many communities. It's hard to imagine there's anyone who grew up in the United States who doesn't recognize the brand or hasn't shopped at Target. This case study is a bit dated, but is such a major case as to be worthy of study despite its age.

In December 2013, during a very heavy Christmas selling season, the retailer announced that a data breach had occurred. It included the theft of about 40 million credit card records. Additionally, the breach resulted in the theft of 70 million records containing personal information such as addresses and phone numbers. The cause of the breach was linked to a vendor who had access to Target's network, through which point of sale (POS) devices were infected with malware. The malware was on thousands of POS systems for weeks. This was one of the largest retail data breaches of its kind.

When the breach was revealed on December 19, the company's stock dropped 11 percent. The stock price largely rebounded within a few months, but the retailer continued to feel the impact for many months after the breach. In February 2014, Target reported it had incurred $61 million in costs related to the breach. In March 2014, the CIO resigned, and Target announced it would hire a new CIO and, for the first time, a dedicated CSO. Additionally, in March 2014, news stories outlined a lawsuit against Target Corporation and Trustwave Holdings Inc., which provides credit card security services to Target. Two banks sued for "monumental" losses. Some estimate that the losses may have exceeded $1 billion for card issuers and $18 billion for banks and retailers combined.

The stakes are high in the case of such a breach. It may put the very survival of a small or midsize company at risk. Even for a large company, the financial impact can be significant. Most important is the impact on the customer. It may be felt for years, given the potential for identity theft and credit problems.

The public may never know exactly what led to the breach. What is known is that there were serious weaknesses in the information security framework and related controls. Take a look at three major impact areas that a security framework, if well implemented, should have addressed:

1. The lack of a dedicated CSO
2. Lack of vendor access management
3. Lack of network POS controls

With no dedicated chief security officer, information security leadership responsibility was spread around the organization, with the CIO responsible for execution.

This lack of a dedicated CSO created an inherent conflict of interest. The CIO in effect had to wear two hats: one to deliver the latest technology to drive sales throughout the store, and the other to protect the security interests of the customers and the company. All CIOs have this challenge of balance. The difference is that within a large organization, the CSO has a seat at the executive table and can challenge CIO decisions. Full-time CSOs can immerse themselves in the information security discipline. That includes gaining a deeper appreciation of emerging security risks than a CIO can typically achieve.

Vendor access must be properly managed if it is to be limited and monitored. If, in fact, a vendor was the source of the malware infection of the POS network, that indicates a failure to manage vendors and their access. In an ideal world, the breach of a vendor system or account should not lead to a breach of an organization's systems. These accounts and connections should be highly controlled. At a minimum, such a breach should be detected and stopped from spreading. But neither preventive nor detective controls seemed to work in this case.

It's fair to conclude that the network for the POS devices was not segmented effectively. Effective segmentation would have offered several key advantages. It limits access to the devices, which reduces the likelihood of malware infection in the first place. It allows a network to be purpose built, meaning that traffic can be more closely monitored to detect unusual activity such as that of malware. Segmentation also limits egress traffic. This means that even when a malware infection occurs, the information it captures cannot leave the network. This layered security approach using segmentation provides a strong security control.

The public may never know for sure what happened in the case of the Target breach. But it's clear that these controls, which are part of most large-company security frameworks, either did not exist or were not effectively implemented.

CHAPTER SUMMARY

Policy framework development is needed for the establishment and ongoing operation of the organization's security program. It establishes the top leadership's intent as to how information security should be managed. This program begins with documentation in the form of policies, standards, baselines, procedures, and guidance for compliance. The library of documents is arranged as a hierarchy with the highest level consisting of a charter. The next level includes policies, followed by an increasing number of standard and baseline documents. These documents are supplemented with guidelines to aid in implementation. Finally, many procedure documents that explicitly describe how to implement a security control or process are included. The library should be developed and managed by dedicated personnel who are experts in the subject matter related to the organization's industry or mission.

Any effective IT security program includes top-down sponsorship to establish and enforce these policies and standards. This framework of documents identifies how an organization manages security risk within its risk appetite and risk tolerance. Because information security never stands still for long, most of the documents in a policy and standards library must be considered living documents that are updated as technology and the environment changes.

KEY CONCEPTS AND TERMS

Compliance
Dormant account
Exception
Granularity

Information security program
charter
ISO/IEC 27000 series
Issue-specific standard

IT policy framework
NIST SP 800-53
Risk appetite
System-specific standard

CHAPTER 6 ASSESSMENT

1. An IT policy framework charter includes which of the following?

   A. The program's purpose and mission
   B. The program's scope within the organization
   C. Assignment of responsibilities for program implementation
   D. Compliance management
   E. A, B, and C only
   F. A, B, C, and D

2. Which of the following is the first step in establishing an information security program?

   A. Adoption of an information security policy framework or charter
   B. Development and implementation of an information security standards manual
   C. Development of a security awareness training program for employees
   D. Purchase of security access control software

3. Which of the following are generally accepted and widely used policy frameworks? (Select all that apply.)

   A. COBIT
   B. ISO/IEC 27002
   C. NIST SP 800-53
   D. NIPP

4. Security policies provide the "what" and "why" of security measures.

   A. True
   B. False

5. _____ are best defined as high-level statements, beliefs, goals, and objectives.

6. Which of the following is *not* mandatory?

   A. Standard
   B. Guideline
   C. Procedure
   D. Baseline

7. Which of the following includes all of the detailed actions and tasks that personnel are required to follow?

   A. Standard
   B. Guideline
   C. Procedure
   D. Baseline

8. Accounts that have not been accessed for an extended period of time are often referred to as _____.

9. List the five tenets of information assurance that you should consider when building an IT policy framework.

10. The purpose of a consequence model is to discipline an employee in order to ensure future compliance with information security policies.

    A. True
    B. False

11. When building a policy framework, which of the following information systems factors should be considered?

    A. Unauthorized access to and use of the system
    B. Unauthorized disclosure of information
    C. Disruption of the system
    D. Modification of information
    E. Destruction of information resources
    F. A, B, and E only
    G. A, B, C, D, and E

12. What is the difference between risk appetite and risk tolerance?

    A. Risk tolerance measures impact and likelihood, whereas risk appetite measures variance from a target goal.
    B. Risk appetite measures impact and likelihood, whereas risk tolerance measures variance from a target goal.
    C. There is no difference between the two.

13. A mitigating control eliminates the risk by achieving the policy goal in a different way.

    A. True
    B. False

ENDNOTES

1. Alberta Health Services, "Policy Development Framework," April 25, 2016, *https://extranet.ahsnet.ca/teams/policydocuments /1/clp-pdf-pol-devt-framework.pdf*, accessed April 18, 2020.

2. University of Huddlesfield, "Policy Framework," *https://www.hud.ac.uk/media/policydocuments /Policy-Framework.pdf*, accessed April 18, 2020.

How to Design, Organize, Implement, and Maintain IT Security Policies

WHAT BINDS WELL-FORMED IT SECURITY POLICIES together is an organization's culture of security. Without such a cultural attitude, written policies are far less effective. Within your organization, you will achieve that, in part, by establishing principles that create a shared vision, by empowering others to act, and by institutionalizing support processes. It's important that the implementation of IT security policies becomes second nature to the organization; that is, business processes should be designed with the controls needed to implement and maintain security policies built in.

For example, consider the issue of emergency access to a server in the middle of the night. Gaining access may require going through a firewall system that will issue an ID and password only when approval by the manager is obtained. In this way, security policies are enforced and cannot be bypassed. However, this process assumes there is an organizational understanding that such controls are important. The extra step of obtaining approval before accessing the server in the middle of the night is of value. Without a security culture, the business may see the process as an unneeded delay, given skilled staff that can be trusted to do the right thing. Defining a shared set of core security principles and vision is vital to how IT security policies are designed and implemented.

This chapter takes a micro look into each document within the collection of policy framework documents.

Chapter 7 Topics

This chapter covers the following topics and concepts:

* Which principles and concepts are important in the design of policy
* How to organize the contents of an IT policy framework
* What to consider when implementing the policy and standards library
* What the importance of the policy change control board is
* How to maintain the policy and standards library over time
* What best practices are for policies and standards maintenance
* What some case studies and examples of IT security policy management and maintenance are

Chapter 7 Goals

When you complete this chapter, you will be able to:

- Describe the characteristics of a "good" policy or standard that meets the organization's needs
- Describe the core security principles that policy writers should keep in mind while developing policies
- Explain the review and approval process for policies, standards, procedures, and guidance documents
- Explain the document publication and training and awareness processes needed for policies and standards
- Explain the role and activities of the policy change control board
- Describe the processes needed for maintaining and updating policies and standards

Policies and Standards Design Considerations

All documents in a policy and standards library are meant for people to read, understand, and implement. Policies and standards are not guidelines that offer suggestions. They are a collection of concrete definitions, procedures, and standards that describe acceptable and unacceptable human behavior. There are consequences for failing to follow approved standards. Developing them is not a trivial undertaking.

 NOTE

Most often, the questions related to where, when, and how are more appropriate for procedures or guidelines rather than policies or standards. Try to keep your policies and standards at the what, who, and why level of detail.

There's little point in writing documents that people cannot understand or that make compliance highly difficult or impossible. The best kinds of documents are clearly worded and address the six key questions of who, what, where, when, why, and how. These questions provide a consistent direction in writing policies and standards. Journalists traditionally ask these six questions as they research and write news stories. Most readers, of news articles and policy documents alike, are busy. They need concise and precise information. Lack of clarity forces readers to make assumptions. Often those assumptions are wrong. When you answer these questions within the first few sections of your documents, you increase the reader's comfort level and increase the likelihood of compliance.

▶ **TIP**

When writing policies and standards, avoid using terms like *should* when you mean *must* or *need to*.

Effective policies are those that employees understand and embrace. It's simply human nature for people to work harder for something they believe in. This depends on a shared belief system. These shared beliefs are collectively described as the **organizational culture**. Some organizations have a strong command and control culture. This dictates that policies and standards are written as strong, imperative statements; for example, "You must log off at the end of each workday." Other organizations use subtler phrases and tone, intended to persuade those who must follow the policy. But it's important to avoid using vague language or loose terms when developing your documents. This includes any terms that are vague. If the employees cannot understand clearly what is intended by the policies, they cannot comply. If you allow people to interpret your requirements on their own, they might look for ways to opt out of them.

The challenge is how to establish, or recognize, a core set of beliefs that can influence how you write policies. One method is to break the problem down into how the security controls are to be implemented and what controls are needed.

Operating Models

An **operating model** can help you understand how the security controls are to be implemented. One issue over which disagreement often arises is how much security should be centralized or decentralized within the business. A discussion of the operating model within the company can identify areas of disagreement and create a common set of beliefs on the proper placement and implementation of controls.

There are different ways to have this broad operational concept conversation. One way is outlined in a book entitled *Enterprise Architecture as Strategy: Creating a Foundation for Business Execution*, by Jeanne W. Ross, Peter Weill, and David C. Robertson. Their approach was to analyze and categorize the primary operating model of the business on the basis of four concepts: *diversified*, *coordinated*, *replicated*, and *unified*. As you can see by **FIGURE 7-1**, these operating model concepts are aligned with how the business chooses to integrate and standardize with an enterprise solution. In general, the higher the level of integration and standardization in an enterprise solution, the easier it is to implement security policies. The more the leaders of the business are deploying their own solution, the harder it is to implement security policies. The following defines each quadrant of Figure 7-1 in the context of IT solutions:

- **Diversified**—In the **diversified operating model**, the technology solution has a low level of integration and standardization with the enterprise. Typically, the exchange of data and use of services outside the business unit itself is minimal.

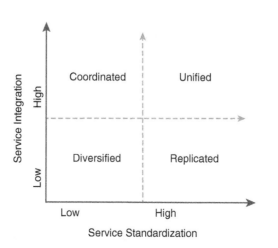

FIGURE 7-1

The four basic business operating models.

- **Coordinated**—In a **coordinated operating model**, the technology solution shares data across the enterprise; however, the level of shared services and standardization are minimal.
- **Replicated**—In a **replicated operating model**, the technology solution shares services across the enterprise; however, the level of data sharing is minimal.
- **Unified**—In a **unified operating model**, the technology solution both shares data and has standardized services across the enterprise.

These are not mutually exclusive. You can certainly have a coordinated model that is also replicated. Typically, you will have both highly integrated and less integrated systems across the enterprise. These choices are made by the business and reflect the beliefs the business holds. For example, if a business makes several changes to an application over a year, it may want more direct control over the technology. The staff may see control as critical to their success. This is especially true if they feel they must make technological changes throughout the year to keep up with the market. This approach can lead to standalone solutions that are business-specific and less integrated with enterprise solutions.

The four concepts align with service integration and service standardization. *Service integration* generally refers to how much shared data is used across a business. *Service standardization*, on the other hand, refers to how much control the business has in setting up its solutions and processes. For example, a real estate business may have a high degree of service integration. The company may share data on new home purchases between the business unit that sold the home and the unit that sells insurance for the home.

Those four models are not the only ways of looking at a business; however, they are useful and clear models. They are a good starting point for considering your organization's business model and how it impacts security policies. The operating model can have a profound effect on how your controls are implemented and how policies are written. The challenge is balancing the needs of the business and the enterprise needs to control security. These deliberate choices the business makes typically reflect the beliefs of the business's leaders.

Principles for Policy and Standards Development

No two organizations or risk assessment outcomes are the same; there are no universal recipes for building an IT security program. Instead, *principles* help you make decisions in new situations using proven experience and industry best practices. By considering several principles, you can derive control requirements and help make implementation decisions.

> **NOTE**
>
> It is important not to underestimate the strong feelings the business has in the level of controls it wants over technology. The challenge is selecting an operating model that the business can commit to and that will ensure that IT security policies are enforced.

Use the following principles to help you develop policies, standards, baselines, procedures, and guidelines. These are the common core security principles recommended for industry best practices, regardless of the organization's business nature:

- **Accountability principle**—The personal responsibility of information systems security should be explicit. Some roles in the organization are accountable only for the work they perform daily. Other roles are accountable for their own work, plus all the work performed by their team of employees.

Accountability helps to ensure that people understand they are solely responsible for actions they take while using organization resources. You can think of accountability as a deterrent control.

- **Awareness principle**—Owners, providers, and users of information systems, as well as other parties, should be informed of the existence and general context of policies, responsibilities, practices, procedures, and organization for security of information systems. Put more simply, it is unlikely that stakeholders will comply with policies they are not aware of.

- **Ethics principle**—The way information systems are designed, and the level of access to data reflected in the security controls, should operate in accordance with the organization's ethical standards. This includes the level of disclosure and access to customer data. This also needs to be entrenched in the organizational culture in order to be effective.

- **Multidisciplinary principle**—Policy and standards library documents should be written to consider everyone affected, including technical, administrative, organizational, operational, commercial, educational, and legal personnel.

- **Proportionality principle**—Security levels, costs, practices, and procedures should be appropriate and proportionate to the value of the data and the degree of reliance on the system. They should also be proportional to the potential severity, probability, and extent of harm to the system or loss of the data. In other words, don't spend $1000 to protect $500 worth of assets.

- **Integration principle**—Your documents should be coordinated and integrated with each other. They should also integrate with other relevant measures, practices, and procedures for a coherent system of security.

- **Defense-in-depth principle**—Security increases when it is implemented as a series of overlapping layers of controls and countermeasures that provide three elements to secure assets: prevention, detection, and response. This is referred to as **defense in depth.** It is both a military concept and an information security concept. Defense in depth dictates that security mechanisms be layered so that the weaknesses of one mechanism are countered by the strengths of two or more other mechanisms. This is a core security concept.

- **Timeliness principle**—All personnel, assigned agents, and third-party providers should act in a timely and coordinated manner to prevent and to respond to breaches of the security.

- **Reassessment principle**—The security of information systems should be periodically reassessed. Risks to technology change daily, and periodic reassessments are needed to ensure that security requirements and practices are kept current with these changes. Standards also need reassessments, at least annually, to ensure they represent the current state of affairs.

- **Privacy principle**—The security of an information system should include secure private information of users of the system. In other words, consider your users or partners when requiring information that could place their privacy rights at risk.

- **Internal control principle**—Information security forms the core of an organization's information internal control systems. Regulations mandate that internal control systems be in place and operating correctly. Organizations rely on technology to maintain business records. It's essential that such technology include internal control mechanisms. These maintain the integrity of the information and represent a true picture of the organization's activities.

- **Adversary principle**—Controls, security strategies, architectures, and policy library documents should be developed and implemented in anticipation of attack from intelligent, rational, and irrational adversaries who may intend harm. This is also the case with threat assessment.
- **Least privilege principle**—People should be granted only enough privilege to accomplish assigned tasks and no more. This is another core principle of security.
- **Separation of duty principle**—Responsibilities and privileges should be divided to prevent a person or a small group of collaborating people from inappropriately controlling multiple key aspects of a process and causing harm or loss. For example, in an accounting department, the person preparing invoices for payment should not be the same person writing the checks for payment.
- **Continuity principle**—Identify your organization's needs for disaster recovery and continuity of operations. Prepare the organization and its information systems accordingly.
- **Simplicity principle**—Try to favor small and simple safeguards over large and complex ones. Security is improved when it's made simpler. Obviously, security should not be over-simplified, but instead made as simple as practically possible.
- **Policy-centered security principle**—Policies, standards, and procedures should be established as the formal basis for managing the planning, control, and evaluation of all information security activities.

In addition to these principles, there are some specific steps that should be taken when developing security policies:

- **Risk identification**—Always begin by identifying the risks that the policies are trying to mitigate.
- **Legal compliance**—Make certain that policies comply with any legal or regulatory requirements.
- **Practicality**—Make sure the policy is something you can implement and enforce.

The Importance of Transparency with Regard to Customer Data

Policies related to the handling and use of customer data should include the concept of transparency. Organizations should be transparent and should notify individuals of the collection, use, dissemination, and maintenance of personally identifiable information (PII). PII is information that can be used to identify a specific person. This can be something used alone, such as a person's name.

> ▶ **TIP**
>
> Whenever customer data is involved, be sure to check with your compliance team on the legal requirements related to handling and use of such data.

A closely related concept is *nonpublic personal information (NPI)*. This is the term the Gramm-Leach-Bliley Act uses to refer to any personally identifiable financial information that a consumer provides to a financial institution.

Transparency with regard to handling of customer data should include the following elements:

- **Individual participation**—Organizations should involve the individual in the process of using PII and seek individual consent. This consent should include the collection, use, dissemination, and maintenance of PII. Organizations should also provide mechanisms for appropriate access, correction, and redress regarding use of PII.
- **Purpose specification**—Organizations should specifically describe the authority that permits the collection of PII and articulate the purpose or purposes for which they intend to use data.
- **Data minimization**—Organizations should collect only PII that is directly relevant and necessary to accomplish the specified purpose(s). Additionally, they should retain PII only for as long as is necessary to fulfill the specified purpose(s). Any excessive data collection or retention only increases the risk to the organization.
- **Use limitation**—Organizations should use PII solely for the purpose(s) specified. If PII is shared, it should be for a purpose for which it was collected. This is now enshrined in laws such as the General Data Protection Regulation (GDPR) in the European Union.

Types of Controls for Policies and Standards

With a shared sense of purpose and beliefs within the business and principles in hand, you can begin to map what you want to accomplish with the security controls. Security controls are measures taken to protect systems from attacks on the confidentiality, integrity, and availability (C-I-A triangle or triad) of the system. Sometimes, safeguards and countermeasures are used synonymously with the word *control*. Controls are chosen after the risk assessment of the assets is complete. Once you have identified and assessed the risks to your assets, you can select the appropriate control to counter the threat, mitigate it, or reduce the risks.

Security Control Types

Security controls can be described according to two different categorization schemes: one based upon what the control is and the other based upon what the control does.

The first category includes administrative, technical, and physical control categories. They describe what the control actually is, such as a named process, a standard, a firewall, or a locked door:

- **Administrative controls**—The policies, standards, and procedures that guide employees when conducting the organization's business. Preemployment screening of personnel and a change management process are also examples of administrative controls.
- **Technical security controls**—The devices, protocols, and other technology used to protect assets. These include antivirus systems, cryptographic systems, firewalls, and more.
- **Physical security controls**—The devices used to control physical access. Examples here are fences, security guards, locked doors, motion detectors, and alarms.

To be effective, security must consider all three approaches. For example, if you wish to secure a server, it should be in a locked server room (physical controls). It should have strong authentication and an encrypted hard drive (technical controls). Finally, there must be effective security policies governing the server (administrative controls).

The second set of controls describes what controls do. These controls include the following:

- **Preventive security controls**—Prevent intentional or unintentional security threats. Examples include network access policies, firewall rules, and locks on wiring closets and server room doors.
- **Detective or response controls**—Act like alarms and warnings. These controls kick in *after* an incident begins. Examples include motion detectors, log files, and files that contain system audit information.
- **Corrective controls**—Help you respond to and fix a security incident. Corrective controls are also used to limit or stop further damage. Some examples include cleaning a virus off a system, closing a firewall port, and blocking an Internet Protocol (IP) address.
- **Recovery controls**—Help you put a system back into operation once an incident ends. Disaster recovery and tape backups fit into this category.

There is significant overlap between security control categories. Some controls can be administrative and preventive or technical and corrective, or any combination. This overlap occurs by design for the purpose of implementing the principle of defense in depth.

You can find catalogs of security controls for virtually every security topic. For example, Control Objectives for Information and related Technology (COBIT) is an IT governance framework developed by ISACA that includes supporting tools to help bridge the gaps between control requirements, technical issues, and business risks. You can visit the ISACA website at *http://www.isaca.org* for more information.

Document Organization Considerations

Although there are many ways to organize a library of policies, one thing they all have in common is the need for a numbering scheme. A numbering scheme helps you organize the material by topic; it becomes a quick reference point for people to use to refer to specific content. You can create your own numbering scheme or use an existing one. Should you decide to use an existing framework like ISO/IEC 27002, you can begin with the taxonomy it provides.

FIGURE 7-2 offers an example that you might consider using for your taxonomy. Think of Figure 7-2 as a sideways tree. The program-level policy or information security charter on the left side is the "root." It establishes the tree and delegates the authority for managing the tree to the information security department of the organization. Let's call it IS (for information security), POL (for policy), and add "001" because it's the first document: IS-POL-001.

NOTE

Taxonomy is the practice and science of classification. A hierarchical taxonomy is a tree structure of classifications for a given set of objects or documents.

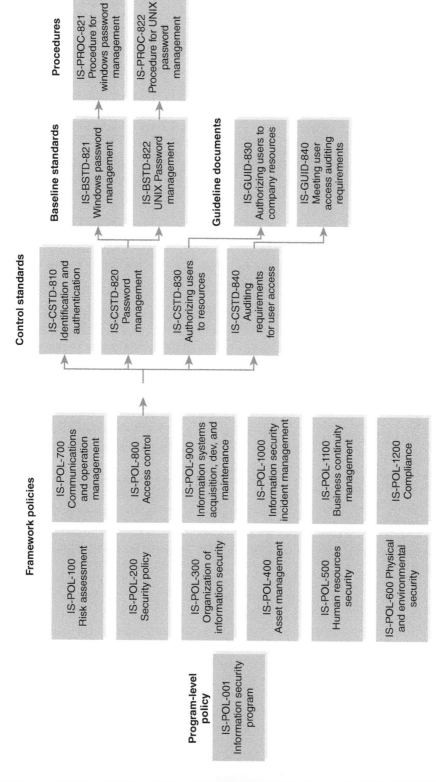

FIGURE 7-2

A possible policy and standards library taxonomy.

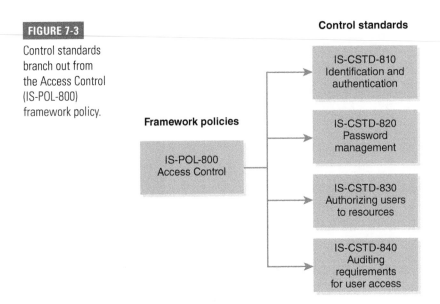

FIGURE 7-3

Control standards branch out from the Access Control (IS-POL-800) framework policy.

Framework policies

To the right, you find a collection of program framework policies. This framework uses ISO/IEC 27002 topics for policy types. They are numbered in groups of 100 to allow for growth. Each of these policies stands on its own and serves as the first major branches of the tree. From these branches, standards and their supporting documents appear.

Looking at the Access Control (IS-POL-800) framework policy as an example, you can see control standards labeled IS-CSTD-810 through 840. The CSTD label is short for Control Standard. **FIGURE 7-3** shows just this part of the policy and standards library.

 TIP

Whatever numbering scheme you adopt, leave plenty of room for adding new documents. Think through a numbering scheme carefully before you decide to use it. Ask yourself how you would add new policies. How would you add new technology areas such as introducing mobility into the organization for the first time?

Baseline standards are then numbered to maintain the consistency of the taxonomy and support the control standards upon which they're based. The baseline standards are specific to technology and numbered as IS-BSTD-821 and 822, where BSTD stands for Baseline Standard. These two standards define the requirements for password management as they pertain to the Windows operating system and the UNIX operating system. In this example, the numbering follows the parent standard's numbering, IS-CSTD-820.

Procedures link to the baseline standards that they support. For example, IS-PROC-821 and 822 are directly mapped to the 821 and 822 baselines. In most cases, there is a one-to-one mapping of baselines and procedures in support of the control standard. **FIGURE 7-4** shows a closeup of baseline standards and procedures in the policy and standards library tree.

Guideline documents are most often tied to a specific control standard, as shown in **FIGURE 7-5**. Guideline documents (GUIDs) are useful where there may not be any

FIGURE 7-4

Baseline standards and procedures provide additional branches of the library tree.

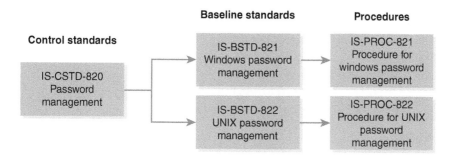

Control standards   **Baseline standards**   **Procedures**

IS-CSTD-820
Password
management

IS-BSTD-821
Windows password
management

IS-PROC-821
Procedure for
windows password
management

IS-BSTD-822
UNIX password
management

IS-PROC-822
Procedure for UNIX
password
management

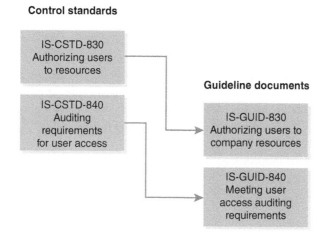

Control standards

IS-CSTD-830
Authorizing users
to resources

IS-CSTD-840
Auditing
requirements
for user access

Guideline documents

IS-GUID-830
Authorizing users to
company resources

IS-GUID-840
Meeting user
access auditing
requirements

FIGURE 7-5

Guidelines provide
additional branches of the
library tree.

technology for enforcing controls, but the guidelines provide useful information for
process management or controls.

When people look for a specific document, the name of the document should tell them all
they need to know. After they gain some experience with the taxonomy, they'll know where
to look.

Sample Templates

This section looks at some suggested document formats for policies and standards. You can
use these as is or create a template that best reflects your organization's needs.

Sample Policy Template

The following outline of a policy document helps you organize the content for your
program-level policy and framework policies:

POLICY NAME AND IDENTIFYING INFORMATION

1. PURPOSE
   This document establishes a policy for . . .
2. BACKGROUND
   This document was developed because . . .
3. SCOPE
   This policy applies to the use of . . .
4. OPERATIONAL POLICY
   4.1. Section 1
   4.2. Section 2
   4.3. Section 3
   4.4. Section 4
5. ROLES AND RESPONSIBILITIES
   The following entities have responsibilities related to the implementation of this policy:
6. APPLICABLE LAWS/GUIDANCE
7. EFFECTIVE DATES
   This policy becomes effective on the date that [xxx], Chief Information Officer (CIO), signs it and remains in effect until officially superseded or canceled by the CIO.
8. INFORMATION AND ASSISTANCE
   Contact the . . . for further information regarding this policy.
9. APPROVED
   [Director of Information Security Policies]   Date of Issuance
10. ASSOCIATED RESOURCES
    This policy is augmented by . . .

> ▶ **TIP**
>
> Never use individual (personal) names in a policy or standard. For Role and Responsibilities, use the name of the department, unit, or specific role that is accountable. Individuals join and leave the company.

The following is a sample policy statement for access control that would appear in the "Operational Policy" section of a framework policy:

> Personnel must be positively authenticated and authorized prior to being granted access to <Organization> information resources. Access based on an individual's role must be limited to the minimum necessary to perform his or her job function.
>
> Access to critical information resources must be controlled through a managed process that addresses authorizing, modifying, and revoking access, and periodic review of information system privileges."

Sample Standard Template

The following outline of a standards document helps you organize the content for your control and baseline standards:

STANDARD NAME AND IDENTIFYING INFORMATION

1. PURPOSE
   This document establishes a standard for . . .

2. BACKGROUND

   This document was developed to support . . .

3. SCOPE

   This standard applies to the use of . . .

4. STANDARD STATEMENT(S)

   4.1. Section 1

   4.2. Section 2

   4.3. Section 3

   4.4. Section 4

5. ROLES AND RESPONSIBILITIES

   The following entities have responsibilities related to the implementation of this standard:

6. GUIDANCE

   Links to guidance documentation for this standard . . .

7. EFFECTIVE DATES

   This standard becomes effective on the date that [xxx], Chief Information Officer (CIO), signs it and remains in effect until officially superseded or canceled by the CIO.

8. INFORMATION AND ASSISTANCE

   Contact the . . . for further information regarding this standard.

9. APPROVED

   [Director of Information Security Policies]   Date of Issuance

10. ASSOCIATED RESOURCES

    This standard is augmented by . . .

The following are sample statements for access control that would appear in the "Standard Statement(s)" section of a control standard:

Access to all <Organization> information resources must be controlled by using user IDs and appropriate authentication methods as required by the Information Classification Standard and the Information Handling Standard.

Access to all <Organization> information resources connected to the <Organization> network must be controlled by using user IDs and appropriate authentication.

In order to ensure individual accountability, the use of any user ID must be associated with a specific individual. Passwords must never be shared between users.

The following is a sample statement for UNIX account management that would appear in the "Standard Statement(s)" section of a baseline standard:

Default system accounts must be locked (except root). The password field for the account must be set to an invalid string, and the shell field in the password file must contain an invalid shell. /dev/null is a good choice because it is not a valid logon shell.

Sample Procedure Template

The following outline of a procedures document helps you organize the content for any procedures needed to implement baseline standard controls:

PROCEDURE NAME AND IDENTIFYING INFORMATION

EFFECTIVE DATE
Date the procedure becomes effective. This can be the same as or later than the approval date in order to allow time for training and implementation if necessary.

1. PROCEDURE
   Insert procedural steps in the table . . .
   1.1. Section 1.1
   1.2. Section 1.2
   1.3. Section 1.3
   1.4. Section 1.4

2. STANDARD
   Indicate the name and number of the baseline standard to which this procedure relates.

3. FORMS
   List any form numbers and names and their location if there are any needed to conduct this procedure.

4. PROCEDURE HISTORY
   List all previous known versions (including obsolete procedure numbers or titles if known) and their effective dates.

5. INFORMATION AND ASSISTANCE
   Contact the . . . for further information regarding this standard.

6. APPROVED
   [Director of Information Security Policies]   Date of Issuance

7. KEYWORDS
   Indicate any cross references, aliases, phrases, or terms that describe the procedure. Define all acronyms and abbreviations.

8. ASSOCIATED RESOURCES
   This standard is augmented by . . .

The following is a sample procedure snippet for data destruction on media that could appear in the "Procedure" section of a procedure document:

Disk sanitization involves securely erasing all the data from a disk so that the disk is, except for the previous wear, "new" and empty of any previous data. For example, a disk connected to a Linux system may be sanitized by repeating the following command three to seven times (or more):

```
dd if=/dev/random of=/dev/hdb && dd if=/dev/zero of=/dev/hdb
```

This command first writes a random pattern to disk /dev/hdb, then writes all zeros to it. Any disk that needs to be sanitized, including any flash memory device or former PC or Macintosh disk, may be attached to a Linux (or other UNIX) system and erased using the above command, replacing /dev/hdb with the appropriate disk device name.

Sample Guideline Template

Although there are generally no standard templates for guidelines, you can use or adapt the following:

GUIDELINE NAME AND IDENTIFYING INFORMATION

1. PURPOSE

    This document provides guidance and advice in helping to meet the control requirements from Standard(s) . . .

2. BACKGROUND

    This document was developed to support . . . .

3. SCOPE

    This guidance applies to the use of . . . .

4. GUIDANCE SECTION(S)

    4.1. Section 1

    4.2. Section 2

    4.3. Section 3

    4.4. Section 4

5. ROLES AND RESPONSIBILITIES

    The following entities have responsibilities related to the implementation of this standard: . . .

6. EFFECTIVE DATES (may or may not be needed)

7. INFORMATION AND ASSISTANCE

    Contact the . . . for further information regarding this document.

8. APPROVED

    [Director of Information Security Policies]   Date of Issuance

9. ASSOCIATED RESOURCES

    This guideline is augmented by . . .

The following is a sample guideline snippet for the use of encryption within a university setting. This text could appear in the "Guidance Section" section of a guideline document:

University personnel and student organizations:

- Should use industry-standard encryption algorithms to protect their data.
- Should not attempt to develop their own proprietary encryption algorithms and should carefully scrutinize any claims made by vendors about the security of proprietary encryption algorithms.

Considerations for Implementing Policies and Standards

Implementing your policies and libraries entails four major steps:

1. Building consensus on intent
2. Reviews and approvals for your documents
3. Publication of the documents
4. Awareness and training

Building Consensus on Intent

Separating the writing of the actual policy language from the discussion of the intent of the policy change is a good way to build a consensus. During this step, you should discuss the drivers for the change in terms of the operating model and principles. This reinforces the shared beliefs and helps promote the desired culture. As much as possible, it is desirable to have a consensus on at least the purpose of a policy. You may or may not be able to achieve consensus on all the detailed items in a policy, but at least the purpose should be one that has broad support.

This separation also has the added advantage of reducing the time it takes to develop the actual policy language. Too often time is wasted disagreeing with policy language when, in fact, the real disagreement is on the need for the policy. If you have agreement on the need for the security control and the intended outcome, then writing the policy language is easier. The actual writing simply documents this agreement. This approach also makes the review and approval easier, because there's already an awareness of the need for the policy change and an understanding of its intent.

Throughout your research and interview processes with operational users and their managers, you should have prepared them for changes that the information security (IS) department will be mandating. This give-and-take process helps to improve the quality of the document content. It also helps with buy-in from those who are subject to the rules and controls you'll be implementing based on the risk analysis and assessment work completed.

Reviews and Approvals

Once they are written, you need to share your documents again with those who helped you develop them. Let those employees review the policy documents' language well before you implement them. These reviews allow you to assess the impact of the policy or standard on the organization before deploying it in a potentially disruptive fashion.

These reviews sometimes require you to revise parts of a policy or standard to allow for current conditions. Or, you may need to postpone implementing some controls until the environment is better prepared for compliance. Early in your overall policy development project, you should work with your organization's audit group to determine how soon after policy publication they will audit based on the policy. By allowing a grace period for compliance, you are helping to ensure that the policies will be enforceable. A grace period gives personnel time to implement any project, processes, or internal communications necessary for compliance.

Allow sufficient time to gather and address concerns, as well as sufficient time for the business to prepare its employees for the change. Once you gain the concurrence of those subject to the policies, it's vital to gain approval from their managers or their management team. Often, executive managers appoint delegates for standards reviews and rely on recommendations before they approve or reject changes. If you've done a good job with those subject to the specific standards, approvals should be timely.

▶ **TIP**

If you cannot implement controls immediately, postpone the implementation date. Let people know that new controls are coming at a future specific date. Depending on the size of the organization, the grace period can be from a few months to one year.

Ultimately, your goal is to gain senior executive approval of the policy or standard. The executive approver may be the chief information security officer (CISO), if the role exists. That person is unlikely to give approval if all parties have not reviewed the document. Internal reviews within the IS department should help mitigate some of the executive approver's concerns once the document reaches him or her for approval. Here are some suggested people who should be given the opportunity to become a second or third layer of review:

* **Technical personnel**—You may need to call upon the expertise of technical staff with specific security and/or technical knowledge in the area about which you are writing.
* **Legal**—The legal department should have input into the policy development process. They can provide advice on current legislation that requires certain types of information to be protected in specific ways. Your legal department should also review policy and standards documents once they are complete. Given the dynamic nature of the legal system, with changes occurring frequently, this is a critical step.
* **Human resources (HR)**—The HR department may need to review and/or approve your policy or standard if your document addresses topics covered by existing HR policies. Email usage and physical security are examples. Make sure you reference the HR policy rather than repeat content. Simply repeating content can lead to future inconsistencies.
* **Audit and compliance**—Internal audit personnel will monitor compliance with a policy once it is in force. If you work with external compliance groups, consult with them as needed. Although the internal audit team members generally will not be the ones to approve policy changes, they can express an opinion or concerns that should be addressed.

Although these review steps may seem onerous, early buy-in is needed to ensure there are no surprises when policy changes take effect. It's better to put in the time and effort early in the process to avoid rework later.

Once policies and standards are approved, you need to distribute them in ways that work best in your organization.

Publishing Your Policy and Standards Library

Publishing your policy and standards library depends on the communications tools available in your organization. Many organizations use some form of an intranet for internal communications. Different departments may have their own subsection of the intranet, and IS should have its own. An intranet generally has a front page or portal that announces new content on the site. It also includes news, other announcements, access to standard forms, and so on.

Sometimes, intranet sites use a back-office engine for managing content, like Microsoft SharePoint Server. Departments can use SharePoint for the documents and contact information they wish to share, and then publish the content to the intranet for anyone to access.

If your organization uses a content management tool for departmental websites, you might consider using that for publishing your documents. Documents must be readily obtainable at any time, with a copy placed on the internal network shared drives or the organization intranet. Some of the best practices for publishing your documents are to create separate webpages for each document and to provide a link to the document itself on that webpage. The page should contain:

- Identifying information
- Overview of the document
- Last revision date and the name or initials of the person who revised the document
- Next scheduled document review date
- Keywords for the intranet search engine to simplify locating your documents
- Links to related documents
- A link to an Adobe Portable Document Format (PDF) version of the document

NOTE

You might consider a roadshow prior to the publication of major policy changes. In this context, a **roadshow** refers to showing up at a large gathering of employees and explaining the change. This could be as simple as being a guest at a normally scheduled department meeting or calling a town-hall meeting to announce the upcoming changes. This approach is usually more appropriate for larger organizations.

The medium you choose for developing your policy content may determine the level of difficulty you'll encounter in the review cycle. Word processing documents are appealing because they're easy to use and convenient. However, for review purposes, word processing documents aren't always efficient. When you're ready with a final draft, you can create a set of PDF documents that comprise the policy and standards library. You then publish the library in a way that's best for your organization.

A class of software, called Governance, Risk, and Compliance (GRC), is available to support policy management and publication. Functions that are commonly found in a GRC tool include:

- Assessing the proper technical and nontechnical operation of controls, and mitigating/remediating areas where controls are lacking or not operating properly (governance)
- Assisting in quantification, analysis, and mitigation of risk within the organization (risk)
- Authoring, distribution, and policy and controls mapping to the governing regulation, as well as tracking exceptions to those policies/regulations (compliance)

GRC tools are typically delivered as modules that plug in to a central GRC engine. Usually, you can license a policy and standards module. With this module, you can use the workflow features to develop and share your documents for reviews and approvals, publish the library as webpages, and search for relevant documents. Some organizations use the tools for:

- Awareness training using quizzes
- Emails to users that notify them of new content or changes to existing policies
- Emails that notify people that new content is ready for them to review or approve

- Tracking changes to documents to ensure that important content is not lost or erroneously changed

The following GRC tools, as well as several others, are widely used:

- RSA Archer GRC, *http://www.emc.com/security/rsa-archer.htm*
- Broadcom Control Compliance Suite, *https://www.broadcom.com/products/cyber-security/information-protection/control-compliance-suite*
- Modulo Risk Manager, *https://www.enisa.europa.eu/topics/threat-risk-management/risk-management/current-risk/risk-management-inventory/rm-ra-tools/t_modulo.html*
- Quantitative GRC Software Suite, *https://quantivate.com*
- LogicManager, *https://www.logicmanager.com*
- ZenGRC, *https://go.reciprocitylabs.com*

 NOTE

As part of a continuous improvement effort, plan to review and update published policies and other framework documents periodically. You'll learn about document review and maintenance later in this chapter.

Awareness and Training

Implementation requires educating personnel not only on each of the core elements, but also on changing their role to emphasize protecting data and systems. Ongoing security awareness training, including training on new policies, is a critical aspect of policy implementation.

An awareness program can motivate employees and promote the shared beliefs discussed earlier in this chapter. Motivating employees is as important as mastering a technology. A motivated employee can deal with the unexpected. This is particularly important when dealing with unexpected security events. Remember, it's not getting employees to learn the policy that's important; it's motivating employees to execute the policy. Additionally, this communication creates a foundation for other discussions, such as performance appraisals and process improvement. Consequently, a security awareness program is one of the key factors for the successful implementation of an organization-wide security policy. Awareness tools should describe and outline the specific mandate for all employees to secure organization assets. It should also explain the core elements of the security policies and standards. The program is aimed at generating an increased interest in the information security field in a way that's easy to understand.

Gaining management awareness and buy-in should be your first step. Without management support and commitment, it's unlikely that your efforts to educate the masses later on will succeed. As you're selling the program to your executive sponsor(s) and gaining approval for issuing your documents, use that time to leverage their authority with managers and direct reports to ensure compliance. With that level of buy-in secure, the task of gaining buy-in from the rest of the organization is made that much easier.

Awareness programs are often divided into two parts: awareness and training. The purpose of awareness is to provide employees with a better understanding of security risks. The importance of security primarily focuses on the daily operation of the organization. Training should cover many potential security problems in detail, as well as introduce a set of easy-to-understand rules to reduce the risk of problems.

Here are a few techniques that many others have found useful in getting the message out:

- The mantra for any awareness and training must be "Security is everyone's responsibility."
- It's vital that employees clearly understand that uneducated and untrained employees can endanger sensitive information and render useless any technical security measure or process in place.
- It's vital to have a good strategy that draws people and motivates them to learn how they can improve information security. Everyone has a particular learning style. Some people are visual learners. Others learn by listening. Still others need hands-on exercises that make it personal to them. Mixing up the modes of learning by using different media, different messages, and content-communications tools helps ensure that most people will understand and retain the information.
- People tend to be interested in stories about computer security, especially computer crimes. Making use of this may help people understand that they are going to be the new "gatekeepers" of critical organization data. Use stories and examples from within your organization, too. Don't focus only on the horror stories of bad security practices. Show and tell people about the benefits of being good corporate citizens and the potential rewards for compliance.
- As much as possible, use examples that make security a personal choice. Develop scenarios where people need to make a choice as to what they might do in a particular situation. Relate these situations to actual ones people might encounter from day to day.

Furthermore, you can help people perceive actual personal benefits from the security program, such as the new skills they will gain. For example, mention to them how this information can help them increase the security of their personal computers at home and their own information.

Varying the methods of education can increase the success of your awareness and training program. Ensure you have a fresh, ever-evolving, and dynamic education program. The following sections offer suggestions for broadening awareness and educating staff about security.

Security Newsletter

One interesting and valuable way to reach and educate your staff is a security newsletter. The main idea is to provide users with an interesting and engaging way of understanding the points outlined in the policy and standards library. You can send it via email or post it on your intranet. To be effective, it must be brief and interesting to read. Lengthy newsletters are less likely to be read. It is often effective to tie the newsletter to some breach or security issue that has been in the news recently.

 TIP

Rather than a formal newsletter, you could set up an Information Security Awareness area on your intranet. You could maintain several pages of information that are linked and easily updated.

If you develop your newsletter in-house, you may need to ask for help from others in the information security group. Also consider getting input from people outside the group who have security-related perspectives to share with the rest of the organization. An alternative is to subscribe to third-party security newsletters that you tailor to your organization.

The following sections describe parts of a typical security newsletter.

Security Articles Sometimes people appreciate reading detailed, in-depth information on a specific topic that helps them understand the subject more clearly. For example, if in a security awareness campaign you covered email threats, you could include an associated article in the next newsletter while the topic is still fresh in the employees' minds. Essentially, articles go deeper than the newsletter, and provide more detail for those who wish to deep-dive into a topic.

The following are possible article topics:

- **Password security**—Discuss the importance of passwords and their crucial role in the protection of data. Other articles might include how to properly maintain user IDs and passwords, password creation and maintenance, and best practices.
- **Acceptable Internet use**—Discuss the possible dangers posed by Internet connectivity and information that employees should be aware of while browsing the web from work.
- **Why are they targeting us?**—This could be an interesting topic to describe the motivation of different attackers and the purpose behind attacks. This can provide users a better understanding of the importance of having proper information security measures implemented.
- **Your role in the protection of the organization**—Think of as many scenarios as you see fit. The idea for these articles is to explain the most important aspects of information security in an informal yet effective way. You could cover social aspects combined with brief technical explanations if needed.

Technical TIP

Create a social network of **evangelists** throughout your organization. Some organizations have had success with identifying a specific security evangelist within each working group or department. These people will act as advocates for information security and help their specific departments or groups answer questions related to their obligations for compliance. You can start with people who show an above-average level of security interest or skills. Identify and promote these groups as a social network that speeds the adoption of security. Start by tracking the people who stand out during awareness sessions or other training opportunities.

What Is...? This section of the newsletter educates or informs staff and acts as an information security glossary. It includes various security terms explained in a nontechnical, easy-to-understand way. General security topics such as Trojan horses, worms, and firewalls can be covered individually, as well as other topics or concepts that you think are useful, must-know, or can help with compliance to standards and policies.

Ask Us You can include an "Ask Us" section in your newsletter. Over time, you can create a frequently asked questions (FAQ) document that summarizes the questions and answers to give users a richer experience when interacting with the IS department.

The questions and corresponding answers could be included in the next issue of the newsletter, so that it will not only be a collective information source to a large group of people, but also stimulate the asking of further questions.

Security Resources A "Security Resources" section might include short news pieces that cover some aspect of information security in an easy-to-understand form. The idea is to help users understand the importance of security awareness via security news, news of the latest security breaches, losses suffered by companies due to security problems, and so on.

Contacts Make sure to include the contact details for the IS department so that users will know precisely whom to contact in case of a problem. Publish the intranet uniform resource locator (URL) to your site everywhere you can to help remind people that help may be a click away.

Policy Change Control Board

Changing policies is like any other change process. When changing technology, organizations usually have a change control board (CCB), sometimes referred to as a change advisory board (CAB). Changing policies should be no different. Effective oversight of the policy change ensures that security is implemented in a thoughtful way. Oversight of the policy change process usually falls under an existing committee. The committee members are often senior leaders who represent both the technology and the business interests. These individuals as leaders ensure that the right balance between protecting the organization and operating needs is maintained.

It's important that changes not be made unilaterally or cause unexpected consequences. To avoid these situations, form a policy change control board or committee. You can organize this group ad hoc, meeting as needed for reviews and approvals. It can also be a standing committee or working group that meets regularly to address changes, additions, and enhancements to policies and standards. You can develop a standard that creates the board and establishes membership requirements. Minimally, you should include people from information security, compliance, audit, HR, leadership from other business units, and project managers (PMs). PMs set the agenda for the meetings, take meeting minutes, assign action items, and follow up on deliverables.

The objectives of the policy change control board are to:

 NOTE

Security personnel need to be aware of policy and standards change requirements. They also need to understand the impact of the change on the IT environment. Because systems, applications, and networks are integrated, a change to one component can affect other components.

- Assess policies and standards and make recommendations for change
- Coordinate requests for change (RFCs)
- Ensure that changes to existing policies and standards support the organization's mission and goals
- Review requested changes to the policy framework
- Establish a change management process for policies and standards

A policy does not exist in a vacuum. If implemented well, it's part of the day-to-day transactions and activity of a business. In that respect, there must be a process to track major events, such as what went right and what went wrong. For example, if there was a breach, a post-breach review would examine which controls should have prevented the event or mitigated the impact. Which policies were not effective in preventing the breach? The policy and standards change-management process ensures that policies and standards are refreshed when needed. It deals with new developments in technology and changes in the business environment. When potential changes are identified, change management determines whether the changes should be made or a new policy or standard is needed. There must also be a "lessons learned" process that allows for problems to be resolved and changes made to the policies and standards being designed.

> **NOTE**
>
> A "lessons learned" process ensures that mistakes are made once and not repeated. **Lessons learned** can come from anyone and anywhere.

The policy change control board assesses and approves RFCs. An RFC typically responds to known problems but can also include improvements. A challenge when handling an RFC is to determine whether it should be approved or whether a transitional policy or standard will resolve the issue.

Business Drivers for Policy and Standards Changes

Additionally, there are business drivers for policy and standards changes, which may include the following:

- **Business exceptions**—As the business changes, new systems or processes are introduced. They may vary from what a policy or standard requires.
- **Business innovations**—New opportunities for revenue growth or cost reduction can lead to innovative changes that were previously not considered. Standards may need to adapt to these innovations or be adjusted to permit innovations.
- **Business technology innovations**—New technology often comes with unknowable risks until you gain experience using it. Standards may need revisions to allow for the use of the new technology or for use in new ways that were not envisioned when the standards were developed.
- **Strategic changes**—An organization may change its business model and come under new regulatory requirements. For example, an organization might purchase a bank to reduce the costs of credit card processing. In this case, changes to an existing standard are far-reaching and may affect every standard in place.
- **Legal changes**—There can be new laws or changes to existing laws that require business policy to change. The most obvious recent example of this is the GDPR in Europe. Any organization that does business in Europe must implement policies to adhere to GDPR.
- **Regulatory changes**—If an organization's operations require compliance with some regulation, then any change in that regulation will likely lead to an update or change to organizational policies. Payment Card Industry Data Security Standard (PCI-DSS) is a good example. If an organization processes credit card data, then when PCI-DSS is updated or changed, the organization must make relevant changes to its own policies.

Some change requests result in a complete redevelopment of the policy and standards library, or at least in one facet of the policy and standards development cycle.

Maintaining Your Policy and Standards Library

The policy and standards library is like a tree, and over time, requires pruning and maintenance. The policy change control board helps determine what changes should be made to which documents. Other needs for changes can come about from issues related to specific users or groups, and documents may need trivial or isolated changes. One of the tasks of the board is to determine which requests they will address and which ones are normal maintenance requests.

 TIP

Establish a frequently asked questions (FAQ) site to clarify minor points in the policy. Over time, as you see the types of questions and answers that resonate with the end user, you can move those answers into the actual policy language itself.

Updates and Revisions

An update many be considered a nonsubstantive edit. Examples include updating a position title or a department name, correcting a typo, and repairing broken website links.

Revisions may be of minor or major significance:

- A minor revision usually has low significance. An example is clarifying the wording within a sentence or paragraph.
- A major revision significantly changes the policy. Examples include new requirements, new limitations, or expanded responsibilities. These types of changes should be sent to the policy change control board for consideration.

Throughout the chapter, you were provided with some best practices for developing your documents, numbering them appropriately, publishing your documents, and spreading the word about them. If you follow this guidance, the change process should take minimal effort. If every change requires a complete revisiting of the library, you have a much bigger problem on your hands.

Assuming that you follow the same development and review cycles for your updates and gain the necessary buy-in from those who are affected by changes, the most time-consuming activity will be communicating your changes to the organization. Using the techniques and tools for communication and media, you should be able to rely on the same processes you developed for ongoing awareness and training.

To help you determine what changes or maintenance you'll need to perform, use the information provided by:

- **Exceptions and waivers**—Look for common problems related to compliance. If the standard cannot be met very often, it's because there is a problem with the standard (or policy).
- **Requests from users and management**—Make it easy to obtain feedback on people's actual experience with complying with the standards. Major requests should be formally documented and sent to the policy change control board. However, don't ignore the feedback about what's causing people concern or prompting questions about the document.

- **Changes to the organization**—Companies come and go. Mergers and acquisitions happen constantly. Should you find yourself in a situation where your organization has bought or sold a division and you need to revisit the policies and standards for the combined organization, use the tools and techniques you've learned in this chapter to help resolve conflicts or fill in gaps that come about from the change.

Best Practices for Policies and Standards Maintenance

The following list of activities and advice comes from leading practices in policy and standards development and management experts. It was culled from years of experience and is offered so that you can avoid many of the pitfalls others have experienced when developing a library:

- Ask yourself the key questions of who, what, where, when, why, and how as you set out to research and develop policies and standards.
- Base your decisions on core information security principles to support business objectives. Because there are no universal recipes for developing policies and standards, you need to rely on principles to advance the cause.
- Establish a cohesive and coherent document organization taxonomy that leaves you with room for growth and changes.
- Use common templates for each type of document and stick with them. Nothing leads to confusion more than different document styles that are intended to meet the same purposes.
- Use a collaboration tool for developing documents that allows others access to drafts early in the development cycle. It should be easy to solicit reviews and comments.
- Establish a repeatable review process for your draft documents. The process should consider a representative sample of people who will be affected by new policies and security controls.
- Publish your library in a form that your organization is already using. Introducing new technology for distributing policies and standards at the same time you publish the documents may cause unnecessary confusion.
- Use a broad variety of communications and awareness media and techniques to reach a wide audience. Keep your message consistent and easy to understand.
- Establish a policy change control board to help identify major changes to the library and to keep it up to date.
- Create a "lessons learned" process to improve the policy through feedback and review of major events.

Case Studies and Examples of Designing, Organizing, Implementing, and Maintaining IT Security Policies

The following three case studies review how to develop or implement a policy framework. You will look at cases from the private sector and the public sector.

Private Sector Case Study 1

The Cyprus Shipping Chamber wanted to address the security requirements of smart shipping. Having digital records, interconnected ships, and electronic data exchange increased the efficiency of shipping, but also increased risk.[1]

In order to facilitate addressing these new security challenges, the company employed a case study approach. It took a case study of a specific subset of the company and used that as a template to study security. This can be an effective way to examine security policies. The approach includes:

- Framing specific organizational concerns so they could be examined effectively
- Examining each organization security concern using a scenario
- Taking that information to facilitate development of security policies

Private Sector Case Study 2

During an internal review, American Imaging Management (AIM) decided it needed to improve its due diligence practices. AIM decided to expand its corporate security program. The company began by performing a risk assessment on its current security program.

The assessment used the ISO 27001 gap assessment methods. When complete, AIM delivered a recommended course of action. These activities were intended to address and remediate areas that were either under- or overcontrolled.

Using the Plan-Do-Act-Check cycle from the ISO standards, AIM's activities included:

- Defining more detailed roles and responsibilities
- Identifying all relevant security requirements (legislative, regulatory, and contractual)
- Defining all supporting policies, standards, and procedures
- Defining and establishing a security awareness program
- Expanding the organization's vulnerability management program
- Collaborating with the business continuity/disaster recovery (BC/DR) team to integrate security program objectives
- Improving the incident response program
- Implementing an internal security control audit program

By the end of the project, AIM was able to create a road map for building a security program that could be registered to the ISO 27001 standard.

Public Sector Case Study

To improve security in California's IT infrastructure, the Office of the State Chief Information Officer (OCIO) issued a new policy that includes employee remote access security standards for working from home or off-site. The policy also requires that state agencies complete a compliance form.

The policy was issued to help state agencies develop secure remote access for employees and minimize security risks. The corresponding standard highlights important measures that IT agencies must adopt to certify their remote access programs. It includes controls related to the use of up-to-date operating system software and security software for every remote connection.

The standard also requires that all computing equipment connected to the state's IT infrastructure network for remote access purposes be state-owned and securely configured. Remote access users can only connect through secure encrypted channels—virtual private networks—authorized by agency management. The security measures also apply to paper files and mobile devices like tablets and smart phones.

According to the information policy letter, agency heads must comply with the following:

- Make sure authorized users permitted to use remote access are trained for their roles and responsibilities, security risks, and the requirements in the standard
- Adopt and implement the requirements in the standard and certify their agency's compliance
- Annually complete and submit the Agency Telework and Remote Access Security Compliance Certification form to the Office of Information Security

California was among the first governments in the country to establish enterprise-wide policies for remote access, joining states such as Virginia and Arizona, and the federal government.

CHAPTER SUMMARY

This chapter addressed techniques for designing, organizing, implementing, and maintaining an IT security policy and standards library. The importance of understanding the organizational culture and creating shared beliefs was discussed. You learned how to understand a business's perspective and mindset through an understanding of its operating model. You learned characteristics of policies and standards that make them easy to understand. Core security principles were covered, which are important to remember when developing security documents. Training and awareness programs help you enforce policies and get buy-in from employees.

You also learned about the review and approval processes that are part of creating and maintaining library documents. A policy change control board, for example, is an efficient way to maintain policies and standards. It also helps minimize unforeseen impacts on the organization. Additionally, you learned the importance of creating a "lessons learned" process to keep the policies current. Finally, you learned about some leading practices that others have found useful for developing and maintaining a policy and standards library.

KEY CONCEPTS AND TERMS

Coordinated operating model	Lessons learned	Roadshow
Defense in depth	Operating model	Taxonomy
Diversified operating model	Organizational culture	Unified operating model
Evangelists	Replicated operating model	

CHAPTER 7 ASSESSMENT

1. When writing policies and standards, you should address the six key questions: who, what, where, when, why, and how.

   A. True
   B. False

2. Which of the following are important to consider *before* a policy?

   A. Operating model
   B. Intent
   C. Policy change control board
   D. A and B
   E. B and C
   F. A, B, and C

3. Guideline documents are often tied to a specific control standard.

   A. True
   B. False

4. Which of the following is *not* an administrative control?

   A. Development of policies, standards, procedures, and guidelines
   B. Screening of personnel
   C. Change control procedures
   D. Logical access control mechanisms

5. Which of the following are common steps taken in the development of documents such as security policies, standards, and procedures?

   A. Design, development, publication, coding, and testing
   B. Feasibility, development, approval, implementation, and integration
   C. Initiation, evaluation, development, approval, publication, implementation, and maintenance
   D. Design, coding, evaluation, approval, publication, and implementation

6. The sole purpose of an operating model is to define how all the businesses technology will be implemented.

   A. True
   B. False

7. Exceptions or waivers to security policies are a bad idea and should never be approved.

   A. True
   B. False

8. Which type of control is associated with responding to and fixing a security incident?

   A. Deterrent
   B. Compensating
   C. Corrective
   D. Detective

9. List examples of physical security control items.

10. A process to refresh policies as needed based on a major event uses the principle called _____.

11. A(n) _____ is a plan or course of action used by an organization to convey instructions from its senior-most management to those who make decisions, take actions, and perform other duties on behalf of the organization.

12. The principle that states security is improved when it is implemented as a series of overlapping controls is called _____.

13. Security principles are needed in the absence of complete information to make high-quality security decisions.

   A. True
   B. False

14. "Access to all Organization information resources connected to the <Organization> network must be controlled by using user IDs and appropriate authentication" is a statement you might find in a procedure document.

    A. True
    B. False

15. Which of the following does a policy change control board do? (Select two.)

    A. Assesses policies and standards and makes recommendations for change
    B. Determines the policies and standards library numbering scheme
    C. Implements technical controls as business conditions change
    D. Reviews requested changes to the policy framework

ENDNOTES

1. Cyprus Shipping Chamber, "Cyber Security Case Study," July 2017, *https://csc-cy.org/wp-content/uploads/2018/06/Cyprus-Shipping-Chamber-Cyber-Security-Case-Study.pdf*, accessed April 20, 2020.

IT Security Policy Framework Approaches

AN INFORMATION TECHNOLOGY (IT) security policy framework supports business objectives and legal obligations. It also promotes an organization's core values. It defines how an organization identifies, manages, and disposes of risk. A core objective of a security framework is to establish a corporate culture that values security, which creates an organization's risk culture.

Selecting the right information security framework is important. There are a variety of frameworks in the industry to choose from. A number of these are industry-specific. Others offer a comprehensive view of IT that cuts across all industries. Which one is right for your organization will depend on the organization's needs, the employees' experience, and the regulators that have jurisdiction. It must also be noted that nothing prevents you from taking elements from diverse frameworks and combining them for your organization. This is obviously more work than simply applying an existing framework, but in some situations, a hybrid solution may be the appropriate choice.

Regulators will have an interest in how the organization's leadership manages risk. One way to demonstrate this is to adopt and effectively execute security policy frameworks. Additionally, selecting frameworks that are common within your industry increases the likelihood of success by allowing your organization to share experiences and incorporate learning from across the industry.

You can look at a security framework as a systematic way to identify, mitigate, and reduce risks. The data can be at rest or moving through a process. In this context, risk represents an event that could affect the completion of these processes. For an organization truly to have control over these risks, a strong system of internal security controls must be in place. Everyone in the organization should understand and adhere to its security policies. These security policies and controls must extend beyond the IT department and into the business process.

The framework manages risk at an enterprise level. It helps an organization deal with conflicting priorities, resource constraints, and uncertainty. An effective IT security policy framework also enables management to deliver value to the business.

This chapter reviews various security policy frameworks. It discusses policy strengths and their positioning in the market. Additionally, this chapter examines key elements from the frameworks such as roles, responsibilities, separation of duties, governance, and compliance.

Chapter 8 Topics

This chapter covers the following topics and concepts:

- How to choose an IT security policy framework
- How to set roles, responsibilities, and accountabilities for personnel
- Why separation of duties within an organization is important
- What a structured approach to security policy governance and compliance entails
- What the best practices are for IT security policy framework approaches
- What are some case studies and examples of IT security policy framework approaches

Chapter 8 Goals

When you complete this chapter, you will be able to:

- Compare and contrast multiple frameworks
- Identify the top security policy frameworks
- Understand the type of roles needed to support these frameworks
- Explain the responsibilities of these roles
- Describe how roles create a separation of duties
- Describe how roles create a layered approach to security
- Understand the need for and importance of governance and compliance
- Understand how these frameworks are applied in the real world through case studies

IT Security Policy Framework Approaches

How do you choose among the many IT security policy frameworks promoted by government agencies, corporations, and many others? There's no simple answer. Your choice will depend on your industry, as well as your management view of risk and any bias within your organization. You should focus on selecting the standards that are widely accepted.

No security framework can prevent all security breaches. At some point, a **security event** will happen. It could be as simple as someone sharing a password with someone else or loaning a security badge to a colleague to provide (unauthorized) access to a restricted data center. Or it could be a criminal stealing customer data. Whatever the security event, an assessment of why the breach occurred and what controls failed should be conducted. Depending on the severity of the security event, regulators may ask for answers. Adopting the right security policy framework helps demonstrate to regulators that your organization followed industry norms. Equally important, the effective adoption of a security framework demonstrates

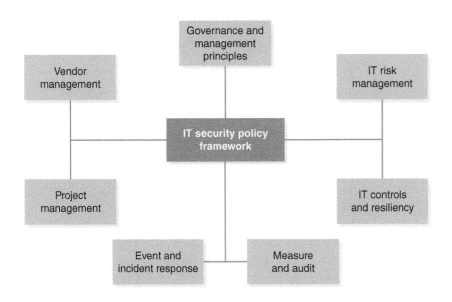

FIGURE 8-1

Simplified IT security policy framework domain model.

that when a security event occurs, the organization can effectively respond to minimize impact to the customers and shareholders.

FIGURE 8-1 depicts a simplified framework domain model. Notice that a significant portion is dedicated to the governance and management of risks. This establishes the principle that managing risks and understanding business are core competencies. More comprehensive frameworks recognize that the effectiveness of controls relies on the understanding of the business process. Understanding the business process allows you to better identify risks and design effective controls.

> ● **NOTE**
>
> *Security event* is a term used to indicate any undesirable event that occurs outside of normal daily security operations. Typically, a security event relates to a breakdown in controls as defined by the security policies.

Your first step is to determine the scope of coverage for your framework. Then, you can use it as a filter to make sense of the various frameworks to choose from. Even a simplified framework domain model can help you recognize your organization's key areas of concern. You can create a framework that addresses specific weaknesses and aligns to your business requirements. Once you understand those requirements, you can use the following steps to select industry frameworks to consider:

1. Review industry regulatory requirements. For example, a government agency is required to implement the Federal Information Security Management Act of 2002 (FISMA).
2. Look to your auditors and regulators for guidance. For example, major external audit firms may have adopted **Committee of Sponsoring Organizations (COSO)** and **Control Objectives for Information and related Technology (COBIT)** as part of their controls testing.
3. Select frameworks that have maintained broad support in the industry over time. These are the frameworks that could be considered industry best practices.

Find out which frameworks are used by peer organizations. This can validate your approach. Many industries tend to share the same risks and leverage the same frameworks. **TABLE 8-1** contains a sample of IT security policy frameworks. These frameworks that are

TABLE 8-1 Sample of IT Security Policy Frameworks

FRAMEWORK	SPONSORING ORGANIZATION	DESCRIPTION
COSO	COSO *http://www .coso.org*	COSO is a framework for validating internal controls and managing enterprise risks. COSO is heavily focused on financial operations and risk management. It's a widely recognized standard for providing reasonable assurance that an organization's financial controls are working appropriately.
COBIT	Information Systems Audit and Control Association (ISACA) *http://www .isaca.org*	COBIT is a framework and supporting tool set that align business and control requirements with technical issues. COBIT is an international governance and controls framework and a widely accepted standard for assessing, governing, and managing IT security and risks. COBIT is extended with a series of other ISACA publications such as risk IT, which extends COBIT for IT risk management. COBIT maps to many major frameworks such as COSO, ISO, and ITIL.
ISO	**International Organization for Standardization (ISO)** *http://www .iso.org*	ISO has produced a vast array of standards supporting a number of different industries and business models. The ISO standards related to information security and IT risk are widely accepted as the leading international standards. The following is a sample of key ISO publications: ISO 20000—IT service management system ISO 27001—Information security management ISO 27002—Code of practice for information security management ISO 38500—Corporate governance of information security ISO 9000—Quality management
ITIL	Information Technology Infrastructure Library (ITIL) *https://www .axelos.com /best-practice -solutions/itil*	ITIL is a widely accepted international framework and set of best practices for delivering IT services. ITIL contains a comprehensive list of concepts, practices, and processes for managing IT services.

NIST	**National Institute of Standards and Technology (NIST)** *http://csrc.nist.gov /publications /PubsSPs .html*	The Federal Information Security Management Act (FISMA) requires federal agencies to follow a common set of security standards. These standards are provided by NIST and are known as the Federal Information Processing Standards (FIPS).
PCI DSS	Payment Card Security Standards Council *https://www .pcisecuritystandards .org/index.php*	The Payment Card Industry Data Security Standard (PCI DSS) is a security framework for any organization that accepts, stores, or processes credit cards.
CIS Critical Security Controls for Effective Cyber Defense	Center for Internet Security *https://www .cisecurity.org /controls/*	First developed in 2008 by the SANS Institute, now managed by the Center for Internet Security.

commonly adopted across an industry define the best practices of an organization. **Best practices** are typically the common practices and the professional care expected for an industry. This is not a comprehensive list; there are other heavily used frameworks, including industry-specific frameworks. The frameworks in Table 8-1 represent different widely adopted framework approaches.

Even the short list of IT security policy frameworks shown in Table 8-1 provides a wide array of approaches and choices. Organizations often combine these frameworks to draw upon each of their strengths.

For example, a single organization could adopt the following:

- COSO for financial controls and enterprise risk management structure
- COBIT for IT controls, governance, and risk management
- ITIL for IT services management
- PCI DSS for processing credit cards
- ISO for broad IT daily operations
- CIS as a broad-based cyberdefense framework

The combination of frameworks in this example provides a comprehensive view of business risk and information security. The combination would represent an organization's security and risk framework. It starts with COSO, which provides a strategic and financial view of risk. COBIT links business requirements with technology controls. ITIL provides best practices for delivery of IT services. PCI DSS provides highly specific technology requirements for handling cardholder data. You could also substitute ISO for any of these layers or mix and match other frameworks to create a comprehensive policy approach.

Let's compare and contrast COBIT and ISO. Although these frameworks may overlap in the topics they cover, they differ greatly in their approach. COBIT covers broad IT management topics and specifies which security controls and management need to be in place. However, COBIT is often silent on how to implement specific controls. ISO, on the other hand, goes into more detail on how to implement controls but is less specific about the broader IT management over the controls. In this way, both frameworks complement each other. As a result, many organizations adopt both.

The power of the frameworks in Table 8-1 is in their flexibility and modularity. They are flexible in that they can align with each other or be implemented by themselves. They are modular in that you can pick and choose the component or set of objectives you wish to implement. An exception to this rule is PCI DSS. An organization required to adhere to PCI DSS must implement all of its requirements.

Risk Management and Compliance Approach

To deliver value, a framework must manage and dispose of risk daily. You will often hear the term *disposal of risk*. Once a risk is identified, you must decide what to do about it; you must decide how to "dispose" of it. This can mean either adding a control so risk no longer exists or accepting the risk. When you accept a risk, it doesn't mean you ignore it. Typically, if you accept the risk, you would consider the need to monitor for it and to create a detective control. In that way, when it does occur, you can detect it and take measures to minimize its impact.

For example, suppose you are concerned about malware. Changing a firewall rule to stop individuals from browsing the Internet would reduce the likelihood of malware. This would be unpopular with employees. Beyond that, though, Internet access may be essential for the business to operate. So, you do your best to prevent as much malware as possible by installing appropriate software on the network and endpoint. Where you cannot prevent a risk, you monitor for suspicious traffic and respond as needed. In essence, you accept that no software can prevent every possible malware attack.

Although the previously mentioned frameworks all have unique approaches, they share some of the same characteristics:

- They are risk-based.
- They speak to the organization's risk appetite.
- They deal with operation disruption and losses.

The risk appetite refers to understanding the level of risk-taking within the business. This approach understands the business and its processes and goals. It's the overall risk the organization is willing to accept. A key measurement is the cost of risk mitigation. The risk appetite is driven by the amount of risk reduction the business is willing to fund.

 NOTE

A framework that is risk-based focuses on the highest risk to the organization's objectives. This includes considering business objectives, legal obligations, and the organization's values.

The goal of these frameworks is to reduce operation disruption and losses. The frameworks reduce surprises. They ensure risks are systematically identified and reduced, eliminated, or accepted.

The ISACA Risk IT framework extends COBIT and is a good example of a comprehensive risk management approach. You

FIGURE 8-2

The Risk IT framework process model is built on three domains.

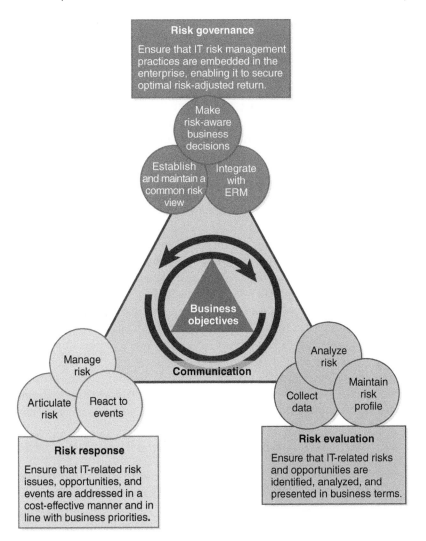

can implement the ISACA Risk IT framework alone or as part of a COBIT implementation. **FIGURE 8-2** is an overview of the Risk IT process model. The Risk IT framework is built on three domains: Risk Governance, Risk Evaluation, and Risk Response. Each of these domains has three process goals. Each process goal is broken down into key activities. For this discussion, this section will focus on domains and process goals.

The **Risk Governance** domain provides the business view and context for a risk evaluation. This ensures that risk activity aligns with the business goals, objectives, and tolerances. This includes aligning to business strategy. This domain ensures that the full range of opportunities and consequences is considered.

The **Risk Evaluation** domain ensures that technology risks are identified and presented to leadership in business terms. Formal risks are analyzed, and processes are created to assess impact. This domain also creates a risk repository of all known risks. This further enhances the risk analysis and reporting.

The **Risk Response** domain ensures risks are reduced and remediated in the most cost-effective manner. This domain coordinates risk responses so that the right people are engaged at the right time. This prevents risks from increasing in magnitude. Processes are established to manage risk throughout the enterprise to an acceptable level.

These domains build on each other, creating flexibility and agility. You can discover a potential threat in the Risk Evaluation domain and quickly assess its impact using the Risk Governance domain. In addition, the framework can quickly identify and coordinate a response to any risk.

The Physical Domains of IT Responsibility Approach

When implementing an IT security policy framework, remember to align the framework to the business process. For example, ISO 27002 provides clear guidance and best practice recommendations on controls. This creates a clear linkage between the control and the business process. This allows you to see all the controls implemented to protect an end-to-end business process. This approach minimizes controls and prevents "silo" thinking about threats. Organizations use the frameworks to reduce costs and to meet regulatory compliance.

For example, assume you are assessing backup and recovery processes. If you follow the process, you can identify risks during the hand-off between technologies. Perhaps you can no longer restore a tape that's been archived for several years. The backup technology in your data center was upgraded to a different format. Taking a look at the off-site inventory independent of the recovery aspect might miss this risk. Mapping out the process that controls the life of a backup tape is a better way to look at controls. A simple mapping might follow the tape from creation to transport, off-site storage, recall, recovery, and destruction.

Roles, Responsibilities, and Accountability for Personnel

It's important to understand the relationship between individuals and organizational roles and committees. Many IT processes pass through numerous hands. Sometimes it goes through a committee or a group of individuals. For example, an organization may have a governance or management oversight to review major projects that have significant budgets. The difference between governance and management oversight is an important distinction. Governance oversight approves the controls and approach by which risk is to be managed. Management oversight executes within the rules set by the governance body. For example, a governance committee may say all projects costing more than $50,000 must be reviewed and approved by the chief information officer and the IT senior leadership team (SLT). It's then up to the CIO to ensure that management processes follow the governance rules. This could mean having the project team present the proposed project in an SLT meeting and getting a formal vote of approval.

 NOTE

Individuals do not work in isolation. They are supported by organizational roles. The organizational roles implement a framework that establishes the standards for identifying and managing risk. Collectively, these roles and the organizational support help define the risk culture.

The Seven Domains of a Typical IT Infrastructure

Managing access to data can be a complex issue. Data can be in emails, in a word-processing document, or on a file server, or it can be accessed through a product application. Regardless, data must be understood and protected. Within the seven domains of a typical IT infrastructure (User, Workstation, LAN, WAN, LAN-to-WAN, Remote Access, and System/Application) are special roles responsible for data quality and handling. The following individuals work with the security teams to ensure data protection and quality:

- Head of information management
- Data stewards
- Data custodians
- Data administrators
- Data security administrators

The **head of information management** role is the single point of contact responsible for data quality within the enterprise. This person deals with all aspects of information. This person establishes guidance on data handling and works closely with the business to understand how information drives profitability. A business person, as opposed to a technologist, typically fills this role.

Data stewards are the individuals responsible for ensuring data quality within the business unit. Data stewards are the owners of the data. They approve access. They work closely with information management to ensure the business gets maximum value from the data. They define the business requirements for data and create descriptions of what the data is and how it will be used.

Data custodians are individuals in IT responsible for maintaining the quality of data. These individuals make decisions on how the data is to be handled given the requirements from the data steward. Whereas the data steward's primary role is to design and plan, the custodian's primary role is implementation.

Data administrators are responsible for executing the policies and procedures such as backup, versioning, uploading, downloading, and database administration.

Data security administrators have a highly restricted role. They grant access rights and assess threats to the information assurance (IA) program.

Organizational Structure

An organizational structure can tell you a lot about how risk is managed. It defines priorities through the teams' specialties. It defines how the organization perceives its threats. It also indicates how agile the response might be. FIGURE 8-3 defines a theoretical information security organization in the private sector. Notice the layer of executive governance of the security function in this example. Executive governance provides oversight for the security process and authority to execute.

The board of directors establishes an **audit committee** to deal with audit issues and nonfinancial risks. The chief information officer (CIO) reports to the audit committee about technology issues. The chief information security officer (CISO) may also report issues directly

FIGURE 8-3

Information security organizational structure.

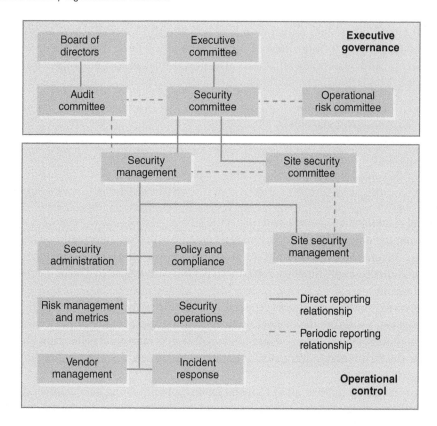

to the audit committee. Alternatively, the CISO may report to the CIO. Then the CIO's role is to report the security issues. The CISO may have a legal requirement to report to the board directly. For example, the Gramm-Leach-Bliley Act (GLBA) requires reporting to the board on the status of the GLBA program. That report is created and presented to the audit committee by the CISO. Keep in mind that the board of directors creates the audit committee. Consequently, issues on security coming to the board would generally go through the audit committee.

The primary issue in an effective audit committee is less about who is on it and more about their autonomy. This means that the audit committee must be free from interference from any part of the organization. Although audit committees are made up of internal employees, it is a good idea to have an outside party perform the actual audit. This does not completely eliminate the chance of influence but does absolutely ameliorate it.

The **executive committee** helps set priorities, removes roadblocks, secures funding, and acts as a source of authority. The **security committee** members are leaders across the organization. This combination ensures buy-in from the business for the information security program. This is typically where a balance is reached between the needs of the business and the needs of the enterprise to implement effective security controls. So, it's important that the line of business (LOB) senior leadership be represented. The higher the level of LOB representation in the committee, the higher the committee's perceived authority. The CISO is usually the chairperson. The CISO sets the committee agenda and facilitates discussions. The security committee reports its issues and budget requests to the executive committee. The executive committee aligns the security committee with the organization's goals and objectives.

The security committee may have a less formal relationship with the audit committee and the **operational risk committee**. The committees will exchange information and on occasion agree to joint initiatives. Although less formal, these are key relationships. For example, the operational risk committee provides important information on the risk appetite of the organization. Knowing the risk appetite can help the security committee understand business requirements and priorities at an operational level. Conversely, the risk committee needs to understand the information security capability and emerging risks. In this way, the risk committee can determine which business activities are riskier than others. Consider a business that wants to sell a product on the Internet for the first time. The risk committee needs to understand the general risks associated with this type of activity and, broadly, the organization's security capability.

The most important role for the risk committee is an objective review of risk. This involves a careful risk analysis. Such an analysis begins with a thorough business impact analysis (BIA) for all business units. As much as possible, quantifiable data should be used. This data includes metrics such as maximum tolerable downtime (MTD), maximum time to recovery (MTTR), and mean time before failure (MTBF). These are common metrics that provide quantifiable data to be used in disaster recovery and business continuity planning; however, they also help influence risk analysis. Not everything will be quantifiable, however. In some cases, that will leave only qualitative analysis. The main issue is that the risk committee remain as objective as possible.

The security management role is held by the CISO. The security committee is the key committee for the CISO. This is where the CISO can set the agenda and direction of the security and risk program.

Security administration in Figure 8-3 refers to centralized access management. Centralized access management involves creating and maintaining user IDs, which includes granting users access rights. This also includes building roles and ensuring appropriate levels of segregation of duties. The team most likely works with project managers and developers to ensure application security requirements are met. Depending on the volume of projects, this function could be separated from security policy management.

The policy and compliance team is responsible for creating, reviewing, approving, and enforcing policy. This team works with legal to capture policy regulatory requirements. The policy and compliance team provides interpretation of policies; approves deviations from policies; interfaces with regulators, providing evidence of compliance; and monitors the effectiveness of and adherence to policies.

The risk management and metrics team reviews the business processes and identifies potential risks and threats. The team works closely with the business to understand potential for fraud. Team members communicate with the other security teams to provide them with their assessment and analysis. They similarly use the other security teams as a source for metrics. By combining various metrics, they develop a scorecard that indicates key risks and the effectiveness of the security function. They also create reports for the CISO to present to various leaders.

A security operations team monitors for intrusions and breaches. Team members monitor firewalls and network traffic. When a breach is discovered, they activate the incident response team (IRT). The IRT responds to breaches and helps the business recover. Furthermore, the IRT assesses how the breach occurred and makes recommendations for improvement. The IRT performs forensic examinations and investigations, and interfaces with law enforcement agencies.

The vendor management team manages security concerns with vendors and third parties. Before data leaves the organization and is processed by a third party, this team performs an assessment on that vendor. Some organizations have adopted the concept of *permission to send*. In other words, data is not allowed to leave the organization until it's been verified that the vendor's control environment meets the organization's own requirements. Only then will permission to send be granted.

Figure 8-3 is a theoretical model based on combining a number of the best practices from various frameworks. This hybrid organizational structure illustrates the need for support from leadership and business. The number of teams and amount of specialization depends on the volume of activity, the complexity of the environment, and funding. The key point is that these teams do not operate in isolation. An organizational framework creates specialties that have the agility to respond quickly while continuously working to reduce risk to the business.

Organizational Culture

The organizational culture influences how IT security policies are implemented. It starts with the tone at the top—how senior leaders deal with the CISO. Security professionals are skilled in gathering threat information and analyzing the impact to the organization. They also are skilled at identifying threats and vulnerabilities and then presenting these findings.

 WARNING

Security frameworks define policy and set behavior expectations. Policies cannot address every situation an employee might encounter. Good training on the policies' core principles, along with common sense, will arm employees with what they need to be successful.

These are important and difficult skills to master. Equally important is the ability to navigate the organizational culture. These soft skills are especially important for a CISO. The CISO must connect and build trust with the business. Without building trust, the IT security team may be viewed as overhead rather than a partner in reducing risk.

As a security professional, you must not talk strictly in threat terms. You must have the ability to connect with line of business leaders and talk about threats in terms of risk to the business. For example, it's more effective to talk about how malware could prevent the service desk from helping a customer than to talk about the technical way in which malware can infect a machine.

Successfully dealing with the organization's culture means understanding how to drive value to the business. This means working with the business to draft comprehensive security strategies to increase the business's capability. For example, the business may strive to be a virtual organization with extensive remote access. This means working on how to extend the perimeter to remote laptops versus focusing on why the risks for such a plan could be too high.

The key point is not to be out of step with the organizational culture. You must drive security solutions into the organization in a way that will resonate and be perceived as delivering value to the business.

Separation of Duties

A fundamental component of internal control is the separation of duties (SOD) for high-risk transactions. The underlying separation of duties concept is that no individual should be able to execute a high-risk transaction, conceal errors, or commit fraud in the normal course of their duties. You can apply separation of duties at either a transactional or an organizational level.

Layered Security Approach

The **layered security approach** involves having two or more layers of independent controls to reduce risk. Layered security leverages the redundancy of the layers so if one layer fails to catch the risk or threat, the next layer should. By this logic, more layers should mean better risk reduction. However, more layers can be burdensome and expensive. There needs to be a balance between cost and return in risk reduction. But in no case should there be a defensive strategy with a single layer.

The classic example of separation of duties is when it's applied at the transactional level. If you have a high-risk transaction, or combination of transactions, then you want to separate them between two or more individuals. For example, suppose a business sets up vendor accounts and issues checks based on the goods received. That business has three distinct processes: setting up a vendor account, receiving goods, and paying the vendor. Having one individual control all three processes may prove too big a temptation for fraud. Such people could set themselves up as vendors and issue checks based on goods never received, as one example. This type of fraud is reduced by assigning responsibility for these processes to separate roles.

Domain of Responsibility and Accountability

Typically, separation of duties applies to transactions within a domain. It's management's responsibility within a domain to identify high-risk transactions and ensure adequate separation of duties. Ensuring adequate separation of duties means that you identify the opportunity for fraud within these transactions. It also means identifying the potential for human error within these transactions. Applying separation of duties can reduce both fraud and human errors.

The concept of separation of duties can also be applied across domains at an organizational level. Some organizational processes and functions come with risk; for example, ensuring an organization is compliant with regulations is vital and a high risk. As in the previous transaction example, you would not have one team responsible for all three tasks of designing, implementing, and validating solutions that ensure compliance. Typically, you

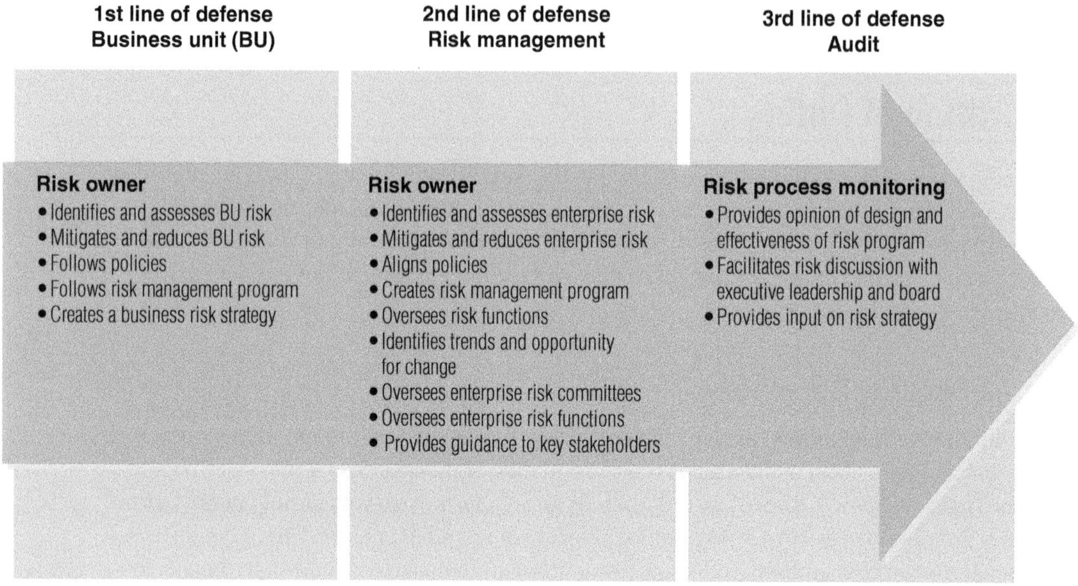

FIGURE 8-4

Three-lines-of-defense model.

1st line of defense **Business unit (BU)**	**2nd line of defense** **Risk management**	**3rd line of defense** **Audit**
Risk owner • Identifies and assesses BU risk • Mitigates and reduces BU risk • Follows policies • Follows risk management program • Creates a business risk strategy	**Risk owner** • Identifies and assesses enterprise risk • Mitigates and reduces enterprise risk • Aligns policies • Creates risk management program • Oversees risk functions • Identifies trends and opportunity for change • Oversees enterprise risk committees • Oversees enterprise risk functions • Provides guidance to key stakeholders	**Risk process monitoring** • Provides opinion of design and effectiveness of risk program • Facilitates risk discussion with executive leadership and board • Provides input on risk strategy

create an organizational separation of duties between those teams that implement and validate compliance. Implementing an organizational separation of duties is less about fraud and more about reducing potential errors in vital processes and functions.

In the financial services sector, some organizations have adopted a three-lines-of-defense model. This risk management model is a good illustration of an organizational layered approach that creates a separation of duties. **FIGURE 8-4** depicts a three-lines-of-defense model to risk management.

First Line of Defense

The first line of defense is the business unit (BU). The business deals with controlling risk daily. They identify risk, assess the impact, and mitigate the risk whenever possible. The business is expected to follow policies and implement the enterprise risk management program. The BU owns the risk and develops short-term and long-term strategies. Ownership means they are directly accountable to ensure the risk is mitigated or reduced.

Second Line of Defense

The second line of defense is the enterprise risk management program. The risk management program can be made of multiple control partners (CPs), depending on the size and complexity of the organization. Operational risk management personnel and compliance personnel are examples of CPs. They are responsible for managing risk across the enterprise. They align controls and policies to ensure that the risk management program aligns with company goals. There is oversight of risk management across multiple risk committees and through various channels of risk reporting to stakeholders.

The second line is responsible for engaging the business to develop a risk strategy and gauging the risk appetite of the organization. Participants have an obligation to report to the board material noncompliance and risks that put the organization's strategic goals in jeopardy. This should not be confused with the multilayered approach; this is a separate concept. In addition to the multilayered approach, enterprise risk management provides an additional line of defense.

Third Line of Defense

The third line of defense is the independent auditor. That role provides the board and executive management independent assurance that the risk function is designed and working well. Additionally, the auditor acts as an advisor to the first and second lines of defense in risk matters. The third line must keep his or her independence but also have input on risk strategies and direction.

Several views exist on how closely involved the third line of defense can be in advising leadership without losing independence. If the third line of defense advises a course of action, is he or she the right person to determine the success of that action? Many audit organizations develop rules to avoid this conflict. Views differ on whether external auditors belong in the third line of defense or actually compose a fourth line.

This model clearly demonstrates how organizational roles can be used to create a separation of duties. In this case, there is oversight, checks, and rechecks across three layers of the organization. In an ideal world, the first line of defense would self-assess and identify all the risks. It's not realistic to expect such precision. The basic idea is that what's not caught in the first line is caught in the second line. What the first and second lines do not catch, the third line catches. By the time you reach the third line, whatever risks still exist should not be significant and should therefore be manageable.

Governance and Compliance

Even in the best of situations, an organization can be challenged to provide evidence that policies are implemented, enforced, and working as designed. The process includes collecting, testing, and reporting evidence. This can be tiresome and time-consuming, especially when an organization struggles to address what may seem to be endless audit findings. These audits can lead to retesting and more control deficiencies and risks identified.

Implementing a governance framework can allow the organization to identify and mitigate risks in an orderly fashion. Once in place, the ability to quickly respond to audit requests drastically improves. The framework provides the ability to measure risk in a few ways:

- In the context of how well the organization has implemented leading practices
- In the context of how much of the organization's risk is covered by the resulting implemented controls

A well-defined governance and compliance framework provides a structured approach to governance and compliance. It provides a common language. It is also a best-practice model for

 NOTE

Controls and risk become more measurable with a framework. Being able to measure the enterprise against a fixed set of standards and controls is powerful. It tells the regulators you are in compliance. It helps prioritize and becomes an unemotional gauge for funding risk remediation efforts. Most important, it helps reduce uncertainty.

8

IT Security Policy
Framework Approaches

organizations of all shapes and sizes. A well-recognized framework standard provides a solid ground for discussing risk. It's a foundation from which information security policies can be governed.

IT Security Controls

Regulatory compliance is a significant undertaking for a number of organizations. Some organizations have full-time teams dedicated to collecting, reviewing, and reporting to show adherence to regulations. This diverts resources that could have been applied to protect the business.

The IT policies framework helps reduce this cost by defining security controls in a way that clearly aligns with policies and regulatory compliance. The better an organization can inventory and map its controls to policies and regulation, the lower its costs to demonstrate compliance. From a controls design view, best practice frameworks provide the mapping to major regulations such as the Sarbanes-Oxley (SOX) Act. As a result, the adoption of these frameworks is a quick way to demonstrate adequate coverage of regulatory IT requirements. However, good design and effective coverage of regulatory requirements don't necessarily guarantee that the controls are working. The more an organization can automate, the lower the cost to demonstrate compliance. This is because automation reduces the time to gather documentation, test controls, and gather evidence. Two key areas of automation are documentation and testing.

Automating documentation for IT security controls simply means capturing the policy and regulatory requirements at the time the control was designed and implemented. The level of automation does not require sophistication. The core requirement of the automation is that the information is searchable. Documenting the information in multiple places in a format that cannot be searched is not automation. When the information is centralized and searchable, it's much easier to explain to a regulator how the organization is compliant. The ability to search a list of controls also makes it easier to determine which controls need to be tested. There's a vast array of low-cost documentation library solutions that can be used for this purpose.

Automating the testing of IT controls is harder but yields the greatest benefit. The type and level of automation will depend on the technology, the control, and the complexity of the IT environment. For example, many tools can compare a file of active employees from an HR database to a list of active accounts. If the control to remove an individual is working, you should not see former employees with active accounts. Providing the same level of assurance manually would be far more costly and prone to errors. Manual verification in a larger population of users would be statistically based. You cannot check every account manually. You would instead sample past and current employees. Depending on the number of errors an auditor finds, an opinion would be made about the overall population of active accounts.

Automated testing tools are often shared across the enterprise to improve operational effectiveness. For example, assume the automated testing of a control identifies a defect. The defect is reported

⚠ **WARNING**

One problem with a statistical sample is that you have to select a sufficient number to make the sample relevant. Auditors follow sampling guidelines to ensure a sufficient number. Another problem is that a statistically based opinion is an educated guess. Even if you use good sampling methods, it's still a guess. The samples selected could have missed a potential problem or weakness. When you automate, you usually do not have that limitation. It is also important that the sample be random. Failure to randomize the sampling can skew the results.

and fixed. During the next test, another defect is found, reported, and fixed. The cycle continues. The individuals responsible for security control often adopt the testing tool to validate their own controls. In the real world, these individuals are motivated to avoid repeated audit findings. As a result, automation of compliance tests builds collaboration and improves operational effectiveness.

Testing for compliance is more complex than the few simple examples provided. Although the complexity and volume are much larger, the key concepts are the same. It's the complexity of the technology and infrastructure that prevents wide-scale automated compliance testing today. Not all controls can be tested automatically. However, the goal should be to design controls that can be tested with automated tools.

> **NOTE**
>
> Automating testing of controls lowers costs by avoiding the need to test a control manually. With limited budgets and time to test, controls should be built so that they can be automated. This can be as easy as a control generating a log file that can be checked later through automation.

IT Security Policy Framework

Business requirements lead to controls, which lead to reduced risk. Regardless of framework, the core objective of reducing risk remains the same. The frameworks listed in Table 8-1 can address many business risks. There are many other types of nontechnology risks, well beyond the scope of these frameworks, such as credit or market risks. These are risks associated with customers being unable to pay, or market changes in which there's no longer a demand for the product or service.

Business risks are defined as six specific risks, as follows:

- **Strategic—Strategic risks** are a broad category focused on an event that may change how the organization operates. Some examples might be a merger or an acquisition, a change in the industry, or a change in the customer. The key point is that it's an event that affects the entire organization.
- **Compliance—Compliance risks** relate to the impact to the business of failing to comply with legal obligations. Noncompliance can be willful, or it can result from being unaware of local legal requirements. This can include regulatory requirements or legally binding contracts. Let's say a company accepts the rules associated with processing credit cards but fails to implement PCI DSS. The card companies, under a binding contract, can force the merchant to stop taking credit cards.
- **Financial—Financial risk** is the potential impact when the business fails to have adequate liquidity to meet its obligations. This is when you fail to have adequate cash flow. For example, the consequences of failure to pay loans, payroll, and taxes would be financial risks. This lack of available funds can be due to a poor credit rating or operations too risky for banks to fund. Regardless of the reason, if you are unable to meet your financial obligations, that would be a financial risk.
- **Operational—Operational risks** are a broad category that describes any event that disrupts the organization's daily activities. The Office of the Comptroller of the Currency (OCC) defines operational risk as "the risk of loss resulting from inadequate or failed internal processes, people and systems, or from external events."[1] In technology terms, it's an interruption of the technology that affects the business process. This can be a coding error, slow network, system outage, or security breach.

- **Reputational**—A *reputational risk* results from negative publicity regarding an organization's practices. This type of risk could lead to a loss of revenue or to litigation. These risks often overlap with other risk categories; for example, a financial issue is likely to have a deleterious impact on the organization's reputation.
- **Other**—*Other risks* is a broad category of non-IT-specific events that introduce risk to the line of business. Typically, this category of risk relates to events that are outside the organization's control. For example, political unrest can occur in another country where the organization has a call center. The political unrest is a non-IT event. Lack of personnel showing up for work could impact IT operations. Although these risks may be outside of the organization's control, they can still be planned for in much the same way natural disasters are planned for.

Best Practices for IT Security Policy Framework Approaches

Governance, risk management, and compliance (GRC) is the discipline that systematically manages risk and policy compliance. *Governance* describes the management oversight in controlling risks. Governance includes the process and committees formed to manage risk. Governance reflects leadership tone at the same time. This means that governance reflects the core values of the organization towards risk, including the ability to enforce policy, the importance given to protecting customer data, and the tolerance for taking risks.

FYI

A study published in 2019 identified the top four best practice frameworks. They are:

- ISO 27000 series
- PCI-DSS
- NIST
- CIS Critical Security Controls

Various experts may disagree on the specific 'best' frameworks. But every list seems to include ISO 27000 and NIST.

Risk management describes the formal process for identifying and responding to risk. The concept beyond this part of GRC is a close alignment of business process and technology. This approach ensures risks are assessed and managed within the context of the business. Risk management also reflects leadership's risk appetite. How far is leadership willing to go to ensure third-party vendor protection of the organization's data? This view of risk can be reflected in leadership acceptance of risk, ranging from accepting vendor representation to insisting on on-site audits.

Compliance refers to the processes and oversight necessary to ensure the organization adheres to policies. Compliance also includes regulatory compliance. An organization's internal policies should address external regulatory concerns. Therefore, for organizations with well-defined policies, the focus is mainly on internal policies. If you can show evidence of adherence to internal policies, you can demonstrate regulatory compliance. The ability to demonstrate regulatory compliance is further enhanced when an organization can demonstrate the adoption of a best practices policy framework.

A framework helps create an enterprise view of risk. Many organizations have complex business and technology environments. The need to align these environments is critical. Organizations also find themselves facing increased pressure from regulators to demonstrate compliance. As a consequence, adoption of best practices provides leaders, regulators, shareholders, and the public the assurance each group requires.

Another framework approach is **enterprise risk management (ERM)**. This framework aligns strategic goals, operations effectiveness, reporting, and compliance objectives. ERM is a methodology for managing a vast array of risks across the enterprise. ERM is not a specific set of technologies. As an example, the ERM function may look at credit or market risk and attempt to determine if the pricing strategy or compensation to the sales force is creating risk to the business. ERM is not an IT security policies framework—it is a good integration point for IT security issues to be considered in context with other risks.

What Is the Difference Between GRC and ERM?

The terms *GRC* and *ERM* are sometimes used interchangeably, but that's incorrect. The difference is not in their goals—they both attempt to control risk. You can view ERM more as a broad methodology that leadership adopts to identify and reduce risks. There are similarities worth noting, because both approaches:

- Define risk in terms of the business threats.
- Apply flexible frameworks to satisfy multiple compliance regulations.
- Eliminate redundant controls, policies, and efforts.
- Proactively enforce policy.
- Seek line of sight into the entire population of risks.

GRC is more a series of tools to centralize policies, document requirements, and assess and report on risk. Because GRC is tools-centric, many vendors have created GRC offerings. It's not surprising that with vendors aggressively selling solutions, GRC has more momentum than ERM. That's not to suggest there aren't tools to support the ERM process. Many of the GRC tools can be used to support the ERM methodology. But as a methodology, ERM adoption is driven by the organization's leadership.

The lines between GRC and ERM do blur. In the real world, ERM teams deal with governance and compliance issues all the time. They use many of the same tools and techniques. More and more, GRC teams are reaching out to risk committees and teams to align efforts at a leadership level.

The important distinction is that ERM focuses on **value delivery**. This shifts the discussion from organizations' budgetary requirements for risk mitigation, compared with how their expenditures enhance value. ERM takes a broad look at risk, whereas GRC is technology-focused. This broad view of risk considers technology as one aspect of risk among many. This can be either a benefit or a drawback depending on the leadership ability to understand IT risk. One of the benefits is that a successful implementation of ERM leads to risk management being fused into the business process and mindset.

Case Studies and Examples of IT Security Policy Framework Approaches

The case studies in this section reflect actual risks that were exploited in the real world. Each case study examines potential causes. By looking at these policies in the context of security policies, you can identify how they might be avoided.

The case studies examined in this section include:

- **Private sector (e-commerce)**—Relates to an e-commerce example, eBay.
- **Private sector (PCI DSS)**—Relates to leveraging PCI DSS to prevent credit card data being stolen
- **Public sector**—Relates to a breach by an NSA contractor that leaked details on the U.S. intelligence Internet surveillance program
- **Critical infrastructure**—Relates to how policies and a security framework could have prevented unauthorized access to U.S. Department of Energy data

Private Sector Case Study

A franchisee of a national hamburger chain in the southern United States was notified by Visa U.S.A, Inc. and the U.S. Secret Service of the theft of credit card information in August 2008. The franchisee has a chain of eight stores with annual revenue of $2 million.

The chain focused on the technology of its point-of-sale (POS) system. A leading vendor that allowed for centralized financial and operating reporting provided the POS system. It used a secure high-speed Internet connection for credit card processing. The company determined that neither the POS nor credit card authorization connection was the source of the breach. Although the POS was infected, the source of the breach was the network. Each of the franchisee's stores provided an Internet hotspot to its customers. It was determined that this Wi-Fi hotspot was the source of the breach. Although considerable care was given to the POS and credit card authorization process, the Wi-Fi hotspot allowed access to these systems. It was determined the probable cause of the breach was malware installed on the POS system through the Wi-Fi hotspot. The malware collected the credit card information, which was later retrieved by the thief.

This was a PCI DSS framework violation. The PCI DSS framework consists of over 200 requirements that outline the proper handling of credit card information. It was clear that insufficient attention was given to the network to ensure it met PCI DSS requirements. For discussion purposes, the focus is on the network. The PCI DSS outlines other standards that may have been violated related to the hardening of the POS server itself. The following four PCI DSS network requirements appear to have been violated:

- Network segregation
- Penetration testing
- Monitoring
- Virus scanning

PCI requires network segments that handle credit cards be segmented. It was unclear whether there was a complete absence of segmentation or if weak segmentation had been breached. PCI DSS outlines the standards to ensure segmentation is effective. If the networks had been segmented, this breach would not have occurred.

PCI requires that all public-facing networks be penetration tested. This type of testing would have provided a second opportunity to prevent the breach. This test would have uncovered such weaknesses within a Wi-Fi hotspot that allowed the public to access back-end networks.

PCI also requires a certain level of monitoring. Given the size of the organization, monitoring might have been in the form of alerts or logs reviewed at the end of the day. Monitoring could include both network and host-based intrusion detection. Monitoring may have detected the network breach. Monitoring may also have detected the malware on the POS system. Both types of monitoring would have provided opportunities to prevent the breach.

PCI also requires virus protection. It was unclear if this type of scanning was on the POS system. If it was not, that would have been a PCI DSS violation. Such scanning provides one more opportunity to detect the malware. Early detection would have prevented the breach.

The PCI DSS requirements are specific and adopt many of the best practices from other frameworks such as ISO. The approach is to prevent a breach from occurring. Early detection of a breach can prevent or minimize card losses. For example, early detection of the malware in this case study would have prevented card information from being stolen. Some malware takes time to collect the card information, which must then be retrieved. Quick reaction to a breach is an opportunity to remove the malware before any data can be retrieved.

Public Sector Case Study

Another older story, but one that is still quite relevant, is that of Edward Snowden. In May 2013, Edward Snowden, a National Security Agency (NSA) contractor, met a journalist and leaked thousands of documents detailing how the United States conducts intelligence surveillance across the Internet. In June 2013, the U.S. Department of Justice charged Snowden with espionage. Not long afterward, Snowden left the United States and finally sought refuge in Russia. The Russian government denied any involvement in Snowden's actions but did grant him asylum.

Although this story reads like a spy novel, it raises a number of information security policy questions. For this discussion, it is not important whether Snowden was a traitor, a spy, or a whistleblower. The issue here is the security policies and controls that allowed a part-time NSA contractor to gain unauthorized access to highly sensitive material. This is particularly important because in April 2014, the Department of Defense announced adoption of the NIST standards. Would the Snowden breach have been prevented if the NIST standards had been adopted earlier?

Given the secret nature of the NSA, the full details of how this breach of sensitive data occurred may never come out. However, reports indicate that Snowden worked part time for an American consulting company that did work for the NSA in Hawaii. There he gained access to thousands of documents that detailed how the U.S. government works with telecommunication companies and other governments to capture and analyze traffic over the

Internet. The details of the scope and nature of this global surveillance program were not publicly known and were considered secret.

It's clear from the reporting that Snowden had excessive access; that is to say, he was granted access beyond the requirements of his job. Additionally, reports indicated that he used other people's usernames and passwords. He obtained these IDs through social engineering. Finally, consider the way in which he accessed and captured the information. Some reports indicate he used inexpensive and widely available software to electronically crawl through the agency's networks. There are also indications that he removed the information on a USB memory stick.

It is noteworthy that there have been two additional data breaches at the NSA since Snowden, both from insiders. Harold Martin III was indicted in 2017 and accused of taking home thousands of pages of classified documents. In March 2019, Mr. Martin pled guilty and was sentenced to 9 years of prison followed by 3 years of probation. Also in 2017, Reality Winner, an NSA contractor, leaked information about an investigation into Russian interference to newspapers. She pled guilty in 2018 and received a 5-year sentence. What these two cases illustrate is that the agency has not made sufficient corrections since the 2013 Edward Snowden case. This illustrates that any organization must take a frank and honest look at security failures. That is the most effective way to learn from those mistakes. Failure to do so can lead to the same security breaches being repeated in the future.

FYI

Social engineering refers to the use of human interactions to gain access. Typically, it means using what amounts to sales techniques to trick an individual into granting access to something you should not have. For example, you might ask to borrow someone's keycard to use the restroom but instead use the keycard to access the data center. Or perhaps you might ask for someone's ID and password to fix his or her computer, and then later use those credentials to access customer information. Or, an outside attacker can use persuasion to convince someone to violate some aspect of security policy.

There were clear NIST framework violations in the Edward Snowden case. For purposes of this discussion, the focus is on the network and social engineering. NIST publications outline other standards that were violated, such as effective security management and oversight.

The following four NIST framework network policies were clearly violated:

- Sharing of passwords
- Excessive access
- Penetration testing
- Monitoring

It's never a good idea to share passwords. This would be a clear violation of security policy, especially by anyone handling classified data. Additionally, the level of access must be considered a policy violation. Any security framework generally prohibits granting access not related to the individual's job function. It's clear from the volume of material involved in the Snowden affair, and its classified nature, that the access he was granted was excessive for the role he performed.

The NIST framework also outlines the guidance on penetration testing. Penetration testing, if done by a competent penetration tester, can be an effective way to measure compliance with security policies. This type of testing and assessment would provide another opportunity to correct the network control deficiencies prior to a breach.

The NIST framework outlines the requirements for effective network monitoring. These requirements require logs to be reviewed in a timely manner. Log reviews are a detective control and essential in identifying potential hackers. Keep in mind, Snowden scanned the internal network for months while downloading vast amounts of data. Hackers tend to probe a network for weaknesses prior to a breach. Assume that some of those links the web crawler attempted to access resulted in an access violation. These violations would have been an indicator of a potential breach in progress. This type of monitoring would have provided another opportunity to correct the network control deficiencies and identify Snowden as an internal hacker.

Finally, consider the lack of controls that allowed Snowden to remove so many documents on a USB memory stick. This unusual activity could have been prevented or, at a minimum, detected, given the volume of material extracted—especially given that many organizations have in place additional controls to monitor contractor activities.

Some of the specifics of the Snowden breach may never be known to the public. Nonetheless, a security policy framework must be a comprehensive way of looking at information risks and ensuring there are layers of controls to prevent data breaches. This case is typical of a breach occurring over many months, indicating the breakdown of multiple controls. It represents both a lack of effective security policies and lost opportunities to detect a breach over several months.

Private Sector Case Study Two

In March 2014, eBay noticed an unexpected database session on its servers. The session was scanning password files. Later, eBay disclosed that users' credentials for 145 million users had been compromised. This is a substantial issue for a company whose entire business model is based on e-commerce. According to eBay, the data stolen did not include credit card information.

The company discovered the breach by first noticing several anomalies on the corporate network. The investigation discovered that the attackers had used employees' passwords to gain initial access to the network. Analysis of the attack indicates attackers may have been in the network for two months or more before a breach was detected. Analysts have speculated that the entire attack may have started with spear phishing campaigns to get employees' credentials.

There are policies that would have, if implemented and adhered to, either prevented this breach or mitigated it substantially:

- Two-factor authentication could have prevented this breach. Even if an attacker obtains a user's password, two-factor authentication would prevent the attacker from gaining access.
- More robust monitoring and alerting of network anomalies would have alerted eBay to the issue much sooner.
- More robust employee education and email policies might have prevented the original spear phishing campaign from being successful.

This case illustrates the pressing need for good security policies that are enforced. Certainly, a wide range of standards apply to eBay, including PCI DSS. It is equally clear that these standards were not adhered to.

Critical Infrastructure Case Study

A more recent example is from August 2019. A story broke regarding a former U.S. Department of Energy contractor named Gary Peter Simon who was accused of accessing the network two months after his contract expired. Mr. Simon is accused of accessing cloud storage and destroying files, altering files, and altering other accounts. Mr. Simon did plead to one count of "intentionally accessing a protected computer without authorization and recklessly causing damage resulting in loss of more than $5,000 during one year." He had accessed the Department of Energy's Strategic Petroleum Reserve Office (SPRO). As of this writing, he has not yet been sentenced.

The real issue with this story is that proper policies and applying a security framework would have entirely prevented this incident. This incident is an ideal case study of why policies are important and how they must be applied.

- An off-boarding process to ensure all access has been revoked for exiting employees would have mitigated this situation.
- Cancelling all access for exiting employees and contractors would have completely prevented this situation.
- A robust intrusion detection system/intrusion prevention system (IDS/IPS) that detects anomalous login attempts (such as those from people no longer authorized) would have identified this situation earlier.

This is a classic case of policies not being implemented properly. Because this was a government office, it was supposed to be applying FISMA, NIST, and related standards. It is clear in this situation that security policies were not followed.

CHAPTER SUMMARY

This chapter examined various IT security policy frameworks. The frameworks share many of the same concepts and goals of controlling risk; however, their approach and scope of coverage differ. The chapter discussed how these differences are not always in conflict, but rather create an opportunity to adopt strengths of multiple frameworks such as COBIT and ISO. The chapter walked through methods to identify which best practice is appropriate for an organization. The implementation approach to each framework will vary by the type of framework and the organization's culture.

The chapter examined separation of duties from a roles and organizational view. The organizational view was used to create three lines of defense to enhance the risk management program. Finally, the importance of the frameworks was highlighted in case studies. These case studies illustrated how implementing a policies framework to control risk prevents breaches and ensures compliance. The case studies also showed how contractors and insiders can be as much of a threat as external hackers.

KEY CONCEPTS AND TERMS

Audit committee

Best practices

Committee of Sponsoring
   Organizations (COSO)

Compliance risk

Control Objectives for
   Information and related
   Technology (COBIT)

Data administrator

Data security administrator

Data steward

Enterprise risk management (ERM)

Executive committee

Financial risk

Governance, risk management,
   and compliance (GRC)

Head of information management

International Organization for
   Standardization (ISO)

Layered security approach

National Institute of Standards
   and Technology (NIST)

Operational risk

Operational risk committee

Risk Evaluation

Risk Governance

Risk Response

Security committee

Security event

Social engineering

Strategic risk

Value delivery

CHAPTER 8 ASSESSMENT

1. The security committee is the key committee for the CISO.

   A. True
   B. False

2. Which of the following is *not* an IT security policy framework?

   A. COBIT
   B. ISO
   C. ERM
   D. OCTAVE

3. Which of the following are PCI DSS network requirements?

   A. Network segregation
   B. Penetration testing
   C. Virus scanning
   D. All of the above
   E. A and B only

4. Which of the following are common IT framework characteristics?

   A. Risk-based management
   B. Aligned business risk appetite
   C. Reduced operation disruption and losses
   D. Established path from requirements to control
   E. All of the above
   F. A and C only

5. Which of the following applies to both GRC and ERM?

   A. Defines an approach to reduce risk
   B. Applies a rigid framework to eliminate redundant controls, policies, and efforts
   C. Passively enforces security policy
   D. Seeks line of sight into root causes of risks

6. The underlying concept of SOD is that individuals execute high-risk transactions as they receive preapproval.

   A. True
   B. False

7. A risk management and metrics team is generally the first team to respond to an incident.

   A. True
   B. False

8. Once you decide not to eliminate a risk but to accept it, you can ignore the risk.

   A. True
   B. False

9. Which of the following is *not* a key area of improvement noted after COBIT implementation?

   A. Value delivery
   B. Decentralization of the risk function
   C. Better resourcing of IT
   D. Better communication

10. A security team's organizational structure defines the team's _____.

11. Implementing a governance framework can allow an organization to systemically identify and prioritize risks.

    A. True
    B. False

12. The more layers of approval required for SOD, the more _____ it is to implement the process.

13. Asking to borrow someone's keycard is an example of _____.

14. All organizations should have a full-time team dedicated to collecting, reviewing, and reporting to demonstrate adherence to regulations.

    A. True
    B. False

ENDNOTES

1. Office of the Comptroller of the Currency, "Supervisory Guidance on Operational Risk Advanced Measurement Approaches for Regulatory Capital," July 2, 2003, *http://www.occ.treas.gov/ftp/release/2003-53c.pdf*, accessed April 30, 2010.

User Domain Policies

A TENET OF TELECOMMUNICATIONS SAYS the more people who access a network, the more valuable the network becomes. This is called Metcalfe's law. Put more formally, Metcalfe's law states that the effect of a telecommunications network is proportional to the square of the number of connected users of the system (n^2). Consider a telephone system as an example. If only two telephones were on the system, the value of the system is limited. Only two people can talk at any given time. But add millions of phones and people, and suddenly the effect of the network rapidly increases. In this case, *effect* and *value* are being used synonymously. Metcalfe's law has been expanded into related areas. For example, David Sarnoff created Sarnoff's law, which states that the value of a broadcast network is proportional to the number of viewers. David Reed created Reed's law, which is a bit more relevant to computer networks. He states that the utility of a network can scale exponentially with the size of the network.

This same principle can also be applied to the introduction of technology. As new technologies introduce new capabilities, the value of the network increases yet again. However, it's also true that the more users and technology involved in a network, the more complex it becomes, and the more potential security risks are introduced. It should also be noted that the more value a network has, the more deleterious an outage will be. This further compounds the security issues.

To illustrate these points, consider what happens when you bring home a new laptop. Typically, a new computer has a new installation of the operating system, preloaded applications, and games. The number of users is one, you. The security risks are low. Then you add technology such as an Internet connection, new social media software, and more users, such as family and friends. The laptop now becomes far more valuable; however, the value comes at a cost of increased security risks. And part of that value, as well as part of that risk, is how connected your laptop is, or how large the network it is connected to is.

This increase in the number of people accessing your network, along with the introduction of new and emerging technology (such as mobile devices), has dramatically increased the number of security risks. As the user population and the diversity of technology increase, so does the need to access information. This need translates into complex security controls that must be maintained. Inevitably, this complex jumble of controls leads to gaps in protection and security risks.

This chapter examines different types of users on networks. It reviews individual need for access and how those needs lead to risks that must be controlled. We will also discuss how security policies mitigate risks in the User domain. The last part of the chapter presents case studies to illustrate the alignment between types of users, risks, and security policies.

Chapter 9 Topics

This chapter covers the following topics and concepts:

- What the weakest link in the information security chain is
- What the different types of users are
- How to govern different types of users with policies
- What acceptable use policies (AUPs) are
- What the significance of a privileged-level access agreement (PAA) is
- What security awareness policies (SAPs) are
- What best practices for User domain policies are
- What the difference between least access privileges and best fit access privileges is
- What are some case studies and examples of User domain policies

Chapter 9 Goals

When you complete this chapter, you will be able to:

- Understand why users are considered the weakest link in implementing security policies and controls
- Understand the different users in a typical organization
- Explain how different users have different information needs
- Define an AUP
- Define a PAA
- Explain how a SAP can reduce risks
- Explain the importance of risk acceptance in understanding security risks
- Identify several best practices related to User domain policies
- Understand through case studies how security policies can reduce risk

The Weakest Link in the Information Security Chain

Security experts consider people the weakest link in security. Unlike automated security controls, different people have different skill levels. People can also let their guard down. They get tired or distracted and may not have information security in mind when they do their jobs. Automated controls have advantages over people. An automated control never sleeps or takes a vacation. An automated control can work relentlessly and execute flawlessly. The major advantage people have over automated controls is the ability to deal with the unexpected. An automated control is limited because it can mitigate only risks that it has been designed for.

This section looks at different ways in which humans earn the distinction of "the weakest link in the security chain." As you'll learn, social engineering, human mistakes, and the actions of insiders account for many security violations. However, lack of leadership support for security policies is another reason security measures fail. As a future security leader, keep in mind why employees at every level must accept and follow security policies.

NOTE

There are many different techniques for social engineering. However, they all rely on a person revealing sensitive information. To be successful, they typically require the attacker to get one or more employees to violate company policy. That's why security awareness training programs should address social engineering.

Social Engineering

People can be manipulated. Social engineering occurs when you manipulate or trick a person into weakening the security of an organization. Social engineering comes in many forms. One form is simply having an adversary befriend an employee. The more intimate the relationship, the more likely the employee may reveal knowledge that can be used to compromise security.

Another method is pretending to be from the IT department. This is sometimes called **pretexting**. An adversary might call an employee and convince him or her to reveal sensitive information. For example, a hacker asks an employee to enter data the hacker knows won't work. The hacker then simply asks for the employee's ID and password to "give it a try." Hackers who use pretexting are usually highly skilled in manipulating people. They can present simple or elaborate stories that seem compelling to an unsuspecting employee.

Another technique is to ask an employee to link to an internal webpage to verify the network performance. On that internal webpage, the user is then prompted to enter an ID and password and provide some random number noting that the response time on the network is good. What the user doesn't realize is that the internal webpage is a fake that has just captured the user's ID and password. As the methods and sophistications of hackers improve, so must the awareness training for the users.

Social engineering accounted for 29 percent of data breaches in 2013, according to a report published in 2014 by Verizon. The 2019 Data Breach Investigations Report from Verizon shows that this problem has not abated. The 2019 report also states that C-level executives are often the target of social engineering. Social engineering is attractive because of the ease with which data can be obtained compared with hacking. Breaking through automated controls like a firewall can take weeks, months, or years. Hackers may never be able to bypass the controls of a well-protected network. If they do, they still might not get access to the information they want. Breaking through a firewall does not necessarily provide access to data on a protected server. And even if hackers access data, they might not be able to send it outside the network. The bottom line for a hacker is that it may be easier to call employees and pose as an IT department employee. This can be accomplished within a short time and takes only one individual letting his or her guard down to succeed.

Phishing

Phishing is closely related to social engineering. It could be considered an email variation of social engineering. A phishing email is an attempt to convince the recipient to click on a link, download an attachment, or perform some similar activity. This is a place where clear policies can aid in mitigating the threat. Employees must be made aware of the dangers of phishing and what to look out for.

Spear phishing is a more refined example of phishing. In spear phishing, the email is more carefully crafted and targeted to a specific audience. For example, the email might state, "We are reaching out to you because you recently bought a new XYZ brand car." Now this virtually guarantees that those who have not recently purchased a new XYZ brand car will ignore the email; however, those who have made such a purchase are far more likely to be lured into clicking a link or downloading an attachment.

Whaling is even more targeted than spear phishing. Consider the following hypothetical scenario. Imagine you are the CISO of a major bank. From observing your social media, the attacker discovers that you are a big fan of deep sea fishing. So, the attacker crafts an email, perhaps even calling you by name. The email pertains to deep sea fishing, maybe an offer for a fishing excursion. Now the majority of people are unlikely to believe the email because it is so tailored; however, you are very likely to open the email. This is the nature of whaling. It is a very targeted attack.

All forms of phishing are essentially variations on social engineering. The 2019 Verizon report states that phishing was part of 32 percent of confirmed breaches and 78 percent of cyber-espionage incidents.

Human Mistakes

One characteristic all humans share is that they all make mistakes. Mistakes come from carelessness, fatigue, lack of knowledge, or inadequate oversight or training. Humans may perceive a security threat that does not exist. And someone might miss a real threat that is obvious to an objective observer.

> **NOTE**
>
> A 2018 report by the information security company Shred-it claimed that employee negligence is the main cause of data breaches. That report stated that 47 percent of business leaders had asserted human error had caused a data breach.[1]

Carelessness can be as simple as writing your password on a sticky note and leaving it on your keyboard. It can also be failing to read warning messages but still clicking OK. Carelessness can occur because an employee is untrained or does not perceive information security as important. Careless employees are prime targets of hackers who develop malicious code. These hackers count on individuals to be their point of entry into the network.

> **NOTE**
>
> When employees feel compelled by management to violate their organization's own established security policies and depart from normal processes, that's a strong indication of the lack of a good risk culture within the organization. In other words, neither employees nor managers have truly "bought in" to the importance of managing security risk.

Another form of carelessness is intimidating people into weakening security controls out of convenience. This can happen when a supervisor or an executive, for example, asks an employee to take shortcuts or to bypass normal control procedures. The employee feels compelled to follow the instructions of his or her superior.

Carelessness can also be a result of a lack of common computer knowledge. Technology often outpaces an employee's skills. Just as some employees acquire solid understanding of a system or application, it's upgraded or replaced. Too much change in an organization is unsettling and can lead to portions of your workforce being inadequately trained. An untrained worker can create

---

[1]https://www.helpnetsecurity.com/2019/06/17/human-error-data-breach/

a security weakness inadvertently, such as by failing to log off a system and leaving information on the screen exposed.

Programmers can also make mistakes. This is particularly a concern when those programmers introduce a coding error into a product with millions of users. That's exactly what happened with OpenSSL, an open source product used by millions to encrypt Internet traffic. In early 2011, code updates were made to OpenSSL that potentially allowed a hacker to read encrypted traffic by obtaining the secret encryption key. The bug was named "Heartbleed." Why is this important? The ability of a hacker to read encrypted messages on the Internet fundamentally undermines the trust needed to conduct business over the Internet. The potential risk is that a hacker can suddenly see IDs, passwords, and the content of messages, such as credit card information. Fortunately, the fix in this case was easy to make. However, the fact such a bug was introduced, affecting potentially millions of users, was a wake-up call. This was not a small event. The sites affected included Google, Yahoo, Facebook, and Netflix, and many others.

FYI

Heartbleed was a security bug in OpenSSL discovered in 2014. Although this example is a bit old, it is famous in the history of security breaches. OpenSSL allows websites to encrypt information from visitors so the data transferred back and forth (including usernames, passwords, and cookies) cannot be seen by others. When you access a website with OpenSSL, the site responds and actively listens for more input. This is known as the *heartbeat routine*. Normally when the heartbeat routine receives input, the website sends back only the amount of data your computer sent. The Heartbleed bug exploits a coding error that allows a hacker to make a request for the server's memory, which includes nonencrypted data such as login credentials. "Heartbleed" is a play on words referring to this coding bug that allows memory bleed in the heartbeat code. What makes this issue more egregious is that because OpenSSL is open source, any of the companies using it could have reviewed the code and found the problem. None did so.

You can use security policies to help developers reduce vulnerabilities during application development. Security policies can establish secure coding standards. The policies require penetration testing for high-risk applications. The best time to reduce risk is when an application is being written. Security policies can define how you perform vulnerability reviews during the development life cycle. Collectively, these policies can help you protect an application against attack.

Insiders

A significant threat to information security comes from the user who is an insider. In more formal terms, this can be referred to as an internal threat vector. Verizon released a 2019 insider threat report that details various threats from insiders. These include careless workers as well as insider agents and disgruntled employees. The term **insider** refers to an employee, consultant, contractor, or vendor. The insider may even be the IT technical people who designed the system, application, or security that is being hacked. The insider knows the organization and the applications. An IT department insider knows what is logged and

Application Code Errors

There are differing views on the number of average errors per line of code written. Some general rules of thumb use 10 to 20 defects per 1000 lines of code; others estimate as many as 50 defects per 1000. Commercial software tends to have fewer errors than code written in-house—as low as 0.5 to 3 defects per KLOC. A KLOC is a unit of measure that stands for 1000 lines of code. For example:

- An application with 2 million lines of code and a rate of 20 defects per KLOC would expect to have 40,000 coding errors.
- This is calculated based on 20 (defects per KLOC) multiplied by 2 million (lines of code) divided by 1000 (the KLOC).

Thousands of new vulnerabilities are discovered in code each year. You can safely assume that the vulnerabilities for new products are not found immediately. The new vulnerabilities discovered each year are a combination of errors in new and existing systems and applications. It should be noted that lines of code are a crude measure of software. Given that one segment of code may be more complex or more critical than another, LOC does not provide details on errors. It is simply a rough estimate.

what is checked and not checked. This person may even have access to local accounts shared between administrators. As a result, the IT insider has an easier time bypassing security controls and hiding his or her tracks. Insiders can hide their tracks by deleting or altering logs and time stamps. Knowing where the logs are kept and how frequently they are checked is a great advantage to an insider.

Regular employees with a long history in the organization may also pose a risk. These employees may be in a position of trust. These individuals have a sense of how the organization responds to incidents and can tailor their attack accordingly.

Insiders are not limited to regular employees; they can also be vendors and suppliers. Suppose, for example, you work for a financial institution. Further suppose it has outsourced the processing of loan applications to India. The workers there have access to detailed confidential financial information of applicants. In March 2012, an undercover reporter in India was able to buy confidential information, including names, addresses, credit card account numbers, and CCV/CVV numbers (card security codes). The reporter obtained everything needed for credit card fraud, in other words. The cost of this information? In some cases, just 3 cents per name. This problem is even worse now. For example, there are Dark Web markets that openly traffic in any insider information, including personal information, credit cards, and similar data.

 NOTE

The motivation of an insider is not always greed. An individual may feel disgruntled for a variety of reasons—from feeling mistreated to being passed over for some promotion. The person may simply have a sense of entitlement, "taking" the rewards he or she feels have been earned.

One motivation is money. Consider someone trying to steal 100,000 credit card numbers. Some estimate stolen credit cards can be sold for $2 to $6 each on the black market. Assume a hacker offers $20,000 to an employee for insider help. The employee copies the card information or provides a way to get into the system. Paying for information becomes a more economical approach than taking the time to hack through automated defenses with uncertain results. The return in this example would be $200,000 to $600,000 for a $20,000 investment.

Insiders breaching security can have a devastating effect on an organization's reputation and viability. A 2018 Accenture survey found that 1 in 5 healthcare employees are willing to sell confidential data.[2] The impact of an insider deliberately selling data can be substantial. This illustrates the issues with insiders and just how widespread the problem can be.

Security policies and controls can help limit damages and threats. Security policies ensure access is limited to individual roles and responsibilities. This means the damage from using an insider's credentials is limited to that function. Additionally, a policy may require that an individual's access be removed immediately upon leaving the organization. These types of user controls can reduce risks.

Seven Types of Users

The User domain, one of seven domains of a typical IT infrastructure, consists of a variety of users. Each user type has unique access needs. As the different types of users in the domain grow, so does the security complexity. At a minimum, each type of user has unique business needs and thus requires unique rights to access certain information. Within each of these major types of users, the rights are further refined into subtypes. Each subtype might be further broken up, and so on. For example, your organization might have many types of administrators. The number depends on the size of the organization, complexity, and team specializations. You may further separate rights between Oracle and Microsoft SQL database administrators. **FIGURE 9-1** is an example of types and subtypes of users.

You can build better security policies and controls by understanding user needs. There is no fixed number of user types possible on a network; for example, a salaried employee may be a full-time experienced professional or a part-time college student. Depending on the business, though, there may be different sets of security issues associated with those two types of employees. To illustrate common user needs, this chapter focuses on seven basic user types, as follows:

- **Employees**—Salaried or hourly staff members of the organization
- **Systems administrators**—Employees who work in the IT department to provide technical support to the systems
- **Security personnel**—Individuals responsible for designing and implementing a security program within an organization
- **Contractors**—Temporary workers who can be assigned to any role; contractors are directly managed by the company in the same manner as employees.
- **Vendors**—These are outside companies, or individuals working for such companies, hired to provide ongoing services to the organization, such as building cleaning. Unlike contractors, vendor employees are directly managed by the vendor company to perform specific services on the organization's network.

---

[2]https://www.beckershospitalreview.com/cybersecurity/1-in-5-health-employees-willing-to-sell -confidential-data-7-survey-insights.html

FIGURE 9-1

Types of users.

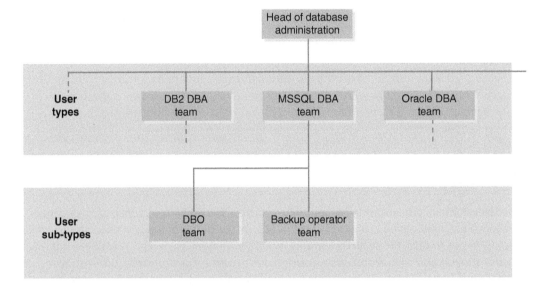

- **Guests and general public**—A class or group of users who access a specific set of applications
- **Control partners**—Individuals who evaluate controls for design and effectiveness

In addition to these (human) user types, all with different access needs, you should also be aware of two other groups. They are really account types, rather than user types. *System accounts* are nonhuman accounts used by the system to support automated service. *Contingent IDs* are nonhuman accounts until they are assigned to individuals, who use them to recover a system in the event of a major outage.

FYI

Contingent accounts, or contingent IDs, are an interesting type of account because they do not truly become user accounts until they are assigned to an individual. That may not happen until a disaster occurs. However, some contingent IDs will be preassigned to individuals, making them a type of user from conception. The point to remember here is that at some point, contingent IDs become a type of user account and must be managed appropriately.

    TABLE 9-1 outlines each of these user types in the context of their business and access needs. The table focuses on nine basic user or account types. The same approach can be applied to any user accessing information on the network.

TABLE 9-1 Access Needs of Typical Domain Users and Account Types

TYPE OF USER	BUSINESS NEED	ACCESS NEED
Employees	Need to access specific applications in the production environment	Access is limited to specific applications and information.
Systems administrators	Need to access systems and databases to support applications	Access is broad and unlimited in context of the role; for example, database administrators may have unlimited access to the database but not the operating system.
Security personnel	Need to protect network, systems, applications, and information	Access to set permissions, review logs, monitor activity, and respond to incidents.
Contractors	Temporary workers needing the same access as full-time workers in the same role	Access is the same as for full-time workers.
Vendors	Need to access network, systems, and applications to perform contracted services	Access is limited to specific portions of the network, systems, and applications.
Guests and general public	Need to access specific application functions	Access is assigned to a type of user and not to the individual.
Control partners	Need to review and assess controls	Access often includes unlimited read access to logs and configuration settings.
Contingent IDs	Need to recover systems and data during an outage	Access is unlimited across both operating systems and databases. Additionally, may also require broad access to network devices (such as firewalls) and data backups.
System accounts	Need to start, stop, and perform automated system services.	Access should be limited to the system function being performed.

User IDs must be managed so that you know who had access to the account when it was used. Suppose a large amount of credit card data was accessed and later found to have been used to commit fraud. Now suppose the log indicates which user ID accessed and stole the data. It would be helpful to know who was assigned to that ID. However, suppose a hundred or even a thousand individuals had access to the user ID. It might be impossible to find out who stole the credit card information. When user IDs are assigned, reassigned, or deleted, records are typically kept. This is sometimes referred to as a **chain of custody**. A chain of custody for a user ID typically refers to knowing at any given point in time who has access to the user ID. Often chain of custody is enforced simply by resetting the password. By resetting the password and giving the new password to a different individual, the ID can be reassigned. This is useful when dealing with temporary access such as a training ID or emergency access ID.

Employees

Employees represent the broadest category of users within an organization. Organizations are composed of departments and lines of business. An employee may be full-time or part-time. An employee may be in a customer-facing role or a corporate function. Regardless of their job in the organization, employees have unique information needs.

Successfully implementing security policies depends on knowing who has access to the organization's information. Security policies require users to have unique identities to access systems, applications, and/or networks. This is typically accomplished by the employee entering a unique user ID and password.

> **TIP**
>
> Before allowing employees to access information, be sure they understand their security responsibilities. Often organizations require formal information security awareness training before an ID is issued.

Employees' access must be managed through the life cycle of their career with the organization. There is always pressure to grant and extend user access to increase productivity. No one wants to wait weeks for a new hire to be granted access.

Additionally, when a change to the business occurs, you might need to change employee access. Although there's significant pressure to grant employees new access rights, the same pressure may not exist to remove access. Consider the following example:

An employee with many years of experience within an organization worked her way to a role with a high level of trust with her management. She entered the organization at an entry-level position. She was eventually promoted to the role of supervisor and then manager. The employee transferred within the department. Throughout the changes in her role, the prior access was never removed. This is someone who understands the inner workings of the department and has intimate knowledge of the technology. She is often asked to train others.

> **⚠ WARNING**
>
> As individuals move from job to job within an organization, their access privileges from previous jobs must be removed. If this is not done, the result may be what is sometimes referred to as *privilege creep*. This, in turn, may make it possible for someone to commit fraud, because there is no longer a separation of duties between jobs such as executing and approving one's own transaction.

Security policies require access to be removed when an individual changes roles. Without good security policies, you may find longtime employees with excessive access rights. They collect new access as they change roles and continue to retain access from their prior roles. Department leadership might not perceive this as a problem, especially when an employee uses this broad access to "save the day" during a crisis. Looking ahead, people may believe there's no time to ask for additional access during an emergency. An individual who is able to execute transitions quickly might prevent the problem from escalating.

Excessive access rights represent a serious security risk. As individuals change roles, their access rights must be adjusted.

Prior access rights that are no longer needed must be removed. New access rights must be properly approved and granted. This is for the employee's protection as much as for the organizations. When a security incident occurs, one of the first steps is to identify who may have had access. This is accomplished by reviewing individual access rights. Employees can avoid suspicion if they have no access to the affected systems, applications, and information. Removing unneeded access also reduces overall security vulnerabilities. In the event an ID and password is compromised, a hacker's access rights would be contained within the employee's current role. Consider the following example:

> In a bank, a teller may be able to initiate the process of sending money between banks from one account to another. This is an important service provided to customers. Before the money is sent, however, the bank manager must approve the transfer. This dual control creates a separation of duties (SOD) to reduce fraud. If the manager was once a teller and retained his access rights, the bank is at risk. The manager in this scenario could start and approve the transfer of money. The ability to perform both roles violates the SOD security policies for these types of transactions. Additionally, having such access becomes an unnecessary temptation for fraud in which employees could target rarely used accounts to wire themselves funds.

Good security policies make clear that individuals have only the access needed for their jobs. Security policies outline how rights are assigned and approved. This includes the removal of prior access that is no longer needed. This accomplishes the following:

- Reduces the overall security risk to the organization
- Maintains separation of duties
- Simplifies investigation of incidents

Systems Administrators

Systems administrators may need unlimited rights to install, configure, and repair systems. With this elevated access comes enormous responsibility to protect credentials. A systems administrator's credentials are a prime target for hackers. As a result, organizations should consider additional layers of authentication for administrators when feasible, such as certificates and two-factor authentication.

Security policies reduce risk by requiring monitoring of the systems administrator's activity. The systems administrator should only use broad access to perform assigned duties. Let's consider a database administrator. She needs access to apply patches, resolve issues, and configure applications. Yet she normally does not access customer personal information stored within the database. Logging administrator activity is one way to verify that access rights are not being abused. Logs record if administrators granted themselves access beyond the scope of their roles. Logs record the names of people who access customer personal information. Although you may not be able to prevent a systems administrator from accessing customer information, you can review the logs to detect the event.

With elevated access, systems administrators could just turn off the logs; however, the act of turning off or altering logs is also trackable. Many systems write an entry when the log service starts and stops. Additionally, logs can be sent to a log server.

A **log server** is a separate platform used to collect logs from platforms throughout the network. Access to log servers is highly restricted. Analyzing logs can help you detect gaps in logs, which are an indication the log service was turned off. Analyzing logs can also help detect if they have been altered. Knowing that your activity is being monitored is a deterrent in itself. Security policies outline the requirements of what is logged and how often the logs are reviewed.

There's a widely accepted approach that states systems administrators' access rights should be limited to their daily routine tasks. Through a separate process, systems administrators' rights can be elevated when they need to install, configure, or upgrade the system. The approach assumes that tasks associated with the elevated rights occur infrequently. Therefore, the additional process is not burdensome. Some systems administrators resist this approach. Having unfettered access makes their job easier in that they don't have to request access before performing certain tasks. It can be hard to predict what their access needs are. As a result, they may feel asking for permission is cumbersome and creates unnecessary delays.

You can consider limiting administrator rights a leading practice in regulated industries. The approach is widely accepted in the financial services industry. Some of the advantages of granting elevated rights to administrators as needed include the following:

- It reduces the overall security risk to the organization. In the event the systems administrator's credentials are compromised, access would be limited.
- It dramatically reduces the volume of logs to be reviewed to detect when an administrator abuses his or her access rights.
- It improves the alignment and understanding between technical tasks and business requirements.
- This approach records the business reason for the elevated rights being granted, which addresses why the security administrator accessed certain files.
  - This information can also be used to identify patterns of control weaknesses.

It's not practical to log every access a busy systems administrator performs daily. The volume of logs would be excessive. Any review of these logs would lack context. It may be possible to see that an administrator accessed a file, but there's no business context for the action. In other words, given the volume of log files, it would be difficult at best to determine which files the person should or should not have accessed that day. The approach described earlier in this section allows you to understand why the access rights were used. By the nature of the request, you know what files the administrator should access and the business reason why. For example, if you found that a security administrator had accessed a financial spreadsheet, was it to fix a corrupted file, or because he or she wanted to illegally access information used to buy or sell stock? When an administrator is fixing a problem, you have a record of the reason why he or she accessed the file. Knowing the business reason gives you the context.

The process for capturing business requirements and elevating privileges is well established. Security policies outline the process of temporarily granting elevated rights, which is often called a

NOTE

A firecall-ID process, along with trouble tickets, can be an important source of information that can be used to detect patterns of problems. Access to this information is important to provide ongoing improvements in the system and application designs.

firecall-ID process. A **firecall-ID process** provides temporary elevated access to unprivileged users. The name implies the urgency behind granting the access to resolve a problem quickly. During a firecall-ID process, the issue or problem is defined in a trouble ticket. The **trouble ticket** is a complete record of what access was granted and the business reason. The ticket is then assigned to someone to fix the problem. When the problem is assigned, the individual is granted elevated privileges. The individual completes the work and then closes the ticket. When the ticket closes, the individual's elevated rights are removed. **FIGURE 9-2** depicts a basic firecall-ID process.

A firecall-ID process is an accepted way to grant temporary access for a number of activities, such as one-time events like special financial reporting. With this approach, you configure more detailed logging without generating excessive volume. This is because you will record more detail, but only when the elevated rights are turned on.

A number of variations to the firecall-ID process are illustrated in Figure 9-2. For example, requiring a help desk manager to approve a ticket may be an optional control that some organizations feel is unnecessary. Another common variation is to allow an administrator to open a trouble ticket, make a repair, and then close a trouble ticket.

This self-service capability may be important when an administrator wants to track unusual events. For example, suppose a database administrator (DBA) has a very stable environment with few outages and problems. To control the risk, the DBA's normal access may not include unlimited access to the database. However, when the database system administrator (DBSA) identifies a problem, he or she may choose to use the firecall-ID process to gain the additional access quickly to repair the database and note the problem.

FIGURE 9-2

Basic firecall-ID process.

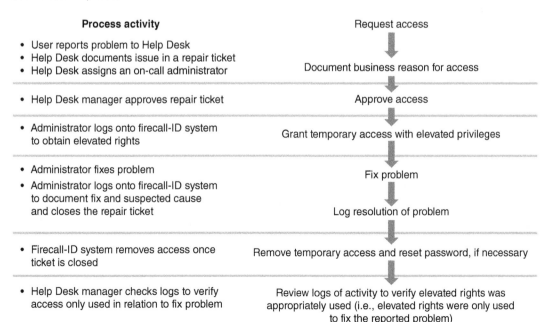

| Process activity | Request access |

- User reports problem to Help Desk
- Help Desk documents issue in a repair ticket
- Help Desk assigns an on-call administrator

Document business reason for access

- Help Desk manager approves repair ticket

Approve access

- Administrator logs onto firecall-ID system to obtain elevated rights

Grant temporary access with elevated privileges

- Administrator fixes problem
- Administrator logs onto firecall-ID system to document fix and suspected cause and closes the repair ticket

Fix problem

Log resolution of problem

- Firecall-ID system removes access once ticket is closed

Remove temporary access and reset password, if necessary

- Help Desk manager checks logs to verify access only used in relation to fix problem

Review logs of activity to verify elevated rights was appropriately used (i.e., elevated rights were only used to fix the reported problem)

Security Personnel

Security personnel are responsible for designing, implementing, and monitoring security programs. In larger organizations, the roles may be separated between those who define and those who implement the policies. Security personnel develop security awareness and training programs. They also align security policies with those of other parts of the organization, such as legal and HR.

Security staff must understand and implement different types of controls, such as management, operational, and technical. They have to wear many hats. On any given day, security staff may handle a variety of tasks. One day they may work with procurement to review a new software package for vulnerabilities. They may be woken up in the middle of the night to respond to a security breach. In many organizations, the security team is understaffed, so they must carefully prioritize the workload to focus on the greatest risks. The following are examples of the diversity of issues that security teams deal with:

- Audit coordination and response, and regulator liaison
- Physical security and building operations
- Disaster recovery and contingency planning
- Procurement of new technologies, vendor management, and outsourcing
- Security awareness training and security program maintenance
- Personnel issues, such as background checks for potential employees and disciplinary actions for current employees
- Risk management and planning
- Systems management and reporting
- Telecommunications
- Penetration testing
- Help desk incident response

Security staff roles and their associated access must be well defined. This includes limiting access to specific duties and, as appropriate, leveraging the firecall-ID process to gain elevated privileges. With this broad access come enormous responsibilities to protect credentials. The credentials of these individuals are also prime targets for hackers.

Contractors

Contractors are temporary workers; however, they can be assigned roles like regular employees. The two major advantages of a contractor are cost and skills. These individuals comply with the same security policies as any other employee. There may be additional policy requirements on a contractor such as a special nondisclosure agreement and deeper background checks.

As short-term employees, contractors may not show the same loyalty to the organization as a long-term employee. Many security experts consider contractors a higher security risk than an employee. This is because the organization often hires these individuals from consulting firms, and the organization does not have full control over the consulting firms' hiring practices or full access to their contractors' job histories or performance reviews.

Contractors allow you to ramp up your workforce during peak periods. Contractors generally save organizations money over the long term. Although you pay contractors more than similar employees' wages, you usually need contractors for shorter periods of time. In addition, contractors generally do not receive paid benefits, such as sick leave and vacation time.

Contractors can bring a variety of special skills to an organization. These skills can be valuable to a specific project or initiative. Maintaining these skills within your full-time staff may not be cost effective. For example, assume you are deploying a new technology to prevent data leakage. The project is to install a leading vendor package designed to prevent sensitive information from being emailed out of the organization. Your staff may be unfamiliar with the package and the technology. You can hire a contractor who has installed this product numerous times. The contractor has knowledge based on prior installations that cannot be achieved through training.

Contractors must be fast learners. Within a short time, they are expected to know your security policies. They also have to adapt to the organization culture. The firm placing the individual often completes background checks for contractors. If that is the case, it's important to verify that the background checks are as thorough as those performed by the hiring organization. The other challenge relates to security awareness. Depending on the length of the engagement, there may be limited time to conduct the same caliber of awareness training as you do with existing employees.

Vendors

Vendor employees need to be managed the same as salaried employees. Their access must be tied to their individual roles. Vendor employees must follow all the same rules and policies as an organization's own employees. A vendor employee may be full-time or part-time. He or she may be in a customer-facing role or a corporate function. Regardless of their jobs in the organization, vendor employees have the same kinds of information needs as an organization's employees.

However, vendor employees are managed directly by the vendor company. Consequently, that company will often manage their access. This adds both complexity and risk. Processes must be in place to ensure that the vendor company is managing its employees effectively. This includes notifying the organization when staffing changes require access changes. Here are some situations for which a vendor must provide notification:

- When individuals are hired or terminated
- When individuals change their roles
- When systems are added to or removed from the organization's network
- When security configuration changes are made to the communications between the vendor and the organization, such as firewall rule changes

A vendor can significantly impact the security readiness of an organization. An organization is only as secure as the vendor systems connected to the organization's own network.

Guests and General Public

Guests and the general public are a special class of users. Unlike other types of users who are assigned unique IDs and passwords, you might not know the identity of an individual accessing a public-facing webpage. This is common on the Internet. There are many applications on the Internet that are freely accessible to the public. When an individual wants access to one of these applications, an ID and password is not needed.

For example, let's assume a website contains a Zip code lookup application in the demilitarized zone (DMZ). You enter a Zip code to find out which city is in the Zip code area. Assume the website is freely available. The cost of the site is supported by advertisers placing ads on the webpage. When someone keys in a Zip code, the corresponding city name appears. This is accomplished through a query to a back-end database that matches the entered Zip code with the appropriate city. Credentials are exchanged between the website server and back-end database server. Rather than seeing an individual accessing the database, the security controls may only see the credentials of the website server. This in itself does not create a security exposure if the application, network, and database are hardened.

The Zip code lookup application ensures that only a five-digit Zip code can be entered, which prevents a **Structured Query Language (SQL) injection** attack. SQL injection is a common form of hacker attack in which a SQL command is placed inside an input field. Hackers hope that when the input field is passed to the database query, they can execute their own commands on the database. Network controls ensure that only traffic from the DMZ application to the database server is permitted. These network controls (such as a firewall) would also ensure that the only traffic permitted is a SQL query from the DMZ application to the specific back-end database server. The back-end database server accepts a connection only from the DMZ application. The back-end database server also permits only one type of SQL query, which reads the Zip code entered and returns the associated city to be displayed. FIGURE 9-3 depicts these layers of controls at the DMZ application, network, and database layers.

In this specific website example, you can see that the application, network, and database would be well protected. It's not so easy in the real world. In the real world, applications share website space and back-end database servers. A breach in one application can lead to a breach in another. Not all applications effectively test and limit what a user can enter. An application's internal controls can be sound, but the application becomes compromised by a vulnerability in the operating system. Security policies outline the types of controls and hardening methods used to protect a server in the DMZ.

Public-facing Internet sites are prime targets for hackers. Hackers may sign up for a legitimate account on your website. Then, using that account, they may try to find ways to expand its authority or gain access to other customers' information. To protect against this, keep the number of system accounts used in the application to a minimum. As much as possible, the DMZ should be used simply to capture and clean customer input and pass the user content to a back-end system. At a high level, think of the DMZ as having two main purposes: cleansing user input and manning secure communications. It's the back-end system behind the firewall that performs additional content verification and the actual processing of the transaction.

When dealing with guests and the general public, you grant access rights to a class of users rather than to individuals. It's important to remember that guests and the general public have different skill sets than your employees do. These individuals have not had

Example of a DMZ application connecting to back-end server.

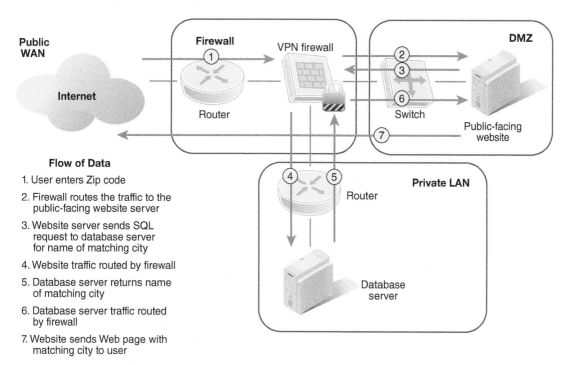

Flow of Data

1. User enters Zip code

2. Firewall routes the traffic to the public-facing website server

3. Website server sends SQL request to database server for name of matching city

4. Website traffic routed by firewall

5. Database server returns name of matching city

6. Database server traffic routed by firewall

7. Website sends Web page with matching city to user

the benefit of security awareness training, either. Assigning guest and public access can be accomplished in several ways. You can assign credentials to applications, servers, or types of database connections. You can also assign rights to a generic user ID or service account. Assigning credentials in the form of a hard-coded ID and password stored within an application is less secure. Security policies typically prohibit this approach to application credentialing. The problem is that if an application is compromised, the ID is also compromised. It also makes it very difficult to change the ID's password without recoding or reconfiguring the application. As a result, a password used in this manner tends not to change very often. This creates a security vulnerability. A much better method of assigning credentials is using a method that does not rely on passwords, such as assigning a certificate. Assigning a certificate to an account, application, or server is fairly easy. The complexity and cost come in setting up the environment to maintain the certificates.

The following are some best practices when dealing with guest and general public access:

- From a policy standpoint, it is important to have a well-defined risk process that performs a detailed assessment of guest and general public access.
- Highly restrict access to specific functions.
- Penetration test all public-facing websites to detect control weaknesses.
- Don't hard-code access credentials within applications.
- Limit network traffic to point-to-point communications.

Control Partners

There are many different types of control partners. The individuals can be auditors, operational risk or compliance processionals, or regulators. Even within these broad types of control partners, there can be subcategories. For example, financial auditors focus on financial operations. They look at the completeness, fairness, and representation in the organization's financial statements. They look at the underlying processes and operations that produced the financial data. Financial auditors look at any potential control weaknesses that may call into question the accuracy of the financial statements.

Technology auditors are often referred to as IT auditors. They look at an organization's technology controls and risks. They assess the controls for design and effectiveness. They ask questions such as "Do the controls address all the vulnerabilities, and are they working well?" They also look at how well an organization assesses technology risk in the context of the business processes.

Although financial and technology audit teams have distinct responsibilities, they often collaborate. This is referred to as an integrated audit. In an **integrated audit**, more than one audit discipline is combined for a single audit. For example, let's assume a company purchases large amounts of equipment for its manufacturing process. The accuracy of the company's financial statements depends in part on properly reporting these expenditures. Financial auditors look at the underlying financial data and accounting methods used to reflect these investments. Financial auditors may look at the depreciation method used. They might even challenge the completeness of the data. On the other hand, IT auditors focus on the underlying technology that captures, records, and calculates the financial results. IT auditors look at the security controls and the integrity of the data.

FYI

The authority to conduct audits depends on the type of organization. For example, government agencies are subject to audits through legal statutes and directives. A private company may be subject to audit requirements set by its board of directors. Many publicly traded companies adopt an audit committee structure. This is a subcommittee of the board of directors formed to focus on audit matters.

Operational risk and compliance teams often have the same need for access as do auditors. The operational risk team reviews the controls to ensure a business is operating within the acceptable risk appetite. This means that the business is not taking on too much risk. Compliance teams ensure that the business is following the law. Like auditors, these teams are specialized. They look at a variety of controls.

In a public company, an auditor reports findings to the business unit management and to the audit committee. Operational risk and compliance reports are often sent to the business and the company's risk committee. This dual reporting serves several goals. It ensures that line management knows about control weaknesses so immediate action can be taken. It also ensures that risks get visibility at the highest level of the organization.

Security policies detail the controls in granting control partners access. For an IT audit this typically means access to security reports, logs, and configuration information. Auditors primarily need read access. Auditors have specialized tools that help analyze samples taken and record their findings. Within these specialized applications they are granted appropriate rights to capture the evidence and write audit reports.

Contingent

Contingent accounts need unlimited rights to install, configure, repair, and recover networks and applications, and to restore data. With this elevated access comes enormous responsibility to protect credentials. These credentials are prime targets for hackers. These IDs are not assigned to individuals until a disaster recovery event is declared. As a result, they must be protected until they are needed.

One challenge is to know whether these IDs will work during a disaster. For example, assume a data center is hit by a hurricane and the systems must be restored across town. That's not the time to find out you don't have access to the backup data. It's important that these contingent IDs be tested at least annually. It's equally important that, during these recovery tests, IDs that are no longer needed be identified and deleted.

System

System accounts often need elevated privileges to start, stop, and manage system services. These accounts can be interactive or noninteractive. The word **interactive** typically refers here to the ability for a person to log on to the account. A system account that is noninteractive is one to which a person cannot log on. An interactive system account has a password that, if known, can be used by a person to log on to the account. System accounts are also referred to as *service accounts*.

Why this distinction between interactive and noninteractive service accounts? These accounts usually have elevated privileges. That makes them targets for hackers. Ideally, you wouldn't want any system accounts to be interactive. That way there would be no passwords to steal, all accounts would be tied to specific applications, and hackers would have less opportunity to get in. But this is not an ideal world. Many system accounts have passwords that can be stolen. Strict controls must be in place to protect passwords for interactive system accounts. A firecall-ID process, as previously described, can provide such controls to restrict access to these sensitive accounts.

Why Govern Users with Policies?

Organizations want a single view of risk. Decision making becomes easier, as does talking with regulators or shareholders. Security policies offer a common way to view and control risks. In addition, regulations require the implementation of security policies. A few examples include the Sarbanes-Oxley (SOX) Act of 2002 and the Health Insurance Portability and Accountability Act (HIPAA). This is not unique to the United States. Global organizations face an array of similar laws and regulations, such as the European Data Protection Directive.

Having well-defined policies that govern user behavior ensures key risks are controlled in a consistent manner. These policies provide evidence of compliance to regulators. Regulators are increasingly looking at how security policies are applied. It's not enough to have written policies. Regulators also want to see evidence that these policies are enforced.

Acceptable Use Policy (AUP)

It is important to set clear expectations for what's acceptable behavior for those using an organization's technology assets. An AUP defines the intended uses of computers and networks, including unacceptable uses and the consequences for violation of policy. An AUP also prohibits accessing or storing offensive content. The following topics are typically found in an AUP:

- Basics of protecting an organization's computers and network
- Managing passwords
- Managing software licenses
- Managing intellectual property
- Email etiquette
- Level of privacy an individual should expect when using an organization's computer or network
- Noncompliance consequences

A good AUP should also be accompanied by awareness training. This training should address realistic scenarios an individual might face. The following situations are a few examples of what might show up in AUP awareness training:

- A coworker asks you to log on to the network or an application because he or she is waiting for access to be approved. What should you do?
- You receive a politically sensitive joke via email. Should you forward the email?
- The person next to you spends many hours a day surfing the Internet for stock tips. What should you do?

The Privileged-Level Access Agreement (PAA)

When administrative rights are breached or abused, the impact can be catastrophic to the organization. A **privileged-level access agreement (PAA)** is designed to heighten the awareness and accountability of those users who have administrative rights. The PAA is a formal agreement signed by an administrator acknowledging his or her responsibilities. The agreement basically says the administrator will protect these sensitive credentials and not abuse his or her authority. The PAA is an enhanced form of security awareness specifically for administrators.

 NOTE

The federal government uses PAAs in the defense industry; however, few organizations outside the defense industry have adopted PAA use.

The PAA is typically a one- to two-page document. It reads as a formal agreement between the administrator and the organization. The PAA generally contains the following from the administrator's perspective:

- Acknowledgment of the risk associated with elevated access in the event the credentials are breached or abused
- Promise not to share the credentials entrusted to his or her care
- Promise to use the access granted only for approved organization business

- Promise not to attempt to "hack" or breach security
- Promise to protect any output from these credentials such as reports, logs, files, and downloads
- Promise to report any indication of a breach or intrusion promptly
- Promise not to tamper with, modify, or remove any security controls without authorization
- Promise not to install any backdoor, malicious code, or unauthorized hardware or software
- Promise not to violate intellectual property rights, copyrights, or trade secrets
- Promise not to access or store inflammatory material, such as pornographic or racist content
- Promise not to browse data that is not directly related to assigned tasks
- Promise to act in good faith and be subjected to penalties under breach of contract and criminal statutes

In many respects, these items are already covered by security policies and awareness training. The PAA reinforces the importance of these terms with administrators.

Security Awareness Policy (SAP)

Security awareness training is often the first view a typical user has into information security. It's often required for all new hires. Think of it as the first impression of management's view of information security. This is management's opportunity to set the tone. Most individuals want to do a good job, but they need to know what the rules and expected behavior are. A good security awareness policy has many benefits, including informing workers of the following:

- Basic principles of information security
- Awareness of risk and threats
- How to deal with unexpected risk
- How to report suspicious activity, incidents, and breaches
- How to help build a culture that is security and risk aware

Security policy is not just a good idea—it's the law! There are many regulations that require security policies and a security awareness program. Many state laws also require security awareness. In most industries, having a security awareness program is considered a best practice. The following list highlights a number of federal mandates that require an organization to have a security awareness program:

- Health Insurance Portability and Accountability Act (HIPAA)
- Gramm-Leach-Bliley Act
- Sarbanes-Oxley Act
- Federal Information Security Management Act (FISMA)
- National Institute of Standards and Technology (NIST) Special Publications 800-53, "Recommended Security Controls for Federal Information Systems"
- 5 Code of Federal Regulations (C.F.R.)
- The NIST Guide for Developing Security Plans for Information Technology Systems

- Office of Management and Budget (OMB) Circular A-130, Appendix III
- The NIST Computer Security Handbook

Laws can outline the frequency and target audience of awareness training. For example, 5 C.F.R. requires security awareness training before an individual can access information. A refresher course must also be taken annually. The following outlines the 5 C.F.R. requirements:

- **All users**—Security basics
- **Executives**—Policy level and governance
- **Program and functional managers**—Security management, planning, and implementation; also risk management and contingency planning
- **Chief information officers (CIOs)**—Broad training in security planning, system and application security management, risk management, and contingency planning
- **IT security program managers**—Broad training in security planning, system and application security management, risk management, and contingency planning
- **Auditors**—Broad training in security planning, system and application security management, risk management, and contingency planning
- **IT function management and operations personnel**—Broad training in security planning and system/application security management, system/application life cycle management, risk management, and contingency planning

For information security policies to deliver value, they must explain how to manage risk and proactively address threats. A well-planned security awareness program can be a cornerstone to accomplish this objective.

Communication of security policy through a security awareness program is vital. Even the best policy is of little use if no one is aware of it. Security awareness changes behavior. Security awareness consists of a series of campaigns aimed at improving understanding of security policies and risks. Security awareness is not a one-time event. It's a campaign that strives to keep reinforcing the message in different ways.

Best Practices for User Domain Policies

A best practice is a leading technique, methodology, or technology that through experience has proved to be reliable. Best practices tend to produce a consistent and quality result. The following short list of best practices focuses on the user and is found in security policies. These best practices go a long way toward protecting users and the organization. Policies should require the following practices:

- **Attachments**—Never open an email attachment from a source that is not trusted or known.
- **Encryption**—Always encrypt sensitive data that leaves the confines of a secure server; this includes encrypting laptops, backup tapes, emails, and so on.
- **Layered defense**—Use an approach that establishes overlapping layers of security as the best way to mitigate threats.
- **Least privilege**—The principle of least privilege is that individuals should have only the access necessary to perform their responsibilities.

- **Best fit privilege**—The principle of best fit access privilege holds that individuals should have the limited access necessary to fulfill their responsibilities and have their access managed efficiently.
- **Patch management**—Be sure all network devices have the latest security patches including user desktop and laptop computers. Patch management is an essential part of a layered defense. Even when you do everything right, there may be a vulnerability in the vendor's system or application. An effective patch management program mitigates many of these risks.
- **Unique identity**—All users accessing information must use unique credentials that identify who they are; the only exception is public access of a publicly facing website.
- **Virus protection**—Virus and malware prevention must be installed on every desktop and laptop computer.

Understanding Least Access Privileges and Best Fit Access Privileges

The difference between **least access privileges** and **best fit access privileges** can be confusing and subtle. Both control risk by limiting access associated with a specific job or role. The difference is that least privileges customize access to the individual, whereas best fit privileges typically customize access to the group or class of users.

For example, suppose you have four accounts receivable specialists. Accounts receivable teams typically collect on invoices due to a company. Of the four specialists, two work on commercial accounts and two work on individual accounts. Their access is the same, except that the commercial receivables specialists also require access to market information about the companies related to the commercial accounts. Under least privileges, you might choose to limit access to the market information to just the commercial receivables specialists. However, this decision comes at a cost. You would have to maintain two sets of access rules for basically the same job.

When you multiply these subtle differences across large populations of users and technologies, these rule differences can be quite complex and expensive to maintain. Best fit privileges would look at the risk of giving access to market data to the two specialists working with noncommercial accounts. If there is little to no risk of fraud or security exposure, then all four specialists may get the same access. Typically, this means assigning access to a receivables specialist role, and then assigning all four individuals to the role. Using this best fit risk-based approach to assigning access can lower support costs and simplify access rules.

Case Studies and Examples of User Domain Policies

The case studies in this section reflect actual risks that were exploited in the real world. Each case study examines potential root causes. By looking at these case studies in the context of security policies, you identify how they can be avoided.

The case studies examined in this section relate to security policy violations, a lack of separation of duties, and poor vendor management. The studies involve the compromise of a government laptop, a Raspberry Pi incident, and unauthorized access to government systems.

Government Laptop Compromised

On October 31, 2012, NASA notified its employees that a laptop containing personal information on more than 10,000 employees was stolen. The theft occurred when a laptop containing the information was taken from a locked car. The laptop had a password, but the hard drive was not encrypted. The NASA announcement included a statement that the IT security policies and practices were under review. Additionally, several immediate actions were undertaken, including requiring that all laptops that leave NASA facilities be encrypted.

Although the details of the theft are unclear, what is clear is that the laptop was left unattended in a locked car. At many organizations, that would be considered a violation of acceptable use policy. Leaving a laptop with sensitive information unattended is not good practice. Typically, such policies require someone to maintain physical possession of devices when they are brought into public spaces, and to carry them into airline cabins rather than leave them in checked bags.

Also, full disk encryption is commonplace in the industry. For NASA not to require full disk encryption and to permit sensitive information to be placed on a laptop is to be out of compliance with industry norms.

In this case, this was a failure of policy as much as individual actions. Had the laptop been fully encrypted, the loss would have been limited to the device itself. Although the theft probably indicated a violation of acceptable use policy, the actual damage resulting in employees having their personal information stolen and the impact on NASA's reputation could have been avoided.

The NASA Raspberry Pi

In April 2018, an attacker was able to gain access to the NASA Jet Propulsion Laboratory by targeting an unauthorized Raspberry Pi. The Raspberry Pi attack went undetected for 10 months. The perpetrator stole approximately 500 megabytes of data.

An audit showed that this was not the only unauthorized device on the network. There have been multiple security incidents at NASA. Many of these threats were due to unauthorized devices on the network. Moreover, the audit found that security log tickets, which included applying a software patch or updating a system's configuration, sometimes went unresolved for more than six months.

This scenario shows a lack of proper device management policies and/or enforcement of such policies. It also shows that security incidents went months without appropriate resolution. Resolution of this scenario would require a substantial overhaul of security policies, audits, and enforcement within the organization.

Defense Data Stolen

Unauthorized access to data can sometimes have substantial national security implications. In 2018, it was reported that Chinese government-backed hackers had compromised the computers of a Navy contractor. They were able to steal a wide range of data, including antiship missile data and over 600 gigabytes of material on a project named "Sea Dragon."

This case is also an excellent example of a failure of policies. Although the data was all quite sensitive, it was stored on unclassified computers. This means that data classification policies were not being followed. This prompted the Pentagon's inspector general's office to begin reviewing contractor cybersecurity issues.

CHAPTER SUMMARY

This chapter examined the risk associated with the User domain, one of the seven domains of an IT infrastructure. As the number of users grows on the network, their diverse needs also grow. Security policies are a structured way of managing the user-related risks in this complex environment. The chapter reviewed the many different types of users and discussed unique roles such as administrator, security, and auditor. With these roles often come elevated privilege and enormous responsibilities.

Security policies are an effective way to reduce risks and govern users. They help identify the higher risk activities such as those performed by systems administrators. The policies are based on principles that help apply security consistently. These principles include core concepts such as least access privileges and best fit access privileges. The principles lay out risk choices and must strike a balance between cost to maintain and risks to control. In the end, security policies can educate users, reduce human error, and be used to better understand how incidents occurred.

KEY CONCEPTS AND TERMS

Best fit access privileges	Interactive	Spear phishing
Chain of custody	Least access privileges	Structured Query Language (SQL) injection
Contingent accounts	Log server	
Contractors	Phishing	Systems administrators
Firecall-ID process	Pretexting	Trouble ticket
Harden	Privileged-level access	Whaling
Insider	agreement (PAA)	
Integrated audit	Security personnel	

CHAPTER 9 ASSESSMENT

1. Pretexting is what happens when a hacker breaks into a firewall.

   A. True
   B. False

2. You can use a(n) _____ process to grant temporary elevated rights.

3. Security awareness is required by which of the following?

  A. Law
  B. Customers
  C. Shareholders
  D. All of the above

4. A(n) _____ looks at risk and issues an independent opinion.

5. A privileged-level access agreement (PAA) prevents an administrator from abusing elevated rights.

  A. True
  B. False

6. Which of the following does an acceptable use policy relate to?

  A. Server-to-server communication
  B. Users accessing the Internet
  C. Encryption when transmitting files
  D. A and B

7. A(n) _____ has inside information on how an organization operates.

8. Social engineering occurs when a hacker posts his or her victories on a social website.

  A. True
  B. False

9. In large organizations, all administrators typically have the same level of authority.

  A. True
  B. False

10. A CISO must _____ risks if the business unit is not responsive.

11. What is the difference between least access privileges and best fit access privileges?

  A. Least access privileges customize access to an individual.
  B. Best fit privileges customize access to a group based on risk.
  C. There is no difference.
  D. A and B

12. System accounts are also referred to as _____ accounts.

13. An interactive service account typically does not have a password.

  A. True
  B. False

IT Infrastructure Security Policies

NFORMATION TECHNOLOGY (IT) infrastructure security policies are represented in many types of policy documents, depending on the organization's network and infrastructure needs. For example, a national telecommunications company's network policies will look different from those of a regional retailer. These differences stem from different cybersecurity risks. They also present organizations with different choices to define and make in their security policies.

However, as much as organizations differ in size and mission, all networks must provide layers of security—from the perimeter through the network layers to, ultimately, the data being accessed. Information security professionals must understand well these common IT infrastructure needs and policies. If you do understand these foundational policy concepts and focus areas, you'll be able to navigate infrastructure policy documents, regardless of how they are organized.

The key purpose of infrastructure security policies is to provide technical knowledge of:

- The interaction among various layers of the network
- The placement of key controls
- The types of risks that will be detected and guarded against

It's important to understand the interactions of these infrastructure layers. The interactions of network layers provide an end-to-end view of infrastructure security. This understanding ensures that the impact of changes to the infrastructure will be well understood and well coordinated. This includes coordination of changes. For example, policies ensure that network and database administrators coordinate activities when a new database server is added to the network. The technical aspect ensures that devices collectively protect data as it flows from one device to another.

Additionally, infrastructure policies ensure that remote access, network, and authentication policies act collectively. Taking this end-to-end view ensures that controls are in place to protect data at rest (in storage) as well as data in transit—as when data passing from an employee's home is encrypted through a virtual private network firewall and securely routed to an internal database server at the organization's headquarters or at some other data center.

This chapter discusses common IT infrastructure policies. It's not possible in one chapter, or even in one book, to cover all the possible security policies an organization needs. So, this chapter illustrates key points by selectively discussing some policies in more detail. The intent is to create an understanding of an IT infrastructure policy's basic structure. In addition, the chapter discusses the most common security policies that relate to different infrastructure domains.

Chapter 10 Topics

This chapter covers the following topics and concepts:

- What the basic anatomy of an infrastructure policy is
- What common Workstation domain policies are
- What common mobile device policies are
- What common LAN domain policies are
- What common LAN-to-WAN domain policies are
- What common WAN domain policies are
- What common Remote Access domain policies are
- What common System/Application domain policies are
- What common telecommunication policies are related to the IT infrastructure
- What some IT infrastructure security policy best practices are
- What some common cloud security policy best practices are
- What some case studies and examples of IT infrastructure security policies are

Chapter 10 Goals

When you complete this chapter, you will be able to:

- Explain the basic anatomy of a policy
- Explain layered security and why it is important
- Understand types of security control requirements for IT infrastructure domains
- Identify the differences between core domain policy requirements
- Describe common policies by domain
- Describe best practices in creating and maintaining domain policies
- Use case study examples to explain how to use domain policies

Anatomy of an Infrastructure Policy

Individual security policies frequently look and feel alike. This makes them easy to read and understand. The challenge is how to organize policies as a collection. Policies need to be easily accessible and align to how an organization manages its IT environment.

There is no limit to the number of ways to organize collections of policies. Three common ways, though, are to organize by functional area, by layers of security, or by domain.

Of course, you don't have to utilize these methods, but they are easy to understand and logical.

Creating policies by functional area of responsibility is a challenge. The advantage of this method is that the policies can be tailored for a specific audience. The disadvantage is that functional areas may change due to organizational realignment. This means policies may have to change, too. Typically, organizing policies by functional area is the approach used in mature companies whose processes rarely change.

Creating policies by layers of security is also a challenge. A core principle in information security is the concept often referred to as *layers of security*, *layered security*, or *defense in depth*. Examples of layers are simple security controls placed within the network perimeter (a firewall), in an operating system (a server), in code (an application), and in secure storage

WARNING

No matter how good any single security control is in place today, you must assume it can and will be hacked at some point. There is someone, or some group, out there with enough time and resources to hack the control. This is why common security practice suggests multiple lines of defense, layers of security, or in-depth security, from the perimeter through the network layers to ultimately protecting the data.

(a database). Ideally, these controls collectively provide layered security. The challenge is that technology is constantly changing and evolving. Additionally, the number of layers depends on the company. For example, should telecommunications be considered a perimeter layer or its own layer? There is no one right answer or industry norm.

Defense in depth is not the only aspect of layered security. It is also important to have multiple controls for the same vulnerability. For example, if your concern is malware, antivirus is one control to mitigate that risk. Email usage policies are, too. External media (USB) policies will also aid in mitigating that risk. The goal is to have multiple, overlapping controls that address the same concern.

The third approach is to organize policies by domains. The seven domains of a typical IT infrastructure are shown in **FIGURE 10-1**. This is one logical way to view requirements and policies. The seven domains are a common taxonomy, or classification system, used across the industry. This taxonomy clearly illustrates how each domain can be used to create a layered security approach. For example, the Workstation domain may involve pirated software. The LAN domain can scan emails for viruses, while the Remote Access domain deals with virtual private network (VPN) tunnels. Different domains can have different security requirements.

The problem with organizing policies by domain is that many issues pertain to multiple domains. For example, virus control is a concern for workstations and servers. The requirements may vary a bit; however, the core need and control solutions are the same. There are few crisp bright lines between these domain areas.

Because there are no clearly drawn lines between domains, you need to ensure that requirements between the domains do not conflict. To give a simple example, a conflict could arise from requiring passwords of six characters on a workstation but eight characters on a server. This minor difference can make it difficult or impossible to implement a single sign-on solution. *Single sign-on* generally refers to the ability to authenticate once to get onto

NOTE

To keep the discussion at a high level, this chapter discusses policies as they align with a typical IT infrastructure. This allows for a discussion of domain requirements that drive policies. It does not mean this is the best way for every organization to organize its policies.

FIGURE 10-1

The seven domains of a typical IT infrastructure.

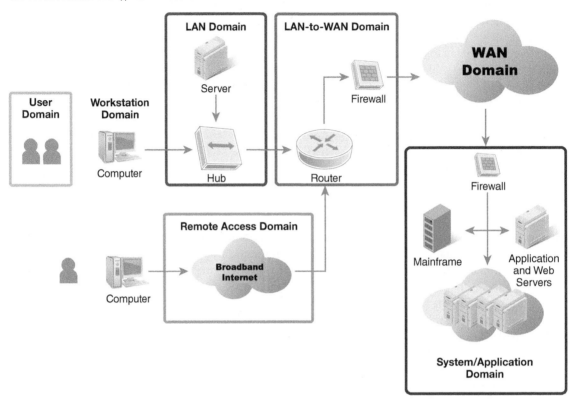

the network and then be automatically authenticated on different devices and applications after that.

A common approach is to organize policies to align with industry-standard frameworks. Examples of these frameworks include those provided by the International Organization for Standardization (ISO) and Control Objectives for Information and related Technology (COBIT). This is the most practical approach. First, many samples are easily accessible over the Internet. Second, once policies align with best practice frameworks, it becomes easier to demonstrate compliance to regulators. Industry-standard frameworks comply with regulations. By adopting the policies that use core concepts from these frameworks, you then demonstrate compliance.

The basic anatomy of a policy starts with understanding the different types of documents that capture the domain security control requirements. Five common documents are:

- **Control standards**—Policy documents describing core security control requirements
- **Baseline standards**—Technical documents describing security controls for a specific technology
- **Procedure documents**—Processes to implement control and baseline standards

- **Guidelines**—Optional documents that include parameters and recommended policies, standards, or procedures
- **A dictionary**—A common taxonomy used in the policies that defines the scope and meaning of terms used

Organizations use different terms to describe control standards. Some describe them as core *policy statements.* A baseline standard is also called a technology *minimum security baseline (MSB).* The key point is that policy documents make a distinction between core policy requirements and requirements unique to technology. For example, a core requirement may be to change passwords every 30 days. You might have two different baseline documents describing how to configure Microsoft and UNIX servers to achieve the core requirement.

The number of documents can also vary greatly between organizations. Some organizations combine related issues into a single policy document; for example, a workstation policy may combine preventing pirated software with virus protection requirements. Other organizations may treat this as two separate policy standards. The number of documents an organization uses depends on its need and capacity to deploy.

The goal is to develop a cohesive set of documents that do not require constant revisions to stay current and relevant. When there is overlap, reference the corresponding document rather than duplicating content. Here are a few common reasons why policy documents vary from one organization to another:

- Organizations use unique sets of technical tools and hardware.
- Risk management practices are often customized to an organization.
- The size of IT departments varies according to business needs.

Format of a Standard

Typically, standard and process documents have a well-defined format. A common format includes the following sections:

- **Document Number**—Uniquely identifies the document and usually categorizes the document as a policy, standard, or procedure, or as guidance
- **Title**—Identifies the topic of the document
- **Version/Date**—Identifies the version and date of the document
- **Purpose**—Provides measurable objectives and goals
- **Background**—Explains why the standard was put in place
- **Standard/Process**—Describes the standard or process to be implemented
- **Roles and Responsibilities**—Identifies who is responsible for implementation and adherence
- **Effective Dates**—States when the standard must be implemented
- **Information and Assistance**—Defines teams within the organization that can explain the standard and assist in coordinating its implementation
- **Approval**—Specifies the approving authority; this can be either an individual executive or a group of individuals such as a standards committee
- **Associated Resources**—Provides any related resources

The exact format may vary among organizations. For example, some organizations may describe whom the standard affects in a separate scope section. In the example listed, this is bundled under Roles and Responsibilities. Other possible sections are Revision History, Key Terms, and Supporting Attachments. The format varies by need and source of material.

Often, samples of policy templates are based on industry-standard frameworks or vendor-supplied samples. These samples usually define the initial format. The format changes over time to adapt to an organization's individual needs.

Standards need to be highly structured to be understood quickly. It is common for an individual to scan a dozen standards looking for a particular piece of information such as scope or responsibility. A well-defined format will allow that individual to quickly sort through a large amount of data and focus on information of interest. Online tools can help make the collection of documents more manageable and searchable. Use online collaboration tools such as Microsoft SharePoint. Many of these tools come out of the box as preconfigured and searchable document libraries.

> **TIP**
>
> It's important to use a consolidated calendar to track the dates when new policies and policy changes take effect. Organizations can have large numbers of policy changes taking effect each month. Having a calendar that is reviewed by stakeholders every month works well to prepare for policy implementation. For example, it helps the developers know what further changes are needed to support the implementation of a new policy.

Workstation Domain Policies

Workstation domain policies relate to any computing device used by an end user. Devices are often a user's desktop or laptop computer. A *workstation* can be any user device that accesses data, such as a smartphone.

These devices might not be operating within a protected office or data center. Encryption is a common method used to protect workstations, laptops, and other devices. By encrypting a device's hard drive, you protect the data, even if the device is lost or stolen. The encryption approach unencrypts the data when the device validates the user's credentials, such as a user ID and password. If the device is lost or stolen and the wrong credentials are entered, the device can then wipe out its data. If someone scans the hard drive without logging in to the device, the data remains encrypted and protected. For some devices, a signal can be sent to the device to wipe its data in the event the device is lost or stolen.

Mobile devices, by their nature, are distributed. This means policies need to address unique monitoring and patching challenges in a distributed environment. How you connect, monitor, and patch a mobile device is a different challenge than doing the same from a desktop in an office or a server in a data center. These challenges are covered in more detail in the next section.

Control Standards

Control standards for workstations establish core security requirements to harden these devices. The standards define how to manage the devices in a distributed environment, and they need to clearly communicate what responsibilities users have versus the responsibilities central administrators have. Workstation policies are often aligned to functional responsibilities.

A Malicious Code Protection standard, for example, is a central responsibility. The standard tries to keep a workstation free from viruses and other malware. The policy is a preventive and detective control. It tries to prevent an infection by installing scanning software. It also requires the user to detect and report symptoms of an infection. Examples of some control statements in this type of policy are as follows:

- Anti-malware software must be used on all devices connected to the organization's network. IT staff is responsible for ensuring that all devices have an approved version of anti-malware software installed. They are also responsible for ensuring a mechanism is in place to keep malware definitions current.
- No executable software, regardless of the source, may knowingly be installed without prior IT staff approval.
- IT staff must verify that all software is free of malicious code before installation.
- Users must not intentionally disable anti-malware software without prior approval.
- IT staff must scan data that will be transferred from the organization's network to a customer. Scanning must indicate that the data is free of malicious code before the transfer may occur.

The Malicious Code Standard is a good example of a policy that protects devices. **TABLE 10-1** outlines other workstation-related control standards. This is not an exhaustive list. This table depicts common control standards that focus on protecting and managing workstation devices. Notice the sheer breadth of policies required to properly secure a workstation.

Baseline Standards

With core policies defined, the focus then turns to how to configure the devices. Baseline standards provide the specific technology requirements for each device. IT staff use documented procedures to implement baseline standards. These configurations by devices ensure the following:

- Secure connectivity for remote devices
- Virus and malware protection
- Patch management capability
- Backup and recovery
- Hardening of the device
- Encryption of the hard drive as needed

This is not an exhaustive list; however, it does depict the configuration considerations for each workstation. This is especially important given the distributed nature of workstations.

You can find a variety of these baseline standards from different organizations around the world. The Center for Internet Security (CIS) offers Security Configuration Benchmarks. These benchmarks include examples for the private sector, government agencies, and

TABLE 10-1 Additional Types of Workstation Domain Control Standards

TYPE OF CONTROL STANDARD	DESCRIPTION
Access control for portable and mobile systems	Establishes restrictions for employer-owned portable and mobile workstations such as laptops and tablets
Acquisitions	Describes security controls for acquiring new devices. This standard might include minimum hardware requirements for security such as cryptographic co-processors.
Configuration management control	Defines the requirements for approving changes to a workstation. This includes configuration and patch management.
Device identification and authentication	Defines how the network identity of the devices will be established.
Session lock	Defines the requirements to prevent access to the workstation after a defined period of inactivity. The session lock remains in effect until the user reauthenticates to the workstation.
Software use	Describes installation of software on workstations. Also describes methods to protect the organization from unapproved software being installed. This usually includes who can install software and the process for approving new software.
System use notification	Describes the onscreen display of system notification messages. This is common to establish a legal notice that you are accessing a protected system. Examples of messages are: • You are accessing an organization-owned workstation. • System usage may be monitored and recorded, and is subject to audit. • Unauthorized use of the system is prohibited and subject to criminal and civil penalties.
Unsuccessful logon attempts	Defines a limit on the number of consecutive invalid access attempts such as three failed logons within 10 minutes per user. Also describes actions the workstation will take when the limit is exceeded, such as locking the account.
Disposal	Describes the proper method of disposing of workstation assets. This includes the wiping of the hard drive and disposal of the physical machine.
Bring your own device (BYOD)	Defines which (if any) personal devices employees are allowed to use to store and access company data. Some companies prohibit using personal devices to access company data. When a company does allow a personal device, it's often the individual's own smartphone, used to access company emails. This will be discussed in more detail in the following section.

educational institutions. You can download the benchmarks from *http://cisecurity.org/en-us/?route=downloads.benchmarks*. CIS also offers auditing tools to its members to assess compliance with these benchmarks.

The following are examples of baseline documents you may need to prepare:

* Host hardening standards for each workstation product family, such as Microsoft Windows, UNIX, Mac OS, and smartphones
* Virus scanner configuration standards
* Patch management agent standards
* Automated backup standards for workstations
* Wireless security standards

Procedures

For each baseline standard, you need a related procedure document. That does not mean every device configuration requires a unique procedure. Many of these configuration activities reuse the same procedure. The key to these procedures is to ensure that the administrators know how to access and apply the baseline configuration. If the tools and methods are substantially different, the process may be unique enough to require its own procedure.

Technical TIP

Monitoring is important whenever baseline standards are implemented. Once configuration baselines are applied, you need to ensure these controls stay in place. One way to achieve this is through monitoring software. Many packages are on the market. Some take a snapshot or signature of the baseline configuration. This monitoring software can detect when devices that are not compliant with the baseline are added to the network or when the baseline security configuration has been changed.

An example of a procedure is a configuration procedure for workstations. This procedure provides the explicit settings for configuration files such as registries. This process might cover Windows, UNIX, Mac OS, and other desktop operating systems.

Guidelines

Guidelines for implementing control standards are useful to planners and managers. It's important to understand the difference between a *guideline* and a *standard*. A guideline is a strong recommendation. A standard is a required control. A guideline recognizes that there are many acceptable ways to approach a problem, but provides one approach considered acceptable to the organization. The following guideline documents are useful when dealing with workstations:

- **Acquisition Guidelines**—Recommendations for sources to acquire new workstations, such as preferred vendors.
- **Guidelines on Active Content and Mobile Code**—Describe the threats and countermeasures over **active content**. These include a discussion on mobile code such as JavaScript and ActiveX controls. Furthermore, they describe the security expectations for the development or use of such code.

Mobile Device Domain Policies

In the previous section, we briefly mentioned mobile devices; however, the use of mobile devices in the workplace is growing and is deserving of more detailed consideration. Mobile devices are part of our lives. Smartphones are the obvious example; however, there are other devices, including smartwatches and tablets. Many people use these devices as an integral part of their daily lives, and they bring them to work. How do you address this on an organizational network? Many questions arise, beginning with whether to allow personal devices to connect.

In most organizations. it is simply impractical to forbid personal devices. Some highly secure defense-related organizations can do this, but for most companies, you will simply have to accept that your employees are likely to be carrying personal devices. These devices pose substantial security risks. They present an entirely new attack vector. These issues must be addressed.

The first issue is defining how these devices can be integrated into the organization. Some established terms accomplish this:

- **Bring your own device (BYOD)**—This is a scenario in which employees bring whatever device they may have purchased and can connect, at least to a guest network. This poses the greatest security risk, but it is quite common.
- **Choose your own device (CYOD)**—This is a situation wherein the organization provides a list of approved devices. If the employee purchases a device from that list, then they can attach the device to the organizational network. This provides some level of security. The company at least knows the device meets minimum security requirements.
- **Company-owned and personally enabled (COPE)**—This is an approach wherein the company provides personal devices, most often phones, to employees who can then also utilize the devices for personal use. This poses the most direct security, because the company has a high degree of control over the device's security. However, when the employee exits, parsing the employee's personal data from company data can be problematic.

There are several approaches that can further mitigate security risks, regardless of the approach implemented. The first is Network Access Control (NAC). NAC functions by scanning a device when it first connects. This scan looks to see if the device meets minimum security requirements and has no obvious malware on it. This can be done in either an agentless or agent manner. The agent approach installs a small software agent on the device in order to scan. This is far more effective, but some people object to the agent being installed.

Another approach is to allow devices to connect to only a guest network, not the corporate network. In this way, the employee still can use the networked device, but it poses far less of a threat to the organization's network. There is still a threat, but no more than from any guest accessing the guest network.

When it comes to mobile devices, one solution doesn't fit all. With mobile devices being so ubiquitous, network security professionals must address them. As with any security issue, an objective threat assessment must be conducted, risks analyzed, and only then can appropriate policies be implemented and enforced.

LAN Domain Policies

The LAN domain refers to the organization's local area network (LAN) infrastructure. A LAN allows two or more computers to connect within a small physical area. The small area can be a home, office, or group of buildings.

LAN security policies focus on connectivity, such as defining how devices attach to the network. The policies also define how to control traffic, such as through segmentation and router filtering.

LAN configuration issues are similar to those for workstations. The primary difference is administration. The LAN domain is often centralized to a small group of network administrators. This means devices are less distributed and are under tighter control.

> **NOTE**
>
> The same individuals who use network policies often write them. This is an advantage because it reduces training and interpretation errors.

Control Standards

Control standards for the LAN domain address a wide array of connectivity issues such as firewall controls, denial of service (DoS) protection, and Wi-Fi security control. Wireless connectivity is also a part of the Workstation domain. This is a good example of a cross-domain security issue. It also underscores the importance of configuring workstations and servers to protect data as it leaves a workstation and travels on a network.

A firewall control standard, for example, describes how LAN firewalls handle network traffic. This kind of traffic filtering includes web, email, and Telnet traffic. The standard describes how to manage and update the firewall. The following are examples of statements adapted from the National Institute of Standards and Technology (NIST) Special Publication 800-41, "Guidelines on Firewalls and Firewall Policy":

The firewall must always block the following types of traffic:

- Inbound traffic from a nonauthenticated system with a destination address of the firewall system. This type of packet usually represents a probe or attack against the firewall.
- Inbound traffic with a source address indicating that the packet originated on a network behind the firewall. This type of packet may represent a spoofing attempt.
- Inbound traffic containing Internet Control Message Protocol (ICMP) traffic. An attacker can use ICMP traffic to map the networks behind some firewalls. Therefore, ICMP traffic should not be allowed from the Internet or any untrusted external network.

FYI

Two terms often used when describing firewalls are *stateful* and *stateless*. A **stateful firewall** watches all the traffic for a given connection. It inspects the packets containing the data and looks for patterns and sequences that don't make sense. This is useful for blocking packets from someone pretending to be someone else in an attempt to hijack your session. A **stateless firewall** looks at each packet independently. It is not aware of what came before and does not try to predict what should come next. It restricts and blocks traffic based on source and destination addresses or other static values. A stateless firewall uses simple rules that do not account for the possibility that a packet might be received by the firewall "pretending" to be something it's not.

Stateless firewalls seldom exist anymore. Even the free firewall that comes with Windows 10 is a stateful packet inspection (SPI) firewall. Most firewalls today are stateful. In fact, many also include even more advanced features such as application firewalls. An application firewall includes additional features to protect a specific application. The classic example is a web application firewall (WAF). A WAF still conducts stateful packet inspection, but it also has specific countermeasures for common web attacks, such as SQL injection and cross-site scripting. Cross-site scripting is often referred to as XSS.

In this example, ICMP represents a protocol within the Internet Protocol (IP). This protocol does not carry data but does carry information about the network. A simple ping command echoes back network information. It is an example of an ICMP.

A DoS protection standard describes controls that protect against or limit the effects of DoS attacks. This standard attempts to prevent using the organization's network as a launching point against another network. Here is an example of control statements from this type of standard:

- Configure routers and firewalls to forward IP packets only if those packets have the correct source IP address for the organization's network.
- Configure access control lists (ACLs) on routers to allow only the traffic you want.
- Only allow packets to leave the network with valid source IP addresses that belong to the organization's network. This will minimize the chance that the organization's network will be the source of a DoS attack.

The firewall and DoS examples illustrate how technical LAN security requirements can be established. These are high-level examples. In the real world, LAN policies are usually long and detailed. **TABLE 10-2** contains additional examples of LAN control standards.

Table 10-2 mentions the term *audit* several times. An **audit** is the act of recording relevant security events that occur on a computing or network device. Why are audits so important? Any security-relevant event needs to be written to a log. Qualified personnel review these logs to determine if a security problem has occurred. These individuals determine who, what, where, and when activity caused the problem. Audit logs determine compliance issues, hardware misconfiguration errors, and application software security problems. They are useful in reconstructing actions that took place during a security incident. Audit logs should be well protected and only accessed by those people authorized by management.

TABLE 10-2 Additional Types of LAN Domain Control Standards

TYPE OF CONTROL STANDARD	DESCRIPTION
Audit events	Describes important events that must be audited and reported, such as breaches to routers, firewalls, and servers
Configuration change control	Describes the change control management process for requesting, approving, and implementing changes on the network
Controlled maintenance	Defines the schedules on LAN-attached devices for routine preventative and regular maintenance
Controls over media	Defines protection, access to media, labeling, storage, transport, sanitization, and disposal
Device identification and authentication	Describes the security requirements for identifying LAN-attached devices for authentication, routing, and filtering
Intrusion detection and prevention	Describes the requirements for host- and network-based intrusion detection and prevention tools
Protection of audit information	Describes the controls needed to protect audit information and tools from unauthorized access, modification, disablement, and deletion
Router security controls	Describes minimal security configuration for all routers and switches
Security assessments	Describes the need to conduct assessments of the security controls in the LAN. These assessments determine the extent to which controls are implemented correctly, operating as intended, and producing the desired outcome
Segmentation	Defines when and how a network is to be partitioned. It also describes how the network traffic is to be controlled passing through the separate network parts (that is, access control between network segments)
Trusted timestamps	Describes the need for trusted timestamps and timeservers for audit record generation, such as Network Time Protocol
Wi-Fi security controls	Defines the authorized uses of Wi-Fi on organization property

Baseline Standards

Two key areas of LAN domain controls are connectivity and controlling network traffic. Baseline standards are particularly important because they establish connectivity between devices. This connectivity is important to ensure data protection in transit. To accomplish this, configure each device with an identity and method of authenticating network traffic it receives. This is no small task given the volume of network traffic generated. The network typically contains mixed traffic, such as sensitive business transactions; routine user-related transactions; and, potentially, hacker traffic. Separating business and routine user transactions depends on properly configuring network devices. These transactions do not attempt to be in conflict and thus are reasonably easy to identify and separate.

A greater challenge is how to configure devices to ensure hackers cannot masquerade as valid transactions. Another concern is hackers monitoring sensitive transactions in the clear. A hacker can configure a network card to "promiscuous mode." When a network card is in promiscuous mode, it captures all the network traffic on a segment. Normally, a network card only captures traffic addressed to its device. In other words, a device in promiscuous mode allows you to listen to all the traffic messages between every device on the segment. With this information, a hacker can create his or her own messages in an attempt to masquerade as valid sensitive transactions.

Network segmentation can be an effective control for limiting traffic and thus help keep hackers out. Network segmentation involves isolating (or segmenting) parts of the network from other parts. This can be achieved in many ways, including adding access lists to routers that limit traffic between segments. Think of it as doors in a house. Suppose you host a graduation party in your home. Half the guests are people you don't know. You might think about locking your bedroom door. You have segmented that room from the rest of the house.

> **NOTE**
>
> To understand policies within a domain, you need a basic understanding of the related technical issues. For example, in the LAN domain, you need a basic understanding of network protocols. You need to understand how to route and filter network traffic. You must also understand the TCP/IP suite.

You can do the same thing with a network. For example, you might choose to segment your network into production and development systems. You might choose to further segment production into product systems, credit card systems, and internal financial systems. The number of network segments you create depends on the level of security you want to achieve.

Another important concern of baseline LAN standards is network traffic monitoring. Regardless of how good firewalls and routers are, they have their limitations. These devices prevent attacks against known and predicted threats. Intrusion systems provide a broad range of protection. They look for patterns of attack. Just as a virus scanner looks for patterns to indicate a file has become infected, an intrusion system looks for network traffic patterns to detect a network attack. An intrusion system can be detective or preventive. An **intrusion detection system (IDS)** recognizes a network attack and sends an alert. An **intrusion prevention system (IPS)** recognizes a network attack, stops the attack, and sends an alert. Audit logs also play an important role in monitoring network traffic. Configuring devices to generate logs about network events helps you to determine later what occurred during an attack.

> **NOTE**
>
> Baseline standards determine how to monitor network traffic. It is important to log network traffic during an event. Use of network IDS or IPS systems is also highly advisable.

The following are examples of baseline standards that configure devices to address connectivity and monitoring activity:

- **Wi-Fi Access Point (AP) Security Standard**—Defines secure wireless connectivity to a network
- **Intrusion Detection System (IDS) and Intrusion Prevention System (IPS) Standard**—Defines configuration of intrusion monitoring for the network
- **Baseline OS Configuration(s) Standard**—Defines hardening of servers, including server authentication and communication protocol
- **Remote Maintenance Standard**—Defines secure connectivity to devices for remote administration

- **Audit Storage and Records Standard**—Defines configuration of auditing tools and logs to record network events
- **Firewall Baseline Security Standard**—Defines configuration of network filters by firewall, version, and manufacturer type
- **Router Baseline Security Standard**—Defines configuration of network filters by router, version, and manufacturer type
- **Server Baseline Configuration(s)**—Defines configuration of servers to support network connectivity such as Dynamic Host Configuration Protocol (DHCP) and authentication protocols

Procedures

Many of the same procedure issues exist between domains, such as configuration and patch management. There is a greater emphasis in the LAN domain on detecting and responding to network attacks. An attack on a workstation is isolated. An attack on the network threatens the entire organization. You can see this difference reflected in several network procedures, as follows:

- **Response to Audit Processing Failures**—Procedure to respond to failure of network monitoring and audit tools such as logs filling up
- **Firewall Port/Protocol Alerts**—Procedure to respond to security alerts, such as the time frame for responses and escalation paths
- **Monitoring Wi-Fi APs**—Procedure for configuring and monitoring Wi-Fi access points
- **Audit Record Retention**—Procedure for preserving audit records

Guidelines

The number of threats against a network can be substantial. The ability to assess these threats takes a combination of technical knowledge and experience. Guidelines can transfer that experience and knowledge by walking an individual through core principles and different ways to look at LAN risks.

These guidelines are useful to planners, systems administrators, network administrators, and their managers. These individuals must assess LAN threats and build appropriate countermeasures. The following guidelines illustrate this point:

- **Security Assessments Guidelines**—Provide guidance on how security assessments should be conducted, how to rate threats, and how to escalate resolution
- **Firewall Architecture and Management Guidelines**—Provide guidance on firewall architectures and their use
- **Router Architecture and Management Guidelines**—Provide guidance on router types and architectures and their use
- **IDS and IPS Architecture and Management Guidelines**—Provide guidance on IDS and IPS architectures and types and their use to reduce false alerts
- **Wi-Fi Security Guidelines**—Provide information on Wi-Fi systems architectures and types and when they should be used

LAN-to-WAN Domain Policies

The LAN-to-WAN domain refers to the technical infrastructure that connects an organization's LAN to a wide area network (WAN). The main concern is controlling network traffic between the outside network, or the WAN, and the private network, or the LAN. The LAN-to-WAN domain denotes, for many organizations, its connection to the Internet. This connection represents significant risk. LAN-to-WAN security standards often focus on how to configure devices to maintain message and transaction integrity. Establishing secure point-to-point communications is an important part of the connectivity through the Internet. The Internet should *never* have a direct connection to the organization's private network without the traffic being heavily filtered and inspected.

An important policy concern is how to filter traffic between the Internet and the internal network. Additionally, many organizations have an Internet presence. This has the additional challenge of serving content on the Internet to customers and businesses. These public-facing websites often provide access to internal resources such as databases for product information. As a result, they are a prime target for hackers.

The LAN-to-WAN key standards define the security requirements to harden Internet-facing servers, filter traffic between these networks, and monitor for breaches in security. Although there are other policy requirements, such as defining what data the public can access, these standards generally represent core requirements.

> **NOTE**
>
> An Internet proxy is a server that acts as an intermediary between users and the Internet. The server receives requests and responses and filters unwanted traffic.

Control Standards

The industry has well-defined standards that require access control to the Internet. As such, the standards tend to be specific about technologies and architecture choices. For example, these standards often require the use of an Internet proxy and specific demilitarized zone (DMZ) architecture.

A content filtering standard can be an effective method of reducing malware attacks. This is achieved by blocking sites known to have malware. This also means blocking sites employees may wish to access. In short, a content filtering standard describes which websites an employee is allowed to access from a company-owned device. The purpose and objective of the filtering needs to be well explained to gain employee support. The standard typically will not list specific sites, but rather types of sites, such as email, gambling, adult material, or political activist websites.

Here are several additional examples of policies that deal with LAN-to-WAN connectivity and filtering:

- **External Information System Services Connect Standard**—Requires that providers of external services establish a secure connection. This standard applies to all external parties such as business partners and outsourced providers. It also establishes service level agreements and sets forth how to measure and report security control compliance.
- **DMZ Control Standard**—Establishes the controls for publicly accessible devices to place them in a DMZ. DMZs are critical because, by definition, outside users can access them rather easily.

- **User Internet Proxy Standard**—Establishes controls for using an Internet access proxy (a **user proxy**) for all inbound and outbound Internet traffic.

Baseline Standards

A LAN-to-WAN domain baseline standard focuses on perimeter devices that separate the WAN from the LAN. The following are some examples:

- **Content-Blocking Tools Configuration Standard**—Requirements that describe what types of web content should be blocked and how updates are approved. Most organizations have at least some content they should block.
- **Intrusion Detection and Prevention Tools Configuration Standard**—Requirements for each product with particular emphasis on those places in the DMZ. Keep in mind that IDS/IPS can also be used within the network, as well as in the DMZ.
- **Proxy Server Configuration Standard**—Requirements for maintaining the **access control list (ACL)** for the device that controls access to the Internet from the LAN.
- **Firewall Configuration Standard**—Describes DMZ and firewall architecture.

Procedures

Many of the same procedures' issues exist between domains such as configuration and patch management. In the case of WAN-to-LAN connectivity, there is a greater emphasis on managing changes and detecting and responding to network attacks. For example, you can view the DMZ as the "front door" to your private network. Changes to configuration in this domain can have a serious impact on the publicly facing website or the ability to prevent an intrusion. It is not uncommon to see procedures in this domain require senior-level approval and extensive testing before changes are applied.

Guidelines

Guidelines in this domain are useful for individuals who must determine how much Internet access should be permitted. Controls and baselines create crisp lines on minimum standards. The guidelines establish additional choices while balancing the additional risk. The following guideline documents are examples:

- **DMZ Guidelines**—Recommend additional services to be placed in the DMZ and, depending on those services, additional security requirements
- **Intrusion Detection and Prevention Systems Guidelines**—Recommend how to design an IDS system of sensors, collection stations, and alert mechanisms to eliminate or reduce false positives
- **Content-Filtering Guidelines**—Recommend content-filtering options, ways to maintain the list of banned sites, and ways to request access to blocked sites when needed

NOTE

LAN policies are also a good place to consider digital rights management (DRM). You want to ensure policies take steps to avoid both copyright infringement and your organization's own confidential data being exfiltrated.

10

WAN Domain Policies

A WAN is a network that covers a large geographical area. The Internet is an example of a WAN. A private WAN can be built for a specific organization to link offices across the country or globally. These types of WANs are constructed using dedicated leased lines, satellites, and/or microwave communications.

Typically, the LAN-to-WAN domain addresses many of the WAN connectivity standards. As a result, this domain's standards tend to focus primarily on the WAN build-out and supporting components. Some organizations may not have any WAN-specific standards or policies. This is because many of the topics are often included in other domains.

Control Standards

When you do see WAN-specific standards, they address WAN management, Domain Name System (DNS), router security, protocols, and web services. The standards might call out specific security requirements for WAN devices such as routers, switches, and wireless devices.

A WAN controls standard might include the following statements:

- The IS department shall approve all access points to the WAN.
- The IS department shall approve all physical and logical connections to the WAN that provide access to individuals or groups.
- The IS department shall approve all WAN-related address changes and configurations.
- Employees who plan to connect to the organization's network must first sign an agreement to abide by the requirements outlined in the WAN Security Standard.

The business executive is often disconnected from the details of security management and any substantive discussion of the WAN. These more technical discussions have been limited in the past to a small group of skilled and technically savvy professionals. However, the increase in security breaches has gotten management's attention. As threats become more prevalent and the infrastructure more complex, a data-level discussion has emerged within the business. "Where is my data?" is the question more and more executives are asking. This question impacts all domains, including the WAN domain. Increasingly, WAN domain policies will include what data may be sent outside the organization's private network. The WAN standards–related questions include:

- What types of connections are required?
- What types of data are allowed to use these connections?
- Who can authorize the creation of a WAN connection?
- Who can authorize the permit to send data outside the network?

Others standards related to the WAN domain may include:

- **WAN Router Security Standard**—Describes the family of controls needed to secure the connection from the WAN router to the internal network.

 NOTE

Enterprise data management (EDM) deals with how to create, integrate, secure, disseminate, and manage data across the enterprise. Larger organizations tend to deal with management of data as its own discipline, cutting across all domains. These organizations may have a dedicated EDM team.

- **Web Services Standard**—Describes which controls are needed for use of **web services** from external partnerships and suppliers. This may include the use of web services security (Security Assertion Markup Language [SAML], Extensible Markup Language [XML] message integrity and confidentiality) and controls over the web services gateway device(s).

Baseline Standards

The lines between baseline and control standards can blur in the WAN domain. The reason is that the topics tend to focus on specific technology solutions such as routers, protocols, and web services. Many organizations tend to focus on a small set of network vendors such as Cisco Systems or Juniper Networks. Because the standards are often written with these technologies in mind, you can find a convergence of control and baseline standards in one document versus two.

Procedures

Procedures in this domain tend to focus on configuration and maintenance of the WAN. This may include specific configuration procedures for WAN devices such as routers and firewalls.

These procedures track closely to change management procedures found in the LAN-to-WAN domain. For most organizations, the network team working on the LAN will be the same network team working on the WAN. As a result, you find the same procedures being used for LANs and WANs.

The Domain Name System (DNS) is the commonly used method of assigning meaningful website names on the Internet. It can also be used to assign meaningful names to any device on a private or public network. Conceptually, think of it as the difference between going to 123 Main St. and going to John's house. In the Internet world, all devices have IP addresses (i.e., 123 Main St.), but it's much easier and faster to remember a DNS name assigned to a website (i.e., John's house). A DNS control procedure might be included in the WAN standard. This standard describes the requirements for obtaining and assigning a domain name for use by external parties. Approvals can be used to track domains and often include:

- An explanation of how the domain will be used
- A justification for using a new domain name
- The server name and IP address where the DNS will be registered
- Information on who will administer the domain name
- The date of last vulnerability scan on the targeted server(s)

Guidelines

Web services are an example of a WAN guideline. It describes when and how web services may be used. DNS management guidelines are another example that offers recommendations on the use of DNS within the LAN and WAN environments.

Remote Access Domain Policies

The Remote Access domain refers to the technology that controls how end users connect to an organization's LAN remotely. An example is someone needing to connect to the office network from his or her home or on the road.

Security standards in this domain focus on remote user authentication and secure connections. Creating a remote computing environment that is secure is a challenge. Beyond authentication and connectivity, you need to secure the remote device. Some standards require all remote users to use employer-owned laptops. This allows the organization to control the remote device itself. These types of business choices drive what standards you see in this domain.

Control Standards

The Remote Access domain standards include standards related to VPN connections and multifactor authentication. For example, a virtual private network standard describes the security requirements for establishing an encrypted session. The following are examples of control statements you might find in this standard. They are adapted from the SANS Institute's "Virtual Private Network Policy" document:

- Employees with VPN privileges must not share their VPN credentials to the organization's internal networks with unauthorized users.
- VPN use must be controlled using one-time password authentication. This may include a token device or a public/private key system with a strong passphrase.
- VPN users will be automatically disconnected from the organization's network after 30 minutes of inactivity.

Other Remote Access domain policies include physical and technical standards. Physical standards might outline the policies for working from home. These policies might require users to lock up company documents at home and ban family members from access to company assets. Other technical security standards might include the need for two-factor authentication.

NOTE

RADIUS is a networking protocol for centralized authentication, authorization, and accounting (AAA) for computers to connect to and use a network service. RADIUS is often used by Internet service providers (ISPs) and organizations to manage access to networks. There are newer protocols like Terminal Access Controller Access Control System Plus (TACACS+) that might be better choices than RADIUS.

Baseline Standards

The control standards establish the broad requirements. Often in this domain, there are multiple technologies involved in establishing a secure connection with a remote user. Here are a few examples of standards that focus on configuration:

- **VPN Gateway Options and Requirements Standard**—Outlines the security configuration features for the specific VPN concentrators used by the organization
- **VPN Client Software Options and Requirements Standard**—Outlines the security configuration features for the specific VPN remote client software
- **RADIUS Server Security Requirements Standard**—Describes the security configuration of the Remote Authentication Dial In User Service (RADIUS)

Procedures

Procedures in this domain are useful to remote users and those responsible for supporting that environment. Because you have a diverse set of users remotely accessing your network from anywhere in the world, support procedures need to be clear and concise. One example is a VPN Configuration and Support Guide, which lists the configuration settings and steps to debug a VPN connection.

Guidelines

Guidelines for implementing control standards are useful to network administrators and access administrators who have responsibilities for remote access. These guidelines may outline various remote computing environments, such as working from home and methods of security. Remote Access domain guidelines often reinforce security awareness training.

System/Application Domain Policies

The System/Application domain refers to the technology and application software needed to collect, process, and store company data. This domain covers a broad range of topics from the systems that process information to data handling. It covers all the security issues associated with applications. Consequently, the types of standards in this domain are diverse.

The document collection in this domain can be quite large. There is a great deal of variation in applications. It's important that the collection be well organized. Here are a few examples of what should be considered in organizing the collection of System/Application domain policies:

- Types of technologies deployed
- Use of technologies, such as application servers versus database servers
- Authentication methods
- Authorization methods
- Testing requirements
- Transition applications from test to production
- Secure coding requirements

Control Standards

With such a diverse set of security issues, many of the standards within this domain focus on classifying assets and assigning accountability. Accountability includes who owns key decisions over the assets and who maintains the security controls. This distinction between the owner and custodian of assets is in many standards. The owner is generally considered the ultimate authority on the use of a resource or data. This means approving the resources and data that are used. A *custodian* is someone with daily operational control over the use of resources and data. The custodian is generally responsible for ensuring that proper approved processes are used to secure and handle the resources and data.

The Information Classification standard, for example, helps employees determine the classification of information. This type of control standard also helps you identify procedures to protect the confidentiality, integrity, and availability of data. The following are example control statements in an information classification standard:

> All the organization's employees and contractors share in the responsibility for ensuring that the organization's information assets receive an appropriate level of protection by observing this Information Classification policy:
>
> * Managers or information "owners" shall be responsible for assigning classifications to information assets according to the standard information classification system presented below.
> * Where practicable, the information category shall be embedded in the information itself.
> * All the organization's associates shall be guided by the information category in their security-related handling of the organization's information.

The Production Data for Testing control standard is an example of a policy dealing with data handling. This standard outlines the controls needed to prevent the use of production data for testing purposes. This standard may require that the data be sanitized or scrubbed before being used for testing.

Other standards related to the System/Application domain include those listed in **TABLE 10-3**.

Baseline Standards

The baseline standards in this domain deal with technology configurations and technical requirements. The following is a sampling of standards:

* **Public Key Infrastructure Certification Authority (CA) Standard**—Describes the public key infrastructure. Also describes how certificates are managed using CAs.
* **Approved Cryptographic Algorithms and Key Lengths Standard**—Describes the encryption algorithms and keys used, such as approved key lengths for symmetric and asymmetric cryptography.
* **Physical Security Baseline Standards**—Describe the physical security technologies deployed. Examples are badge readers, electronic locks, and cameras and other monitoring systems. Each technology needs a baseline standard to describe which features should be implemented for what purposes, and how to handle and manage the information generated by those devices.
* **Developer Coding Standards**—Describe how to write and test the security of applications.

Procedures

For each baseline technical standard, you may need to create a procedure document for administrators and developers to implement the control requirements. You could also have procedures for incident handling, monitoring, and reporting. Some organizations have procedures for using penetration-testing tools.

As with other domains, change management is an important procedure. In this particular domain, the project management life cycle (PMLC) plays a central role. The PMLC typically

TABLE 10-3 Additional Types of System/Application Domain Control Standards

TYPE OF CONTROL STANDARD	DESCRIPTION	EXAMPLES
Separation of environments	Establishes the need to separate the development environment from the production environment Outlines the rules and conditions for promoting application software between environments	Logical or physical access control Prohibition of compilers on production computers
Physical security control standards	Include a number of standards for physical security and data-center access controls	Physical access authorizations Physical access control Monitoring physical access Visitor control Access records Power equipment and power cabling Emergency power, lighting, and shutoff Fire protection Temperature and humidity controls Water damage protection Delivery and removal of assets
Developer-related standards	Specify secure coding and developer standards	Developer workstation and account configuration management—limits or grants the rights to developers to change their workstation configurations Developer security testing control requirements Secure coding standards, including published programming standards and developer training requirements Information accuracy, completeness, validity, and authenticity Malicious code protection Error handling
Authentication	Specifies the authentication method and identity store to be used	Applications may be required to use Active Directory (AD) to authenticate all access to networked devices.

10

outlines the procedures a team follows to implement an IT project, such as developing a new software application. The PMLC is a specific series of steps and procedures. These steps have safeguards that ensure the prior step's deliverables are complete.

Guidelines

With such a diverse set of security issues, the standards cannot define every situation. Guidelines are useful as education vehicles and for offering recommendations. For example, software developers might have guidelines for secure coding of .NET, Java, and other leading languages. The guidelines promote secure coding habits and educate developers on specific threats.

Telecommunications Policies

Telecommunications generally refers to any technology, service, or system that provides transmission of electronic data and information. Telecommunications may be wired or wireless. This includes voice and data networks; telephones, other wireless services; messaging and directory services; high-speed data communications; facsimile devices; personal digital assistants; tablets; network servers; switches; or any other device, service, or system used in the transmission of electronic communication. It's not surprising that such a broad topic crosses over into other domains that deal more with data connectivity. For the purposes of this chapter, the telecommunications discussion focuses on devices such as telephones, fax machines, modems, and smartphones.

Control Standards

An essential control standard in this category is Voice over IP (VoIP). These standards describe the security considerations and controls that apply to a VoIP network. Because of the ease of access to and prolific nature of VoIP connections, there are growing technology risks. The telephone system was once isolated within an organization. Now telephone service uses the same network as any other application. This expanded use of the network brings new security challenges and vulnerabilities. A VoIP standard describes countermeasures to prevent unnecessary risk and the compromising of corporate information.

The following are some control statements that might appear in this standard. They are adapted from the U.S. Federal Aviation Administration's "Voice Over Internet Protocol (VoIP) Security Policy" document:

> **NOTE**
>
> The key point of telecommunication standards is to define the protocols and devices to be used. Once defined, the standards address how to handle data on those devices. Remember, VoIP deals with digital information. These digital conversations can be captured, stored, and played back.

The integration of voice and data into a single physical network is a complex process that may introduce vulnerabilities and risk. To mitigate these risks, the following must be adhered to:

- VoIP systems and networks must adhere to a common security configuration recommended by the organization's security requirements.

* VoIP equipment used to transmit or discuss confidential or restricted information must be protected with FIPS 140-2 encryption standards.
* VoIP systems must follow security guidance on the segregation of data and voice networks.

Fax machine standards are another example of telecommunication policies. This standard outlines the controls necessary for the transmission and receipt of faxed information such as company confidential or restricted information.

> **⚠ WARNING**
>
> Securing the physical fax device is as important as security over a copier. Both have internal memory and may store the last documents printed. If these documents contain sensitive information, access to the physical machine must be controlled.

Baseline Standards

Telecommunications equipment and devices usually have specific technology requirements. The baseline standards focus on securing equipment and on configuration issues. Here are some examples of baseline standards:

* **Smartphone Enterprise Server Configuration Requirements Standard**—Describes security characteristics for the enterprise server that delivers corporate email to smartphones
* **Use of Bluetooth Communications Standard**—Describes controls for the use of Bluetooth technology on employer-issued mobile computing devices
* **VoIP Security Product Requirements Standard**—Documents security controls for specific VoIP equipment selected by the organization
* **Use of other wireless**—Today we have Z-Wave, Zigbee, ANT+, and other wireless protocols. There should be policies regarding the use of these protocols. They are quite common in smart devices.

Procedures

For each baseline technical standard, you may need to create a procedure document for telecommunications personnel to implement control requirements. Procedure documents might give details for reporting a lost or stolen employer-issued smartphone. Other procedure documents outline how to configure an employer-issued mobile device and VoIP product security.

Guidelines

Guidelines for implementing control standards are helpful to personnel who are responsible for the security of telecommunications devices and equipment. Consider using employer-issued mobile phone and other device security guidelines for employees and administrators. Some organizations also use VoIP systems architecture and security guidelines.

Best Practices for IT Infrastructure Security Policies

The volume of infrastructure policies can be quite large, depending on your organization's need. For example, the more diverse the technologies deployed, the greater the number of baseline standards required. It is important to define the requirements for standards in a methodical way.

10

IT Infrastructure Security Policies

This chapter discusses the requirements based on domains. More than one approach works. Many organizations first select a framework, such as ISO or COBIT. They then develop requirements and standards based on the framework.

Do not reinvent the wheel. There are rare instances where you will need to develop original content to create a new policy. More often, you modify an existing sample obtained from a reliable source. Before you create content for a specific topic, see what others have already done and adapt that work to your specific needs. Some sources for security policies and standards include the following:

- The U.S. government offers hundreds of standards through NIST.
- Private organizations, such as SANS, sell prewritten security policies.
- Professional associations offer security policy examples to their membership. Some associations are the Institute of Internal Auditors (IIA) and the Information Systems and Control Association (ISACA).
- Contact the vendors of your IT products to find out if they offer sample security policies.

Do not impose strict access controls on your policies and standards. Make them freely available to everyone expected to follow them. These documents reinforce security awareness messages.

Keep content cohesive. Although standard boilerplate security policies are easily accessible, they can conflict with one another. The conflicts can be at many levels, from approach to specific requirements. When developing a document, focus only on the subject it covers. Compare the content with related topics. If you need to refer to other topics contained in other documents, do not repeat the content. Simply reference the other related documents in the one you have developed. When it's finished, look at it as a complete end-to-end story of how to control risks. This end-to-end view allows you to adjust for inconsistencies and close gaps.

Keep content coherent. Maintain the same "voice" throughout a single document. Do not add more information than is necessary to convey the information. Do not stray from the message.

Make your library as searchable as possible. When implementing your policies, make it easy to locate relevant documents by indexing them with keywords and phrases.

Federate ownership to where it best belongs. Over time, you will find that nonsecurity personnel are adept at producing policy documents. This is especially true for creating procedures they use every day. If you work on building alliances with data center operators and administrators, you can often obtain their help in preparing policy documentation.

Cloud Security Policies

It is becoming increasingly common for organizations to move their data to the cloud. Cloud storage provides a great deal of convenience, and from a disaster recovery perspective, is extremely resilient. However, cloud storage is not without some security risks. Before we discuss cloud security policies, some basics on how clouds function will be necessary.

The term *cloud computing* was popularized when Amazon.com released Elastic Compute Cloud in 2006. Cloud computing uses servers distributed geographically. In some cases, the servers are in other countries. In February 2010, Microsoft released the Microsoft Azure cloud service. Amazon and Apple also provide cloud services for the general public. There are four general types of clouds:

- Public clouds are defined by the NIST as simply clouds that offer their infrastructure or services to either the general public or at least a large industry group.
- Private clouds are those clouds used specifically by a single organization without offering the services to an outside party. There are, of course, clouds that combine the elements of a private and public cloud. These are essentially private clouds that have some limited public access.
- Community clouds are systems wherein several organizations share a cloud for specific community needs. For example, several computer companies might join to create a cloud devoted to common security issues.
- Hybrid clouds, as the name suggests, are some mixture of two or more of these cloud approaches.

Clouds are essentially virtualization taken to a new level. You have probably used a virtual machine on a computer—perhaps VMWare Workstation or Oracle Virtual Box. All virtual systems are one of two types:

- **Type I: bare metal**—These systems are installed directly onto hardware. There is no need for an underlying operating system. The virtual system directly hosts virtual machines.
- **Type II: hosted**—These are virtual systems installed on top of an existing operating system. The aforementioned VMWare Workstation and Oracle Virtual Box are examples of this.

There are several categorizations of virtual systems, and these are often the ways in which people interact with cloud services:

- **Software as a Service (SaaS)**—NIST defines SaaS as "The capability provided to the consumer is to use the provider's applications running on a cloud infrastructure. The applications are accessible from various client devices through either a thin client interface, such as a web browser (e.g., web-based email), or a program interface. The consumer does not manage or control the underlying cloud infrastructure including network, servers, operating systems, storage, or even individual application capabilities, with the possible exception of limited user-specific application configuration settings."
- **Platform as a Service (PaaS)**—NIST defines PaaS as "The capability provided to the consumer is to deploy onto the cloud infrastructure consumer-created or acquired applications created using programming languages, libraries, services, and tools supported by the provider. The consumer does not manage or control the underlying cloud infrastructure including network, servers, operating systems, or storage, but has control over the deployed applications and possibly configuration settings for the application-hosting environment."
- **Infrastructure as a Service (IaaS)**—NIST defines IaaS as "where the consumer is able to deploy and run arbitrary software, which can include operating systems and applications. The consumer does not manage or control the underlying cloud infrastructure but has

control over operating systems, storage, and deployed applications; and possibly limited control of select networking components (e.g., host firewalls)."

Today there are many permutations of these, such as:

- Content as a Service (CaaS)
- Data as a Service (DaaS)
- Desktop as a Service (DaaS)
- Security as a Service (SaaS)

New acronyms are being generated quite regularly; however, they are all focused on the same concept: An underlying IT service is not being installed locally. It is instead virtualized, often via a cloud, and accessed in that manner.

There are some guidelines for cloud security. You don't have to start from nothing. ISO 27017 is guidance for cloud security. It does apply the guidance of ISO 27002 to the cloud, but then adds seven new controls.

- **CLD.6.3.1**—This control addresses agreement on shared or divided security responsibilities between the customer and cloud provider.
- **CLD.8.1.5**—This control addresses how assets are returned or removed from the cloud when the contract is terminated.
- **CLD.9.5.1**—This control states that the cloud provider must separate the customer's virtual environment from other customers or outside parties.
- **CLD.9.5.2**—This control states that the customer and the cloud provider both must ensure the virtual machines are hardened.
- **CLD.12.1.5**—This control states it is solely the customer's responsibility to define and manage administrative operations.
- **CLD.12.4.5**—This control states the cloud provider's capabilities must enable the customer to monitor their own cloud environment.
- **CLD.13.1.4**—This control states the virtual network environment must be configured so that it at least meets basic standards

ISO 27018 is closely related to ISO 27017. ISO 27018 defines privacy requirements in a cloud environment, particularly how the customer and cloud provider must protect personally identifiable information (PII). Regardless of which cloud service an organization uses (IaaS, PaaS, etc.), it is important that security policies are in place for handling cloud security.

Case Studies and Examples of IT Infrastructure Security Policies

The case studies in this section examine how industries and state governments develop and implement infrastructure security standards. These case studies illustrate the influence that industry standards have on internal infrastructure policies. These examples reference leading industry standards to create and implement internal policies. This approach is true for both private and public sector.

State Government Case Study

In 2019, a coordinated attack was launched against government agencies in the State of Texas. Twenty-three state government services were affected, including police departments. The attackers were seeking $2.5 million in ransom.

The first infrastructure issue to address is email. Ransomware is most often delivered as an email attachment. This ransomware was not detected by any of the agencies' email anti-virus programs. Furthermore, various individuals were willing to open the attachment, and thus infect the organization.

The particular ransomware encrypted the files and added a .JSE extension. It is generally referred to as the .JSE ransomware. This is not a currently known strain of ransomware; however, it was delivered to the systems using the Nemucod Trojan. Nemucod is a well-known Trojan. It typically is distributed as JavaScript embedded in a Zip file attached to an email. The emails are usually socially engineered to increase the likelihood of them being opened.

Some reports have indicated a common managed service provider may be the issue. Whether or not those preliminary reports ultimately are determined to be accurate, they do bring up a valid concern. When several organizations have a single point of contact, such as a managed service provider, that point of contact becomes a very enticing target.

There are several items that could have mitigated this attack:

- More effective policies regarding attachments.
- The common security concept of never trusting any data, regardless of environment, should have been applied to the managed service provider as a policy.
- Effective policies regarding employees recognizing social engineering. This can be accomplished by training.

This particular case study is important because all indicators show that ransomware is on the increase. In 2019, several cities in the United States were hit with ransomware attacks. Most analysts predict this will continue.

Public Sector Case Study

The State of Maryland initiative is an example of external influences on infrastructure security policies. The governor of Maryland created a "Best in the Nation Statewide Health Information Exchange and Electronic Health Records" initiative. The state created a statewide technology infrastructure to support the electronic exchange of health records. This infrastructure supports health service providers doing business in Maryland. The goal of the initiative is to reduce costs and improve the quality of patient treatment.

The Information Technology Support Division (ITSD) is the state's IT department. The Department of Health and Mental Hygiene (DHMH) was responsible for meeting the governor's health goals. ITSD was responsible for the technology aspect of the initiative. The ITSD was already supporting the DHMH technology environment.

Some of the core ITSD requirements include:

- Expand network performance and capacity.
- Provide continuous operations.

- Provide a secure infrastructure.
- Provide remote access.
- Provide real-time access to patient medical information.

DHMH developed a staged implementation strategy. The strategy starts with pilot applications. After assessing performance and security, the pilot applications evolve to fully functional operations. This includes ITSD providing continuous security support.

This government initiative directly impacts infrastructure policies. ITSD is responsible for developing and maintaining information security policies, standards, and procedures for DHMH. This new infrastructure affects state-owned computing environments. Although this is not implicitly stated, any private company wishing to participate in and access this network must also adopt these infrastructure standards.

This is also a good example of not reinventing the wheel. It's reasonable to assume that ITSD based the new statewide policies on the Health Insurance Portability and Accountability Act (HIPAA). HIPAA can be viewed as the core security control standards. The implementation of these core controls results in numerous baseline standards for the state's new infrastructure, such as new and modified LAN and WAN security standards.

Critical Infrastructure Case Study

Televent is a company that provides software and services to monitor and support the energy industry in the United States and Canada. On September 10, 2012, the company identified a breach of its internal firewall and network. Televent said the hacker installed malicious software and stole software related to its core offering used by its customers. This is a class of software known as "supervisory, control, and data acquisition," commonly called SCADA. SCADA systems are vital components in managing and controlling of power grids.

These types of successful attacks highlight how vulnerable power grids, and thus the national critical infrastructure, are to hackers. SCADA networks were built originally as closed systems, but over time devices with Internet access have been added to the SCADA networks. For example, individual desktops have Internet access and access to business servers as well as the SCADA network. This makes the SCADA system vulnerable to Internet threats.

In this case, Televent reported that it had disconnected the usual data links between clients and segmented the affected portions of its internal networks.

As with many breaches, the technical details may never be known to the public; however, it is clear that the existing infrastructure policies were not adequate. The measures taken in the breach announcement indicate a lack of adequate policy and/or enforcement in at least these two areas:

- Network segmentation
- Separation between production and test environments

Network segmentation was introduced immediately to isolate the customer support systems from those infected by malicious software. This raises the question of why such segmentation wasn't included as part of the LAN policy in the first place. Such a policy would have ensured the creation of a closed network of people, processes, and technology for the systems providing direct access to the customer network.

It is unclear if the malicious software was placed on production or test systems. Separation between production and test systems is an important control. In this case, the need to segment the network immediately and the loss of software code are good indications that both test and production systems were vulnerable. This would be an indication of a potential lack of control between the test and production environments. System and application domain policies not only should be segmented, but also should highly restrict access between these two environments.

CHAPTER SUMMARY

This chapter discussed security documents that relate to each domain of a typical IT infrastructure. You learned there is more than one approach to creating standards. It is important to separate core policy language from specific technology configuration. One way to approach this is to have two separate documents, such as control standards and baseline standards. Supporting documents include procedures and guidelines. Collectively, these documents represent a comprehensive way of addressing risk.

The chapter examined both the form and substance of many standards. In fact, the volume of policy and standard topics is enormous. No one chapter could cover in detail every aspect of infrastructure policies and related controls. Policies that are well organized are likely to be better understood and more fully adopted. Early adoption of security policies can be a source of pride for both the individual and the team. Organizing this material in a searchable and useful manner is important to drive this understanding. This chapter also discussed how to categorize various documents in the library and how to describe their relationships. Finally, the chapter examined best practices that included a number of sources for policy and standard material. Organizations rarely create new policies from scratch. It is far better to leverage best practices security frameworks and related policies.

KEY CONCEPTS AND TERMS

Access control list (ACL)	Intrusion detection system (IDS)	Stateless firewall
Active content		User proxy
Audit	Intrusion prevention system (IPS)	Web services
Enterprise data management (EDM)	Stateful firewall	Workstation domain policies

CHAPTER 10 ASSESSMENT

1. The steps to implement security controls on a firewall would be documented within which of the following?

   A. Policy
   B. Control standard
   C. Baseline standard
   D. Procedure

2. A DMZ separates a LAN from which of the following?

   A. Phone network
   B. Internet
   C. Cellular network
   D. VoIP network

3. Visitor control is an aspect of which of the following?

   A. Network security
   B. Personnel security
   C. Workstation security
   D. Physical security

4. Which of the following can you use to segment LANs?

   A. Routers and firewalls
   B. Routers and gateways
   C. Gateways and servers
   D. Servers and workstations

5. Without a policy that leads to controls that restrict employees from installing their own software on a company workstation, a company could suffer which of the following consequences?

   A. Malware on the network
   B. Lawsuits from software licensing issues
   C. Loss of productivity
   D. All of the above

6. Good sources for security policies and standards include which of the following?

   A. U.S. government
   B. Private companies selling standards
   C. Professional organizations
   D. Vendors
   E. All of the above

7. Two-factor authentication is a typical control used by employees to remotely access which of the following?

   A. Workstation
   B. LAN
   C. DMZ website
   D. WAN

8. Which document outlines the specific controls that a technology device needs to support?

   A. Control standard
   B. Baseline standard
   C. Procedure
   D. Policy

9. In information security, EDM typically refers to _____.

10. The content for the documents in the policies and standards library should be written so they are _____ and _____.

11. Production data should be sanitized before being used in a test environment.

    A. True   B. False

12. Organizations should always create new policies tailored to their needs rather than adapt industry norms found on the Internet.

    A. True   B. False

13. An owner of the data must obtain approval from the custodian of the resource to use the data.

    A. True   B. False

14. What is the difference between a stateless firewall and a stateful one?

    A. A stateful firewall looks at each packet individually, and a stateless firewall examines the packet in the context of the connection and other packets.
    B. A stateless firewall looks at each packet individually, and a stateful firewall examines the packet in the context of the connection and other packets.
    C. There isn't a difference.
    D. A stateful firewall requires authentication, whereas a stateful firewall does not.

Data Classification and Handling Policies and Risk Management Policies

DATA SUSTAINS AN ORGANIZATION'S business processes and enables it to deliver products and services. Stop the flow of data, and for many companies, business comes quickly to a halt. Data drives online ordering, delivery schedules, allocation of resources, production lines, warehouse management, supply chain, and much more. The economy is driven by data. Those who understand its value and have the ability to manage related risks will have a competitive advantage. If the loss of data lasts long enough, the viability of an organization to survive may come into question. Fortunately, most outages and data disruptions are short in duration. But even short outages and data disruptions can be costly. For example, *Forbes* magazine wrote about a 30-minute outage that Amazon incurred on August 19, 2013. Speculation was that Amazon lost $66,240 per minute during the outage. The problem has not improved even after several years. In September 2019, Yahoo! email was out for many parts of the world for several hours. In July 2019, an article in *The Verge,* titled "Internet Outages Are Getting More Serious,"[1] commented that outages are growing both more widespread and more substantial.

Data classification is a useful way to rank the value and importance of groups of data. The importance of the data and the type of value assigned varies by organization. The value may be monetary, because certain data may be key to driving revenue. The value may be regulatory, because certain data carries legal obligations. The type of data categories (known as *classifications*) may vary greatly depending on the organization's need. Data classification creates a standardized way of assigning data (or groups of data) to a classification. These data classifications then drive how data is appropriately handled. These policies and techniques feed into a risk management approach that helps prevent disruption of services.

This chapter discusses data classification techniques used by the government and within the private sector. It discusses ways of classifying data. It also discusses risk management approaches that include quality assurance, quality control, and key measurements.

Chapter 11 Topics

This chapter covers the following topics and concepts:

- What data classification policies are
- What data handling policies are

---

1. https://www.theverge.com/interface/2019/7/4/20681733/facebook-outage-internet-myanmar-consequences

- Which business risks are related to information systems
- What a risk and control self-assessment (RCSA) is and why it is important
- What risk assessment policies are
- What quality assurance (QA) and quality control (QC) are
- What best practices for risk management policies are
- What some case studies and examples of risk management policies are

Chapter 11 Goals

When you complete this chapter, you will be able to:

- Explain various data classification approaches
- Explain the difference between classified and unclassified data
- Describe common business classification techniques
- Understand the need for policies that govern data in transit and at rest
- Explain common business risks in a disaster
- Describe quality assurance
- Describe quality control
- Explain the difference between QA and QC
- Describe the relationship between QA/QC and risk management

Data Classification Policies

Data classification in its simplest form is a way to identify the value of data. You achieve this by placing a label on the data. Labeling data enables people to find it quickly and handle it properly. You classify data independently of the form it takes. In other words, data stored in a computer should be classified in the same way as data printed on a report.

There is a cost to classifying data. Classifying data takes time and can be a tedious process. This is because there are many data types and uses. It's important not to overclassify. A data classification approach must clearly and simply represent how you want the data to be handled.

When Is Data Classified or Labeled?

Classifying all data in an organization may be impossible. There has been an explosion in the amount of unstructured data, logs, and other data retained in recent years. Trying to individually inspect and label terabytes of data is expensive, time consuming, and not productive.

Different approaches can be employed to reduce this challenge. Here are several approaches used to reduce the time and effort needed to classify data:

- Classify only the most important data, the data that represents the highest risk to the organization. Use a default classification for the remaining data.
- Classify data by storage location or point of origin. For example, all data stored in the financial application database could be considered to be for internal use only and thus classified as "confidential."
- Classify data at time of creation or use; this technique relies on software that "hooks" into existing processes. For example, before an email is sent, a pop-up box requires the email content to be classified.

Regardless of the approach, the reason for classifying the data must determine the way it is secured and handled. The point is not just to classify data. The point is to classify data in order to manage risk.

It is recommended that at minimum, you classify any data that is not public. This leads to which classification system to use. There are a variety of classification systems. The U.S. Department of Defense (DoD) utilizes confidential, secret, and top secret as the baseline classifications for data. The Department of Energy uses Unclassified Controlled Nuclear Information (UCNI), Formerly Restricted Data (FRD), and Restricted Data. Then there are additional categories such as National Security Information (NSI) and Critical Nuclear Weapon Design Information (CNWDI). DoD classification is discussed in more detail later in this chapter.

It is highly unlikely that a civilian company that is not a DoD contractor would require that level of classification. And it would be very difficult to manage. However, at least a "confidential" or "not confidential" would be workable for any organization.

The Need for Data Classification

You can classify data for different purposes depending on the need of the organization. For example, the military would have a very different classification need than the local grocery market. Both handle data, but handling requirements differ greatly. The more sensitive the data, the more important it is to handle the information properly.

An organization has several needs to classify data. The three most common needs are to:

- Protect information
- Retain information
- Recover information

Protecting Information

The need to protect information is often referred to as the *security classification*. An organization has to protect data when its disclosure could cause damage. Data classification drives what type of security you should use to protect the information. Data classification also helps define the authentication and authorization methods you should use to ensure the data does not fall into unauthorized hands.

It is always important to protect your confidential data. In fact, one major aspect of trade secret litigation is whether or not the data owner took reasonable steps to secure that information. I frequently work as an expert witness in such cases, and if you don't take steps to secure confidential data, you may not be able to enforce trade secret protection.

Authentication is the process used to prove the identity of the person. **Authorization** is the process used to grant permission to the person. Both authentication and authorization control access to systems, applications, networks, and data. Authentication makes sure you know who is accessing the data. Authorization makes sure you know the level of access that is permitted—for example, "read" versus "update." When an individual is said to be an *authorized user*, it means that he or she received formal approval to access the systems, applications, networks, and data.

All organizations have some form of data that requires protection. Any organization that has employees has sensitive personal information, which, by law, must be protected.

Retaining Information

An organization must determine how long to retain information. It's not practical to retain data forever. When you purge and delete sensitive data, there's less of a target for a future breach. Therefore, organizations should retain only data that is needed to conduct business. Data retention policies define the methods of retaining data as well as the duration.

You need to retain data for two major reasons: legal obligation and needs of the business. All organizations have some legal requirements to keep records, such as financial and tax records. Generally such records are retained for seven years in the United States. There are also business reasons to keep records, such as customer information, contracts, and sales records. TABLE 11-1 depicts a sample retention classification scheme.

There are records for which there is no legal or business reason to keep them. Many organizations require that such records be deleted at some point. Deleting this information helps the company cut down on storage costs and protects the information from accidental disclosure. The additional benefit of removing unneeded data is the reduction of legal liabilities. There is a general theory that unneeded data creates a liability for a company. The key concept is "what you don't know *can* hurt you." As stated previously, there is an explosion of data across many businesses. Much of this data is unstructured, such as emails, call center recordings, other transactions, and even social media postings. Understanding what's contained in every data file is impossible. This means that an organization may not fully understand the legal obligation or liability associated with handling every data item. In short, the less data retained, the less unknown liability exists.

TABLE 11-1 Data Classification for Retention of Information

DATA CLASS	CLASS DESCRIPTION	RETENTION PERIOD	EXAMPLES
Regulated	Records that are required to be kept by regulations	Seven years	Financial and tax records
Business	General business records needed to support operations	Five years	Customer records Vendor records
Temporary	Temporary records that are not mission-critical	One year	Emails

Storage can be expensive for an organization. A corporate setting can have thousands of employees generating huge volumes of data. Retaining this data takes up valuable resources to back up, recover, monitor, protect, and classify. If you delete unneeded data, these costs are avoided.

Given the volume of data produced, it is inevitable that sensitive data will show up where it's not supposed to. A good example is email. A service agent might try to help a customer by email to resolve a payment problem. Despite the agent's good intentions, the agent might include the customer's personal financial information in the email. Once that data is in the email system, it's difficult to remove. The person receiving the email may have designated others to view the mail. Backups of the desktop and mail system will also have copies of the personal information. Wherever that data resides or travels, the information must now be protected and handled appropriately.

> **NOTE**
>
> According to a legal memorandum by Ater Wynne, LLP, each person in a corporate setting produces about 736 megabytes annually of electronic data. That equates to a stack of books 30 feet tall. Additionally, it's estimated that email accounts for 80 percent of corporate communications in the United States.

As discussed earlier, you can reduce the likelihood of accidental disclosure by routinely deleting data that is no longer needed for legal or business reasons. Classifying what's important ensures that the right data is deleted. Without retention policies, vital records could be lost. The retention policy can use data classification to help define handling methods.

It's important to work with management in determining the retention policy. It's also important to work with legal staff. The legal obligations can change depending on the business context. Assume a service agent with a securities brokerage wrote an email about a customer's stock trade. This type of email correspondence must be retained by law. The Securities and Exchange Commission (SEC) Rule 17a-4 requires all customer correspondence to be retained for three years. This is to ensure a record is kept in case of an accusation of fraud or misrepresentation. The SEC rule also says the correspondence must be kept in a way that cannot be altered or overwritten. This means the retention policy must specify how the data is to be backed up. An example is a requirement that data should be kept on write-once optical drives. Regulations make data classification even more important in defining proper handling methods.

A retention policy can help protect a company during a lawsuit. The courts have held that no sanction will be applied to organizations operating in good faith. This is true even if they lost the records as a result of routine operations. "Good faith" is demonstrated through a retention policy that demonstrates how data is routinely classified, retained, and deleted.

Recovering Information

The need to recover information also drives the need for data classification. In a disaster, information that is mission-critical needs to be recovered quickly. Properly classifying data allows the more critical data to be identified. This data can then be handled with specific recovery requirements in mind. For example, an organization may choose to mirror critical data. This allows for recovery within seconds. In comparison, it can take hours to recover data from a tape backup. **TABLE 11-2** depicts a sample recovery classification scheme.

There are various approaches, sometimes called *classification schemes*, to classifying data. A good rule of thumb is to keep it simple! A dozen classes within each scheme for security,

TABLE 11-2 Data Classification for Recovery of Information

DATA CLASS	CLASS DESCRIPTION	RECOVERY PERIOD	EXAMPLES
Critical	Data that must be recovered immediately to avoid serious impact on the organization	30 minutes	Web site and e-commerce channels Customer records
Urgent	Data that can be recovered later with minimal impact on the organization	48 hours	Email backups
Nonvital	Data not vital to the daily operations of the business	30 days	Historical records Archived contract files

retention, and recovery would be confusing. Employees cannot remember elaborate classification schemes. It's difficult to train employees on the subtle differences among so many classes. A good rule is to use five or fewer classes. Many organizations use three classifications. Some add a fourth classification to align better to their business model and mission. Although a fifth classification is rarer, this may be an indication that an organization has a high enough level of automation and a mature enough risk program to use the additional classification to better manage its data.

In a three-class scheme, the classes represent a lower and upper extreme combined with a practical middle ground. It's also good to keep the class names short, concise, and memorable. Some classification requirements are influenced by specific legal requirements. In other cases, classification requirements will be driven by what the business is willing to pay for. For example, Table 11-2 indicates a recovery time of less than 30 minutes for critical data. This sample recovery scheme may not be appropriate for all organizations; for example, the scheme might be too expensive for an elementary school to implement. In contrast, a Wall Street brokerage firm might find 30 minutes inadequate.

Legal Classification Schemes

A legal classification scheme to label data is driven primarily by legal requirements. Such schemes are often adopted by organizations that have a significant regulatory oversight or have had a significant legal or privacy viewpoint driving the data classification program. Regardless of the reason the organization adopts this approach, it's important that as legal requirements change, the data classifications change with them. For example, the definition of privacy has changed over the years. If the objective of the classification is to maintain individual privacy as legally defined, as the law changes, so must the classification. Consider an individual's home address. In some states the address alone is considered private information. In other states a home address is considered private only when combined with an individual's name. This changing legal landscape can affect how data is classified and handled.

Stanford University offers a good example of a legal classification scheme to label data. The University Privacy Officer is listed as a contact point for questions on the data classification. The Chief Information Security Officer is listed as the key contact point for how the classes of data should be protected. It is a common practice to have privacy and security departments team up to create and manage data classification schemes. Stanford University has adopted the following data classification scheme:

- **Prohibited information**—Information is classified as Prohibited if law or regulation requires protection of the information.
- **Restricted information**—Information is classified as Restricted if it would otherwise qualify as Prohibited, but it has been determined by the university that prohibiting information storage would significantly reduce faculty/staff/student effectiveness.
- **Confidential information**—Information is classified as Confidential if it is not considered to be Prohibited or Restricted but is not generally available to the public.
- **Unrestricted information**—Information is classified as Unrestricted if it is not considered to be Prohibited, Restricted, or Confidential.

You can quickly see how the legal value placed on data determines use of the Prohibited and Restricted classifications. Examples of Prohibited information are Social Security numbers, driver's license numbers, and credit card numbers. Examples of Restricted information are health records and passport numbers.

Military Classification Schemes

A security data classification reflects the criticality and sensitivity of the information. *Criticality* refers to how important the information is to achieving the organization's mission. *Sensitivity* refers to the impact associated with unauthorized disclosure. A specific piece of data can be high on one scale but low on the other. The higher of the two scales typically drives the data classification. As data becomes more important, generally it requires stronger controls. The U.S. military classification scheme is used by several federal agencies.

The U.S. military classification scheme is defined in National Security Information document EO 12356. There are three classification levels:

- **Top Secret** data, the unauthorized disclosure of which would reasonably be expected to cause grave damage to national security
- **Secret** data, the unauthorized disclosure of which would reasonably be expected to cause serious damage to national security
- **Confidential** data, the unauthorized disclosure of which would reasonably be expected to cause damage to national security

Any military data that is considered "classified" must use one of these three classification levels. There is also unclassified data that is handled by government agencies. This type of data has two classification levels:

- **Sensitive but unclassified** is confidential data not subject to release under the Freedom of Information Act.
- **Unclassified** is data available to the public.

Sensitive but unclassified is sometimes called *SBU*. It's also sometimes called *For official use only (FOUO)* in the United States. The term *FOUO* is used primarily within the U.S.

Department of Defense (DoD). Some examples of SBU data are Internal Revenue Service tax returns, Social Security numbers, and law enforcement records.

The Information Security Oversight Office (ISOO) oversees the U.S. government's classification program. The ISOO produces an annual report to the president summarizing the classification program from the prior year. The report outlines what data has been classified and declassified each year. The 2018 report stated that of all the classified data, 38.35 percent was Top Secret, 59.67 percent was Secret, and 1.98 percent was Confidential.

Declassifying data is important. It's not practical to keep data classified forever. First, it's better to focus limited resources on protecting a smaller amount of the most important data. Second, in democracies, we expect the government to be transparent. Unless there's a compelling reason to keep a secret, the expectation is the information will be released to the public.

The government routinely declassifies data. **Declassification** is a term that means to change the classification to "unclassified." The declassification of data is handled in one of three programs run by the ISOO:

- **Automatic declassification** automatically removes the classification after 25 years.
- **Systematic declassification** reviews those records exempted from automatic declassification.
- **Mandatory declassification** reviews specific records when requested.

These three programs declassified 19.8 million pages of information as far back as 2012. As you can see, the government has more and more data to protect. The amount could become overwhelming unless there are policies to reduce the amount of data the government protects.

Business Classification Schemes

The private sector, like the military, uses data classification to reflect the importance of the information. Unlike the government, there is no one data classification scheme. There is no one right approach to classification of data. Also like the military, data classification in business drives security and how the data will be handled.

Although there is no mandatory data classification scheme, there are norms for private industry. Earlier in this chapter, we introduced a flat system with only two levels. If you want more detail, the following four classifications are often used:

- Highly sensitive
- Sensitive
- Internal
- Public

Highly sensitive classification refers to data that is mission-critical. You use criticality and sensitivity to determine what data is mission-critical. This classification is also used to protect highly regulated data. This could include Social Security numbers and financial records. If this information is breached, it could represent considerable liability to the organization. Mission-critical data is information vital for the organization to achieve its core business. As such, an unauthorized breach creates substantial risk to the enterprise.

Access to highly sensitive data is limited. Organizations often apply enhanced security and monitoring. Monitoring can include detailed logging of when records are accessed. Additional security controls may be applied, such as encryption.

Sensitive classification refers to data that is important to the business but not vital to its mission. If information is breached, it could represent significant financial loss. However, the breach of the information would not cause critical damage to the organization. This data might include client lists, vendor information, and network diagrams.

Access to sensitive data is restricted and monitored. The monitoring may not be as rigorous as with highly sensitive data.

The key difference between highly sensitive and sensitive is the magnitude of the impact. Unauthorized exposure of highly sensitive data may put the business at risk. Unauthorized exposure of sensitive data may result in substantial financial loss, but the business will survive.

Internal classification refers to data not related to the core business. The data could be routine communications within the organization. The impact of unauthorized access to internal data is a disruption of operations and financial loss.

Access to internal data is restricted to employees. The information is widely available for them, but the data is not released to the public or individuals outside the company.

Public classification refers to data that has no negative impact on the business when released to the public. Access to public data is often achieved by placing the data on a public website or through press releases. The number of individuals who are permitted to make data public is limited.

Many laws and regulations require you to know where your data is. These laws require you to protect the data commensurate to the risk to your business. Data classification is an effective way of determining risk. The organization is at greater risk when mission-critical data is breached. By classifying the data, you are able to find it quickly and define proper controls.

Developing a Customized Classification Scheme

You can often create a customized classification scheme by altering an existing one. Federal agencies cannot customize a scheme. This is because their classification schemes are mandated by law. Many security frameworks provide guidance and requirements to develop a classification. Some sources of guidance and requirements include the International Organization for Standardization (ISO), Control Objectives for Information and related Technology (COBIT), and Payment Card Industry Data Security Standard (PCI DSS).

Sometimes customizing a classification scheme is minor. This might include modifying the label but not changing the underlying definition; for example, the "highly sensitive" classification could equate to private, restricted, or mission-critical. It's not the name that matters but the definition. Classification names can vary depending on the organization and the perspective of the creator. "Private" classification in one organization could mean "highly sensitive" in another. In still another it might mean "sensitive."

When developing a customized data classification scheme, keep to the basics. You should consider the following general guidelines:

1. Determine the number of classification levels.
2. Define each classification level.
3. Name each classification level.
4. Align the classification to specific handling requirements.
5. Define the audit and reporting requirements.

You determine the number of classification levels by looking at how much you want to separate the data. One approach is to separate the data by aligning it to critical business processes. This helps you understand the business to better protect the assets. For example, a power plant may want to isolate its supervisory control and data acquisition (SCADA) systems. SCADA data helps run the facility. Special security and controls may be placed on these systems and data. This can be achieved by classifying the SCADA data differently than other types of data.

The definition of each classification level depends on how you want to express the impact of a breach. Federal agencies determine impact based on confidentiality, integrity, and availability. They assign a rating of low, moderate, or high impact to each of these. By applying a formula, they can determine an impact. Organizations outside the government have adopted similar approaches. **TABLE 11-3** depicts the basic impact matrix described in National Institute of Standards and Technology (NIST) Federal Information Processing Standard (FIPS) 199.

The FIPS-199 publication uses phrases such as "limited adverse effect" to denote low impact. For moderate and high impact, it uses "serious adverse effect" and "severe or catastrophic adverse effect."

In the business world, impact definitions closely align with measured business results. For example, low risks can be defined as causing "operations disruptions and minimal financial loss." An organization understands these terms because a financial scale can be used. For example, a low impact may result when $1 to $20,000 is at risk; a moderate impact might be defined as $20,000 to $500,000; and a high-impact risk might be defined as $500,000 and above. The exact amounts vary depending on the size of the organization and its risk tolerance. Applying specific dollar amounts to impacts makes the definitions clearer.

The name of each classification level is usually taken from the definition itself. The important point is to select a name that resonates within the organization. You may also consider using a name that peer organizations adopt. This can help facilitate the exchange

TABLE 11-3 Classification for Security of Information

	POTENTIAL IMPACT		
SECURITY OBJECTIVE	**LOW**	**MODERATE**	**HIGH**
Confidentiality			
Integrity			
Availability			

of approaches within the industry. The name can reflect leadership's view of risk, such as classifying data as "proprietary" versus "sensitive."

To align the classification to specific handling requirements is a critical step. Once you determine the classification level, you must apply the appropriate security control requirements. Consider combining the levels where there's little to no difference in security requirements.

Audit and reporting requirements depend on industry and regulatory requirements. Many organizations are subject to privacy law disclosures. You should consider these reporting requirements when classifying data. For example, sensitive data for audit and reporting requirements can be assigned a special classification. This classification can include additional logging and monitoring capability.

Classifying Your Data

You need to consider two primary issues when classifying data. One issue is data ownership, and the other is security controls. These two issues help you derive maximum value from the data classification effort.

The business is accountable to ensure data is protected. The business also defines handling requirements. IT is the custodian of the data. It's up to the business to ensure adequate controls are funded and they meet regulatory requirements. The COBIT framework recommends that a data owner be assigned. The data owner is the person who would be accountable for defining all data handling requirements with the business. The data owner determines the level of protection and how the data is stored and accessed. Ultimately, the data owner must strike a balance between protection and usability. The data owner must consider both the business requirements and regulatory requirements.

The position of the data owner should be senior enough to be accountable. The data owner has a vested interest in making sure the data is accurate and properly secure. The data owner needs to understand the importance and value of the information to the business. He or she also needs to understand the ramifications that inaccurate data or unauthorized access has on the organization.

The data owner guides the IT department in defining controls and handling processes. The IT department designs, builds, and implements these controls. For example, if cardholder data is being collected, the data owner should be aware of PCI DSS standards. The IT department would advise the data owner on the technology requirements. Responsibility stays with the data owner to fund the technology. The duties and responsibilities of the data owner should be outlined in the security controls or in security policies.

Determining the security controls for each classification level is a core objective of data classification. It would make no sense to identify data as "highly sensitive" or "Top Secret," and then allow broad access. The data owner and IT department determine what controls are appropriate. The following is a sampling of the security controls to be considered:

- Authentication method
- Encryption
- Monitoring
- Logging

TABLE 11-4 Data Classification and Security Controls

DATA CLASSIFICATION	SECURITY CONTROLS		
	AUTHENTICATION	MONITORING	LOGGING
Highly sensitive	Two factor	Real-time alerts	Detailed logs
Sensitive	Two factor	Daily log review	Supports monitoring and for forensic use
Internal	ID/password	Log review in response to event	For forensic use
Public	ID/password for internal network access None for external public access	None	Log who updates the data and when it is updated

It's up to the business to ensure adequate controls are funded and they meet regulatory requirements. But beyond regulatory requirements, there are some basic guidelines. It should be readily apparent that the more sensitive the data, the stronger encryption, more detailed logging, and more monitoring that are needed.

Today, encryption is relatively easy to implement. Even Microsoft Windows has Bit-Locker for drive encryption and Encrypted File System (EFS) for individual file encryption. There are also a wide range of open source encryption solutions for files or entire drives. Communications on a network can be encrypted with Transport Layer Security (TLS) with minimal effort. Otherwise, the security policies are viewed as unrealistic and may even be ignored. TABLE 11-4 depicts a simple approach to linking data classifications to security controls.

Data Handling Policies

One of the difficult exercises when defining access requirements is understanding exactly who has a clear need to use the information. It's important that data handling policies assign responsibility for how the data is to be used. For example, data handling policies should limit what data is allowed to be printed. Another data handling concern is protecting data when it's moved. The concern is that the data gets used in a way that is no longer protected.

As with data classification, the data owner must strike a balance between protection and usability. The data owner must consider both the business and regulatory requirements.

The Need for Policy Governing Data at Rest and in Transit

A discussion on how best to protect data at rest and in transit inevitably leads to the subject of encryption. There certainly is more to protecting data than just encrypting it. There's an array of factors that must be considered, such as authentication, authorization, logging, and monitoring. However, the one topic that gets much attention is encryption. That's due in part to the emergence of state privacy laws. The majority of states today have privacy laws that fall under two types of encryption requirements:

* Laws that require private data to be encrypted
* Laws that require notification of breaches when private data is not encrypted

Both requirements are driving businesses to adopt encryption. There are differences among state laws as to the level of encryption that's required. For example, the California privacy law requires notification when private information that has not been encrypted is breached. The Massachusetts privacy law requires encryption of data, at rest or in transit, when it leaves the confines of a company's network. Nevada privacy law mandates the use of PCI DSS, which requires cardholder data to be encrypted both inside and outside the company's network.

> **NOTE**
>
> The term *data at rest* refers to data that is in storage. This includes data on a server, laptop, CD, DVD, or universal serial bus (USB) thumb drive. Any data that is stored is considered data at rest. The term *data in transit* refers to data that is traversing the network. That includes data on a private network, the Internet, and wireless networks. If the data is moving over any type of network, the data is in transit.

Regardless of your opinion about whether encryption is a good idea, encryption is a mandate for many organizations. You need to ensure that IT security policies addressing where and how encryption will be used are well defined within those policies.

Security policies need to be clear about when you should use encryption. The policies should also state the level of encryption that is acceptable. Sometimes when people discuss encrypting data within the network, they raise passionate arguments about the value of the protection obtained by encrypting data. Some argue there's little value because absent stealing the physical hard drive, the data is automatically decrypted. Others argue that it's another layer of control preventing access because the decryption process is controlled. Both are right. Sometimes the data is automatically decrypted, and other times it is not.

FIGURE 11-1 illustrates both points of view. There are two scenarios presented. In both scenarios, a hacker breaches the environment. In scenario #1, a breach of the application leads to unencrypted data being exposed. In this case, encryption was of no value in protecting the information. In scenario #2, a breach of the operating system leads to a database file being stolen. In this case, the data remained encrypted, which significantly helped prevent the data from being exposed. Encryption of data within the network can offer valuable protection depending on the type of breach. The key factor is whether the encryption key becomes exposed in the process.

Now take a look at how this works in more detail. In scenario #1, a breach of the application allows the hacker to retrieve unencrypted data. The critical point here is that the application and/or database server has access to the encryption key. In this example, the database is decrypting the data. Alternatively, it could be the application that is decrypting the data. Either way, you are in essence asking the application to get the information and decrypt it for you. However, in scenario #2, the hacker has breached the operating system (OS), bypassing the application and database server. In this scenario, the hacker only has access to the file system. In other words, the hacker can retrieve the database files, but they remain encrypted. Thus, no data has been breached.

FIGURE 11-1

Database encryption attack scenarios.

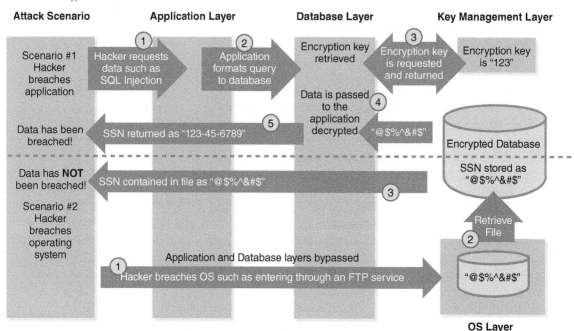

Encrypting data within the network does protect against many attacks but does not protect against a breach of the application. What makes scenario #2 a viable solution is that the key management layer is outside the application and database layer. Without the encryption key, the data is unreadable. It would not make sense to encrypt the data on the server and leave the encryption key on the same server. That's like leaving your car key in the ignition of your car. For encryption to be effective, security policies must establish core requirements and standards, such as:

- Encryption keys must be separated from encrypted data.
- Encryption keys must be retrieved through a secure process.
- Administrator rights at the OS layer do not give access to the database.

What's generally accepted as best practice is that whenever sensitive data leaves the confines of the organization's private network, the information should be encrypted. This is not consistently applied within many organizations. For example, suppose an organization encrypts all laptop hard drives; however, the organization may fail to encrypt email, USB drives, or CD/DVD drives. In this case, it's common to deploy a patchwork of encryption solutions. Many organizations fail to comply completely with encryption requirements. The use of the term *best practice* in this context recognizes that the level of success among organizations varies. This lack of full compliance to implement encryption is due to:

- Confusion over the laws
- Cost to comply
- Lack of a standardized approach among vendor products

The IT industry is quickly adapting. New vendor products offer encryption solutions. Today the encryption of mobile hard drives and encryption over the Internet are commonplace. For example, it's common in many organizations to encrypt the hard drive of mobile devices, such as laptops and smartphones. This protects the sensitive information contained inside the device. If the device is lost or stolen, the information cannot be read. Also, encryption over the Internet is commonplace. For example, employees routinely connect to an office through virtual private network (VPN) solutions that encrypt all the traffic between the employees and the private network. Organizations with consumers who buy online routinely encrypt the consumers' website sessions so they can enter their credit card information safely.

Beyond mobile devices and traversing the Internet, sensitive information leaves the confines of a private network in other forms. These include backup tapes, CDs, thumb drives, and any other storage media. Encrypting backup tapes protects the data both at rest and as it's being transported. If a tape is lost or stolen, the information is not breached. This is because the data cannot be decrypted without the key. Encrypting backup tapes is commonplace in industries such as financial services. Also, keep in mind that not all backups are well managed through elaborate data center processes. Many small offices make backups on very portable media such as mini tapes or portable hard drives. These backups also need to be protected. There's a lack of consensus on best solutions to protect CD/DVD drives, thumb drives, and email.

The IT security policies must state clearly how data is to be protected and handled. An organization can choose to lock out CD/DVDs or USB ports from writing data. An organization can also attempt to encrypt any information written to the drives. Both solutions have complexity, benefits, and drawbacks. It's the chief information security officer's (CISO's) role to bring the organization to a consensus. Some organizations choose to accept the risk. That is becoming harder to do as privacy laws become more stringent.

Policies, Standards, and Procedures Covering the Data Life Cycle

Data has a life cycle like any IT asset. It's created, accessed, and eventually destroyed. Between these states, it changes form. It is transmitted, stored, and physically moved. Security policies, standards, and procedures establish different requirements on the data depending on the life-cycle state. The main objective is to ensure that data is protected in all its forms. It should be protected on all media and during all phases of its life cycle. The protection needs to extend to all processing environments. These environments collectively refer to all applications, systems, and networks.

Policies state that users of information are personally responsible for complying with policies, standards, and procedures. All users are held accountable for the accuracy, integrity, and confidentiality of the information they access. Policies must be clear as to the use and handling of data. For discussion purposes, this section outlines some of the policy considerations for data handling at different points:

- **Creation**—During creation, data must be classified. That could be simply placing the data within a common storage area. For example, a human resources (HR) system creates information in the HR database. All information in that database can be assigned a common data classification. Security policies then govern data owner, custodians, and accountabilities. Security procedures govern how access is granted to that data.

- **Access**—Access to data is governed by security policies. These policies provide special guidance on separation of duties (SOD). It's important that procedures check SOD requirements before granting access. For example, the ability to create and approve a wire transfer of large sums out of a bank typically requires two or more people. The SOD would have one person create the wire and one person approve it. In this case, the procedure to grant authority to approve wires must also include a check to verify that the same person does not have the authority to create a wire. If the person had both authorities, that person could create and approve a large sum of money to him- or herself.

- **Use**—Use of data includes protecting and labeling information properly after its access. The data must be properly labeled and safeguarded according to its classification. For example, if highly sensitive data is used in a printed report, the report must be labeled "highly sensitive." Typically, labeling a report "highly sensitive" means there will be data handling issues related to storage.

- **Transmission**—Data must be transmitted in accordance with policies and standards. The organization may have procedures and processes for transmitting data. All users must follow these procedures. This ensures that the data is adequately protected using approved technology, such as encryption.

- **Storage**—Storage devices of data must be approved. This means that access to a device must be secured and properly controlled. For example, let's say mobile devices are encrypted. Once a device is approved and configured, access can be granted through normal procedures. Storage handling also relates to physical documents. "Highly sensitive" documents, for example, need to be locked up when not in use. They should be shared only with those individuals authorized to view such material.

- **Physical transport**—Transport of data must be approved. This ensures that what leaves the confines of the private network is protected and tracked. The organization has an obligation to know where its data is. Also, it needs to know that data is properly protected. When possible, the data should be encrypted during transport. In the event of data media being lost or stolen, the data will then be protected. Many organizations use preapproved transport companies for handling data. These services provide the tracking and notification of arrival needed to meet the companies' obligations.

- **Destruction**—Destruction of data is sometimes called *disposal*. When an asset reaches its end of life, it must be destroyed in a controlled procedure. The standards that govern its destruction make sure that the data cannot be reconstructed. This may require physical media to be placed in a disposal bin. These bins are specially designed to allow items to be deposited but not removed. The items are collected and the contents shredded. All users are required to follow procedures that have been approved for the destruction of physical media and electronic data.

IT security policies, standards, and procedures must outline the clear requirements at each stage of the data's life cycle. The policies must be clear on the responsibilities of the user to follow them. They also need to outline the consequences of noncompliance or purposely bypassing these controls.

Identifying Business Risks Related to Information Systems

Risk management policies establish processes to identify and manage risks to the business. As risks vary depending on the organization, so do the risk policies that must be considered. Common across many organizations are risk policies that consider the value of the data (that is, data classification), types of risks, impact to the business, and effective measurement through quality control and quality assurance.

No matter the size of your organization, understanding data is vital to its success. It's a simple fact that good decisions are more likely to come from good data. Data classification lets you understand how data relates to the business. Data classification drives how data is handled and thus is the foundation required for data quality. A well-defined data classification approach helps achieve good data quality. This is because data classification enables you to stratify data by usage and type. Understanding your data allows you to reduce risks and minimize costs.

Types of Risk

Much IT risk is operational risk. Operational risk is a broad category. It includes any event that disrupts the activities the organization undertakes daily. In technology terms, it's an interruption of the technology that affects the business process. It could be a coding error, a network slowdown, a system outage, or a security breach. Data classification helps focus resources on those assets needed to recover the business; for example, data classification identifies what data is critical to resuming minimal operations. FIGURE 11-2 illustrates that point, with Tier 1 representing mission-critical applications. With mission-critical applications, data should be mirrored so it can be recovered quickly.

Notice the transition between Tier 1 and Tier 2. This is represented by the dotted line cutting across the curved line. In this case, only a small percentage of data needs to be recovered for minimum operations. Conversely, for optimized operations, a significant amount of data needs to be recovered. This is represented by the path of the curved line in Tier 3. However, this large amount of data is not as vital in the short term. Data classification allows you to stratify this data so the mission-critical data can be found quickly and recovered.

Physical, environmental, and technical hazards can disrupt IT operations. A physical hazard can be any physical threat, such as a fire within the data center. An environmental hazard can be an environmental event, such as a storm or an earthquake. A technical hazard is a general category that covers other types of hazards. Data classification helps plan for many hazards. Such hazards might necessitate selecting a mirroring solution that copies mission-critical data across two data centers in two different locations.

Financial risk is the potential impact when the business fails to meet its financial obligations. Financial risk is often driven by a lack of adequate liquidity and credit for the business to meet its obligations. Financial decisions depend on financial data being accurate and available. Data classification builds processes that ensure the integrity of the information. When data is properly classified, you can identify financial information clearly. In addition, you can apply appropriate protection and handling methods.

FIGURE 11-2

Data classification of volume versus time to recover.

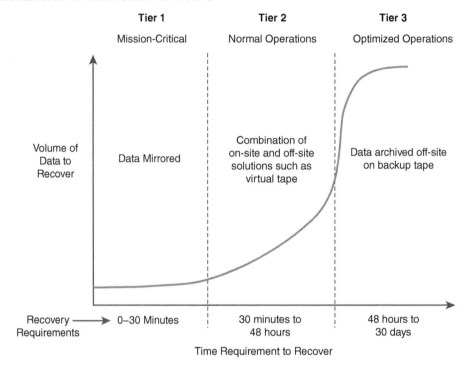

Strategic risks may change how the organization operates. Some examples are mergers and acquisitions, a change in the industry, or a change in the customer. Understanding the sensitivity and criticality of your data brings you closer to understanding your customer and products. Stratifying your data through classification helps you understand what your core business truly is and what it is not.

The key takeaway is recognizing that the process of data classification is more than a label or tag. It's a review of how data drives your business. The benefit of data classification is identification of critical information assets and properly protecting those assets. The residual benefit is that you will understand your business and customers better.

Development and Need for Policies Based on Risk Management

Establishing a new risk-based management approach can be a daunting challenge. The objective of a risk-based approach is to focus on the greatest threats to an organization. IT security policies that are risk-based will focus on the greatest threats to business processes and promote a risk-aware culture. Policies, processes, and controls have more value when they reduce real business risk.

Compliance is more than adhering to laws and regulations. Regulators also want an organization to demonstrate that it can systematically identify and reduce risk. Policies based on risk management principles can achieve this. Security policies steer the organization within regulatory boundaries. Policies also need to reflect the organization's risk culture, tolerance, appetite, and values. For example, the Health Insurance Portability and Accountability Act (HIPAA) requires a risk management and analysis approach. This promotes a thorough understanding of the risks. This understanding leads to the selection of appropriate safeguards. These safeguards are based on the level of risks faced by the organization.

Developing tools to make mathematical calculations of these factors provides a means of assessing the risk in an objective fashion. Table 11-4 is a simple example of this approach. Tools can inform the organization's leadership of trends and emerging risks. But in the end they are only tools. There is no substitute for common sense. As much as they enlighten us, they can also cloud our judgment when they are followed blindly. An experienced leader knows to dig deeper when a model is saying something that doesn't make sense.

The use of security policies based on sound risk management will help to educate the organization on tradeoffs that are implicit in the risk-reduction decisions. The following are some benefits of a risk management approach to security policies. Such an approach:

- Identifies possible costs and benefits of decisions
- Considers actions that may not be apparent to the leaders and forces alternative thought
- Provides analytic rigor to ensure an objective consideration of risk

Risk management that is rigorous and well executed helps leaders make choices that reduce risk over the long term. This is critically important. Reducing risks is not a one-time activity. Risk management is a continuous dialogue. As time passes, other pressing needs compete for resources, and support for the risk reduction effort wavers. An effective risk management system explains the risks in the context of the business. It justifies its priority and funding.

Risk management is a process of governance. It's also a continuous improvement model. **FIGURE 11-3** depicts a simple continuous improvement model for risk management. The following steps are cycled through each time a new risk is discovered:

1. Prioritize the risk; align the risk to strategic objectives.
2. Identify an appropriate risk response; sometimes this may require adjusting policies.
3. Monitor the effectiveness of the response and gauge the reduction in risk.
4. Identify residual and new risks whereby the cause of the risk is determined.
5. Assess the risk to measure the impact to the organization.

This risk management continuous improvement model can be used to start a risk management program. In a startup, you would begin by prioritizing all known risks. This means aligning the risks to strategic objectives. This process may cause a change in the risk management programs or policies themselves. This is vital to ensure the program drives value into the business.

Controlling risks to the business extends beyond daily operations. It is important that you understand risks that can affect how to recover and sustain your business.

Risk management continuous improvement model.

Risk and Control Self-Assessment

A **risk and control self-assessment (RCSA)** is an effective tool in the risk management arsenal. It allows the organization to understand its risks and their potential effects on the business. It's a formal exercise many organizations conduct annually.

An RCSA can be a time-consuming exercise requiring engagement from the business's senior leadership and technology teams; however, the benefits are enormous. By the end of the day a common view emerges on the challenges and risks that face an organization, including:

- What the major known risks are
- Which of these risks will limit the ability of the organization to complete its mission
- What plans are in place to deal with these risks
- Who "owns" the management and monitoring of these risks

The RCSA process is often not well understood or leveraged. It contains the business leaders' view of their risks. Consequently, they are an ideal source of information to support your risk management program. If you demonstrate how managing risks to data reduces the risks identified in the RCSA, you will get the attention of management and increased opportunity to win their support.

The RCSA contains detailed risk information that shows the impact on an organization in the event that key processes and technology are not available. You use the RCSA to develop risk management plans, such as where to place quality assurance and quality control routines. The RCSA also contains multiple scenarios. Each scenario details the risks and effects on the business. The main intent of an RCSA is to ensure that these risks are identified and assigned to an individual executive to manage.

The RCSA approach is not a standard used across all industries. Although any organization can use the RCSA, and many use some form of it under a different name, it's only one of many approaches used to manage risk. Which approach to use is less important than having a systematic approach to managing risk in the first place. That said, the RCSA can provide an organization with a new opportunity to identify and plan for unexpected or emerging risks. These may include new operational risks resulting from shifts in the regulatory or market environment. Additionally, this approach can be used to align thinking about risk and awareness of it across the enterprise.

Risk Assessment Policies

A risk assessment is one of the most important activities that an organization performs. A risk assessment defines threats and vulnerabilities and determines control recommendations. It allows the organization to make informed decisions to invest in risk reduction. Risk-based decisions are the basis of most IT security policies.

Risk Exposure

A **risk exposure** is the impact to the organization when an event occurs. There are several ways to calculate risk exposure. Ideally, you want to quantify it within business terms, such as putting a dollar value on the losses. A generally accepted formula can be used to calculate exposure, as follows:

$$\text{Risk exposure} = \text{Likelihood the event will occur} \times \text{Impact if the event occurs}$$

For example, if there's a 50-percent chance that a $2 million loss may occur, the risk exposure would be $1 million (0.5 × $2 million = $1 million). This calculation, plus other assessments, can lead to understanding the total risk exposure of a business unit.

You can use different analytical methods to determine likelihood and impact. These methods fall into two types: quantitative and qualitative. Quantitative methods involve using numerical measurements to determine risks. Measurements may include a range of measurements, such as asset value and frequency of the threat. A shortcoming of quantitative methods is a lack of reliable data. This can be overcome by reaching a consensus on the use of industry benchmarks.

Qualitative analysis involves professional judgment. This means making a well-educated guess, so to speak. Qualitative techniques may include questionnaires, interviews, and working groups. Qualitative analysis can be used to adjust measurement created through quantitative methods.

These are very powerful tools that allow you to have an engaged conversation on risk with the business. When presented with the risk exposure, the business can accept the risk or fund its mitigation. It's important that you discuss with the business any assumptions made in determining the likelihood or impact. This serves two purposes: It validates your assumption, and it also builds credibility for the analysis. This avoids the situation where the analysis is discarded as unrealistic.

Prioritization of Risks, Threats, and Vulnerabilities

When you combine the risk exposure and business impact analysis (BIA), you can see the direct impact on the business. This view of risk allows you to prioritize the risks. A risk management program creates a balance between reducing the most likely events and mitigating risks with the greatest impact. Controls addressing one risk can impact other risks.

Security policies and controls can reduce reputational, operational, legal, and strategic risk. This is accomplished by limiting vulnerabilities and reducing breaches, which builds consumer confidence.

Risk Management Strategies

Once you identify a risk, you choose a strategy for managing it. There are four generally accepted risk management strategies, as follows:

- **Risk avoidance**—Not engaging in certain activities that can incur risk. This is difficult in most situations.
- **Risk acceptance**—Accepting the risk involved in certain activities and addressing any consequences that result.
- **Risk transference**—Sharing the risk with an outside party.
- **Risk mitigation**—Reducing or eliminating the risk by applying controls.

Risk avoidance is primarily a business decision. You need to look at the risks and benefits to determine how important they are to the viability of the business. This is quite difficult to implement. For example, there is risk of malware if you use email; however, simply not using email is not a viable option.

Risk acceptance is either a business or technology decision. The business needs to know about risks that impact its operations. If the business does not think it is feasible or cost-effective to manage the risk in other ways, it must choose to accept the risk. There are a host of daily technology risks that are accepted by the IT department. Hopefully, these risks have a low probability of impacting the business. From a practical standpoint, not all risks can be formally accepted by the business. The key is to have a process by which risks are assessed and rated. This rating can be used to determine who has the authority to accept each risk.

Risk transference is taking the consequences of a risk and moving the responsibility to someone else. The most common type of risk transference is the purchase of insurance. For example, you might purchase data breach insurance that would pay your expenses in the event of a data breach. Transferring a risk does not reduce the likelihood that a risk will occur. It removes the financial consequences of that risk.

There is no one list of mitigation strategies. The mitigation strategy depends on the risks, threats, and vulnerabilities facing the organization. A grocery market protecting customer credit cards has a different set of threats than a nuclear power plant. Their mitigation strategies will also differ.

However, all mitigation strategies have a common objective: prevention. The prevention of risks is less costly than dealing with their aftermath. To be effective, you must have a process in place to identify risks before they threaten the business. Risk management policies promote a series of efforts that allow an organization to be always self-aware of risks. The following is a sampling of those efforts:

- Threat and vulnerability assessments
- Penetration testing
- Monitoring of systems, applications, and networks
- Monitoring of vendor alerts on vulnerabilities
- Active patch management
- Effective vendor management and oversight
- Aggressive risk and security awareness

These methods reduce risk. They also provide a source of new information about the environment. This information can be used to design better solutions and understand limits of the existing environment. You can measure the impact of these effects in reduced risk to data integrity, confidentiality, and availability.

Vulnerability Assessments

Vulnerability assessments are a set of tools used to identify and understand risks to a system, application, or network device. *Vulnerabilities* is a term that identifies weaknesses in the IT infrastructure, or control gaps. If these weaknesses or control gaps are exploited, it could result in an unauthorized access to data.

There are a number of tools and techniques to perform vulnerability assessments. Here are a few examples:

- A vulnerability scan of a network
- A scan of the source code of an application
- A scan of an operating system's open ports

It's important to understand that these are tools, not assessments. They are valuable tools identifying potential weaknesses; however, the assessment comes from the analysis of the results. The assessment must address the vulnerability. It must also address the impact to the business and cost of remediation.

Security policies define when and how to perform a vulnerability assessment. The following are typical steps to be followed:

1. Scope the assessment.
2. Identify dependencies.
3. Perform automated testing.
4. Analyze and generate reports.
5. Assign a rating.

You need to scope the assessment and understand the environment prior to any assessment work. This work involves both technical and business aspects. You need to understand what business processes are being used on the internal networks plus what processes are being used externally through the firewall. Based on this information, you can assess the security policies, standards, and procedures. This should provide a comprehensive baseline to compare the assessment results against.

A comprehensive vulnerability assessment looks at the processes end-to-end. This is more effective than just looking at processes on an isolated component. For example, assume your organization has a network of car dealerships across the state. Also assume there is a VPN available to cross-check inventory and delivery of new cars. You conduct a vulnerability assessment. The assessment finds a control weakness that could prevent a car dealership from receiving new cars. That is a much more meaningful conclusion than, "XYZ server has open ports."

Next, you identify dependent processes and technology that support each primary process. For example, remote access from home may be dependent on the **security token**. A security token is either a hardware device or software code that generates a "token" at logon. A token is usually represented as a series of numbers. A security token is extremely difficult (and some say impossible) to replicate. When assigned to an individual as part a required logon, the token provides assurance as to who is accessing the network. The home environment and the security token each creates a potential vulnerability. The home and token both need to be discussed beyond the firewall.

It is important to understand how information is used. For example, the assessment should address employee access, use, and dissemination of information. Network and application diagrams are good sources of information.

The use of automated testing tools is best practice. They can scan a large volume of vulnerabilities within seconds. The key takeaway is that the results must be examined and put into the context of the process and risk.

Automated testing tools call for you to rank threats in order of greatest risk. Classifying risks allows the organization to apply consistent protection across its asset base.

During analysis and reporting, you bring the data together and determine the business impact. Using the BIA results helps align risks to the business. For example, if the assessment includes a process that the business has already declared mission-critical, then the assessment can reflect that fact. This approach helps you assess vulnerabilities that deserve priority attention.

With the vulnerability analysis completed, it's time to assign a rating. A vulnerability assessment rating describes the vulnerability in relation to its potential impact on the organization. The rating typically follows the same path as any risk rating adopted with other risk teams. You typically calculate the exposure, as discussed earlier in the section entitled "Risk Exposure." Based on the risk exposure, you assign a value. Then, using a scale, you can assign a rating such as low, moderate, or high, as discussed in Table 11-4.

You do not have to apply a report rating. You could rate the report based on risk exposure. More organizations tend to use the low, moderate, and high ratings. The feeling is that these ratings can more accurately reflect the risk by applying professional judgment.

Vulnerability Windows

Vulnerabilities are weaknesses in a system that could result in unauthorized access to data. All software has some vulnerability. The goal is to produce code with the lowest number of vulnerabilities possible. That means designing code well and reducing defect rates. Equally important is closing vulnerabilities quickly once they are discovered. For commercial software, closing vulnerabilities often comes in the form of the vendor issuing a patch or an update release.

At some point vulnerabilities become known. This is called zero day. From that point to the point where a security fix can be distributed is the vulnerability window. For example, assume a new virus is found on a desktop. Your virus scanner and other preventative measures did not detect and prevent the virus. You discovered this vulnerability on March 1. You notified the vendor of the vulnerability on March 2. The vendor issued a new signature file to detect and prevent the virus on March 15. On the same day, you upgraded all the virus scanners with the new signature file. In this example you have a vulnerability window from March 1 to March 15. The zero day is March 1, which is the day the vulnerability became known.

Vulnerability can last for years when the distributed fix does not fix the root cause. When a vulnerability is exposed through a specific type of attack, you create a security fix. Later, however, you may discover that a different type of attack exploited the same vulnerability. It turns out that the original fix did not address the root cause of the vulnerability. The security fix of the first attack only cut off the original avenue of attack. This avenue of attack is also known as an *attack vector*. The fix did not resolve the root cause of the vulnerability.

Reducing the vulnerability window is important for an organization. It reduces the possibility of unauthorized data access and disclosure of information. That means working quickly with vendors and in-house development teams to identify fixes.

Common Vulnerability Scan Tools

There are a number of common tools one can utilize to conduct vulnerability scans. A few are discussed here:

- **Nmap**—This is a common port scanner. It scans for open ports, running services, and so forth. It is a free download.
- **Nessus**—This is the most widely used vulnerability scanner. It is not a free tool; there are various licensing models. However, it is a powerful tool.
- **OWASP ZAP**—The Open Web Application Security Project Zed Attack Proxy is a free download that will scan websites for the common vulnerabilities. Specifically, it searches for the OWASP top 10 vulnerabilities.

Patch Management

The objective of a patch management program is to quickly secure against known vulnerabilities. Patches are produced by the vendors of systems, applications, and network devices. The objective to patch quickly seems straightforward; however, implementing patches can be challenging. For a large organization with a diverse set of technologies, there may be a continual flood of vendor patches. The dilemma is that failing to apply the patch leaves a security vulnerability that a hacker can exploit. Applying every patch that comes your way may lead to incompatibilities and outages.

Security policies outline the requirements for patch management. These include defining how patches should be implemented. The security policies also define how the patches should be tracked.

The key to success in patch management is to have a consistent approach to applying patches. This approach includes:

- Vetting
- Prioritization
- Implementation
- Post-implementation assessment

Vetting the patch is important to understanding the impact to your environment. Not all patches will apply to your environment. You must determine what security issues and software updates are relevant. An organization needs a point person or team responsible for tracking a patch from receipt to implementation. An asset management system helps inventory all systems, applications, and network devices. This is used to track what assets have been patched.

Each patch needs to be tested to ensure its authenticity. It also needs to be checked as to whether it is compatible with the organization's applications. Regardless of how well you tested the patch, systems may encounter an incompatibility. When that occurs, you will need to work with the vendor to resolve the issue. You could also find an alternative way to mitigate the vulnerability.

 NOTE

The implementation should include a back-out plan, in the event the patch creates major problems. It's not unusual to test patches on small populations of users before they become more widely distributed.

You need to determine the priority of the patch before you implement it. Security policies should provide guidance on how long any security vulnerability can go without being mitigated. The patch team should have clear guidance about how quickly critical patches must be applied. Critical patches are those that mitigate a risk that is actively spreading within the company. Generally, critical patches are applied within hours or days.

Once you assess the priority, you can schedule the patch. You typically schedule patches monthly or quarterly. You make all patches viewable, such as on a Microsoft SharePoint site, by key stakeholders. These stakeholders could be systems, application, and network administrators. This gives them the ability to review and comment on patch deployment. Security policies should identify the notification period before patches are applied.

At this stage the patch process is most visible to the organization. You need to assess the security of the patch management application itself periodically. By its nature, the patch management application needs elevated rights. The patch may need to be applied to every system, application, and network device. A breach of the patch management application can be devastating to an organization.

These patch management tools also provide a vital task of discovery. These tools can examine any device on the network and determine its patch level. Some of these tools are used for dual purposes, such as patch and asset management.

Perform a post-implementation assessment to ensure that the patch is working as designed. Patches can have unintended consequences. Problems with patches need to be tracked and the patch backed out, if necessary.

Quality Assurance Versus Quality Control

One method of measuring the effective of risk management is through quality assurance (QA) and quality control (QC) functions. These functions both measure defects, but in different ways. The idea is simple: If you are managing risks well, you should see fewer problems and fewer defects.

Given the number of definitions used in the industry to describe QA and QC, the differences can be confusing. The American Society for Quality (ASQ), a global association, defines these terms as follow:

- **Quality assurance**—The act of giving confidence, the state of being certain, or the act of making certain
- **Quality control**—An evaluation to indicate needed corrective responses; the act of guiding a process in which variability is attributable to a constant system of chance causes

Other standards such as COBIT adopt similar definitions. Although the wording differs, the underlining core meaning is the same. The QA function "makes certain." That is achieved at the time of the transaction for process execution. Implied is that each transaction or process at a certain stage is validated to create that assurance. In contrast, the QC function "evaluates" the "responses" over time. Implied is that each transaction or process has already been executed.

In short, typically QA is a real-time preventive control. If a transaction or process fails a QA test, the defect is immediately caught. At that point, the defect can be corrected or rejected. In contrast, a QC function typically looks at defects over time and over a broader group of samples, as a detective control. In this way the QC process can capture lessons learned and improve the QA process.

As an example, consider an auto factory. The QA process tests various parts after they are installed, such as by turning on the radio to make sure it works. This will catch improper wiring of the radio. In contrast, the QC process looks at all the dealership reports of radio repairs and tests why the QA process failed to catch the defect. Assume most of the need for radio repairs results from a wire that comes loose over time. The QC process could note that additional testing of the wire connection is required in addition to turning on the radio.

Best Practices for Data Classification and Risk Management Policies

Risk management policies provide the framework for assessing risk across data classification and RCSA activities. The resulting risk assessment looks at how risk is managed end to end. This means that the risk assessment can examine how data classification affects data handling and the RCSA process. It can also identify control gaps between the quality assurance and quality control processes. Risk management policies identify the criteria and content of assessments. Risk management requirements may vary by industry and regulatory standards.

When creating a data classification scheme, you must keep the following in mind:

- Keep the classification simple—no more than three to five data classes.
- Ensure that data classes are easily understood by employees.
- Data classification must highlight which data is most valuable to the organization.
- Classify data in the most effective manner that classifies the highest-risk data first.

The takeaway is that there is no one common approach to defining risk and controls within an organization. Many of the same elements are there but repackaged in a different form. Regardless of what the plan is called, it's important that the risk management policies promote a thorough understanding of the business. They should include a definition of its risks and the ability to ensure data is properly handled.

Case Studies and Examples of Data Classification and Risk Management Policies

The following case studies and examples examine the implementation of several risk-management-related policies. The case studies focus on the risks and policies outlined in this chapter. Risk management policies represent a broad category of risks. These case studies and examples focus on a single policy group, such as disaster recovery, and represent successful implementations.

Private Sector Case Study 1

In May 2017, the virus WannaCry spread across the world quite rapidly. This ransomware utilized the EternalBlue exploit to compromise Microsoft Windows computers. What made this particular attack noteworthy was that it exploited a vulnerability in Windows for which a patch had been available for almost two months. Any organization that was affected by WannaCry clearly did not have a good patch management process.

This case illustrates the need for appropriate patch management. Patches are not usually applied instantly. The patches need to be tested to ensure they won't disrupt existing applications. However, there really is no valid reason for a patch to not be applied two months after its release. Although WannaCry is a well-known example, there are many malware outbreaks and breaches that could have been prevented or mitigated with effective patch management.

Public Sector Case Study

The University of Texas posted a data classification standard on its website. The standard classified data as Category I, II, and III. Category I was defined as data that is protected by law or university regulations. Some of the examples cited were HIPAA, the Sarbanes-Oxley (SOX) Act, and the Gramm-Leach-Bliley Act (GLBA). Category II was defined as other data needing to be protected. Examples cited were email, date of birth, and salary. Category III was defined as data having no requirements for confidentiality, integrity, and availability. These three requirements defined the categories to which the university's data was assigned. The university cited security policies as the authority for the standard.

This is an example of a customized data classification scheme. The university tailored the scheme based on a review of critical data. The university determined that three classification levels were sufficient to meet regulatory requirements. In this case, the university called the data classification a standard. It could as easily have been labeled a policy. In either case, it clearly defined classification levels. It defined roles and responsibilities. It also defined scenarios, such as handling data on a professor's blog. It was a good example of how data assessment and regulatory compliance can come together to create a data classification standard.

Private Sector Case Study 2

In July 2019 it was discovered that an outside individual gained access to Capital One credit card customer data. Reports are that 30 gigabytes of data were downloaded, affecting more than 100 million people. The data included more than 140,000 Social Security numbers of U.S. citizens and 1 million social insurance numbers of Canadian citizens. On July 29, 2019, the FBI arrested Paige Thompson in connection with the breach.

Thompson was a software engineer who formerly worked for Amazon Web Services, which hosted the Capitol One database. She publicly exposed the data she collected and admitted to the incident via Twitter and Slack. The FBI agent who investigated the breach said in court papers that Thompson had gained access to the sensitive data through a "misconfiguration" of a firewall on a web application.

This incident highlights several failures of policy:

- Monitoring internal access to identify when someone is accessing data outside the scope of their job duties
- Ensuring proper configuration of all servers
- Encrypting data at rest

All of these issues were not addressed at Capital One and/or Amazon, thus making this breach possible.

CHAPTER SUMMARY

You learned in this chapter how you can use data classification to identify critical data and protect it. The chapter reviewed military and business classification schemes and examined how these schemes apply to data handling policies. It examined the need to have policies govern data at rest and in transit. The chapter also discussed how data classification helps reduce business risks.

The chapter included discussion of risk management. It discussed how the risk control and self-assessment process (RCSA) can be leveraged to help gain support from executive management. The chapter also explored the differences between quality assurance and quality control. Also, you read in this chapter about how to use QA and QC techniques to measure the effectiveness of risk management policies.

KEY CONCEPTS AND TERMS

Authorization

Automatic declassification

Confidential

Declassification

Highly sensitive classification

Internal classification

Mandatory declassification

Public classification

Risk and control self-assessment (RCSA)

Risk exposure

Secret

Security token

Sensitive but unclassified

Sensitive classification

Systematic declassification

Top Secret

Unclassified

CHAPTER 11 ASSESSMENT

1. Which of the following is *not* a common need for most organizations to classify data?

   A. Protect information
   B. Retain information
   C. Sell information
   D. Recover information

2. Authorization is the process used to prove the identity of the person accessing systems, applications, and data.

   A. True
   B. False

3. You need to retain data for what major reasons?

   A. Legal obligation
   B. Needs of the business
   C. Recovery
   D. A and B
   E. A, B, and C

4. What qualities should the data owner possess?

   A. Is in a senior position within the business
   B. Understands the data operations of the business
   C. Understands the importance and value of the information to the business
   D. Understands the ramifications of inaccurate data or unauthorized access
   E. All of the above

5. In all businesses, you will always have data that needs to be protected.

   A. True
   B. False

6. Risk exposure is best-guess professional judgment using a qualitative technique.

   A. True
   B. False

7. The lowest federal government data classification rating for classified material is _____.

8. Federal agencies can customize their own data classification scheme.

   A. True
   B. False

9. What is a process to understand business leaders' perspective of risk called?

   A. QA
   B. QC
   C. RCSA
   D. D. RA

10. Quality assurance is typically a detective control.

    A. True
    B. False

11. Generally, having 5 to 10 data classifications works best to cover all the possible data needs of an organization.

    A. True
    B. False

12. Risk exposure can be expressed in the following manner: _____ = _____ × _____.

13. Data in transit is what type of data?

    A. Data backup tapes being moved to a recovery facility
    B. Data on your USB drive
    C. Data traversing a network
    D. Data being stored for later transmission

14. Encryption protects data at rest from all types of breaches.

    A. True
    B. False

Incident Response Team (IRT) Policies

NO MATTER HOW WELL YOUR DATA is protected, eventually there will be an incident. That incident could be a breach of your system security, an authorized user inadvertently damaging data, or a natural disaster. It could be the result of an operating system vulnerability or a host of problems outside your control. The fact is that no security program can be 100% effective, as much as we might wish it. Thus, it is critical to have incident response policies to deal with incidents that will inevitably occur. What is certain is that at some point, most organizations will have to respond to a security incident. The speed and effectiveness of the response will limit the damage and reduce any losses. When an incident occurs, an organization needs to respond quickly through a well-thought-out process. An effective response can control the costs and consequences resulting from the incident.

In addition to major incidents, there is the routine response to less substantial incidents. Fortunately, responding to routine security events does not typically rise to the level of a recovery event. However, security events do have the potential to create outages that require activation of a business continuity plan. Whether this activation is due to a security event or natural disaster, security response teams need to be aware of how recovery plans are built and executed.

Well-prepared organizations create an incident response team (IRT). This team and its supporting policies ensure that an incident is quickly identified and contained. It's also the IRT's responsibility to perform a careful analysis of the cause of the incident. Understanding the nature of an incident can help prevent future attacks. An IRT is the first responder to major security incidents within an organization. It's not unusual for an attack to be active when the team responds. To ensure the IRT members are effective at what they do, the organization needs to provide the policies, tools, and training necessary for their success.

This chapter will focus on the incident response team. It will define an incident and related policies. It will discuss how to create an IRT and the various roles and responsibilities within an IRT. The chapter will examine key activities that are performed during an incident. It will also discuss specific policies and procedures ranging from reporting and containing to analyzing an incident. Additionally, this chapter will look at key aspects and documents related to disaster recovery and business continuity. This understanding is high level and foundational in the event a security incident triggers the activation of a recovery plan. Finally, the chapter will review best practices and explore some case studies.

Chapter 12 Topics

This chapter covers the following topics and concepts:

- What an incident response policy is
- How to classify incidents
- What a response team charter is
- Who makes up an incident response team (IRT)
- Who is responsible for actions during an incident
- Which procedures must be followed to respond to an incident
- What best practices to follow for incident response policies
- What business impact analysis (BIA) policies are
- How business continuity plan (BCP) policies protect information
- How disaster recovery plan (DRP) policies protect information
- What some case studies and examples of incident response policies are

Chapter 12 Goals

When you complete this chapter, you will be able to:

- Explain the purpose of an incident response policy
- Define what an incident is
- Explain various incident classification methods
- Understand key components of an IRT charter
- Describe IRT member roles and responsibilities
- Understand major procedures for responding to an incident
- Explain best practices for incident response
- Describe a BIA, a BCP, and a DRP
- Describe the relationship among a BIA, a BCP, and a DRP
- Apply knowledge learned in case studies to real-world issues

Incident Response Policy

An **incident response team (IRT)** is a specialized group of people whose purpose is to respond to major incidents. The IRT is typically a cross-functional team. This means the people on the team have different skills. They are pulled together in a coordinated effort. In many organizations, the IRT is formed to respond to major incidents only. Minor incidents are often managed as part of normal operations. When the team is called together, the IRT is said to be "activated."

It would not be practical to activate the IRT for minor incidents. Policy infractions, for example, are handled by an individual's manager or, if need be, by someone in the security department. Suppose an employee shares his or her password with a second employee. This might occur when that second employee has been approved but is waiting for access to be granted. An incident report may be required in this case, but the IRT would not be activated. Normally, incident response teams are only activated for incidents that require a response that is both immediate and requires the resources of multiple individuals focused on the incident.

The incident response policy must be clear and concise to prevent ambiguity in the response process. The policy must define what an incident is versus an infraction. The policy must define the criteria for activating the IRT. There should be a centralized incident notification process so that appropriate individuals are aware of incidents. These individuals can then decide about whether to declare a disaster. Most important, the policy and related processes must enable the IRT to respond to incidents quickly. From the point an incident is detected to the point the IRT is activated, as little time should pass as possible. Organizations cannot afford to be slow to respond to an active attack.

There are many types of security incidents. When to declare an incident and activate an IRT depends on the organization's policy. This chapter focuses on major information security breaches. Major breaches can include incidents such as systems breached from the outside, internal fraud, or a denial of service attack.

What Is an Incident?

An **incident** is any event that violates an organization's security policies. An incident may disrupt normal operations of an application, system, or network. An incident may result in a reduction in quality of service and in service outages. These outages may require the activation of a recovery plan. An incident may also result in unauthorized access to or modification of data.

Examples of security incidents include:

- Unauthorized access to any computer system
- A deliberately caused server crash
- Copying customer information from a database
- Unauthorized use of computer systems for gaming

It is important that a formal incident definition is included in the incident response policy. This definition is then used to support processes for declaring an incident and activating the IRT.

Incident Classification

The classification of incidents is part of the incident response policy. The classification approach can be documented as an incident response policy or a standard. In the case of a security breach, that naturally means some vulnerability in your systems or security has been exploited. By classifying the incident, you can better understand the threat and the weakness. Knowing the type of attack can help you determine how to respond to stop the damage. It can also help you analyze the control weaknesses in your environment. This helps reduce the risk of future attacks. There's no one standard approach to follow in classifying incidents; however, an industry often adopts similar approaches among companies. The key point is to select an approach that meets your legal and regulatory obligations. This should be an approach that provides enough detail to analyze an incident. This analysis will help you improve weaknesses that lead to incidents.

As an example, the Payment Card Industry Data Security Standard (PCI DSS) requires merchants who accept credit cards to report security incidents involving cardholder data. This report should be issued whenever a breach is detected that violates the PCI DSS. One method of classifying a breach is by attack method. The PCI Security Standards Council publishes lists of common security issues. Some of these are attack types; some of them are vulnerabilities. The following are examples of the sorts of things that the PCI Security Standards Council identifies as methods to gain unauthorized access to systems and sensitive information:

- **SQL injection**—A technique that introduces modified Structured Query Language (SQL) into a website. This attack depends on the website allowing unfiltered input.
- **Improperly segmented network environment**—Related attacks rely on the lack of partitioning or on isolating high-risk assets on their own network segments. For example, in a flat network, all portions of the network are accessible from anywhere on the network. A breach in one part of the network exposes the entire network to potential access.
- **Malicious code or malware**—Programs (such as viruses, worms, Trojan applications, and spyware) added to the platform without a user's knowledge. These programs can damage systems, delete files, encrypt files and demand ransom, or exfiltrate confidential data.
- **Insecure remote access**—Attacks gaining access through remote services such as point-of-sale (POS) devices, vendor networks, and employee remote access tools.
- **Insecure wireless**—Attacks accessing the network through wireless points of entry. The wide variety of networked devices that are now wireless ready has increased the risk in recent years. Such devices include copiers, fax machines, inventory systems, POS terminals, web cameras, and more.

Another example is the federal government. Under the Federal Information Security Management Act (FISMA), the government uses the National Institute of Standards and Technology (NIST) Special Publication 800-61. This publication classifies incidents into the following events on a system or network:

- **Malicious code**—This is a broad category for all code that causes some harm, including computer viruses, Trojan horses, and spyware.
- **Denial of service**—An attacker crafting packets to cause networks and/or computers to crash.
- **Unauthorized access**—An exploit to gain access.
- **Inappropriate usage**—Any use of the computer that violates company policies. This can also facilitate other attacks. For example, visiting websites that are not allowed or inserting portable USB storage that is not approved can lead to malware.

It's important to use a classification that has meaning to both internal and external stake-holders. In both the PCI DSS and FISMA approaches, incidents must be reported. These breaches are classified within categories that help assess the threat level. Also, they use a taxonomy, or classification system, that is easily understood by external stakeholders. It's not uncommon to find similarities among many incident-classification approaches. They all share the goal of providing a common language to describe security incidents.

The incident classification is also used to assess the severity of the incident; that is, is an incident minor or major? On this basis, you determine whether the IRT should be activated. What is considered a major incident versus a minor one depends on the organization's view of risk. Major incidents are generally viewed as incidents that have significant impact on the organization. The impact can be measured in several ways. It might be financial. It may be measured based on disruption of service or legal liability. From a practical standpoint, many major incidents are easier than minor incidents to identify. They might cause effects such as a significant number of users unable to process transactions or unauthorized access to millions of customers' personal data. Any incident related to the protection of human life is considered a major incident. What is considered a minor incident depends on how much risk the organization is willing to accept.

FYI

Incidents can turn into court cases. It's important that the actions of the IRT be clear and show reasonable due care. **Due care** refers to the effort made to avoid harm to another party. It's a legal term that essentially refers to the level of care that a person would reasonably be expected to exercise under particular circumstances. All documents produced during an incident should be written in a straightforward, professional manner.

The Response Team Charter

Typically, organizations require a charter before an IRT can be formed. A charter is an organizational document that outlines the mission, goals, and authority of a team or committee. It's important that legal review the IRT charter for any language that might create a liability. Always assume an outside party may eventually view the charter.

The first step in writing a charter is to determine the type of IRT model to adopt. This part of the charter determines the authority, approach, and deliverable of the IRT. There are several types of IRT models:

- **IRT provides on-site response**—The IRT has full authority to contain the breach.
- **IRT acts in a support role**—The IRT provides technical assistance to local teams on how to contain the breach.
- **IRT acts in a coordination role**—The IRT coordinates among several local teams on how to contain the breach.

Many IRTs provide on-site response. In this case, the IRT is given complete authority to contain the threat. This typically means an IRT member is on-site with hands on the keyboard providing technical response. This IRT model requires its members to have full authority to direct local resources. The IRT members make key decisions in consultation with upper management. The IRT members may be required to have a specific local expert execute a task; however, the expert executes the task under the direction of the IRT member.

When the IRT is in a support role, its members become a resource for the local team. The local team has the responsibility to respond to an incident leveraging the IRT's skills. This model is useful in limited circumstances where the local site team has appropriate skills to respond to an incident. This model may also be viable when the application or system is specialized. For example, in a situation in which a system is used in a narrowly defined profession such as engineering software, the local team would be better equipped to deal with the incident.

When the central IRT is in a coordination role, it becomes a facilitator among parties involved in the incident response. This model is useful when the response covers multiple geographical regions. In this case, you might have to coordinate with IRTs in each location. In this model, the central IRT functions as the lead to facilitate the immediate response. The central IRT also coordinates the root cause analysis.

Once you determine the type of IRT model you'll use, you need to construct the actual charter. This includes setting specific goals. The goals must be simple and realistic. Overly ambitious goals create both a credibility and an execution problem. It's important during an incident that the team focuses on specific achievable goals. These goals can include response times to incidents and level of cost containment. These goals will be used to create policies and processes and influence the selection of tools. For example, if the charter requires an on-site response in 30 minutes or less, the goal will drive a certain staffing level.

The structure of the charter document itself is simple and concise. A typical charter includes the following sections:

- **Executive summary**—Provides background on incident response and the importance it has to the organization. This section defines why the IRT exists and the types of incidents it handles.
- **Mission statement**—Defines the overall goals of the IRT. It also describes what the IRT is responsible for achieving. The mission statement is used to gauge the effectiveness of the IRT.
- **Incident declaration**—Defines an incident. It also describes how an incident is declared. This section becomes the basis for creating a process to activate the IRT team.
- **Organizational structure**—Documents how the IRT is aligned within the organization. It also indicates how the members are managed during an incident.
- **Role and responsibilities**—Describes the purpose and types of activities for each IRT member. This is important in the selection of the right team members. It's essential to remember that you need to fill these roles with capable individuals.
- **Information flow**—Defines how information will be disseminated. It establishes the central team responsible for collecting, analyzing, and communicating incident information to the upper levels of management. This ensures the IRT is accountable for being the central point of contact.
- **Methods**—Defines the way the goals will be achieved. This may include a list of services the IRT team will provide.
- **Authority and reporting**—Describes what authority the team has. This section defines the source of the IRT's authority. For example, the authority can be assigned by upper management in response to specific regulatory requirements.

A charter would not contain a detailed line budget. Funding should be included in the department budget as an annual expense. This avoids having to rewrite the charter every time there are changes in the budget.

Incident Response Team Members

The IRT members typically represent a cross-functional team. These team members are from several departments and bring together multiple disciplines. Being part of this designated team allows members to coordinate their efforts. They can also train together on how to respond to an incident. The team can offer a centralized, full-time service depending on the size of the organization and volume of incidents.

The IRT is composed of a core team supplemented with specialties, when needed. These specialties are brought in based on the type of incident. Usually, full-time IRT departments exist to support very large organizations and the government.

Most organizations activate the IRT when a major incident occurs. In this case, the management of the process comes out of the information security team. Members outside the security team have normal job responsibilities. In the event of an incident, the team is pulled together to deal with the immediate threat. Once the threat is stopped, the team's mission shifts to incident analysis. This analysis determines the cause of the incident and formulates recommendations. Once the final report on the incident is issued, the team is disbanded.

The IRT usually includes members of the information security team along with representatives from other functional areas. Common IRT members include:

- **Information technology subject matter experts (SMEs)**—The **information technology subject matter experts** have intimate knowledge of the systems and configurations. These individuals are typically developers and system and network administrators. They have the technical skills to make critical recommendations on how to stop an attack. The SMEs chosen for each incident response effort will vary depending upon the type of incident and affected system(s).
- **Information security representative**—The **information security representative** provides risk management and analytical skills. He or she may also have specialized forensic skills needed to collect and analyze evidence.
- **Human resources (HR) representative**—The **human resources representative** provides skills on how to deal with employees. Breaches do not always come from outside attackers. When internal employees are involved, the HR representative can advise the team on proper methods of communicating and dealing with the employees. They are experts on HR policies and disciplinary proceedings or employee counseling.
- **Legal representative**—The **legal representative** understands laws and regulatory compliance. This person can be a valuable advisor in ensuring compliance. His or her work will involve reviewing the incident response plans, policies, and procedures. During an incident, the legal representative can help facilitate communication with law enforcement. This person can examine the ramifications of decisions. The representative can also provide expert guidance on legal issues, such as the notification of employees or customers affected by a breach.

NOTE

Many organizations choose to route all communication with law enforcement agencies through their legal counsel. If an incident involving criminal conduct is mishandled, the organization can conceivably be liable. It's important that all action be documented. This will help the company be seen as acting in good faith.

Legal representatives can also advise IRT members on how to conduct themselves to preserve attorney–client privilege. When investigations are conducted by a legal representative as part of his or her duties to an organization, the communication is considered confidential and not subject to certain disclosure.

- **Public relations (PR) representative**—The **public relations representative** can advise on how to communicate with the public and customers who might be impacted by the incident. This is valuable to ensure that accurate information gets out and damaging misconceptions are prevented.
- **Business continuity representative**—The **business continuity representative** understands the organization's capability to restore the system, application, network, or data. This individual also has access to call lists needed to contact anyone in the organization during off hours.
- **Data owner**—The data owner understands the data and the business. As data owner, he or she understands how the data should be handled. The data owner understands the control environment. Because data owners are business leaders, they also understand the data's impact to the business.
- **Management**—Management plays a key decision-making role. Management approves the response policy, charter, budget, and staffing. Management also makes the decision to turn to law enforcement and outside agencies. Ultimately, management is held accountable for the outcome of the incident response effort.

"Emergency services" is a broad category related to any outside agency. These agencies might include police, fire, and state and federal law enforcement. They bring government authority. They can also be useful in tracking down the identity of the attacker, in the case of a cyberbreach.

As can be seen from this list, the IRT has a vast array of skills available. You can add members as needed to deal with an incident. The team's effectiveness will be determined by how quickly a coordinated and focused effort can be deployed. When the incident is a cyberattack, it is usually good to involve the appropriate authorities as soon as possible. Both the Federal Bureau of Investigation (FBI) and the U.S. Secret Service investigate cybercrimes. The sooner you involve them, the better.

Responsibilities During an Incident

The IRT is the single point of contact during an incident. It provides management with information as to what has occurred and what actions are being taken. It serves as the repository for all related incident information. Keeping a repository to determine the root cause of the incident is an important team function.

During an incident, a core team is formed to respond to the threat. **FIGURE 12-1** depicts a typical IRT core team. Not all members of the core team will be activated for every security event. Some security events are small and localized and thus need a smaller core team. Other events are major and impact the entire enterprise, requiring maximum effort by all core team members. At the time of a security event, the IRT manager determines which

FIGURE 12-1

Core incident response team.

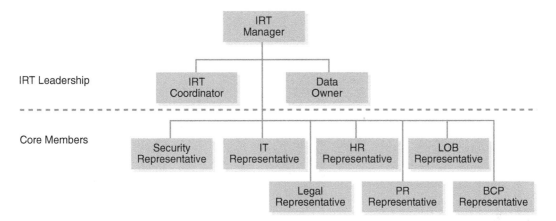

resources are needed to address the specific incident. Additionally, notice that upper management is not considered part of the core team. Instead, upper management is a consumer of the results of the core IRT. Upper management is, however, a critical decision maker in responding to an incident.

Users on the Front Line

It's the responsibility of all users in an organization to support the efforts of the IRT. When the IRT responds to an incident, time is of the essence. It's important that the users on the front line provide quick response to requests for information. Such requests may include preserving evidence. The users may be requested to document events and assist in gathering evidence.

The users on the front line also play an important role in detecting an incident. You increase the likelihood that incidents are detected early when an alert user reports suspicious activity.

System Administrators

The system administrator may be a core member of the IRT team. System administrators help analyze the threat and recommend immediate response. These individuals know the technology and technical infrastructure. They know how it's been customized. They are in a good position to assist with the response.

System administrators have the authority to make critical changes to repel an attack. The term *system administrator* can mean system, application, and network administrator. These individuals have the skills to identify anomalies to the configuration and the ability to respond. For example, they can disconnect devices from the network.

System administrators would also be critical to recovery of the environment. Administrators typically perform reconstruction. This is an important task that often needs to be performed to resume operations.

Information Security Personnel

The information security team has several roles during an incident. Team members may be the first to recognize the security breach. This is because the security team monitors the environment for signs of security breaches, such as intrusion detection alerts. In addition, information security staff members understand the layers of security. They understand the points of potential breach.

The incident response process is typically designed and managed by information security personnel. Security personal are either directly or indirectly involved in most IRT activities. These activities include:

- Discovery
- IRT activation
- Containment
- Analysis and threat response
- Incident classification
- Forensics
- Clean-up and recovery
- Postevent activities

The information security team often provides management and oversight of an incident response. They are facilitators and subject matter experts on security and risk. As such, they may or may not be the individuals tasked with performing the activities listed. In some organizations, these functions are performed by information security personnel. The security team is often responsible only for ensuring the activity occurs. For example, forensic investigations demand a highly specialized skill set. They require significant training and special tools. Forensic investigations are often needed to find out what the root cause of the incident is, even if criminal charges are unlikely to be filed. However, if the attack can be traced to a specific attacker, failure to follow standard criminal procedures can render the evidence unusable. Many organizations do not have the skills and tools to do a forensic review. Some organizations have only basic capabilities. Information security personnel often arrange for a forensic review through an outside firm.

Security personnel also ensure reviews are conducted after an incident to ensure lessons are learned and adopted. The role information security personnel most often perform is writing the final incident report to management. This role makes sense because in their oversight role they see all the issues. They track the timeline of the event. They can see the big picture and combine all the incident issues into a single document.

Management

Management provides authority and support for the IRT's efforts. When parts of the organization are not supporting or reacting quickly enough, it is management's responsibility to remove barriers.

Management also makes key decisions on how to resolve the incident. It's important to remember that the IRT recommends and management approves. If a purely technical decision needs to be made, the IRT operates independently. But a decision that significantly affects the business should be escalated to management, if possible. Management should empower the IRT with enough authority to take drastic action quickly when time is critical. One of the decisions to be made will be when to notify law enforcement, in the event of a cyberattack.

Support Services

This is a broad category that refers to any team that supports the organization's IT and business processes. The help desk, for example, would be a support services team.

During an incident, the help desk may be in direct contact with customers who are being impacted by the attack. The help desk, at that point, becomes a channel of information on the incident. It's vital that the help desk provide a script of key talking points during an incident. Such a script can be very short and only refer questions to another area. Or the script can give more detail with the intent of keeping the public informed. These scripts should be developed and distributed by the PR department.

Other Key Roles

The **IRT manager** is the team lead. This individual makes all the final calls on how to respond to an incident. He or she is the interface with upper management. The IRT manager makes clear what decisions management needs to make. This person also advises management of the ramifications of not making a decision.

The **IRT coordinator** role is to keep track of all the activity during an incident. This person acts as the official scribe of the team. All activity flows through the IRT coordinator, who maintains the official records of the team. It's a critical position because what is recorded becomes the basis for the reconstruction of the event to determine a long-term response.

> ⚠️ **WARNING**
>
> Absent effective communication to management during a security event, there's a risk that various levels of leadership will take actions that make the impact of the breach worse or delay its recovery. The IRT manager must be proactive and have well-established channels of communication with management. This communication includes letting management know the status of the incident and what steps are being taken.

Business Impact Analysis (BIA) Policies

A **business impact analysis (BIA)** is the first step in building a security response and business continuity plan (BCP). Not all security events will require a recovery plan; however, if a security incident creates outages, you need to know which processes are most important to the business and provide for their recovery first. You can use the BIA to coordinate the security and business responses to minimize losses.

Many BIAs are based on building out multiple scenarios. Each scenario is a likely incident, and the impact of that incident is analyzed. This includes natural disasters such as a fire in the server room, as well as computer hardware failure or cyberattacks. The BIA will include the probability of each event as well as the damage from such an event.

The main intent of a BIA is to identify which assets are required for the business to recover and continue doing business.

> ⬛ **NOTE**
>
> The BIA is created by the line of business with the participation of the security team. The BIA is used for both information security and non–information security purposes. For example, it's used to help identify market risks.

TIP

Keep in mind that the BIA process is used to recover from a variety of incidents, not just security breaches. As a result, you need to pick and choose the information most relevant for the IRT's needs.

This identification of key assets and business priorities can then be used by the IRT manager to drive key decision making during an incident. These assets include critical resources, systems, facilities, personnel, and records. Additionally, the BIA identifies recovery times.

Once the data is collected, you need to perform an analysis. Compile all requirements and integrate the knowledge into the incident response processes.

Component Priority

Use the BIA to identify adverse effects on the organization. During this process you identify key components. A *component* can be a function/process or a system such as a database server. How detailed the component definition is depends on the organization. It must be of enough detail that the impact on the business is clear and a recovery strategy can be selected.

The source for this information is the business itself. A BIA cannot be conducted in isolation. It is the business that must establish the priority of components. This phase of the BIA has the following objectives:

- Identify all business functions and processes within the business.
- Define each BIA component.
- Determine the financial and service impact if the component were not available.
- Establish recovery time frames for each component.

There are specific metrics that are collected or computed for each component. One such metric is the maximum tolerable downtime (MTD). This is the amount of time that a component can be out of service without catastrophic damage to the organization. Related to that is the issue of mean time to recovery (MTTR), sometimes called mean time to repair. It is an arithmetic mean (average) of the time needed to get that component back online or replaced. These two metrics will feed into metrics like the recovery time objective, which will be discussed a bit later in this chapter.

Component Reliance

One of the most important parts of the BIA is the determination of dependencies—which components depend or rely on other components. This includes dependency on other BIA components. The BIA must also identify specific resources, such as technology and facilities. Other dependencies may include specific skills in short supply.

The key objectives of this phase of the BIA are to:

- Identify dependencies, such as other BIA components
- Identify resources required to recover each component
- Identify human assets needed to recover these components

Impact Report

Once you complete the assessment, you compile the results, formulating recommendations and integration points into the IRT process.

With this in hand, the business can make decisions. The BIA impact report is not just issued unilaterally by one office or group. You should develop it as a collaborative effort among key stakeholders. These stakeholders include executive leadership, risk teams, IT, and the business. The process of producing the report creates the consensus. Most important, the collaboration process builds the political will to implement the BIA recommendations.

The key objectives of this phase of the BIA are to:

- Validate findings of the BIA report
- Create consensus for its findings and recommendations
- Provide a foundation for other assessments
- Start educating individuals who are key to recovery

The BIA final report is an essential component of an organization's business continuity. It becomes the key document in planning the IRT process. It sets the organization's priorities for IRT responses and for funding IT resiliency efforts. *Resiliency* is a term used in IT to indicate how quickly the IT infrastructure can recover from an outage.

Development and Need for Policies Based on the BIA

The BIA describes the mission-critical functions and processes. This report leads to further assessments that identify threats and vulnerabilities. You typically produce a BIA annually. Next, you compare the findings to existing security policies. This comparison identifies gaps that may be opportunities to improve policies.

As a business changes over time, the BIA is an excellent way to understand the business. This top-priority list of business processes helps focus security efforts to protect the most vital assets of the business. It also drives security decisions on how these assets are to be protected and recovered.

Procedures for Incident Response

There are a number of key steps necessary to effectively handle an incident. These steps are outlined in the incident response procedures.

FIGURE 12-2 depicts the basic steps of an incident response procedure. Notice the model is built as a continuous improvement model. This means that as lessons are learned from incidents, they are used to improve the incident response program itself. Notice that the controls in place before the incident are improved by people outside the IRT. Implementation of control recommendations is typically not handled by the IRT members. Each of the steps in Figure 12-2 is discussed in this section of the chapter. The important takeaway is that incident response is not a one-time process. It takes significant time and effort to create and support an IRT. The organization's commitment and appropriate delegation of authority are essential to responding to incidents quickly and effectively.

FIGURE 12-2

Incident response continuous improvement model.

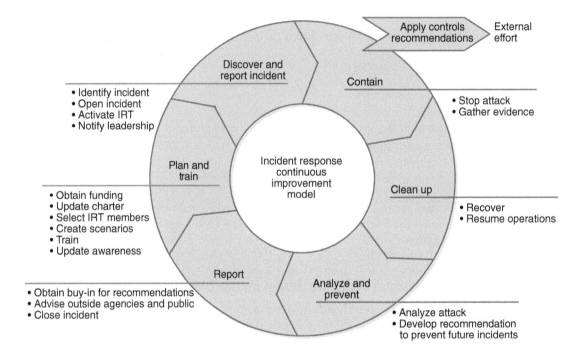

Discovering an Incident

Discovering an incident quickly is a complex undertaking. It requires a solid understanding of normal operations. It also requires continuous monitoring for anomalies. It requires that alert employees report unusual events that can be indicators of an incident. An enterprise awareness effort must teach employees how to report suspicious activity.

The signs of an incident can be obvious or subtle. The number of possible signs is enormous. The following is a small sampling:

- Suspicious activity of a coworker is noticed, and accounts within the department's control do not balance.
- An intrusion detection sensor alerts that a buffer overflow occurred.
- The antivirus software alerts infection across multiple machines.
- Users complain of slow access.
- The system administrator sees a filename with unusual characters.
- The system administrator sees an unknown local account on a server.
- The logs on a server are found to have been deleted.
- Logs indicate multiple failed logon attempts.

These signs do not necessarily mean that an incident has occurred; however, each needs to be investigated to make sure there has been no breach. Some incidents are easy to detect.

On the other hand, small, unexplained signs may only hint that an incident has occurred. Such a small sign might be a configuration file that has been changed. A well-trained and capable staff is necessary to evaluate the signs of an incident.

Reporting an Incident

It's important to establish clear procedures for reporting incidents. This includes methods of collecting, analyzing, and reporting data. When you receive a report of an incident, classify it. This process is often called *triage*. Triage is an essential part of the incident response process. The triage process creates an immediate snapshot of the current situation. This is used to assess the severity of the threat. When the incident reaches a certain severity, the IRT is activated. This is the official declaration of an incident.

It's important to note that many security incidents are isolated occurrences, such as computer viruses. These are easily handled with well-established procedures. When an incident is reported, the triage process must be staffed with well-trained individuals who can classify the incident and its severity. A sample severity classification is as follows:

- **Severity 4**—A small number of system probes or scans are detected, or an isolated instance of a virus is found. The event is handled by automated controls. No unauthorized activity is detected.
- **Severity 3**—A significant number of system probes or scans are detected, or widespread virus activity is detected. The event requires manual intervention. No unauthorized activity is detected.
- **Severity 2**—Limited disruptions to business as usual (BAU) operations are detected. Automated controls failed to prevent the event. No unauthorized activity is detected.
- **Severity 1**—A successful penetration or DoS attack is detected with significant disruption of operations, or unauthorized activity is detected.

There's no one standard approach to assessing the severity of a reported incident. You may choose to allow the existing procedures to handle severity 3 and 4. The IRT may be activated to handle severity 1 and 2. You want to have a clear definition of terms. Severity 1 uses the phrase "significant interruption of operations." That definition might vary among organizations. You do not want to interpret definitions so strictly that the definitions lose common sense. For example, consider a breach of the scheduling system for lawn care at a major organization. Yes, it's a successful penetration. However, it is doubtful it would trigger a severity 1. Although it may seem like a silly example, that's the problem you have with acting on pure definitions. Definitions cannot cover every situation. The best practice is to use professional judgment in assigning severity classifications. Definitions should provide guidance but not prescriptive rules.

A severity classification alone is not used in determining a response. You should also consider the incident classification to understand the nature of the attack. For example, there is a substantial difference between a server being down due to a denial of service and an unauthorized access to your credit database containing

 NOTE

During the early stage of an attack, you don't know what the final impact and damage to the organization will be. During triage, the focus is on understanding the nature of the attack and containment. Severity and incident classifications can help you to quickly come to a decision on how to contain the threat.

millions of customer records. Both incidents may mean access to data is temporarily disrupted, but the latter incident is clearly more serious.

A senior leader in the information security team is typically called to make the formal declaration decision. This person is the chief information security officer or a delegate. His or her responsibility is to ensure the analysis is sound and appropriate to declare an event. Once an incident is formally declared, the IRT response timeline starts. Triage captures all the actions taken to that point. The process activates the IRT plan and notifies upper management. The documentation includes what the basis for the severity was.

Containing and Minimizing the Damage

There are several quick actions you can take to contain the incident. This might include blocking the Internet Protocol (IP) from which the attack is being launched. It also might include disabling the affected user ID or removing the affected server from the network. Regardless of the specific method, the first issue is always to contain the attack. That must always be the priority.

Before a response can be formulated, a decision needs to be made. This involves balancing the needs of the business and the need to pursue the attacker. The BIA can help facilitate that decision. Depending on the impact documented in the BIA and the assets at risk, you can decide to allow the breach to continue to gather information on the hacker or to stop the breach immediately. In simple terms, if low-value assets are being attacked, then you could choose to allow the breach to continue in order to gather information on the attacker. If high-value assets are being attacked, you must stop the breach immediately.

FYI

An organization can use different terms to represent the IRT process and core team. The terms may be different, but the core objectives are the same: Services are to be protected and restored when needed, financial losses are to be minimized, and lessons are to be learned.

You will obviously not know the type of incident in advance. Therefore, you may find that getting preapproval from management to act is difficult to impossible. A decision on what action to take should come from upper management. However, management needs to understand the damage that will occur by allowing the attacker to continue. Having a protocol with management can establish priorities and expedite a decision. The BIA scenario discussion can help expedite leadership understanding of the organization's priorities and choices. Business leaders should understand in advance the types of decisions they will be asked to make and the range of implications involved.

The IRT will work to classify the attack. It will also work to determine the best means to stop it. You should document each step of the decision-making process. The IRT will also determine if forensics skills are required and if it is appropriate to inform law enforcement.

It's important to have a set of responses prepared in advance. The initial analysis provides the picture of the threat to prioritize a sequence of prerehearsed steps. This could range from taking the server offline to blocking outside IP addresses. These predetermined responses should be well documented. Documentation should include what level of authority is needed to execute. For example, management may grant the IRT permission to block overseas IP addresses. Blocking domestic IP addresses, however, may need management approval. In that case, management should be alerted early when domestic IP addresses are involved. Such an alert would advise management of the situation and ensure someone is available to make a quick decision.

An important part of containment is evidence-gathering. Parts of the IRT team will be focused on stopping the attack while others take snapshots of logs, configuration, and other evidence. Remember, a successful breach is a crime scene. If there's a chance you can prosecute the attacker, it's important to gather as much evidence as possible. You should also disturb the environment as little as possible. This is very difficult when you're trying to stop an attack. However, it's important to be aware of the need to collect evidence.

Cleaning Up After the Incident

A core mission of the IRT is to ensure efficient recovery of the operations. Obviously, recovery is focused on getting affected systems back in service, but that is not the only thing that recovery accomplishes. Recovery includes ensuring that the vulnerabilities that permitted the incident have been mitigated. Find out precisely what happened and how it can be prevented or at least mitigated in the future. Mitigation includes both lessening the probability of such an incident reoccurring and lessening the impact.

The recovery phase begins once the threat has been contained. You can implement an effective recovery strategy together with the business continuity plan (BCP) representative. This may require restoring servers and rebuilding operating systems from scratch. The next step would then be to test the affected machines and data. The testing should include looking for any signs of the original incident, such as virus or malware. Once you test the servers and systems, you can certify them to be put back into production.

During the containment phase, you have little time to gather evidence. You have more time in the clean-up phase; however, management may pressure you to resume operations. Forensically image the damaged computer(s), if possible, for further analysis after operations have resumed. That way you know the exact state prior to recovery. There are forensic tools that can perform this function for you.

It should be noted that imaging suspect machines as early as possible is going to be critical if you wish to perform a forensic investigation later. And in the case of law enforcement becoming involved, having forensic images will facilitate their investigation. It is important that you maintain chain of custody from the beginning of the imaging process, in case a criminal case develops. That process is not terribly complicated. You document when the device is imaged, by whom, using what tool. Then you store the image in a secure location and document everyone who has access to that location. That should be as few people as possible. It should be noted that imaging a drive can be a slow process. It often takes several hours to image a machine's hard drive. It is recommended that even if an organization does not intend to keep full-time forensic specialists on staff, that at least some members of the IRT have some basic forensics training.

If your organization is successfully attacked, it may be attacked again. It's important that the security controls are hardened to withstand another attack. It is often a good idea to install additional monitoring after systems are brought back online. You can use the additional monitoring to validate that the systems have been hardened. You can also use additional monitoring to change how management approaches future attempts to breach the same systems.

Documenting the Incident and Actions

As a focal point for the enterprise, the IRT can gather information across the organization. The IRT assesses the information gathered during and after the incident to gain insights into the threat. It's important that all status reports be issued through the IRT manager. Status reports are internal communications between the IRT and management. However, you should assume that others may end up viewing them. They might even end up in a court of law. You should avoid speculation in these reports. The reports should stay with the basic facts. These include what you know and what you are doing about it.

You should start incident analysis immediately upon declaring an incident. Quickly determine the type of threat. Then determine the scope of the incident and the extent of damage. This will allow you to determine the best response. During this analysis you are collecting information to contain the incident. You are also collecting it for future forensic analysis.

Collecting forensic evidence is an important part of the IRT's responsibility. This means collecting and preserving information that can be used to reconstruct events. Analysis depends on gathering as much information as possible about the following:

- What led up to the event
- What happened during the event
- How effective the response was

There are specific tools and techniques used to collect forensic evidence. It's important that a trained specialist collects the information. This is because the evidence may end up being used in a court of law. The gathering of information must follow strict rules that the court finds acceptable.

Part of these rules involves a *chain of custody*. This was mentioned a bit earlier. It's important not only that the information be gathered a certain way, but also that the information be stored securely after it's collected. *Chain of custody* is a legal term referring to how evidence is documented and protected. Evidence must be documented and protected from the time it's obtained to the time it's presented at court. In forensics it is difficult to have too much documentation.

 TIP

You should only use an established forensic tool software package when gathering evidence to be submitted to a court. Examples of such tools are OSForensics by Passmark Software, Forensics Toolkit by Access Data, Blackbag Forensics, or EnCase Forensic by Guidance Software.

There is a basic approach to proving that digital evidence has not been tampered with. It is to take a physical image of machines and calculate a hash value. A physical image is a bit by bit copy of the storage for the machine. The hash value is obtained by running a special algorithm. This algorithm generates a mathematical value based on the exact content of the bit image of the machine. The hash value is essentially a fingerprint of the image. Imaging software will hash the original and the image and compare the two hashes. If one bit of data on the bit image copy is altered in any way, the hash value would change.

The IRT coordinator should maintain an evidence log. All evidence associated with the investigation should be logged in and locked up. If any evidence needs to be examined, it's logged out and then logged back in. Where possible, once evidence is logged in, only copies should be logged out for further review. It is important to maintain a chain of custody to be sure the material is not altered or tampered with.

Analyzing the Incident and Response

The goal of the analysis is straightforward: It is to identify the weakness in your control. Knowing the weakness allows you to continuously improve your security. It helps prevent the incident from occurring again. As you examine your control, you may find other weaknesses unrelated to the incident. Ideally, you want to be able to identify the following:

- The attacker
- The tool used to attack (if possible)
- The vulnerability that was exploited
- The result of the attack
- The control recommendation that would prevent such an attack from occurring again

Each incident is different and may require a different set of techniques to arrive at these answers. There are some steps you can take to help the analysis:

- **Update your network diagram and inventory**—Be sure to have a current network diagram and inventory of devices available.
- **Profile your network**—Map the network traffic by time of day and keep trending information.
- **Understand business processes**—Understand normal behavior within the network and business.
- **Keep all clocks synchronized**—Be sure the logs all have a synchronized timestamp.
- **Correlate central logs**—Be sure logs are centrally captured and easily accessible.
- **Create a knowledge base of threats**—Create and maintain a library of threat scenarios.

Understanding the environment makes it easier to detect suspicious activity. As you become more familiar with the business processes, you can consider new threat scenarios. These new threat scenarios then need to be fed back into the BIA process. Over time, this builds institutional knowledge on what risks the business faces and how to properly respond.

The key point is to use these incident analyses to be proactive in defending against threats. The reports examine how to close a security weakness as well as why the security weaknesses were not originally considered and closed. Reports improve the risk assessment process as much as they help close a specific vulnerability.

Creating Mitigation to Prevent Future Incidents

Part of the analysis is to trace the origin of the attack. This is important for preventing future incidents. This activity involves finding out how hackers entered the application, systems, or network. The analysis should create a storyboard and timeline of events. The storyboard is a complete picture of the incident. This includes actions taken by the hacker, employees, and IRT.

The IRT may engage outside help in identifying the attacker. This outside help may include consulting firms that specialize in forensic investigations. It may also include various law enforcement agencies. These outside resources have established contacts with Internet service providers (ISPs). They can track down online users. Although the exact identity of the hacker may not always be determined, these firms can often identify the point of origin. In other words, you may never know the hacker's real name; however, there's a good chance you will know the country and city of origin. These firms can also provide a profile of the attacker. Such a profile might include the attacker's level of skill and potential motive. The attacker might be a high school student. It might also be a foreign government. This information could be valuable to know in determining a response.

It is vital that an organization learn from incidents to improve its controls. Sometimes that may mean changing its policies and procedures. Other times it may mean improving security awareness to reduce human error. It can also mean making changes in your security configuration standards.

A final IRT incident report should be published for executive management. This report will bring everyone up to date on the risk that was exploited. It will also show how it was mitigated. The report should answer the following:

- How the incident was started
- Which vulnerabilities were exploited
- How the incident was detected
- How effective the response was
- What long-term solutions are recommended

After a major incident, you should hold a lessons-learned meeting with key stakeholders. This meeting will review key points in the IRT incident report. A lessons-learned meeting should also be held periodically for minor incidents. You can use an annual trending report as an effective measure of progress in reducing risk.

The lessons learned should include how to improve the incident response process. These lessons can be used to help training. They can also help improve IRT skills. Skills can be improved using methods such as additional training. They can also be improved through testing using new scenarios built from the lessons learned.

Handling the Media and Deciding What to Disclose

The PR department will play an important role in communicating the incident to the media and impacted parties. The PR department can correct misinformation that could damage the company's reputation. The decision to release information to the public is often handled through a press release.

The PR department is also a point of contact for press inquiries. If a reporter contacts the PR department, it's important that the PR department have the latest information on the incident. How much information to release is a decision for management. It is the role of the IRT management to make sure the PR representative has the core facts. It's then up to management and the PR department to work out the type of disclosure that's appropriate for the situation.

Notification may be required that will impact consumers. Many privacy laws require consumers to be notified if their personal information has been breached. Once again, the PR department will work with management and legal to determine what needs to be disclosed to stay in compliance. Note that any attempt to cover up a breach is likely to cause additional harm. In many cases, such a coverup may be illegal. Even if it is not, strictly speaking, illegal, it is likely to damage an organization's reputation should it come to light.

Business Continuity Planning Policies

A **business continuity plan (BCP)** policy creates a road map for continuing business operations after a major outage or disruption of services. BCP policies establish the requirement to create and maintain the plan. The BCP policies give guidance for building a plan. These include elements such as key assumptions, accountability, and frequency of testing. BCP policies must clearly define responsibilities for creating and maintaining a BCP. The BCP identifies responsibilities for its execution.

The plan must cover the business's support structure, which includes things like facilities, personnel, equipment, software, data files, vital records, and relationships with contractors and service providers. When you must have minimum downtimes, BCP planning and documentation must have a high degree of precision.

But suppose a recent risk assessment has identified serious control weaknesses based on poor physical security at the vendor's facilities. Well-defined BCP policies would require a gap analysis along with the risk assessment. This approach allows you to assess the vendor weaknesses as part of the BCP process. These weaknesses can become scenarios discussed in the BIA. In this example, you may choose to continue this strategic relationship but consider how to mitigate the vendor's physical security risk.

As previously mentioned, the BIA is the initial step in the business continuity planning process. The purpose of a BIA is to identify the company's critical processes and assess the impact of a disruptive event. The desired results of the BIA include:

- A list of critical processes and dependencies
- A workflow of processes that include human requirements for recovering key assets
- An analysis of legal and regulatory requirements
- A list of critical vendors and support agreements
- An estimate of the maximum allowable downtime

TIP

Compare the business impact assessment and the business continuity plan. The two should closely align. For example, if the business identifies a critical asset or process in the BIA, then it should be a recovery priority in the BCP. Gaps or discrepancies should be reported to appropriate management.

NOTE

A BCP is about getting essential business operations up and running, which include technology components. A disaster recovery plan, which you'll learn about later in this chapter, is about full recovery as if the incident never happened. Think of BCP as just enough to keep the organization running.

The BIA is the foundation on which a BCP is developed. The individuals accountable for the BCP should be key stakeholders in the BIA process. These include the auditors who must assess the adequacy of the planning process. Poor-quality results in the BIA will lead to poor-quality BCP planning.

Dealing with Loss of Systems, Applications, or Data Availability

The list of critical systems, applications, and user access requirements comes from the BIA. The BIA also includes maximum downtime. This drives the selection of recovery methods and techniques. As the recovery window is shortened, there must be more reliance on technology. People can react only so fast. Speed of reaction can be a problem if a disaster strikes while individuals are most distracted, such as during a long holiday weekend. Key staff may be away for the holidays and out of communication. In that case, you should rely more heavily on automation and well-documented plans that others can execute in the absence of that staff.

In the case of a long holiday weekend, it may take hours to connect with key personnel who have a reasonable understanding of the event. At worst, it may take days. Coping with the loss of systems and technology requires effective planning. It also requires coordination, often with a greater reliance on manual processes. These manual processes must be well defined.

The BCP policies require the same level of care for the information. Assume a clinic faces a disaster. It chooses to capture information by hand. The information captured needs the same level of care as if the information were entered into a computer. The information may be covered by HIPAA and thus require the same diligence in security and handling. The BCP is not just about recovery; it must detail the access controls needed to protect the information during recovery. These controls might include securely storing and transporting the information.

Response and Recovery Time Objectives Policies Based on the BIA

The **recovery time objective (RTO)** is the length of time within which a business process should be recovered after an outage or downtime. Put another way, how soon will you have a given system back online? This should be set with the previously discussed maximum tolerable downtime (MTD) in mind.

It's important to understand that the RTO relates to the business process. It does not relate to the dependent components, such as the technology. The RTO is the measurement of how quickly individual business processes should be recovered. The RTO is a natural extension of the BIA. It identifies the maximum allowed downtime for a business process. The maximum allowed downtime is based on the business tolerance for loss. This, in turn, becomes the RTO. That is why the business continuity planner is part of the BIA process.

The continuity planner understands the capabilities of the organization to recover from a disaster. The planner should be able to catch an unrealistic RTO set by the business during the BIA process. For example, the business may state that it requires near real-time recovery of its applications in the event of a disaster. Few organizations can achieve that goal. The

BCP planner facilitates a candid discussion on the cost of recovery and the organization's capabilities. The continuity planner can also push requirements that increase costs.

RTO policies often include a discussion of **recovery point objectives (RPOs)**. The RPO is the maximum acceptable level of data loss from the point of the disaster. Consider an example wherein the company backs up a server every hour. In the event of a hard drive crash, the company could lose up to 59 minutes' worth of data. The organization must ask whether this is acceptable. If it is not, then backup strategies must be re-examined.

The RPO can be shorter than the RTO. In that case, the business is saying the business process can be down longer. However, when business operations resume, the business needs the data from an earlier point, such as the point of outage. It's important to understand that the RPO relates to the data, not to a single RTO. When you look at the RTO and RPO, the requirements to recover a business successfully emerge. These requirements drive the selection of recovery technology and design of the BCP.

 NOTE

The BIA becomes the requirements document for the BCP and RTO. You rarely change the BIA requirements during the BCP process unless new data is discovered.

Best Practices for Incident Response Policies

Incident response policies recognize that an organization needs to build strong external relationships. The policies need to identify which role is responsible for maintaining these relationships. For example, the legal department often maintains relationships with outside law firms.

The IRT may wish to establish a formal contract with consulting firms that specialize in incident response. These firms can provide a depth of knowledge on specific attacks. Such knowledge may not be available within the organization. Because consulting firms respond to multiple incidents across many customers, they can respond to incidents rapidly.

Incident response policies and capabilities need to be tested. Testing can also act as training for the IRT. Training ensures the staff has the required skill set to respond quickly to an incident. Ideally, the test should not be announced, so the activation process can also be tested.

The effectiveness of the IRT and its related policies needs to be measured. This is to ensure that the IRT is achieving its stated goals. The measurement should be published annually with a comparison to prior years. The measurements should include the goals in the IRT charter, plus additional analytics to indicate the reduction of risk to the organization. This might include:

- Number of incidents
- Number of repeat incidents
- Time to contain per incident
- Financial impact to the organization

Disaster Recovery Plan Policies

The **disaster recovery plan (DRP)** consists of the policies and documentation needed for an organization to completely recover from some incident. The business impact analysis drives the requirements for the business continuity plan. The BCP drives the requirements for the disaster recovery plan. These include software, data, and hardware. The DRP essentially is more detailed than the BCP. The DRP must not only get essential systems online, but in fact get *all* systems back online.

Disaster recovery planning considers people, processes, and technology. In many cases, laws and regulations outline the requirements for a DRP. For healthcare organizations, the Health Insurance Portability and Accountability Act of 1996 (HIPAA) requires a DRP. In developing a DRP, it's important to work with your organization's legal department to ensure requirements are being met. As another example, the Occupational Safety and Health Administration (OSHA) requires organizations with 10 employees or more to have a DRP. The law is meant, in part, to protect employees' health and safety during a disaster.

Disaster Declaration Policy

The disaster declaration policy outlines the process by which a BCP and/or DRP is activated. It's not unusual to have an IT disruption event that is localized in the technology infrastructure.

If an event causes major business outages, the BCP would be activated. Localized technology outages often impact the business. They may not rise to the level of a disaster. Still, in those cases, the DRP portion of the BCP plan would be activated. A server may go down, or a critical file may be deleted. This can disable a vital application in a smaller organization. In a large organization, however, many of these events occur each month. They are considered routine and would not trigger a DRP.

> **NOTE**
>
> It's important to note that technology outages occur often, not just when there's a security breach. Often the recovery plan is created independent of the cause, and then integrated into the IRT process as appropriate.

The disaster declaration policy defines the roles and responsibilities for assessing and declaring a disaster. Once a DRP is activated, a number of processes and capabilities are launched. You can handle many of these activities, such as notification to staff, through automated systems. The activation of a DRP for a large, complex organization costs thousands of dollars. In this case, the decision about who can declare a disaster is tightly controlled. Once the plans are activated, you want the process to be as automatic as possible. It should be second nature for those involved.

Once a disaster is declared, it's very hard to stop its early ramp-up stages. These might include notifying key leaders and staging recovery capability. The process for declaring the disaster is contained in the disaster declaration policy. The following is a sampling of activations the plan might also include:

- Emergency notification of personnel, stakeholders, and strategic vendors
- Alternative site activation
- Activation of the emergency control center
- Transport and housing arrangements
- Release of prepositioned assets

Many of these activities will overlap with BCP activities. The difference is that they focus on the recovery of the IT infrastructure, as opposed to business operations.

Assessment of the Disaster's Severity and of Potential Downtime

Not all disasters are alike. There's a difference between losing your entire data center to a flood and having a DOS attack that disables a few dozen servers. But both would activate a DRP.

Assessment of the severity occurs throughout the life of a disaster. It starts with the disaster declaration and is continually updated. You forward the information to the emergency control center. Here it's included in the decision-making process. Performing this continued assessment of the potential downtime is important. It ensures the right resources are being allocated to the problem. Many critical business decisions during a disaster rely on the assessment of the problem's severity. A small sampling includes:

- Allocation of resources
- Notification to customers
- Assessment of financial losses and costs

Allocation of resources gets the right people to focus on the right problem. Consider a major outage of a vital vendor application. Your IT team estimates the outage at an hour or so. Then you reassess and estimate the potential downtime to be several days. The leadership in the emergency control center may be more patient in the first case. In the second case, the leadership may be on the phone with the vendor and begin flying in additional resources.

Having realistic estimates of downtime is important for customer relations. Overly optimistic recovery estimates often lead to loss of credibility. Suppose air travelers are told they face a flight delay of 20 minutes, but then their plane doesn't leave until 3 hours later. This can cause a big public relations problem when it occurs repeatedly. The best professional judgment on potential downtime is expected in a DRP. Unrealistic estimates can overcomplicate and undermine the recovery process. It's important to keep a complete history and basis for the estimates throughout the recovery process. You can use this information in postdisaster assessments to improve your process.

Assessments during a disaster are needed to determine financial losses and costs. An extended outage may require the infusion of capital to sustain an organization throughout the disaster. The amount of capital required will depend on the duration of the outage. Accurately estimating potential downtime is important to controlling those costs. It's important to remember this is not just about a security breach or event. Equally, you need to look at a security event as a business disruption. Business relies on an end-to-end process working. From a technology perspective this means that the system, application, and data must all be in place and working. If any one of these components is not recovered or is out of alignment, the process fails. Disaster recovery policies define what to back up, and how often, and how to recover data in case of a disaster. The DRP must align well with the BCP and the BIA.

There are unique requirements for backup and recovery for systems, applications, and data. Systems and applications are easier to recover in some ways. They change less frequently and often rely on software from vendors. Having multiple sources to recover systems and applications makes recovery easier.

The customization of systems and applications is a different story. These customization settings are commonly referred to as *configuration*. They must also be captured and available during a recovery. The configuration for operating systems and databases includes security controls. The DRP needs to ensure these controls are not disabled during a disaster. A subset of the DRP is a security plan that outlines how security controls will be monitored and maintained during a disaster. The plan may restrict access to key staff to improve performance and stability. Approval for access may have to go through the emergency control center. It may require CISO approval.

The key point is that security planning and execution during a disaster are important considerations when building a DRP. Recovery of mission-critical data can be more challenging than recovery of systems and applications. The value of data is often time dependent. Data backups taken at the point of the disaster are typically more valuable than data backups from the prior month. The BIA process and data classification effort identify the data that must be recovered.

Case Studies and Examples of Incident Response Policies

The case studies in this chapter examine various organizations that had formal incident response teams established by policies. The case studies examine how effective these teams were during a security breach.

Private Sector Case Study

An online forensic case study was published about a multibillion-dollar publicly traded company. The company is a leader in the IT infrastructure market. The company was not named in the article.

The problem: The company's servers had been compromised to be the jumping-off point to attack a host of other companies.

The company was notified by another company of what was being attacked. The company's administrator activated an IRT to assess the threat. The administrators were unable to find that a breach had occurred. They called in a consulting firm named Riptech, which specialized in intrusions and forensic analysis. Riptech discovered that a server had been compromised. The firm wanted to monitor the intruder's activities. However, Riptech was advised by in-house counsel that the company was not comfortable allowing the breach to continue. Riptech managed to trace the attack to a North Dakota high school.

This case study illustrated weaknesses in the company's incident response policies and plans. It did point to the skills and tools available to the company. In addition, information response policies were clear on the role and skill requirements to form an IRT. The team did appear to be cross-functional, because the legal department was clearly engaged. Also, the IRT was activated quickly. However, the administrators were unable to find the breach.

The incident is a good example of working with legal specialists to determine the appropriate response. Although Riptech preferred to track down the attacker, the company's legal counsel was concerned over the potential liability of permitting a breach. The decision was to protect the organization and stop the intrusion.

The case study illustrates how forensic tools are used to gather evidence. A bitmap copy of the infected systems was made prior to the systems being restored. This preserved the affected server. The image could then be used as evidence or for further analysis of the incident.

The case study also illustrates the public relations approach that was taken. Because there was no breach of data, the company decided not to publicly acknowledge the attack. The article indicated the concern was public perception. The organization did not want it known that a teenager was able to breach its system.

The final incident report issued by Riptech outlined a series of control weaknesses that allowed the breach. The consulting firm helped the company restore its system and mitigate the threat in the future.

Public Sector Case Study

In August 2019, various government facilities in Texas were hit with ransomware. Twenty-three towns and cities in Texas were hit with a coordinated cyberattack. City government services were unavailable due to ransomware. The response team included state officials and the FBI. The FBI identified the malware as the Odinokibi virus, which had first been seen in April 2019.

The incident response process identified that the most likely attack vector used by the ransomware was a communication channel managed by a third party. The initial entry appears to have been a phishing email. This is the first takeaway from this incident: Only by identifying how the incident occurred can steps be taken to reduce the chances of a repeat.

It also happens that the state of Texas had been working for some time to have a centralized incident response system. This included coordination of the incident response across affected cities and involving the FBI and the Secret Service early on. Due to the improved incident response, most of the cities were fully operational again within a matter of days, and none paid the ransomware. Furthermore, there was an immediate statewide push for more cybertraining and improving both defenses and incident response. This is an example of an effective incident response policy.

Critical Infrastructure Case Study

A case study was published by the Carnegie Mellon CERT program. It described how one of the largest banks in the country started an IRT. The case study concealed the bank's name, referring to it as AFI. The case study described the process that AFI went through to create the team and related policies.

The need for an IRT was clear to the security manager. He had observed security incidents being handled inconsistently. This was a problem because the bank was governed by certain regulations. The approach was to involve several of the risk groups and key stakeholders. The effort was jump-started by using best practices. It took several years to deploy globally. This was because of the size and complexity of the organization. The effort was initially understaffed. The effort that would be required was underestimated. Requirements were not clearly understood.

This case study is a good example of how regulated industries are required to have effective information response policies. This is also an example of an IRT that is filled with appropriately skilled individuals. There was no indication in the case study that an external firm was engaged to assist the company. It would be a best practice to engage an outside firm to help plan such an effort when internal skills are not available.

CHAPTER SUMMARY

You learned in this chapter what incident response policies are needed to respond effectively to security breaches. It's important that policies define what an incident is. They should also state clearly how to classify an event. You also learned how to build a team charter. The chapter examined the difference between on-site response teams and teams that facilitate responses. The chapter discussed key roles and responsibilities within the team during an incident. The chapter discussed how incident plans are built, including the importance of a BIA assessment. Additionally, the chapter discussed the alignment among the BIA, BCP, and DRP.

The chapter also examined typical procedures you should follow during an incident. It examined key decisions that are needed at each step in responding to an incident. This includes containing the incident and gathering evidence. The chapter also discussed best practices and the importance of using outside firms to supplement an organization's skill sets. Finally, the chapter explored how these principles are applied in the real world. Implementing well-defined incident response policies takes significant time and effort. However, the value in containing threats and limiting damage to an organization outweighs the costs.

KEY CONCEPTS AND TERMS

Business continuity plan (BCP)
Business continuity representative
Business impact analysis (BIA)
Disaster recovery plan (DRP)
Due care
Human resources representative

Incident
Incident response team (IRT)
Information security representative
Information technology subject matter experts
IRT coordinator

IRT manager
Legal representative
Public relations representative
Recovery point objectives (RPOs)
Recovery time objective (RTO)

CHAPTER 12 ASSESSMENT

1. All incidents, regardless of how small, should be handled by an incident response team.

A. True

B. False

2. Which of the following should *not* be in an information response team charter?

A. Mission

B. Organizational structure

C. Detailed line budget

D. Roles and responsibilities

3. Which of the following IRT members should be consulted before communicating to the public about an incident?

   A. Management
   B. Public relations
   C. IRT manager
   D. All of the above

4. As defined by this chapter, what is *not* a step in responding to an incident?

   A. Discovering an incident
   B. Reporting an incident
   C. Containing an incident
   D. Creating a budget to compare options
   E. Analyzing an incident response

5. A method outlined in this chapter to determine if an incident is major or minor is to classify an incident with a(n) _____ rating.

6. When containing an incident, you should always apply a long-term preventive solution.

   A. True
   B. False

7. The IRT starts recording events once a(n) _____.

8. During the containment step, you should also gather as much evidence as reasonably possible about the incident.

   A. True
   B. False

9. To clean up after an incident, you should always wipe the affected machine clean and rebuild it from scratch.

   A. True
   B. False

10. What value does a forensic tool bring?

    A. Gathers evidence
    B. Helps evidence to be accepted by the court
    C. Can take a bit image of a machine
    D. All of the above

11. How important is it to identify the attacker before issuing a final IRT report?

    A. Critically important; do not issue the report without it.
    B. Moderately important; nice to have but issue the report if not available.
    C. Not important; focus on the incident and do not include identity of attacker even if you have it.
    D. Important; allow law enforcement to brief management about attacker's identity.

12. When analyzing an incident, you must try to determine which of the following?

    A. The tool used to attack
    B. The vulnerability that was exploited
    C. The result of the attack
    D. All of the above

13. Which IRT member is responsible for handling the media?

14. The business impact analysis (BIA) is created after the business has created a business continuity plan (BCP).

    A. True
    B. False

15. What is the difference between a BCP and a DRP?

    A. A BCP focuses on the business recovery, and a DRP focuses on technology recovery.
    B. A DRP focuses on the business recovery, and a BCP focuses on technology recovery.
    C. There is no difference. The two terms mean the same thing.

16. The BIA assessment is created by the IRT team primarily for use during a security incident.

    A. True
    B. False

PART THREE

Implementing and Maintaining an IT Security Policy Framework

IT Security Policy Implementations

I NFORMATION SECURITY POLICIES are the foundation upon which you build good security habits. IT security policies define what business and technology risks will be controlled and how they will be controlled. Users can turn to policies for guidance in their daily work. Policies are a useful tool for creating a risk culture that protects information. Policies are also part of the artifacts that are examined in any audit. The adoption and effective implementation of these policies are evidence to regulators, customers, and shareholders that due care is being taken to protect the company and its customers' personal information. The stakes are high. Well-implemented security policies build brand confidence and help an organization achieve its goals. Poorly implemented security policies lead to breaches, fines, and damage to brand value, and they undermine confidence in the organization.

Everyone must follow the policies if they are to be effective. A security policy implementation needs user acceptance to be successful. Absent user acceptance, the policies may not be implemented consistently. They may sometimes be seen as optional. You can gain user acceptance, in part, by effectively communicating policies that are also easy to understand. A security awareness program, in addition to other methods, helps users understand policies and why they're important. The implementation of security policies also requires management support. Thorough planning allows you to overcome challenges and gain that support.

This chapter examines a simple process approach to implementing IT security policies. It walks you through this high-level process and explores the major issues encountered while implementing security policies. You will read how to overcome challenges and the importance of a communication plan. The chapter also examines best practices for implementing security policies. Finally, the chapter presents case studies that reinforce important topics and concepts.

Chapter 13 Topics

This chapter covers the following topics and concepts:

- What a simplified implementation process looks like
- What is meant by "target state"
- How to win executive support, and why it matters

- What good policy language is
- What's involved in employee awareness and training
- How to educate employees through proper dissemination of information
- What policy implementation issues you should anticipate
- What the roles of governance and monitoring in security policy implementation are
- Which best practices to follow when implementing IT security policies
- What some case studies and examples of successful IT security policy implementations are

Chapter 13 Goals

When you complete this chapter, you will be able to:

- Describe a simple implementation process
- Explain key process steps and related concerns
- Identify key organizational and cultural issues in implementing policies
- Describe why executive support is so important
- Define what a communications plan is
- Explain the importance of a communications plan
- Explain the difference between awareness of and training in security policies
- Describe examples of policy training
- Describe what a brown bag session is and what its benefits are
- Explain techniques for overcoming objections
- Describe different ways to disseminate policy material
- Explain the technical and nontechnical barriers to implementing IT security policies
- Understand best practices to follow when implementing IT security policies
- Use case studies of successful IT security policy implementations as examples for your organization

Simplified Implementation Process

There are many approaches to implementing IT security policies. The approach can vary based on any number of factors, such as organizational need, level of technical complexity, industry, culture, and maturity of change process. Assume, for example, you have an organization adding mobile solutions for the first time. This may be a major project for an organization with no prior experience in this area. It should have a detailed IT security plan that includes looking at business risks, cyberthreats, compliance requirements, policy changes, employee awareness, training, policy implementation, governance, and more. The addition of new mobile solutions could be expensive and time consuming.

Now consider an organization with years of experience at implementing mobile solutions. Also assume you wish to make a change to security policies. In many ways the process is the same. You still want to look at the policy change from the perspective of business risks, cyberthreats, compliance requirements, policy changes, employee awareness, training, policy implementation, and governance. However, the scale and effort in the second case would be smaller. Introducing change into a mature organization with extensive mobile experience significantly reduces the time needed to consider the risks and implications of a policy change. In fact, although the thought process may be the same, the experience and knowledge could mean some of these steps are less formal. In both cases, it's good practice to think through the risks and needs consistently and document them well.

FIGURE 13-1 shows a simple process flow for implementing IT security policies. As you can see by the figure, implementing a security policy is much more than writing and publishing a document. In fact, writing and publishing a policy document is a small part of a larger process. Creating an IT security policy is less about the document and more about the control environment the policy creates. A policy is a way of implementing a control, such as a way to prevent or detect a type of security breach. So simply publishing a policy in itself doesn't prevent or detect a security breach. The policy implementation must

> **NOTE**
>
> **Control environment** is a term for the overall way in which the organization's controls are governed and executed, including how effectively the controls are implemented, the risk culture of the organization, and management's attitude.

13

IT Security Policy
Implementations

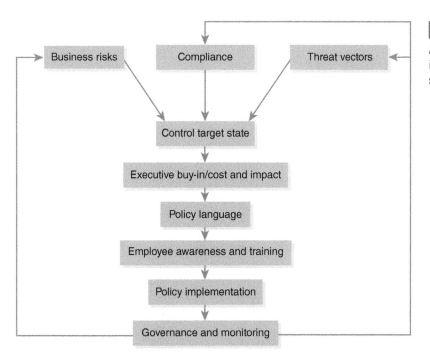

FIGURE 13-1

A process flow for implementing IT security policies.

be a series of steps that ensures the policy is put into practice. Put another way, a policy that is not adhered to is not useful. A proper implementation process educates, creates support for, and integrates the policy into the day-to-day operations. The policy must also minimize costs and impact on the business.

Target State

Target state is a general term used in technology to describe a future state in which specific goals and objectives have been achieved. It is the state you want the system to be in. In security policy terms, this future state generally describes which tools, processes, and resources (including people) are needed to achieve the goals and objectives. So, describing policy in terms of goals and objectives is important to get agreement on the target state.

> **NOTE**
>
> **Threat vector** is a general information security term to describe a tool or path by which a hacker can gain unauthorized access. For example, accessing a website through the Internet and adding SQL injection code into an input field on a webpage would be considered a threat vector.

There are different ways to describe policy goals and objectives. The value of the policy will often be judged by how well you can describe the goals and objectives. The more persuasive the descriptions, the more people will value the policy. One of the more effective techniques is to describe goals and objectives in the following ways:

- **Business risk**—Describes how the policy will reduce risk to the business and, more specifically, how it will reduce risk to an acceptable level.
- **Compliance**—Describes how the policy will ensure the business is compliant with laws and regulations. This is particularly important with regulated industries such as health care and credit cards.
- **Threat vectors**—Describe how the policy will prevent, mitigate, or detect IT security threats.

Business risk can be expressed in terms of how the policy either enables the business or reduces business disruptions. This risk can also be described in business risk terms such as expressed in the risk and control self-assessment (RCSA). The RCSA is typically produced annually by the business and describes its top risks, controls, and barriers to their objectives.

For example, assume a company wants to start selling product over the Internet to overseas customers. In this case, there might be an elevated risk of fraud. Some overseas regions, such as Eastern Europe, Africa, Malaysia, Indonesia, Turkey, and Pakistan, are considered higher-risk areas. In the event of fraud, options for recovery and legal action by the merchant are limited. Taking additional security measures to prevent or detect that fraud would be seen by the business as added value. For example, a company may choose to limit sales to specific countries or regions where the perceived risk is lower, such as Western Europe or Japan. This can be accomplished, in part, by blocking certain IP addresses.

Compliance relates to the legal and regulatory mandates a business must follow. Certain security policies are required by laws and regulations. Describing how the security policies help the organization to meet legal mandates is another valuable addition to the business. It should be noted that compliance to a regulation or industry standard is a minimum level of security, not ideal. Organizations sometimes make the error of assuming that if they are in compliance with a given standard, then they are secure. Compliance should be viewed as just a baseline, minimum level of security.

Threat vectors are a business concern. A threat vector is the way in which an attack is launched. Often these are more technical threats that the business might not understand well. Describing a SQL injection attack, for example, might not have much meaning to the business executive. However, describing the results and impact to the business will be important to him or her. You can explain a SQL injection attack, for instance, as leading to the theft of customer credit card information or the takedown of the company's website.

There should also be a policy regarding the company cybersecurity team keeping updated on current threats. This is a part of what is generally referred to as cyberthreat intelligence. Several services and websites can help a cybersecurity professional stay current with threats. A few are listed here:

* SANS Internet Storm Center: https://isc.sans.edu
* Cyware: https://cyware.com/category/cyber-threat -intelligence-news
* Threatpost: https://threatpost.com
* Cyber Threat Intelligence Feeds: http://thecyberthreat.com /cyber-threat-intelligence-feeds/

 TIP

Brown bag sessions are good opportunities for senior leaders to convey expectations related to information security policies. This is especially true for the chief information security officer (CISO). Such sessions provide a nonthreatening forum for the CISO to connect with various levels within the organization.

Regardless of the method used, the target state must describe in clear terms the technology, tools, and resources needed to implement the process. Additionally, to sell the need for the policy, the target state must describe the value in terms of the goals and objectives it will achieve.

Target state describes how policy implementation is closely tied to technology controls. You can have the best policies, but if they cannot be implemented, they're useless. The following section outlines several common technology challenges that can hinder the implementation of security policies.

Distributed Infrastructure

Security policies apply throughout the enterprise. As such, they rely on a centralized view and control of risks. You design a central set of policies and apply them across the enterprise. However, today's technology is highly decentralized. Smart devices are mobile. Users' laptops and desktops have tremendous computing power. Remote offices have servers and complex data closets supporting local networks. These are just a few examples. Today, many organizations also have substantial resources stored in a cloud.

All these add up to what's known as **distributed infrastructure**. That's a term for an organization's collection of computers—including laptops, tablets, and smartphones—networked together and equipped with distributed system software so that they work together as one, even from various locations.

For many organizations, the amount of technology outside the data center is significant. How do you implement centralized security policies in a decentralized environment? It's challenging. The target state must describe how to accomplish this. You first look at the administration of the distributed infrastructure.

Fortunately, although many technologies are distributed, many administration tools are centralized. Centralized administration tools allow for policies to be centrally distributed. A classic example is malware protection. Most organizations use a central malware management tool that keeps malware scanners up to date. The updating typically occurs when the desktop or laptop is connected to the network. An agent on the devices communicates with the central server and downloads the latest updates.

A distributed infrastructure is typically managed through an agent or an agentless central management tool. An **agent** is a piece of code that sits on the distributed device. As in the case of the virus scan, the agent software periodically reports back to the central management tool. An agent typically has multiple functions. The most common function is to report the state of the device back to the central server. It also receives commands and updates. In the case of the malware scan, the agent would report any malware detected and receive updates to the scanner.

An **agentless central management tool** has the ability and permission to reach out and connect to distributed devices. Unlike in the malware example, where the agent software pulls the updates onto the device, the agentless software is centrally housed. It pushes the changes to the device. Agentless management products use standard interfaces within the operating system or devices. They then authenticate, which grants them rights to perform their function. For example, Intelligent Platform Management Interface (IPMI) can be used as an agentless interface to Dell's Open-Manage IT Assistant tool. This tool can be used to monitor and maintain a server's performance.

A current inventory is key to implementation in a highly distributed infrastructure. You need to know how many devices are on the network. You also need to know which devices adhere to security policies. Many organizations use discovery and inventory tools to capture and track this information. These tools track devices connecting and disconnecting from the network. They can also capture key security control information.

The combination of a good inventory count and good configuration information allows you to implement security policies in a distributed infrastructure. This is because you can assess the population of network devices and compare compliance with security policies. For example, a typical policy might state that all desktops must have updated virus protection. The inventory might indicate 2000 desktops. The central malware management tool might indicate that about 1800 desktops have updated malware protection. You can now assess the effectiveness of the security policy implementation. Approximately 90 percent of your desktops comply with the policy.

Outdated Technology

Another challenge for describing a target state is how to deal with outdated technology. **Outdated technology** is hardware or software that, because obsolete, makes it difficult to implement best practices consistently. Outdated technology generally does not adhere to current best practices. When that occurs, you must decide how to address the lack of security controls within policies. You have four basic choices:

1. Replace the outdated technology.
2. Write security policies to best practices and issue policy waivers for outdated technology that inherently cannot comply.
3. Write security policies to the lowest, most common standard that the technology can support, even if it's outdated.
4. Write different sets of policies for the outdated technologies.

The ideal solution is to replace all outdated technology; however, that's not always an option, especially in a declining economy when many organizations are cutting costs. You should, however, be aware that if you are using outdated technology, there are security threats you cannot defend against. Continuing to use outdated technology is always a last option.

Of the three remaining choices, none is good. Generally, the least objectionable choice is option 2. The technology that is not outdated will conform to policies. The technology that cannot conform is typically granted a waiver with additional hardening to mitigate risk as much as possible. Waivers provide transparency on the risks the business is accepting. At a minimum, any waiver granted should require annual renewal. This will provide an opportunity to review the waiver and the risk—and the additional cost it introduces into the control environment.

It's sometimes less expensive to replace technology than to upgrade its security. FIGURE 13-2 illustrates that point. Assume you had outdated technology in your network. One response would be to improve segmentation controls to compensate. If you had outdated technology in the segment's network controls, you would place more reliance on operation system controls. If your operating system technology was outdated, you would place greater reliance on application controls. Any combination of the enhanced controls might mitigate some of the risk of outdated technology. Of course, all these additional layers of controls would increase costs to the organization.

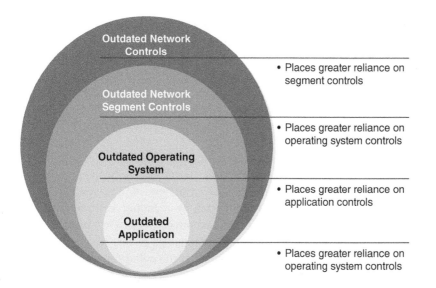

FIGURE 13-2

Expanded layers of control required for outdated technology.

Outdated technology creates security vulnerabilities. Vendors usually do not support outdated technology, so new security vulnerabilities will not be patched. Even adding additional layers of security can only go so far. There's significant risk to having outdated operating systems. Once the operating system is breached, it's likely the application will be breached.

Lack of Standardization Throughout the IT Infrastructure

Another technical challenge is the lack of standardization within the infrastructure. This can have several causes, but two common causes are 1) a lack of consistency with configurations; or 2) deployment of a diverse population of technologies.

The lack of a consistent configuration is a problem that arises when similar technologies are used in different ways by different lines of business. Each line of business has its own technologists applying different standards to similar technology. Assume, for instance, you have a company with physical stores and an online presence. Both lines of business have an inventory application that the public cannot access. The application may be on the same operating system and perform the same basic functions. Yet the configuration may look completely different if two different groups of administrators maintain the application.

This diversity in security approaches can be overcome in time, but it may create delays in the implementation of the security policies and increase costs. Both administration groups need to agree on a common approach to security. An implementation plan is needed so both types of configurations can migrate to the new policy in an orderly fashion.

When you have a diverse number of technologies deployed, security policies must be more generic. The policies must ensure that as much of the technology as possible can comply. That means that if one set of technologies has a weakness, the policy may choose to apply the weaker standard across the broadest set of technologies. Security policies often consider minimum standards. So, although one set of technologies has a weakness, the remaining technologies can add security beyond what's called for in the policies. The drawback is that policies are mandatory. By removing a security requirement from policy, there's no certainty that those additional controls will ever be applied.

Consequently, having a diverse population of technologies creates a set of tradeoffs. You want security policies to be as inclusive of the technology within the organization as possible. That may mean lowering some of the security standards at times. One option is to publish a security policy with an effective date that's in the future. This gives the organization time to upgrade technology and configurations. Whatever approach is selected, it's important that security policies be realistic in their expectations. Security policies should not be a theoretical exercise or an ideal state. They should reflect realistic expectations on how the organization needs to control risks.

Executive management support is critical in overcoming hindrances. A lack of support makes implementing security policies impossible. It takes a strong partnership between management and the IT security team to implement security policies. Consequently, it's vitally important to gather support for the security program by including senior management in building the target state. Listen carefully to the executives' needs. For example, if executives are particularly concerned about regulatory compliance, be sure the policies address compliance thoroughly. The more you can convey that the policy target state solves real problems for executives, the more likely they will be to support it.

Executive Buy-in, Cost, and Impact

Ultimately you will need senior managers' formal buy-in and support for any costs they need to incur. When dealing with executive management, define expectations clearly. Senior executives generally have little time to create specific strategies. They expect well-defined security approaches and recommendations. You might need their input on undecided key issues. However, executives expect you to do your homework and to engage their teams. You should have already spoken to their staffs and worked out most of the details. When a CISO is in front of an executive to talk about implementing security policies against a target state, it should be a short conversation. The conversation should focus on "This is our recommended approach" and "This is what I need." The executive will want to know the following, at a minimum:

- The level of commitment being asked of his or her team
- The impact of the policies on the current environment
- The value the policy brings; in other words, what risks the policy addresses
- The metrics of success—how success will be measured

Also, be sure to establish lines of communication. You'll want to spread the word on both major successes and setbacks throughout the implementation. Keep the lines to executives open. They want to avoid surprises. If something is not going well, they prefer to hear it from you first. They will also use success as a barometer for future requests.

Executive Management Sponsorship

Without **executive management sponsorship**, users will be less likely to be eager to participate in awareness training and to support the policy implementation. Support for a policy implementation takes time away from an individual's regular job. Many organizations are understaffed and overcommitted. Security policy implementation may not be seen as valuable or urgent. Executive management sponsorship changes that perception.

You should expect to fund the implementation with a defined budget. Buying tools and creating training materials are start-up costs. These costs may not be in the current budget. Additionally, you should expect a formal communication from management supporting the program. This communication can be a simple email that emphasizes the importance of team participation. This tone at the top is important to overcome common objections, such as, "I'm too busy right now."

Efforts to gather support should not be limited to a single executive. A security policy implementation spans the enterprise. This means you should seek multiple executive supporters. Remember, awareness is ongoing and extends well beyond the classroom. Awareness and a communications plan should be executed throughout the policy implementation process. For example, partnering with corporate communications or marketing departments allows the security message to be included in company newsletters and bulletins. The IT security team provides the content, whereas the communication and marketing department professionally packages the message. Executive sponsorship in those areas can extend the message's reach. These executives can advise the IT security team on how best to market through existing communication channels.

Overcoming Nontechnical Hindrances

It's not just technical challenges that can delay security policies from being implemented. It's important to remember that human factors matter, too. Success depends on how well people accept the policies.

Distributed Environment

Many organizations operate in a distributed environment. Organizations are typically divided by lines of business, product, or geography. In a distributed environment, an organization is run by different individuals with different business objectives. Therefore, different parts of an organization can have different views of risk. This diverse set of leaders can delay security policy implementation.

The first challenge is to get senior leadership to agree on a common set of security policies. The second challenge is agreeing on an implementation timeline.

User Types

A diverse set of views is not just reflected by leaders. The organization's general population also harbors a diverse set of views. The workplace has many types of users. Remember that you operate in an existing culture. That culture might not share the principles stated in the security policies. Even in the best of circumstances, it takes time for security policies to change the culture. In the meantime, you must recognize the type of culture and users that exist at the time the security policies are being implemented.

This sometimes means working in a culture that thinks of information security as an afterthought. Users in this environment may do the minimum to get by. You have to educate them on security policies and help them shed bad habits. Security awareness that targets specific habits can help. It's important that these users and habits be identified early. Plan specific communication events that focus on policy value and awareness training to change existing habits.

Some users think information security is a technology problem, not their problem. They might not object to the rollout of new policies, but they might undermine the policies' effectiveness by doing the bare minimum. This type of user attitude can best be managed through effective leadership. When a user knows that his or her job responsibilities include implementing security policies, such attitudes begin to change.

Organizational Challenges

Organizational challenges depend on the culture and industry. For example, the financial services industry puts significant resources into implementing security policies. In these organizations, the focus is on how to implement security policies to meet compliance laws and regulations.

Other, less-regulated organizations may question whether they should implement security policies at all. Understanding and overcoming these objections is an important part of obtaining buy-in. The following is a list of organizational challenges you might face when implementing security policies:

- Unclear accountability
- Lack of budget

- Lack of priority
- Tight schedules

Management is ultimately accountable for protecting information. Thus, management has a key role to play in implementing the proper policies. Implementations require management to be accountable for their success. The challenge is when leaders perceive policy implementation as an IT function. Leaders must support the implementation and provide the right message to all their subordinate teams.

> **NOTE**
>
> Security policies reflect a core set of principles. When you have different views of risk, it becomes a challenge to agree on these core values. It also becomes a challenge to decide how to enforce the policies.

Another organizational challenge is a lack of budget. Implementing security policies across the enterprise requires resources and funding. It may be a challenge to obtain funding without management support. The implementation of policies is more than sending out emails and posting a policy on a server. It takes time and funding to create training programs, to brief departments, to train users, and to hold town hall meetings. A **town hall meeting** is a gathering of teams to make announcements and discuss topics. These types of efforts take time and funding on both the IT and business side. It's even more challenging when the business is asked to allocate funds from its own budget. Competing for limited funds is always a challenge in an organization. Information security has to compete for organizational priority.

Implementing security policy is no different from any other activity. An organization faces many conflicting priorities. It may face business challenges that drive its priorities. For example, a priority may be to expand customer services. An organization may need to reduce defects in its product line. The key point is that organizations have limited resources. Often, there are more priorities than resources available. The challenge is to avoid security policies becoming low-priority items. Ideally, security policy should be seen as supporting or enabling the business's highest priorities.

For the implementation of security policies to be effective, it must be taken as a serious organizational commitment. You accomplish this, in part, by avoiding direct conflicts with other priorities. You should time the implementation of security policies so it doesn't conflict with other events. For example, assume you know over the next three months that a new product will be released. You may want to hold off implementing major security policies until after the product launch. Companies in this situation may not have the bandwidth to deal effectively with both efforts.

Yet you don't always have the luxury of waiting to implement policies. You may be under a regulatory requirement to meet specific timelines. When you do have flexibility, plan the timing of the implementation to ensure the organization can properly focus on the effort. Even in the best of circumstances, you often face tight implementation schedules. Once an organization has agreed on the content of security policies, the tendency is to implement them quickly, so the organization can move on to other priorities. Tight schedules may also be a byproduct of how well you communicated the benefits. For example, an organization that is facing significant audit findings may view the implementation of security

> **NOTE**
>
> Policies are, by definition, organizational directives. Assigning specific tasks and responsibilities during implementation is important. This becomes even more important when dealing with large, complex organizations. An implementation plan must define clear accountabilities for everyone from the leadership level to the IT security team.

policies as an important step in controlling those risks. This results in significant pressure to implement quickly. It's important that an implementation plan recognize the time and effort required to reach and train everyone involved in the changes.

Policy Language

Writing policy statements is like writing a legal contract. First, two parties must agree on what they want to achieve, and then they must put it in a contract. If the two parties can't agree on what they want to achieve, they can never agree on the contract language. In writing security policies, too, this first step is often missed. When this occurs, the resulting policy language can lack context, and the goals may seem confusing. In contrast, following an implementation process (as previously depicted in Figure 13-1) means getting agreement on a target state with funding and executive support.

Writing policies supporting an agreed-upon target state is much easier and provides a way to quickly gain approval for supporting policy language. Still, don't underestimate the time it takes, especially in a large organization. Words can have different meanings to different people. You want to create a clear and concise policy in language that is easily understood.

Don't use imprecise language such as "should" or "expected." For example, consider a policy that states, "You should use an eight-character password." Do you have to? It sounds more like a suggestion than a rule. A clearer policy statement would be, "You must use an eight-character password."

Be sure to assign clear accountability to specific roles. You must assume at some point that a policy will not be followed. The language must indicate who is accountable. For example, assume the policy language states, "Management is responsible for reviewing an employee's access every 90 days." Who is "management"? The manager? The line supervisor? The executive over the department? This language can be confusing. A better policy language statement would be, "All employees with direct reports must review their direct reports' access every 90 days." You can now go to a system of record (such as a corporate directory) and determine who should be performing what reviews.

Be sure to be precise about which resources the policy covers. Avoid requiring specific products in a policy. Policies should focus on *what* needs to be achieved and not *how*. Often, technology policy can have broad implications across multiple technical environments. A lack of precision and a failure to state a solution can be confusing and limiting. For example, assume a policy states, "All servers must use EFS when storing credit card information." Encrypting File System (EFS) is a feature of Microsoft Windows that can be used to encrypt information on a hard drive. This policy is not precise and limits encryption to a specific vendor product. It's not unusual to put technical limits on solutions, such as requiring a minimum of 256-bit encryption. But it's not a good idea to require specific vendor products in policy.

Here's why: First, EFS is a Windows product. How do you store credit card information if you're using a UNIX or Linux platform? Second, the policy objective should not be the use of EFS. The objective should be the encryption of the credit card information. This allows the flexibility to use the appropriate solution or tool.

Additionally, the policy as written is unclear. Does it allow credit card information to be stored on laptops? If a server is the only place you are allowed to store credit card information, the policy must state that clearly. A better policy statement would be, "Only production servers may be allowed to store credit card information. Additionally, all credit card information must be encrypted when stored." You can still limit which technologies can be used by adding, "Only an approved encrypted solution may be used." That addition allows control over which specific encryption products can be used by calling for a defined approval process.

The key point is to be sure that there's clear agreement on the target state. Use that agreement to write the supporting language in policy. When writing policy, use precise language that clearly defines the outcome and assigns accountability.

Employee Awareness and Training

The goal of employee awareness and training is to ensure that individuals have the knowledge and skills needed to implement the security policies. The primary objective of a security awareness program is to educate users. A well-executed awareness and training program can do much more. Some additional benefits include:

- Reinforcing core organizational values
- Giving management an opportunity to demonstrate support
- Creating opportunities for employees to acquire new skills, leading to increased job satisfaction

Awareness includes teaching employees about policies and core security concepts. Effective security awareness helps drive acceptance. When users understand policies, they can be held accountable for observing the policies. This promotes a long-term security culture shift. With so much at stake, it's important to have a well-thought-out approach to education.

Typically, an organization offers security awareness training. This is broken down into two components:

- **Awareness**—To increase understanding of the importance and value of security policies
- **Training**—To provide the skills needed to comply with security policies

Awareness should be an ongoing effort that reinforces key concepts. The awareness component is important, because it sets the tone and goals for security policy implementation. By setting realistic goals, you build credibility for the policies. Awareness also promotes candid conversations. Security awareness is, in part, about effective marketing and messaging.

The training component is more straightforward than creating awareness. In security training, you review security policies in detail. You discuss how the policies apply to individual roles. You set expectations on behavior. Security training focuses on mechanics—what is expected to be done and when. Often, in security policy training, you will discuss the supporting processes. For example, you might discuss restricting security administrator accounts. This can lead to a discussion on how to grant rights.

13

IT Security Policy
Implementations

Technical TIP

You should expect some level of participation by executives during training. An executive may simply stop by to kick off a session. A few opening remarks in a training session can send a powerful message throughout the organization. Also, consider videotaping a message from a senior leader as an effective communication technique. This avoids the problem of scheduling his or her time for multiple training sessions.

Organizational and Individual Acceptance

Users are more likely to accept what they understand. Security awareness is the first step in getting people to think about security. Security awareness training gives you an opportunity to explain the value of security policies. When security policies help users do their work, they are more likely to consider the policies to have value. Consequently, the goal of the security awareness program should be to gain support as well as to teach material. You need to tailor training to the users. For example, the type of training senior leaders receive would be different from individual user training.

Collectively, user behavior defines the organization's acceptance of security policies. When security policies are widely accepted, they become part of the culture. That tends to reduce risk, resulting in a lower number of security incidents. The converse is also true. When security policies are not widely accepted, there's an increase in security incidents. It's important that users embrace security policies to ensure the policies are used and thus effective.

Motivation

Ideally, awareness should excite and inspire, as well as train; however, motivation is a broader topic. How individuals are motivated varies by person. One clear motivation is self-interest. When management rigorously enforces security policies, that becomes a powerful motivator. This can be demonstrated by how management holds users accountable for failing to follow policies. Users need to know that management is serious about implementing security policies. This clear message of rewards and discipline is important in motivating users.

> **TIP**
>
> Best practices and standards often include information on how to create a security awareness training policy. Following this guidance can ensure that you meet regulatory requirements. For example, FISMA security awareness compliance is based on NIST Special Publications 800-16 and 800-50.

Untrained or unmotivated employees can make poor decisions. Poor decisions can lead to security incidents, even when individuals are trained. Poor decisions can occur anywhere within the organization. A user can fall prey to social engineering pretexts. A user can fail to report a control weakness. Management can fail to act when a report is received. Risk experts can fail to correctly assess the extent of the vulnerability. Senior leaders can fail to fund the mitigation. Regardless of the failure, there's a danger that policies will be perceived as ineffective when security incidents rise.

The key point is that effective security policy implementation depends on acceptance. Acceptance depends on the individuals who perceive value in the policy. Ultimate acceptance depends on the value being demonstrated by lowered risk to the organization. Security awareness and training is an opportunity to communicate value and get employees motivated.

Developing an Organization-Wide Security Awareness Policy

Effective security awareness training must reach everyone in the organization. This includes anyone with access to data, including employees, contractors, and vendors. The form of security awareness training may vary depending on the type of user. For example, security awareness training for a vendor might be handled by its parent company. The contract with the vendor should specify the type of awareness training the client requires.

Typically, the vendor is responsible for training its employees. This is different from contractors. Contractors usually go through the same type of training as the contracting company's regular employees. In this case, the contracting organization is responsible for security awareness training.

Contractor training may be condensed, however. If a contractor will be on-site for only a short time—three weeks, for example—it does not make sense to require weeks of security awareness training.

The security awareness policy ensures that education reaches everyone. For example, the policy might require that all users receive security awareness training before being granted access to data. This might include completing basic security awareness training during employee orientation. This ensures newly hired individuals receive training before handling sensitive information.

The security awareness policy typically outlines the frequency and type of training required. Awareness training is conducted at least annually. A security awareness training policy may require the following types of training:

- **New employee and contractor**—At time of hire before access to data is granted
- **Promotion**—As individuals are promoted into significantly different roles
- **All users**—Annual refresher training
- **Postincident**—After major security incidents, when lack of education was noted
- **Vendor**—As defined in the contract

It's important that you know your audience. You should tailor training to resonate with them. For example, humor is often an effective tool in awareness training. Humor can capture an individual's attention. It can also elicit cooperation and make the topic fun. Although that may be appropriate in larger audiences, it may not be the best choice when training executives. As a general rule, you want to tailor your approach on the basis of:

- **Job level**—The higher people are in the organization, the more strategic their training needs to be.
- **Level of awareness**—Some users need more training on basic security concepts.
- **Technical skill level**—Individuals who are technically savvy may be able to understand threats more easily.

The security awareness policy determines the type of awareness training that's provided. The policy also defines the audience that receives the training. For example, the policy could require senior management to receive strategic security and policy training. Middle management might be required to take policy and basic security training.

 NOTE

All users must receive some type of security awareness training. The policy should define how such training will be delivered.

Training should focus on individual roles and responsibilities. Middle managers need to understand basic security concepts and the risks they may encounter running daily operations. Senior managers are less likely to encounter those risks when they focus on strategic issues in running the organization. Basic security training might include discussion of how to implement encryption methods. This is a real issue that middle management may face. Senior management would have little interest in, or bandwidth for, dealing with basic security issues.

TABLE 13-1 Simple Security Policy Awareness Requirements

TYPES OF USERS	SECURITY BASIC REQUIREMENTS	LEGAL AND REGULATORY REQUIREMENTS	DETAIL POLICY REVIEW	LOGGING AND MONITORING POLICIES	SUSPICIOUS ACTIVITY REPORTING
Senior management	X	X			X
Middle management	X	X	X		X
End users	X				X
IT custodian	X		X	X	X

The scope of security awareness training is not one-size-fits-all. One approach to security policy awareness training is to define the user population and types of security awareness training offerings. This allows you to require specific training to address individual needs. TABLE 13-1 is a simple example of this concept. Notice that there are four basic user types defined. The security awareness policy would define each of these user types to ensure individuals in these roles can be quickly enrolled in training. The columns represent the type of training offered. The type and level of training would vary depending on the organization's needs. Notice the emphasis on reporting suspicious activity. This is reflected by the fact that all users are required to receive this type of training.

 NOTE

The security awareness policy must require specific training across the organization. This ensures expectations are set consistently. The message and type of training can vary by role.

In many organizations, this type of training is tracked through an online course registration tool. The application allows an individual to enroll in available training sessions. The application can also automatically assign required courses to individuals and track attendance. Online course registration tools help enforce the security awareness policy. These tools can also show evidence of enforcing the policy.

Conducting Security Awareness Training Sessions

The goal of formal security awareness training is to build knowledge and skills to help workers perform their roles in a way that protects assets and complies with policies. Security awareness training is not just about echoing back the trained material. The measure of success is how effectively the workers apply their training on the job.

There are two common ways of formally delivering security awareness training: in the classroom and through **computer-based training (CBT)**. Both methods are widely used, and both have strengths and weaknesses. Large organizations often use a combination of methods. There are also a host of informational methods. They can be as simple as a manager emailing a policy to the team, asking everyone to read the material. Information dissemination methods are discussed later in this chapter.

In the classroom setting, a trained instructor usually conducts security awareness training. The advantage of having an instructor deliver the training is flexibility. Suppose some training materials were developed under the assumption that the audience has a certain technical skill set. If a session is delivered and the audience doesn't have the necessary background, an experienced instructor can adjust the delivery accordingly. An instructor in a classroom can answer questions and connect with the class.

There are also drawbacks to a classroom setting. The first is cost. Classroom sessions can be expensive because of facility and travel costs. You need to find a suitable classroom and arrange for everyone's attendance. Conference rooms can be effective but are sometimes a poor choice, depending on class size and number of interruptions. It's not uncommon for individuals to be pulled out of training sessions held within the office setting. Alternatively, arranging for a conference room at a local hotel or alternative location comes at a price. Attendance could mean flying individuals to a training location or flying an instructor to remote offices. Another issue is the skill set of the instructor. Experienced instructors are typically in short supply. It takes a specific skill set to facilitate a training session.

> **NOTE**
>
> Many organizations use a combination of approaches, offering classroom training and CBT.

The CBT approach can be a lower-cost alternative to classroom training. A number of factors can drive a cost difference between CBT and classroom training. Some of these factors are size of the organization, location, and travel. Larger organizations can find it expensive to hold enough classes to cover enough of the employee population to be effective. Besides, the cost of travel and classroom space at some remote office locations can be high. With CBT you can reach an unlimited number of workers with a consistent set of messages. Online courses also allow workers to learn at their convenience. This can include taking a course at night or on weekends, away from the pressures and distractions of the office.

FYI

A classroom session can be a positive experience where individuals exchange ideas and make a personal connection with other students and the instructor. Another significant benefit is that the instructor can gauge the audience's acceptance of the material. Through questions and discussions, an instructor can determine how well the audience has understood the message. Based on this feedback, the instructor can adjust the training to be more effective.

Online courses offer quizzes throughout each session to automatically score competency. An online training tool can also require review of material the attendee found challenging. CBT offers statistical tracking of who takes courses and which part of the material individuals are struggling with.

The CBT approach has drawbacks, though. It can only measure what individuals know about the material. Unlike an instructor, it cannot measure how well the material is being accepted. A strength and weakness of CBT is the consistent format in which it's presented. The message in the material is consistently delivered; however, some CBT has limited or no opportunity to tailor the message to a specific audience. Finally, CBT is impersonal. Unlike classroom instruction, CBT offers little opportunity to connect with others in the organization.

> **NOTE**
>
> Simply knowing the subject material doesn't mean you are able to teach the material. It's important that the core message not change as the material is adjusted to fit the audience. Delivering a consistent message is important.

It's important to get feedback on the training by the attendees as soon as possible. This feedback should focus on how well the material is being accepted beyond what knowledge was conveyed. In other words, it's important to know the attendee is using the knowledge rather than simply memorizing the material. Some suggested ways of getting feedback include:

- Anonymous surveys after the session
- Focus groups
- Interviews of attendees
- Exit interviews of individuals leaving the company
- Monitoring compliance through incident reports

Human Resources Ownership of New Employee Orientation

New employees can often be reached through the human resources (HR) department. The HR department usually manages the onboarding of new employees. HR usually has an array of employment documents new employees must complete, from benefits forms to ID badge acknowledgments. HR also provides a series of training sessions to help new employees ease into the organization's culture. Most organizations add security awareness training to the list of items the HR department provides to new employees. It's cost efficient, because it simply adds material to new employee training HR conducts. You don't have to pull new employees offline into a separate training session. It's also practical from a timing perspective. You don't want new employees to access sensitive data until they receive training. You want to get to the employees as early as possible.

TIP

The security awareness training that all employees must take should be delivered during new-employee orientation. Additional training can be handled after the employee is on the job.

Review of Acceptable Use Policies (AUPs)

A core topic in security awareness training is reviewing the acceptable use policy (AUP). It's not uncommon to require employees to sign the AUP. This acknowledges they have received and read the policy. The AUP clearly defines what's considered acceptable and unacceptable use of technology. The AUP, for example, specifies that the organization's computers should be used for business purposes only. It may also exclude specific types of usage such as gambling or accessing offensive material. The AUP also defines personal responsibilities, such as protecting one's own password.

One of the more critical training points in an AUP is to prohibit sharing of an individual's ID and password. Sharing such information can place sensitive data at risk from unauthorized access. It also undermines the concept of nonrepudiation. Assume a supervisor asked a user to share his or her password. This is a violation of the AUP by both the employee and the supervisor. In the real world, if the employee promptly reported the violation, no action would be taken against him or her. Although it may be a violation by the employee, the supervisor is the source of the breach. It's not always reasonable to expect an employee to stand up against a supervisor, manager, or executive; however, failure to report the violation might be considered significant cause to discipline the employee. In either case, the supervisor should be disciplined for requiring the employee to provide that information. The level of discipline depends on the organization. If the violation leads to a fraud or security breach, there's a strong case to be made for terminating the supervisor.

The AUP does more than protect passwords. It also addresses other high-risk behaviors, which should be included in security training:

* Handling and sharing of sensitive customer information
* Transmission of information outside the company
* Handing of company intellectual property

 NOTE

The acceptable use policy (AUP) is a document that clearly defines a core set of user responsibilities and expectations. It also discusses the consequences of failing to comply. The document is meant to be enforceable. A violation of the policy could lead to disciplinary action, including termination. As a result, the AUP language is precise.

Information Dissemination—How to Educate Employees

Educating users can be a formal or informal process. Formal methods are those that communicate policies in a formal training environment, such as a classroom or CBT. The advantage of formal training is that you know who's taking the training, and you can measure, to some extent, its effectiveness.

Remember that people learn in different ways. It's a good idea to select multiple methods to disseminate security policy messages and materials. Because people learn differently, this increases your odds of reaching everyone. For example, those that find computer-based training less appealing may find a department newsletter more relevant to their job.

It's also important to understand the culture and the audience in the organization. If an organization has many remote offices, face-to-face presentations of the material will be less practical. In addition, some organizations distribute too many newsletters. Some users simply stop reading newsletters due to the volume. As a consequence, newsletters may not be the best choice for communicating critical information. The following is a list of potential ways to disseminate security policy information:

* Telephone town hall meetings
* Emails
* Newsletters
* The company intranet
* Posters
* Face-to-face presentations
* Giveaways such as pins, mugs, sticky notes, and so on
* Contests that include prizes

Any communication method that keeps the security message "alive" is effective. You are usually limited by time and money; however, communicating the policy message does not have to be expensive. It's limited only by imagination. You could sponsor a security policy awareness contest. It might be as simple as asking individuals to answer security policy trivia questions online. The

NOTE

Security awareness is more than just formal training. It's reinforcing the message and keeping information security in everyone's mind. The policies themselves are good resources for individuals.

winner gets a basket of goods worth less than $20. For just a few dollars, you can apply creative ideas to engage employees and reinforce key messages.

To successfully disseminate security policy messages, you need a communications plan. A **communications plan** outlines what information is to be shared. A communications plan defines the message, the people, and the method of delivery. By laying out an entire communications plan, you can quickly assess if the right message is reaching everyone.

When developing a communications plan, you should ask yourself the following key questions:

- **Who communicates?**—Are the right people delivering the message to build credibility for the effort?
- **What is the target audience?**—Is everyone receiving the appropriate message?
- **What is communicated?**—Is the right message being delivered?
- **How is it communicated?**—Are we delivering the message in the most efficient manner?
- **When is it communicated?**—Is the communication well timed?
- **What collateral is used?**—Is the message being delivered consistently?
- **What objective is achieved?**—Are specific goals being achieved?

TABLE 13-2 depicts a simple communications plan that has two events. Both events are to be communicated by senior management. The first communication event prepares middle management for the announcement to staff. One can anticipate questions during a policy launch. Leadership needs to be well prepared to answer questions from staff, which makes the policy rollout more effective. The second communication event is the actual kick-off of the security awareness effort.

A communications plan can help rationalize the implementation strategy. For example, your strategy may call for everyone to receive at least three communications during the first

TABLE 13-2 Simple Communications Plan

WHO COMMUNICATES	TARGET AUDIENCE	WHAT	HOW	WHEN	COLLATERAL	OBJECTIVE
Senior management	Middle management	Key messages to be conveyed to staff	Leadership staff meeting	Before xx/xx/xx	Management talking points	Ensure key leaders have talking points to answer staff questions after kick-off email
Senior management	All employees	Security awareness program announcement	Email broadcast	xx/xx/xx	Kick-off email	Program kick-off

six months of the security awareness program. If that's the case, by scanning the Target Audience column in the communications plan, you can quickly determine if the goal is being achieved.

Hard Copy Dissemination

Hard copies of policies are rarely sent out today. The challenge in sending out volumes of paper is the cost and accuracy of the material. All of the security policies, standards, processes, and guidelines in an enterprise can be thousands of pages long. That doesn't include the supporting materials, such as executive summaries, slide decks, and spreadsheets. Consequently, it's not practical to disseminate the material in print form. Printing costs would be high, and it would take time, money, and effort to disseminate. In addition, as soon as changes to the material are made, the printed material is out of date. Putting policies on an internal intranet website is very effective. These can be easily updated and are readily available to all employees.

 TIP

Regardless of form, include your communication channels in your communications plan.

 TIP

Determining which materials are candidates for hard copy publishing will depend on the organization. The rule of thumb is to avoid sending hard copies where possible. When this is not possible, keep hard copies to a small amount of material with a limited distribution.

Posting Policies on the Intranet

The best method for communicating security policies is through a document-handling server such as an intranet. These servers offer multiple benefits, such as:

* Costs to disseminate material are low.
* Policies are kept current.
* Policies are searchable.
* Changes to policies can be highlighted.
* You can link to supporting material.

Many organizations already have an intranet. Consequently, the incremental costs for housing security policies are minimal. Centralized security policy management helps you keep policies current.

A significant advantage of electronic over hard copies is the ability to search for documents. Anyone who has browsed the Internet is familiar with search engines. You can enter key phrases and get a list of related documents. The same technology applies to an intranet. Your internal policies can be quickly searched for key phrases. In seconds, thousands of pages can be searched. For example, assume a business has decided to work with a vendor to process sensitive information. A quick search of policies using the keyword "vendor" may return a half-dozen documents. The topics may range from the need for a vendor assessment to secure connection requirements.

Another powerful tool of document-handling servers is the ability to track changes. When a modified policy is released, it's helpful to know the exact wording that was changed. Policies often include a high-level explanation of the changes but few details. The ability to view the actual word-level changes in the policy is a powerful tool. This allows you to better assess the impact of the change on your existing controls.

Another significant benefit is the ability to link policies to supporting materials. The supporting materials can be executive summaries, slide decks, or a wide array of educational material. You can link any supporting material that makes it easier to understand the policy. For example, suppose you are reading a security policy on database logging, but you don't quite understand the material. You notice a slide deck linked to the policy. After clicking on it, you are presented with a tutorial created by the database administrator explaining how to apply the policy.

Using Email

Although the level of sophistication on how policies are disseminated varies between organizations, most organizations still rely on email. Organizations depend on email to approve policies and keep management informed on implementation activities.

Email also plays a central role in most communications plans. Email allows you to notify a large population about major events. It also allows you to track everyone who has read the notification. This is a good tool for ensuring that individuals are properly notified of policy releases. Email also allows you to send out surveys and follow up on how well the implementation is being perceived.

Brown Bag Lunches and Learning Sessions

A brown bag session is a training event. An expert on a topic is invited to share his or her thoughts, ideas, and experiences. The term *brown bag* came about because sessions were usually held at lunchtime, and people brought their own lunches in brown bags. Nowadays these sessions may or may not be held over lunch, and if they are, lunch may even be catered. As a broad term, *brown bag* can be applied to a wide variety of less formal training situations.

The core concept of a brown bag usually applies to a small group of people that has access to one or more experts. Participants ask the experts questions. The experts guide the conversation. There may or may not be a formal presentation. The key idea is that the sessions are less scripted than a formal classroom setting.

The level of success of these sessions depends on the expert. A brown bag session provides an opportunity to persuade and influence both the experts and the attendees. Regardless of your position on a topic, a brown bag session is a good opportunity to create a personal connection.

Brown bag sessions can also be divided by type of security policy. For example, a new policy on acceptable email use might be of particular concern to customer service. A security team member might be the selected expert to help explain why the new policy has been implemented and talk through how email communication with customers might change.

Policy Implementation Issues

When implementing policy, it's important is to consider the organization's structure in relation to its business, size, and technology. Another important consideration is the fit to its leaders. If a leader holds team meetings or town halls, the implementation plan might consider using these events to discuss the policy change. A different leader may be more hierarchical in his or her approach, holding a series of group meetings. What's most important is recognizing these differences and adjusting your security policy approach accordingly.

Depending on the policy change, one method is to find an early adopter. An **early adopter** implements the security policy ahead of rollout as a type of pilot. In this way you can demonstrate the value of the policy and use the positive experience of the early adopter to overcome concerns and objections. An early adopter of security policies will help lead an organization's successful implementation. Early adoption of security policies can be a source of pride for both an individual and the team.

When you navigate an organizational structure to build support for implementation, keep in mind that you are talking to people, not boxes on an organizational chart. It's important to listen, accept suggestions, and realize you will need to overcome concerns and user apathy towards information security. It will be important to build support with executive leaders throughout the implementation process, especially with those with differing views of risk and different management styles.

Encourage management to be personally involved in the implementation. They know their teams. A good manager will listen to the employees' issues and feed back to the security team concerns and ways to overcome objections. Security awareness and messaging is not a one-time event. It's important to reinforce the message as much as possible. If you can engage employees and show them why security is relevant to their jobs, there's a greater chance your employees will adhere to policies. Security awareness programs help keep workers engaged with the information security message, thereby helping to prevent apathy.

Remember, motivating employees is as important as mastering a technology. A motivated employee can deal with the unexpected. This is particularly important when dealing with unexpected security incidents.

Changing an organization's culture and users' perceptions is not a one-time event. Simply releasing security policies does not change attitudes. Security is a tough sell because the benefits are not always obvious. Cultural change comes from having a clear value message that is demonstrated daily. It also requires collaboration and an understanding of the business. Culture is changed in small increments. That's why you need a well-planned, step-by-step approach to implementing policies. Three common messages to deliver during an implementation are:

- Personal accountability
- Directives and enforcement
- The value of security policy

Although "selling security" has an upside, security is, in the end, mandatory in most organizations. A soft sell goes only so far in motivating employees, because the consequences may not seem real. The more abstract the perceived argument as to why information security is important, the less convincing it becomes.

It's important to discuss personal accountability and the consequences of not implementing policy. The consequences can range from loss of data to lack of regulatory compliance. This message can resonate with executives, especially those who operate in a regulated industry. In highly regulated companies, executives can be held personally accountable for failure to implement effective controls. The Sarbanes-Oxley Act is an example of this type of regulation.

After a period of "selling" the implementation, there often comes a management directive and enforcement. Management will require policies to be implemented. Management sets the tone within an organization through how it enforces its policies. Inevitably, someone will fail to follow policy. The level of tolerance and how aggressively policies are enforced sets the tone. It also shapes whether policies are perceived as important.

Mandates by management and aggressive implementation are often needed to meet tight deadlines. This is particularly important in meeting regulatory mandates. For example, in banking, strong authentication for some transactions is a legal mandate. This might translate into requiring two-factor authentication to access a bank account online. The implementation of these policies can help the online banking manager achieve his or her goals of reducing online fraud and becoming compliant with regulations.

Finally, keep in mind that the business and the IT team are both often overworked and overcommitted. Information security is sometimes seen as an additional layer of complexity. Some people perceive security policies as a roadblock to the delivery of services. These perceptions of security policies are inaccurate. Security policies can enable organizations to expand by creating reliable controls that protect vital systems and applications.

Implementation is as much about changing attitudes as it is about implementing controls. Overcoming perceptions and changing culture are goals of security policies. In other words, it is about implementing in a way that wins hearts and minds. You need to be transparent about what risks security policies can and cannot reduce. Most important, security policies need to be viewed as a useful tool.

President Theodore Roosevelt's famous counsel was "speak softly and carry a big stick." This is good advice for implementing security policies. Do everything possible in the early stages to win the hearts and minds. In later stages, you need clear and concise statements of management mandates and of accountabilities.

Governance and Monitoring

The Control Objectives for Information and related Technology (COBIT) 5.0 framework defines governance thus: "Governance ensures that enterprise objectives are achieved by evaluating stakeholder needs, conditions and options; setting direction through prioritization and decision making; and monitoring performance, compliance and progress against agreed-on direction and objectives."

Governance policy ensures that policies are used, adopted, and effective. To monitor policy adoption and effectiveness, organizations should create a governance policy committee, usually made up of security teams and business-side leaders. Typically, governance is organized around a series of regularly scheduled committee meetings. A policy governance committee might meet weekly or monthly; there is no set standard. A governance committee must meet as often as needed to ensure that enterprise objectives are achieved.

Monitoring performance depends on the types of reports and information the committee is provided. If there's a lack of adoption, you would expect to see that reflected in the type of audit findings issued. If there's a lack of awareness, you might see that in annual awareness testing or survey scores. Ultimately, effectiveness might be measured in how many breaches have been successful or, conversely, in how many security attacks have been successfully defended against.

Regardless of the effectiveness measurements used, governance is an ongoing evaluation of stakeholder needs, conditions, and options to achieve desired policies. This means that governance sets direction through prioritization and decision making. Remember, a governance meeting is typically made up of management leaders. These leaders can act when policies are not working as designed. They can also act should new threats emerge. That's why most implementation processes (such as in Figure 13-1) take the lessons learned from the monitoring to reassess business risk, compliance, and threat vectors. This reassessment of the organization's needs can lead to changes in the target state and thus changes in the IT security policy.

As a management group, the governance committee can help drive organizational and cultural change. The upside is gains in efficiency, coordination, transparency, and agility. It can be hard to standardize business processes across a company. But if you do, you can drive efficiency and predictability companywide. This can simplify your environment and make responding to attacks much easier.

For policies to prevent security breaches, everyone must follow them. This requires that everyone in the organization be accountable for implementing security policies. This requires executive commitment. It will be a cultural change for any organization that views security policies as an abstract concept or an additional layer of complexity. Security policies that hold everyone in the organization accountable help promote this cultural change. For this to happen, the goal should be to make security policies:

- A routine part of daily interaction
- The recipient of support from organizational committees
- A matter of instinctive reaction

These goals are measurable indicators of a shift in organizational thinking and risk culture. Security policies cannot outline every potential situation. You cannot expect people to memorize volumes of material. Information overload is a real concern when implementing security policies. When information security policies are large, complex documents, they become hard to understand. They are also hard to teach, so security policies must include core concepts that can be applied to a wide range of situations. In this way, the policies' tenets can be easily recalled.

The advantage of core values that management understands well is that they can be applied to unexpected situations. You can measure (and thus, monitor) routine daily interaction to see if policies are being followed. For example, you can review business deployment plans. Usually it becomes obvious if security policies were clearly considered in these plans' formulation. When security is considered as a **bolt-on**, or afterthought, cultural change has not occurred. You can also gauge the level of interaction based on the number of requests from the business side to interpret security policies. When information security is at the forefront of everyone's mind, the business side often asks for clarification on policy details when implementing new processes. The natural source for this interpretation is the IT security team. If the volume of requests for interpretation is low, it's a good indicator that active conversations on security risks are not occurring. When you have a large number of initiatives, you should expect lots of questions on policies.

You can measure committee support by the conversations that occur between members. A quick indicator is to look at the minutes of committee meetings, such as the operational risk committee or the audit committee. Such committees should all be dedicating time to discussing information security and policies. These committees should also be discussing enforcement. They will want to know how to manage overall risk to the organization. If these committees spend little or no time on these topics, it's a good indicator they have delegated the conversation to lower ranks. A risk-aware culture has senior management equally engaged in these discussions. The chief information security officer (CISO) can help overcome organizational apathy toward security policies by attending key committee meetings. The CISO can promote candid discussions on policies and risks.

A culture shift occurs when users instinctively react to situations consistent with the core values of the security policies. This personal accountability can help promote security thinking across a broad range of situations. It could be as simple as asking a stranger in the office for his or her identification. It could be questioning the need for access, even though a procedure allows it. This can be measured in several ways. For example, an organization with a high number of security policy exceptions might not appreciate the importance of security.

Best Practices for IT Security Policy Implementations

A proper implementation process educates, creates support, and integrates the policy into day-to-day operations. Having a standard process approach that ensures that business risks, compliance, and threat vectors are considered in all policy changes is a best practice.

The goal of employee awareness and training is to ensure that individuals have the knowledge and skills needed to implement security policies. The primary objective of a security awareness program is to educate users. Creating awareness should be an ongoing effort that reinforces key security concepts. The awareness component is important because it sets the tone and goals for security policy implementation.

In writing policy, don't use imprecise language such as "should" or "expected." Assign clear accountability to specific roles. Specify precisely which resources are covered by the policy. Avoid requiring specific technologies in a policy.

As noted earlier, implementing a security policy is much more than simply writing and publishing a document. In fact, writing and publishing a policy document is but a small part of a larger process. Creating an IT security policy is less about the document and more about the control environment the policy creates. A policy is a means of implementing a control—such as a way to prevent or detect a specific type of security breach. So simply publishing a policy in itself doesn't prevent or detect a security breach. The policy implementation must be a series of steps that ensure that the policy is put into practice. The following sources can be of help:

- SANS Institute, Building and Implementing an Information Security Policy: https://www .sans.org/reading-room/whitepapers/policyissues/paper/509
- ComputerWorld, 10 Steps to a Successful Security Policy: https://www.computerworld .com/article/2572970/10-steps-to-a-successful-security-policy.html

- SANS, Information Security Policy—A Development Guide for Large and Small Companies: https://www.sans.org/reading-room/whitepapers/policyissues/paper/1331
- PCI Security Standards Council, Best Practices for Implementing a Security Awareness Program: https://www.pcisecuritystandards.org/documents/PCI_DSS_V1.0_Best_Practices _for_Implementing_Security_Awareness_Program.pdf
- United States Postal Service, Developing a Successful Enterprise Information Security Policy: https://www.uspsoig.gov/sites/default/files/document-library-files/2017 /IT-WP-17-001_0.pdf

Case Studies and Examples of IT Security Policy Implementations

Unlike previous chapters, rather than provide individual case studies, this section will give general guidelines on implementing security policies from respected resources. This will provide you with the broadest possible understanding of security policy implementation.

CIO Magazine

In 2019, *CIO Magazine* published an article on how to implement a successful security policy.[1] This article begins by advising that one assess the current state of security. That is usually good advice in any security situation. The article also recommends implementing monitoring. This is the best way to have an ongoing understanding of what is happening on the network.

Only after those preliminary steps does one set security measures and controls. The article provides good general guidelines on how to do this. This includes the use of live documents that are easy to update and thus always current. The article also recommends end-to-end security. Most notably, *CIO Magazine* recommends working to foster a dynamic security culture.

SANS

The SANS Institute has a white paper on building and implementing a security policy.[2] This document actually provides examples of how to structure specific security policies. One of the examples is given in **FIGURE 13-3**.

Public Sector Case Study

This is an older case, but it is still important because of the significant impact it has. In November 2012, South Carolina state officials disclosed a massive data breach at the Department of Revenue. Few details on the breach were disclosed, but it involved exposing more than 3.6 million taxpayers' personal information records and 650,000 business tax–related records. The breach occurred in September 2012. It's clear that massive amounts of personal information were stolen.

---

[2]https://www.sans.org/reading-room/whitepapers/policyissues/paper/509

FIGURE 13-3

Like *CIO Magazine*, SANS recommends monitoring as a key mechanism for understanding what is occurring on the network. Just as importantly, the white paper provides a list of resources to assist you.

Section:	Overview/Policy Stance.
Summary:	Explain you chosen policy stance.
Notes:	Choosing a stance to adopt in relation to the planning, implementation and monitoring of your security policy is critical. Defining the potential stances has, once again, been done for you in that there are accepted standards as follows:

Promiscuous: Everything is permitted, which in effect equates to having no security in place.

Permissive: Everything not explicitly prohibited is permitted. This is considered a high-risk stance since the default is 'to allow'. In order for security to be effective under this stance, your prohibited list & associated configurations must be fully up to date at all times.

Prudent: Everything not explicitly permitted is prohibited. This is considered the best option for commercial organisations, since the default action is 'deny'. (Forgetting to expressly permit something carries minimal risk.)

Paranoid: Nothing is permitted. Whilst this is the option of choice for military, health service and security service type organisations it compromises the 'Availability' target and is therefore often not acceptable in a commercial organisation.

A former top official with the FBI estimated the cost to the state at more than $350 million, based upon past FBI experience, including the cost of offering free credit monitoring to affected individual taxpayers and businesses.

The root cause of the breach cited in news reports was the lack of mandatory security policies across 100 state agencies, boards, commissions, and colleges and universities.

All state agencies have some type of computer security system in place. It's fair to assume they all have some level of security policy in place. But it is clear these policies were discretionary. That meant an approach to information security across state government that was at best inconsistent. Nor did the state appear to have a comprehensive approach to sharing best practices for information security or for coordinating response to these types of data breaches.

In the case of the South Carolina Department of Revenue, the policies clearly were neither adequate nor consistent. Additionally, reports indicate the source of the hack was in Eastern Europe. The hacker or hackers gained access through a phishing email. Phishing emails try to trick a user to open an email and execute a link or program with malware. Security awareness is a strong control that educates users on how to protect themselves from such attacks, including how to recognize such attacks and why not to open suspect links. If a phishing email was a source of the attack, it might be an indication that the security awareness program at this state agency was inadequate.

CHAPTER SUMMARY

You learned in this chapter how to approach the implementation of security policies. This included standardizing a process approach. You learned the importance of executive buy-in and users' acceptance of policies. The goal is to have the policies become second nature to users over time. When users embrace security policies as part of their daily routines, you begin to see a cultural change. You learned about the importance of security awareness training. It ensures that everyone understands the policies. It also increases the chance policies will be used. You can hold users accountable if they understand the policies.

The chapter also examined the importance of governance and monitoring. It discussed how security policies are published and disseminated. You explored various communication methods. You learned the importance of a communications plan and how it's used to coordinate a consistent message. Finally, the chapter examined how to overcome technical and nontechnical hindrances. This included a discussion of best practices.

KEY CONCEPTS AND TERMS

Agent	Control environment	Target state
Agentless central management tool	Distributed infrastructure	Threat vector
	Early adopter	Town hall meeting
Bolt-on	Executive management	
Communications plan	sponsorship	
Computer-based training (CBT)	Outdated technology	

CHAPTER 13 ASSESSMENT

1. Which of the following indicates that the culture of an organization is adopting IT security policies?

   A. Security policies are part of routine daily interaction.
   B. Security policies are supported by organizational committees.
   C. Security policies' core values are demonstrated in workers' instinctive reactions to situations.
   D. All of the above

2. Effective security policies require that everyone in the organization be accountable for policy implementation.

   A. True
   B. False

3. A control environment is defined as:

   A. An inventory of the security policy controls
   B. A well-defined framework to track control exceptions
   C. The overall way in which the organization's controls are governed and executed
   D. None of the above

4. Deliberate acts and malicious behavior by employees are easy to control, especially when proper deterrents are installed.

   A. True
   B. False

5. Which of the following is *not* an organizational challenge when implementing security policies?

   A. Accountability
   B. Surplus of funding
   C. Lack of priority
   D. Tight schedules

6. Which type of plan is critical to ensuring security awareness reaches specific types of users?

   A. Rollout plan
   B. Media plan
   C. Executive project plan
   D. Communications plan

7. Why should a security policy implementation be flexible to allow for updates?

   A. Unknown threats will be discovered.
   B. New ways of teaching will be introduced.
   C. New technologies will be introduced.
   D. A and C
   E. A, B, and C

8. Which of the following is the *least* objectionable when dealing with policies with regard to outdated technology?

   A. Write security policies to best practices and issue a policy waiver for outdated technology that inherently cannot comply.
   B. Write security policies to the lowest, most common security standard the technology can support.
   C. Write different sets of policies for outdated technologies.
   D. All of the above

9. What is a strong indicator that awareness training is *not* effective?

   A. A firewall breach
   B. Sharing your password with a supervisor
   C. Sharing a laptop with a coworker
   D. A fire in the data center

10. A target state is generally defined as:

    A. A future state
    B. A way to describe specific policy goals and objectives
    C. A way to describe what tools, processes, and resources (including people) are needed to achieve the goals and objectives
    D. All of the above
    E. None of the above

11. Classroom training for security policy awareness is always the superior option to other alternatives, such as online training.

    A. True
    B. False

12. To get employees to comply and accept security policies, the organization must understand the employees' _____.

13. A brown bag session is a formal training event with a tightly controlled agenda.

    A. True
    B. False

14. What is the best way to disseminate a new policy?

    A. Hardcopy
    B. Intranet
    C. Brown bag session
    D. All of the above

15. A formal communication plan is _____ when implementing major security policies.

    A. Always needed
    B. Optional
    C. Never needed

ENDNOTES

1. Lago, Cristina, "How to Implement a Successful Cybersecurity Plan," July 10, 2019, *https://www.cio.com/article/3295578/how-to -implement-a-successful-security-plan.html*, accessed May 8, 2020.

IT Security Policy Enforcement

THE ENFORCEMENT OF A SECURITY POLICY begins when the hard work of creating the policy and providing initial security awareness is done. All the effort put into creating the policy is of little value if it's not followed. Essentially, a policy that is not enforced is the same as no policy at all. A compliance program is essential to ensure that policies are adopted and deliver intended value. Quality assurance and quality control reviews (sometimes referred to as compliance reviews) and vulnerability assessments are three important components of a compliance program.

A quality assurance (QA) review ensures that the security policy is adopted before an action is taken. For instance, ensuring that security is properly coded before a piece of software is moved to production is an illustration of quality assurance. In contrast, quality control (QC) reviews and vulnerability assessments are performed after the environment is built. A QC review determines if policies are being followed. The vulnerability assessment is used to measure the effectiveness of the policies. If everyone follows the policies, then the number of vulnerabilities declines. If the number of vulnerabilities does not decline, the fault lies with either individuals or poorly designed policies. Vulnerability assessments need to be aligned with business goals. The level of enforcement needs to align to the level of risk.

How you implement a compliance program will depend in part on your organization's governance and management structure. This organizational structure defines how a company sets and follows a strategic course. The structure also can be leveraged to enforce IT security policies.

This chapter reviews the organizational and technical methods of enforcing security policies. It discusses the importance of executive support for the enforcement process. It discusses specific roles in the organization. The chapter also discusses legal considerations when enforcing security policies. It then ends by illustrating the points made through a discussion of best practices and case studies.

Chapter 14 Topics

This chapter covers the following topics and concepts:

- Who is responsible for IT security policy enforcement
- What rights an organization has to monitor user actions

- How security policies balance legal requirements and risk management
- What the difference is between laws and policies
- How policies can be enforced manually and automatically
- Who is legally accountable for IT security policies
- Who is ultimately accountable for risks, threats, and vulnerabilities
- What some case studies and examples of successful IT security policy enforcement are

Chapter 14 Goals

When you complete this chapter, you will be able to:

- Describe the differences between governance and management processes
- Explain what a pervasive control is
- Describe the basic layers of controls within an organization to enforce policies
- Explain the role of executive management and the chief information security officer (CISO) in enforcement
- Describe how monitoring can help policy enforcement
- Explain the difference between automated and manual policy enforcement
- Explain who is ultimately accountable for enforcement of security policies
- Describe legal implications when enforcing policies
- Describe best practices for enforcing policies

Organizational Support for IT Security Policy Enforcement

 NOTE

The introduction of new policies forces change within the existing culture. Unfortunately, security policy changes are needed. For example, new threats emerge and new policies are required to address them. It is also true that many people tend to resist change. It's important that change be discussed well in advance of introducing new policies. Individuals must internalize and embrace policies for them to be effective.

Abuse of a company's technology can leave it at risk. Failure to follow policies can lead to regulatory noncompliance. Failure to follow up and resolve issues can result in lawsuits. These situations can lead to more regulatory sanctions and expensive legal fees.

Enforcement of security policies needs to be ingrained in an organization. Many people must participate—enforcing policies is not a one-person role. Enforcement of policies is achieved through layers. This includes organizational committees enforcing policies and monitoring workers' actions. Each layer validates that security policies are being followed. The goal is to build awareness and enforcement throughout the organization over time. IT security policy compliance is everyone's role.

An organization needs to decide what it wants to accomplish through policy enforcement. The organization can choose to focus on a limited number of areas such as access control, **data leakage** protection, and virus protection. Alternatively, the organization can use policies to enforce change in the culture. Certainly, enforcing security policies changes habits and thus the culture. Whatever the specifics, policy enforcement must have a goal. The most obvious is to ensure compliance with policies—but that is somewhat circular. Sometimes companies have ineffective policies. This often stems from not thinking clearly about policy goals. If your goal is good password management, but your policy requires a 50-character random password, that will almost guarantee employees write down their password because they cannot remember it. In this case, you have actually subverted your real goal by enforcing this unreasonable policy.

When introducing change, remember that it may create conflict. Security policies may conflict with how people naturally react. For example, you've been trained on social norms such as the simple act of opening the door for someone. You probably see these acts as being polite. Yet a security policy prohibits opening a door or allowing someone behind you to gain entry. You're expected to deny access to uncredentialed workers and perhaps even to a well-liked coworker. Policies may require you to deny access to senior executives. These seem like small issues, but they can create internal conflict and uneasiness in workers. These conflicts are inevitable. Workers who take a commonsense approach may have their thinking challenged. Nevertheless, part of enforcement is recognizing the conflicts and working with employees to overcome them.

> **NOTE**
>
> The person primarily responsible for setting goals in security should be the chief information security officer (CISO). The CISO's key task is to build support for implementing security policies and programs within the executive ranks. The CISO's ability to build personal relationships with executives and gain their trust is the most effective tool for implementing security.

Executive Management Sponsorship

Executive management today is pulled in many directions. It's a fast-paced world, for some industries more so than others. To be effective, executives need to be surrounded by employees with a strong sense of clarity, purpose, and action. Effective leaders have the ability to encourage people to achieve the leaders' goals. They lead the organization in the right direction in order to achieve a specific goal. They use their values, knowledge, and skills to motivate and get others to excel. Effective executives persuade people to do the right thing for a better future.

Executive management support is not just about budgets and mandates. When you have executive management support, you have powerful allies. Executives can overcome objections and persuade an organization to adopt policies. They can coach the chief information security officer (CISO) on how to avoid pitfalls.

Executive support is key to security policy enforcement. At some point in the enforcement process you need to change workers' behaviors. This can require disciplinary action. Even taking workers aside and coaching them runs the risk of negatively impacting a department. It is important that you lay the foundation for such discussions in advance. You accomplish this through the executive of the department. This executive can send a clear message that there's zero tolerance for ignoring security policies. The executive must be clear that

▶ **TIP**

Work with the people who report directly to executive management before presenting any proposal. Direct reports are often trusted advisers. Even if you have a good idea, the executives often defer decisions until they can discuss the issue with advisers. By presenting your proposal to the adviser first, you avoid delays. Advisers can also be strong advocates for you with the executive.

violations of policies will be taken seriously. This type of message establishes a tone at the top.

Governance Versus Management Organizational Structure

Enforcement is most effective when it comes from the employees' own leadership. Information security teams often do not enforce policies directly. Security teams do not directly manage all employees and thus, typically cannot "order" an employee to comply with policies. So how do security policies get enforced? Usually security teams monitor for compliance and then report noncompliance to leadership. It's then up to leadership to direct employees and ensure the right behavior occurs. This can include disciplinary action up to and including termination (firing) in the case of a serious violation of security policies.

It's important to remember that the employees look to executive management for direction. The executive leaders are expected to lead by example. This means they follow the same policies as employees. When they exempt themselves, they devalue the importance of the policies.

Executive management should take an active interest in key performance indicators and show continued support for the program. They should be visible in approving any deviation from policies and approve it only when necessary. This visibility sends a powerful message about the importance of security policies and risk management. When an incident does occur, this preparation creates less chance of pushback. The executive is more likely to enforce policies to support his or her personal credibility. Once executives put their own credibility behind policies, they are less likely to allow violations to occur.

Finding the right level of leadership to take action can be a challenge. It's generally more effective to have leadership governance and management committees responsible for IT security policy enforcement. There is a difference between governance and management within an organization. To see this difference, consider Control Objectives for Information and related Technology (COBIT) 5.0 definitions, as illustrated in **FIGURE 14-1**. As you see by the figure, governance sets strategic direction, and management executives run day-to-day operations. Governance, as defined by COBIT 5, "ensures that enterprise objectives are achieved" and directs management to execute. It's these governance processes that balance competing interests such as the business needs to make a profit and the customer needs to buy services at a fair price. Governance sets the direction for management to follow. It's then up to management to achieve its goals "in alignment with the direction" set by the governance processes. Management is responsible for running day-to-day operations. Both organizational structures monitor activity.

Governance committees are more likely to monitor activity after the fact and in the aggregate to assess whether goals are being achieved. Management committees are likely to monitor activities before, during, and after as part of running the operations. What does this mean for the compliance program? It means that you need to monitor the effectiveness of quality assurance within management processes.

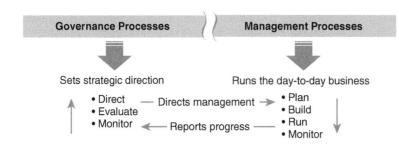

FIGURE 14-1

How governance and management work together within the COBIT 5.0 framework.

Management committees are responsible for running the business. As they run these processes, they need to be checking whether security is in place. For example, as they create an ID, they also need to ensure it has the right kind of access before it is issued. Before moving code into production, management needs to make sure it has all the security features turned on.

Both management and governance committees would be interested in results from QC reviews and compliance assessment. Remember, governance generally deals with issues in the aggregate. What that means is that governance cares about the accumulation of issues that would impact the organization's goals. For example, governance might care that 30 percent of the online systems fail a Payment Card Industry Data Security Standard (PCI DSS) vulnerability assessment. Governance committees tend to focus on total amount of PCI DSS testing rather than any one specific test. The 30-percent failure rate might indicate potential risk of fines, or the risk that a hacker could disrupt the company's ability to accept credit cards. These risks could impact the company's goals and objectives.

Management would also be interested in the PCI DSS assessment. Management would want to know a range of details, such as which vulnerabilities failed and on which systems. Management would want to know why the QA processes were not able to detect the problem before the systems went into production. Management processes typically deal with the detail needed to run the business day-to-day, whereas governance deals with setting strategic direction.

Both management and governance committees are generally provided monitoring reports from the compliance program. These compliance reports provide the information needed for leadership to take action. Additionally, the management processes are generally used to identify root causes and recommendations for fixing any noncompliance problems.

To continue the 30-percent PCI DSS assessment example, management might identify a root cause for the high rate of failure. The problem may be due to outdated technology. Management may recommend an increased budget to replace the outdated technology. Governance processes consider the recommendation and the impact of the situation on the organization's goals, and they approve funding for the technology replacement.

The Hierarchical Organizational Approach to Security Policy Implementation

The organization itself has a role in enforcing policies. This is typically handled through **gateway committees**. These committees are executive management processes to review technology activity. They often provide approvals before a project or activity can proceed to the next stage. This is why they are referred to as "gateways." They are literally the gateway for new technology projects entering the organization.

Some organizations combine different functions into one oversight board. Larger organizations often separate committee functions. The names of these committees depend on the organization. Regardless of how these committees are combined or divided, the membership should include senior leaders across the organization.

Don't get confused by committee names or the number of committees in an organization. The key is to understand how committees within an organization view risk and enforce policies. The following are committee roles and responsibilities found in most organizations:

- **Project committee**—Approves project funding, phases, and base requirements
- **Architecture review committee**—Approves standard technologies and architectures
- **External connection committee**—Approves external data connections
- **Vendor governance committee**—Approves new vendors and oversight of existing vendors
- **Security compliance committee**—Approves controls for compliance with laws and regulations such as Sarbanes-Oxley (SOX)
- **Operational risk committee**—Approves risk tolerance and oversight of risk exposure to the business

 TIP

Committees often have charters. These are formal documents that outline the mission and goals of the committee. These charters are valuable sources of information as to the function of the committee.

These committees have line of sight into all major projects and initiatives within the organization. Each committee looks at risk from a different perspective; however, they all play a role in enforcing security policies.

Project Committee

The **project committee** reviews project concepts, designs, and testing phases. It approves when a project can go into production. The number of phases requiring the committee's approval depends on the project life cycle (PLC). The intent is to identify project problems early to reduce costly mistakes. This external project review is an ideal time to examine any security policy issues.

This committee has the authority to stop a project that fails to adhere to policy. This is a powerful organizational enforcement mechanism. At a minimum, the committee asks the project team about any known security policy deviations. Additionally, representatives from the security team are members of the committee. They can ask focused security policy questions. For example, they may ask PCI DSS compliance questions about a new online credit card processing system being deployed. The security or audit staff often perform an assessment of a project. That assessment would be submitted to the committee for resolution of any security policy issues.

Architecture Review Committee

The **architecture review committee** promotes standard use of technology and architecture. By creating architectural models to be followed, the organization can more rapidly deploy consistent technology solutions. These models usually have much of the security policies embedded in their design. Consequently, deploying standard sets of technology ensures highly reliable and compliant solutions.

This committee has the authority to stop a project that fails to adhere to these technology standards. The committee can enforce security policies. This is accomplished by deploying technology solutions that are compliant with security policies. Additionally, the committee needs to resist adopting technology that deviates from the security policies. When noncompliant technology needs to be adopted, the risk must be accepted by the business. The committee presents the risk and technology recommendation to the business.

External Connection Committee

The **external connection committee** defines how data is transmitted outside the organization. This includes how and what data is sent and received. This committee works closely with the vendor governance committee to make sure no external connections to unauthorized parties are approved. A focus of the committee is the security and reliability of these third-party connections. For organizations with little external connection, these responsibilities may be rolled into other committees, such as the architectural review committee. Another focus is defining what data may be

 TIP

Sending sensitive or confidential data outside the organization to a third party must be considered a major decision and event. Make sure the third party has adequate controls in place before turning on the external connection.

sent to a third party. The committee generally does not give blanket approval for all types of data to be sent once a secure connection is built.

This committee typically enforces communication and encryption security requirements. No connections that violate these policies are approved.

Vendor Governance Committee

The **vendor governance committee** has both a business and a technology role. The business role is the oversight of the vendor relations. This role ensures that vendors deliver on commitments. In other words, this committee ensures that the vendor meets the service level agreement (SLA) in the contract. The committee also examines concerns about product quality.

The technical role of the committee is to ensure that the vendor complies with contracted policies. These contracted policies should be at least as restrictive as your own policies. For example, assume you identified a security policy requirement to log access to a file. This is to be compliant with a regulation. Just because that file is now transmitted to a vendor to be processed doesn't mean the security policy requirement for logging ceases to exist.

Vendor contract requirements must require a level of care for data equal to or better than the organization's. Vendor governance policies must require the organization to put in place a way of ensuring such care is taken. It's not adequate to simply sign a contract. Accountability for that data remains with the organization. For example, under the Gramm-Leach-Bliley Act (GLBA), a bank is responsible for protecting an individual's personal financial records. The bank is still accountable if a vendor on the bank's behalf processes that data.

The bank must ensure the vendor has adequate controls in place. This can be accomplished by auditing the vendor. You can also ask the vendor to provide evidence of a recent audit. The contract itself, which is a promise by the vendor, is not considered evidence that the vendor is adequately handling the bank's data.

Security Compliance Committee

The **security compliance committee** typically has many roles. One of the key roles is to determine when policy violations occur. The security compliance committee reviews risk and vulnerability assessments. The committee often focuses on pervasive controls. A **pervasive control** is a common control that is used across a significant population of systems, applications, and operations. For example, assume the same ID and password can be used across many systems and applications. That control would be considered pervasive in the environment. The security compliance committee role is to ensure those controls conform to the security policies. The committee may also be a gateway for projects to ensure that controls follow policies.

It is important that pervasive controls comply with security policies. These controls have significant impact on securing systems and applications. If there is a weakness in one of these controls, a weakness exists throughout the infrastructure. These controls are also critical to compliance testing. For example, many organizations rely on these controls for SOX compliance. When these controls do not work, organizations can find themselves out of compliance with key regulations.

Operational Risk Committee

The operational risk committee, often referred to as *ops risk*, has both a business and a technology role. The committee's primary role is to manage risk to the business. The operational risk function makes sure the business is operating within risk appetite and risk tolerance. For example, ensuring proper segregation of duties can ensure that some risks are properly controlled.

To illustrate this point: You would not want the same person to be able both to set up a vendor and to order and accept goods from that vendor. If you did, that person could set up a fake vendor. The person could then order goods without receiving anything, but would trigger an invoice, which the company would then pay. This means the company would have paid a fake vendor who supplied no goods. The dishonest employee, in other words, would have created a channel to divert funds from the company to a partner in crime, or even to his or her own bank account.

The ops risk committee has an enforcement role for security policies. The committee is responsible for ensuring that the policies are adequate to control key business risks. Security policies, by definition, control business risk. This means the committee is required to approve any deviations from security policies, thus accepting the accompanying risk.

The operational risk committee views risk as an individual event and as a portfolio of risks. By looking at risk both ways, the committee can determine a risk tolerance for the organization. For example, suppose the committee finds isolated instances of policy violation. Perhaps it's too expensive to replace outdated technology. These isolated instances may be acceptable risks individually; however, the combination of so many isolated cases may undermine a key compliance program. The committee needs to look at accepting risk both from the specific event and as part of a larger portfolio of risk.

The CISO or delegate is typically a committee member. He or she plays an important role by explaining the level of risks accepted by the committee on behalf of the business. Other members of this committee are typically business leaders. These leaders help enforce security policies within the business.

Organizations vary in size and management approach. As a result, the number of committees and their responsibilities can vary. Some organizations combine the functions of several of these committees. The key point is that these responsibilities need to be formally assigned to some committee within the organization.

Front-Line Managers' and Supervisors' Responsibility and Accountability

Once policies are established, management must figure out how to implement them. This includes making the policies operational. For line management that means the following:

- Ensuring everyone on the front-line team is trained
- Taking on the role as the go-to person for questions
- Applying the policies consistently
- Gathering metrics on the policy's effectiveness
- Ensuring everyone follows the policy

Front-line managers and supervisors work with employees every day. They see what works and what does not. They need to work with their teams to make sure everyone understands the new policies. Managers ensure everyone has gone through awareness training. They also answer any outstanding questions. If they don't know the answers, they find out where to get the information. They are responsible for ensuring their team is ready to implement policies. They also ensure the policy rollout is on schedule within their team's responsibility.

Front-line managers and supervisors are directly accountable to ensure that employees are implementing the policies consistently. This oversight includes gathering metrics on how well the implementation is working. Sometimes policies have unintended consequences. These individuals need to document the situation when policies don't work out as designed. They are responsible for notifying management of issues and problems.

Inevitably, something will go wrong. If someone fails to follow policy, managers are responsible for finding out why and resolving the problem. Sometimes that includes disciplining an employee. Other times, it is more a matter of finding out why the employee wasn't successful and overcoming the problem with coaching or additional training.

The result of these managers' and supervisors' efforts is enforced policies. These efforts ensure policies are implemented and are working properly.

Grass-Roots Employees

Employees react to the environment around them. It's rare that a worker comes to work with the intent not to follow a security policy. Obviously, it is possible that employees with malicious intent could exist in an organization; however, this is not the primary cause for failure to adhere to policies. Often it is that they don't fully understand the policy, or it is very inconvenient to adhere to. The problem is exacerbated if policy enforcement is either nonexistent or inconsistent.

This means that employees have great influence over coworker actions. If one employee is violating some policy with apparent impunity, it becomes more likely that other employees will consider violating that policy. This peer pressure provides a grass-roots enforcement method. In close-knit teams, peer pressure can be a tremendous asset. Such pressure is most effective when employees know that infractions will bring scrutiny and lead to embarrassment in front of the group. The key is management's response to security policy violations. The peer pressure is more likely to be applied when the response of management is visible. This is similar to driving on a road in the United States. If you see several other drivers exceeding the speed limit by 10 miles per hour without consequence, you may feel emboldened to speed yourself.

Enforcement need not always be punitive. Rewards can also be a means of policy enforcement. If someone is exemplary at following some critical policy, they should be recognized. If a given team or department goes for an extended period of time without any incidents, they should be rewarded. The specific criteria and mechanisms for reward will vary among organizations.

Employees are key to understanding how to align policies to business. They understand the level of risk for a particular business function. Based on that risk, appropriate enforcement can be applied from employees, front-line managers, and supervisors.

Policies evolve as the business evolves. The risk management process must have a feedback loop from employees to ensure that the policies still make sense for the business.

An Organization's Right to Monitor User Actions and Traffic

The prevailing legal view is that employers have the right to monitor workers' activities on company computers. This right is not absolute. In other words, it's important that an organization act in accordance with its policies and the law. The policies must be clear and concise. This does not mean you need a policy that creates a right to monitor employees. That right is already written in law. The Electronic Communication Privacy Act (ECPA) gives employers the right to monitor employees in the ordinary course of business. These broad rights include monitoring telephone calls and computer usage such as email. Having such a policy reduces an employee's argument that he or she perceived a right to privacy. It's always best that organizations put in writing their intent to monitor workers' activities on computers.

There are a number of good reasons to monitor workers' computer activities. The following is a list of some of those reasons:

- Maintaining a productive workforce
- Detecting when security policies are not being followed
- Maintaining the security of sensitive data
- Ensuring quality and protecting the organization's reputation
- Avoiding liability from pirated intellectual property such as software and music

Employers argue that because the computers are their property, they have the right to any information they contain. This is especially true when policy requires employee notification that computers are for company use only. All files contained in the computer potentially represent a record of the company's business.

Not only does productivity drop when workers spend many hours writing personal emails, but there's also a danger of viruses or security breaches. Companies argue that they have a have right to inspect all files on the computer, even when the file is a personal email sent from a work computer.

The acceptable use policy (AUP) typically includes statements regarding the employer's intent to monitor. Employees typically read and sign this document. Many of these documents state that the employee should not expect any right to privacy while using company computers.

However, the right is not absolute. Assume you are a worker planning on suing your company. You use a company laptop to sign on to a personal email account to exchange messages with your attorney. It's not a company email account, but rather a personal account such as Yahoo! or Gmail. After you leave the company and file your lawsuit, the company scans your laptop and finds portions of your communications. The company has a clear policy stating you have no right to privacy on company equipment. Did the company violate your privacy? Yes. Take a look at a specific court case to understand why.

The situation was reported in a *New York Post* article written in April 2010 and several online law sites such as the Sacramento Bankruptcy Lawyer blog. This is an older case, but in the legal world precedence is very important. The case, *Marina Stengart v. Loving Care Agency, Inc.*, involved Marina Stengart, a woman who worked for a health company from home. She had exchanged emails with an attorney regarding a possible lawsuit against her company. Ms. Stengart had used her employer-issued laptop computer to access her web-based email. After leaving the company, she turned in her laptop. Her former employer scanned her laptop and found her conversations with her attorney. In this case, the court held there was a reasonable expectation of privacy on behalf of Ms. Stengart.

This was a significant case because until that time it was assumed that with the right policy in place, an organization could monitor any activity on a company device. When the lines between a worker's personal and professional life blur, the court rulings become less clear. Organizations that allow the use of employee-owned devices may find themselves in the same situation. Some organizations, for example, allow personal smartphones to be used to send and received company emails. Even when these devices have the same encryption and other controls, the legal lines between work and personal life are blurred. Although this is done to reduce costs, it can quickly create legal entanglements.

There is little dispute that organizations can monitor employer-owned computers used during work hours through company accounts. There are typically three areas of monitoring employee actions:

* Internet
* Email
* Computers

Although the following sections will provide general guidance, it should be remembered that this author is not an attorney. Before implementing any employee monitoring process, it is advised that you consult with an attorney who specializes in privacy law or human resources law.

Internet Use

Internet use is typically monitored for access to inappropriate sites such as those that contain pornographic or obscene material. Access is also monitored for unauthorized access to subscription-only sites. Access to competitor sites or copyrighted material can be monitored. Uploading confidential material is a potential problem.

Most recently concerns have increased around social networking sites. These are sites that build online communities of people who share interests and information. The concern is that workers in these social communities begin exchanging information about the company. This information runs the gamut from entirely innocent remarks to negative commentary on the company all the way to divulging company secrets. The question for companies is how much of this activity should be monitored. Many organizations block these sites. This solves the problem of access while on the company network during work hours. The problem becomes more challenging when it comes to monitoring employee activity during off-hours. This problem is complicated by the fact that social networking sites meant for business do exist. The classic example is LinkedIn. Depending on the employee's role, he or she may have a legitimate reason for visiting LinkedIn; for example, someone working in the human resources or recruiting department may need to access profiles on LinkedIn.

Organizations do routinely monitor for any negative publicity on social networking sites, blog spaces, and the Internet in general. If it's determined that an individual's public posting reflects negatively on the organization, then the employee will be asked to remove the posting. Usually that's as far as things will go for minor infractions. Unless you have a highly sensitive job dealing with national security secrets, most organizations are reluctant to monitor employee activity after hours. Employers do take action against employees who post extremely negative comments about their organization. This is what happened to a web designer who lost her job after posting negative comments about her bosses. She also mentioned her company by name.

Email Use

Email use is typically monitored for viruses and malware. Companies also monitor email for data leakage protection (DLP) and sensitive information. DLP monitoring may look for large files being emailed outside the organization. It can also scan emails for sensitive information such as account numbers and Social Security numbers. Email can also be monitored for abusive or threatening language.

Company email accounts are difficult to permanently delete. It may be illegal to delete some emails and records that are part of a lawsuit. Once a lawsuit is filed, the expectation is that all records related to the case will be preserved. That includes keeping emails. For many organizations, this process of identifying which records to keep or not keep is managed by the legal department. The attorney will identify which materials and individuals are involved, and then direct the technology and security teams to preserve the records in a secure location. This may mean saving an individual's email messages. Additionally, the court may order the retention of emails. For example, in 2012 in the case of *E.E.O.C. v. Original Honeybaked Ham Co.*, the court ordered broad retention and discovery of text messages and email. The case concerned allegations of sexual harassment, a hostile environment, and retaliation. Again, some of the legal cases mentioned in this chapter may seem outdated, but that is not how the legal system works. Legal precedents can be from several years back.

Every organization should have an email policy. This builds on the AUP and talks specifically about the proper use of emails. The email policy should require disclaimers and warn individuals that their email is subject to monitoring. With these measures in place, the courts have put few limits on organizations that act in good faith, such as in the court case in 2001 of *Fraser v. Nationwide Mutual Insurance Company* (135 F. Supp. 2d 623 (E.D. Pa. 2001)). In this case, a worker emailed a competitor company with the objective of stealing customers. The court noted that "an employer can do anything with e-mail messages sent and received on company computers." The court went on to note that "as long as it has notified employees that they have no expectation of privacy," email can be monitored at any time without notice.

It should be noted that there is an additional motivation for monitoring workplace email: to prevent issues that involve harassment. Is someone in your organization sending inappropriate emails or offensive content? If you do not monitor emails, you may not know the answer to that until either a complaint is lodged or, more egregiously, a harassment lawsuit is filed.

Computer Use

An employee's computer is generally monitored for viruses and malware. It's also typically monitored for pirated software and excessive use such as game playing, as well as for unauthorized files that have been removed from secure servers. The extent of the monitoring depends on the concerns of the organization.

With the right policies, companies can protect themselves against these risks. There are a few restrictions on monitoring company equipment on a company network. The basic policies that should be in place to allow monitoring to be enforced are transparency and clarity. The basic steps are to make sure you have informed the workers that such monitoring can take place. Be clear, through an AUP, what the expected behavior is while using the organization's computers.

Compliance Law: Requirement or Risk Management?

Security policies, by their nature, attempt to comply with all regulatory requirements to be met by the organization. The word *attempt* is used to reflect the balance policies create. The policies must balance achievable goals, best practices, and interpretation of regulations. This balance requires compromise. That's why the legal department is a key stakeholder in creating security policies. The legal department ensures the security policies are defensible with regulators and in the courts.

The regulators look first at the organization's policies. They assess if the policies are reasonable and conform to guidance. The regulators ensure core requirements are met regardless of whether the organization feels they are achievable. However, even regulators must interpret legal language, and they may do it differently than your organization.

For example, under the Graham-Leach-Bliley Act (GLBA), organizations must notify regulators promptly of any unauthorized access that breaches customer financial records. You need to figure out what constitutes an unauthorized access or breach. There are clear examples, such as an outside hacker. There are also gray areas. If a teller accesses an account out of curiosity, would that be a reportable breach under GLBA? It could be. Regulators provide threshold guidance. It's doubtful a bank would notify a regulator over one customer account accessed inappropriately by an internal employee. It's not uncommon for a threshold to be set at 1000 or more records. That doesn't mean the breach of a single account isn't important. Thresholds are a practical way of assessing the magnitude of a breach. Even a

TIP

Regulators use approved documents and processes to assess an organization's security policies. These guidance documents are usually publicly available. You can compare them with your own security policies to ensure that they meet all requirements. Guidance documents also provide evidence to the regulator of conformance.

single account breach can have significant impact. Assume, for example, that a single account breach identified pervasive control weakness. *Pervasive control* is a term used to mean a control that is widely used across the enterprise. As such, that single account breach can identify a control weakness that could have led to a much bigger breach.

Pervasive control weaknesses are of interest to a regulator. For example, assume that a retail account statement was found in the possession of an employee who had no authorization to have the document. Suppose it was later found that the employee picked it up out of a trash bin on a loading dock. Although only a single document was removed, the breach indicates a much bigger problem. If there was a general lack of controls for secure disposal of customer account documents, then that would be considered a pervasive control weakness.

Regulatory guidance addresses most gray areas in the law. The key point is that organizations need to establish a risk management program that ensures security policies address legal requirements. The risk management program also ensures these policies are enforced. It is important to provide regulators with evidence that the security policies help manage risk as well as prevent breaches.

What Is Law and What Is Policy?

Organizations enforce policies and report on compliance. Organizations generally do not internally enforce laws. In other words, security policies are not a legal interpretation of the law. Security policies are interpretations of legal requirements that lead to compliance.

A **law** is any rule prescribed under the authority of a government entity. A regulatory agency may be granted the authority under the law to establish **regulations**. Regulations inherit their authority from the original law.

The distinction among laws, regulations, and security policies is as follows:

- Laws establish the legal thresholds.
- Regulatory requirements establish what an organization has to do to meet the legal thresholds.
- Security policies establish how the organization achieves the regulatory requirements.

Consider an example in the security world that relates to the interpretation of information security regulations. The Gramm-Leach-Bliley Act (GLBA) was intended to ensure the security and confidentiality of customer information. GLBA Section 501(b) requires that the board or its designated committee adequately oversee the financial institution's information security program. What does "adequately oversee" mean? The Federal Deposit Insurance Corporation (FDIC) issued a regulatory ruling that the organization's board must receive a formal report at least annually. Many organizations interpret that to be a formal report to the audit committee by both the CISO and auditors. The point is that organizations can achieve regulatory compliance in different ways. Often you write policies to achieve regulatory requirements. Most of the time, you do not write policy to specific language of the law.

A violation of a policy is not necessarily a violation of law; however, it might be. Legal interpretation of statutes is a different skill set from policy interpretation. Often, the legal threshold to violate a law is high. It considers circumstance and intent. Only a court or regulatory body can determine if there are sufficient grounds for determining a violation of the law.

Although it is important to remain aware of the current laws and regulations, they should not be your sole driver. There are many risks to the business that are not addressed by laws and regulations. Regulations are written to address a specific area of concern that may have been a result of a public incident or class-action suit. Although ensuring adherence to regulations is a must, there's no substitute for common sense. The key point is that law always trumps policies with the regulators and the courts. Laws and regulation do not cover all risks.

What Security Controls Work to Enforce Protection of Personal Data?

Organizations have the ability to accept risk. They can accept risks that could potentially impact the business. These organizations do not, however, have the right to accept risk on behalf of the customer. In other words, they cannot put their customer at risk by mishandling their data.

The risk management approach used to assess and accept business risk cannot be applied equally to customers' personal data. Any organization that collects, stores, processes, and transmits personal information must be compliant with privacy laws.

These privacy laws establish specific controls. Privacy laws do vary from state to state. Some common security controls include:

- Notification when a breach occurs
- Encrypting data when it leaves the organization's network
- Ensuring that each user has a unique identity when accessing the data
- Granting access for business purposes only
- Destroying data when no longer needed
- Having appropriate policies and security awareness in place

It is important to find out what privacy laws exist when you are doing business. On the basis of these laws, you can determine a common set of core controls. These common controls need to be in the security policies. Effectively destroying data is often overlooked. Yes, shredding documents is a good idea; however, an incinerator is an even more effective approach. Computer storage media must be completely, forensically wiped. In some cases, it is the appropriate approach to simply destroy the computer media rather than try to wipe it for reuse.

What Automated Security Controls Can Be Implemented Through Policy?

Automating as many security controls as possible is the best way to ensure adoption, enforcement, and effectiveness. By far, this is the preferred approach when possible. Automated controls work the same way every time. That means controls are consistently applied and often executed faster than humans can achieve. Human judgment is expensive and inconsistent. You must train individuals to know what to do. Even then, consistency depends on alert individuals who don't get tired or distracted. Consequently, automated controls are cost efficient for large volumes of work that need to be performed consistently.

Another advantage is reporting and monitoring. Automated controls can easily be configured to log and track activity. The same level of data collection performed by a person would be time consuming and subject to errors. The time component is important. Automated controls tend to be in real time, allowing processes to have self-service capability and reporting instantly.

For example, access to a low-risk application may be preapproved. As a result, an individual might be able to go to a self-service site that reviews the request and automatically grants access. With a manual process, a request would have to be submitted to someone to determine whether it is approved.

It's not uncommon for manual access requests to take days or weeks, depending on staffing availability, backlog, implementation complexity, and the number of approvals required. Automation can significantly reduce that time in the following areas:

- **Appropriate request**—Automated controls can validate that the request is complete and does not violate any policy requirements such as segregation of duties.
- **Approval workflow**—Automated controls can route a request to those who must approve it as quickly as possible; electronic approval is a common practice for many security requests.
- **Implementation**—Automatic controls can implement a change once it's approved.

An automated control is configured into a device to enforce a security policy. Here's a short list of several common automated controls:

- Authentication methods
- Authorization methods
- Data encryption
- Logging events
- Data segmentation
- Network segmentation

The number of automated controls is limited only by the technology's capability. Continued improvement in technology allows for more automation. The biggest challenge isn't the automation but the deployment.

Consider an example where a policy says that a user must change his or her password every 30 days. A central authentication server exists within the environment. The challenge is how to configure every device to use the authentication server. The IT environment can have thousands of devices. Each may have to be configured. Once configured, these devices have to be monitored to ensure the configuration is not changed. As new devices are added, the same configuration has to be applied to every device from servers to smartphones. The configuration of an automated control may be simple. Applying it consistently becomes the major challenge. The problem gets more complicated as the number of automated controls increases. The diversity of the technology in the environment can make supporting the automated controls more complex. Consequently, automation is the practical solution to implement this security policy.

Many commercial products come with enterprise management software to solve this automation challenge. Central policy management software is designed specifically for this purpose. These types of applications create policy rules on a central server. These rules are then sent to the various devices via an agent or agent-less architecture.

Automated policy management tools take security policies and implement them as configuration updates. Once the device is configured, the automated control enforces the policy. The enforcement can be a preventive or detective control. Either way, the control is automated. The control either prevents an event that is outside policy or detects that an event occurred. Our example of a policy that requires a password to be changed every 30 days is typically a preventive control. The central authentication server forces users to change their password at the end of 30 days.

Policy management tools also correlate large amounts of data. They can discover devices on the network. They can track which device has the policies applied. These tools can also monitor for policy violations. The tool can identify devices that do not have the policy applied. These tools identify the existing configuration to compare with the desired policy state. Deviation from policies can be corrected automatically. This is a powerful tool. Auditors and regulators often request extracts from the policy management tools. This extract can help them assess the level of policy compliance.

> **TIP**
>
> Many administrator tools can support policy management. You can use administrator tools as a first step in policy management.

What Manual Security Controls Assist with Enforcement?

Not all controls can or should be automated. Manual controls are appropriate for low volume work. They're also appropriate for work that requires human judgment. Examples of manual controls are:

- Background checks
- Log reviews
- Access rights reviews
- Attestations

In each of these cases, volumes are low, and human judgment is important to the process. It is important that manual processes be clear. This means that both the step is clear and the criteria for the judgment are clear.

Take a look at background checks as a manual control. The process should be clear as to how to collect the information for the background check. The criteria should also be defined. For many jobs, minor traffic violations are acceptable. For other jobs, such as commercial drivers, any traffic violation may be considered unacceptable. A clearly defined security policy ensures everyone is treated equally on background checks. This can avoid legal problems.

> **TIP**
>
> All too many companies either do not perform background checks or do so inadequately. The number of people who exaggerate or outright lie about credentials on their resume/application is surprising. Beyond that, this author is personally aware of two instances of an employee at a company with access to sensitive, even financial data, wherein the employee had a felony criminal record. In both cases, the employer had inadequate background checks.

A human can review logs for unusual activity that is difficult to automate. For example, when a programmer is granted elevated rights to fix a production problem, logs are often reviewed to determine if the programmer performed an activity that exceeded the scope of the fix. For instance, the log review may change if the programmer changed account data in a database. These types of changes to fix an application may be unusual and require management follow-up.

Access rights include a review by the business to ensure adequate separation of duties. This type of review is manual and requires knowledge of how the business operates. Based on this knowledge, a reasonable balance is struck between operational efficiency and reducing risks.

An *attestation* is a formal management verification. Management is attesting that a condition exists. Some regulations require management to attest that security policies and controls are in place; for example, SOX requires this type of attestation from senior management.

When someone makes an attestation, they are personally liable for the accuracy of the statement. This is a way the law holds management accountable to ensure appropriate controls are put in place. Making a false statement is often a crime; however, making a statement you believe is true that later turns out to false may be defendable. How defendable depends on the information on which you based the statement. It's not if you knew but whether you should have known. In other words, simply asking someone if the controls are in place is not sufficient.

Legal Implications of IT Security Policy Enforcement

Technology makes it easy to transact business. Computers provide an effective method of communication and record keeping. Technology offers the ability to automatically keep an audit trail. This ease of use and creation of massive amounts of data have security policy enforcement implications. Data must be preserved and retrievable for a host of legal reasons.

Failure to properly retain records can lead to significant fines. This is especially true for data related to a lawsuit. Destroying records can jeopardize a company's case. It can also lead to criminal charges. Even the innocent destruction of data can lead to accusations of negligence, withholding or hiding information, and altering or destroying evidence. So how long should you retain data? That depends on the content, organization, and location. For example, the Texas state Government Code, Section 441.158, requires local governments to retain records on annexation permanently. On the other hand, certain minutes of government meetings need be retained for only two years. Such legal distinctions must be assessed by a legal department and incorporated into policies and security practices to ensure the data is adequately archived.

In general, destroying records prematurely can actually cause far more problems than it might solve. If you have a reasonable expectation that some civil litigation is imminent, you have a duty to retain relevant records. Failure to do so could have substantial consequences. Older data should be destroyed only in accordance with well-established policies and only if there is no reasonable expectation that the data may be required in some context such as a legal proceeding.

It's important to enforce security policies on data retention. This includes the preservation of data. The security policies must ensure that record keeping is accurate and securely maintained. Electronic discovery (e-discovery) is a part of the legal process. It's used to gather computer-generated information for a legal action. This can be far more complicated than the discovery of paper documents because of the massive amount of data an organization holds.

FIGURE 14-2 illustrates this point. Consider a simple loan document. Notice from the figure that information from the original document is used to generate a monthly statement. The statement now contains personal financial information. That document, in turn, may be used to generate a late notice. The notice may be tied to an email correspondence with the customer. And so on. The personal financial information could even be sent to an external collection agency. The data most likely is stored in multiple systems. This is depicted to the far left—note the information is flowing through loan, customer service, collection, and accounts receivable applications.

Over the years, hundreds of documents can be generated in multiple systems. You can quickly see the problem when an organization is required under e-discovery to produce documents and identify everyone who accessed these documents. The effort to retrieve this information is significant.

The legal implication of policy enforcement is not just about protecting data. There's a host of issues that need to be considered when writing security policies. You may not be able to terminate a user based on a violation of security policy. It depends on how the policy was written, HR policy, and the security awareness training provided.

FIGURE 14-2

Illustration of how data quickly expands.

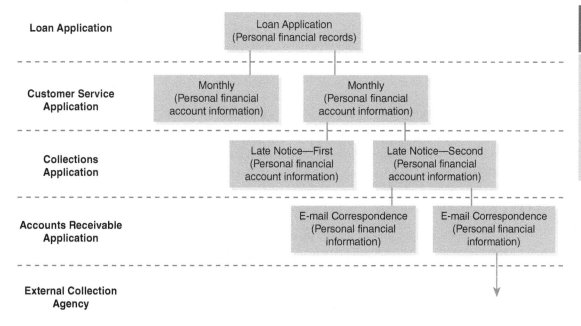

Even the deployment of security devices can have legal implications. For example, a **honeypot** is a network security device that acts as a decoy. Its sole purpose is to look like a tempting target to a hacker. When a hacker attempts to break into the honeypot, it records the hacker's actions. This can be used as evidence of an attack. A honeypot also allows you to analyze the attack methods in great detail. This information can be used to harden other devices. This type of device has legal implications, however. Other security devices such as a firewall can be used to stop a hacker; however, a honeypot, by its nature, attempts to lure the hacker. Even more legal complications arise when a honeypot is put in the DMZ and publicized. This type of deployment raises the question of whether the organization is encouraging an illegal act.

Smartphones not owned by the organization are a challenge, even if the organization has a policy stating they can configure and wipe the device. Who has control when employees use smartphones for company business? It's especially hard to tell when an employee leaves the firm and disconnects the device from the organization's control. How does the organization ensure the device is wiped? There are legal implications for wiping devices not owned by the organization. Policy alone cannot provide sufficient legal authority to access the device unless an employee has granted such rights through some binding agreement.

The key point is that legal implications with security policies come in many forms. It's important that you build a good working relationship with the legal department. It can ensure that security policies can be enforced without causing legal problems.

Who Is Ultimately Accountable for Risks, Threats, and Vulnerabilities?

Executive management is ultimately accountable for controlling risks. Executives must explain why major security breaches occurred. They must rebuild trust with the public. They also have to rebuild confidence with shareholders and regulators.

To be accountable means to face consequences for failure to act. Some organizations find it difficult to apply consequences to top leadership. Worse yet are organizations that identify so many leaders as accountable that, for all practical purposes, no one is accountable.

As a result, not all organizations are capable of holding their leaders accountable. Accountability can come from external forces such as:

- **Public opinion**—This can turn against a company, leading to a loss of trust that damages or even destroys it. This can damage an organization's reputation.
- **Shareholders**—Vote and are active at the shareholder level
- **Regulators**—Hold the organization accountable for violation of law
- **Courts**—Hold executives personally accountable

Executive management is ultimately responsible for ensuring that data is protected. That means executives are accountable for selecting key leaders such as the CISO. It also means they need to support the security program. This support includes proper funding, removing barriers, and providing visible support. All levels of management are held accountable to ensure the security program is understood and properly implemented.

This support also means defining clear roles and responsibilities for implementing security policies. Employees are responsible for understanding their roles and the security policies. They are accountable for following those policies.

The organization holds much of the liability. The organization is ultimately in control of the data. There's an obligation on the organization's part to hire competent staff. It's also the organization's obligation to give this staff appropriate resources, training, and supervision. Employees can still be held liable for violation of the law. Employees can be prosecuted for illegal acts, but often it's the organization that is ultimately held accountable. It's executive management that is held accountable for allowing such acts to occur.

The information security organization plays a key role in controlling risk. It is accountable for identifying risks, threats, and vulnerabilities. Many times, it's the IT organization that executes assessments. The IT teams also implement mitigating solutions. The information security organization is a **subject matter expert (SME)**. It is often responsible for establishing the policies and procedures to be executed by the IT teams. The teams also review the assessment results.

Where Must IT Security Policy Enforcement Come From?

Multiple layers in the organization enforce security policies. Everyone has a role to play in identifying and managing risks. The following is a sampling of key roles to enforce security policies:

- **General counsel**—Enforces legally binding agreements
- **Executive management**—Implements enterprise risk management
- **Human resources (HR)**—Enforces disciplinary actions
- **Information systems security organization**—Enforces security policies at a program level
- **Front-line manager/supervisor**—Enforces security policies at an employee level

This is not a comprehensive list. For example, the **general counsel** works with law enforcement to prosecute employees who violate the law. The key point is to notice that every layer of the organization enforces security policies. Enforcement is not a single team's responsibility.

FYI

Although enforcement of security policies may align with different layers of the organization, ultimate accountability for identifying and escalating security noncompliance lies with the chief information security officer (CISO). The CISO "owns" the information security program (and related controls) across the enterprise. If the policies and controls are not effective, the CISO must escalate the matter to senior leadership. Senior leadership must enforce security policies through the CISO's guidance.

The general counsel enforces legal binding agreements. This enforcement takes the form of dealing with opposing legal counsel or filing lawsuits on the organization's behalf to resolve contract disputes. This includes agreements with vendors and outsourcers. The legal department is involved when the contracts are first written. These contracts often define the security policy to be followed. Ideally, any concerns with these contract policies are quickly resolved without involving the legal department; however, when security policy issues cannot be resolved, then the legal department is called. The legal department can either enforce the contract or terminate it. In extreme cases the department can file a lawsuit to recover damages due to the breach of contract. Regardless of the remedy, ultimate enforcement of legal provision falls on the legal department. Beyond this role, general counsel provides legal advice to management on writing and enforcing policies internally.

Executive management often focuses on implementing enterprise risk management. Executive committees (ECs) exist in many organizations. The EC brings multiple lines of business together to resolve strategic business issues. This is also true for enterprise risk management. The approval and enforcement of security policies is an EC responsibility. When two or more executives have differing views on security policies, the CISO tries to facilitate a solution. When the solution cannot be found, often the issue is brought to executive management through the EC. It is this committee's role to enforce security policies at the enterprise and executive level.

HR is a key player in the enforcement of disciplinary actions. The HR area defines the processes to discipline employees. These processes are one tool for enforcing security policies. The discipline could be a simple coaching session or a formal warning. Many HR teams have specific guidelines to be followed. This ensures security violations are handled in a consistent and fair manner. The visibility of a fair process is important in encouraging appropriate behavior.

The information systems security organization enforces security policies at a program level. The team is accountable for identifying violations of policies. It also needs to bring violations to the attention of management. Keep in mind that employees do not report to the security staff. Employees receive direction from their own management. The security staff is not a corporate police officer enforcing policies as corporate law. This perception is exactly what a security team should avoid. Security teams report risks. They also report facts on incidents. It is the employee's management that takes appropriate action.

The front-line manager/supervisor enforces security policies at an employee level. These individuals represent the employee's chain of command. It is these individuals that are responsible for the employee's day-to-day work. This includes ensuring that employees follow policy.

Best Practices for IT Security Policy Enforcement

The information security team should develop a close relationship with the legal team. They need to understand each other's processes and priorities. Teams should communicate their roles and responsibilities to one another. This helps them understand the various ways they can help enforce policies.

The information security team should review the current legislation that governs their business. This helps them understand what the law requires and what their legal team recommends.

The legal department should review all new or major changes to policies. The legal department needs to be briefed on how the policies will be enforced. This includes a discussion of both automated and manual controls. If your organization does not have an in-house legal department, then it is advised that you retain outside counsel to review your policies.

Enforcement of policies is based on a risk assessment. All policies should be followed; however, those that mitigate the greatest risk to the business should be targeted first. Excessive enforcement of policies with little or no effect on the business damages credibility.

It's important to ensure that consequence and enforcement are properly socialized throughout organization. This can be accomplished through both awareness and executive messaging. Information security policy enforcement is primarily a risk management function.

Wherever possible, use automated controls to enforce policies. If the organization is concerned about social networking sites, then block them. If the organization is concerned about personal email, then block those sites. When sites are blocked, an employee must overtly disable or bypass a control to gain access. The overt act of disabling or bypassing the control would be a significant violation of policy. There should be zero tolerance for such acts. However, automated controls must be reviewed from time to time. There are numerous instances of automated controls inadvertently blocking legitimate traffic.

As much as possible, make a clear distinction between home and work life. Be sure that policies are clear about the use of company equipment. This includes clearly stating that there's no expectation of privacy. Also state that all company equipment can be monitored. Personal devices connected to the network should be prohibited.

Security policies should not be solely based on enforcing laws. Developments in computer technology occur very frequently. With every new product or upgrade, new vulnerabilities are discovered. Often, we are not aware of the vulnerability until it is exploited. When enough exploits occur, laws are sometimes created. Because the legal system is reactionary in nature, it does not have the ability to keep up with exploits. Laws take time to be formulated and approved, and then they must be interpreted and regulated.

The CISO position continues to evolve from a technical management position to one that combines both technical and executive functions. In many organizations, the CISO role reports directly to one or more top leadership roles. The CISO must rely on the organization to enforce policy. The role needs to build relationships and consensus. The enforcement of security policies is about influencing behavior and changing culture. Executive management must set the tone and enforce policy consistently across all lines of business. There must be a consequence for noncompliance. Management must engage in making employees aware of the importance of security policies. There must be escalating levels of disciplines for noncompliance. This includes termination of employees who commit serious violations.

Case Studies and Examples of Successful and Unsuccessful IT Security Policy Enforcement

The following case studies discuss various enforcement problems with IT security policies. The first two illustrate a lack of enforcement. This lack of enforcement allowed data security breaches to occur. The third talks about how a policy was effectively enforced. Although data was inappropriately downloaded in the third case study, the study shows how changes in policy could improve the culture.

Private Sector Case Study

In 2017, it was widely reported that the credit reporting agency Equifax had been breached. The personal information of 147 million people was exposed. Among the data accessed were credit card numbers for approximately 209,000 U.S. consumers. This was a substantial breach. The event occurred in mid-May through July and was discovered July 29, 2017. What later became known was that in several instances, Equifax used default usernames and passwords—specifically, "admin" and "admin". These discoveries were made after the major breach; they were not the cause of the breach. Researchers at a cybersecurity firm found that they were able to uncover personal employee information housed on Equifax's South American site, including names, emails, and Social Security equivalents of over 100 individuals.

This is an example of failure to enforce security policies. Almost all organizations, particularly sizable ones, have specific policies against using default passwords. The Payment Card Industry Data Security Standard (PCI DSS) specifically warns against having any default accounts or passwords. However, this was clearly not enforced at Equifax.

Public Sector Case Study 1

In January 2019, it was discovered that the Oklahoma Department of Securities had been exposed for nearly a week before a breach was discovered by a research firm. Three terabytes of data were unprotected. The data included files on sensitive criminal investigations.

The department handles all securities-related data for the State of Oklahoma. The data revealed included investigations related to securities issues. It was also found that email archives going back 17 years as well as Social Security numbers were in the exposed data. Passwords for remote access to agency computers were also exposed. The data involved spanned from 1986 to 2016. The breach was due to an open rsync server. Rsync is often used for backups, thus backup data was exposed. It appears it was not secured.

This is an example of poor policy enforcement. The rsync server should have had much more robust security. Furthermore, having that much data exposed via the breach of a single server is itself disconcerting. This indicates a lack of the basic principle of defense in depth.

Public Sector Case Study 2

This is an older case but one that still is relevant. In July 2013, the U.S. Department of Energy system suffered a data breach. It resulted in unauthorized access to more than 104,000 individual personal records. The records included Social Security numbers, birthdates and locations, bank account numbers, and security questions and answers.

According to the Department of Energy Inspector General's report, there were "early warning signs" that personnel-related information systems were at risk. Yet no actions were taken to improve security. The Inspector General's report went on to identify "a number of technical and management issues" that were root causes. Additionally, the report cited "numerous contributing factors related to inadequate management processes."

Although the details of the breach were not made public, it's clear from the language and tone of the report that a lack of management process led to the security breach. Given that this agency is governed by the National Institute of Standards and Technology (NIST) standards, adequate security policies were most likely not the issue. That suggests the problem was lack of governance or management process to enforce the NIST standards.

It is interesting that the report indicates there were "early warning signs" of the security risks. In the absence of specifics, here are a couple of possibilities, among many, to consider:

First, the management processes may have failed to identify the security control weaknesses. This could happen if the breach was the result of a management process that did not adequately rate risks. For example, patch management processes must identify critical patches for issues that could lead to a breach. If this process fails to properly risk-rank a patch, then applying the patch could be significantly delayed and needlessly expose the systems to the risk. Regardless, management processes must enforce both ranking and installing patches to prevent data breaches.

A second possibility to consider is a lack of effective governance and management oversight. Had the risk been properly identified and raised with management, the lack of action could have been an indication that management was not enforcing policies. Given that lack of management action is cited as a cause, then lack of policy enforcement as required by NIST standards might be a root cause.

CHAPTER SUMMARY

The chief information security officer (CISO) "owns" the information protection program for the organization. He or she must monitor the adoption and effectiveness of the security policies. The CISO must ensure that noncompliance is escalated to senior leadership for enforcement. Still, it's everyone's responsibility to enforce security policies. This is accomplished by the collective action of leaders. Enforcement starts with executive support. This support goes beyond granting permission to implement security policies. Executive support also means personal commitment by the managers to use their position and skills to influence the direction of their teams. Once executives put their own credibility behind policies, they are less likely to allow violations to occur.

The organization also enforces policies through committees. These committees act as a gateway to check that security policies are being followed. This may mean monitoring employee use of the computer. When behavior does not conform to policies, it is the role of front-line managers and supervisors to act.

This chapter examined the relationship among organizational layers (governance and management), laws, regulations, and policies. It defined what is law and what is policy. It examined different methods of enforcing policies. It also examined the strengths and weaknesses of automated and manual controls. Finally, the chapter examined the legal implication of enforcing security policies.

KEY CONCEPTS AND TERMS

Architecture review committee
Data leakage
External connection committee
Gateway committees
General counsel

Honeypot
Law
Pervasive control
Project committee
Regulations

Security compliance
  committee
Subject matter expert (SME)
Vendor governance
  committee

CHAPTER 14 ASSESSMENT

1. Which of the following is *not* an organizational gateway committee?

A. Architecture review committee
B. Internal connection committee
C. Vendor governance committee
D. Security compliance committee

2. _____ often focuses on enterprise risk management across multiple lines of business to resolve strategic business issues.

3. The security compliance committee has one role, which is to identify when violations of policies occur.

A. True
B. False

4. Which of the following is *not* an access control?

A. Authentication
B. Authorization
C. Decryption
D. Logging

5. In which of the following areas might a company monitor its employees' actions?

A. Internet
B. Email
C. Computers
D. A and B
E. A, B, and C

6. _____ establish how the organization achieves regulatory requirements.

7. Laws define the specific internal IT processes needed to be compliant.

A. True
B. False

8. What is *not* required in modern-day CISO positions?

A. Must rely on the organization to enforce policy
B. Needs to have strong law enforcement background
C. Needs to build relationships and consensus
D. Must influence behavior and change culture to enforce policy

9. What is an example of a manual control?

A. Background checks
B. Authentication
C. Access rights reviews
D. A and C
E. A, B, and C

10. A breach of a single customer record cannot be considered a pervasive control weakness.

A. True—you must lose a significant amount of data for it to be considered a pervasive control weakness.
B. False—any breach can be a pervasive control weakness, depending on the control that failed.

11. Connecting a personal device to the company network can create legal implications.

A. True
B. False

12. Line management does which of the following to make policies operational?

- A. Acts as go-to people for addressing questions
- B. Applies policies consistently
- C. Gathers metrics on the policies' effectiveness
- D. A and C
- E. A, B, and C

13. In which process would you place quality assurance controls?

- A. Governance processes
- B. Management processes
- C. Both governance and management processes
- D. Neither governance nor management processes

14. Which of the following is *not* reviewed when monitoring a user's email and Internet activity?

- A. Data leakage
- B. Viruses and malware
- C. Unauthorized access to sites
- D. Network performance

15. When testing for security in an application code, the quality assurance process tests _____ the code is in production and quality control tests _____ the code is in production.

16. The operational risk function is responsible for ensuring that the business operates within risk _____ and risk _____.

IT Policy Compliance and Compliance Technologies

MAINTAINING COMPLIANCE with laws and regulations in a complex IT environment is difficult. The vast array of regulations a company must comply with is constantly increasing and changing. Consider, too, that it's not usual for different regulating agencies to issue conflicting rules. This means sometimes you have to manage to the intent of regulations as much as managing them to the letter. At the center of most regulations' intent is data protection. Stop the flow of data, and just as quickly you will disrupt the delivery of products and services. If the loss of data lasts long enough, the viability of the organization itself comes into question.

Laws that require notifying consumers of data breaches are a good example of conflicting regulatory rules. Each state has its own set of laws and regulations that indicate who is covered by the law and what event triggers the notification. For example, the State of Alaska (under Alaska Statute Title 45.48.010) requires notification of a data breach for any organization with 10 or more employees that maintains unencrypted personal information about Alaska residents. However, there's a provision in the law waiving the notification requirement if there's a reasonable determination that no harm will come to the consumer. In contrast, the State of Illinois (815 Ill. Comp Stat. Ann. 530/1–/30) requires notification of data breaches for any entity that collects data on Illinois residents. Notification is triggered upon discovery of the breach. No exemption is cited.

The exact language of the laws is not important for this discussion. It is important for you to comply with specific laws, but this discussion is more general. The point is that two breach notification laws that look at the same event and the same data require potentially two different actions. In the case of Alaska, no notification may be needed. In the case of Illinois, the size of the company makes no difference. Initial reaction might be, Why the concern? Two states and two laws. But the Internet has made businesses borderless. Just consider the confusion of reporting if an Alaskan company that ships product from a warehouse in Illinois had a data breach. Which law applies? Not to mention the question about whether the order that contained the personal information was received and stored in a third state. A company now must navigate a maze of jurisdictions and conflicting laws.

That's how vital data is for many organizations today. Now consider the regulatory view of how to process, manage, and store data properly. To address this challenge across a changing landscape of regulation requires a solid set of information security policies and the right tools. A lot of time and energy go into ensuring that security policies cover what is important to an organization. These policies help an organization comply with laws, standards, and industry best practices. Implemented properly, they reduce outages and increase the organization's capability to achieve its mission. The alternative could be fines, lawsuits, and business disruptions.

A comprehensive security policy is a collection of individual policies covering different aspects of the organization's view of risk. For management, security policies are valuable for managing risk and staying compliant. The policies define clear mandates from many regulators on how risks should be controlled. IT security policies can help management identify risks, assign priorities, and show, over time, how risks are controlled. This is a valuable tool for management. This is an example of how to build value that solves a real problem for management. For example, a company wanting to offer services to the government may have to prove it's compliant with the Federal Information Security Management Act (FISMA). In that case, implementing National Institute of Standards and Technology (NIST) standards clearly demonstrates to regulators how risks are controlled in accordance with FISMA requirements. As policies are perceived as solving real business problems, management and users are more likely to embrace the policies. This is an important step toward building a risk-aware culture. Even if your organization is not under FISMA, it is a comprehensive law and worth reviewing to gain some suggestions.

Many tools are available to ease the effort to become and stay compliant. These tools can inventory systems, check configuration against policies, track regulations and changes, and much more. Combining policy management with the right set of tools creates a powerful ability to help ensure compliance. The most important way to stay compliant is to be aware of your environment, manage to a solid set of policies, and use tools that will be effective in keeping you up to date with changes. If you are able to achieve this, then you show regulators that you not only have good policies, but also use them effectively to manage changing risks.

Chapter 15 Topics

This chapter covers the following topics and concepts:

- What a baseline definition for information systems security is
- How to track, monitor, and report IT security baseline definitions and policy compliance
- What automating IT security policy compliance involves
- What some compliance technologies and solutions are
- What best practices for IT security policy compliance monitoring are
- What some case studies and examples of successful IT security policy compliance monitoring are

Chapter 15 Goals

When you complete this chapter, you will be able to:

- Explain a baseline definition for information systems security
- Define the vulnerability window and information security gap

- Describe the purpose of a gold master copy
- Discuss the importance of tracking, monitoring, and reporting IT security baseline definitions and policy compliance
- Compare and contrast automated and manual systems used to track, monitor, and report security baselines and policy compliance
- Describe the requirements to automate policy distribution
- Describe configuration management and change control management
- Discuss the importance of collaboration and policy compliance across business areas
- Define and contrast Security Content Automation Protocol (SCAP), Simple Network Management Protocol (SNMP), and Web-Based Enterprise Management (WBEM)
- Describe digital signing
- Explain how penetration testing can help ensure compliance
- List best practices for IT security policy compliance monitoring

FYI

A **security baseline** defines a set of basic configurations to achieve specific security objectives. These security objectives are typically represented by security policies and a well-defined security framework. The security baseline reflects how you plan to protect resources that support the business.

Creating a Baseline Definition for Information Systems Security

Taking your policies and building security baselines is a good way to ensure compliance. For example, suppose you have about 200 servers and an Active Directory (AD) server that enforces password rules. Configuring the servers to use AD to authenticate ensures that their passwords meet standard requirements. Additionally, if the password rules within the policy are compliant with NIST standards, then AD might be an effective tool to enforce that aspect of regulatory compliance. So, a baseline is a good starting point for enforcing compliance.

Within IT, a baseline provides a standard focused on a specific technology used within an organization. When applied to security policies, the baseline represents the minimum security settings that must be applied.

For example, imagine that an organization has determined every system needs to be hardened. The security policy defines specifically what to do to harden the systems. For example, the security policy could provide the following information:

- **Protocols**—Only specific protocols listed within the security policy are allowed. Other protocols must be removed.

- **Services**—Only specific services listed in the security policy are allowed. All other services are disabled.
- **Accounts**—The administrator account must be renamed. The actual name of the new administrator may be listed in the security policy, or this information could be treated as a company secret.

The security policy would have much more information, but these few items give you an idea of what is included. The point is that baselines can be complex, referencing multiple policies. A server baseline, for example, may be configured to enforce both passwords and monitoring standards.

Baselines have many uses in IT. Anomaly-based intrusion detection systems (IDSs) use baselines to determine changes in network behavior. Server monitoring tools also use baselines to detect changes in system performance. This chapter focuses on the use of baselines as part of enforcing compliance with security policies and detecting security events.

An anomaly-based IDS, at least in part, operates by detecting changes in the network's behavior. You start by measuring normal activity on the network, which becomes your baseline. The IDS then monitors activity and compares it against the baseline. As long as the comparisons are similar, activity is normal. When the network activity changes so that it is outside a predefined threshold, activity is abnormal. It should be noted that IDSs and intrusion prevention systems (IPSs) use signature matching in addition to anomaly detection.

Abnormal activity doesn't always mean a security event. An alert could be what's referred to as a "false positive." That means the alert was triggered by activity that appears unusual but after closer examination can be explained. Consider an online retailer's spike in activity during the holiday season, for instance, or the introduction of a new application on the network, generating new transactions. Much of this abnormal activity can be anticipated or detected. The IDS can be configured to ignore it.

However, the point of an IDS device is to detect security threats. For example, if a worm infected a network, it would increase network activity. The IDS recognizes the change as an anomaly and sends an alert. The anomaly-based IDS can't work without first creating the baseline. You can also think of an anomaly-based IDS as a behavior-based IDS because it is monitoring the network behavior.

Administrators commonly measure server performance by measuring four core resources: the processor, the memory, the disk, and the network interface. When these are first measured and recorded, it provides a performance baseline. Sometime later, the administrator measures the resources again. As long as the measurements are similar, the server is still performing as expected; however, if there are significant differences that are not explainable, the change indicates a potential problem. For example, a denial of service (DoS) attack on the server may cause the processor and memory resource usage to increase.

A security baseline is also a starting point. For example, a security baseline definition for the Windows operating system

 TIP

Some people argue that one should only use an intrusion prevention system (IPS)—one that actually stops the suspected malicious activity. However, the issue of false positives means this is not always advisable. One has to weigh the impact of failing to stop a real attack (false negative) against accidentally shutting down legitimate traffic (false positive) in order to choose between IDS and IPS. It should be noted that IDS and IPS usually require some effort to get configured properly.

identifies a secure configuration for the operating system in an organization. As long as all Windows systems use the same security baseline, they all start in a known secure state. Later, you can compare the security baseline against the current configuration of any system. If it's different, something has changed. The change indicates the system no longer has the same security settings. If a security policy mandated the original security settings, the comparison shows the system is not compliant.

Policy-Defining Overall IT Infrastructure Security Definition

Many organizations use **imaging** techniques to provide baselines. An image can include the full operating system, applications, and system settings. This includes all the desired security and configuration settings required for the system.

FIGURE 15-1 shows an example of how imaging is accomplished. You start with a clean system, referred to as a *source computer*. You install the operating system and any desired applications on the source computer. Next, you configure specific settings needed by users. Then you configure the security settings to comply with the security policy; for example, you could remove unneeded protocols, disable unused services, and rename the administrator account. You can lock this system down with as much security as you need or desire.

Next, you capture an image of the system. You can think of this as being like taking a snapshot. Imaging captures the entire software contents of the system at that moment. Symantec Ghost is a popular imaging program used to capture images of any operating system. This is particularly easy when using virtual systems. Most virtualization software includes snapshot capability.

Once you've captured the image, you can deploy it to other systems. The original image is often referred to as the *gold master*. Each system that receives the image will have the same operating system and applications. It will also have the same security and configuration settings.

This baseline improves security for systems. It also reduces the total cost of ownership. Imagine that the security policy required changing 50 different security settings. Without

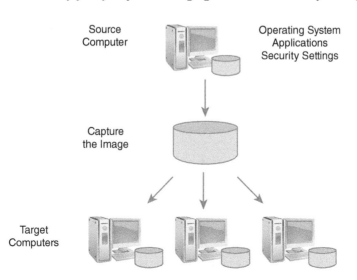

Source Computer

Operating System
Applications
Security Settings

Capture the Image

Target Computers

FIGURE 15-1

Using imaging technologies.

15

IT Policy Compliance and Compliance Technologies

the baseline, these settings would have to be configured separately across potentially hundreds or thousands of servers. The time involved to configure them separately may be substantial. Additionally, there's no guarantee that all the settings would be configured exactly the same on each system when done manually.

If all the systems are configured the same, help desk personnel can troubleshoot them more quickly. This improves availability. Imagine if hundreds (or thousands) of different systems were configured in different ways. Help desk personnel would first need to determine the normal configuration when troubleshooting problems. Once they determined normal operation, they would then determine what's abnormal in order to fix it. Each time they worked on a new system, they'd repeat the process. Worse yet, the same servers configured radically differently mean lack of consistency and lack of compliance with security standards.

However, if all the systems are the same, help desk personnel need to learn only one system. This knowledge transfers to all the other systems. Troubleshooting and downtime are reduced. Availability is increased. Compliance with security policies is consistently enforced.

Vulnerability Window and Information Security Gap Definition

The **vulnerability window** is the gap between when a new vulnerability is discovered and when software developers start writing a patch. Attacks during this time are sometimes referred to as *zero-day vulnerabilities*. This means that there have been zero days that the vendor is aware of the vulnerability. These are a serious concern because there is not yet any patch or remediation available for this vulnerability. You don't know when the vulnerability window opens, because you don't know when an attacker will find the vulnerability. However, most vendors will start writing patches as soon as they learn about the vulnerability.

For example, Microsoft announced on April 26, 2014, a zero-day vulnerability that resided in all versions of Internet Explorer. By May 1, a patch was released.

There are other examples. In 2019, there was a vulnerability found in Windows task scheduler. It affected Windows 10 and Windows server 2019. The Task Scheduler service runs at the maximum level of privilege defined by the local machine, namely NT AUTHORITY\SYSTEM. There was a weakness in the task schedule that allowed attackers to elevate privileges. It was eventually found and given the designation CVE-2019-1069.

Similarly, there's a delay between the time a patch is released and when an organization patches its systems. Even if you start with a baseline, there is no way that it will always be up to date or will meet the needs for all your systems. The difference between the baseline and the actual security needs represents a security gap. For example, you may create an image on June 1. One month later, you may deploy the image to a new system. Most of the configuration and security settings will be the same; however, there may have been some changes or updates that occurred during the past month. These changes present attackers with a vulnerability window and must be plugged.

If your organization uses change management procedures, you can easily identify any changes that should be applied to the system. If you don't have a change management procedure, you will have a significant gap in security policies. Change management is fundamental to network administration, software development, and security.

In addition to change management, patch management is an important security practice. Software vulnerabilities are routinely discovered in operating systems and applications. Vendors release patches or updates to plug the vulnerability holes; however, if the patches aren't applied, the system remains vulnerable. Keeping systems patched helps an organization avoid significant attacks and outages.

Within a Microsoft domain, **Group Policy** deploys many settings. Group Policy allows an administrator to configure a setting once, and it will automatically apply to multiple systems or users. If Group Policy is used to change settings, the changes will automatically apply to the computer when it authenticates on the domain. Additional steps are not required.

Tracking, Monitoring, and Reporting IT Security Baseline Definition and Policy Compliance

A baseline is a good place to start. It ensures that the systems are in compliance with security requirements when they are deployed. However, it's still important to verify that the systems stay in compliance. An obvious question is to ask how the systems may have been changed so they aren't in compliance. Administrators or technicians may change a setting to resolve a problem; for example, an application may not work unless security is relaxed. These changes may weaken security so that the application works. Malicious software (malware) such as a virus may also change a security setting.

It doesn't matter how or why the setting was changed. The important point is that if it was an unauthorized change, you want to know about it. You can verify compliance using one or more of several different methods. These methods simply check the settings on the systems to verify they haven't been changed. Several common methods include:

* Automated systems
* Random audits and departmental compliance
* Overall organizational report card for policy compliance

Automated Systems

Automated systems can regularly query systems to verify compliance. For example, the security policy may dictate that specific protocols be removed or specific services be disabled. For instance, the policy may require password-protected screen savers. An automated system can query the systems to determine if these settings are enabled and match the gold master.

Many automated tools include scheduling abilities. You can schedule the tool to run on a regular basis. Advanced tools can also reconfigure systems that aren't in compliance. All you have to do is review the resulting report to verify systems are in compliance. For example, assume your company has 100 computers. You could schedule the tool to run every Saturday night. It would query each of the systems to determine their configuration and verify compliance. When the scans are complete, the tool would provide a report showing all of the systems that are out of compliance, including the specific issues. If your organization is very large, you could configure the scans to run on different computers every night.

Microsoft provides several automated tools you can use to manage Microsoft products. Although Microsoft isn't the only tool developer to choose from, it does have a large installed base of computers in organizations. It's worthwhile knowing which tools are available. These include:

- **Systems Management Server (SMS)**—This is an older server product but is still used in many organizations. It combines and improves the capabilities of several other products. It can query systems for vulnerabilities using standard methods. It can deploy updates. It adds capabilities to these tasks, such as the ability to schedule the deployment of updates and the ability to push out software applications.
- **System Center Configuration Manager (SCCM)**—SCCM is an upgrade to SMS. It can do everything that SMS can do and provides several enhancements. SCCM can deploy entire operating system images to clients.

In addition to the Microsoft products, there is a wide assortment of other automated tools. These can run on other operating systems and scan both Microsoft and other operating systems such as UNIX and UNIX derivatives. Many scanner types and versions are available. The following are several that are on the market today:

- **Nessus**—Nessus is considered by many to be the best vulnerability scanner. Nessus was being used by more than 75,000 organizations worldwide before it switched from a free product to one you had to purchase in 2008. For several years there was a free personal edition, but no more. However, it is considered by many to be well worth the cost.
- **Nmap**—Nmap is a network scanner that can identify hosts on a network and determine services running on the hosts. It uses a ping scanner to identify active hosts. It uses a port scanner to identify open ports and likely protocols running on these ports. It is also able to determine the operating system.
- **eEye Digital Security Retina**—Retina is a suite of vulnerability management tools. It can assess multiple operating systems such as Microsoft, Linux, and other UNIX distributions. It also includes patch deployment and verification capabilities.
- **Security Administrators Integrated Network Tool (SAINT)**—SAINT provides vulnerability assessments by scanning systems for known vulnerabilities. It can perform penetration testing that attempts to exploit vulnerabilities. SAINT runs on a UNIX/Linux platform, but it can test any system that has an Internet Protocol (IP) address. It also provides reports indicating how to resolve the detected problems.
- **Symantec Altiris**—Altiris includes a full suite of products. It can manage and monitor multiple operating systems. This includes monitoring systems for security issues and deployed patches.
- **OpenVAS**—This is a widely used vulnerability scanner. It will also check for missing patches and updates.

It's also possible to use logon scripts to check for a few key settings. For example, a script can check to see if antimalware software is installed and up to date, or if the system has current patches. The script runs each time a user logs on.

Some organizations quarantine systems that are out of compliance. In other words, if a scan or a script shows the system is not in compliance, a script modifies settings to restrict the computer's access on the network. The user must contact an administrator to return the system to normal.

FYI

Although vulnerability scanners continue to be important tools, they do have their limitations. First, they are only as good as their testing scripts and approach. No scanner can find all vulnerabilities. The way to deal with this is to use multiple vulnerability scanners, rather than rely on a single vendor.

SCAP Compliance Tools

The Security Content Automation Protocol (SCAP) is presented later in this chapter. SCAP is one of the programs of the National Institute of Standards and Technology (NIST). SCAP defines protocols and standards used to create a wide variety of automated scanners and compliance tools.

NIST accredits independent laboratories. These independent laboratories validate SCAP-compliant tools for the following automated capabilities:

- **Authenticated configuration scanner**—The scanner uses a privileged account to authenticate on the target system. It then scans the system to determine compliance with a defined set of configuration requirements.
- **Authenticated vulnerability and patch scanner**—The scanner uses a privileged account to authenticate on the target system. It then scans the system for known vulnerabilities. It can also determine if the system is patched, based on a defined patch policy.
- **Unauthenticated vulnerability scanner**—The scanner doesn't use a system account to scan the system. This is similar to how an attacker may scan the system. It scans the system over the network to determine the presence of known vulnerabilities.
- **Patch remediation**—This tool installs patches on target systems. These tools include a scan or auditing component. The patch scanner determines a patch is missing, and the patch remediation tool applies the missing patch.
- **Misconfiguration remediation**—This tool reconfigures systems to bring them into compliance. It starts by scanning the system to determine if a defined set of configuration settings is accurate. It then reconfigures any settings that are out of compliance.

You can read more about the SCAP validation program on NIST's site here: *http://scap.nist.gov/validation /index.html.*

Random Audits and Departmental Compliance

You can also perform random audits to determine compliance. This is often useful when IT tasks have been delegated to different elements in the organization. For example, a large organization could have a decentralized IT model. A central IT department manages some core services such as network access and email, and individual departments manage their own IT services. The organization still has an overall security policy; however, the individual departments are responsible for implementing them. In this case, the central IT department could randomly audit the departments to ensure compliance. Some larger organizations employ specialized security teams. These teams have a wide variety of responsibilities in the organization such as incident response and boundary protection. They could also regularly scan systems in the network and randomly target specific department resources.

It's important to realize the goal of these scans. It isn't to point fingers at individual departments for noncompliance. Instead, it's to help the organization raise its overall security posture. Of course, when departments realize their systems could be scanned at any time, this provides increased motivation to ensure the systems are in compliance.

Overall Organizational Report Card for Policy Compliance

Many organizations use a report card format to evaluate policy compliance. These report cards can be generated from multiple sources such as a quality assurance program. Organizations can create their own grading criteria; just as in school, a grade of A is excellent whereas a grade of F is failing. The included criteria depend on the organization's requirements. For example, the following elements can be included in the calculation of the grade:

- **Patch compliance**—This compares the number of patches that should be applied versus the number of patches that are applied. A time period should be considered. Patches that close major vulnerabilities might be considered critical and must be applied sooner. For example, the organization could state a goal of having 100 percent of critical patches deployed within seven days of their release. The only exception would be if testing of a patch verified that the patch caused problems.
- **Security settings**—The baseline sets multiple security settings. These should all stay in place. However, if an audit or scan shows that the settings are different, it represents a conflict. Each security setting that is not in compliance is assigned a value. For example, every setting that is different from the baseline could represent a score of 5 percent. If scans detect three differences, the score could be 85 percent (100 percent minus 15 percent).
- **Number of unauthorized changes**—Most organizations have formal change control processes. When these are not followed, or they do not exist, changes frequently cause problems. These problems may be minor problems affecting a single system or major problems affecting multiple systems or the entire network. Every unauthorized change would represent something less than 100 percent; for example, 15 unauthorized changes within a month could represent a score of 85 percent, or a grade of B in this category.

FYI

One approach for deciding whether a patch is critical is to determine its risk score. You can look at the likelihood and impact to the organization if an attack were to happen without the patch having been applied. This approach applies numerical values to likelihood and impact (say from 0 to 9), with the higher number indicating an attack is very likely and, if successful, would have significant impact to the organization. With these values assigned, risk can be scored as Risk = Likelihood × Impact. The higher the risk score, the more critical the patch. This system is referred to as the OWASP Risk Rating Methodology. More information is available at *www.owasp.org*.

Once you identify the rules or standards, you could use a spreadsheet to calculate the grades. An administrator could pull the numbers from the scans and enter them into the spreadsheet monthly. You could use individual grade reports for each department that manages IT resources and combine them into a single grade report for the entire organization.

Automating IT Security Policy Compliance

The one thing that computers are good at is repetition. They can do the same task repeatedly and always give the same result. Conversely, people aren't so good at repetitious tasks. Ask an administrator to change the same setting on 100 different computers and it's very possible that one or more of the computers will not be configured correctly. Additionally, automated tasks take less labor and ultimately cost less money. For example, a task that takes 15 minutes to complete and needs to be done 100 times will take 25 labor hours ($15 \times 100/60$). If an administrator took 2 hours to write and schedule a script, it results in a savings of 23 labor hours. Depending on how much your administrators are paid, the savings can be significant.

Many security tasks can also be accomplished with dedicated tools. For example, the "Automated Systems" section earlier in this chapter lists several different tools with a short description of some of their capabilities. However, if you plan to automate any tasks related to IT security policy compliance, you should address some basic concerns. These include:

- Automated policy distribution
- Configuration and change management

Technical TIP

Open source configuration management software has become widely available and accepted in many organizations. Many of the open source solutions support newer technologies such as integrating with cloud providers. For example, a product named *Chef* offers configuration management for network nodes either on premises or in the cloud.

Automated Policy Distribution

Earlier in this chapter, imaging was described as a method to start all computers with a known baseline. This is certainly an effective way to create baselines. However, after the deployment of the baseline, how do you ensure that systems stay up to date? For example, you could deploy an image to a system on July 1. On July 15, the organization approves a change. You can modify the image for new systems, but how do you implement the change on the system that received the image on July 1, as well as on the other existing systems? Additionally, if you didn't start with an image as a baseline, how do you apply these security settings to all the systems on the network?

The automated methods you use are dependent on the operating systems in the organization. If the organization uses Microsoft products, you have several technologies you can use. Some, such as SMS and SCCM, were mentioned previously. Another tool is Group Policy.

Group Policy is available in Microsoft domains. It can increase security for certain users or departments in your organization. You could first apply a baseline to all the systems with an image. You would then use Group Policy to close any security gaps or increase security settings for some users or computers. This method can also ensure regulatory and standards compliance such as with those controls required to protect credit cards under the Payment Card Industry Data Security Standard (PCI DSS).

Consider FIGURE 15-2 as an example. The organization name is ABC Corp and the domain name is ABCCorp.int. The Secure Password Policy is linked to the domain level to require secure passwords for all users in the domain. The organization could define a password policy requiring all users to have strong passwords of at least six characters. If the

FIGURE 15-2

Using Group Policy in a Microsoft domain.

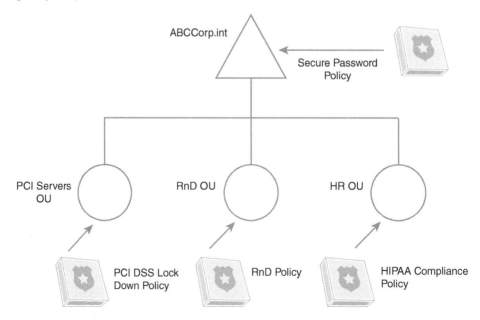

organization later decides it wants to change this to a more secure eight-character policy, an administrator could change the Secure Password Policy once and then it would apply to all users in the domain. It doesn't matter if there are 50 or 50,000 users—a single change applies to all equally.

All the PCI DSS server objects are placed in the PCI Servers organizational unit (OU). A policy named PCI DSS Lock Down Policy is linked to this OU. It configures specific settings to ensure these servers are in compliance with PCI DSS requirements.

Human resources (HR) personnel handle health data covered by the Health Insurance Portability and Accountability Act (HIPAA). These users and computers can be placed in the HR OU. The HIPAA Compliance Policy includes Group Policy settings to enforce HIPAA requirements. For example, it could include a script that includes a logon screen reminding users of HIPAA compliance requirements and penalties.

The figure also shows a research and development OU, named RnD OU, for that area. Users and computers in the research and development department would be placed in the RnD OU. The RnD policy could include extra security settings to protect data created by the RnD department.

Group Policy not only configures the changes when systems power on, but also provides automatic auditing and updating. Systems query the domain every 90 to 120 minutes by default. Any Group Policy changes are applied to affected systems within two hours. Additionally, systems will retrieve and apply security settings from Group Policy every 16 hours even if there are no changes.

> **TIP**
>
> Figure15-2 represents a simplistic view of Group Policy in a Microsoft domain. It doesn't show the Default Domain or the Default Domain Controllers policies that are both created by default and add basic security to a domain. Additionally, an organization will likely have more than just three organizational units (OUs).

Training Administrators and Users

These tools and technologies aren't always easy to understand. They include a rich set of capabilities that require a deep understanding before they can be used effectively. It takes time and money to train administrators and users how to get the most out of these tools.

Training should be considered when evaluating tools. Determine if training is available and its cost. Almost all the companies that sell these tools also sell training. You can send administrators to train at a vendor location. If you have enough employees who require training, you can conduct it on-site.

The important point to remember is that even the most "valuable" tool is of no value if it's not used.

Organizational Acceptance

Organizational acceptance is also an important consideration. Resistance to change can be a powerful block in many organizations. If the method you're using represents a significant change, it may be difficult for some personnel to accept. As an example, using a baseline of security settings can cause problems. Applications that worked previously may no longer work. Websites that were accessible may no longer be. There are usually work-around steps that will resolve the problem, but it will take additional time and effort.

> **NOTE**
>
> Automated solutions providing configuration management must be well protected. By their nature, these solutions require administrator authority across any device they manage. Consequently, any hacker who gets into a configuration management system might then gain administrator access to your production environment.

15

To illustrate, assume that a baseline is being tested for deployment. Administrators in one department determine that the baseline settings prevent an application from working. There are three methods for resolving the problem. First, the administrators could weaken security by not using the baseline settings; however, weakening security is not a good option. Second, the department may decide it can no longer use the application. If the application is critical to its mission, this may not be a good option. Third, a work-around method can be identified that doesn't bypass the original baseline settings, but also allows the application to work. The third option will require digging in to resolve the problem. If the administrators are already overburdened, or don't have the knowledge or ability to resolve the problem, they may push back. This requires a climate of collaboration to address the problem.

Vulnerability scanning is a common tool and part of normal security operations. Ideally, it quickly and routinely identifies vulnerabilities to be fixed. Penetration testing takes that capability to the next level. A **penetration test** is designed to actually exploit weaknesses in the system architecture or computing environment. Typically, a penetration test involves a team pretending to be hackers, using vulnerability scanners, social engineering, and other techniques to try to hack the network or system.

Testing for Effectiveness

Not all automated tools work the same. Before investing too much time and energy into any single tool, it's worthwhile testing them to determine their effectiveness. Some of the common things to look for in a tool include:

- **Accurate identification**—Can the tool accurately identify systems? Does it know the difference between a Microsoft server running Internet Information Services (IIS) and a Linux system running Apache, for example?
- **Assessment capabilities**—Does it scan for common known vulnerabilities? For example, can it detect weak or blank passwords for accounts?
- **Discovery**—Can the system accurately discover systems on the network? Can it discover both wired and wireless systems?
- **False positives**—Does it report problems that aren't there? For example, does it report that a patch has not been applied when it has?
- **False negatives**—Does it miss problems that exist? In other words, if a system is missing a patch, can the tool detect it?
- **Resolution capabilities**—Can the tool resolve the problem, or at least identify how it can be resolved? Some tools can automatically correct the vulnerability. Other tools provide directions or links to point you in the right direction.
- **Performance**—The speed of the scans is important, especially in large organizations. How long does the scan of a single system take? How long will it take to scan your entire network?

Audit Trails

If a tool makes any changes on the network, it's important that these changes are recorded. Changes are recorded in change management logs that create an audit trail. The tool making the change can record changes it makes on any systems; however, it's common for logs to be maintained for individual systems being changed, separate from the change management log.

Logs can be maintained on the system or off-system. The value in having off-system logs is that if the system is attacked or fails, the logs are still available. Additionally, some legal and regulatory requirements dictate that logs be maintained off-system.

Audit trails are especially useful for identifying unauthorized changes. Auditing logs the details of different events. This includes who, what, where, when, and how. If a user made a change, for example, the audit log would record who the user was, what the user changed, when the change occurred, and how it was done.

Imagine a security baseline is deployed in the organization. You discover that one system is regularly being reconfigured. The security tool fixes it, but the next scan shows it's been changed again. You may want to know who is making this change. If auditing is enabled, it will record the details. You only need to view the audit trail to determine what is going on.

 TIP

Some auditing is enabled by default on systems. However, you may need to enable additional auditing to determine details on specific events.

Configuration Management and Change Control Management

The Information Technology Infrastructure Library (ITIL) includes five books that represent the ITIL life cycle, as shown in **FIGURE 15-3**. A central part of ITIL is Service Transition. This relates to the transition of services into production. It includes configuration management and change management.

ITIL isn't an all-or-nothing approach. Organizations often adopt portions of ITIL practices without adopting others. Configuration management and change management are two elements within the Service Transition stage that many organizations do adopt.

Configuration management (CM) establishes and maintains configuration information on systems throughout their life cycle. This includes the initial configuration established in

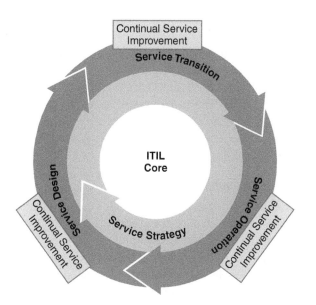

FIGURE 15-3

The ITIL life cycle.

the baseline. It also includes recording changes. The initial public draft of NIST SP 800-128 defines CM as a collection of activities. These activities focus on establishing the integrity of the systems by controlling the processes that affect their configurations. It starts with the baseline configuration. CM then controls the process of changing and monitoring configuration throughout the system's lifetime.

Change management is a formal process that controls changes to systems. One of the common problems with changes in many organizations is that they cause outages. When an unauthorized change is completed on one system, it can negatively affect another system. These changes aren't done to cause problems. Instead, well-meaning technicians make a change to solve a smaller problem and unintentionally create bigger problems. Successful change management ensures changes have minimal impact on operations. In other words, change management ensures that a change to one system does not take down another system.

Change management is also important to use with basic security activities such as patching systems. Consider for a moment what the worst possible result of a patch might be. Although patches are intended to solve problems, they occasionally cause problems. The worst-case scenario is when a patch breaks a system. After the patch is applied, the system no longer boots into the operating system.

If a patch broke your home computer, it would be inconvenient; however, if a patch broke 500 systems in an organization, it could be catastrophic. Patches need to be tested and approved before they are applied. Many organizations use a change management process before patching systems.

NOTE

It's important that change management be tied to an external process such as emergency fixes, often referred to as firecall systems. A firecall system allows for quick access to fix an issue. For example, if a website is down, an emergency ticket may be opened in a firecall system to grant access to the server hosting the website.

NOTE

NIST SP 800-128, "Guide for Security Configuration Management of Information Systems," covers configuration management in much more depth.

Configuration Management Database

A configuration management database (CMDB) holds the configuration information for systems throughout a system's life cycle. The goal is to identify the accurate configuration of any system at any moment.

The CMDB holds all the configuration settings, not just the security settings. However, this still applies to security. The security triad includes confidentiality, integrity, and availability. Many of the configuration settings ensure the system operates correctly. A wrongly configured system may fail, resulting in loss of availability.

Tracking, Monitoring, and Reporting Configuration Changes

Many organizations use a formal process for change requests. It's not just a technician asking a supervisor if he or she can make a change. For example, a web application could be used to submit changes. Administrators or technicians submit the request via an internal webpage. The webpage would collect all the details of the change and record them in the change control work order database. Details may include the system, the actual change, justification, and the submitter.

Key players in the organization review the change requests and provide input using the same intranet web application. These key players may include senior IT experts, security experts, management personnel, and disaster recovery experts. Each will examine the change as it relates to his or her area of expertise and determine if it will result in a negative impact. If all the experts agree to the change, it's approved.

> **NOTE**
>
> Change management reviews must also consider regulatory and compliance matters. Implementing a change could result in compliance violations. For example, suppose an organization makes a change on how the network is segmented. If this change resulted in credit card systems no longer being segmented, then the change might result in a **PCI DSS** violation.

Collaboration and Policy Compliance Across Business Areas

It's always important for different elements of a business to get along. One element of the business should not make changes without any thought to how it may affect other areas. Collaboration is also important within IT and security policy compliance.

Some security policies must apply to all business areas equally. However, other policies can be targeted to specific departments. If you look back to Figure 15-2, this shows an excellent example of how different requirements are addressed within a Microsoft domain. Group Policy applies some settings to all business areas equally. Additionally, it can configure different settings for different departments or business areas if needed.

In Figure 15-2, different policies were required for PCI DSS servers, HR personnel, and research and development personnel. Each of these business areas has its own settings that don't interfere with the other units.

No matter how hard you try to communicate through the approval process, inevitably some miscommunication will occur. Someone will be caught off guard by a change, or two changes will conflict. You might find multiple changes need to be backed out, but the resources are not available as expected to perform the recovery. Or the miscommunication will occur because the full scope of the change was not fully understood.

There's no magic formula to solving all these problems. A good rule of thumb is to overcommunicate and build change into a predictable schedule and set of resources. For example, maybe routine (noncritical) patches are always applied the first Saturday of every month. Create a SharePoint site to house the descriptions of the changes. Commit to having descriptions of the changes available the week prior. Send reminder emails to both approvers and stakeholders. In short, be transparent and make a best effort to communicate accurately and often. This provides every opportunity for stakeholders to be engaged and offer comment.

Version Control for Policy Implementation Guidelines and Compliance

Another consideration related to automating IT security policy compliance is version control. First, it's important to use version control for the security policy itself. In other words, if the security policy is changed, the document should record the change. A reader should be able to determine if changes have occurred since the policy was originally released, with an idea of what those changes were.

Version control requirements for a document can be as simple as including a version control page. The page identifies all the changes made to the original in a table format. It would often include the date and other details of the change. It may also include who made the change.

It's also important to record the actual changes to systems. However, these changes are also recorded in the change control work order database and the CMDB discussed in the previous section.

Compliance Technologies and Solutions

Organizations use both emerging and existing technologies to ensure compliance. One particular challenge is how to update and track regulatory changes and new rules, including how to use them to coordinate policy management and compliance training.

This section presents some of the notable technologies. They are:

- Committee of Sponsoring Organizations (COSO) Internal Control—Integrated Framework
- Security Content Automation Protocol (SCAP)
- Simple Network Management Protocol (SNMP)
- Web-Based Enterprise Management (WBEM)
- Digital signatures

COSO Internal Control—Integrated Framework

The COSO Internal Control—Integrated Framework was developed by the Committee of Sponsoring Organizations of the Treadway Commission. That led to the term *COSO*. The organization was formed in 1992 with the main idea of creating a framework of controls to ensure a company's financial reports were accurate and free from fraud. The COSO framework has evolved over the years with the latest version published in May 2013. Since 1992, both technology in general and the Internet in particular have evolved. Not surprisingly, technology and information security have become major parts of the COSO controls framework.

In fact, COSO, like Control Objectives for Information and related Technology (COBIT), is often used by auditors, compliance professionals, and risk professionals. COSO is widely used and recognized as a major U.S. standard that has been adopted worldwide. Because COSO controls apply both to business functions (such as financial accounting) and to technology (such as information security), they make a powerful framework. The framework can describe how controls should be built, in both business and technology terms. This has enormous benefits for the security team. The security team can build controls in a way that the business side is more likely to understand. That makes it a little easier to talk the language of the business side. That, in turn, leads to greater business support for adopting the security controls.

The COSO control framework works well with other frameworks, such as COBIT. In fact, COBIT 5 leverages both COSO and International Organization of Standardization (ISO) principles and extends the work into many information security areas not handled by COSO. So rather than competing, these frameworks actually complement each other.

COSO outlines how controls should be built and managed in order to ensure compliance with many major regulations today. For example, the governance body for the Sarbanes-Oxley (SOX) Act of 2002 recommends the COSO internal framework as a means of compliance with SOX. In other words, if you implement the COSO control framework, you will be compliant with SOX regulations.

FYI

The MITRE Corporation is a private company that performs a lot of work for U.S. government agencies. For example, MITRE maintains the Common Vulnerabilities and Exposures (CVE) for the National Cyber Security Division of the U.S. Department of Homeland Security. Many of the original employees came from the Massachusetts Institute of Technology (MIT), and they work on research and engineering (RE). However, MITRE is not an acronym. Additionally, MITRE is not part of MIT.

Consequently, COSO is a powerful framework to ensure that risks are well managed and the right controls are built to keep systems compliant with many laws and regulations.

> **NOTE**
>
> More information on the COSO internal controls framework can be found at *www.coso.org.*

SCAP

The **Security Content Automation Protocol (SCAP)**, pronounced "S-cap," is a technology used to measure systems and networks. It's actually a suite of six specifications. Together these specifications standardize how security software products identify and report security issues. SCAP is a trademark of NIST.

NIST created SCAP as part of its responsibilities under the Federal Information Security Management ACT (FISMA). The goal is to establish standards, guidelines, and minimum requirements for tools used to scan systems. Although SCAP is designed for the creation of tools to be used by the U.S. government, private entities can use the same tools.

The six specifications are:

- **eXtensible Configuration Checklist Description Format (XCCDF)**—This is a language used for writing security checklists and benchmarks. It can also report results of any checklist evaluations.
- **Open Vulnerability and Assessment Language (OVAL)**—This is a language used to represent system configuration information. It can assess the state of systems and report the assessment results.
- **Common Platform Enumeration (CPE)**—This provides specific names for hardware, operating systems, and applications. CPE provides a standard system-naming convention for consistent use among different products.
- **Common Configuration Enumeration (CCE)**—This provides specific names for security software configurations. CCE is a dictionary of names for these settings. It provides a standard naming convention used by different SCAP products.
- **Common Vulnerabilities and Exposures (CVE)**—This provides specific names for security-related software flaws. CVE is a dictionary of publicly known software flaws. The MITRE Corporation manages the CVE.

- **Common Vulnerability Score Systems (CVSS)**—This provides an open specification to measure the relative severity of software flaw vulnerabilities. It provides formulas using standard measurements. The resulting score is from zero to 10, with 10 being the most severe. There is a formula that includes several separate criteria that all influence the final score.

SCAP isn't a tool itself. Instead, it's the protocol used to build the tools. Compare this to Hypertext Transfer Protocol (HTTP), the protocol that transmits traffic over the Internet so that applications can display data in user applications. Web browsers can display pages written in Hypertext Markup Language (HTML) and Extensible Markup Language (XML). However, HTTP can't display the traffic itself. Instead, web browsers such as Edge, Firefox, or Chrome are the tools that use HTTP to transmit and receive HTTP traffic and display the HTML-formatted pages. Similarly, SCAP-compliant tools use the underlying specifications of SCAP to scan systems and report the results. There are a wide variety of tool purposes. These include the ability to audit and assess systems for compliance with specific requirements. They can scan systems for vulnerabilities. They also can detect systems that don't have proper patches or are misconfigured.

Some of the tools currently available are:

- BigFix Security Configuration and Vulnerability Management Suite (SCVM)
- Retina by eEye Digital Security
- HP SCAP Scanner
- SAINT vulnerability scanner
- Symantec Control Compliance Suite—Federal Toolkit
- Tripwire Enterprise

■ NOTE

NIST has established a formal validation program for NIST products. You can view a full list of SCAP validated products at http://nvd.nist.gov/scapproducts.cfm.

If you want to read more about SCAP, read NIST SP 800-126. This is the technical specification for SCAP version 1.3. At this writing, NIST SP 800-126 rev 3 is in draft. It is the technical specification for SCAP version 1.1. You can access NIST SP 800-126 and other NIST 800-series special publications at *http://csrc.nist.gov/publications /PubsSPs.html*.

SNMP

The **Simple Network Management Protocol (SNMP)** is used to manage and query network devices. SNMP commonly manages routers, switches, and other intelligent devices on the network with IP addresses. SNMP is a part of the TCP/IP suite of protocols, so it's a bit of a stretch to call it an emerging technology. However, SNMP has improved over the years. The first version of SNMP was SNMP v1. It had a significant vulnerability: Devices used community strings for authentication. The default community string was "Public," and SNMP sent it over the network in clear text. Attackers using a sniffer such as Wireshark could capture the community string even if it was changed from the default. They could then use it to reconfigure devices.

SNMP was improved with versions 2 and 3. Version 3 provides three primary improvements:

- **Confidentiality**—Packets are encrypted. Attackers can still capture the packets with a sniffer; however, they are in a ciphered form, which prevents attackers from reading them.
- **Integrity**—A message authentication code (MAC) (not to be confused with Media Access Control) is used to ensure that data has not been modified. The MAC uses an abbreviated hash. The hash is calculated at the source and included in the packet. The hash is recalculated at the destination. As long as the data has not changed, the hash will always provide the same result. If the hash is the same, the message has not lost integrity.
- **Authentication**—This provides verification that the SNMP messages are from a known source. It prevents attackers from reconfiguring the devices without being able to prove who they are.

WBEM

Web-Based Enterprise Management (WBEM) is a set of management and Internet standard technologies. It standardizes the language used to exchange data among different platforms for management of systems and applications. Just as SCAP provides the standards used to create tools, WBEM also provides standards used in different management tools. The tools can be graphical user interface (GUI)–based tools; some tools are command line tools that don't use a GUI.

WBEM is based on different standards from the Internet and from the Distributed Management Task Force (DMTF), Inc. DMTF is a not-for-profit association. Members promote enterprise and systems management and interoperability. These standards include:

> **NOTE**
>
> WBEM uses HTTP, which is commonly used on the Internet. However, WBEM also can operate on internal networks using HTTP.

- **CIM-XML**—The Common Information Model (CIM) over XML protocol. This protocol allows XML-formatted data to be transmitted over HTTP. CIM defines IT resources as related objects in a rich object-oriented model. Just about any hardware or software element can be referenced with the CIM. Applications use the CIM to query and configure systems.
- **WS-Management**—The Web Services for Management protocol. This protocol provides a common way for systems to exchange information. Web services are commonly used for a wide assortment of purposes on the Internet. For example, web services are used to retrieve weather data or shipping data on the Internet. Clients send web service queries and receive web service responses. The WS-Management protocol specifies how these queries and responses retrieve data from devices. It can also be used to send commands to devices.
- **CIM Query Language (CQL)**—This language is based on the Structured Query Language (SQL) used for databases, and the W3C XML Query language. The CQL defines the specific syntax rules used to query systems with CIM-XML and WS-Management.

Digital Signing

A digital signature is a value that identifies a file's origin. Usually the data in the file is first hashed using a cryptographic hash, then signed (i.e., encrypted with the sender's private key).

Digital signing technologies provide added security for files. A file signed with a digital signature provides authentication and integrity assurances. It also provides nonrepudiation; in other words, it provides assurances that a specific sender sent the file. It also provides assurances that the file has not been modified.

A public key infrastructure (PKI) is needed to support digital signatures. A PKI includes certificate authorities (CAs) that issue certificates. The certificate includes a public key matched to a private key. Anything encrypted with the private key can be decrypted with the public key. Additionally, anything encrypted with the public key can be decrypted with the private key.

Digital signatures provide added security for many different types of policy compliance files. For example, consider patches and other update files. You would download these files and use them to patch vulnerabilities. If an attacker somehow modified the patch, instead of plugging a vulnerability, you would be installing malware. Similarly, many definition updates for security tools are digitally signed.

If a file is digitally signed, you know it has not been modified. The following steps show one way that a digital signature is used for a company named Acme Security. The company first obtains a certificate from a CA with the following steps:

1. Acme Security creates a public and private key pair.
2. Acme Security includes the public key that is part of its certificate request to the CA with the company's request. It keeps the private key private and protected.
3. The CA verifies Acme Security is a valid company and is who it says it is. The CA then creates a digital certificate for Acme Security. The certificate includes the public key provided by Acme Security.

   At this point, the company is able to digitally sign files. Consider Figure 15-4 as you follow the steps for creating and using a digital signature.
4. Acme Security creates the file.
5. Acme Security hashes the file. The hash is a number normally expressed in hexadecimal. There are many hashing algorithms, but SHA-2 is one of the most widely used.
6. Acme Security encrypts the hash with its private key. The result is a string that appears to be random gibberish. Remember, something encrypted with a private key can only be decrypted with the matching public key. Said another way, if you can decrypt data with a public key, you know it was encrypted with the matching private key.
7. Acme Security packages the file and the digital signature together and sends them to the receiving client. The digital certificate could be sent at the same time or separately.
8. The receiving client uses the certificate to verify that Acme Security sent the file. Additionally, the client checks with the CA to verify the certificate is valid and hasn't been revoked.
9. The client decrypts the signature with the public key from the certificate. That gives them the hash. They then generate their own hash of the file and compare it to the hash they received. Both should match perfectly.

 NOTE

No matter how many times you calculate a hash, it will always be the same as long as the source is the same. This is similar to counting the number of apples in a bowl. As long as the number of apples stays the same, you'll always come up with the same number. If someone takes an apple away or adds an apple, the resulting number will change.

Digital signatures aren't a new technology; however, their use with security tools and downloads has significantly increased over the years. A digital signature provides you with an additional tool to verify authentication and integrity for downloaded files. It is likely that drivers you use for devices like printers are digitally signed.

Best Practices for IT Security Policy Compliance Monitoring

When implementing a plan for IT security policy compliance monitoring, you can use several different best practices. The following list shows some of these:

- **Start with a security policy**—The security policy acts as the road map. This is a written document, not just some ideas in someone's head. Without the written document, the actual security policy becomes a moving target, and monitoring for compliance is challenging if not impossible.
- **Create a baseline based on the security policy**—Use images whenever possible to deploy new operating systems. These images will ensure that systems start in a secure state. They also accelerate deployments, save money, and increase availability.
- **Track and update regulatory and compliance rule changes**—Formally track regulatory and rule changes as a routine. Map changes to these rules to policies and configurations controls. Then update security policies and technology as needed.
- **Audit systems regularly**—After the baseline is deployed, regularly check the systems. Ensure that the security settings that have been configured stay configured. Well-meaning administrators can change settings. Malware can also modify settings. However, auditing will catch the modifications.
- **Automate checks as much as possible**—Use tools and scripts to check systems. Some tools are free. Other tools cost money, but all are better than doing everything manually. They reduce the amount of time necessary and increase the accuracy.
- **Manage changes**—Ensure that a change management process is used. This allows experts to review the changes before they are implemented and reduces the possibility that the change will cause problems. It also provides built-in documentation for changes.

Case Studies and Examples of Successful IT Security Policy Compliance Monitoring

The following sections show different case studies and examples related to IT security policies and compliance monitoring. Private sector and public sector case studies and examples are included.

Private Sector Case Study 1

In this example, a large sales organization with a dedicated IT staff suffered a major outage due to a minor change to a printer. The lack of compliance with change management policies was a contributing cause for the outage.

The organization had a subnet hosting multiple servers and a printer. Routers connected this subnet to other subnets on the network. All systems were working until a new server was added to the network with the same IP address as the printer. This IP address conflict prevented the printer from printing and prevented the new server from communicating on the network. This problem is like having two identical street addresses in the same Zip code. At best, each address will get some mail, but not all of it. Similarly, on a network, each IP address will receive some traffic, but not all traffic that is expected. At best, you will see inconsistent performance.

The problem with the new server wasn't discovered right away. However, a technician began troubleshooting a problem with the printer on the same subnet. While troubleshooting, the technician suspected a problem with the IP address. The technician changed the IP address for the printer to 10.1.1.1, as shown in **FIGURE 15-4**. This change didn't solve the problem, but the technician forgot to change the IP address back to normal. As you can see in the figure, the change caused a conflict between the printer and the default gateway. The printer and the near side of the router both had the same IP address, and neither was working.

The default gateway is the path for all server communications out of the subnet. Because there was a conflict with the default gateway, none of the servers on the subnet was able to get traffic out of the subnet. They were all operating, but clients outside of the subnet couldn't use them. With several servers no longer working, the problem was quickly escalated. Senior administrators were called in and discovered the problems. They corrected the IP address on the printer and provided some on-the-job training to the original technician.

Notice how this problem started with a small error. The new server was added using an IP address that was already used by the printer. After the printer IP address change, all the servers on the subnet lost network access. Change management and configuration management processes would have ensured this new server was added using a configuration that didn't interfere with other systems. Additionally, change management would have prevented the change to the printer's IP address.

FIGURE 15-4

Misconfigured printer results in outage for multiple servers.

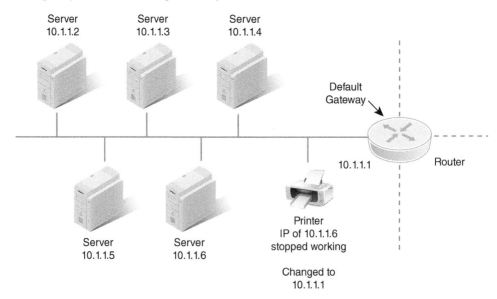

As it turns out, this was the turning point for this company. It was one of a long string of problems caused by unauthorized changes. Management finally decided to implement a formal change management process and hired an outside consultant to help them.

Private Sector Case Study 2

In 2018, there was a breach of the Marriott hotel chain. Personal and financial information of 500 million guests over a four-year period was exposed. The breach involved unauthorized access to a database on or around September 10, 2018.

The hotel chain revealed that for many of those records, the data could include birth date and passport number. In some cases, the data also included payment card numbers and payment card expiration dates, but the payment card numbers were encrypted using Advanced Encryption Standard encryption (AES-128). Thus, it is unlikely the attackers could decrypt that data.

Thus, this case study has mixed results. The breach itself was egregious. However, the fact that credit card information was encrypted, as per PCI DSS, may ameliorate the impact of the breach. Conversely, many security analysts opine that the breach should have been detected sooner.

Nonprofit Sector Case Study

This is an older case study, but still relevant today. In June 2013, it was reported that Stanford University's Lucile Packard Children's Hospital had had a data breach. An employee reported on May 8, 2013, that an unencrypted laptop containing medical information on pediatric patients had been stolen. The laptop contained personal information on 13,000 patients, including their names, ages, medical record numbers, and surgical procedures, as well as the names of physicians involved in the procedures, and telephone numbers. The computer involved was no longer in use; it was, in fact, nonfunctioning. But it had not been properly disposed of when it was taken out of service.

This was the fifth major data breach for the hospital within a space of four years. In January 2013, to give another example, the hospital reported that a laptop containing medical information for 57,000 patients had been stolen from a physician's car.

These events show a lack of compliance with HIPAA regulations. Encrypting laptops with sensitive information is a de facto standard in the healthcare industry. It's also a requirement for many regulations, including those of HIPAA.

So how could this happen when the regulations and industry best practices are clear? That there were five major breaches within such a brief period suggests a systemic failure of the university to define its security policies, train its staff, and then hold them accountable with strict enforcement.

The Stanford episodes highlight three areas worth thinking about:

- Policy enforcement
- Awareness training
- Equipment disposal

With HIPAA standards and industry best practices so clear, you might assume that policy enforcement was lacking. There should have been a complete inventory of laptops and a crosscheck to ensure they were all encrypted.

Enforcement needs to be aggressive. Some organizations are very strict about enforcing these policies. For example, all laptops are required to be encrypted before they are issued. Scans are performed regularly to ensure laptops remain encrypted. When a device is found to be unencrypted (as in the case of an older or "legacy" device), the user is given a short window—a matter of days—to have it encrypted. A user who fails to comply loses access, and leadership is notified to take management action. Having a consequence for failing to follow security policy is an important enforcement tool.

University officials cited new and improved "HIPAA training" being put in place. This again might suggest that policies were in place but were not followed. Congress enacted HIPAA in 1996. The law's requirements are well defined and known. The need to put new HIPAA training in place suggests a lack of employee awareness. If this is one of the causes, it illustrates that having a good policy is not enough. Compliance with the policy depends on a skilled workforce that embraces its implementation as part of day-to-day duties.

Equipment disposal seems the most puzzling part of the story. Why a broken device was still in the possession of the end user is confusing. As soon as a device is disabled, it should be immediately turned over to IT personnel and the information contained within properly disposed of. In this case, the delay in turning over the old device seems inappropriate. The employee had been issued a new device and the old laptop was considered "nonfunctional."

Many organizations in such a case would insist on receiving the damaged device before issuing a new one. This is a good policy.

It is also interesting that university officials emphasized that the "nonfunctioning" laptop had "a seriously damaged screen." The screen has nothing to do with the data contained within the laptop. Offering screen damage as a reason to be less concerned about the theft of the device raises questions about officials' understanding of the threat. The hard drive is what matters. A laptop screen can be replaced or, even more easily, bypassed with an external monitor. Or the hard drive can be quickly moved to another machine.

> **NOTE**
>
> Always remember, breaches are about the data. Regardless of the damage to a physical device, as long as the hard drive is intact, the data on a stolen machine is at risk. That's why encrypting the hard drive of a portable device is considered an industry best practice in many cases.

CHAPTER SUMMARY

This chapter covered some of the technologies used to ensure IT policy compliance. Imaging technologies can deploy identical baseline images for new systems. The chapter discussed the importance of a gold master image. However, the baseline is up to date only for a short period of time. As patches are released or other changes are approved, the baseline becomes out of date. The difference between the baseline and the required changes represents a vulnerability or a security gap. This gap must be closed to ensure systems stay secure.

Many automated tools are available to IT administrators today. These tools can examine systems to ensure the baseline security settings have not changed. They can also scan systems for vulnerabilities such as ensuring the computers have current patches. Many tools include the ability to scan for issues and deploy changes to correct the issues. NIST published standards for SCAP in SP 800-126. These standards have resulted in a wealth of available tools to increase security for networks today. You also learned about how penetration testing is an important test of the effectiveness of controls. Finally, the case studies in this chapter illustrated how the lack of compliance can lead to significant impact to an organization.

KEY CONCEPTS AND TERMS

Configuration management (CM)
Gold master
Group Policy
Imaging
Penetration test

Security baseline
Security Content Automation
    Protocol (SCAP)
Simple Network Management
    Protocol (SNMP)

Vulnerability window
Web-Based Enterprise
    Management (WBEM)

CHAPTER 15 ASSESSMENT

1. A(n) _____ is a starting point or standard. Within IT, it provides a standard focused on a specific technology used within an organization.

2. An operating system and different applications are installed on a system. The system is then locked down with various settings. You want the same operating system, applications, and settings deployed to 50 other computers. What's the easiest way?

   A. Scripting
   B. Imaging
   C. Doing it manually
   D. Spreading the work among different departments

3. After a set of security settings has been applied to a system, there is no need to recheck these settings on the system.

   A. True
   B. False

4. The time between when a new vulnerability is discovered and when software developers start writing a patch is known as a(n) _____.

5. Your organization wants to automate the distribution of security policy settings. What should be considered?

   A. Training of administrators
   B. Organizational acceptance
   C. Testing for effectiveness
   D. All of the above

6. Several tools are available to automate the deployment of security policy settings. Some tools can deploy baseline settings. Other tools can deploy changes in security policy settings.

   A. True
   B. False

7. An organization uses a decentralized IT model with a central IT department for core services and security. The organization wants to ensure that each department is complying with primary security requirements. What can be used to verify compliance?

   A. Group Policy
   B. Centralized change management policies
   C. Centralized configuration management policies
   D. Random audits

8. Change requests are tracked in a control work order database. Approved changes are also recorded in a CMDB.

   A. True
   B. False

9. An organization wants to maintain a database of system settings. The database should include the original system settings and any changes. What should be implemented within the organization?

   A. Change management
   B. Configuration management
   C. Full ITIL life cycle support
   D. Security Content Automation Protocol

10. An organization wants to reduce the possibility of outages when changes are implemented on the network. What should the organization use?

    A. Change management
    B. Configuration management
    C. Configuration management database
    D. Simple Network Management Protocol

11. A security baseline image of a secure configuration that is then replicated during the deployment process is sometimes called a _____.

    A. Master copy
    B. Zero-day image
    C. Gold master
    D. Platinum image

12. Microsoft created the Web-Based Enterprise Management (WBEM) technologies for Microsoft products.

    A. True
    B. False

13. A common method of scoring risk is reflected in the following formula:
    $$Risk = \underline{\hspace{2cm}} \times \underline{\hspace{2cm}}.$$

14. What is a valid approach for validating compliance to security baseline?

    A. Vulnerability scanner
    B. Penetration test
    C. A and B

15. It is important to protect your gold master because an infected copy could quickly result in widespread infection with malware.

    A. True
    B. False

16. A(n) _____ can be used with a downloaded file. It offers verification that the file was provided by a specific entity. It also verifies the file has not been modified.

17. If an organization implements the COSO internal control framework, then it cannot implement another control framework like COBIT.

    A. True
    B. False

Answer Key

CHAPTER 1   Information Systems Security Policy Management

1. C   2. Standards   3. A   4. D and E   5. Procedure   6. D   7. C
8. Human   9. E   10. B   11. E

CHAPTER 2   Business Drivers for Information Security Policies

1. C   2. A   3. A   4. Preventive   5. C   6. B   7. D   8. A   9. D   10. D
11. A   12. B   13. B   14 . D   15. D

CHAPTER 3   Compliance Laws and Information Security Policy Requirements

1. B   2. E   3. E   4. D   5. Cyberterrorism or cyberwarfare   6. B
7. CIPA   8. B   9. B   10. B   11. D   12. D

CHAPTER 4   Business Challenges Within the Seven Domains of IT Responsibility

1. B   2. A   3. C   4. C   5. LAN-to-WAN domain   6. A   7. Segmented
network   8. A   9. B   10. B   11. D   12. B   13. C   14. B   15. C
16. Concentrators   17. C   18. IDs and passwords

CHAPTER 5   Information Security Policy Implementation Issues

1. E   2. B   3. Be in the background; precisely what is asked of them
4. The cost of business   5. B   6. A   7. C   8. A   9. A   10. B
11. Security policy   12. A   13. D   14. A   15. C   16. C

CHAPTER 6   IT Security Policy Frameworks

1. F   2. A   3. A, B, and C   4. A   5. Policies   6. B   7. C   8. Dormant
accounts   9. Confidentiality, integrity, availability, authorization, and
nonrepudiation   10. B   11. G   12. B   13. B

CHAPTER 7   How to Design, Organize, Implement, and Maintain IT Security Policies

1. A   2. D   3. A   4. D   5. C   6. B   7. B   8. C   9. Answers may include
devices and processes used to control physical access; examples include
fences, security guards, locked doors, motion detectors, and alarms
10. Lessons learned   11. Policy   12. Defense in depth   13. A   14. B
15. A and D

| CHAPTER 8 | IT Security Policy Framework Approaches |

1. A   2. C   3. D   4. E   5. A   6. B   7. B   8. B   9. B   10. Priorities or specialties   11. A   12. Expensive or burdensome   13. Social engineering 14. B

| CHAPTER 9 | User Domain Policies |

1. B   2. Firecall-ID   3. A   4. Auditor   5. B   6. B   7. Insider   8. B 9. B   10. Escalate   11. D   12. Service   13. B

| CHAPTER 10 | IT Infrastructure Security Policies |

1. D   2. B   3. D   4. A   5. D   6. E   7. B   8. B   9. Enterprise data management   10. Cohesive, coherent   11. A   12. B   13. B   14. B

| CHAPTER 11 | Data Classification and Handling Policies and Risk Management Policies |

1. C   2. B   3. E   4. E   5. A   6. B   7. Confidential   8. B   9. C   10. B 11. B   12. Risk exposure [=] Likelihood the event will occur [×] Impact if the event occurs   13. C   14. B

| CHAPTER 12 | Incident Response Team (IRT) Policies |

1. B   2. C   3. D   4. D   5. Severity   6. B   7. Incident is declared   8. A 9. B   10. D   11. B   12. D   13. Public relations   14. B   15. A   16. B

| CHAPTER 13 | IT Security Policy Implementations |

1. D   2. A   3. C   4. B   5. B   6. D   7. D   8. A   9. B   10. D   11. B 12. Motivations or needs   13. B   14. B   15. A

| CHAPTER 14 | IT Security Policy Enforcement |

1. B   2. Executive management   3. B   4. C   5. E   6. Security policies 7. B   8. B   9. D   10. B   11. A   12. E   13. B   14. D   15. Before, after 16. Appetite, tolerance

| CHAPTER 15 | IT Policy Compliance and Compliance Technologies |

1. Baseline   2. B   3. B   4. Vulnerability window or security gap   5. D 6. A   7. D   8. A   9. B   10. A   11. C   12. B   13. Likelihood [×] Impact 14. C   15. A   16. Digital signature   17. B

Standard Acronyms

ABAC	attribute-based access control	**CAP**	Certification and Accreditation Professional
ACD	automatic call distributor		
AES	Advanced Encryption Standard	**CAUCE**	Coalition Against Unsolicited Commercial Email
ALE	annual loss expectancy		
ANSI	American National Standards Institute	**CBA**	cost-benefit analysis
		CBF	critical business function
AO	authorizing official	**CBK**	common body of knowledge
AP	access point	**CCC**	CERT Coordination Center
API	application programming interface	**CCNA**	Cisco Certified Network Associate
APT	advanced persistent threat	**CDR**	call-detail recording
ARO	annual rate of occurrence	**CERT**	Computer Emergency Response Team
ATM	asynchronous transfer mode		
AUP	acceptable use policy	**CFE**	Certified Fraud Examiner
AV	antivirus	**C-I-A**	confidentiality, integrity, availability
B2B	business to business		
B2C	business to consumer	**CIPA**	Children's Internet Protection Act
BBB	Better Business Bureau		
BC	business continuity	**CIR**	committed information rate
BCP	business continuity plan	**CIRT**	computer incident response team
BGP4	Border Gateway Protocol 4 for IPv4		
		CISA	Certified Information Systems Auditor
BIA	business impact analysis		
BU	business unit	**CISM**	Certified Information Security Manager
BYOD	bring your own device		
C2C	consumer to consumer	**CISSP**	Certified Information System Security Professional
CA	certificate authority		
CAC	Common Access Card	**CMIP**	Common Management Information Protocol
CAN	controller area network		
CAN-SPAM	Controlling the Assault of Non-Solicited Pornography and Marketing Act	**CMMI**	Capability Maturity Model Integration
		CND	computer network defense
		CNE	computer network exploitation

COBIT	Control Objectives for Information and related Technology	**EDI**	Electronic Data Interchange
COPPA	Children's Online Privacy Protection Act	**EIDE**	Enhanced IDE
		ELINT	electronic intelligence
COS	class of service	**EPHI**	electronic protected health information
COSO	Committee of Sponsoring Organizations	**EULA**	End-User License Agreement
CPs	control partners	**FACTA**	Fair and Accurate Credit Transactions Act
CRC	cyclic redundancy check	**FAR**	false acceptance rate
CSA	Cloud Security Alliance	**FCC**	Federal Communications Commission
CSF	critical success factor		
CSI	Computer Security Institute	**FDIC**	Federal Deposit Insurance Corporation
CSP	cloud service provider		
CTI	Computer Telephony Integration	**FEP**	front-end processor
CVE	Common Vulnerabilities and Exposures	**FERPA**	Family Educational Rights and Privacy Act
DAC	discretionary access control	**FIPS**	Federal Information Processing Standard
DBMS	database management system		
DCS	distributed control system	**FISMA**	Federal Information Security Management Act
DDoS	distributed denial of service		
DEP	data execution prevention	**FRCP**	Federal Rules of Civil Procedure
DES	Data Encryption Standard	**FRR**	false rejection rate
DHCPv6	Dynamic Host Configuration Protocol v6 for IPv6	**FTC**	Federal Trade Commission
		FTP	File Transfer Protocol
DHS	Department of Homeland Security	**GAAP**	generally accepted accounting principles
DIA	Defense Intelligence Agency	**GDPR**	General Data Protection Regulation
DISA	direct inward system access		
DLP	data loss protection OR data leakage protection	**GIAC**	Global Information Assurance Certification
DMZ	demilitarized zone	**GigE**	Gigibit Ethernet LAN
DNS	Domain Name Service OR Domain Name System	**GLBA**	Gramm-Leach-Bliley Act
		HIDS	host-based intrusion detection system
DoD	Department of Defense	**HIPAA**	Health Insurance Portability and Accountability Act
DoS	denial of service		
DPI	deep packet inspection	**HIPS**	host-based intrusion prevention system
DR	disaster recovery		
DRP	disaster recovery plan	**HTML**	Hypertext Markup Language
DSL	digital subscriber line	**HTTP**	Hypertext Transfer Protocol
DSS	Digital Signature Standard	**HTTPS**	Hypertext Transfer Protocol Secure
DSU	data service unit		

HUMINT	human intelligence		**MAC**	mandatory access control
IA	information assurance		**MAN**	metropolitan area network
IaaS	Infrastructure as a Service		**MAO**	maximum acceptable outage
IAB	Internet Activities Board		**MASINT**	measurement and signals intelligence
ICMP	Internet Control Message Protocol		**MD5**	Message Digest 5
IDEA	International Data Encryption Algorithm		**modem**	modulator demodulator
IDPS	intrusion detection and prevention system		**MP-BGP**	Multiprotocol Border Gateway Protocol for IPv6
IDS	intrusion detection system		**MPLS**	multiprotocol label switching
IEEE	Institute of Electrical and Electronics Engineers		**MSTI**	multiple spanning tree instance
			MSTP	Multiple Spanning Tree Protocol
IETF	Internet Engineering Task Force		**NAC**	network access control
IGP	interior gateway protocol		**NAT**	network address translation
IMINT	imagery intelligence		**NFIC**	National Fraud Information Center
InfoSec	information security		**NIC**	network interface card
IP	intellectual property OR Internet Protocol		**NIDS**	network intrusion detection system
IPS	intrusion prevention system		**NIPS**	network intrusion prevention system
IPSec	Internet Protocol Security			
IPv4	Internet Protocol version 4		**NIST**	National Institute of Standards and Technology
IPv6	Internet Protocol version 6			
IRT	incident response team		**NMS**	network management system
ISACA	Information Systems Audit and Control Association		**NOC**	network operations center
			NSA	National Security Agency
IS-IS	intermediate system-to-intermediate system		**NVD**	national vulnerability database
(ISC)²	International Information System Security Certification Consortium		**OPSEC**	operations security
			OS	operating system
			OSI	open system interconnection
ISO	International Organization for Standardization		**OSINT**	open source intelligence
			OSPFv2	Open Shortest Path First v2 for IPv4
ISP	Internet service provider			
ISS	Internet systems security		**OSPFv3**	Open Shortest Path First v3 for IPv6
ITIL	Information Technology Infrastructure Library			
			PAA	privileged-level access agreement
ITRC	Identity Theft Resource Center		**PaaS**	Platform as a Service
IVR	interactive voice response		**PBX**	private branch exchange
L2TP	Layer 2 Tunneling Protocol			
LAN	local area network		**PCI**	Payment Card Industry

PCI DSS	Payment Card Industry Data Security Standard	**SCADA**	supervisory control and data acquisition
PGP	Pretty Good Privacy	**SCSI**	small computer system interface
PHI	protected health information	**SDLC**	system development life cycle
PII	personally identifiable information	**SDSL**	symmetric digital subscriber line
		SET	secure electronic transaction
PIN	personal identification number	**SGC**	server-gated cryptography
PKI	public key infrastructure	**SHA**	secure hash algorithm
PLC	programmable logic controller	**S-HTTP**	secure HTTP
POAM	plan of action and milestones	**SIEM**	Security Information and Event Management system
PoE	power over Ethernet		
POS	point-of-sale	**SIGINT**	signals intelligence
PPTP	Point-to-Point Tunneling Protocol	**SIP**	Session Initiation Protocol
		SLA	service level agreement
PSYOPs	psychological operations	**SLE**	single loss expectancy
RA	registration authority OR risk assessment	**SLT**	senior leadership team
		SMFA	specific management functional area
RAID	redundant array of independent disks		
		SNMP	Simple Network Management Protocol
RAT	remote access Trojan OR remote access tool	**SOX**	Sarbanes-Oxley Act of 2002 (also Sarbox)
RCSA	risk and control self-assessment		
RFC	Request for Comments	**SPOF**	single point of failure
RIPng	Routing Information Protocol next generation for IPv6	**SQL**	Structured Query Language
		SSA	Social Security Administration
RIPv2	Routing Information Protocol v2 for IPv4	**SSCP**	Systems Security Certified Practitioner
ROI	return on investment	**SSID**	service set identifier (name assigned to a Wi-Fi network)
RPO	recovery point objective		
RSA	Rivest, Shamir, and Adleman (algorithm)	**SSL**	Secure Sockets Layer
		SSL-VPN	Secure Sockets Layer virtual private network
RSTP	Rapid Spanning Tree Protocol		
RTO	recovery time objective	**SSO**	single system sign-on
SA	security association	**STP**	shielded twisted pair OR Spanning Tree Protocol
SaaS	Software as a Service		
SAN	storage area network	**TCP/IP**	Transmission Control Protocol/Internet Protocol
SANCP	Security Analyst Network Connection Profiler		
		TCSEC	Trusted Computer System Evaluation Criteria
SANS	SysAdmin, Audit, Network, Security		
		TFA	two-factor authentication
SAP	service access point OR security awareness policy	**TFTP**	Trivial File Transfer Protocol
		TGAR	trunk group access restriction

TNI	Trusted Network Interpretation	**VPN**	virtual private network
TPM	technology protection measure OR trusted platform module	**W3C**	World Wide Web Consortium
		WAN	wide area network
UC	unified communications	**WAP**	wireless access point
UDP	User Datagram Protocol	**WEP**	wired equivalent privacy
UPS	uninterruptible power supply	**Wi-Fi**	wireless fidelity
USB	universal serial bus	**WLAN**	wireless local area network
UTP	unshielded twisted pair	**WNIC**	wireless network interface card
VA	vulnerability assessment	**WPA**	Wi-Fi Protected Access
VBAC	view-based access control	**WPA2**	Wi-Fi Protected Access 2
VLAN	virtual local area network	**XML**	Extensible Markup Language
VoIP	Voice over Internet Protocol	**XSS**	cross-site scripting

Glossary of Key Terms

A

Acceptable use policies (AUPs) | Formal written policies that describe proper and unacceptable behavior when using computer and network systems. For example, an acceptable use policy may set rules on what type of website browsing is permitted or if personal emails over the Internet are allowed.

Access control list (ACL) | An implementation technique to control access to a resource by maintaining a table of authorized user IDs.

Active content | Software or plug-ins that run within a client browser, usually on certain websites. Examples include Java applets, JavaScript, and ActiveX controls.

Agent | In the context of distributed infrastructure, a piece of code that sits on a distributed device, such as the laptop or tablet of a mobile sales representative, to manage it. An agent typically reports the state of the device to the central server, reports any malware detected, and receives commands and updates.

Agentless central management tool | In the context of distributed infrastructure, a piece of software housed on the central server that "pushes" changes, such as updates, to remote devices.

Apathy | A state of indifference, or the suppression of emotions such as concern, excitement, motivation, and passion.

Application software | Generally any business software that an end user (including customers) touches is considered an application. This includes email, word processing, and spreadsheet software.

Architecture operating model | A framework for helping an organization understand how security controls are to be implemented. One common issue for the organization is that of centralization or decentralization of security within the business. An architecture operating model discussion can identify areas of disagreement and create a common set of beliefs on the proper placement and implementation of controls.

Architecture review committee | A gateway committee that approves standard technologies and architectures.

Attribute-based access control (ABAC) | An authorization control that relies on dynamic roles rather than the static roles of role-based access control. In ABAC, you build an expression of attributes describing the role that is dynamically built at run time.

Audit | The act of recording relevant security events that occur on a computing or network device (server, workstation, firewall, etc.). Can also refer to a review of business and financial processes and files by an auditor.

Audit committee | A committee that deals with audit issues and nonfinancial risks.

Auditor | An individual accountable for assessing the design and effectiveness of security policies. Auditors may be internal or external to an organization.

Authentication | The process of determining the identity of an individual or device.

Authorization | The process of granting permission to some people to access systems, applications, and data.

Automated control | A security control that stops behavior immediately and does not rely on human decisions.

Automatic declassification | Automatically removing a classification after a certain period of time, such as 25 years.

Availability | Ensuring accessibility of information to authorized users when required.

B

Best fit access privileges | An approach to granting systems access. Best fit privilege provides a group or class of users only the access they need to do their job. Compare with least access privileges, an approach that typically customizes access to individual users.

Best practices | Leading techniques, methodologies, or technologies that through experience have proved to be very reliable. Best practices tend to produce consistent and quality results.

Bolt-on | In terms of information security, refers to adding information security as a distinct layer of control. Bolt-on security is the opposite of integrated security, in which information security controls are an integral part of the process design and not a separate distinct layer.

Breach | A confirmed event that compromises the confidentiality, integrity, or availability of information.

Bring your own device (BYOD) | A policy of allowing employees, contractors, and others to sign on to their organization's network with their own phones, computers, and other devices rather than equipment belonging to the organization.

Business as usual (BAU) | A term used with reference to an organization's budget, to mean normal spending. Integrating the costs of governance into an organization's BAU budget makes these costs seem like a normal operating expense rather than something exceptional.

Business continuity plan (BCP) | A plan on how to continue business after a disaster. A BCP includes a disaster recovery plan (DRP) as a component.

Business continuity representative | An individual who understands the organization's capability to restore the system, application, network, or data. This individual also has access to call lists to contact anyone in the organization during off hours.

Business impact analysis (BIA) | A formal analysis to determine the impact on an organization in the event that key processes and technology are not available.

Business process reengineering (BPR) | A management technique used to improve the efficiency and effectiveness of a process within an organization.

C

Chain of custody | A legal term referring to how evidence is documented and protected. Evidence must be documented and protected from the time it's obtained to the time it's presented in court.

Change agent | A person who challenges current thinking.

Change management | The practice of managing upgrades to an IT system, including understanding the impact of change and knowing how to recover if something goes wrong.

Chief information officer (CIO) | The person who determines the overall strategic direction and business contribution of the information systems function in an organization; often the one within the organization designated as accountable for information security.

Chief information security officer (CISO) | The person within an organization responsible for securing anything related to digital information; this person often has a role in ensuring the organization's compliance with the information security provisions of laws such as the Gramm-Leach-Bliley Act. Sometimes referred to simply as *information security officer (ISO)*.

Chief privacy officer (CPO) | Most senior leader responsible for managing risks related to data privacy.

Committee of Sponsoring Organizations (COSO) | An organization that developed a framework for validating internal controls and managing enterprise risks; focuses on financial operations and risk management.

Communications plan | Outlines what information is to be shared and how the information will be disseminated.

Compensating control | A security control that achieves the desired outcome and policy intent, but doesn't necessarily achieve it the way the policy says to do it. The outcome is the same, however.

Compliance | The ability to reasonably ensure conformity and adherence to organization policies, standards, procedures, laws, and regulations.

Compliance officer | An individual accountable for monitoring adherence to laws and regulations.

Compliance risk | Relates to the impact on the business for failing to comply with legal obligations.

Computer-based training (CBT) | Training done partly or fully on computer-based channels of communication, such as the Internet or through training software.

Confidential | A level of government classification that refers to data in which unauthorized disclosure would reasonably be expected to cause some damage to the national security.

Confidentiality | Limiting access to information/data to authorized users only.

Confidentiality agreement (CA) | Legally binding agreements on the handling and disclosure of company material.

Configuration management (CM) | A collection of activities that track system configuration. It starts with a baseline configuration. It continues through a system's life cycle, including changing and monitoring configurations.

Consumer rights | Established rules on how consumers and their information should be handled during an e-commerce transaction.

Contingent accounts | Accounts used to recover a system in case of disaster; such accounts need unlimited rights to install, configure, repair, and recover networks and applications, and to restore data. This elevated level of access makes such accounts prime targets for hackers.

Continuous improvement | An ad hoc, ongoing effort to improve business products, services, or processes.

Contractors | Temporary workers who can be assigned to any role.

Control environment | The overall way in which an organization's controls are governed and executed.

Control Objectives for Information and related Technology (COBIT) | A widely accepted framework that brings together business and control requirements with technical issues.

Control partners | People within an organization whose responsibility it is to offer an opinion on the soundness and impact of security policy. Control partners often work in the areas of internal audit or operational risk, or the compliance or legal departments of their organizations.

Coordinated operating model | An operating model in which the technology solution shares data across the enterprise, but there is only minimal sharing and standardization of services.

Corrective control | A security control that restores a system or process.

Critical infrastructure | Assets that are essential for the society and economy to function, such as key elements of the transportation, energy, communications, banking, and other systems.

Cyberterrorism | An attack that attempts to cause fear or major disruptions in a society through attacking government computers, major companies, or key areas of the economy.

Data administrator | Implements policies and procedures such as backup, versioning, uploading, downloading, and database administration.

Data at rest | The state of data stored on any type of media.

Data classification | Level of protection based on data type.

Data custodian | An individual responsible for the day-to-day maintenance of data and the quality of that data. May perform backups and recover data as needed. A data custodian also grants access based on approval from the data owner.

Data encryption | When data is encrypted, the actual information can be viewed only when the data is decrypted with a key.

Data in transit | The state of data when traveling over or through a network.

Data leakage | Unauthorized sharing of sensitive company information, whether intentional or accidental.

Data leakage protection (DLP) | A formal program that reduces the likelihood of accidental or malicious loss of data. May also stand for *data loss protection*.

Data loss protection (DLP) | A formal program that reduces the likelihood of accidental or malicious loss of data. May also stand for *data leakage protection*.

Data manager | An individual who establishes procedures on how data should be handled.

Data owner | An individual who approves user access rights to information that is needed to perform day-to-day operations.

Data privacy | The laws that set expectations on how your personal information should be protected and places limits on how the data should be shared.

Data security administrator | One who grants access rights and assesses information security threats to the organization.

Data steward | Owner of data and approver of access rights; responsible for data quality.

Data user | The end user of an application. A data user is accountable for handling data appropriately by understanding security policies and following approved processes and procedures.

Declassification | The process of changing the status of classified data to unclassified data.

Defense in depth | The approach of using multiple layers of security to protect against a single point of failure.

Demilitarized zone (DMZ) | Taken from the military, a buffer between two opposing forces. With regards to networks, it is the segment that sits between the public Internet and a private local area network (LAN). A DMZ is built to protect private LANs from the Internet. It uses a series of firewalls, routers, IDSs, and/ or IPSs. The DMZ is where public web servers, email servers, and public DNS servers are located.

Detective control | A manual security control that identifies a behavior after it has happened.

Digital assets | Any digital material owned by an organization, including text, graphics, audio, video, and animations.

Disaster recovery plan (DRP) | A plan to recover an organization's IT assets during a disaster, including software, data, and hardware.

Discovery management | In the context of workstation central management systems, refers to processes that determine what is installed on a workstation. It could also refer to knowing what information sits on a workstation.

Distributed infrastructure | A term for an organization's collection of computers, including laptops, tablets, and smartphones, networked together and equipped with distributed system software, so that they work together as one, even though they are in various locations.

Diversified operating model | An operating model in which the technology solution has a low level of integration and standardization within the enterprise. Typically, the exchange of data and use of services outside the business unit itself are minimal.

Division of labor | How various tasks are grouped into specialties to enhance the depth and quality of work product.

Domain | A logical piece of our technology infrastructure with similar risks and business requirements.

Dormant account | An account that hasn't been used for an extended period of time.

Due care | A legal term that refers to effort made to avoid harm to another party. It essentially refers to the care that a person would reasonably be expected to see under particular circumstances.

Early adopter | One who adopts a security policy early on as a type of pilot. Early adopters provide useful feedback to the IT team, and can serve as role models of good practice for other users within the organization.

Email policy | A policy that discusses what's acceptable when using the company email system.

Enterprise data management (EDM) | The discipline of creating, integrating, securing, disseminating, and managing data across the enterprise. Larger organizations may have a dedicated EDM team.

Enterprise risk management (ERM) | A framework that aligns strategic goals, operations effectiveness, reporting, and compliance objectives; not technology specific.

Entitlement | A fine-grained granting of access to information resources, often facilitated through use of an application gateway. For example, an application can allow a user to approve a payment but limit the amount to less than $1000.

Escalation | In the context of information security, refers to a process by which senior leaders through a chain of command are apprised of a risk. An escalation continues one level of organizational structure at a time until the issue is addressed or the escalation reaches the highest level of the organization.

Evangelists | People with enthusiasm for a cause or project. Evangelists often gain acceptance for a project from a wide audience.

Evidence | 1. Information that supports a conclusion. 2. Material presented to a regulator to show compliance.

Exception | A deviation from a centrally supported and approved IT security standard. Exceptions can come about because of a lack of preparedness by the organization to comply with a standard or due to the use of a technology that has not been sanctioned by the standards.

Executive | A senior business leader accountable for approving security policy implementation, driving the security message within an organization, and ensuring that policies are given appropriate priority.

Executive committee | A committee that helps align the security committee to organization goals and objectives.

Executive management sponsorship | Getting senior management to participate in training to improve the effectiveness of security policies.

External connection committee | A gateway committee that approves external data connections.

File Transfer Protocol (FTP) | A protocol used to exchange files over a local area network (LAN) or wide area network (WAN).

Financial risk | Events that could potentially impact the business when it fails to provide adequate liquidity to meet its obligations.

Firecall-ID process | Granting elevated rights temporarily to enable a person to resolve a problem quickly. Provides emergency access to unprivileged users.

Firewall | A device that filters the traffic in and out of a local area network (LAN). Many firewalls can do deep packet inspection, in which they examine the content, as well as the type, of the traffic. A firewall can be used internally on the network to further protect segments. Firewalls are most commonly used to filter traffic between the public Internet and an internal private LAN.

Flat network | A network with little or no controls that limit network traffic.

Flat organizational structure | An organization with few layers separating the leaders from the bottom ranks of workers.

Full disclosure | The concept that an individual should know what information about them is being collected. An individual should also be told how that information is being used.

Gateway committees | Committees that review technology activity and provide approvals before the project or activity can proceed to the next stage.

General counsel | The highest ranking lawyer in an organization, who usually reports to the president or chief executive officer. He or she is asked to give legal opinions on various organization issues, participate in contract negotiations, and act as a liaison with outside law firms retained by the organization.

Globalization | The development of a world economy held together by advanced technology for communications, transportation, and finance.

Gold master | A master image that is copied for deployment. Use of golden images saves time by eliminating the need for repetitive configuration changes and performance tweaks. It ensures all images imaged using a copy of the gold master are configured the same.

Governance | The act of managing implementation and compliance with organizational policies.

Governance, risk management, and compliance (GRC) | A set of tools that bring together the capabilities to systematically manage risk and policy compliance.

Granularity | The level of detail a set of security policies goes into. The more granular a policy, the easier it is to enforce and to detect violations. But less granular policies may be more helpful in responding to new threats.

Group Policy | An automated management tool used in Microsoft domains. Administrators can configure a setting one time in Group Policy and it will apply to multiple users and computers.

Guideline | A parameter within which a policy, standard, or procedure is recommended when possible but is optional.

Harden | To eliminate as many security risks as possible by reducing access rights to the minimum needed to perform any task, ensuring access is authenticated to unique individuals, removing all nonessential software, and other configuration steps that eliminate opportunities for unauthorized access.

Head of information management | A role that deals with all aspects of information such as security, quality, definition, and availability; responsible for data quality.

Help desk management | In the context of workstation central management systems, services that provide support to the end user. This includes allowing the help desk technician to remotely access the workstation to diagnose problems, reconfigure software, and reset IDs.

Hierarchical organizational structure | An organization with multiple layers of reporting, which separates leaders from the bottom ranks of workers.

Highly sensitive classification | A classification level used to protect highly regulated data or strategic information.

Honeypot | A network security device that acts as a decoy to analyze hacker activity.

Human resources representative | An individual who is an expert on HR policies and disciplinary proceedings or employee counseling.

Imaging | A technology used to create baselines of systems. An image is captured from a source computer. This image can then be deployed to other systems. Images include the operating system, applications, configuration settings, and security settings.

Incident | An event that violates an organization's security policies.

Incident response team (IRT) | A specialized group of people whose purpose is to respond to major incidents.

Information assurance | The implementation of controls designed to ensure confidentiality, integrity, availability, and nonrepudiation.

Information security | The act of protecting information or data from unauthorized use, access, disruption, or destruction.

Information security officer (ISO) | *See* chief information security officer.

Information security program charter | A capstone document that establishes the reporting lines and delegation of responsibilities for information security to management below the organization's chief information officer (CIO) or other executive leader.

Information security representative | In the context of an IRT team, an information security representative provides risk management and analytical skills. A representative may also have specialized forensic skills for collecting and analyzing evidence.

Information security risk assessment | A formal process to identify threats, potential attacks, and impacts to an organization.

Information systems security (ISS) | The act of protecting information systems or IT infrastructures from unauthorized use, access, disruption, or destruction.

Information systems security management life cycle | The five-phase management process of controlling the planning, implementation, evaluation, and maintenance of information systems security.

Information systems security policies | Collections of documents that outline the controls, actions, and processes to be performed by an organization to protect its information systems.

Information technology and infrastructure library (ITIL) | A framework that contains a comprehensive list of concepts, practices, and processes for managing IT services.

Information technology subject matter expert | An individual who has intimate knowledge of the systems and configurations of an organization. This individual is typically a developer, system administrator, or network administrator. He or she has the needed technical skills to make critical recommendations on how to stop an attack.

Insider | An employee, consultant, contractor, or vendor. The insider may even be one of the IT technical people who designed the system, application, or security that is being hacked. The insider knows the organization and the applications.

Integrated audit | An audit in which two or more audit disciplines are combined to conduct a single audit.

Integrity | The act of ensuring that information has not been improperly changed.

Intellectual property (IP) | Any product of human intellect that is unique and not obvious with some value in the marketplace.

Interactive | Refers to system accounts (also known as service accounts) to which it is possible for someone to log on. System accounts, because of their high level of access, are attractive to hackers.

Interactivity makes these accounts more vulnerable to hackers. Noninteractive system accounts are much more secure.

Internal classification | A classification level for data that would cause disruption to daily operations and some financial loss to the business if leaked.

International Organization for Standardization (ISO) | An organization that creates widely accepted international standards on information security and IT risks.

Internet filters | Software that blocks access to specific sites on the Internet.

Intrusion detection system (IDS) | A series of software agents, appliances, and servers that monitors for network activity that is deemed a threat, alerts administrators, and logs the information. IDSs operate by matching signatures of known possible network attack traffic or by building over time a baseline of normal behavior, and then alerting on traffic that is anomalous to that normal pattern of behavior.

Intrusion prevention system (IPS) | A system that intercepts potentially hostile activity prior to it being processed.

Inventory management | In the context of workstation central management systems, refers to tracking what workstation and related network devices exist. This usually takes place whenever a workstation connects to the local area network (LAN).

IRT coordinator | The person who keeps track of all the activity of the IRT during an incident. He or she acts as the official scribe of the team. All activity flows through this person. The person records who's doing what.

IRT manager | The IRT manager is the team lead. This individual makes all the final calls on how to respond to an incident. He or she is the interface with management.

ISO/IEC 27000 series | Information security standards published by the International Organization for Standardization (ISO) and by the International Electrotechnical Commission (IEC). ISO/IEC 27002, for example, provides best practice recommendations on information security management for those who are responsible for initiating, implementing, or maintaining an information security management system.

Issue-specific standard | A standard that focuses on areas of current relevance and concern to an organization. Such standards are used to express security control requirements, typically for nontechnical processes, and are used to guide human behavior.

IT policy framework | A logical structure that is established to organize policy documentation into groupings and categories that make it easier for employees to find and understand the contents of various policy documents. Policy frameworks can also be used to help in the planning and development of the policies for an organization.

Label | A mark or comment placed inside the document itself indicating a level of protection.

LAN domain | This domain refers to the organization's local area network (LAN) infrastructure. A LAN allows two or more computers to be connected within a small area. The small area could be a home, office, or group of buildings.

LAN-to-WAN domain | This domain refers to the technical infrastructure that connects the organization's local area network (LAN) to a wide area network (WAN), such as the Internet. This allows end users to surf the Internet.

Law | Any rule prescribed under the authority of a government entity. Establishes legal thresholds.

Layered security approach | Having two or more layers of independent controls to reduce risk.

Least access privileges | The principle of granting users only the systems access they need to accomplish their jobs. Typically this is done by customizing access to individuals. Compare with *best fit access privileges*, an approach that typically customizes access to a group or class of users.

Legal representative | An individual who has an understanding of laws and regulatory compliance.

Lessons learned | Knowledge gained from a particular experience, such as the implementation of a policy change. Lessons learned can be shared with others, turned into standard procedure, and applied to similar situations in the future.

Log management | In the context of workstation central management systems, refers to extracting logs from the workstation—typically, moving the logs to a central repository. Later these logs are scanned to look for security weakness or patterns of problems.

Log server | A separate platform used to collect logs from platforms throughout the network.

Mandatory declassification | A process of reviewing specific records when requested and declassifying them if warranted.

Manual control | A security control that does not stop behavior immediately and relies on human decisions.

Matrix relationships | The complex relationships between multiple stakeholders in an organization.

Mitigating control | A security control after the fact. It assumes the absence or breakdown of a primary control. A mitigating control addresses the security issue at hand, but may not achieve a policy's full intent.

Multifactor authentication | Authentication of users on a network by more than one factor, such as a combination of password and access code.

Nation-states | Sovereign countries with their own national governments.

National Institute of Standards and Technology (NIST) | An organization that creates security guidelines on security controls for federal information systems.

Need to know | A principle that restricts information access to only those users with an approved and valid requirement.

NIST SP 800-53 | A publication for the U.S. National Institute of Standards and Technology (NIST), titled "Recommended Security Controls for Federal Information Systems and Organizations."

Nondisclosure agreement (NDA) | Legally binding agreement on the handling and disclosure of company material. This is also known as a confidentiality agreement.

Nonrepudiation | The concept of applying technology in such a way that an individual cannot deny or dispute they were part of a transaction.

Operating model | An organized, planned approach for operations.

Operational deviation | The difference between what policies and procedures state should be done and what is actually performed.

Operational risk | An event that disrupts the daily activities of an organization.

Operational risk committee | A committee that provides important information on the risk appetite of the organization and various businesses.

Opt-in | The practice of agreeing to use of personal information beyond its original purpose. An example of opt-in is asking a consumer who just sold his or her home if the real-estate company can share the consumer's information with a moving company.

Opt-out | The practice of declining permission to use personal information beyond its original purpose. For example, a consumer who just sold his or her home may decline permission for the real estate company to share his or her information with a moving company.

Organizational culture | The traditions, customs, patterns of behavior, values, and beliefs shared by members of an organization. Anyone seeking to introduce change into an organization, such as a new set of security policies, must know and take account of organizational culture.

Outdated technology | Hardware or software that makes it difficult to implement best practices consistently.

Patch management | Refers to making sure that devices on the network, such as workstations and servers, have current patches from the vendor. It's particularly important to apply security patches in a timely way to address known vulnerabilities.

Payment Card Industry Data Security Standard (PCI DSS) | A worldwide information security standard that describes how to protect credit card information. If you accept Visa, MasterCard, or American Express, you are required to follow PCI DSS.

Penetration test | A test designed not just to identify, but also to actually exploit weaknesses in system architecture or the computing environment.

Personal privacy | In e-commerce, broadly deals with how personal information is handled and what it is used for.

Personally identifiable information (PII) | Sensitive information used to uniquely identify an individual in a way that could potentially be exploited.

Pervasive control | A common control, such as the same ID and password, that is used across a significant population of systems, applications, and operations.

Phishing | Use of any communication to attempt to get information from the target. Email is commonly used.

Policy | A document that states how the organization is to perform and conduct business functions and transactions with a desired outcome.

Policy definitions document | A glossary for an organization's security policies, ideally clear and concise, often used by auditors and regulators when evaluating the soundness of an organization's controls.

Policy framework | A structure for organizing policies, standards, procedures, and guidelines.

Policy principles document | A document that communicates general rules that cut across the entire organization. The principles focus on key risks or behaviors and express core values of the organization that often include the areas where there will be zero tolerance for transgression.

Pretexting | When a hacker outlines a story in which the employee is asked to reveal information that weakens the security.

Preventive control | An automated security control that stops a behavior immediately.

Privacy policy | Places importance on privacy in the business and discusses the regulatory landscape and government mandates. This policy often talks about physical security and the importance of "locking up" sensitive information.

Privileged-level access agreement (PAA) | Designed to heighten the awareness and accountability of those users with administrator rights.

Procedure | A written statement describing the steps required to implement a process.

Project committee | A gateway committee that approves project funding, phases, and base requirements.

Public classification | A classification level for data that has no negative impact on the business if released to the public.

Public record | Any record required by law to be made available to the public. These types of records are made or filed by a governmental entity.

Public relations representative | In the context of an IRT team, it is an individual who can advise on how to communicate to the public and customers that might be impacted by the incident. This person is valuable in ensuring that accurate information gets out and damaging misconceptions are prevented.

Quality assurance | A kind of preventive, before-the-fact control within an organization that prevents mistakes from happening.

Quality control | A kind of detective, after-the-fact control that affords an organization opportunities to learn from its mistakes.

Recovery point objectives (RPOs) | The maximum acceptable levels of data loss after a disaster.

Recovery time objective (RTO) | A measure of how quickly a business process should be recovered after a disaster. The RTO identifies the maximum allowed downtime for a given business process.

Reduction in force | Laying off employees or downsizing to save money.

Regulations | Established rules of what an organization has to do to meet legal requirements.

Remote Access domain | This domain refers to the technology that controls how end users connect to the organization's local area network (LAN). A typical example is someone needing to connect to the office from his or her home.

Remote authentication | Enhanced authentication over what's typically found in the office. Usually it requires more than an ID and password, such as a security token or smartcard.

Replicated operating model | An operating model in which the technology solution shares services across the enterprise, but the level of data sharing is minimal.

Residual risk | The risk that remains after all the controls have been applied.

Risk | The likelihood or probability of an event and its impact.

Risk and control self-assessment (RCSA) | A tool that allows an organization to understand its risks and their potential impact on the business. It is a formal exercise many organizations conduct annually.

Risk appetite | Understanding risks and determining how much potential risk and related problems the business is willing to accept.

Risk assessment | *See* information security risk assessment.

Risk culture | The way an organization normally deals with risk; for instance, whether by following security policies consistently or not. The leaders of an organization are usually a strong influence on its risk culture.

Risk evaluation | A domain in the ISACA Risk IT framework that calls for analyzing risk and determining impact on the business.

Risk exposure | The level of damage and likelihood of a risk being realized.

Risk governance | A domain in the ISACA Risk IT framework that ensures that risk management activity aligns with the business's goals, objectives, and tolerances.

Risk response | A domain in the ISACA Risk IT framework that specifies the ability to react so that risks are reduced and remedied in a cost-effective manner.

Risk tolerance | The dominant view within an organization of how much risk is acceptable.

Roadshow | In the information security context, a presentation before a large group on a topic such as a new security policy. A roadshow may involve gathering all employees of a company into a large auditorium, or simply showing up as a guest speaker at a department's regular staff meeting.

Role-based access control (RBAC) | A system of granting users access to a network on the basis of their role rather than their individual identity. An accounting firm may have a role of "accountant," for instance, and all newly hired accountants may be assigned the same package of access privileges.

Router | Connects local area networks (LANs) or a LAN and a wide area network (WAN).

 S

Secret | A level of government classification that refers to data, the unauthorized disclosure of which would reasonably be expected to cause serious damage to the national security.

Security awareness program | Training about security policies, threats, and handling of digital assets.

Security baseline | Defines a set of basic configurations to achieve defined security objectives. These defined security objectives are typically represented by security policies and a well-defined security framework.

Security committee | A committee that acts as a steering committee for the information security program.

Security compliance committee | A gateway committee that approves uses of specific controls for compliance.

Security content automation protocol (SCAP) | A group of specifications that standardize how security software products measure, evaluate, and report compliance. NIST created SCAP, and several private companies created SCAP-compliant tools.

Security control mapping | When related to compliance, it's the mapping of regulatory requirements to policies and controls.

Security event | Any undesirable event that occurs outside the normal daily security operations. Typically, a security event relates to a breakdown in controls as defined by the security policies.

Security management | Refers to managing security in an organization, usually IT security. This can include making sure end users have limited rights and access controls are in place, among many other techniques and processes.

Security personnel | Individuals responsible for designing and implementing a security program within an organization.

Security policies | A set of policies that establish how an organization secures its facilities and IT infrastructure. Can also address how the organization meets regulatory requirements.

Security policy compliance | Adherence to the organization's set of rules with regard to security policies.

Security token | A hardware device or software code that generates a token (usually represented as a series of numbers) at logon. A security token is extremely difficult and some say impossible to replicate. When assigned to an individual as part of his or her required logon, it provides assurance of who is accessing the network.

Segmented network | A network that limits how computers are able to talk to each other.

Segregation of duties (SOD) | Another term for *separation of duties*.

Sensitive but unclassified | A level of government classification that refers to data that is confidential and not subject to release under the Freedom of Information Act.

Sensitive classification | A classification level for data that would mean significant financial loss if leaked.

Separation of duties (SOD) | A requirement that high-risk tasks be divided so that it takes more than one person to perform them. The idea is to prevent employees from concealing errors or fraud in the normal course of their duties.

Service level agreement (SLA) | The portion of a service contract that formally defines the level of service. These agreements are typical in telecommunications contracts for voice and data transmission circuits.

Shareholder | A person who buys stock in a company (investor).

Simple Network Management Protocol (SNMP) | A protocol used to query and manage network devices. SNMP v1 had known vulnerabilities such as transmitting the community name in clear text. SNMP v2 and v3 improved security and performance of SNMP.

Sniffer | A network device that can read communications traffic on a local area network (LAN).

Social engineering | Manipulating or tricking a person into weakening the security of an organization.

Span of control | Relates to the number of areas of control achieved through the number of direct reports found in an organization.

Spear phishing | Phishing that is targeted at a small group.

Standard | An established and proven norm or method. This can be a procedural standard or a technical standard implemented organization-wide.

Stateful firewall | A firewall that watches all the traffic for a given connection. It inspects packets containing data, looking for patterns and sequences that don't make sense. This is useful to block packets from someone pretending to be someone else in an attempt to hijack your session.

Stateless firewall | A firewall that restricts and blocks traffic based on source and destination addresses or other static values. It looks at each data packet independently.

Statement on Standards for Attestation Engagements No. 16 (SSAE16) | A standard created by the American Institute of Certified Public Accountants for auditing an organization's control environment, including information security controls.

Strategic risk | An event that may change how the entire organization operates.

Structured Query Language (SQL) | A standardized language used to access a database.

Structured Query Language (SQL) injection | A type of attack in which the hacker adds SQL code to a Web or application input box to gain access to or alter data in the database.

Switch | A piece of equipment that is similar to a hub but can filter traffic. You can set up rules that control what traffic can flow where. Unlike hubs, which duplicate the traffic to all ports, a switch typically routes traffic only to the port where the system is connected. This reduces network traffic, thus reducing the chance of someone intercepting the traffic.

System access policy | Rules of conduct on how and when access to systems is permitted. This policy covers end user credentials like IDs and passwords. The policy may also be specific to the business or application, such as the use of role-based access control (RBAC).

System software | Software that supports the running of the applications.

System/Application domain | This domain refers to the technology needed to collect, process, and store the information. It includes controls related to hardware and software.

Systematic declassification | A process of reviewing records exempted from automatic declassification and then removing the data from classification.

Systems administrators | IT staff who provide administrative support to the systems and databases.

System-specific standard | A standard that focuses on specific technology or systems being used within an organization. These are used to express the security control implementation requirements for some specific technology.

Target state | A term used in technology to describe a desired future state of information security, including policy goals and objectives and the tools, processes, and resources needed to achieve them.

Taxonomy | The practice and science of classification. A hierarchical taxonomy is a tree structure of classifications for a given set of objects or documents.

Threat | A human or natural event that could impact the system.

Threat vector | A general information security term to describe a tool or path by which a hacker can gain unauthorized access.

Tone at the top | The message from an organization's leadership on a given subject. When senior executives voice support for a policy, they are said to be setting the tone at the top.

Top Secret | A level of government classification that refers to data, the unauthorized disclosure of which would reasonably be expected to cause grave damage to the national security.

Town hall meeting | A gathering of teams to make announcements and discuss topics.

Trouble ticket | A complete record of what access was granted and the business reason behind it in order to resolve a problem.

Two-factor authentication | Requires end users to authenticate their identity using at least two of three different types of credentials. The three most commonly accepted types of credentials are something you know, something you have, and something you are.

Unclassified | A level of government classification that refers to data available to the public.

Unified operating model | An operating model in which the technology solution both shares data and has standardized services across the enterprise.

User domain | This domain refers to any user accessing information. This includes customers, employees, consultants, contractors, or any other third party. These users are often referred to as *end users*.

User proxy | An application firewall that is used to control the flow of traffic to and from the Internet to user workstations attached to a local area network (LAN). The proxy intercepts the user's request for an Internet resource, initiates a new connection, and proxies the result back to the requestor.

Value delivery | Focusing resources to deliver the greatest benefits.

Vendor governance committee | A gateway committee that approves new vendors and has oversight of existing vendors. This includes making sure new vendors meet minimum security policy requirements such as having a formal contract in place and adequate proof of security controls.

Virtual private network (VPN) | A VPN is set up between two devices to create an encrypted tunnel. All communications are protected from eavesdropping and considered highly secure.

Vulnerability | A weakness in a system that can be exploited.

Vulnerability window | The time in which a vulnerability can be exploited (i.e. before it is patched).

WAN domain | This domain includes wide area networks (WANs), which are networks that cover large geographical areas. The Internet is an example of a WAN. A private WAN can be built for a specific company to link offices across the country or globally.

Web graffiti | Alterations to a webpage that result from a website defacement attack. Website graffiti can contain abusive language or even pornographic images.

Web services | Automated information services over the Internet using standardized technologies and formats/protocols that simplify the exchange and integration of data. Web services help organizations to interoperate regardless of the types of operating systems, programming languages, and databases being used.

Web-Based Enterprise Management (WBEM) | A set of standards and technologies used to query and manage systems and applications in a network. It is used on the Internet and internal networks. WBEM capabilities are built into GUI-based applications and command line applications.

Website defacement | An attack on a website in which the site's content is altered, usually in a way that embarrasses the website owner.

Whaling | Phishing targeted at a single high value victim.

Workstation domain | This domain refers to any computing device used by end users. This usually means a desktop or laptop that is the main computer for the end user.

References

Accredited Standards Committee X9 Incorporated, *http://www.x9.org*, accessed March 8, 2010.

Alberta Health Services, "Policy Development Framework," April 25, 2016, *https://extranet .ahsnet.ca/teams/policydocuments/1/clp-pdf-pol-devt-framework.pdf*, accessed April 18, 2020.

Allbusiness, "Boston Attorney General Investigates E-Mail Destruction," January 1, 2010, *http://www.allbusiness.com/government/government-bodies-offices-public/13829522-1 .html*, accessed May 14, 2010.

American Speech-Language-Hearing Association, "Health Information Technology for Economics and Clinical Health (HITECH) Act," *https://www.asha.org/Practice /reimbursement/hipaa/HITECH-Act/*, accessed April 10, 2020.

ArticleInput.com, "A Few Facts on Information Security and Accountability," 2009, *http://www .articleinput.com/e/a/title/A-few-facts-on-information-security-and-accountability/*, accessed March 10, 2010.

Asia-Pacific Economic Cooperation, "APEC Privacy Framework," *https://www.apec.org /Publications/2005/12/APEC-Privacy-Framework*, accessed April 11, 2020.

Baker & Hostetler LLP, "State Data Breach Statute Form," *http://www.bakerlaw.com/files /Uploads/Documents/Data%20Breach%20documents/State_Data_Breach_Statute_Form.pdf*, accessed June 2, 2014.

Barrett, Jim, "Electronic Discovery Employment Roundtable," AterWynne LLP, October 19, 2006, *http://www.aterwynne.com/files/ERT_%20Electronic%20discovery.PDF*, accessed March 26, 2010.

Bloch, Michael, Sven Blumberg, and Jürgen Laartz, "Delivering Large-Scale IT Projects on Time, on Budget, and on Value," McKinsey & Company, Insights & Publications, October 2012, *http://www.mckinsey.com/insights/business_technology/delivering_large-scale_it_projects _on_time_on_budget_and_on_value*, accessed March 10, 2014.

Bloomberg, "Kerviel's New Lawyers Will Focus on SocGen Conduct," July 30, 2008, *http://www .bloomberg.com/apps/news?pid=20601085&sid=aWbERdIeyYO4&refer=europe*, accessed April 12, 2010.

Calfa, Jimena, "Difference between QA and QC," American Society for Quality, October 13, 2011, *http://www.onquality.info/2011/10/difference-between-qa-and-qc.html*, accessed May 1, 2014.

Caputo, Kim, *CMM Implementation Guide: Choreographing Software Process Improvement.* New York, NY: Addison-Wesley Professional, 1998.

Carroll, Rory, "Snowden Used Simple Technology to Mine NSA Computer Networks," *The Guardian*, February 9, 2014, *http://www.theguardian.com/world/2014/feb/09/edward -snowden-used-simple-technology-nsa*, accessed March 20, 2014.

"Case Study: Using Security Awareness to Combat the Advanced Persistent Threat," 13th Colloquium for Information Systems Security Education, June 2009, *http://www.cisse2009 .com/colloquia/cisse13/proceedings/PDFs/Papers/S03P02.pdf*, accessed May 20, 2010.

Center for Strategic and International Studies, "Significant Cyber Incidents," *https://www.csis .org/programs/technology-policy-program/significant-cyber-incidents*, accessed April 10, 2020.

CERT, "Creating a Financial Institution CSIRT: A Case Study," *http://www.cert.org/csirts/AFI _case-study.html*, accessed May 2, 2010.

Ch., Radoslave, "Cloud Computing Statistics 2020," Techjury, March 28, 2019, *https://techjury .net/stats-about/cloud-computing/*, accessed April 13, 2020.

Chaudhuri, Saabira, "Cost of Replacing Credit Cards After Target Breach Estimated at $200 Million," *The Wall Street Journal*, February 18, 2014, *http://online.wsj.com/news /articles/SB10001424052702304675504579391080333769014?mg=reno64-wsj&url =http%3A%2F%2Fonline.wsj.com%2Farticle%2FSB10001424052702304675504579391080 333769014.html*, accessed June 29, 2014.

Chef, "Why Chef?," *https://www.chef.io/why-chef/*, accessed May 30, 2014.

Cheng, Andria, "Two Months After Damaging Data Breach, Target Stock Has Its Best Day in 5 Years," Market Watch *Wall Street Journal*, February 26, 2014, *http://blogs.marketwatch .com/behindthestorefront/2014/02/26/two-months-after-damaging-data-breach-target -stock-has-its-best-day-in-5-years/*, accessed March 10, 2014.

CIPP Guide, "OMB Memorandum 07-16 Safeguarding Against and Responding to the Breach of Personally Identifiable Information," *https://www.cippguide.org/2010/05/04/omb -memorandum-07-16-safeguarding-against-and-responding-to-the-breach-of-personally -identifiable-information/*, accessed April 15, 2020.

Clay, Kelly, "Amazon.com Goes Down, Loses $66,240 Per Minute," *Forbes*, August 19, 2013, *http://www.forbes.com/sites/kellyclay/2013/08/19/amazon-com-goes-down-loses-66240 -per-minute*, accessed May 1, 2014.

Columbus, Louis, "Public Cloud Soaring to $331B by 2022 According to Gartner," *Forbes*, *https://www.forbes.com/sites/louiscolumbus/2019/04/07/public-cloud-soaring-to-331b-by -2022-according-to-gartner/#39bdacfb5739*, accessed April 13, 2020.

Committee of Sponsoring Organizations of the Treadway Commission, "COSO Internal Control— Integrated Framework Executive Summary," May 14, 2013, accessed May 20, 2014.

"Compliance E-mail Retention System Crucial under SEC17a-4," SEC17a-4Compliance.com, *http://www.sec17a-4compliance.com/ediscovery*, accessed May 9, 2010.

Constantin, Lucian, "DDoS Attack Against Spamhaus Was Reportedly the Largest in History," Infoworld, March 27, 2013, *http://www.infoworld.com/d/networking/ddos-attack-against -spamhaus-was-reportedly-the-largest-in-history-215352?page=0,0*, accessed June 29, 2014.

Conway, Tara, Susan Keverline, Michelle Keeney, Eileen Kowalski, Megan Williams, Dawn Cappelli, Andrew P. Moore, Stephanie Rogers, and Timothy J. Shimeall, "Insider Threat Study: Computer Sabotage in Critical Infrastructure Sectors," U.S. Secret Service and Carnegie Mellon University CERT Program, May 2005, *http://www.cert.org/insider_threat /insidercross.html*, accessed April 12, 2010.

Cyprus Shipping Chamber, "Cyber Security Case Study," July 2017, *https://csc-cy.org/wp -content/uploads/2018/06/Cyprus-Shipping-Chamber-Cyber-Security-Case-Study.pdf*, accessed April 20, 2020.

"Diagnosing Cornell's Security Breach," *Cornell Daily Sun*, June 24, 2009, *http://cornellsun.com /node/37476*, accessed May 14, 2010.

Digitalmedialawyerblog.com, "TJX Data Security Breach Saga Continues: Financial Institution Class Action against TJX Survives Based on Unfair Competition Claim Predicated on Statements in FTC Complaint against T.J. Maxx / Marshalls' Parent Company," August 10, 2009, *http://www.digitalmedialawyerblog.com/2009/08/tjx_data_security_breach_saga .html*, accessed March 4, 2010.

Dilanian, Ken, and Richard A. Serrano, "Snowden Leaks Severely Hurt U.S. Security, Two House Members Say," *Los Angeles Times*, January 9, 2014. *http://articles.latimes.com/2014/jan/09 /nation/la-na-snowden-intel-20140110*, accessed March 20, 2014.

E-CommerceAlert.com, "The Risk of At-Work Surfers," November 23, 2004, *http://www .e-commercealert.com/article645.shtml*, accessed April 24, 2010.

Egress.com, "IT Leaders and Employees Differ on Data Ethics, Ownership and Root Causes of Insider Breaches," May 22, 2019, *https://www.egress.com/en-US/news/insider-data-breach -survey-2019-na*, accessed April 15, 2020.

"The Eight Classic Types of Workplace Behavior," *HR Magazine*, September 2000. *http:// findarticles.com/p/articles/mi_m3495/is_9_45/ai_65578688/*, accessed March 7, 2010.

EMA, "EMA's 2008 Survey of IT Governance, Risk and Compliance Management in the Real World," 2008, *http://eval.symantec.com/mktginfo/enterprise/other_resources/b-whitepaper _ema_symantec-it-grc_an_06-2008.en-us.pdf*, accessed April 30, 2010.

Erikson, Chris, "Re: Privacy," *New York Post*, April 12, 2010, *http://www.nypost.com/f/print /news/business/jobs/re_privacy_zUsPRscheD905WKCSVv2qM*, accessed May 12, 2010.

eSecurity Planet, "A Case Study in Security Incident Forensics and Response," March 5, 2001, *http://www.esecurityplanet.com/trends/article.php/10751_688797/article.htm*, accessed May 2, 2010.

eSecurity Planet, "How To Set Social Networking Policies for Employees," April 20, 2010, *http://www.esecurityplanet.com/views/article.php/3877481/How-To-Set-Social-Networking -Policies-for-Employees.htm*, accessed May 14, 2010.

Espelund, Leif, "Predictions 2013: Continued Exponential Data Growth Will Result in Increased Investment in Data Management & Big Data," March 7, 2013, *http://www.symform.com/blog /exponential-data-growth-2013/*, accessed March 10, 2014.

ETSI, "Cyber," *https://www.etsi.org/committee/1393-cyber*, accessed April 11, 2020.

eWeek, "Microsoft Responds: WMF Vulnerability," February 2, 2006, *http://www.eweek .com/c/a/Windows/Microsoft-Responds-WMF-Vulnerability/*, accessed March 28, 2010.

"Executive Order—Improving Critical Infrastructure Cybersecurity," The White House, Office of the Press Secretary, February 12, 2013, *https://obamawhitehouse.archives.gov/the-press -office/2013/02/12/executive-order-improving-critical-infrastructure-cybersecurity*, accessed April 11, 2020.

Fadilpašić, Sead, "DDoS Attacks Are Getting Even Larger," ITProPortal, September 13, 2018, *https://www.itproportal.com/news/ddos-attacks-are-getting-even-larger/*, accessed April 14, 2020.

Federal Deposit Insurance Corporation, "501(b) Examination Guidance," FIL-68-2001, Financial Guidance Letters, August 24, 2001, *http://www.fdic.gov/news/news/financial /2001/fil0168.html*, accessed May 20, 2010.

Federal Deposit Insurance Corporation, "FFIEC Supplement to Authentication in an Internet Banking Environment," June 29, 2011. *http://www.fdic.gov/news/news/financial/2011 /fil11050.html*, accessed June 30, 2014.

Federation of American Scientists, "National Security Information EO 12356," April 2, 1982, *http://www.fas.org/irp/offdocs/eo12356.htm*, accessed March 27, 2010.

Glaser, John, "Management's Role in IT Project Failures: Senior Managers Obviously Have Great Interest in Seeing That Projects Become Successful. Yet Despite Best Intentions, All Too Often They Wind Up Playing a Pivotal Role in Ensuring Project Failure," Allbusiness.com, October 2004, *http://www.allbusiness.com/technology/technology-services/237595-1.html*, accessed April 26, 2010.

Globalscape, "Stolen Laptops Cause Data Breach for Coca-Cola," January 27, 2014. *http://www .globalscape.com/blog/2014/1/27/stolen-laptops-cause-data-breach-for-cocacola*, accessed May 1, 2014.

Goodin, Dan, "New Advanced Malware, Possibly Nation Sponsored, Is Targeting US Utilities," Ars Technica, *https://arstechnica.com/information-technology/2019/08/new-advanced -malware-possibly-nation-sponsored-is-targeting-us-utilities/*, accessed April 10, 2020.

Gorman, Siobhan, August Cole, and Yochi Dreazen, "Computer Spies Breach Fighter-Jet Project," *Wall Street Journal*, April 21, 2009. *http://online.wsj.com/article/SB124027491029837401 .html*, accessed April 11, 2010.

"Governor O'Malley's 15 Strategic Policy Goals," State of Maryland StateStat, *http://www.gov .state.md.us/statestat/gdu.asp*, accessed March 14, 2010.

Gralla, Preston, "Windows Market Share Dips Again; World and Microsoft Survive," ComputerWorld Blogs, January 4, 2010, *http://blogs.computerworld.com/15344/windows _market_share_dips_again_world_and_microsoft_survive*, accessed April 2010.

Grier, Sam, "ISACA Releases the Risk IT Framework Draft," IT Manager's Inbox, *http:// itmanagersinbox.com/1007/isaca-releases-the-risk-it-framework-draft/*, accessed April 30, 2010.

Halock Security Labs, "Building a Security Program Using ISO 27001," *http://www.halock.com /Downloads/Case_Study/AIM%20Case%20Study.pdf*, accessed March 17, 2010.

Harress, Christopher, "Obama Says Cyberterrorism Is Country's Biggest Threat, U.S. Government Assembles 'Cyber Warriors,'" *International Business Times*, February 18, 2014, *http://www.ibtimes.com/obama-says-cyberterrorism-countrys-biggest-threat-us -government-assembles-cyber-warriors-1556337*, accessed June 29, 2014.

Health Management Technology, "Organized Security," 2010, *http://www.healthmgttech.com /index.php/solutions/hospitals/organized-security.html*, accessed March 8, 2010.

Healthitlawblog.com, "Rising Numbers and Costs of Data Breaches," January 28, 2010, *http://www.healthitlawblog.com/tags/data-breach/*, accessed March 4, 2010.

Help Net Security, "Average DDoS Attack Sizes Decrease 85% Due to FBI's Shutdown of DDoS -for-Hire Websites," March 21, 2019, *https://www.helpnetsecurity.com/2019/03/21 /average-ddos-attack-sizes-decrease/*, accessed April 14, 2020.

Help Net Security, "Top 10 Information Security Threats for 2010," January 14, 2010, *http:// www.net-security.org/secworld.php?id=8709*, accessed April 10, 2010.

Higgins, Kelly Jackson, "Violation of Sensitive Data Storage Policy Led to Exposure of Info on 3.3 Million Student Loan Recipients," DarkReading, March 29, 2010, *http://www. darkreading.com/insiderthreat/security/privacy/showArticle.jhtml?articleID=224200648*, accessed May 14, 2010.

HostingFacts, "Internet Stats and Facts (2020)," *https://hostingfacts.com/internet-facts-stats/*, accessed April 10, 2020.

Hu, Vincent C., David Ferraiolo, Rick Kuhn, Adam Schnitzer, Kenneth Sandlin, Robert Miller, and Karen Scarfone, "Guide to Attribute Based Access Control (ABAC) Definition and Considerations," National Institute of Standards and Technology, January 2014, *http:// nvlpubs.nist.gov/nistpubs/specialpublications/ NIST.sp.800-162.pdf*, accessed March 11, 2014.

IBM, "IBM Security Solutions X-Force(r) 2009 Trend and Risk Report: Annual Review of 2009," 2010, *http://www-935.ibm.com/services/us/iss/xforce/trendreports/*, accessed April 10, 2010.

Industry.bnet.com, "Financial Roundup: Total Bank Losses to $3.6 Trillion, Mortgage Lender Breaks, Half of CDOs in Default," February 13, 2009, *http://industry.bnet.com/financial -services/1000403/financial-roundup-total-bank-losses-to-36-trillion-mortgage-lender -breaks -half-of-cdos-in-default/*, accessed March 6, 2010.

Information Security Oversight Office, "Information Security Oversight Report 2009," March 10, 2010, *http://www.archives.gov/isoo/reports/2009-annual-report.pdf*, accessed March 27, 2010.

Internet Security Systems, "Computer Security Incident Response Planning," *http://documents .iss.net/whitepapers/csirplanning.pdf*, accessed May 1, 2010.

Internet World Stats, *https://www.internetworldstats.com/stats.htm*

ISACA, "COBIT 4.1," 2007, *http://www.isaca.org/Knowledge-Center/COBIT/Pages/Overview .aspx*, accessed February 13 and March 24, 2010.

ISACA, "COBIT 5 Design Paper Exposure Draft," 2010, *http://www.isaca.org/Content Management/ContentDisplay.cfm?ContentID=56448*, accessed April 30, 2010.

ISACA, "COBIT 5 Introduction," *http://www.isaca.org/cobit/documents/cobit5-introduction.ppt*, accessed June 30, 2014.

"ISO/IEC 27002:2005 Information Technology—Security Techniques—Code of Practice for Information Security Management," InsecT Ltd., 2010, *http://www.iso27001security.com /html/27002.html*, accessed March 8, 2010.

ITIL, *http://www.itil-officialsite.com/home/home.asp*, accessed March 22, 2010.

Jansen, Wayne, and Karen Scarfone, "Guidelines on Cell Phone and PDA Security," NIST SP 800-124, NIST Computer Security Division, October 2008, *http://csrc.nist.gov /publications/nistpubs/800-124/SP800-124.pdf*, accessed March 8, 2010.

Jarmom, David, "A Preparation Guide to Information Security Policies," SANS Institute, 2002, *http://www.sans.org/reading_room/whitepapers/policyissues/preparation-guide -information-security-policies_503*, accessed March 7, 2010.

Javaid, Adeel, "Code Error Caused Million Hearts to Bleed," Linkedin.com, April 11, 2014, *http://www.linkedin.com/today/post/article/20140411161121-71158614-code-error -caused-million-hearts-to-bleed*, accessed May 1, 2014.

JobStreet, "Salary Report, Position Title: Call Center Agent, Country: Philippines," 2010, *http://myjobstreet.jobstreet.com/career-enhancer/basic-salary-report.php?param=Call%20 Center%20Agent%7C000%7Cph%7C%7Cph*, accessed March 24, 2010.

Johnson, Arnold, Kelley Dempsey, Ron Ross, Sarbari Gupta, and Dennis Bailey, "Guide for Security Configuration Management of Information Systems," National Institute of Standards and Technology Special Publication 800-128 initial public draft (NIST SP 800-128). Gaithersburg, MD: United States Department of Commerce, 2010.

K&L Gates, "Court Orders Broad Discovery of Class Members' Social Media, Text Messages & Email," November 13, 2012, *http://www.ediscoverylaw.com/2012/11/articles/case -summaries/court-orders-broad-discovery-of-class-members-social-media-text-messages -email/*, accessed May 22, 2014.

Kaplan, Dan, "U.S. House to Toughen Internal Cybersecurity Policy," *SC Magazine*, December 16, 2009, *http://www.scmagazineus.com/us-house-to-toughen-internal-cybersecurity-policy /article/159785/*, accessed May 2, 2010.

Karvy, "Unlearnt Lessons from Barings," *http://www.karvy.com/articles/baringsdebacle.htm*, accessed April 11, 2010.

Keeper Security, "2018 State of Cybersecurity in Small & Medium Size Businesses," Ponemon Institute, 2018, *https://keepersecurity.com/assets/pdf/Keeper-2018-Ponemon-Report.pdf*, accessed April 15, 2020.

Kemp, Simon, "Digital 2019: Global Internet Use Accelerates," We Are Social, *https://wearesocial .com/blog/2019/01/digital-2019-global-internet-use-accelerates*, accessed April 10, 2020.

Krebs, Brian, "Chinese Hackers Blamed for Intrusion at Energy Industry Giant Telvent," Krebs on Security, September 26, 2012, *http://krebsonsecurity.com/2012/09/chinese-hackers -blamed-for-intrusion-at-energy-industry-giant-telvent/*, accessed May 1, 2014.

Lago, Cristina, "How to Implement a Successful Cybersecurity Plan," July 10, 2019, *https://www.cio.com/article/3295578/how-to-implement-a-successful-security-plan.html*, accessed May 8, 2020.

Leapfrog, "What Percentage of Your Company's Budget Should Be Allocated for IT Operations," July 30, 2019, *https://leapfrogservices.com/percentage-companys-budget-allocated/*, accessed April 14, 2020.

Legal Center for Foster Care and Education, "The Uninterrupted Scholars Act: How Do Recent Changes to FERPA Help Child Welfare Agencies Get Access to School Records?," 2013, *http://www.fostercareandeducation.org/portals/0/dmx/2013/02/file_20130211_145758_xjnFqt_0.pdf*, accessed June 30, 2014.

Legal Information Institute, "Intellectual Property," *https://www.law.cornell.edu/wex/intellectual_property*, accessed April 15, 2020.

LeMay, Renai, "Nessus Security Tool Closes Its Source," CNET News, October 6, 2005, *http://news.cnet.com/Nessus-security-tool-closes-its-source/2100-7344_3-5890093.html*, accessed May 15, 2010.

Leyden, John, "The Enemy Within," The Register, December 2005, *http://www.theregister.co.uk/2005/12/15/mcafee_internal_security_survey/*, accessed May 1, 2010.

MachroTech, "E-commerce Quick Facts," 2002, *http://www.machrotech.com/services/ecommerce-marketsize-statistics.asp*, accessed April 30, 2010.

Malcolm, Hadley, "Target Tech Chief Resigns Amid Security Overhaul," *USA Today*, March 6, 2014, *http://www.usatoday.com/story/money/business/2014/03/05/target-tech-chief-resigns-data-breach/6070263/*, accessed March 10, 2014.

Marr, Bernard, "How Much Data Do We Create Every Day? The Mind-Blowing Stats Everyone Should Read," *Forbes*, *https://www.forbes.com/sites/bernardmarr/2018/05/21/how-much-data-do-we-create-every-day-the-mind-blowing-stats-everyone-should-read/#3ad8b75b60ba*, accessed April 13, 2020.

Marzigliano, Leonard T., "Defense Department Adopts NIST Security Standards," *Information Week*, March 14, 2014, *http://www.informationweek.com/government/cybersecurity/defense-department-adopts-nist-security-standards/d/d-id/1127706*, accessed March 20, 2014.

McAfee, "12 Must-Know Statistics on Cloud Usage in the Enterprise," March 9, 2017, *https://www.skyhighnetworks.com/cloud-security-blog/12-must-know-statistics-on-cloud-usage-in-the-enterprise/*, accessed April 13, 2020.

McCann, Erin, "Stanford Reports Fifth Big HIPAA Breach," *HealthcareITNews*, June 13, 2013, *http://www.healthcareitnews.com/news/stanford-reports-fifth-big-hipaa-breach*, accessed May 13, 2014.

McCue, T.J., "Cloud Computing: United States Businesses Will Spend $13 Billion On It," *Forbes*, January 29, 2014, *http://www.forbes.com/sites/tjmccue/2014/01/29/cloud-computing-united-states-businesses-will-spend-13-billion-on-it/*, accessed June 30, 2014.

MediaValet, "What Is a Digital Asset," *https://www.mediavalet.com/blog/what-is-a-digital-asset-2/*, accessed April 15, 2020.

Meier, J.D., "Diversification, Coordination, Replication, and Unification," MSDN Blogs, February 24, 2013, *http://blogs.msdn.com/b/jmeier/archive/2013/02/24/diversification-coordination-replication-and-unification.aspx*, accessed March 30, 2014.

Meltzer, Joshua, "The Internet, Cross-Border Data Flows and International Trade," *The Brookings Institution: Issues in Technology Innovation*, No. 22, February 2013, *http://www.brookings.edu/~/media/research/files/papers/2013/02/25%20international%20data%20flows%20meltzer/internet%20data%20and%20trade%20meltzer.pdf*, pg. 2, accessed June 29, 2014.

Merchant University, "PCI Compliance & Fines," *http://www.merchantuniversity.org/101 -education/security-pci-101/pci-compliance-fines.aspx*, accessed June 29, 2014.

Microsoft, "Microsoft Security Advisory 2963983: Vulnerability in Internet Explorer Could Allow Remote Code Execution," April 26, 2014, *https://technet.microsoft.com/en-us/library /security/2963983.aspx*, accessed May 28, 2014.

Milford, Kim, Tracy Mitrano, and Steve Shuster, Educause electronic presentation, *http://net .educause.edu/ir/library/powerpoint/SPC0662.pps*, accessed March 17, 2010.

Montgomery College, "Remote Access Standard," August 12, 2008, *http://cms.montgomery college.edu/WorkArea/linkit.aspx?LinkIdentifier=id&ItemID=846*, accessed April 14, 2010.

Moscaritolo, Angela, "Record-Breaking DDoS Attack Nears 400 Gbps," *PC Magazine*, February 11, 2014, *http://www.pcmag.com/article2/0,2817,2453157,00.asp*, accessed June 29, 2014.

NACS, "Nevada Mandates PCI DSS," June 24, 2009, *http://www.nacsonline.com/NACS/News /Daily/Pages/ND0624094.aspx*, accessed March 26, 2010.

Nash, Kim S., "Information Technology Budgets: Which Industry Spends the Most?," CIO, November 2, 2007, *http://www.cio.com/article/151301/Information_Technology_Budgets _Which_Industry_Spends_the_Most_*, accessed March 10, 2014.

Nash, Troy, "An Undirected Attack Against Critical Infrastructures: A Case Study for Improving Your Control System Security," US-CERT Control Systems Security Center, Lawrence Livermore National Laboratory, September 2005, *http://www.us-cert.gov/control_systems /pdf/undirected_attack0905.pdf*, accessed April 11, 2010.

National Cybersecurity Alliance and Symantec, "2012 NCSA/Symantec National Small Business Study," October 2012, *https://www.staysafeonline.org/stay-safe-online/resources/*, accessed June 30, 2014.

National Institute of Standards and Technology, "Contingency Planning Guide for Information Technology Systems," NIST Special Publication 800-34, June 2002, *http://csrc.nist.gov /publications/nistpubs/800-34/sp800-34.pdf*, accessed March 26, 2010.

National Institute of Standards and Technology, "Federal Desktop Core Configuration (FDCC)," 2010, *http://nvd.nist.gov/fdcc/index.cfm*, accessed May 12, 2010.

National Institute of Standards and Technology, "National Institute of Standards and Technology Special Publications (800 Series)," *http://csrc.nist.gov/publications/PubsSPs .html*, accessed March 8, 2010.

National Institute of Standards and Technology, "Standards for Security Categorization of Federal Information and Information Systems," NIST Special Publication 199, February 2004, *http:// csrc.nist.gov/publications/fips/fips199/FIPS-PUB-199-final.pdf*, accessed March 26, 2010.

Newman, Jared, "The Target Credit Card Breach: What You Should Know," *Time*, December 19, 2013, *http://techland.time.com/2013/12/19/the-target-credit-card-breach-what-you-should -know/*, accessed June 29, 2014.

Nextgov, "VA Investigating Security Breach of Veterans' Medical Data," March 9, 2010, *http:// www.nextgov.com/nextgov/ng_20100309_9888.php*, accessed May 14, 2010.

Nichols, Russell, "California Issues Telework Policy to Curb Cyber-Security Risks," *Government Technology*, March 3, 2010, *http://www.govtech.com/gt/748172*, accessed March 17, 2010.

Nova Scotia, "Wide Area Network Security Policy," 2010, *http://www.gov.ns.ca/treasuryboard /manuals/PDF/300/30408-04.pdf*, accessed April 15, 2010.

Office of Homeland Security, "Recommended Practice: Developing an Industrial Control Systems Cybersecurity Incident Response Capability," October 2009, *http://csrp.inl.gov /Documents/final-RP_ics_cybersecurity_incident_response_100609.pdf*, accessed May 2, 2010.

Office of the Comptroller of the Currency, "Supervisory Guidance on Operational Risk Advanced Measurement Approaches for Regulatory Capital," July 2, 2003, *http://www.occ.treas.gov/ftp /release/2003-53c.pdf*, accessed April 30, 2010.

Office of the Director of National Intelligence, "Information Sharing and the Private Sector," *http://www.ise.gov/pages/partner-private.aspx*, accessed March 10, 2010.

Online Trust Alliance, "2014 Data Protection and Breach Readiness Guide," April 7, 2014, *https://www.otalliance.org/resources/data-breach-protection*, accessed June 30, 2014.

Ooma, "Call Anywhere in the U.S. with No Monthly Fee," *http://www.ooma.com*, accessed March 27, 2010.

Open Web Application Security Project, "OWASP Risk Rating Methodology," May 13, 2014, *https://www.owasp.org/index.php/OWASP_Risk_Rating_Methodology*, accessed May 30, 2014.

PCI Security Standards Council, *https://www.pcisecuritystandards.org*, accessed June 30, 2014.

Ponemon Institute, "2011 Cost of Data Breach Study," March 2012, *http://www.ponemon.org/local/upload/file/2011_US_CODB_FINAL_5.pdf*, accessed June 29, 2014.

Prince, Brian, "Stolen Credit Card Data Goes for Cheap on Cyber-Black Market," *eWeek*, August 20, 2009, *http://www.eweek.com/c/a/Security/Stolen-Credit-Card-Data-Goes-for-Cheap-on-CyberBlack-Market-891275/*, accessed March 24, 2010.

Privacy Rights Clearinghouse, "Chronology of Data Breaches," December 31, 2013, *http://www.privacyrights.org/data-breach*, accessed June 30, 2014.

Purcell, James, "Security Control Types and Operational Security," GIAC, February 12, 2007, *http://www.giac.org/resources/whitepaper/operations/207.php*, accessed March 15, 2010.

"Putting Big Data to Work for Your Business," *Aon One*, Q1, April 2013, *http://one.aon.com/putting-big-data-work*, accessed March 13, 2014.

Quinn, Stephen, David Waltermire, Christopher Johnson, Karen Scarfone, and John Banghart, "The Technical Specification for the Security Content Automation Protocol (SCAP)," National Institute of Standards and Technology Special Publication 800-126. Gaithersburg, MD: U.S. Department of Commerce, 2009.

Ranum, Marcus J., *The Myth of Homeland Security*. Indianapolis: Wiley, 2004.

Risk Based Security, Inc., "Data Breach QuickView: An Executive's Guide to 2013 Data Breach Trends," 2013, *https://www.riskbasedsecurity.com/reports/2013-DataBreachQuickView.pdf*, accessed July 2, 2014.

Robinson, Jasmin, Tamma Sorbello, and Kerrie Unsworth, "Innovation Implementation: The Role of Technology Diffusion Agencies," *Journal of Technology, Management and Innovation*, 3, no. 3 (2008): 1–10. *http://www.scielo.cl/scielo.php?pid=S0718-27242008000100001&script=sci_arttext*, accessed March 6, 2010.

Rupert, Brad, "IT Guidance to the Legal Team," SANS Institute Reading Room, April 15, 2009, *http://www.sans.org/reading_room/whitepapers/legal/guidance-legal-team_33308*, accessed May 14, 2010.

SANS, "CyberLaw 101: A Primer on US Laws Related to Honeypot Deployments," SANS Institute Reading Room, 2007, *http://www.sans.org/reading_room/whitepapers/honors/cyberlaw-101-primer-laws-related-honeypot-deployments_1746*, accessed May 14, 2010.

SANS, "Database Credentials Policy," Security Policy Templates, 2010, *https://assets.contentstack.io/v3/assets/blt36c2e63521272fdc/blt2b856a20ea955f3c/5e9dd82045a2a97194a1da17/database_credentials_policy.pdf*, accessed April 15, 2010.

SANS, "Developing a Security-Awareness Culture—Improving Security Decision Making," July 2004, *http://www.sans.org/reading_room/whitepapers/awareness/developing-security-awareness-culture-improving-security-decision-making_1526*, accessed May 1, 2010.

SANS, "Employee Internet Use Monitoring and Filtering Policy," SANS Technology Institute Student Projects, November 2007, *http://www.sans.edu/resources/student_projects/200711_004.pdf*, accessed April 15, 2010.

SANS, "Information Security Policy—A Development Guide for Large and Small Companies," SANS Institute Reading Room, 2007, *http://www.sans.org/reading_room/whitepapers*

/policyissues/information_security_policy_a_development_guide_for_large_and_small _companies_1331?show=1331.php&cat=policyissues, accessed March 7, 2010.

SANS, "Virtual Private Network Policy," 2010, http://www.sans.org/security-resources/policies /Virtual_Private_Network.pdf, accessed April 15, 2010.

Schulz, David, "College Rupture Impacts 300,000 Students & Staff: Why Is This Breach Different from All Other Breaches?," Privacy Writes, October 15, 2012, http://www.501cybersecurity .com/2012/10/may-september-college-rupture-impacts-300000-students-staff-why-is-this -different/, accessed June 30, 2014.

SecTools.org, "Top 10 Vulnerability Scanners," http://sectools.org/vuln-scanners.html, accessed May 15, 2010.

Smith, Tim, "Lack of Security Policy Cited in S.C. Breach," USA Today, November 14, 2012, http://www.usatoday.com/story/news/nation/2012/11/14/lack-computer-security-policy -sc-hacking/1704529/, accessed May 1, 2014.

Stanford University, "Disk and Data Sanitization Policy and Guidelines," July 2005. http://www .stanford.edu/group/security/securecomputing/data_destruction_guidelines.html, accessed March 17, 2010.

Stanford University Information Security Office, "Data Classification, Access, Transmittal, and Storage," http://www.stanford.edu/group/security/securecomputing/dataclass_chart.html, accessed May 1, 2014.

State of Maryland, Department of Health and Mental Hygiene, "Information Resources Management Administration," http://dhmh.maryland.gov/irma/, accessed March 8, 2010.

State of Tennessee, Department of Finance and Administration, Office for Information Resources, Information Security Program, "Enterprise Information Security Policies," April 4, 2008, http://www.tennessee.gov/finance/oir/security/PUBLIC-Enterprise-Information -Security-Policies-v1-6.pdf, accessed March 8, 2010.

Stempel, Jonathan, "Target, Security Auditor Trustwave Are Sued Over Data Breach," Reuters, March 26, 2014, http://www.reuters.com/article/2014/03/26/us-target-trustwave-lawsuit -idUSBREA2P0B020140326, accessed March 27, 2014.

SUNY Levine Institute, "Advances in Information Technology," http://www.globalization101.org /advances-in-information-technology/, accessed June 29, 2014.

Target Corporation, "Corporate Fact Sheet," http://pressroom.target.com/corporate, accessed March 10, 2014.

Target Corporation, "Corporate Overview," http://investors.target.com/phoenix.zhtml?c =65828 &p=irol-homeprofile, accessed June 29, 2014.

TechEncyclopedia, "Definition of System Software," Techweb.com, 2010, http://www .techweb.com/encyclopedia/defineterm.jhtml?term=systemsoftware, accessed March 25, 2010.

Telecommunications Industry Association, http://www.tiaonline.org/index.cfm, accessed March 8, 2010.

Teschner, Charles, Peter Golder, and Thorsten Liebert, "Bringing Back Best Practices in Risk Management: Banks' Three Lines of Defense," Booz & Company, October 17, 2008, http:// www.booz.com/global/home/what_we_think/reports_and_white_papers/ic-display /42753543, accessed April 30, 2010.

Texas State Library and Archives Commission, "Local Schedule GR, Retention Schedule for Records Common to All Local Governments," July 4, 2012, https://www.tsl.texas.gov/slrm /recordspubs/gr.html, accessed May 22, 2014.

TexasWorkForce, "Monitoring Employees' Use of Company Computers and the Internet," http://www.twc.state.tx.us/news/efte/monitoring_computers_internet.html, accessed May 14, 2010.

University of Guelph, "Information Technology Security Policy Framework," January 27, 2010, *http://www.uoguelph.ca/cio/sites/uoguelph.ca.cio/files/CIO-ITSecurity-00-PolicyFramework -2009Approved.pdf*, accessed April 30, 2010.

University of Huddlesfield, "Policy Framework," *https://www.hud.ac.uk/media/policy documents/Policy-Framework.pdf*, accessed April 18, 2020.

University of Montana, "Guidelines for Appropriate Use of External Communication Systems," June 29, 2009, *http://www.umt.edu/it/policies/externalwebsystems.aspx*, accessed March 15, 2010.

University of Texas, "Data Classification Standard," September 14, 2007, *http://www.utexas.edu /its/policies/opsmanual/dataclassification.php*, accessed March 28, 2010.

U.S. Department of Energy, "DNS Policies & Procedures," *http://cio.energy.gov/policy-guidance /952.htm*, accessed April 15, 2010.

U.S. Department of Energy, Office of Inspector General, Special Report: IG-0900, "Department of Energy's July 2013 Cyber Security Breach," December 6, 2013, *http://energy.gov/ig /downloads/special-report-ig-0900*, accessed May 20, 2014.

U.S. Department of Health and Human Services, "New Rule Protects Patient Privacy, Secures Health Information," January 17, 2013, *http://www.hhs.gov/news/press/2013pres/01 /20130117b.html*, accessed June 30, 2014.

U.S. Department of Transportation, Federal Aviation Administration, "Voice Over Internet Protocol (VoIP) Security Policy," September 21, 2009, *http://www.faa.gov/documentLibrary /media/Order/1370.108.pdf*, accessed April 15, 2010.

U.S. Department of the Treasury, Comptroller of the Currency, "Report to the Congress on Review of Regulations Affecting Online Delivery of Financial Products and Services," November 2001, *http://www.occ.treas.gov/netbank/729jrptnov1601.doc*, accessed May 20, 2010.

U.S. Department of Veterans Affairs, "Federal Information Security Management Act Audit for Fiscal Year 2012," June 27, 2013, *http://www.va.gov/oig/pubs/VAOIG-12-01712-229.pdf*, accessed June 30, 2014.

U.S. Securities and Exchange Commission, Office of Inspector General, Office of Audits, "Audit of the SEC's Compliance with the Federal Information Security Modernization Act for Fiscal Year 2017," *https://www.sec.gov/files/Audit-of-the-SECs-Compliance-with-FISMA-for-Fiscal -Year-2017.pdf*, accessed April 10, 2020.

VendorSafe Technologies, "Case Study: Fast Food Franchise Security Breach (Multiple Locations)," October 2008, *http://www.vendorsafe.com/images/pdfs/CaseStudy _FastFood.pdf*, accessed April 30, 2010.

Verizon, "2013 Data Breach Investigations Report," *http://www.verizonenterprise.com /resources/reports/rp_data-breach-investigations-report-2013_en_xg.pdf*, accessed June 30, 2014.

Verizon Business RISK Team, "2009 Data Breach Investigations Report," 2009, *http://www .verizonbusiness.com/resources/security/reports/2009_databreach_rp.pdf*, accessed on April 11, 2010.

Verizon Business RISK Team, "2009 Data Breach Investigations Supplemental Report," 2010, *http://www.bankinfosecurity.com/external/rp_2009-data-breach-investigations -supplemental-report_en_xg.pdf*, accessed April 11, 2010.

Vijayan, Jaikumar, "Computer Theft May Have Exposed Patient Data Across Five States," Computerworld, January 4, 2007, *http://www.computerworld.com/s/article/9007199 /Computer_theft_may_have_exposed_patient_data_across_five_states?intsrc=hm_list*, accessed March 25, 2010.

Vijayan, Jaikumar, "NASA Breach Update: Stolen Laptop Had Data on 10,000 Users," *Computerworld*, November 15, 2012, *http://www.computerworld.com/s/article/9233701 /NASA_breach_update_Stolen_laptop_had_data_on_10_000_users?taxonomyId=17&page Number=2*, accessed May 1, 2014.

Visa, "Security Incident Response Procedure," 2007, *http://www.visa-asia.com/ap/sea /merchants/riskmgmt/includes/uploads/SecurityIncidentRespProcd.pdf*, accessed May 3, 2010.

Visa, "What to Do If Compromised: Visa Inc. Fraud Control and Investigations Procedures Version 3.0," May 2011, *http://www.visacemea.com/ac/ais/uploads/cisp_what_to_do_if _compromised.pdf*, accessed June 30, 2014.

Wack, John, Ken Cutler, and Jamie Pole, "Guidelines on Firewalls and Firewall Policy," NIST SP 800-41, U.S. Department of Commerce, January 2002, *http://www.ffiec.gov/.../nis-guide _on_firewall_and_firewall_pol_800_41.pdf*, accessed April 15, 2010.

Waldron, Harry, "SEC Approves Sarbanes-Oxley Changes for Section 404," Microsoft Most Valuable Professional, May 23, 2007, *http://msmvps.com/blogs/harrywaldron/archive /2007/05/23/sec-approves-sarbanes-oxley-changes-for-section-404.aspx*, accessed June 30, 2014.

Walker, Richard W., "Negligent Employees Cause Most Data Breaches; Mobile Is Key Factor," BreakingGov, March 22, 2012, *http://breakinggov.com/2012/03/22/negligent-employees -cause-most-data-breaches-mobile-is-key-fact/*, accessed June 29, 2014.

White House, Office of the Press Secretary, "Executive Order—Improving Critical Infrastructure Cybersecurity," February 12, 2013, *http://www.whitehouse.gov/the-press-office/2013/02/12 /executive-order-improving-critical-infrastructure-cybersecurity*, accessed June 29, 2014.

Yu, Roger, and Mike Snider, "Bans on Streaming at Work Target Bandwidth-Eating Sites," *USA Today*, April 3, 2012, *http://usatoday30.usatoday.com/tech/news/story/2012-04-03 /employers-ban-streaming-video/53980384/1*, accessed June 30, 2014.

Zeno, Thomas, and Lindsay Holmes, "Data Security Laws and Penalties: Pay IT Now or Pay Out Later," Tech Republic, December 4, 2013, *http://www.techrepublic.com/blog/data-center /data-security-laws-and-penalties-pay-it-now-or-pay-out-later/*, accessed May 18, 2014.

Zimmermann, Stephanie, "Could Target-Style Data Breach Happen to Me?," ABC News, February 13, 2014, *http://abcnews.go.com/Blotter/target-style-data-breach-happen /story?id=22483195*, accessed June 29, 2014.

Index